# The Complete Dog Book

Official Publication of the American Kennel Club

# THE
# COMPLETE
# DOG BOOK

The photograph, history and official standard of every breed
admitted to AKC registration, and the selection, training,
breeding, care and feeding of pure-bred dogs.

1992
18th Edition—First Printing

**HOWELL BOOK HOUSE**
New York

Maxwell Macmillan Canada
Toronto

Maxwell Macmillan International
New York   Oxford   Singapore   Sydney

Howell Book House                    Maxwell Macmillan Canada, Inc.
Macmillan Publishing Company         1200 Eglinton Avenue East
866 Third Avenue                     Suite 200
New York, NY 10022                   Don Mills, Ontario M3C 3N1

Macmillan Publishing Company is part of the
Maxwell Communication Group of Companies.

The American Kennel Club seal design is registered in the United States
Patent and Trademark Office as a trademark and a service mark owned by
The American Kennel Club, 51 Madison Avenue, New York, New York.

Library of Congress Cataloging-in-Publication Data
The Complete dog book : the photograph, history, and official standard
of every breed admitted to AKC registration, and the selection,
training, breeding, care, and feeding of pure-bred dogs. — 18th ed.
        p.      cm.
"Official publication of the American Kennel Club."
Includes index.
ISBN 0-87605-464-5
1. Dogs.   I. American Kennel Club.
SF427.C69   1992
636.7'088'8—dc20      91-42714      CIP

Macmillan books are available at special discounts for bulk
purchases for sales promotions, premiums, fund-raising, or
educational use. For details, contact:
        Special Sales Director
        Macmillan Publishing Company
        866 Third Avenue
        New York, NY 10022

10  9  8  7  6  5  4  3  2  1

Printed in the United States of America

# Contents

*Color Display of Pure-bred Dogs (2) Falls Between Pages 500 and 501*

Breed standards as approved on May 1, 1992.
New standards, and revisions of standards, are published when approved in the American Kennel Club's official monthly magazine, *Pure-Bred Dogs—American Kennel Gazette.*
Each breed standard is copyrighted by the American Kennel Club.

THE COMPLETE DOG BOOK, *18th Edition*

### *Editors:*

**AKC:** John J. Mandeville, Vice-President
W. Terry Stacy, Vice-President
Eliz. M. Bodner, DVM, Editor-in-Chief, *Pure-Bred Dogs—AK Gazette*
Dr. James Edwards, Director of Judging Research and Development
Joan Alt . . . Marie Fabrizi . . . Janet Ford . . . Hilde Weihermann

**Howell Book House:** Ab Sidewater, Editor Emeritus
Sean P. Frawley, Publisher
Kathy Nebenhaus, Editor

# Introduction to the 18th Edition

The American Kennel Club is particularly pleased to present this 18th edition of *The Complete Dog Book*, the official book of AKC breed standards. It is, in many respects, the most important new edition yet.

The years since the previous edition in 1985 have seen the most extensive effort in AKC history to improve the clarity, completeness, and format of the standards—an effort so successful that two-thirds of the 134 breeds currently recognized by the AKC have new, revised, or reformatted standards in this 18th edition.

For those new to a serious interest in dogs, we explain that each standard is a description of the ideal specimen of the breed—a pattern in words to be used as a goal for breeders and as a guide for judges. The AKC's By-Laws (Article IV, Section 5) prescribe that "It shall be the duty and privilege of each parent member Specialty Club to define precisely the true type of the breed of pure-bred dogs which it was organized to promote and improve," subject to approval by AKC's Board of Directors.

Many of the standards have stood the test of time, coming down to us through the generations, retaining a vitality and validity without having to be changed at all. Some other standards have been changed frequently. And some others, unfortunately, have remained unchanged despite major shortcomings, complete omissions, or outright errors.

In 1986, a Delegate Advisory Committee to AKC's Board Committee on Judging Research and Development studied the standards in depth and strongly recommended that a program be undertaken to improve them. In conjunction with their study, the committee contacted every parent club to find out what they thought of making all standards conform to a standardized format and using standardized terminology. The response was overwhelmingly in support. Accordingly, the all-out program was launched with the momentous result seen in these pages.

First published in 1929, *The Complete Dog Book* has become the best selling dog book of all time. This pleases us, but also gives us a responsibility. With each new edition we aim to improve it and increase its usefulness. In preparing this 18th edition we have not only completely updated it, but have expanded it.

With the help of authorities, we have reviewed and improved upon the chapters providing guidance on owning, caring for and training dogs. The information on AKC services has been brought up to the minute and includes the new address for registration processing, current fees, and note of such new performance events as Herding Trials and Lure Coursing. There are many great new pictures and the new drawings in illustration of dog anatomy are truly spectacular.

We hope you'll find this to be the invaluable guide its name implies—truly *The Complete Dog Book*.

ROBERT G. MAXWELL
*President*

# Before You Buy Your Dog

For you who are about to purchase a dog, or to receive one as a gift, some considerations are in order, especially if this is to be your first.

To begin with, the family's receptiveness to having the dog must be established. The attitudes, habits and dispositions of all who will have responsibility for the dog must be taken into account. A new puppy is a delight, but there will be need for housebreaking, training to the leash and the obeying of commands, and of course, his daily care. From the time each puppy acquires a master, its health, happiness and welfare are largely determined by the mutual understanding and devotion that develops between them.

Ordinary common sense is important in selecting and caring for a dog. One cares for a dog from the heart, but one must care for a dog from the brain as well. All puppies seem irresistible, but the full grown animal must be visualized. Adult height, length, weight, appetite, disposition, amount of grooming required, must all be carefully considered before bringing home a cuddly ball of fur that can grow up to be a 100-pound terror. Consider, too, any limitations imposed by your environs; if it is to be a city dog, for example, the necessary excursions for exercise and elimination might prove a problem.

What breed is right for you?

In this book you will find a picture, history, and the official standard of the breeds currently accepted for registration by the American Kennel Club. There are dogs of all sizes, shapes and colors. There are old breeds, and relatively new breeds—breeds that have served man as hunter, guard, tracker, shepherd, sled dog, and above all as companion. Studying these pages can be a great aid in choosing the breed whose background inheritance, size and temperament best suits *your* needs and desires.

If you are able to supplement your study with attendance at a dog show, a field trial, an obedience trial, or a visit to a kennel, so much the better. There you will be able to see both puppies and mature adults of the breed that interest you.

Probably the most important consideration in buying a puppy is that it be from someone in whom you can put full confidence. A reliable seller can be of great assistance in the decisions you must make.

For example, one of the questions most frequently asked of sellers is "What is the best breed for a child?" The answer is that it is not so much the breed as it is the individual dog that is the factor, and whether or not the child can

1

properly handle him. The dependable breeder can help a lot in making this determination.

You should determine in advance whether you want a male or a female. Other than the fact that a bitch, unless you have her spayed (which makes her ineligible for conformation showing), comes in season approximately twice a year and at that time must be carefully isolated from males, she is to be considered as desirable a pet as the male, if not more so. She is not as prone to fight with other dogs, and is less liable to stray.

If you are buying your dog with the expectancy of entering it at shows or field trials some day, or if you plan to breed, the pedigree of the puppy you select takes on greater importance, and you should learn as much as you can concerning the dog's ancestry.

A word of caution regarding dogs bought to be watchdogs. It is usually a natural thing for a dog of any breed to sound an alarm when anything strange occurs, or a stranger appears on the premises, and for most homes this is protection enough. However, dogs are available that have been specially trained to be guard or attack dogs, such as are used for professional police work. In acquiring such a dog, be aware that *a dog trained to this extent is safe only in the custody of a person equally well-trained.*

Do not buy a puppy under six weeks of age—eight weeks would probably be better. The important thing is to know that the puppy is fully weaned, and strong enough to be on its own away from the mother.

The puppy should be healthy, normal and alert. Never select from a litter in which disease seems to be present, and certainly never a puppy that seems ill with runny nose, watery eyes or fever. A cowed, trembling, shy puppy, or one that seems snappy and bad-tempered, should be avoided.

From the beginning, you should have a local veterinarian to whom you can turn. He can give you specific recommendations for the area in which you live, and can advise you on the vaccinations that are essential, from the outset, to provide immunity from the diseases that are fatal to so many puppies. The veterinarian will guide and help you in keeping your dog healthy, as well as in caring for him in sickness.

Because it has been subject to past misinterpretation, you should know that the designation "AKC Reg." following the name of a kennel simply means that the kennel's name is thus protected for the sole use of its owner in naming dogs to be registered or shown. It does not signify any special stamp of approval on the kennels—the American Kennel Club does not register or rate kennels as such. Nor does the AKC buy or sell dogs.

The American Kennel Club does register individual dogs, and in buying a pure-bred dog you should assure yourself of the following safeguards:

When you buy a dog that is represented as being eligible for registration with the American Kennel Club, you are entitled to receive an AKC application form properly filled out by the seller, which—when completed by you and submitted to the AKC with the proper fee—will enable you to effect the registration of the dog. When the application has been processed, you will receive an AKC registration certificate.

Under AKC rules, any person who sells dogs that are represented as being AKC registrable, must maintain records that will make it possible to give full identifying information with every dog delivered, even though AKC papers may not yet be available. *Do not accept a promise of later identification.*

The Rules and Regulations of the American Kennel Club stipulate that whenever someone sells or delivers a dog that is said to be registrable with the AKC, the dog must be identified either by putting into the hands of the buyer a properly completed AKC registration application, or by giving the buyer a bill of sale or a written statement, *signed by the seller,* giving the dog's full breeding information as follows:

—**Breed, sex and color of the dog**
—**Date of birth of the dog**
—**Registered names of the dog's sire and dam**
—**Name of the breeder**

If you encounter any problems in acquiring the necessary registration application forms, it is suggested that you write the American Kennel Club, 5580 Centerview Drive, Raleigh, NC 27606, *giving full particulars* and the difficulty will be reviewed. All individuals acquiring a dog represented as being AKC registrable should realize it is their responsibility to obtain complete identification of the dog as described above sufficient to identify in AKC records, or THEY SHOULD NOT BUY THE DOG.

REGISTRATION FEE: $7.00
EACH SUPPLEMENTAL TRANSFER: $3.00
FEES SUBJECT TO CHANGE WITHOUT NOTICE

MAIL APPLICATION WITH FEE TO:
AMERICAN KENNEL CLUB
5580 CENTERVIEW DRIVE
RALEIGH, NC 27606

The person who owns the dog at the time this
application is submitted to the AKC has the right
to name it. Names are subject to AKC approval. DO NOT use a
number as part of a name. AKC may assign a number suffix. Names
should be unique.

**DOG'S NAME**

## AKC DOG REGISTRATION APPLICATION

DO NOT WRITE IN SPACE ABOVE

| Y | A | N | K | E | E | | D | O | O | D | L | E | | D | A | N | D | Y | | | |

Select an **unusual** name. Limit name to one letter per box. Skip a box between words.
— SEE REVERSE SIDE FOR BALANCE OF APPLICATION —

BB 108

I hereby give permission to use my AKC registered Kennel Name

IN NAMING

SIGNATURE OF OWNER OF KENNEL NAME

THIS DOG

BREED **LABRADOR RETRIEVER**
SIRE **FLD CH BLACK BART**  SE654321  (6–86)

DAM **SUSIE CUE**  SM069393/02  (11–91)

BREEDER **JOHN Q PUBLIC**

LITTER OWNER
**JOHN Q PUBLIC**
**123 W MAIN ST**
**ELMHURST, MO  63749**

**DATE OF BIRTH**
**JULY 13 1991**

AUG 9 1991
ISSUED

**NOT VALID AFTER**
**ONE YEAR FROM**
**DATE ISSUED**
© 1990 The American Kennel Club, Inc.

LITTER NUMBER  **SM123321/01**

Owner of litter
must insert **DOG'S SEX**  ► MALE

**COLOR**
▼
CIRCLE the COLOR which best describes the dog.

(007)  **BLACK**
071  **CHOCOLATE**
232  **YELLOW**

THE AKC RESERVES THE RIGHT TO CORRECT OR REVOKE FOR CAUSE ANY REGISTRATION CERTIFICATE ISSUED. ANY MISREPRESENTATION ON THIS APPLICATION IS CAUSE FOR
CANCELLATION AND MAY RESULT IN LOSS OF ALL AKC PRIVILEGES FOR THOSE INDIVIDUALS WHO VIOLATE THE INTEGRITY OF THIS APPLICATION.
• IF NOT USED INDICATE SEX ABOVE AND RETURN TO AKC WITH EXPLANATION •

The individual registration application, properly filled out on front and back, covering
the transfer of ownership from a puppy's breeder to its new owner.

INSTRUCTIONS: PLEASE TYPE — OR USE PEN. **NO PENCIL**. Erasures or Corrections may cause return of application for an explanation.

**SEC. A.** TO BE COMPLETED IN FULL AND SIGNED BY OWNER OF LITTER (AND CO-OWNERS, IF ANY)

**Check one**
**and only**
**one box**

1 ☐ I (we) still own this dog, and I (we) apply for a LIMITED REGISTRATION—OFFSPRING WILL NOT BE ELIGIBLE FOR REGISTRATION
and to have ownership recorded in my (our) name(s).

2 ☐ I (we) still own this dog, and I (we) apply for full registration and to have ownership recorded in my (our) name(s).

3 ☒ I (we) certify that this dog was transferred DIRECTLY TO THE FOLLOWING PERSON(S) ON  | 10 - 22 - 91 |
mo.  day  year

MUST be
filled in
by owner(s)
of Litter

PRINT NAME(S) OF PERSON(S) TO WHOM
DOG WAS DIRECTLY TRANSFERRED  SUE SMITH

ADDRESS  631 N. HARRISON , KIRKWOOD, MO 63122

I CERTIFY, BY MY SIGNATURE, THAT I AM IN GOOD STANDING WITH THE AMERICAN KENNEL CLUB.

Signature  John Q Public
OWNER OF LITTER AT BIRTH

Signature
CO-OWNER (IF ANY) OF LITTER AT BIRTH

**SEC. B.** TO BE COMPLETED and SIGNED BY THE PERSON(S) NAMED IN SEC. A ABOVE, PROVIDED the person(s) owns the dog at the time this application is submitted to the A.K.C. If the person(s)
named in SEC. A has transferred the dog to some other person(s), obtain a Supplemental Transfer Statement form from the A.K.C. Instructions for its completion and use are on the form.

I apply to The American Kennel Club to have Registration Certificate for this dog issued in my/our name(s), and certify that I/we acquired it on the date set forth above DIRECTLY from the person(s)
who signed Sec. A above, and that I/we still own this dog. I agree to abide by American Kennel Club rules and regulations.

New Owner's
Signature  Sue Smith

New Co-Owner's
Signature

**New owner**
**must complete**
**this Section**

PRINT

Name  SUE SMITH
Address  631 N. HARRISON
City  KIRKWOOD  State  MO  Zip 63122

Complete
only if
co-owner
is named
in Section A

PRINT

Name
Address
City  State  Zip

Fees must accompany application. See top left corner of the reverse side for the required fees. Make checks payable to the American
Kennel Club — DO NOT SEND CASH. Application becomes the property of the American Kennel Club when submitted.

## SUPPLEMENTAL TRANSFER STATEMENT
### NOT VALID unless attached to the AKC Dog Registration Application

SEC. A MUST BE COMPLETED AND SIGNED PERSONALLY BY PERSON OR PERSONS WHO TRANSFER THE DOG.*

I certify that on (month) 10 (day) 31 (year) 91 I delivered or shipped the (breed) Labrador Retriever

DO NOT WRITE IN SPACE ABOVE

**INVALID IF SIGNED IN BLANK**

(sex) M (color and markings) BIK from litter No. SM123321/01 DIRECTLY TO:

PRINT NAME(S) MARY JONES

ADDRESS 3 MAIN ST KIRKWOOD, MO

I CERTIFY, BY MY SIGNATURE, THAT I AM IN GOOD STANDING WITH THE AMERICAN KENNEL CLUB.

SIGNED *Sue Smith* SIGNED _____

FORMER OWNER – PERSON TRANSFERRING DOG          FORMER CO-OWNER (if any)

SEC. B MUST BE COMPLETED AND SIGNED PERSONALLY BY NEW OWNER (AND NEW CO-OWNER, IF ANY) NAMED IN SEC. A ABOVE, provided he still owns the dog and wants registration certificate issued in his name. If the dog has again been transferred, do not use this Sec. B, but make out Sec. A on another of these forms.

I apply to The American Kennel Club to have Registration Certificate for this dog issued in my/our name(s), and certify that I/we acquired it on the date set forth above DIRECTLY from the person(s) who Signed Sec. A above, and that I/we still own this dog. I agree to abide by the American Kennel Club rules and regulations.

New owner's personal signature *Mary Jones*

New co-owner's signature if jointly owned _____

PRINT

Name MARY JONES

Address 3 MAIN ST.

City, State, Zip KIRKWOOD, MO 64541

Name _____

Address _____

City, State, Zip _____

*READ INSTRUCTIONS ON REVERSE SIDE

R 48-18 (2/91)

---

If, prior to registering the puppy in her own name, the new owner decides she doesn't want the puppy and transfers it to another person, a supplemental transfer statement must be completed and sent along with the original application. If the person who acquires the dog sends in these two forms to the American Kennel Club, along with the required fee, an individual registration certificate will be made out and issued in the name of the new owner.

---

## AMERICAN KENNEL CLUB

| | |
|---|---|
| NAME **YANKEE DOODLE DANDY** | No. SM123321/01 |
| BREED **LABRADOR RETRIEVER** (108) | SEX **MALE** |
| COLOR **BLACK** | DATE OF BIRTH **JULY 13 1991** |
| SIRE **FLD CH BLACK BART** SE654321 (6–86) | |
| DAM **SUSIE CUE** SM069393/02 (11–91) | |
| BREEDER **JOHN Q PUBLIC** | |
| OWNER **MARY JONES** 3 MAIN STREET KIRKWOOD, MO 64541 | CERTIFICATE ISSUED **DEC 1 1991** |

IF A DATE APPEARS AFTER THE NAME AND NUMBER OF THE SIRE AND DAM, IT INDICATES THE ISSUE OF THE STUD BOOK REGISTER IN WHICH THE SIRE OR DAM IS PUBLISHED.

THIS CERTIFICATE ISSUED WITH THE RIGHT TO CORRECT OR REVOKE BY THE AMERICAN KENNEL CLUB

See Transfer Instructions on Back of Certificate

### REGISTRATION CERTIFICATE

Beagle, Boston Terrier

Chesapeake Bay Retriever, Cocker Spaniel

Alaskan Malamute, Collie

Black and Tan Coonhound, American Foxhound

The four stamps shown here were designed by Roy Anderson, and issued by the United States Postal Service on September 7, 1984, in commemoration of the 100th anniversary of the American Kennel Club. This marked the first time that the Post Office has specifically honored the pure-bred dog on American stamps.

—Photo, copyright © United States Postal Service, 1984.

# The American Kennel Club

The American Kennel Club, established September 17, 1884, is a non-profit organization devoted to the advancement of pure-bred dogs. It maintains a registry of recognized breeds; adopts and enforces rules and regulations governing dog shows, obedience trials, and field trials; and fosters and encourages interest in, and the health and welfare of, pure-bred dogs.

The AKC does not have individual memberships. Rather, it is composed of almost 500 autonomous dog clubs throughout the United States. Each club exercises its voting privilege through a representative known as a "delegate." The delegates are the legislative body of the AKC, making the rules, and electing directors from among their number.

The Board of Directors, thus elected, is responsible for managing the AKC, appointing key staff, and making regulations and policies in conformity with the rules prescribed by the delegates.

The Stud Book, ancestry record of every dog that has been registered since the inception of the American Kennel Club, now represents an enrollment of more than 36,000,000 dogs, and about 1,250,000 new registrations are being added each year.

The American Kennel Club's main executive offices are located in New York City. Registration processing, related services, and data processing are located in Raleigh, North Carolina. In addition to the principal executive offices, the following departments are located at 51 Madison Avenue, New York, NY, 10010: Dog Events, Event Plans, Event Records, Performance Events, Judges, Clubs, the Inspection and Investigation Department, and the editorial and subscription fulfillment office of AKC's official magazine *Pure-Bred Dogs—American Kennel Gazette*.

Located in Raleigh are all registration functions including: Customer Service, Correspondence, and Certified Pedigrees. All inquiries concerning registration of a dog or litter should be directed to American Kennel Club, 5580 Centerview Drive, Raleigh, NC 27606.

The official magazine of the AKC, published monthly, is *Pure-Bred Dogs—American Kennel Gazette*. In addition to articles and photos of every phase of pure-bred dog interest, and news of the various breed clubs, each issue includes official notice of: all forthcoming events approved to be held under AKC rules; listing of all new champions and obedience degree winners; and all actions taken by the Club's Board of Directors. Official record of awards at AKC events is published in a separate monthly, *The American Kennel Club Show, Obedience and Field Trial Awards*.

At its headquarters in New York City, the American Kennel Club maintains a reference library of more than 15,000 volumes. One of the most complete collections of its kind in the world, the Library contains many rare, out-of-print editions (some published as early as 1576). It includes as well the works of modern authorities on the breeds, books and magazines in English and practically all foreign languages. On file are the stud books of many other accredited registration agencies here and abroad. Included in the Library's collection are famous prints and oil paintings by old masters and modern artists, as well as a unique file of pictures for the study of every known breed of dog. The public is invited to use the facilities of the Library, which is open for reference purposes Mondays through Fridays from 9 A.M. to 4 P.M.

The following booklets, covering AKC rules and regulations, are currently available upon written request to the American Kennel Club, 5580 Centerview Drive, Raleigh, NC 27606. There is no charge for individual copies, but when ordered in quantity there is a charge of 25 cents for each copy.

- Rules Applying to Registration and Dog Shows (E 37-17)
- Obedience Regulations (E 36-7)
- Registration and Field Trial Rules (S 55-9)
- Beagle Field Trial Rules (S 56-9)
- Basset Hound Field Trial Rules (S 56 A-9)
- Regulations for Junior Showmanship (E 76-5)
- Match Regulations (E 87)

Various information booklets are also available from AKC, free when ordered individually, but 50 cents each when ordered in quantity. Presently they include booklets on: The Formation of Dog Clubs, Guidelines for Dog Show Judges, Guidelines for Obedience Judges, The Status of a Judge of Licensed Field Trials, Dogs: General Information from the American Kennel Club, et al.

*The Complete Dog Book* is an official publication of the American Kennel Club. AKC also publishes a *Dog Care and Training* book in paperback (Howell Book House, $11.50). Other official publications available for purchase from the AKC include the monthlies, *Pure-Bred Dogs—American Kennel Gazette* ($4.75 a single copy, $28. a year) and *The American Kennel Club Show, Obedience and Field Trial Awards* ($6.50 a single copy, $40. a year). A special combination offer brings you both for $62. a year. Also published monthly is the Stud Book Register ($12.50 a copy, $75. a year). A directory of AKC judges is available for $5.

AKC also provides a certified pedigree service for all registered dogs: 3 generations, $15.; 4 generations, $25.

AKC offers an extensive series of videos, most of which are $35. Included are:

**Obedience**
- 200?
- *Exercise Finished*: A Day with an Obedience Judge

## General Interest

- *In the Ring with Mr. Wrong*
- *AKC and the Sport of Dogs*
- *The Quest for a Quality Dog Show*
- *Gait: Observing Dogs in Motion*
- *Dogsteps—A Study of Canine Structure and Movement* by Rachel Page Elliott, 1 hour and 9 minutes . . . $49.95. (*Dogsteps* also available in PAL for $100.)

## Hunting Tests

- *Love 'Em, Hunt 'Em, Test 'Em*: The AKC Hunting Tests for Retrievers
- *High on Hunting Spaniels*: The AKC Hunting Tests for Flushing Spaniels
- *The Point Is*: The AKC Hunting Tests for Pointing Breeds

## Field Trials

- *Carrying the Line*: A Look at Beagle Field Trials
- *With Courage and Style*: The Field Trial Retriever

AKC has produced educational videos on almost all registered breeds:

- Brittany
- Pointer
- German Shorthaired Pointer
- German Wirehaired Pointer
- Chesapeake Bay Retriever
- Curly-Coated Retriever
- Flat-Coated Retriever
- Golden Retriever
- Labrador Retriever
- English Setter
- Gordon Setter
- Irish Setter
- American Water Spaniel
- Clumber Spaniel
- Cocker Spaniel
- English Cocker Spaniel
- English Springer Spaniel
- Field Spaniel
- Irish Water Spaniel
- Sussex Spaniel
- Welsh Springer Spaniel
- Vizela
- Weimaraner

- Afghan Hound
- Basenji
- Basset Hound
- Beagle
- Black and Tan Coonhound
- Bloodhound
- Borzoi
- Dachshund
- Greyhound
- Ibizan Hound
- Norwegian Elkhound
- Otterhound
- Pharaoh Hound
- Rhodesian Ridgeback
- Saluki
- Scottish Deerhound
- Whippet

- Akita
- Alaskan Malamute
- Bernese Mountain Dog
- Boxer
- Bullmastiff
- Doberman Pinscher

- Giant Schnauzer
- Great Dane
- Great Pyrenees
- Komondor
- Kuvasz
- Mastiff
- Newfoundland
- Portuguese Water Dog
- Rottweiler
- Saint Bernard
- Samoyed
- Siberian Husky
- Standard Schnauzer

- Airedale Terrier
- American Staffordshire Terrier
- Australian Terrier
- Bedlington Terrier
- Border Terrier
- Bull Terrier
- Cairn Terrier
- Dandie Dinmont Terrier
- Smooth Fox Terrier
- Wire Fox Terrier

- Irish Terrier
- Kerry Blue Terrier
- Lakeland Terrier
- Manchester Terrier
- Miniature Schnauzer
- Norfolk Terrier
- Norwich Terrier
- Scottish Terrier
- Sealyham Terrier
- Skye Terrier
- Smooth Fox Terrier
- Soft Coated Wheaten Terrier
- Staffordshire Bull Terrier
- Welsh Terrier
- West Highland White Terrier
- Wire Fox Terrier

- Affenpinscher
- Brussels Griffon

- Chihuahua
- Chinese Crested
- English Toy Spaniel
- Italian Greyhound
- Maltese
- Miniature Pinscher
- Papillon
- Pekingese
- Pomeranian
- Pug
- Shih Tzu
- Silky Terrier
- Yorkshire Terrier

- Bichon Frise
- Boston Terrier
- Bulldog
- Chow Chow
- Dalmation
- Finnish Spitz
- French Bulldog

- Keeshound
- Lhasa Apso
- Poodle
- Schipperke
- Tibetan Spaniel
- Tibetan Terrier

- Australian Cattle Dog
- Bearded Collie
- Belgian Sheepdog
- Belgian Tervuren
- Bouvier des Flandres
- Briard
- Cardigan Welsh Corgi
- Collie
- German Shepherd Dog
- Old English Sheepdog
- Pembroke Welsh Corgi
- Puli
- Shetland Sheepdog

Videos may be ordered by sending a check to the American Kennel Club, Attention Videos, 51 Madison Avenue, New York, NY 10010. Videos may also be ordered by phone charge at 212-696-8392.

## Clubs

No matter what your interest in dogs, the chances are good that there's a dog club near you where you can meet people who share your interests. Believe it or not, at latest count in early 1991, there were more than 4,000 different dog clubs in the United States which are holding events under AKC *Rules* and *Regulations.* So the odds are there's a club near you.

AKC recognizes nine different types of clubs: All-breed clubs, specialty (breed) clubs, obedience clubs, tracking clubs, field trial clubs, hunting test clubs, herding clubs, coonhound clubs, and lure coursing clubs.

The largest group of clubs is the specialty or breed clubs. There are more than 1,700 specialty clubs in the United States. There are two types of specialty clubs. The first is the national (or parent) breed club—an example would be the Golden Retriever Club of America. AKC only recognizes one club as the national or parent breed club for each recognized breed. The second type of specialty (breed) club is the local specialty; for example, the Golden Retriever Club of Greater Los Angeles or the Kansas City Golden Retriever Club.

It is this extensive network of serious fanciers of the respective breeds that you should be contacting to help you choose your dog. You may obtain detailed information about the clubs nearest you by contacting AKC Customer Service, 5580 Centerview Drive, Raleigh, NC 27606, phone number 919-233-9767.

## The Dog Museum

The tradition of the dog in art dates back thousands of years; there is now a substantial and distinguished body of books and art on canine themes. In order to broaden public appreciation of these treasures, in June 1980 the American Kennel Club established the American Kennel Club Foundation, the primary goal of which was to set up a national repository for books and art objects relating to the dog. The Foundation moved quickly toward the establishment of The Dog Museum of America, the first public repository for the display and study of canine art. The Museum formally opened, in space provided for it by AKC, in September 1982.

Renamed the Dog Museum, and relocated to St. Louis, Missouri in Queeny Park, the museum opened to the public in its permanent home in historic Jarville House in 1987.

The museum is open Tuesday–Saturday 9:00 AM – 5:00 PM and Sunday from Noon to 5:00 PM. It is closed Mondays and holidays.

Judging of the preliminary heats at the American Kennel Club's first National Invitational Dog Championship, which was broadcast on network television in April 1992.

# The Dog Sport

The American Kennel Club was founded in 1884 by amateur sportsmen interested in establishing a uniform set of rules for the holding of dog shows. From that day to this the Board of Directors, responsible for the operation of AKC, has been made up of dedicated amateur sportsmen.

Each year, more than 10,000 competitive events are held under American Kennel Club rules. These competitions fall into three categories: dog shows, field trials, and obedience trials. In each of these categories, there are formal "licensed" events ("point shows" at which championship points or credit toward field or obedience titles may be earned) and informal events ("match shows" at which no points or credits are earned.)

## Dog Shows

Most numerous of the competitive events held under AKC rules are dog shows. At these, the accent is on *conformation*. Judges examine the dogs and place them in accordance with how close (in the judge's opinion) they measure up to the ideal called for in the official standards of their breeds—the standards published in this book.

There are two types of conformation dog shows—specialty and all-breed. Specialty shows are limited to dogs of a designated breed or grouping of breeds; for example, the Poodle Club of America Specialty is for Poodles only. All-breed shows, as the name indicates, are for all-breeds.

The shows held under AKC rules are put on by individual clubs; the specialty shows by breed clubs, and the all-breed shows by all-breed clubs.

For each breed recognized by AKC, there is a national parent club. In addition to the parent club, many breeds have local specialty clubs serving specific geographical areas.

The parent clubs have a unique and vital responsibility. They are the custodians of the official standards of their breeds. Any revision, clarification or addition to a breed standard must come through the parent club. Only after such changes have been approved by the parent club's membership can they be submitted to the AKC's Board of Directors for final approval.

The standard is, or course, the official guide by which dogs are judged at dog shows. In August 1987, the Board of Directors of the American Kennel Club approved a program to improve standards. The program had three goals:

1. *To have all standards follow a consistent format for order.*
2. *To be certain standards are complete on the basics.*
3. *To make certain terminology is correctly used.*

The standard format contains ten major headings and a few required subheads. The format is:

I. **General Appearance**
II. **Size, Proportion, Substance**
III. **Head**
   *Expression*
      *Eyes*
      *Ears*
   *Skull*
   *Muzzle*
   *Bite*
IV. **Neck, Topline, Body,**
   *Neck*
   *Topline*
   *Body*
   *Tail*
V. **Forequarters**
VI. **Hindquarters**
VII. **Coat**
VIII. **Color**
IX. **Gait**
X. **Temperament**

Judging at a conformation show is a process of elimination that ultimately results in one dog being selected as Best of Breed; if it's an all-breed show, further eliminations climax with one dog being selected Best in Show.

Most dogs in competition at conformation shows are competing for points toward their championship. To become an official American Kennel Club champion of record, a dog must earn fifteen points. Essentially, these points are based upon the number of dogs in actual competition—the more dogs, the more points. However, the number of dogs required for points varies with the breed, its sex, and the geographical location of the show in accordance with a schedule annually set up by AKC to help equalize competition from breed to breed and area to area.

A dog can earn from one to five points at a show. Wins of three, four or five points are termed "majors." The fifteen points required for championship must be won under at least three different judges, and must include two majors won under different judges.

At a show there are five regular classes in which dogs seeking points compete. (Dogs competing for points are frequently referred to as "class dogs.") These classes are:

Puppy—frequently subdivided into *Puppies—6 to 9 months* and *Puppies—9 · to 12 months*
*Novice*
*Bred-by-Exhibitor*
*American-Bred*
*Open*

Only one male and one female of each breed can win points at each show—as we shall see. There is no intersex competition in these classes—the dogs (males) compete against other dogs, and the bitches (females) against other bitches.

Judging in every breed is the same. The judge begins with the Puppy dog class. In each class the dogs are evaluated and the prime four are placed First, Second, Third and Fourth. However, only the first place winner in each class remains in competition—the others are eliminated.

After the judge has judged the Puppy dogs, Novice dogs, Bred-by-Exhibitor dogs, American-Bred dogs and Open dogs, the winners (first place) from each class are brought back to compete against each other. This is called the Winners class. The dog selected best is the Winners Dog. He is the male who receives the points at the show.

Following selection of the Winners Dog, the dog that placed second to him in his original class of competition is brought into the ring to compete with the other class winners for Reserve Winners Dog. The Reserve will receive the points if for any reason the Winner's win is disallowed by AKC.

The same process is repeated in bitches, with a Winners Bitch—the only bitch of the breed to receive points at the show—and a Reserve Winners Bitch being selected.

The judge must now judge one more class and make three more awards. The Best of Breed class has in it all the champions of record competing, male and female, and the Winners Dog and Winners Bitch. The judge goes over all the dogs and selects one Best of Breed. Then, between the Winners Dog and Winners Bitch, the judge selects a Best of Winners. If either the Winners Dog or Winners Bitch is selected Best of Breed, it automatically, of course, becomes Best of Winners. (If the points at the show for the defeated Winner were higher than those of the Best of Winners, the latter now gets the same higher total.) The judge then finishes the breed judging by selecting a Best of Opposite Sex to the Best of Breed.

At an all-breed show, this same process of elimination takes place in every breed. Then each Best of Breed winner competes in its group (see Contents pages for listing of dogs by groups.) Four placements are awarded in each group, but only the first place winner remains in competition. Finally the seven group

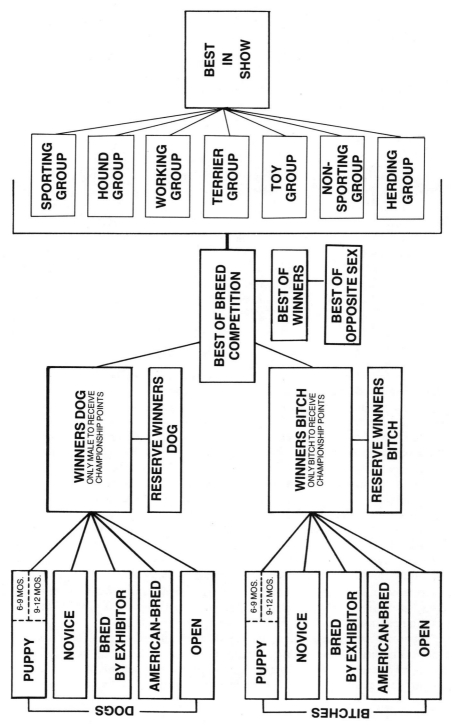

winners are brought into the ring and a Best in Show winner is selected. At the largest all-breed shows nearly 4,000 contestants are narrowed down to the Best in Show winner in the course of one day's judging.

## Canine Good Citizens

The American Kennel Club sponsors a program administered by dog clubs throughout the United States to encourage all dog owners to train their dogs. The program is called the Canine Good Citizen.

In it, dog owners have their dogs evaluated on a pass/fail basis for ten different activities that a good canine citizen would be expected to be capable of performing. Dogs who pass are awarded a Canine Good Citizen Certificate.

Included are such things as allowing a stranger to approach, walking naturally on a loose lead, walking through a crowd, sitting for examination, reacting to a strange dog and reacting to a distraction such as a door suddenly closing or a jogger running by the dog.

When you've got your boisterous pup in shape you might want to try a Canine Good Citizen test. Look for notices in your local paper or contact the AKC for the name of the club nearest you that sponsors these evaluations. And for those of you who would like to try actual Obedience competition, there are thousands of Obedience Trials held each year by AKC clubs.

## Obedience Trials

Obedience trials are tests of man and dog. In obedience, the dog must perform a prescribed set of exercises which the judge grades or—as it is called by obedience enthusiasts—scores. The dog's conformation has no bearing on its being able to compete in obedience. Dogs that would be disqualified from the show ring under a breed standard, even spayed bitches and neutered dogs, may compete in obedience trials.

Obedience is divided into three levels, each more difficult than the preceding one. At each level a competitor is working for an AKC obedience degree or title. The three levels and titles are: *Novice*—Companion Dog (C.D.); *Open*—Companion Dog Excellent (C.D.X.); and *Utility*—Utility Dog (U.D.).

*Novice* work embraces the basics that all dogs should be taught to make them good companions. The six exercises in Novice work are: heel on leash, stand for examination, heel free, recall, long sit, long down. *Open* work consists of seven exercises: heel free, drop on recall, retrieve on flat, retrieve over the high jump, broad jump, long sit, and long down. *Utility* work consists of: signal exercise, two scent discrimination tests, directed retrieve, directed jumping and group examination.

To receive an obedience title a dog must earn three "legs." To get credit for a leg, a dog must score at least 170 points out of a possible 200 (the passing score and grand total are the same at each level, although the exercises vary), and get more than fifty percent on each exercise.

**Three phases of the great sport of dogs:** *Above:* **Final judging at a large show.** *Opposite,* *top:* **An Old English Sheepdog competing in Obedience.** *Opposite, below:* **Competing at a National Open championship field trial.** *—Photos by Gilbert, Abrams and Shafer.*

Only dogs that have earned the Utility Dog title can earn points toward an Obedience Trial Championship. Championship points are recorded for dogs earning a First or Second place in Open B or Utility Class (or Utility B, if divided) according to the schedule of points established by the AKC Board of Directors. To become an Obedience Trial Champion a dog must win 100 points that include a First place in Utility (or Utility B, if divided) with at least 3 dogs in competition, a First place in Open B with at least 6 dogs in competition, and a third First place in either of these competitions. The three First places must be won under three different judges.

### Tracking

Tracking tests, held under AKC regulations, require a dog to follow a trail by scent. A dog passing such a test earns a Tracking Dog title (TD). Mastery of a more advanced test entitles a dog to use the letters TDX for Tracking Dog Excellent after its name.

### Field Trials and Hunting Tests

Field trials are held separately for pointing breeds, retrievers and spaniels, as well as Beagles, Basset Hounds and Dachshunds. Field trials are practical demonstrations of the dog's ability to perform, in the field, the functions for which they were bred. The titles that are awarded are Field Champion and Amateur Field Champion.

Retrievers, pointing breeds and spaniels are also eligible to participate in Hunting tests. Here, owners of these breeds can obtain an evaluation of their dogs' hunting ability. A dog's performance is evaluated at three levels, and again, each succeeding level is increasingly difficult. Dogs successfully completing the respective levels earn the titles Junior Hunter, Senior Hunter and Master Hunter.

### Herding

The herding program is divided into Testing and Trial sections.

In the Testing section, dogs can earn the titles of Herding Test Dog (HT) and Pre-Trial Tested Dog (PT). The former is awarded to dogs that show an inherent herding ability and are trainable in herding. The PT title, on the other hand, is earned by dogs with some training in herding, and can, therefore, herd a small group of livestock through a simple course.

Trials offer four titles, beginning with the Herding Started (HS), Herding Intermediate (HI), and Herding Excellent (HX) titles. After earning an HX, dogs can then accumulate the necessary fifteen championship points for the Herding Championship (HCH). Such a dog is proficient in herding and capable of controlling even the most difficult livestock in diverse situations. The trials are run on three distinct courses, which differ in both physical appearance and style of herding.

**Pembroke Welsh Corgi herding sheep.** —*Callea Photo*

**Lure coursing, an activity filled with excitement, is based on the ancient function of the sighthounds.** —*Photo, Debbie Strzelecki*

## Lure Coursing

Like the herding program, Lure Coursing is new to the family of AKC performance events, becoming an official program in 1991.

Lure coursing is to sighthounds what field trials are to scent hounds and sporting breeds: the chance for dogs to prove themselves at what they were originally bred to do. For the sighthounds, this means running down their fleet-footed prey, sometimes over great distances.

In a lure coursing event the hounds chase a lure of three plastic bags, white or black. The hounds are judged in five categories: overall ability, follow, speed, agility, and endurance. Hounds earn title of Junior Courser (JC) Senior Courser (SC), and Field Champion (FC).

## Junior Showmanship

A club that is approved to hold a licensed or member all-breed show or a specialty show held apart from an all-breed show, may also be approved to offer Junior Showmanship competition at its show.

Junior Showmanship is judged solely on the ability and skill of the handler. Dogs are handled as in the breed ring although the dog's conformation should not be considered by the judge. Dogs entered in this competition must also be eligible to compete in dog shows or obedience trials.

Junior Showmanship is usually divided by class, age and occasionally by sex. Competition is for Juniors 10 through 16 years inclusive. The Novice class is for those who have not won three (3) first place awards in that class and the Open class is for those who have won three (3) first place awards in the Novice class.

## Titles

Dogs compete in the various competitions offered under the *Rules* and *Regulations* of the American Kennel Club for 22 different titles. When a dog completes the requirements for one of the titles, official note of the title is made on the dog's AKC records. Thereafter the notation of title will always appear with the dog's name in AKC's records. Seven of the titles are indicated before the dog's name (prefixes), and 15 appear after the dog's name (suffixes). The titles and their abbreviations are:

## Breed, Obedience, Herding and Lure Coursing Titles (Prefixes)

| | |
|---|---|
| CH | Champion |
| FC | Field Champion (Field Trial/Lure Coursing) |
| AFC | Amateur Field Champion |
| OTCH | Obedience Trial Champion |
| HCH | Herding Champion |
| DC | Dual Champion (CH & FC) |
| TC | Triple Champion (CH, FC, & OTCH) |

## Obedience, Hunting and Herding and Lure Coursing Titles (Suffixes)

| | | | |
|---|---|---|---|
| CD | Companion Dog | HT | Herding Tested |
| CDX | Companion Dog Excellent | PT | Pre-Trial Tested |
| UD | Utility Dog | HS | Herding Started |
| TD | Tracking Dog | HI | Herding Intermediate |
| TDX | Tracking Dog Excellent | HX | Herding Excellent |
| JH | Junior Hunter | JC | Junior Courser |
| SH | Senior Hunter | SC | Senior Courser |
| MH | Master Hunter | | |

# The Dog's Anatomy

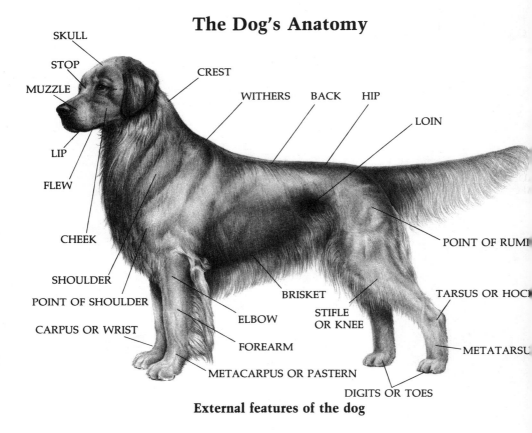

SKULL

STOP

MUZZLE

CREST

WITHERS    BACK    HIP

LOIN

LIP

FLEW

CHEEK

POINT OF RUMI

SHOULDER

POINT OF SHOULDER

BRISKET

TARSUS OR HOC

CARPUS OR WRIST

ELBOW

STIFLE
OR KNEE

FOREARM

METATARSU

METACARPUS OR PASTERN

DIGITS OR TOES

**External features of the dog**

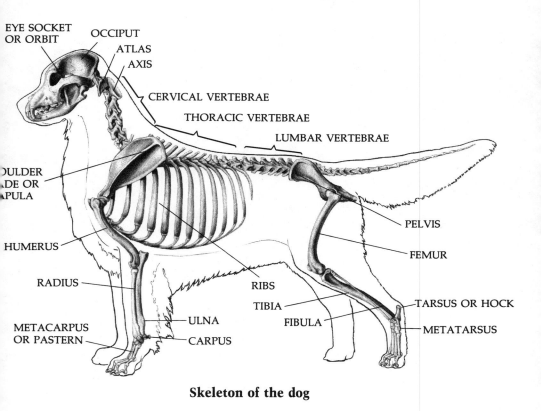

EYE SOCKET OR ORBIT
OCCIPUT
ATLAS
AXIS
CERVICAL VERTEBRAE
THORACIC VERTEBRAE
LUMBAR VERTEBRAE
SHOULDER BLADE OR SCAPULA
HUMERUS
RADIUS
METACARPUS OR PASTERN
ULNA
CARPUS
RIBS
TIBIA
FIBULA
PELVIS
FEMUR
TARSUS OR HOCK
METATARSUS

**Skeleton of the dog**

*A glossary of dog terminology, with some illustrative drawings, is presented on pages 655 to 683. Drawings by Stephen J. Hubbell*

**The English Setter, ADONIS
No. 1 in the American Kennel Club stud book**

*—Courtesy, New Bedford Standard-Times*

Records of breedings of dogs in the United States existed long before the American Kennel Club was founded in 1884, but these were mainly private records kept by individuals. In 1876, Arnold Burges, a well known sportsman and editor of *The American Sportsman*, published a book called "The American Kennel and Sporting Field" which included pedigrees for 332 dogs as well as reports of early shows and field trials. In Chicago, the National American Kennel Club published the first volume of its stud book in 1878. In 1885 Volume II was published by Dr. N. Rowe for the Club and in 1886 Volume III was published by him as an individual at his own expense. Another stud book was issued by Forest and Stream Publishing as the "American Kennel Register" in April 1883.

Two years after its formation, AKC decided that a reliable record of pedigrees was vital to the advancement of the sport of pure-bred dogs and negotiated with the two existing stud books. The American Kennel Register declined to sell or transfer its records to AKC, but Dr. Rowe was amenable and handed over his three volumes listing 5,397 dogs. Adonis, pictured here, had the honor of being dog number I, since his name came first alphabetically. (Adonis also appears first in Burges' list but with a different dam.) These first three volumes were accepted by AKC as the basis for its Stud Book Register, which has been published continuously since 1887.

# THE BREEDS

## Histories and Official Standards

$A$ll of the breeds currently recognized for registration by the American Kennel Club are presented here in the order (within their Groups) in which they appear in the dog show catalogs. A photograph, brief history and the official AKC standard is included for each breed.

In most instances the information for the histories has been provided by the parent club of the breed. For the benefit of those unacquainted with dog shows, it should be explained that the official standard for each breed, or revision of the standard, originates with the parent club and not—as many suppose—with the American Kennel Club. The membership of the parent club must approve the standard or revision by vote, and only then can it be submitted to the Board of Directors of the American Kennel Club for approval.

The standard portrays what, in the minds of compilers, would be the ideal dog of the breed. Ideal in type, in structure, in gait, in temperament—ideal in every aspect. Thus, the standard is not the representation of any actual dog, but a concept. It is against this concept that a dog show judge must measure every competitor of that breed. The dog most closely approaching that ideal in the judge's determination, is the dog that wins.

The date shown at end of each standard represents the date of approval of the latest revision. (Where no date is shown, it indicates that there has been no change in the standard since the first printing of *The Complete Dog Book* in 1929.)

The pictures presented are intended primarily as an aid for the novice. Much care has been taken to select photographs that do credit to the breeds—in many instances the picture has been provided by the parent club—but it should not be inferred that the dogs pictured are perfect depictions of their standards or entirely without fault. Rarely indeed, even when we include the immortals, is there a dog that measures up 100% to every specification of its standard.

A complete list of the breeds in Group order is included in the Contents; a listing in alphabetical order is provided in the presentation of First Registrations starting on 30.

# Disqualifications Applying to All Breeds

For convenience in consulting the standards, the disqualifications (for show purposes) specified within a breed standard are presented in italicized type at the end of the particular standard. It should be noted however, that in addition to these disqualifications, there are the following disqualifications that apply to ALL BREEDS:

*A dog which is blind, deaf, castrated, spayed, or which has been changed in appearance by artificial means except as specified in the standard for its breed, or a male which does not have two normal testicles normally located in the scrotum, may not compete at any show and will be disqualified except that a castrated male may be entered in the Veteran Dog Class or as stud dog in the Stud Dog Class, and a spayed bitch may be entered in the Veteran Bitch Class or as brood bitch in the Brood Bitch Class. Neutered dogs and spayed bitches would be allowed to compete in Veterans Classes only at independent specialties and/or those all-breed shows which do not offer any competitive classes beyond Best of Breed. A dog will not be considered to have been changed by artificial means because of removal of dewclaws or docking of a tail, if it is a breed in which such removal or docking is a regularly approved practice which is not contrary to the standard. (Note: Spayed bitches and monorchid or cryptorchid dogs may compete in obedience trials.)*

*A dog that is lame at any show may not compete and shall not receive any award at the show. It shall be the judge's responsibility to determine whether the dog is lame.*

*No dog shall be eligible to compete at any show, and no dog shall receive any award at any show in the event the natural color or shade of natural color, or the natural markings of the dog, have been altered or changed by the use of any substance, whether such substance has been used for cleaning purposes or for any other reason. Such cleaning substances are to be removed before the dog enters the ring.*

*Any dog whose ears have been cropped or cut in any way shall be ineligible to compete at any show in any state where the laws prohibit the same, except subject to the provisions of such laws.*

*No dog shall be eligible to compete at any show, no dog shall be brought into the grounds or premises of any dog show, and any dog which may have been brought into the grounds or premises of a dog show shall immediately be removed, if it:*

*(a)* shows clinical symptoms of distemper, infectious hepatitis, leptospirosis or other communicable disease, or

*(b)* is known to have been in contact with distemper, infectious hepatitis, leptospirosis or other communicable disease within thirty days prior to the opening of the show, or

*(c)* has been kenneled within thirty days prior to the opening of the show on premises on which there existed distemper, infectious hepatitis, leptospirosis, or other communicable disease.

## YEAR EACH BREED WAS FIRST REGISTERED BY THE AKC, AND NAME AND NUMBER OF FIRST DOG

| BREED | YEAR | NAME AND NUMBER OF FIRST DOG |
|---|---|---|
| Affenpinscher | 1936 | Nollie v Anwander A-107711 |
| Afghan Hound | 1926 | Tezin 544928 |
| Airedale Terrier | 1888 | Pin 9087 |
| Akita | 1972 | Akita Tani's Terukoshi WC-292650 |
| Alaskan Malamute | 1935 | Rowdy of Nome 998426 |
| American Staffordshire Terrier | 1936 | Wheeler's Black Dinah A-86066 |
| Australian Cattle Dog | 1980 | Glen Iris Boomerang, C.D.X. WE-507650 |
| Australian Terrier | 1960 | Canberra Kookaburra R-258126 |
| Basenji | 1944 | Phemister's Bois A-738970 |
| Basset Hound | 1885 | Bouncer 3234 |
| Beagle | 1885 | Blunder 3188 |
| Bearded Collie | 1976 | Cannamoor Cartinka WD-439250 |
| Bedlington Terrier | 1886 | Ananian 4475 |
| Belgian Malinois (*Registered as Belgian Sheepdog until 1959*) | | |
| Belgian Sheepdog | 1912 | Rumford Dax 160405 |
| Belgian Tervuren (*Registered as Belgian Sheepdog until 1959*) | | |
| Bernese Mountain Dog | 1937 | Quell v Tiergarten A-156752 |
| Bichon Frise | 1972 | Sha-Bob's Nice Girl Missy NS-077900 |
| Black and Tan Coonhound | 1945 | Grand Mere Big Rock Molly A-898800 |
| Bloodhound | 1885 | Carsdoc 3237 |
| Border Terrier | 1930 | Netherbyers Ricky 719372 |
| Borzoi | 1891 | Princess Irma 20716 (*Originally registered as Russian Wolfhound*) |
| Boston Terrier | 1893 | Hector 28814 |
| Bouvier des Flandres | 1931 | Hardix 780160 |
| Boxer | 1904 | Arnulf Grandenz 78043 |
| Briard | 1928 | Dauphine de Montjoye 635613 |
| Brittany (*Registered as Spaniel (Brittany) until September 1982*) | 1934 | Edir du Mesnil 949896 |
| Brussels Griffon | 1910 | Dolley's Biddy 137219 |
| Bulldog | 1886 | Bob 4982 |
| Bullmastiff | 1934 | Fascination of Felons Fear 914895 |
| Bull Terrier | 1885 | Nellie II 3308 |
| Cairn Terrier | 1913 | Sandy Peter out of the West 173555 |
| Chihuahua | 1904 | Midget 82291 |
| Chinese Crested | 1991 | Maya of Rivercrest D 413100 |
| Chinese Shar Pei | | |
| Chow Chow | 1903 | Yen How 74111 |
| Collie | 1885 | Black Shep 3249 |
| Dachshund | 1885 | Dash 3223 |

| BREED | YEAR | NAME AND NUMBER OF FIRST DOG |
|---|---|---|
| Dalmatian | 1888 | Bessie 10519 |
| Dandie Dinmont Terrier | 1886 | Bonnie Britton 4472 |
| Doberman Pinscher | 1908 | Doberman Intelectus 122650 |
| English Toy Spaniel | 1886 | Mildmay Park Beauty 4456 |
| Finnish Spitz | 1991 | Hammerfest's Loveable Sister D87106/01 |
| Foxhound (American) | 1886 | Lady Stewart 4320 |
| Foxhound (English) | 1909 | Auditor 129533 |
| Fox Terrier | 1885 | Cricket 3289 |
| French Bulldog | 1898 | Guguss II 49705 |
| German Shepherd Dog | 1908 | Queen of Switzerland 115006 |
| Giant Schnauzer | 1930 | Bella v Fuchspark Potzhauss 72173 |
| Great Dane | 1887 | Don Caesar 6046 |
| Great Pyrenees | 1933 | Blanchette 866751 |
| Greyhound | 1885 | Baron Walkeen 3241 |
| Harrier | 1885 | Jolly 3236 |
| Ibizan Hound | 1978 | Asuncion HC 522350 |
| Irish Terrier | 1885 | Aileen 3306 |
| Irish Wolfhound | 1897 | Ailbe 45994 |
| Italian Greyhound | 1886 | Lilly 4346 |
| Japanese Spaniel (name changed to Japanese Chin— 1977) | 1888 | Jap 9216 |
| Keeshond | 1930 | Bella v Trennfeld 751187 |
| Kerry Blue Terrier | 1922 | Brian of Muchia 349159 |
| Komondor | 1937 | Andrashazi Dorka A-199838 |
| Kuvasz | 1931 | Tamar v Wuermtal 791292 |
| Lakeland Terrier | 1934 | Egton What a Lad of Howtown 938424 |
| Lhasa Apso | 1935 | Empress of Kokonor 987979 |
| Maltese | 1888 | Topsy 12056 |
| Manchester Terrier | 1886 | Gypsy 4485 (Toy) |
| Mastiff | 1885 | Bayard 3271 |
| Miniature Bull Terrier | 1991 | Navigation Pinto RM023801 |
| Miniature Pinscher | 1925 | Asta von Sandreuth 454601 |
| Miniature Schnauzer | 1926 | Schnapp v Dornbusch of Hitofa 551063 |
| Newfoundland | 1886 | Fly 4447 |
| Norfolk Terrier (Registered as Norwich Terrier until 1979) | 1979 | Bar Sinister Little Ruffian RA475550 |
| Norwegian Elkhound | 1913 | Koik 170389 |
| Norwich Terrier | 1936 | Witherslack Sport A-58858 |
| Old English Sheepdog | 1888 | Champion of Winkleigh 9252 |
| Otter Hound | 1910 | Hartland Statesman 135334 |
| Papillon | 1915 | Joujou 192537 |
| Pekingese | 1906 | Rascal 95459 |
| Petit Basset Griffon Vendéen | 1990 | Axmos Babette de la Garonne HDB93000 |

| BREED | YEAR | NAME AND NUMBER OF FIRST DOG |
|---|---|---|
| Pharaoh Hound | 1983 | Fqira HD-027750 |
| Pointer | 1878 | Ace of Spades 1187 |
| Pointer (German Shorthaired) | 1930 | Greif v.d. Fliegerhalde 723642 |
| Pointer (German Wirehaired) | 1959 | Eiko vom Schultenhof S-963376 |
| Pomeranian | 1888 | Dick 10776 |
| Poodle | 1887 | Czar 7597 |
| Portuguese Water Dog | 1983 | Renascenca do Al-Gharb WF-382950 |
| Pug | 1885 | George 3286 |
| Puli | 1936 | Torokvesz Sarika A-107734 |
| Retriever (Chesapeake Bay) | 1878 | Sunday 1408 |
| Retriever (Curly-Coated) | 1924 | Knysna Conjurer 398399 |
| Retriever (Flat-Coated) | 1915 | Sand Bridge Jester 190223 |
| Retriever (Golden) | 1925 | Lomberdale Blondin 492685 |
| Retriever (Labrador) | 1917 | Brocklehirst Floss 223339 |
| Rhodesian Ridgeback | 1955 | Tchaika of Redhouse H-520551 |
| Rottweiler | 1931 | Stina v Felsenmeer 805867 |
| St. Bernard | 1885 | Chief 3280 |
| Saluki | 1929 | Jinniyat of Grevel 674570 |
| Samoyed | 1906 | Moustan of Argenteau 102896 |
| Schipperke | 1904 | Snowball 83461 |
| Scottish Deerhound | 1886 | Bonnie Robin 4345 |
| Scottish Terrier | 1885 | Prince Charlie 3310 |
| Sealyham Terrier | 1911 | Harfats Pride 151623 |
| Setter (English) | 1878 | Adonis #1 |
| Setter (Gordon) | 1878 | Bank 793 |
| Setter (Irish) | 1878 | Admiral 534 |
| Shetland Sheepdog | 1911 | Lord Scott 148760 |
| Shih Tzu | 1969 | Choo Lang of Telota TA-573228 |
| Siberian Husky | 1930 | Fairbanks Princess Chena 758529 |
| Silky Terrier | 1959 | Winsome Beau Ideal T-610051 |
| Skye Terrier | 1887 | Romach 6184 |
| Soft Coated Wheaten Terrier | 1973 | Holmenocks Gramachree C.D. RA-44600 |
| Spaniel (American Water) | 1940 | Tidewader Teddy A-426838 |
| Spaniel (Clumber) | 1878 | Bustler 1353 |
| Spaniel (Cocker) | 1878 | Capt 1354 |
| Spaniel (English Cocker) [*Separated from Spaniel (Cocker) in 1946*] | | |
| Spaniel (English Springer) | 1910 | Denne Lucy 142641 |
| Spaniel (Field) | 1894 | Colehill Rufus 33395 |
| Spaniel (Irish Water) | 1878 | Bob 1352 |
| Spaniel (Sussex) | 1878 | Jack (alias Toby) 1363 |
| Spaniel (Welsh Springer) | 1914 | Faircroft Bob 185938 |
| Staffordshire Bull Terrier | 1974 | Tinkinswood Imperial RA-161150 |
| Standard Schnauzer | 1904 | Norwood Victor 77886 |
| Tibetan Spaniel | 1983 | Tritou Charlotte NS-789150 |
| Tibetan Terrier | 1973 | Amanda Lamleh of Kalai NS-107000 |
| Vizsla | 1960 | Rex Z Arpadvar SA-63201 |

| BREED | YEAR | NAME AND NUMBER OF FIRST DOG |
|---|---|---|
| Weimaraner | 1943 | Adda v Schwarzen Kamp 646165 |
| Welsh Corgi (Cardigan) | 1935 | Blodwen of Robinscroft 965012 |
| Welsh Corgi (Pembroke) | 1934 | Little Madam 939536 |
| Welsh Terrier | 1888 | T'Other 9171 |
| West Highland White Terrier | 1908 | Talloch 116076 |
| Whippet | 1888 | Jack Dempsey 9804 |
| Wirehaired Pointing Griffon | 1887 | Zolette 6773 (*Russian Setter*) |
| Yorkshire Terrier | 1885 | Belle 3307 |

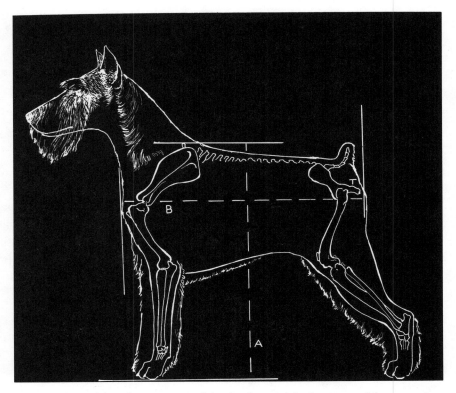

How height and length are measured in the dog. Height is measured from a point horizontal with the withers straight down to the ground (line A). Length is measured from point of shoulder to point of buttock (line B). *Reproduced by permission from "Illustrated Discussion of the Miniature Schnauzer Standard," drawing by Loraine L. Bush.*

# SPORTING DOGS

## Brittany

Named for the French province in which it originated, the Brittany was, from 1934 to 1982, registered by the American Kennel Club as the Spaniel, Brittany. Although until then called a spaniel, in its manner of working game the Brittany is setterlike. In appearance it is smaller than the setters but leggier than the spaniels, with a short tail and a characteristic high ear set. Effective September 1, 1982, its official AKC name was changed to Brittany.

While it is generally conceded that the basic stock for all bird dogs is the same, most of the actual facts concerning the development and spread of the various breeds are lost in antiquity. Early written records are confusing. Dogs are referred to as being of *Bretagne* or *Brittania*, which may have referred to the British Isles rather than the French province, for Brittany was called Armorique until the 5th century. Oppian, who lived about 150 A.D., wrote of the uncivilized people of Brittany (or Britain?) and reported that their dogs' scenting ability surpassed all others, a characteristic many present-day Brittanys retain.

It would seem probable that the dogs of Brittany and Wales had the same progenitors and developed along similar paths, quite possibly interbreeding. The two lands are geographically close and there was much commerce between them. One need only look at today's Welsh Springer and Brittany to recognize their similar physical characteristics.

The first accurate records to pinpoint the actual Brittany-type dog are the paintings and tapestries of the 17th century. The frequency with which this type appears suggests it was fairly common. Oudry (1686–1745) shows a liver and white dog pointing partridge and this same type of dog is common in the Flemish paintings of the school of Jan Steen. Other painters show this same type of dog, so it must have been common along the northern coast of France and in Holland, even stretching into Germany where it developed into the Wachtelhund, a modern breed much like the Brittany in appearance and ability.

Legend has it that the first tailless ancestor of the modern Brittany was bred about the mid-1800s at Pontou, a little town situated in the Valley of Douron, the result of a cross between a white-and-mahogany bitch owned by an old hunter of the region, and a lemon-and-white dog brought to Brittany by an English sportsman for the woodcock shooting. Of two tailless specimens produced in this litter, only one was considered worth keeping. His work in the field has been described as wonderful and because of it he became a popular stud. All his litters contained puppies either without tails or with short stubs.

There is nothing written before 1850 that can be interpreted unequivocally as referring to the Brittany. In that year the Reverend Davies wrote of hunting in Carhaix with small bob-tailed dogs not as smooth-coated as the Pointer, that worked well in the brush. They pointed, retrieved their game well and were particularly popular with poachers, as the nature of that profession required that the dogs be easy to handle. The description fits the Brittany to perfection.

It was speculated (and in at least one case confirmed) that matings of the native spaniels of Brittany were made around 1900 with English pointing dogs whose owners vacationed in France primarily for the woodcock shooting. These matings were believed to have been effective in intensifying the pointing qualities of the spaniel while the basic features of the dogs remained essentially Breton.

The Brittanys became a recognized breed when, in 1907, Boy, an orange-and-white, was registered as the first l'epagneul Breton (queue courte naturelle), a nomenclature that was soon shortened to simply l'epagneul Breton. Prior to this date, Brittanys had competed in classes for miscellaneous French Spaniels.

The first standard was outlined in 1907. This early standard required that the tail always be short at birth and that, in order to discourage further cross-breeding, black-and-white dogs be disqualified. The requirement for the natural bob-tail was soon dropped.

The breed was introduced into the United States in 1931 and officially recognized by the American Kennel Club in 1934. The first standard was a direct translation from the French and not particularly comprehensible. The first major accomplishment of the American Brittany Club upon its formation in 1942 was to replace the original standard with a clear and concise one.

The Brittany's steady gain in popularity in the United States has been due to its merits as a shooting dog. Its smaller size and natural proclivity for hunting close fill the need of the modern American bird hunter. Its superb nose and desire to please are two of its major assets. Its size makes it better adapted to city living than some of the larger bird dogs, and its close range makes it more adaptable to today's hunting areas, crisscrossed with numerous roads and fences.

Many American Brittany breeders have strived to maintain the dual concept, i.e. to breed a dog that is good looking as well as being a good hunter. The most popular formal competition has been in field trials, sponsored by the parent club and its many chapters. Interest in showing Brittanys was initially somewhat limited, but there has been an upsurge over recent years. In the first 30 years of competition in this country, over 150 dogs of the breed gained the coveted title of Dual Champion (a champion in both the field and show).

## Official Standard for the Brittany

**General Appearance**—A compact, closely knit dog of medium size, a leggy dog having the appearance, as well as the agility, of a great ground coverer. Strong, vigorous, energetic and quick of movement. Ruggedness, without clumsiness, is a characteristic of the breed. He can be tailless or has a tail docked to approximately four inches.

**Size, Proportion, Substance—***Height*—17½ to 20½ inches, measured from the ground to the highest point of the shoulders. Any Brittany measuring under 17½ inches or over 20½ inches shall be disqualified from dog show competition. *Weight*—Should weigh between 30 and 40 pounds. *Proportion*—So leggy is he that his height at the shoulders is the same as the length of his body. *Body Length*—Approximately the same as the height when measured at the shoulders. Body length is measured from the point of the forechest to the rear of the rump. A long body should be heavily penalized. *Substance*—Not too light in bone, yet never heavyboned and cumbersome.

**Head—***Expression*—Alert and eager, but with the soft expression of a bird dog. *Eyes*—Well set in head. Well protected from briars by a heavy, expressive eyebrow. A prominent, full or popeye should be heavily penalized. It is a serious fault in a dog that must face briars. Skull well chiseled under the eyes, so that the lower lid is not pulled back to form a pocket or haw that would catch seeds, dirt and weed dust. Preference should be for the darker colored eyes, though lighter shades of amber should not be penalized. Light and mean-looking eyes should be heavily penalized. *Ears*—Set high, above the level of the eyes. Short and triangular, rather than pendulous, reaching about half the length of the muzzle. Should lie flat and close to the head, with the tip rounded very slightly. Ears well covered with dense, but relatively short hair, and with little fringe. *Skull*—Medium length, rounded, very slightly wedge-shaped, but evenly made. Width, not quite as wide as the length and never so broad as to appear coarse, or so narrow as to appear racy. Well defined, but gently sloping stop. Median line rather indistinct. The occiput only apparent to the touch. Lateral walls well rounded. The Brittany should never be "appleheaded" and he should never have an indented stop. *Muzzle*—Medium length, about two thirds the length of the skull, measuring the muzzle from the tip to the stop, and the skull from the occiput to the stop. Muzzle should taper gradually in both horizontal and vertical dimensions as it approaches the nostrils. Neither a Roman nose nor a dish-face is desirable. Never broad, heavy or snipy. *Nose*—Nostrils well open to permit deep breathing of air and adequate scenting. Tight nostrils should be penalized. Never shiny. Color: fawn, tan, shades of brown or deep pink. A black nose is a disqualification. A two-tone or butterfly nose should be penalized. *Lips*—Tight, the upper lip overlapping the lower jaw just to cover the lower lip. Lips dry, so that feathers will not stick. Drooling to be heavily penalized. Flews to be penalized. *Bite*—A true scissors bite. Overshot or undershot jaw to be heavily penalized.

**Neck, Topline, Body**—*Neck*—Medium length. Free from throatiness, though not a serious fault unless accompanied by dewlaps, strong without giving the impression of being overmuscled. Well set into sloping shoulders. Never concave or ewe-necked. *Topline*—Slight slope from the highest point of the shoulders to the root of the tail. *Chest*—Deep, reaching the level of the elbow. Neither so wide nor so rounded as to disturb the placement of the shoulders and elbows. Ribs well sprung. Adequate heart room provided by depth as well as width. Narrow or slab-sided chests are a fault. *Back*—Short and straight. Never hollow, saddle, sway or roach backed. Slight drop from the hips to the root of the tail. *Flanks*—Rounded. Fairly full. Not extremely tucked up, or flabby and falling. Loins short and strong. Distance from last rib to upper thigh short, about three to four finger widths. Narrow and weak loins are a fault. In motion, the loin should not sway sideways, giving a zig-zag motion to the back, wasting energy. *Tail*—Tailless to approximately four inches, natural or docked. The tail not to be so long as to affect the overall balance of the dog. Set on high, actually an extension of the spine at about the same level. Any tail substantially more than four inches shall be severely penalized.

**Forequarters**—*Shoulders*—Shoulder blades should not protrude too much, not too wide apart, with perhaps two thumbs' width between. Sloping and muscular. Blade and upper arm should form nearly a ninety degree angle. Straight shoulders are a fault. At the shoulders the Brittany is slightly higher than at the rump. *Front Legs*—Viewed from the front, perpendicular, but not set too wide. Elbows and feet turning neither in nor out. Pasterns slightly sloped. Down in pasterns is a serious fault. Leg bones clean, graceful, but not too fine. Extremely heavy bone is as much a fault as spindly legs. One must look for substance and suppleness. Height at elbows should approximately equal distance from elbow to withers. *Feet*—Should be strong, proportionately smaller than the spaniels', with close fitting, well arched toes and thick pads. The Brittany is "not up on his toes." Toes not heavily feathered. Flat feet, splayed feet, paper feet, etc., are to be heavily penalized. An ideal foot is halfway between the hare and the cat foot. Dewclaws may be removed.

**Hindquarters**—Broad, strong and muscular, with powerful thighs and well bent stifles, giving the angulation necessary for powerful drive. *Hind Legs*—Stifles well bent. The stifle should not be so angulated as to place the hock joint far out behind the dog. A Brittany should not be condemned for straight stifle until the judge has checked the dog in motion from the side. The stifle joint should not turn out making a cowhock. Thighs well feathered but not profusely, halfway to the hock. Hocks, that is, the back pasterns, should be moderately short, pointing neither in nor out, perpendicular when viewed from the side. They should be firm when shaken by the judge. *Feet*—Same as front feet.

**Coat**—Dense, flat or wavy, never curly. Texture neither wiry nor silky. Ears should carry little fringe. The front and hind legs should have some feathering, but too little is definitely preferable to too much. Dogs with long or profuse feathering or furnishings shall be so severely penalized as to effectively eliminate them from competition. *Skin*—Fine and fairly loose. A loose skin rolls with briars and sticks, thus diminishing punctures or tearing. A skin so loose as to form pouches is undesirable.

**Color**—Orange and white or liver and white in either clear or roan patterns. Some ticking is desirable. The orange or liver is found in the standard parti-color or piebald patterns. Washed out colors are not desirable. Tri-colors are allowed but not preferred. A tri-color is a liver and white dog with classic orange markings on eyebrows, muzzle and cheeks, inside the ears and under the tail, freckles on the lower legs are orange. Anything exceeding the limits of these markings shall be severely penalized. Black is a disqualification.

**Gait**—When at a trot the Brittany's hind foot should step into or beyond the print left by the front foot. Clean movement, coming and going, is very important, but most important is side gait, which is smooth, efficient and ground covering.

**Temperament**—A happy, alert dog, neither mean nor shy.

### DISQUALIFICATIONS

*Any Brittany measuring under 17½ inches or over 20½ inches.*
*A black nose.*
*Black in the coat.*

Approved April 10, 1990

# Pointer

The Pointer comes by his name honestly. He was the first dog, so far as we know, used to stand game in the sense in which we use the term today, and was developed as a distinct breed much earlier than any of the setters. For years it was believed the first Pointers used in England were importations from Spain and Portugal, but that theory has been pretty thoroughly disproved and it seems far more likely that Pointers came into general use in Spain, Portugal, throughout eastern Europe and in the British Isles at approximately the same time. Whether or not the dogs from which they sprung were native to all these places no one can say, but it can be stated with confidence that the *development* of the English Pointer took place within the confines of Great Britain, most probably in England itself. Later on Spanish Pointers were brought in, but from the first they were considered as a different strain, if not a different breed, from the English dogs.

The first Pointers of which there is any dependable record appeared in England about 1650, some years before the era of wing-shooting with guns, and the use to which they were put is interesting. Coursing with Greyhounds was a favorite sport of those times and the earliest accounts of Pointers reveal that they were taken afield to locate and point hares. When the hare had been found, the Greyhounds were brought up and unleashed, the game was kicked from cover and the fun began. But early in the 18th century, at least by 1711, wing-shooting had come into vogue and, from that day on, the "shorthair" has been considered by the majority of sportsmen the equal, if not the superior, of any of the gun dogs.

As to the Pointer's lineage, as usual we find it something of an enigma, but there is no question that the Foxhound, Greyhound and Bloodhound all had a share in his making. Individuals of the three breeds were probably crossed with the inevitable "setting spaniel," which played such a prominent part in the creation of all our modern bird dogs.

During the first years of the 18th century the Spanish Pointer began to appear in England, and he, too, was used for a cross, but as he was exceedingly heavy and very slow in comparison with the English, French, and German Pointers, subsequent breeding operations not only left him out but definitely attempted to correct the faults he had introduced. It appears that his real value was not to improve type but to fix and intensify the pointing instinct, in which, we are told, he was peculiarly strong.

If this was the purpose it seems to have been successful. Remarkable (and incidentally quite unbelievable) stories are to be found in British sporting papers of the early 19th century, relating the prodigies performed by certain English Pointers of a former day. Col. Thornton's Pluto and Juno, for example, are said to have held a point on a covey of partridges for an hour and a quarter by the watch. But when we find so solid an authority as Stonehenge telling as gospel truth the now famous yarn of the sportsman who lost his Pointer on the moors, and returning a year later, discovered the skeleton of the dog pointing a skeleton bird, we realize that the statements of these pre-Victorian worthies must be taken with considerably more than a pinch of salt.

During the 19th century the English Pointer was repeatedly crossed with the various setters as they came into existence and favor. This, it seems, was partly to improve his disposition, for an old-time writer, commenting on the breed says: "They have a ferocity of temper which will not submit to correction or discipline, unless taken in hand very young." While the Pointer of today is anything but ferocious, it may be that this characteristic, tempered by judicious breeding and in combination with the natural independence that made him object to correction and discipline, has made him the superlative field-trial dog he is today. He certainly possesses the competitive spirit to a greater degree than is usually found in the other bird dogs, a quality that makes him especially suited to public performance.

The modern Pointer is a specialist and looks the part. He is every inch a gun dog. Clean-limbed, lithe, and muscular without being coarse, full of nervous energy and "hunt," put together for speed and endurance, courageous, and with the ability to concentrate on his job, he is an ideal dog for the man or woman who is looking for results when afield. His short hair makes him neat and clean around the house and his disposition makes him adaptable for the kennel. He requires less personal attention than some other gun dogs and he is willing to work satisfactorily for someone other than his own master and handler.

In addition to all this, he has another characteristic—tendency towards early development. As a breed, Pointers seem to acquire the hunting instinct at a tender age, puppies of two months frequently pointing and even backing. For this reason they are especially suited for derby and puppy stakes.

For show purposes, his short coat makes his outline, conformation, and quality easily seen at a glance, and he is a superb poser. His color, usually white with rich liver markings is striking and he has an ideal bench temperament. Lemon and white, orange and white, black and white and sometimes solid black are other colorings.

The Pointer is peculiarly fortunate in one all-important respect. He has always been bred for type as well as field ability, hence we have in this case no divergence between the two insofar as appearance goes. From the beginning type has been carefully developed and intelligently preserved. An illustration for Col. Thornton's book *A Tour Through Scotland* shows Captain Fleming of Barochan out hawking. This picture was drawn or painted about 1786, yet a Pointer that is among the dogs shown would pass muster today as an excellent specimen.

## Official Standard for the Pointer

**General Appearance**—The Pointer is bred primarily for sport afield; he should unmistakably look and act the part. The ideal specimen gives the immediate impression of compact power and agile grace; the head noble, proudly carried; the expression intelligent and alert; the muscular body bespeaking both staying power and dash. Here is an animal whose every movement shows him to be a wide-awake, hard-driving hunting dog possessing stamina, courage, and the desire to go. And in his expression are the loyalty and devotion of a true friend of man.

**Temperament**—The Pointer's even temperament and alert good sense make him a congenial companion both in the field and in the home. He should be dignified and should never show timidity toward man or dog.

**Head**—The skull of medium width, approximately as wide as the length of the muzzle, resulting in an impression of length rather than width. Slight furrow between the eyes, cheeks cleanly chiseled. There should be a pronounced stop. From this point forward the muzzle is of good length, with the nasal bone so formed that the nose is slightly higher at the tip than the muzzle at the stop. Parallel planes of the skull and muzzle are equally acceptable. The muzzle should be deep without pendulous flews. Jaws ending square and level, should bite evenly or as scissors. Nostrils well developed and wide open. *Ears*— Set on at eye level. When hanging naturally, they should reach just below the lower jaw, close to the head, with little or no folding. They should be somewhat pointed at the tip—never round—and soft and thin in leather. *Eyes*—Of ample size, rounded and intense. The eye color should be dark in contrast with the color of the markings, the darker the better.

**Neck**—Long, dry, muscular and slightly arched, springing cleanly from the shoulders.

**Shoulders**—Long, thin, and sloping. The top of blades close together.

**Front**—Elbows well let down, directly under the withers and truly parallel so as to work just clear of the body. Forelegs straight and with oval bone. Knee joint never to knuckle over. Pasterns of moderate length, perceptibly finer in bone than the leg, and slightly slanting. Chest, deep rather than wide, must not hinder free action of forelegs. The breastbone bold, without being unduly prominent. The ribs well sprung, descending as low as the elbow-point.

**Back**—Strong and solid with only a slight rise from croup to top of shoulders. Loin of moderate length, powerful and slightly arched. Croup falling only slightly to base of tail. Tuck-up should be apparent, but not exaggerated.

**Tail**—Heavier at the root, tapering to a fine point. Length no greater than to hock. A tail longer than this or docked must be penalized. Carried without curl, and not more than 20 degrees above the line of the back; never carried between the legs.

**Hindquarters**—Muscular and powerful with great propelling leverage. Thighs long and well developed. Stifles well bent. The hocks clean; the legs straight as viewed from behind. Decided angulation is the mark of power and endurance.

**Feet**—Oval, with long, closely-set, arched toes, well-padded, and deep. Catfoot is a fault. Dewclaws on the forelegs may be removed.

**Coat**—Short, dense, smooth with a sheen.

**Color**—Liver, lemon, black, orange; either in combination with white or solid-colored. A good Pointer cannot be a bad color. In the darker colors, the nose should be black or brown; in the lighter shades it may be lighter or flesh-colored.

**Gait**—Smooth, frictionless, with a powerful hindquarters' drive. The head should be carried high, the nostrils wide, the tail moving from side to side rhythmically with the pace, giving the impression of a well-balanced, strongly-built hunting dog capable of top speed combined with great stamina. Hackney gait must be faulted.

**Balance and Size**—Balance and over-all symmetry are more important in the Pointer than size. A smooth, balanced dog is to be more desired than a dog with strongly contrasting good points and faults. Hound or terrier characteristics are most undesirable. Because a sporting dog must have both endurance and power, great variations in size are undesirable, the desirable height and weight being within the following limits:

Dogs:         Height—25–28 inches
                 Weight—55–75 pounds
Bitches:     Height—23–26 inches
                 Weight—45–65 pounds

Approved November 11, 1975

# Pointer, German Shorthaired

The German Shorthaired Pointer combines in field-dog requirements those qualities which have long popularized the various breeds of hunting dogs. So successfully have keen scenting powers, linked with high intelligence, been fused into the breed through judicious crossing of the descendants of the old Spanish Pointer, English Foxhound, and local German tracking hounds, and so varied are this dog's field accomplishments, that its adaptability has earned it the reputation of being an all-purpose dog. In fact, the term was applied to it by the Germans before United States sportsmen started importing the breed to any extent in the early 1920s.

It is indeed rare to find wrapped up in one package a staunchly pointing bird dog, a keen-nosed night trailer, a proven duck dog, a natural retriever on land and water, pleasing conformation and markings, great powers of endurance, and an intelligent family watchdog and companion. Indicative of this dog's versatility is its successful work on pheasant, quail, grouse, partridge, jacksnipe, woodcock, duck, rabbits, coon, and possum. It is also used to trail and handle deer. With a water-repellent coat and webbed feet, it retrieves well from rough terrain or icy waters.

The origin of the German Shorthaired Pointer, as indeed with most breeds,

**45**

cannot be described precisely. Prior to the establishment of the *Klub Kurzhaar* stud book in the 1870s, few records are available, though the German hunting fraternity had already spent many years in attempting to produce a truly versatile utility dog-of-all-work, using of necessity the stock that was locally available. The main source of basic foundation stock seems to have been the German Bird Dog, a not very admirable step down by inheritance from the old Spanish Pointer. Its utility was further improved by introducing local types of scent hounds—track and trail dogs, that were also dependable in water and that were used by the German foresters. These *Schweisshunde (Schweiss*—scent; *Hunde*—dogs) were of many and diverse types. They had originated principally down through the centuries from the hounds introduced from Eastern countries after the Crusades, and had been developed particularly in France, so that they became the forebears of practically all present-day scenting hounds.

The Germans still were not satisfied. Since obedience was of paramount importance, these early dogs were selectively bred for biddability. Steps were taken later to improve stance, style, and, above all, *nose*. Fine Pointers were brought from England and were used to lend elegance to the manner of working—*die hohe nase* (the high nose) being the major aim. This was accomplished, and the breeders then had only the problem of ridding their developing *Kurzhaar* of its unwanted Pointer characteristics—aversion to water and lack of aggressiveness toward predators. These objectives were achieved long before the turn of the century. A dog breeding true to type was developed, giving the world at long last a magnificent utility dog combining these virtues with the good looks, sound temperament, and longevity that have made the German Shorthaired Pointer a favorite with sportsmen everywhere.

The German Shorthaired Pointer was first admitted to the stud book of the American Kennel Club in March, 1930. The first AKC licensed Specialty Show for German Shorthaired Pointers was held by the German Shorthaired Pointer Club of America at the International Kennel Club show in Chicago on March 29–30, 1941; the first AKC licensed Field Trial for the breed was also held by the parent club at Anoka, Minnesota, on May 21, 1944.

## Official Standard for the German Shorthaired Pointer

The Shorthair is a versatile hunter, an all-purpose gun dog capable of high performance in field and water. The judgment of Shorthairs in the show ring should reflect this basic characteristic.

**General Appearance**—The overall picture which is created in the observer's eye is that of an aristocratic, well-balanced, symmetrical animal with conformation indicating power, endurance and agility and a look of intelligence and animation. The dog is neither unduly small nor conspicuously large. It gives the impression of medium size, but is like the proper hunter, "with a short back, but standing over plenty of ground."

Tall leggy dogs, or dogs which are ponderous or unbalanced because of excess substance should be definitely rejected. The first impression is that of a keenness which denotes full enthusiasm for work without indication of nervous or flighty character. Movements are alertly coordinated without waste motion. Grace of outline, clean-cut head, sloping shoulders, deep chest, powerful back, strong quarters, good bone composition, adequate muscle, well-carried tail and taut coat, all combine to produce a look of nobility and an indication of anatomical structure essential to correct gait which must indicate a heritage of purposefully conducted breeding. Doggy bitches and bitchy dogs are to be faulted. A judge must excuse a dog from the ring if it displays extreme shyness or viciousness toward its handler or the judge. Aggressiveness or belligerence toward another dog is not to be considered viciousness.

**Symmetry**—Symmetry and field quality are most essential. A dog in hard and lean field condition is not to be penalized; however, overly fat or poorly muscled dogs are to be penalized. A dog well-balanced in all points is preferable to one with outstanding good qualities and defects.

**Head**—Clean-cut, neither too light nor too heavy, in proper proportion to the body. Skull is reasonably broad, arched on side and slightly round on top. Scissura (median line between the eyes at the forehead) not too deep, occipital bone not as conspicuous as in the case of the Pointer. The foreface rises gradually from nose to forehead. The rise is more strongly pronounced in the dog than in the bitch as befitting his sex. The chops fall away from the somewhat projecting nose. Lips are full and deep, never flewy. The chops do not fall over too much, but form a proper fold in the angle. The jaw is powerful and the muscles well developed. The line to the forehead rises gradually and never has a definite stop as that of the Pointer, but rather a stop-effect when viewed from the side, due to the position of the eyebrows. The muzzle is sufficiently long to enable the dog to seize properly and to facilitate his carrying game a long time. A pointed muzzle is not desirable. The entire head never gives the impression of tapering to a point. The depth is in the right proportion to the length, both in the muzzle and in the skull proper. The length of the muzzle should equal the length of skull. A pointed muzzle is a fault. A dish-faced muzzle is a fault. A definite Pointer stop is a serious fault. Too many wrinkles in forehead is a fault. *Ears*— Ears are broad and set fairly high, lie flat and never hang away from the head. Placement is just above eye level. The ears, when laid in front without being pulled, meet the lip angle. In the case of heavier dogs, the ears are correspondingly longer. Ears too long or fleshy are to be faulted. *Eyes*—The eyes are of medium size, full of intelligence and expression, good humored and yet radiating energy, neither protruding nor sunken. The eye is almond shaped, not circular. The eyelids close well. The best color is dark brown. Light yellow (Bird of Prey) eyes are not desirable and are a fault. Closely set eyes are to be faulted. China or wall eyes are to be disqualifies. *Nose*—Brown, the larger the better, nostrils well-opened and broad. Spotted nose not desirable. Flesh colored nose disqualifies. *Teeth*—The teeth are strong and healthy. The molars intermesh properly. The bite is a true scissors bite. A perfect level bite (without overlapping) is not desirable and must be penalized. Extreme overshot or undershot bite disqualifies.

**Neck**—Of proper length to permit the jaws reaching game to be retrieved, sloping downwards on beautifully curving lines. The nape is rather muscular, becoming gradually larger towards the shoulders. Moderate houndlike throatiness permitted.

**Chest**—The chest in general gives the impression of depth rather than breadth; for all that, it should be in correct proportion to the other parts of the body with a fair depth. The chest reaches down to the elbows, the ribs forming the thorax show a rib spring and are not flat or slabsided; they are not perfectly round or barrel-shaped. Ribs that are entirely round prevent the necessary expansion of the chest when taking breath. The back ribs reach well down. The circumference of the thorax immediately behind the elbows is smaller than that of the thorax about a hand's-breadth behind elbows, so that the upper arm has room for movement.

**Back, Loins and Croup**—Back is short, strong and straight with slight rise from root of tail to withers. Loin strong, of moderate length and slightly arched. Tuck-up is apparent. Excessively long, roached or swayed back must be penalized.

**Forequarters**—The shoulders are sloping, movable, well-covered with muscle. The shoulder blades lie flat and are well laid back nearing a 45° angle. The upper arm (the bones between the shoulder and elbow joints) is as long as possible, standing away somewhat from the trunk so that the straight and closely muscled legs, when viewed from the front appear to be parallel. Elbows which stand away from the body or are too close indicate toes turning inwards or outwards, which must be regarded as faults. Pasterns are strong, short and nearly vertical with a slight spring. Loose, short-bladed or straight shoulders must be faulted. Knuckling over is to be faulted. Down in the pasterns is to be faulted.

**Hindquarters**—The hips are broad with hip sockets wide apart and fall slightly toward the tail in a graceful curve. Thighs are strong and well-muscled. Stifles well bent. Hock joints are well angulated and strong, straight bone structure from hock to pad. Angulation of both stifle and hock joint is such as to combine maximum combination of both drive and traction. Hocks turn neither in nor out. A steep croup is a fault. Cowhocked legs are a serious fault.

**Feet**—Are compact, close-knit and round to spoon-shaped. The toes sufficiently arched and heavily nailed. The pads are strong, hard and thick. Dewclaws on the forelegs may be removed. Feet pointing in or out is a fault.

**Coat and Skin**—The skin is close and tight. The hair is short and thick and feels tough to the hand; it is somewhat longer on the underside of the tail and the back edges of the haunches. It is softer, thinner and shorter on the ears and the head. Any dog with long hair in body coat is to be severely penalized.

**Tail**—Is set high and firm, and must be docked, leaving 40% of length. The tail hangs down when the dog is quiet, is held horizontally when he is walking. The tail must never be curved over the back toward the head when the dog is moving. A tail curved or bent toward the head is to be severely penalized.

**Bones**—Thin and fine bones are by no means desirable in a dog which must possess strength and be able to work over any and every country. The main importance is not laid so much on the size of bone, but rather on their being in proper proportion to the body. Bone structure too heavy or too light is a fault. Dogs with coarse bones are handicapped in agility of movement and speed.

**Weight and Height**—Dogs, 55 to 70 pounds. Bitches, 45 to 60 pounds. Dogs, 23 to 25 inches. Bitches, 21 to 23 inches at the withers. Deviations of one inch above or below the described heights are to be severely penalized.

**Color**—The coat may be of solid liver or any combination of liver and white, such as liver and white ticked, liver spotted and white ticked, or liver roan. A dog with any area of black, red, orange, lemon or tan, or a dog solid white will be disqualified.

**Gait**—A smooth lithe gait is essential. It is to be noted that as gait increases from the walk to a faster speed, the legs converge beneath the body. The tendency to single track is desirable. The forelegs reach well ahead as if to pull in the ground without giving the appearance of a hackney gait, and are followed by the back legs which give forceful propulsion. Dragging the rear feet is undesirable.

### DISQUALIFICATIONS

*China or wall eyes.*
*Flesh colored nose.*
*Extreme overshot or undershot.*
*A dog with any area of black, red, orange, lemon or tan,*
*or a dog solid white.*

Approved October 14, 1975

# Pointer, German Wirehaired

Hunting has been called our earliest sport, but it is more than that. It was a way of life in ancient times when the ax, the club, and the spear were the sole weapons man had with which to find food for himself and his brood. Throughout the course of time he hunted with traps and pitfalls, hawks and falcons, nets and snares, bows and arrows. Later, the princes, the nobles, and the big landowners hunted not for food but for sport, but to the rank and file such privilege was denied.

However, around 1850 the incidence of political revolt, together with improvements in the shotgun and the cartridge, spurred the business of hunting to such degree that everybody, regardless of class distinction, took to the hunt. The number of sportsmen more than doubled as game bird shooting grew popular. More dogs were needed, hence more were bred. And slowly but surely the hunting dog became something of a specialist. One kind grew adept at ranging woods and fields where it pointed birds for the huntsman to shoot, others learned to retrieve from land and from water, and as time went on each attained proficiency in its special department.

Continental sportsmen were hard to please; they were not satisfied with a gun dog that would hunt only one kind of game. They envisioned an all-purpose dog, and so it happened that in various European countries retrieving Pointers began to emerge. One of these, native to Germany, was the *Deutsch-Drahthaar* which, literally translated, means German Wirehair.

In order to understand the heritage of this breed we must bear in mind that there existed abroad a wide variety of retrieving Pointers, all of them more or less interbred. The early Deutsch-Drahthaar Club, in fact, at first catered to all varieties of wirehaired pointing dogs. Later, however, they thought it best to separate their activities into four subdivisions catering to the advancement of the Deutsch-Drahthaar, the Pudelpointer, the Stichelhaar, and the Griffon.

Most of the early wirehaired Pointers represented a combination of Griffon, Stichelhaar, Pudelpointer, and German Shorthair. The Pudelpointer was a cross between a Poodle dog and an English Pointer bitch, while the Griffon and the Stichelhaar were composed of Pointer, Foxhound, Pudelpointer, and a Polish water dog. Thus it is easy to appreciate the different hunting skills incorporated in the wirehaired Pointers of a century or more ago.

Admirable breeders and trainers, the Germans demanded a great deal of their sporting dogs. They had no patience with specialists, preferring instead an extra-rugged hunter capable of working on any kind of game and on any terrain. In the German Wirehaired Pointer, this is exactly what they got, for they molded into the one breed the distinctive traits of Pointer, Foxhound, and Poodle. Through these avenues of diversified accomplishment they created an all-purpose dog approximating their ideal. He pointed and retrieved equally well on land and in water. He was keen-nosed and constitutionally tough. What is more, he had the courage as well as the coat fit to brave any sort of cover.

Coat has always been emphasized throughout the development of the breed, as indicated by a statement made by members of the Drahthaar Club back in 1902, when they said: *"The breeding of a correct wire coat is the most important feature."* There was ample reason for this emphasis on coat, considering the work that the German Wirehair was called upon to do. In short, he was designed as an all-weather as well as an all-purpose dog, and he had to negotiate underbrush that would have punished severely any dog not so characteristically armored.

The coat is weather-resisting in every sense of the term, and it is to large extent water-repellent. It is straight, harsh, wiry, and quite flat-lying. One and one half to two inches in length, it is long enough to shield the body from rough cover, yet not so long as to hide the outline. A heavy growth on the brow guards the eyes from injury, and a short beard and whiskers combine to save the foreface from laceration by brush and briar. A very dense undercoat insulates the body against the cold of winter, but it sheds out to such a degree as to be almost invisible in summertime.

Although it had become a favored sporting dog in Germany many years earlier, the Drahthaar was not admitted into the German Kartell for dogs until 1928. The breed was imported to the United States in the 1920s. In 1953, the German Drahthaar Club of America was formed. The breed was admitted into

AKC's stud books in 1959 as the German Wirehaired Pointer, and the name of the national club was changed to the German Wirehaired Pointer Club of America.

## Official Standard for the German Wirehaired Pointer

**General Appearance**—The German Wirehaired Pointer is a well muscled, medium sized dog of distinctive appearance. Balanced in size and sturdily built, the breed's most distinguishing characteristics are its weather resistant, wire-like coat and its facial furnishings. Typically Pointer in character and style, the German Wirehaired Pointer is an intelligent, energetic and determined hunter.

**Size, Proportion, Substance**—The *height* of males should be from 24 to 26 inches at the withers. Bitches are smaller but not under 22 inches. To insure the working quality of the breed is maintained, dogs that are either over or under the specified height must be severely penalized. The body is a little longer than it is high, as ten is to nine. The German Wirehaired Pointer is a versatile hunter built for agility and endurance in the field. Correct size and balance are essential to high performance.

**Head**—The head is moderately long. *Eyes* are brown, medium in size, oval in contour, bright and clear and overhung with medium length eyebrows. Yellow eyes are not desirable. The *ears* are rounded but not too broad and hang close to the head. The *skull* broad and the occipital bone not too prominent. The *stop* is medium. The *muzzle* is fairly long with nasal bone straight, broad and parallel to the top of the skull. The *nose* is dark brown with nostrils wide open. A spotted or flesh colored nose is to be penalized. The *lips* are a trifle pendulous but close to the jaw and bearded. The *jaws* are strong with a full complement of evenly set and properly intermeshing teeth. The incisors meet in a true *scissors bite.*

**Neck, Topline, Body**—The *neck* is of medium length, slightly arched and devoid of dewlap. The entire *back line* showing a perceptible slope down from withers to croup. The skin throughout is notably tight to the body.
    The *chest* is deep and capacious with ribs well sprung. The *tuck-up* apparent. The back is short, straight and strong. Loins are taut and slender. Hips are broad with the croup nicely rounded. The *tail* is set high, carried at or above the horizontal when the dog is alert. The tail is docked to approximately two-fifths of its original length.

**Forequarters**—The shoulders are well laid back. The forelegs are straight with elbows close. Leg bones are flat rather than round, and strong, but not so heavy or coarse as to militate against the dog's natural agility. Dewclaws are generally removed. Round in outline, the feet are webbed, high arched with toes close, pads thick and hard, and nails strong and quite heavy.

**Hindquarters**—The angulation of the hindquarters balances that of the forequarters. The thighs are strong and muscular. The hind legs are moderately angulated at the stifle and hock and, as viewed from behind, parallel to each other. Dewclaws are generally removed. Feet as in front.

**Coat**—The functional wiry coat is the breed's most distinctive feature. A dog must have a correct coat to be of correct type. The coat is weather resistant and, to some extent, water-repellent. The undercoat is dense enough in winter to insulate against the cold but is so thin in summer as to be almost invisible. The distinctive outer coat is straight, harsh, wiry and flat lying, and is from one to two inches in length. The outer coat is long enough to protect against the punishment of rough cover, but not so long as to hide the outline of the dog. On the lower legs the coat is shorter and between the toes it is of softer texture. On the skull the coat is naturally short and close fitting. Over the shoulders and around the tail it is very dense and heavy. The tail is nicely coated, particularly on the underside, but devoid of feather. Eyebrows are of strong, straight hair. Beard and whiskers are medium length. The hairs in the liver patches of a liver and white dog may be shorter than the white hairs. A short smooth coat, a soft woolly coat, or one excessively long is to be severely penalized. While maintaining a harsh, wiry texture, the puppy coat may be shorter than that of an adult coat. Coats may be neatly groomed to present a dog natural in appearance. Extreme and excessive grooming to present a dog artificial in appearance should be severely penalized.

**Color**—The coat is liver and white, usually either liver and white spotted, liver roan, liver and white spotted with ticking and roaning or solid liver. The head is liver, sometimes with a white blaze. The ears are liver. Any black in the coat is to be severely penalized.

**Gait**—The dog should be evaluated at a moderate gait. The movement is free and smooth with good reach in the forequarters and good driving power in the hindquarters. The topline should remain firm.

**Temperament**—Of sound, reliable temperament, the German Wirehaired Pointer is at times aloof but not unfriendly toward strangers; a loyal and affectionate companion who is eager to please and enthusiastic to learn.

Approved July 9, 1985
Reformatted May 14, 1989

# Retriever, Chesapeake Bay

**W**hile the Chesapeake Bay Retriever originated in this country, he came from stock destined to sail from England. There is no complete and authentic record of his development; at the same time his breed origin as here described is probably correct and at the present time is the one generally accepted. Theories regarding later development are entirely supposition, lacking, as yet, definite proof.

In the year 1807 an English brig was wrecked off the coast of Maryland and crew and cargo were rescued by the American ship *Canton.* Also rescued were two Newfoundland puppies, a dingy red dog named "Sailor" and a black bitch called "Canton" after the rescuing boat. Presented to the gentlemen who gave hospitality to the sailors of the wrecked brig, the two dogs were found to possess wonderful qualities as retrievers. Many of the nondescript dogs then used for retrieving were bred to them, although we do not know whether Sailor and Canton themselves were ever mated together. Eventually other outcrosses were used, and of these, the English Otter Hound has been claimed as one of the most influential. However, such a cross would probably have produced different results, since the Chesapeake shows no trace of hound. It is more likely that the Flat-Coated and Curly-Coated Retrievers constituted the most important outcrosses, if any were ever purposely made.

By the time of the AKC's establishment in 1884, a definite Chesapeake type had been developed and was known for its prowess in the rough, icy waters of the Chesapeake Bay, where the dogs were often called upon to retrieve 100 or 200 ducks in a day. Anthony Bliss, in his history of the breed, noted that there were several differences between this type and the present-day Chesapeake. For one, the breed was found in one color only—dark brown, shading into a sort of reddish sedge. (The deadgrass color came into popularity in the Midwest later.) Also, heads were inclined to be of a more wedge-shaped type, and coats were longer and thicker.

Today, under leadership of its parent club—the American Chesapeake Club, founded in 1918—the breed is active in all areas of AKC competition. The club held its first licensed retriever trial in 1932. Over recent years it has become increasingly important at the shows and in obedience and tracking trials. The Chesapeake is still a remarkable water dog and the club issues Working Dog (WD) or Working Dog Excellent (WDX) certificates to dogs who have passed retrieving tests on land and water.

## Official Standard for the Chesapeake Bay Retriever

**Head**—Skull broad and round with medium stop, nose medium short muzzle, pointed but not sharp. Lips thin, not pendulous. Ears small, set well up on head, hanging loosely and of medium leather. Eyes medium large, very clear, of yellowish or amber color and wide apart.

**Neck**—Of medium length with a strong muscular appearance, tapering to shoulders.

**Shoulder, Chest and Body**—Shoulders, sloping and should have full liberty of action with plenty of power without any restrictions of movement. Chest strong, deep and wide. Barrel round and deep. Body of medium length, neither cobby nor roached, but rather approaching hollowness, flanks well tucked up.

**Hindquarters and Stifles**—Hindquarters should be as high or a trifle higher than the shoulders. They should show fully as much power as the forequarters. There should be no tendency to weakness in either fore or hindquarters. Hindquarters should be especially powerful to supply the driving power for swimming. Back should be short, well-coupled and powerful. Good hindquarters are essential. Stifles should be well-angulated.

**Legs, Elbows, Hocks and Feet**—Legs should be medium length and straight, showing good bone and muscle, with well-webbed hare feet of good size. The toes well rounded and close, pasterns slightly bent and both pasterns and hocks medium length—the straighter the legs the better, when viewed from front or rear. Dewclaws, if any, must be removed from the hind legs. Dewclaws on the forelegs may be removed. A dog with dewclaws on the hind legs must be disqualified.

**Tail**—Tail should extend to hock. It should be medium heavy at base. Moderate feathering on stern and tail is permissible. Tail should be straight or slightly curved. Tail should not curl over back or side kink.

**Coat and Texture**—Coat should be thick and short, nowhere over 1½ inches long, with a dense fine woolly undercoat. Hair on face and legs should be very short and straight with tendency to wave on the shoulders, neck, back and loins only. The curly coat or coat with a tendency to curl not permissible.

The texture of the dog's coat is very important, as the dog is used for hunting under all sorts of adverse weather conditions, often working in ice and snow. The oil in the harsh outer coat and woolly undercoat is of extreme value in preventing the cold water from reaching the dog's skin and aids in quick drying. A Chesapeake's coat should resist the water in the same way that a duck's feathers do. When he leaves the water and shakes himself, his coat should not hold the water at all, being merely moist. Color and coat are extremely important, as the dog is used for duck hunting. The color must be as nearly that of his surroundings as possible and with the fact that dogs are exposed to all kinds of adverse weather conditions, often working in ice and snow, the color of coat and its texture must be given every consideration when judging on the bench or in the ring.

**Color**—Any color varying from a dark brown to a faded tan or deadgrass. Deadgrass takes in any shade of deadgrass, varying from a tan to a dull straw color. White spot on breast, toes and belly permissible, but the smaller the spot the better. Solid and self-colored dogs are preferred.

**Weight**—Males, 65 to 80 pounds; females 55 to 70 pounds. **Height**—Males, 23 inches to 26 inches; females, 21 inches to 24 inches. Oversized or undersized dogs are to be severely penalized.

**Symmetry and Quality**—The Chesapeake dog should show a bright and happy disposition and an intelligent expression, with general outlines impressive and denoting a good worker. The dog should be well proportioned, a dog with a good coat and well balanced in other points being preferable to the dog excelling in some but weak in others.

Courage, willingness to work, alertness, nose, intelligence, love of water, general quality, and, most of all, disposition, should be given primary consideration in the selection and breeding of the Chesapeake Bay dog.

### POSITIVE SCALE OF POINTS

| | | | |
|---|---|---|---|
| Head, incl. lips, ears & eyes | 16 | Elbows, legs and feet | 12 |
| Neck | 4 | Color | 4 |
| Shoulders and body | 12 | Stern and Tail | 10 |
| Hindquarters and stifles | 12 | Coat and Texture | 18 |
| | | General conformation | 12 |
| | | *Total* | 100 |

*Note:*—The question of coat and general type of balance takes precedence over any scoring table which could be drawn up.

### APPROXIMATE MEASUREMENTS

|  | *Inches* |
|---|---|
| Length head, nose to occiput | 9½ to 10 |
| Girth at ears | 20 to 21 |
| Muzzle below eyes | 10 to 10½ |
| Length of ears | 4½ to 5 |
| Width between eyes | 2½ to 2¾ |
| Girth neck close to shoulder | 20 to 22 |
| Girth at flank | 24 to 25 |
| Length from occiput to tail base | 34 to 35 |
| Girth forearms at shoulders | 10 to 10½ |
| Girth upper thigh | 19 to 20 |
| From root to root of ear, over skull | 5 to 6 |
| Occiput to top shoulder blades | 9 to 9½ |
| From elbow to elbow over the shoulders | 25 to 26 |

### DISQUALIFICATIONS

*Black colored.*
*Dewclaws on hind legs.*
*White on any part of body, except breast, belly or spots on feet.*
*Feathering on tail or legs over 1¾ inches long.*
*Undershot, overshot or any deformity.*
*Coat curly or tendency to curl all over body.*
*Specimens unworthy or lacking in breed characteristics.*

Approved November 9, 1976

# Retriever, Curly-Coated

In the absence of very early records, the correct origin of the Curly-Coated Retriever must remain a matter of conjecture, but there appears little doubt that he is one of the oldest of all breeds now classified as Retrievers. He is popularly believed to be descended from the 16th century English Water Spaniel, and from the retrieving setter. Some maintain the Irish Water Spaniel was his ancestor and it is more than probable that a cross was made with this Spaniel from time to time, the liver color being a recognized color for the Curly as well as the black.

Whichever Spaniel was his progenitor, it is certain that added to the mixture of Water Spaniel and retrieving setter was the small or St. John's Newfoundland, which, according to records, first arrived in England in 1835 as a ship's dog on board the boats that brought salted cod from Newfoundland. The St. John's dog, curiously enough, is sometimes called a Labrador by early writers, a fact which has given rise to some confusion with respect to the modern Labrador.

In the early 1880s the Curly is said to have been crossed again with the Poodle (the one-time retriever of France), this cross taken with the object of giving his coat a tight curl.

The popular gun dog following the Old English Water Spaniel, the Curly was first exhibited in 1860 at England's Birmingham show. In 1889 specimens were exported to New Zealand, where they have long been used for retrieving duck and California quail. In Australia, too, where they are used in the swamps and lagoons of the Murray River on duck, they are much admired as steady and tender-mouthed retrievers quite unsurpassed in the water.

The first breed club for the Curly Coated Retriever was formed in England in 1896. The breed was introduced to the United States as early as 1907, but first AKC registration was in 1924.

Many assert that the Curly Retriever is temperamentally easy to train. He is affectionate, enduring, hardy, and will practically live in the water. Moreover, his thick coat enables him to face the most punishing covert. He is a charming and faithful companion and an excellent guard.

## Official Standard for the Curly-Coated Retriever

**General Appearance**—A strong smart upstanding dog, showing activity, endurance and intelligence.

**Head**—Long and well proportioned, skull not too flat, jaws long and strong but not inclined to snipiness, nose black, in the black coated variety, with wide nostrils. Teeth strong and level. *Eyes*—Black or brown, but not yellow, rather large but not too prominent. *Ears*—Rather small, set on low, lying close to the head, and covered with short curls.

**Coat**—Should be one mass of crisp curls all over. A slightly more open coat not to be severely penalized, but a saddle back or patch of uncurled hair behind the shoulder should be penalized, and a prominent white patch on breast is undesirable, but a few white hairs allowed in an otherwise good dog. Color, black or liver.

**Shoulders, Chest, Body and Loins**—Shoulders should be very deep, muscular and obliquely placed. Chest, not too wide, but decidedly deep. Body, rather short, muscular and well ribbed up. Loin, powerful, deep and firm to the grasp.

**Legs and Feet**—Legs should be of moderate length, forelegs straight and set well under the body. Quarters strong and muscular, hocks low to the ground with moderate bend to stifle and hock. Feet round and compact with well-arched toes.

**Tail**—Should be moderately short, carried fairly straight and covered with curls, slightly tapering towards the point.

Approved November 9, 1976

# Retriever, Flat-Coated

When it became possible for man to kill game on the wing many different breeds of dogs were used to find and retrieve it and any such dog was regarded as a retriever. Eventually, by selective breeding for the perfection of this skill, the Retriever Proper, a large black dog, had come into existence in Britain by the early part of the 19th century. It was not accepted as a pure breed, but regarded as a mongrel because of its cross-bred origin from various breeds such as the Large Newfoundland, the setter, the sheepdog and spaniel-like Water dogs.

The last named were invaluable as retrievers to fishermen and were the subjects of trade between Britain and the North American continent, particularly with the cod fishery off Newfoundland during the 19th century. It was at this time that the term "Labrador" dog came into use and was applied indiscriminately to a number of different types of dogs associated with this area. These dogs, found in St. John's, Newfoundland, and called the small Labrador dog, the Lesser Newfoundland or St. John's Newfoundland, contributed towards the Wavy-coated (and subsequently the Flat-coated) retriever, but they must have had considerable British stock as ancestors. They should not be confused with the modern day Labrador Retriever as they differed in coat, size and structure.

The first British dog show was held in 1859, but classification for retrievers, comprising Curly-coated and Wavy or Smooth-coated, was not available until the following year. Records of awards and pedigrees, if known, were kept from the beginning of shows and published in the Kennel Club Stud Book in 1874.

From 1864 on, two bitches of a working strain of retrievers belonging to J. Hull, a gamekeeper, figured in the awards. These were "Old Bounce," out of his bitch "Boss" and by Blaydon's "Black Sailor," and "Young Bounce," her daughter, by Mr. Chattock's "Cato." It was this stock that produced an important nucleus to the development of the breed. The greatest credit for the integration of these retrievers into a stable type goes to S. E. Shirley, founder of the Kennel Club in 1873.

Subsequently the breed gained enormously in popularity and numerous important breeders made their contribution to the quality and elegance of the Flat-coated Retriever as well as to his excellent working abilities. The breed's most famous patron was H. R. Cooke, who for over 70 years kept the breed in his fabulous "Riverside" kennel—a kennel perhaps unique among those for any breed of dog in numbers, quality and awards won in the field and on the show bench.

The liver-colored Flat-Coat became more popular after J. H. Abbott's liver-colored dog "Rust" won at the Retriever Society's official field trials in 1900. His prestigious win proved that this color was finally considered acceptable.

The Flat-Coated Retriever was admitted to AKC registration in 1915. By 1918, the breed's popularity was overtaken by the modern Labrador Retriever, and by the end of the 1920s by the Golden Retriever. At times, particularly during the two World Wars, registrations dwindled to dangerous levels. After World War II it was not easy to pick up the threads of disappearing lines. S. O'Neill, one of the greatest authorities on the breed, must be credited with a valuable contribution to this end. He showed selfless devotion in putting the breed on as sound a footing as possible and in advising new patrons on correct type. Stock continued to build up gradually until about the mid-1960s when an appreciable increase in number and popularity took place in Britain and a keen demand for the breed appeared in Europe and America.

The parent club in the United States is the Flat-Coated Retriever Society of America, a flourishing and well-integrated club, whose members are very enthusiastic and anxious to further the best interests of the breed.

His fall from popularity has kept the Flat-Coat out of the hands of the commercial breeder and under control of those interested in retaining his great natural working abilities. He is unafraid of thick covert and cold water, shows drive and perseverance when out hunting and retrieves tenderly to hand. He has a delightful and inimitable character and temperament, is highly intelligent and companionable and retains his youthful outlook on life into old age, tail-wagging being the hallmark of the breed. Apart from these virtues he is a handsome fellow.

# Official Standard for the Flat-Coated Retriever

**General Appearance**—The Flat-Coated Retriever is a versatile family companion hunting retriever with a happy and active demeanor, intelligent expression, and clean lines. The Flat-Coat has been traditionally described as showing *"power without lumber and raciness without weediness."*

The distinctive and most important features of the Flat-Coat are the silhouette (both moving and standing), smooth effortless movement, head type, coat and character. In silhouette the Flat-Coat has a long, strong, clean, "one piece" head, which is unique to the breed. Free from exaggeration of stop or cheek, the head is set well into a moderately long neck which flows smoothly into well laid back shoulders. A level topline combined with a deep, long rib cage tapering to a moderate tuck-up create the impression of a blunted triangle. The brisket is well developed and the forechest forms a prominent prow. This utilitarian retriever is well balanced, strong, but elegant; never cobby, short legged or rangy. The coat is thick and flat lying, and the legs and tail are well feathered. A proud carriage, responsive attitude, waving tail and overall look of functional strength, quality, style and symmetry complete the picture of the typical Flat-Coat.

Judging the Flat-Coat moving freely on a loose lead and standing naturally is more important than judging him posed. Honorable scars should not count against the dog.

**Size, Proportion, Substance**—*Size*—Individuals varying more than an inch either way from the preferred height should be considered not practical for the types of work for which the Flat-Coat was developed. Preferred height is 23 to 24½ inches at the withers for dogs, 22 to 23½ inches for bitches. Since the Flat-Coat is a working hunting retriever he should be shown in lean, hard condition, free of excess weight. *Proportion*—The Flat-Coat is not cobby in build. The length of the body from the point of the shoulder to the rearmost projection of the upper thigh is slightly more than the height at the withers. The female may be slightly longer to better accommodate the carrying of puppies. *Substance*—Moderate. Medium bone is flat or oval rather than round; strong but never massive, coarse, weedy or fine. This applies throughout the dog.

**Head**—The long, clean, well molded head is adequate in size and strength to retrieve a large pheasant, duck or hare with ease. *Skull and Muzzle*—The impression of the skull and muzzle being "cast in one piece" is created by the fairly flat skull of moderate breadth and flat, clean cheeks, combined with the long, strong, deep muzzle which is well filled in before, between and beneath the eyes. Viewed from above, the muzzle is nearly equal in length and breadth to the skull. *Stop*—There is a gradual, slight, barely perceptible stop, avoiding a down or dish-faced appearance. Brows are slightly raised and mobile, giving life to the expression. Stop must be evaluated in profile so that it will not be confused with the raised brow. *Occiput* not accentuated, the skull forming a gentle curve where it fits well into the neck. *Expression* alert, intelligent and kind. *Eyes* are set widely apart. Medium sized, almond shaped, dark brown or hazel; not large, round or yellow. Eye rims are self-colored and tight. *Ears* relatively small, well set on, lying close to the side of the head and thickly feathered. Not low set (houndlike or setterish). *Nose*—Large open nostrils. Black on black dogs, brown on liver dogs. *Lips* fairly tight, firm, clean and dry to minimize the retention of feathers. *Jaws* long and strong, capable of carrying a hare or a pheasant. *Bite*—Scissors bite preferred, level bite acceptable.

Broken teeth should not count against the dog. *Severe Faults*—Wry and undershot or overshot bites with a noticeable gap must be severely penalized.

**Neck, Topline, Body**—*Neck* strong and slightly arched for retrieving strength. Moderately long to allow for easy seeking of the trail. Free from throatiness. Coat on neck is untrimmed. *Topline* strong and level. *Body*—*Chest (Brisket)*—Deep, reaching to the elbow and only moderately broad. *Forechest*—Prow prominent and well developed. *Rib cage* deep, showing good length from forechest to last rib (to allow ample space for all body organs), and only moderately broad. The foreribs fairly flat showing a gradual spring, well arched in the center of the body but rather lighter towards the loin. *Underline*—Deep chest tapering to a moderate *tuck-up*. *Loin* strong, well muscled and long enough to allow for agility, freedom of movement and length of stride, but never weak or loosely coupled. *Croup* slopes very slightly; rump moderately broad and well muscled. *Tail* fairly straight, well set on, with bone reaching approximately to the hock joint. When the dog is in motion, the tail is carried happily but without curl as a smooth extension of the topline, never much above the level of the back.

**Forequarters**—*Shoulders* long, well laid back shoulder blade with *upper arm* of approximately equal length to allow for efficient reach. Musculature wiry rather than bulky. *Elbows* clean, close to the body and set well back under the withers. *Forelegs* straight and strong with medium bone of good quality. *Pasterns* slightly sloping and strong. *Dewclaws*—Removal of dewclaws is optional. *Feet* oval or round. Medium sized and tight with well arched toes and thick pads.

**Hindquarters**—Powerful with angulation in balance with the front assembly. *Upper thighs* powerful and well muscled. *Stifle*—Good turn of stifle with sound, strong joint. *Second thighs* (Stifle to hock joint)—Second or lower thigh as long as or only slightly longer than upper thigh. *Hock*—Hock joint strong, well let down. *Dewclaws*—There are no hind dewclaws. *Feet* oval or round. Medium sized and tight with well arched toes and thick pads.

**Coat**—Coat is of moderate length, density and fullness, with a high lustre. The ideal coat is straight and flat lying. A slight waviness is permissible but the coat is not curly, woolly, short, silky or fluffy. The Flat-Coat is a working retriever and the coat must provide protection from all types of weather, water and ground cover. This requires a coat of sufficient texture, length and fullness to allow for adequate insulation. When the dog is in full coat the ears, front, chest, back of forelegs, thighs and underside of tail are thickly feathered without being bushy, stringy or silky. Mane of longer heavier coat on the neck extending over the withers and shoulders is considered typical, especially in the male dog, and can cause the neck to appear thicker and the withers higher, sometimes causing the appearance of a dip behind the withers. Since the Flat-Coat is a hunting retriever, the feathering is not excessively long. *Trimming*—The Flat-Coat is shown with as natural a coat as possible and must not be penalized for lack of trimming, as long as the coat is clean and well brushed. Tidying of ears, feet, underline and tip of tail is acceptable. Whiskers serve a specific function and it is preferred that they not be trimmed. Shaving or barbering of the head, neck or body coat must be severely penalized.

**Color**—Solid black or solid liver. ***Disqualification***—Yellow, cream or any color other than black or liver.

**Gait**—Sound, efficient movement is of critical importance to a hunting retriever. The Flat-Coat viewed from the side covers ground efficiently and movement appears balanced, free flowing and well coordinated, never choppy, mincing or ponderous. Front and rear legs reach well forward and extend well back, achieving long clean strides. Topline appears level, strong and supple while dog is in motion.

### SUMMARY

The Flat-Coat is a strong but elegant, cheerful hunting retriever. Quality of structure, balance and harmony of all parts both standing and in motion are essential. As a breed whose purpose is of a utilitarian nature—structure, condition and attitude should give every indication of being suited for hard work.

**Temperament**—Character is a primary and outstanding asset of the Flat-Coat. He is a responsive, loving member of the family, a versatile working dog, multi-talented, sensible, bright and tractable. In competition the Flat-Coat demonstrates *stability* and a desire to please with a confident, happy and outgoing attitude characterized by a wagging tail. Nervous, hyperactive, apathetic, shy or obstinate behavior is undesirable. ***Severe Fault***—Unprovoked aggressive behavior toward people or animals is *totally* unacceptable. ***Character***—Character is as important to the evaluation of stock by a potential breeder as any other aspect of the breed standard. The Flat-Coat is primarily a family companion hunting retriever. He is keen and birdy, flushing within gun range, as well as a determined, resourceful retriever on land and water. He has a great desire to hunt with self-reliance and an uncanny ability to adapt to changing circumstances on a variety of upland game and waterfowl.

As a family companion he is sensible, alert and highly intelligent; a lighthearted, affectionate and adaptable friend. He retains these qualities as well as his youthfully good-humored outlook on life into old age. The adult Flat-Coat is usually an adequate alarm dog to give warning, but is a good-natured, optimistic dog, basically inclined to be friendly to all.

The Flat-Coat is a cheerful, devoted companion who requires and appreciates living with and interacting as a member of his family. To reach full potential in any endeavor he absolutely must have a strong personal bond and affectionate individual attention.

### DISQUALIFICATION

*Yellow, cream or any color other than black or liver.*

Approved September 11, 1990

# Retriever, Golden

In the early 1800s game was plentiful in England and Scotland, and hunting was both a sport and a practical way of obtaining food. Retrievers came into prominence because of the desire for a medium-sized dog that would do well in wild-fowling, both water fowl and upland game.

The most complete records of the development of the Golden Retriever are included in the record books that were kept from 1835 until about 1890 by the gamekeepers at the Guisachan (pronounced Gooeesicun) estate of Lord Tweedmouth at Inverness-Shire, Scotland. These records were released to public notice in *Country Life* in 1952, when Lord Tweedmouth's great-nephew, the sixth Earl of Ilchester, historian and sportsman, published material that had been left by his ancestor. They provided factual confirmation to the stories that had been handed down through generations.

The delightful story that had the "six circus-performing Russian Trackers" as antecedents for Golden Retrievers is only that—a story, one which gained wide circulation but has no basis in fact.

It is known that in developing the Golden Retriever a Tweed Water Spaniel was used. Also, a small, lighter-built Newfoundland. There were other

**65**

crosses—Irish Setters, other water spaniels. Water retrieving was very important and hunters needed a strong dog that could withstand cold water, would
be a good swimmer and could fend with the heavy vegetation in which upland
game was found.

Lord Tweedmouth bought his first Yellow Retriever, Nous (i.e. Wisdom) in
Brighton in 1865. Nous was said to have been bred by the Earl of Chichester.
A photograph of Nous in about 1870 shows a biggish Golden with a wavy coat.
Some paintings in the British Museum show dogs similar in type. Portrait
painters often painted individuals and families with their favorite dogs.

The location of Guisachan on the Tweed River at Beauly, near Inverness,
had a direct bearing on the program pursued by Lord Tweedmouth to produce the characteristics he desired in his Yellow Retrievers. Along the shores
of this river was the Tweed Water Spaniel, the hardy type of spaniel used for
retrieving. The dog was descended from the ruggedly built water dogs which
for years had been used along the British seacoast by families who depended
upon the courage, intelligence and ability of these animals to retrieve game
under all sorts of conditions. According to Dalziel, author of *British Dogs*
(1881), Tweed Water Spaniels were light liver in color, so close in curl as to
give the idea that they had originally been a cross from a smooth-haired dog,
long in tail, ears heavy in flesh and hard like a hound's—but only slightly
feathered, forelegs feathered behind, hind legs smooth, head conical and lips
slightly pendulous.

Though this variety of water spaniel has long since sunk into obscurity, its
influence on the development of Golden Retrievers cannot be overlooked. The
gamekeepers' books at Guisachan indicate that Nous was mated to a Tweed
Water Spaniel named Belle in about 1867–68. Belle was liver-colored. At that
time, liver was a term to describe any shade of brown to fawn or sand color.
Nous and Belle produced four yellow puppies: Crocus, Cowslip, Primrose and
Ada. Cowslip proved important in Lord Tweedmouth's plan to develop a Yellow Retriever. She was later bred to a Tweed Water Spaniel and a bitch puppy
retained. In time, this dog was bred to a descendant of Ada. Yellow puppies
were entered in the records from the breedings, breedings that included an Irish
Setter and another Tweed Water Spaniel. It is believed that a Bloodhound was
also used. Line breeding, not often used at this time, was a factor in developing
the Golden Retriever, as Nous and Cowslip appear several times in the pedigrees.

Yellow or Golden Retrievers became popular in England toward the end of
the 19th century. The first win of a field trial by a Golden Retriever took place
in 1904.

Golden Retrievers were first shown in England at the Crystal Palace show
in 1908, and were listed as Flat Coats (Golden). Others (also grouped with
other retrievers as Flat Coats) were exhibited in 1909 and 1913. In 1913 they
were given separate status by color and shown as Golden or Yellow Retrievers.
Some enthusiasts formed the Golden Retriever Club (of England).

Travelers had taken some of the dogs with them on visits to America, and it is known that there were Golden Retrievers in the United States and Canada during the 1890s. Goldens from Great Britain and Canada were brought to both the East and West Coasts of the United States in the 1920s and 1930s.

The first registration of a Golden Retriever by the American Kennel Club was in November 1925. While there had been Goldens registered before that date, they had been registered as Retrievers with some description as to color. In Canada, their first registration as a separate breed was in 1927.

Goldens were furthered in the United States in the 1930s and 1940s. (The Golden Retriever Club of America was formed in 1938.) The dogs were predominantly used as hunters, though some were shown on the bench. The owners made a great effort and were conscientious breeders for they wanted sound, good looking dogs as hunters for the game that was then plentiful. More and more of these breeders began exhibiting their dogs in the show ring.

On the whole, the darker dogs were favored but there were some medium gold colors as well. Both dark and light dogs were run in English field trials and seen in the show rings in Scotland and England. The same was true in the United States and Canada, and remains true today. Balance, soundness, gait, trainability and temperament have ever been the first considerations for the knowledgeable fancier.

In England and Scotland the standard was changed in 1936 to allow the lighter as well as the darker colors. As more and more dogs were imported from England and Scotland to fill the American demand, the lighter colors were brought over along with the darker. While there have been some that have won, the very light dog is not well favored in the show rings in the United States, and such winners might have been the exceptions that won because of other qualities. There is a swing away from the very light dog by the American public, and as a rule they have not been favored by field trial people and hunters.

Golden Retriever clubs in the United States and other countries are taking active steps in maintaining the breed at its best. Today, Golden Retrievers are used successfully in field trials, hunting, obedience, as personal companion dogs and as guide dogs for the blind. The excellent nose which makes for good game finding and tracking has been useful in other areas, including narcotics detection.

The first three dogs of any breed to achieve the AKC Obedience Champion title, first available in July 1977, were all Golden Retrievers. The first (Ch. Moreland's Golden Tonka) was a bitch, the others were males. Both males and females have done well in field trials and hunting. Their size, their biddable temperament and their desire to please, are all part of why Golden Retrievers have increased so rapidly in popularity.

# Official Standard for the Golden Retriever

**General Appearance**—A symmetrical, powerful, active dog, sound and well put together, not clumsy nor long in the leg, displaying a kindly expression and possessing a personality that is eager, alert and self-confident. Primarily a hunting dog, he should be shown in hard working condition. Overall appearance, balance, gait and purpose to be given more emphasis than any of his component parts. *Faults*—Any departure from the described ideal shall be considered faulty to the degree to which it interferes with the breed's purpose or is contrary to breed character.

**Size, Proportion, Substance**—Males 23–24 inches in height at withers; females 21½–22½ inches. Dogs up to one inch above or below standard size should be proportionately penalized. Deviation in height of more than one inch from the standard shall *disqualify*.

Length from breastbone to point of buttocks slightly greater than height at withers in ratio of 12:11. Weight for dogs 65–75 pounds; bitches 55–65 pounds.

**Head**—Broad in *skull* slightly arched laterally and longitudinally without prominence of frontal bones (forehead) or occipital bones. *Stop* well defined but not abrupt. *Foreface* deep and wide, nearly as long as skull. *Muzzle* straight in profile, blending smooth and strongly into skull; when viewed in profile or from above, slightly deeper and wider at stop than at tip. No heaviness in flews. Removal of whiskers is permitted but not preferred. *Eyes* friendly and intelligent in expression, medium large with dark, close-fitting rims, set well apart and reasonably deep in sockets. Color preferably dark brown; medium brown acceptable. Slant eyes and narrow, triangular eyes detract from correct expression and are to be faulted. No white or haw visible when looking straight ahead. Dogs showing evidence of functional abnormality of eyelids or eyelashes (such as, but not limited to, trichiasis, entropion, ectropion, or distichiasis) are to be excused from the ring. *Ears* rather short with front edge attached well behind and just above the eye and falling close to cheek. When pulled forward, tip of ear should just cover the eye. Low, hound-like ear set to be faulted. *Nose* black or brownish black, though fading to a lighter shade in cold weather not serious. Pink nose or one seriously lacking in pigmentation to be faulted. *Teeth* scissors bite, in which the outer side of the lower incisors touches the inner side of the upper incisors. Undershot or overshot bite is a *disqualification*. Misalignment of teeth (irregular placement of incisors) or a level bite (incisors meet each other edge to edge) is undesirable, but not to be confused with undershot or overshot. Full dentition. Obvious gaps are serious faults.

**Neck, Topline, Body**—*Neck* medium long, merging gradually into well laid back shoulders, giving sturdy, muscular appearance. No throatiness. *Backline* strong and level from withers to slightly sloping croup, whether standing or moving. Sloping backline, roach or sway back, flat or steep croup to be faulted. *Body* well balanced, short coupled, deep through the chest. *Chest* between forelegs at least as wide as a man's closed hand including thumb, with well developed forechest. Brisket extends to elbow. *Ribs* long and well sprung but not barrel shaped, extending well towards hindquarters. *Loin* short, muscular, wide and deep, with very little tuck-up. Slabsidedness, narrow chest, lack of depth in brisket, excessive tuck-up to be faulted. *Tail* well set on, thick and muscular at the base, following the natural line of the croup. Tail bones extend to, but not below, the point of hock. Carried with merry action, level or with some moderate upward curve; never curled over back nor between legs.

**Forequarters**—Muscular, well coordinated with hindquarters and capable of free movement. *Shoulder blades* long and well laid back with upper tips fairly close together at withers. *Upper arms* appear about the same length as the blades, setting the elbows back beneath the upper tip of the blades, close to the ribs without looseness. *Legs,* viewed from the front, straight with good bone, but not to the point of coarseness. *Pasterns* short and strong, sloping slightly with no suggestion of weakness. Dewclaws on forelegs may be removed, but are normally left on. *Feet* medium size, round, compact, and well knuckled, with thick pads. Excess hair may be trimmed to show natural size and contour. Splayed or hare feet to be faulted.

**Hindquarters**—Broad and strongly muscled. Profile of croup slopes slightly; the pelvic bone slopes at a slightly greater angle (approximately 30 degrees from horizontal). In a natural stance, the femur joins the pelvis at approximately a 90-degree angle; *stifles* well bent; *hocks* well let down with short, strong *rear pasterns. Feet* as in front. *Legs* straight when viewed from rear. Cow-hocks, spread hocks, and sickle hocks to be faulted.

**Coat**—Dense and water-repellent with good undercoat. Outer coat firm and resilient, neither coarse nor silky, lying close to body; may be straight or wavy. Untrimmed natural ruff; moderate feathering on back of forelegs and on underbody; heavier feathering on front of neck, back of thighs and underside of tail. Coat on head, paws, and front of legs is short and even. Excessive length, open coats, and limp, soft coats are very undesirable. Feet may be trimmed and stray hairs neatened, but the natural appearance of coat or outline should not be altered by cutting or clipping.

**Color**—Rich, lustrous golden of various shades. Feathering may be lighter than rest of coat. With the exception of graying or whitening of face or body due to age, any white marking, other than a few white hairs on the chest, should be penalized according to its extent. Allowable light shadings are not to be confused with white markings. Predominant body color which is either extremely pale or extremely dark is undesirable. Some latitude should be given to the light puppy whose coloring shows promise of deepening with maturity. Any noticeable area of black or other off-color hair is a serious fault.

**Gait**—When trotting, gait is free, smooth, powerful and well coordinated, showing good reach. Viewed from any position, legs turn neither in nor out, nor do feet cross or interfere with each other. As speed increases, feet tend to converge toward center line of balance. It is recommended that dogs be shown on a loose lead to reflect true gait.

**Temperament**—Friendly, reliable, and trustworthy. Quarrelsomeness or hostility towards other dogs or people in normal situations, or an unwarranted show of timidity or nervousness, is not in keeping with Golden Retriever character. Such actions should be penalized according to their significance.

### DISQUALIFICATIONS

*Deviation in height of more than one inch from standard either way.
Undershot or overshot bite.*

Approved October 13, 1981
Reformatted August 18, 1990

# Retriever, Labrador

The Labrador Retriever did not, as his name implies, come from Labrador, but from Newfoundland, although there is no indication of by what means he reached the latter place. However, in 1822 a traveler in that region reported a number of "small water dogs" and said: "The dogs are admirably trained as retrievers in fowling, and are otherwise useful . . . The smooth or short-haired dog is preferred because in frosty weather the long-haired kind become encumbered with ice on coming out of the water."

Early in the 19th century the Earl of Malmesbury reputedly saw one of the dogs that had been carried to England by fishermen and immediately arranged to have some imported. In 1830 the noted British sportsman Colonel Hawker referred to the ordinary Newfoundland and what he called the St. John's breed of water dog, mentioning the former as "very large, strong of limb, rough hair, and carrying his tail high." Referring to what is known now as the Labrador, he said they were "by far the best for any kind of shooting. He is generally black and no bigger than a Pointer, very fine in legs, with short, smooth hair and does not carry his tail so much curled as the other; is extremely quick running, swimming and fighting . . . and their sense of smell is hardly to be credited. . . ."

The dogs were not at first generally known in England as Labradors. In fact, the origin of the name is shown in a letter written in 1887 by an Earl of Malmesbury in which he said: "We always call mine Labrador dogs, and I have kept the breed as pure as I could from the first I had from Poole, at that time carrying on a brisk trade with Newfoundland. The real breed may be known by its close coat which turns the water off like oil and, above all, a tail like an otter."

The Labrador gradually died out in Newfoundland on account of a heavy dog tax which, with the English quarantine law, practically stopped the importations into England. Thereafter many Labradors were interbred with other types of retrievers. Fortunately, however, the Labrador characteristics predominated. And finally fanciers, desiring to stop the interbreeding, drew up a standard so as to discourage crossing with other retrievers.

There is a stud book of the Duke of Buccleuch's Labrador Retrievers which made it possible to work out pedigrees of the two dogs that did most to produce the modern Labrador, Mr. A. C. Butter's Peter of Faskally, and Major Portal's Flapper. These pedigrees go back as far as 1878.

The Labrador Retriever was first recognized as a separate breed by the English Kennel Club in 1903. The first registration of Labradors by the American Kennel Club was in 1917—Brocklehirst Nell, a Scottish bitch import. From the late 1920s through the 1930s there was a great influx of British dogs (and Scottish retriever trainers) that was to form the backbone of the breed in this country.

In England, no Labrador can become a bench show champion unless he has a working certificate, too—testament that he has also qualified in the field. In America, the Labrador became primarily a retriever trial and shooting dog, but the dual concept of retriever excellence combined with good looks, style and proper type was established early. The fanciers of the 1930s who started the retriever trials—The Labrador Retriever Club (U.S.) was organized in 1931—also exhibited their field dogs at the bench shows with marked success.

The Labrador Retriever's capabilities, fine temperament, and dependability have established it as one of the prime breeds for service as a guide dog for the blind, or for search and rescue work.

## Official Standard for the Labrador Retriever

**General Appearance**—The general appearance of the Labrador should be that of a strongly built, short-coupled, very active dog. He should be fairly wide over the loins, and strong and muscular in the hindquarters. The coat should be close, short, dense and free from feather.

**Head**—The skull should be wide, giving brain room; there should be a slight stop, *i.e.* the brow should be slightly pronounced, so that the skull is not absolutely in a straight line with the nose. The head should be clean-cut and free from fleshy cheeks. The jaws should be long and powerful and free from snipiness; the nose should be wide and the nostrils well developed. Teeth should be strong and regular, with a level mouth. The ears should hang moderately close to the head, rather far back, should be set somewhat low and not be large and heavy. The eyes should be of a medium size, expressing great intelligence and good temper, and can be brown, yellow or black, but brown or black is preferred.

**Neck and Chest**—The neck should be medium length, powerful and not throaty. The shoulders should be long and sloping. The chest must be of good width and depth, the ribs well sprung and the loins wide and strong, stifles well turned, and the hindquarters well developed and of great power.

**Legs and Feet**—The legs must be straight from the shoulder to ground, and the feet compact with toes well arched, and pads well developed; the hocks should be well bent, and the dog must neither be cowhocked nor be too wide behind; in fact, he must stand and move true all round on legs and feet. Legs should be of medium length, showing good bone and muscle, but not so short as to be out of balance with rest of body. In fact, a dog well balanced in all points is preferable to one with outstanding good qualities and defects.

**Tail**—The tail is a distinctive feature of the breed; it should be very thick towards the base, gradually tapering towards the tip, of medium length, should be free from any feathering, and should be clothed thickly all round with the Labrador's short, thick, dense coat, thus giving that peculiar "rounded" appearance which has been described as the "otter" tail. The tail may be carried gaily but should not curl over the back.

**Coat**—The coat is another very distinctive feature; it should be short, very dense and without wave, and should give a fairly hard feeling to the hand.

**Color**—The colors are black, yellow, or chocolate and are evaluated as follows:
  (a) *Blacks:* All black, with a small white spot on chest permissible. Eyes to be of medium size, expressing intelligence and good temper, preferably brown or hazel, although black or yellow is permissible.
  (b) *Yellows:* Yellows may vary in color from fox-red to light cream with variations in the shading of the coat on ears, the underparts of the dog, or beneath the tail. A small white spot on chest is permissible. Eye coloring and expression should be the same as that of the blacks, with black or dark brown eye rims. The nose should also be black or dark brown, although "fading" to pink in winter weather is not serious. A "Dudley" nose (pink without pigmentation) should be penalized.
  (c) *Chocolates:* Shades ranging from light sedge to chocolate. A small white spot on chest is permissible. Eyes to be light brown to clear yellow. Nose and eye-rim pigmentation dark brown or liver colored. "Fading" to pink in winter weather not serious. "Dudley" nose should be penalized.

**Movement**—Movement should be free and effortless. The forelegs should be strong, straight and true, and correctly placed. Watching a dog move towards one, there should be no signs of elbows being out in front, but neatly held to the body with legs not too close together, and moving straight forward without pacing or weaving. Upon viewing the dog from the rear, one should get the impression that the hind legs, which should be well muscled and not cowhocked, move as nearly parallel as possible, with hocks doing their full share of work and flexing well, thus giving the appearance of power and strength.

**Approximate Weights of Dogs and Bitches in Working Condition**—Dogs—60 to 75 pounds; bitches—55 to 70 pounds.

**Height at Shoulders**—Dogs—22½ inches to 24½ inches; bitches—21½ inches to 23½ inches.

Approved April 9, 1957

# Setter, English

From the best authorities on the subject, it appears that the English Setter was a trained bird dog in England more than 400 years ago. A perusal of some of the old writings leads us to believe that the English Setter had its origin in some of the older of the land spaniels that originated in Spain. We are indebted, however, to Hans Bols, who, in *Partridge Shooting and Partridge Hawking*, written in 1582, presents quite definite pictorial evidence that the setter and the spaniel breeds were quite different in appearance, and even at that time the tails of the spaniels appeared to have been docked as they are today and the tails of setters left as nature intended them.

There is some evidence in the earlier writings of sportsmen that the old English Setter was originally produced from crosses of the Spanish Pointer, the large Water Spaniel, and the Springer Spaniel, and by careful cultivation attained a high degree of proficiency in finding and pointing game in open country. We can see from examination of the sketches in many of the old writings that this setter-spaniel was an extremely handsome dog, many having a head much longer and with a more classical cut than that of the spaniel, while others had the short spaniel-like head, lacking the well-defined profile of the skull and foreface of the modern dogs. Also most of these older setters had coats which were quite curly, particularly at the thighs. It can be seen from this brief review that even our oldest authorities were not entirely in accord as to the origin of this breed.

There is little doubt that the major credit for the development of the modern setter should go to Edward Laverack, who about 1825 obtained from the Rev. A. Harrison, "Ponto" and "Old Moll." The Rev. Harrison had apparently kept this breed pure for 35 years or more. From these two Laverack, through a remarkable process of inbreeding, produced Prince, Countess, Nellie, and Fairy, which were marvelous specimens of English Setters.

The first show for English Setters was held at Newcastle-on-Tyne on January 28, 1859, and from this time on dog shows flourished throughout England, gradually increasing in popularity.

Along about 1874, Mr. Laverack sold a pair of dogs to Charles H. Raymond of Morris Plains, N.J. During the next ten years the English Setter became more and more popular and it was around this time that many Setters bred by R. L. Purcell Llewellin were imported into this country and Canada.

In considering the so-called Llewellin strain, it is recorded in the writing of Dr. William A. Bruette that about the time the Laverack strain was at its zenith in England, Mr. Llewellin purchased a number of Laverack's best show dogs of the pure Dash-Moll and Dash-Hill Laverack inheritance and crossed them with some entirely new "blood" which he obtained in the north of England, represented by Mr. Statter's and Sir Vincent Corbet's strain, since referred to as the Duke-Rhoebes, names of the two most prominent members of the strain. The results of these crosses were eminently successful, particularly at field trials; they swept everything before them. Their reputation spread to America and many were purchased by sportsmen in different sections of the United States and Canada, so that this line of breeding soon became firmly established on this side of the Atlantic.

Probably the name that stands out most conspicuously in the foundation of the field-trial setter in America is Count Noble. This dog was purchased from Llewellin by Dave Sanborn of Dowling, Michigan, who, after trying him out on the prairies, was upon the point of returning him to England, but was persuaded not to do so by the late B. F. Wilson of Pittsburgh. On the death of Sanborn, Count passed into the hands of Wilson, who gave him an opportunity to demonstrate his sterling qualities from coast to coast. The body of this famous dog was mounted at his death and is now in the Carnegie Museum at Pittsburgh, where it is visited annually by many sportsmen.

The English Setter has retained its popularity since its introduction to this country primarily because of its usefulness and beauty. As a result of intelligent breeding it has been brought to a high state of perfection and a representative entry is always to be found at all bench shows and field trials.

The mild, sweet disposition characteristic of this breed along with the beauty, intelligence, and aristocratic appearance it makes in the field and in the home has endeared it both to the sportsman as well as all lovers of a beautiful, active, and rugged outdoor dog. A lovable disposition makes it an ideal companion; it is, however, a dog that requires considerable exercise and therefore is better suited to ownership in the suburbs than in the city.

## Official Standard for the English Setter

**General Appearance**—An elegant, substantial and symmetrical gun dog suggesting the ideal blend of strength, stamina, grace, and style. Flat-coated with feathering of good length. Gaiting freely and smoothly with long forward reach, strong rear drive and firm topline. Males decidedly masculine without coarseness. Females decidedly feminine without overrefinement. Overall appearance, balance, gait, and purpose to be given more emphasis than any component part. Above all, extremes of anything distort type and must be faulted.

**Head**—Size and proportion in harmony with body. Long and lean with a well defined stop. When viewed from the side, head planes (top of muzzle, top of skull and bottom of lower jaw) are parallel. *Skull*—oval when viewed from above, of medium width, without coarseness, and only slightly wider at the earset than at the brow. Moderately defined occipital protuberance. Length of skull from occiput to stop equal in length of muzzle. *Muzzle*—long and square when viewed from the side, of good depth with flews squared and fairly pendant. Width in harmony with width of skull and equal at nose and stop. Level from eyes to tip of nose. *Nose*—black or dark brown, fully pigmented. Nostrils wide apart and large. *Foreface*—skeletal structure under the eyes well chiseled with no suggestion of fullness. Cheeks present a smooth and clean-cut appearance. *Teeth*—close scissors bite preferred. Even bite acceptable. *Eyes*—dark brown, the darker the better. Bright, and spaced to give a mild and intelligent expression. Nearly round, fairly large, neither deepset nor protruding. Eyelid rims dark and fully pigmented. Lids fit tightly so that haw is not exposed. *Ears*—set well back and low, even with or below eye level. When relaxed carried close to the head. Of moderate length, slightly rounded at the ends, moderately thin leather, and covered with silky hair.

**Neck and Body**—*Neck*—long and graceful, muscular and lean. Arched at the crest and clean-cut where it joins the head at the base of the skull. Larger and more muscular toward the shoulders, with the base of the neck flowing smoothly into the shoulders. Not too throaty. *Topline*—in motion or standing appears level or sloping slightly downward without sway or drop from withers to tail forming a graceful outline of medium length. *Forechest*—well developed, point of sternum projecting slightly in front of point of shoulder/upper arm joint. *Chest*—deep, but not so wide or round as to interfere with the action of the forelegs. Brisket deep enough to reach the level of the elbow. *Ribs*—long, springing gradually to the middle of the body, then tapering as they approach the end of the chest cavity. *Back*—straight and strong at its junction with loin. *Loin*—strong, moderate in length, slightly arched. Tuck up moderate. *Hips*—croup nearly flat. Hip bones wide apart, hips rounded and blending smoothly into hind legs. *Tail*—a smooth continuation of the topline. Tapering to a fine point with only sufficient length to reach the hock joint or slightly less. Carried straight and level with the back. Feathering straight and silky, hanging loosely in a fringe.

**Forequarters—*Shoulder*—**shoulder blade well laid back. Upper arm equal in length to and forming a nearly right angle with the shoulder blade. Shoulders fairly close together at the tips. Shoulder blades lie flat and meld smoothly with contours of body. ***Forelegs*—** from front or side, forelegs straight and parallel. Elbows have no tendency to turn in or out when standing or gaiting. Arm flat and muscular. Bone substantial but not coarse and muscles hard and devoid of flabbiness. ***Pasterns*—**short, strong and nearly round with the slope deviating very slightly forward from the perpendicular. ***Feet*—**face directly forward. Toes closely set, strong and well arched. Pads well developed and tough. Dewclaws may be removed.

**Hindquarters—**Wide, muscular thighs and well developed lower thighs. Pelvis equal in length to and forming a nearly right angle with upper thigh. In balance with forequarter assembly. Stifle well bent and strong. Lower thigh only slightly longer than upper thigh. Hock joint well bent and strong. Rear pastern short, strong, nearly round and perpendicular to the ground. Hind legs, when seen from the rear, straight and parallel to each other. Hock joints have no tendency to turn in or out when standing or gaiting.

**Coat—**Flat without curl or woolliness. Feathering on ears, chest, abdomen, underside of thighs, back of all legs and on the tail of good length but not so excessive as to hide true lines and movement or to affect the dog's appearance or function as a sporting dog.

**Markings and Color—*Markings*—**white ground color with intermingling of darker hairs resulting in belton markings varying in degree from clear distinct flecking to roan shading, but flecked all over preferred. Head and ear patches acceptable, heavy patches of color on the body undesirable. ***Color*—**orange belton, blue belton (white with black markings), tricolor (blue belton with tan on muzzle, over the eyes and on the legs), lemon belton, liver belton.

**Movement and Carriage—**An effortless graceful movement demonstrating endurance while covering ground efficiently. Long forward reach and strong rear drive with a lively tail and a proud head carriage. Head may be carried slightly lower when moving to allow for greater reach of forelegs. The back strong, firm, and free of roll. When moving at a trot, as speed increases, the legs tend to converge toward a line representing the center of gravity.

**Size—**Dogs about 25 inches; bitches about 24 inches.

**Temperament—**Gentle, affectionate, friendly, without shyness, fear or viciousness.

Approved November 11, 1986

# Setter, Gordon

Beauty, brains, and bird sense are the outstanding qualities of the handsome black-and-tan Setter from Scotland whose ancient lineage dates back at least to 1620 when Markham, a writer of the time, praised the "black and fallow setting dog" as "hardest to endure labor." Popular among hunters of Scotland for decades, the black-and-tan (or occasionally black-white-and-tan) Setter came into prominence in the kennels of the fourth Duke of Gordon in the 1820s. Commenting on these kennels, a writer familiar with the Duke's Gordons describes them much as a sportsman would describe a Gordon of today: "The Castle Gordon Setters are as a rule easy to break and naturally back well. They are not fast dogs but they have good staying powers and can keep on steadily from morning until night. Their noses are first class and they seldom make a false point or what is called at field trials a sensational stand. . . . When they stand you may be sure there are birds." A later and illustrious authority, Idstone notes: "I have seen better Setters of the black and tan than of any other breed."

Attracted quite as much by the Gordon's beauty as by his superior hunting ability, George Blunt in 1842 imported a brace from Castle Gordon to America. Drawings of the pair, Rake and Rachel, show Rake to be a mostly white, curly-coated dog with a black saddle; Rachel was black with tan markings, and was given to Daniel Webster. In following years other importations from Great Britain and the Scandinavian countries, and the perfecting of the American strains, helped the Gordon achieve great popularity as a pet and faithful gun dog, particularly in the period when game was marketed commercially and a real "meat" dog assured a full bag at the end of the day's shooting.

In 1891 Henry Malcolm formed the first Gordon Setter Club of America, though the breed was not officially recognized by the AKC as the Gordon Setter until a year later.

With the coming of the field-trial form of competition, Gordon popularity waned for a time, as the dog's habit of quartering thoroughly and working close to the gun placed him at a disadvantage where flashing speed was demanded, though as a one-man shooting dog the Gordon knows no peer. Currently, several regional clubs hold field trials and the Gordon is being encouraged to develop greater range and speed while maintaining his superiority as a methodical, dependable bird finder.

The Gordon's characteristic eagerness to work for a loving master has never changed over the centuries, nor have his keen intellect and retentive memory, which enable him to improve with age with no need for retraining each season. Gordon breeders, backed by a strong national club, make no distinction between field or show types. As a rule, bench-show champions are used regularly for hunting and give a good account of themselves in the field, as do the field trial winners at the bench show.

The oft-quoted comment that the Gordon's coloring makes him difficult to see in the field has doubtless been made by those who have never seen him there. Against the tan fall sedge grass or early snow, a black dog is highly conspicuous, and when this black dog is difficult to distinguish against his background it is then too dark to shoot with safety.

A true Setter, the Gordon is distinctive, resembling the English or Irish Setters only in general type. In field-trial competition the smaller, but not light-boned, Gordon has been more favored while the larger dog is preferred for bench work. The official standard of the breed allows considerable range in sizes primarily because individual sportsmen from various corners of the nation prefer their Gordons of a size to suit their local hunting terrain. There is general agreement, however, on the aristocratic beauty of the Gordon, with his silky black coat, rich mahogany markings, his well-feathered legs and gaily carried tail. The finely chisled, somewhat heavy head with long, low-set ears is distinctive for its intelligent expression. His good-sized, sturdy build with plenty of bone and substance and his upstanding, stylish gait give him the necessary stamina to match his ardor for the long days in the field.

The quality that endears the Gordon to the pet owner or to the sensitive sportsman is his devoted loyalty to members of the household. Wary of the unwanted intruder, the Gordon is not the chum of every passer-by, but lives for the pleasure of being near his owners. This almost fanatical devotion has helped make the Gordon not only a responsive gun dog, but a mannerly, eager-to-please dog in the home.

## Official Standard for the Gordon Setter

**General Appearance**—The Gordon Setter is a good-sized, sturdily built, black and tan dog, well muscled, with plenty of bone and substance, but active, upstanding and stylish, appearing capable of doing a full day's work in the field. He has a strong, rather short back, with well sprung ribs and a short tail. The head is fairly heavy and finely chiseled. His bearing is intelligent, noble, and dignified, showing no signs of shyness or viciousness. Clear colors and straight or slightly waved coat are correct. He suggests strength and stamina rather than extreme speed. Symmetry and quality are most essential. A dog well balanced in all points is preferable to one with outstanding good qualities and defects. A smooth, free movement, with high head carriage, is typical.

**Size, Proportion, Substance**—*Size*—Shoulder height for males, 24 to 27 inches; females, 23 to 26 inches. Weight for males, 55 to 80 pounds; females, 45 to 70 pounds. Animals that appear to be over or under the prescribed weight limits are to be judged on the basis of conformation and condition. Extremely thin or fat dogs are discouraged on the basis that under or overweight hampers the true working ability of the Gordon Setter. The weight-to-height ratio makes him heavier than other Setters. *Proportion*— The distance from the forechest to the back of the thigh is approximately equal the height from the ground to the withers. The Gordon Setter has plenty of bone and substance.

**Head**—Head deep, rather than broad, with plenty of brain room. *Eyes* of fair size, neither too deep-set nor too bulging, dark brown, bright and wise. The shape is oval rather than round. The lids are tight. *Ears* set low on the head approximately on line with the eyes, fairly large and thin, well folded and carried close to the head. *Skull* nicely rounded, good-sized, broadest between the ears. Below and above the eyes is lean and the cheeks as narrow as the leanness of the head allows. The head should have a clearly indicated stop. *Muzzle* fairly long and not pointed, either as seen from above or from the side. The flews are not pendulous. The muzzle is the same length as the skull from occiput to stop and the top of the muzzle is parallel to the line of the skull extended. *Nose* broad, with open nostrils and black in color. The lip line from the nose to the flews shows a sharp, well-defined, square contour. *Teeth* strong and white, meeting in front in a scissors bite, with the upper incisors slightly forward of the lower incisors. A level bite is not a fault. Pitted teeth from distemper or allied infections are not penalized.

**Neck, Topline, Body**—*Neck* long, lean, arched to the head, and without throatiness. *Topline* moderately sloping. *Body* short from shoulder to hips. Chest deep and not too broad in front; the ribs well sprung, leaving plenty of lung room. The chest reaches to the elbows. A pronounced forechest is in evidence. Loins short and broad and not arched.

Croup nearly flat, with only a slight slope to the tailhead. *Tail* short and not reaching below the hocks, carried horizontal or nearly so, not docked, thick at the root and finishing in a fine point. The placement of the tail is important for correct carriage. When the angle of the tail bends too sharply at the first coccygeal bone, the tail will be carried too gaily or will droop. The tail placement is judged in relationship to the structure of the croup.

**Forequarters**—Shoulders fine at the points, and laying well back. The tops of the shoulder blades are close together. When viewed from behind, the neck appears to fit into the shoulders in smooth, flat lines that gradually widen from neck to shoulder. The angle formed by the shoulder blade and upper arm bone is approximately 90 degrees when the dog is standing so that the foreleg is perpendicular to the ground. Forelegs big-boned, straight and not bowed, with elbows free and not turned in or out. Pasterns are straight. Dewclaws may be removed. Feet catlike in shape, formed by close-knit, well arched toes with plenty of hair between; with full toe pads and deep heel cushions. Feet are not turned in or out.

**Hindquarters**—The hind legs from hip to hock are long, flat and muscular; from hock to heel, short and strong. The stifle and hock joints are well bent and not turned either in or out. When the dog is standing with the rear pastern perpendicular to the ground, the thighbone hangs downward parallel to an imaginary line drawn upward from the hock. Feet as in front.

**Coat**—Soft and shining, straight or slightly waved, but not curly, with long hair on ears, under stomach and on chest, on back of the fore and hind legs, and on the tail. The feather which starts near the root of the tail is slightly waved or straight, having a triangular appearance, growing shorter uniformly toward the end.

**Color and Markings**—Black with tan markings, either of rich chestnut or mahogany color. Black pencilling is allowed on the toes. The borderline between black and tan colors is clearly defined. There are not any tan hairs mixed in the black. The tan markings are located as follows: (1) Two clear spots over the eyes and not over three-quarters of an inch in diameter; (2) On the sides of the muzzle. The tan does not reach to the top of the muzzle, but resembles a stripe around the end of the muzzle from one side to the other; (3) On the throat; (4) Two large clear spots on the chest; (5) On the inside of the hind legs showing down the front of the stifle and broadening out to the outside of the hind legs from the hock to the toes. It must not completely eliminate the black on the back of the hind legs; (6) On the forelegs from the carpus, or a little above, downward to the toes; (7) Around the vent; (8) A white spot on the chest is allowed, but the smaller the better. Predominantly tan, red or buff dogs which do not have the typical pattern of markings of a Gordon Setter are ineligible for showing and undesirable for breeding.

**Gait**—A bold, strong, driving free-swinging gait. The head is carried up and the tail 'flags' constantly while the dog is in motion. When viewed from the front the forefeet move up and down in straight lines so that the shoulder, elbow and pastern joints are approximately in line. When viewed from the rear the hock, stifle and hip joints are approximately in line. Thus the dog moves in a straight pattern forward without throwing the feet in or out. When viewed from the side the forefeet are seen to lift up and reach forward to compensate for the driving hindquarters. The hindquarters reach well forward and stretch far back, enabling the stride to be long and the drive powerful. The overall appearance of the moving dog is one of smooth-flowing, well balanced rhythm, in which the action is pleasing to the eye, effortless, economical and harmonious.

**Temperament**— The Gordon Setter is alert, gay, interested, and aggressive. He is fearless and willing, intelligent and capable. He is loyal and affectionate, and strong-minded enough to stand the rigors of training.

### DISQUALIFICATION

*Predominantly tan, red or buff dogs which do not have the typical pattern of markings of a Gordon Setter.*

Approved October 9, 1990

# Setter, Irish

The Irish Setter first came into popular notice early in the 18th century and less than a hundred years later his reputation was firmly established, not only in his native Ireland but throughout the British Isles. Speculations as to his origin are little more than guesswork, various breeds having been named as his progenitors, but none that can boast a clear title to the honor. Among the conjectures is that he was developed from an Irish Water Spaniel-Irish Terrier cross, but it is far more believable that an English Setter-Spaniel-Pointer combination, with a dash of Gordon thrown in, was the true formula.

The Irish Red Setter was the name originally chosen by the Irish Setter Club of America to designate the breed in this country. His earliest ancestors in the Emerald Isle, on the contrary, were rarely self-colored dogs. By far the larger number were red and white, the white frequently predominating over the red, and even today many individuals across the water are parti-colored. In America, however, solid reds or reds with small and inconspicuous white markings are the only ones accepted as typical. The Irishman's rich mahogany coat is thoroughly distinctive and has done much to make its wearer the bench-show favorite he is today.

The solid red Setter, as distinguished from the red and white, first appeared in Ireland in the 19th century. Jason Hazzard of Timaskea, County Fermanagh, Sir St. George Gore, and the Earl of Enniskillen all bred self-colored dogs, and it is a matter of record that in 1812 the Earl would have nothing else in his kennels. A few years later Stonehenge wrote: "The blood red, or rich chestnut or mahogany color is the color of an Irish Setter of high mark. This color must be unmixed with black; and studied in a strong light, there must not be black shadows or waves, much less black fringes to the ears, or to the profile of the form." The mention of black in the above is significant as indicating the possibility of the Gordon cross already mentioned. Today this color is absolutely taboo and even a few black hairs are faulted at the shows.

So much for the external appearance of the Irish Setter; now for more important, if less obvious characteristics. The breed is essentially a sporting one, and it is as a gun dog, after all, that this flashy red fellow must stand or fall. The first individuals imported into this country were brought over for use on game and, in spite of the fact that our ruffed grouse, quail, and prairie chicken were new and strange to them, they made good immediately. Elcho, imported in 1875 and one of the first of his breed to make a reputation for himself and his progeny in the United States, was not only a sensational success on the bench, but a thoroughly trained and capable shooting dog. To quote A. F. Hochwalt, in his book *The Modern Setter*, "All through the early field-trial records we find the Irish Setter holding his own with the 'fashionable blue bloods.' Had the Irish Setter fanciers continued on, their favorite breed would no doubt now be occupying a place as high in field trials as the other two breeds"; by which he means, of course, the English Setter and Pointer.

But the Irish Setter men didn't continue on, insofar as field trials were concerned, with the result that the Llewellin Setter and the Pointer have practically cornered the market in public competition in that field. Yet, in spite of this handicap, the red dog from Erin has lost none of the attributes of the good hunting companion, and given a fair chance, can and does demonstrate his quality as a high-class gun dog on all kinds of game. Strange as it may seem, his good looks have been his undoing in a way. His fatal gift of beauty, together with his gaiety, courage, and personality, have made him an ideal show dog. For this reason many fanciers have yielded to the temptation to breed for the bench only and to sacrifice to this most worthwhile object, field ability equally worthwhile and in no way incompatible with proper color, good size, and correct breed type.

Just a word regarding the characteristic personality of the red dog. First and foremost, he is typically Irish, with a devil-may-care something about him that not only makes him tremendously likeable but also adds to his value as a bird dog in rough country and briars. He is bold and at the same time gentle and lovable and loyal. He is tough—good and tough. He can stand continued work in the brush, is almost never stiff or sore, has the best of feet and running gear, and almost never gets "sour" when corrected in his work. He is not an early developer and frequently requires more training than some other breeds, but he is not as a rule headstrong in the sense that he is hard to handle in the brush. His outstanding fault as a field-trial performer is that he is not independent enough and pays too much attention to his handler. In reply to the criticism that he develops slowly, it is only fair to say that, once trained on birds, he is trained for the rest of his life and does not require a repetition of the process every fall. When you own a good Irishman, you own him for many years, every day of which you can be proud of his appearance, his personality, and his performance.

## Official Standard for the Irish Setter

**General Appearance**—The Irish Setter is an active, aristocratic bird dog, rich red in color, substantial yet elegant in build. Standing over two feet tall at the shoulder, the dog has a straight, fine, glossy coat, longer on ears, chest, tail and back of legs. Afield, the Irish Setter is a swift-moving hunter; at home, a sweet natured, trainable companion.

At their best, the lines of the Irish Setter so satisfy in overall balance that artists have termed it the most beautiful of all dogs. The correct specimen always exhibits balance, whether standing or in motion. Each part of the dog flows and fits smoothly into its neighboring parts without calling attention to itself.

**Size, Proportion, Substance**—There is no disqualification as to size. The make and fit of all parts and their overall balance in the animal are rated more important. 27 inches at the withers and a show weight of about 70 pounds is considered ideal for the dog; the bitch 25 inches, 60 pounds. Variance beyond an inch up or down is to be discouraged. *Proportion*—Measuring from the breastbone to rear of thigh and from the top of the withers to the ground, the Irish Setter is slightly longer than it is tall. *Substance*—All legs sturdy with plenty of bone. Structure in the male reflects masculinity without coarseness. Bitches appear feminine without being slight of bone.

**Head**—Long and lean, its length at least double the width between the ears. Beauty of head is emphasized by delicate chiseling along the muzzle, around and below the eyes, and along the cheeks. *Expression* soft, yet alert. *Eyes* somewhat almond shaped, of medium size, placed rather well apart, neither deep set nor bulging. Color, dark to medium brown. *Ears* set well back and low, not above level of eye. Leather thin, hanging in a neat fold close to the head, and nearly long enough to reach the nose. The *skull* is oval when viewed from above or front; very slightly domed when viewed in profile. The brow is raised, showing a distinct stop midway between the tip of the nose and the well-defined occiput (rear point of skull). Thus the nearly level line from occiput to brow is set a little above, and parallel to, the straight and equal line from eye to nose. *Muzzle* moderately deep, jaws of nearly equal length, the underline of the jaws being almost parallel with the top line of the muzzle. *Nose* black or chocolate; nostrils wide. Upper lips fairly square but not pendulous. The *teeth* meet in a scissors bite in which the upper incisors fit closely over the lower, or they may meet evenly.

**Neck, Topline, Body**—*Neck* moderately long, strong but not thick, and slightly arched; free from throatiness and fitting smoothly into the shoulders. *Topline* of body from withers to tail should be firm and incline slightly downward without sharp drop at the croup. The *tail* is set on nearly level with the croup as a natural extension of the topline, strong at root, tapering to a fine point, nearly long enough to reach the hock. Carriage straight or curving slightly upward, nearly level with the back. *Body* sufficiently long to permit a straight and free stride. *Chest* deep, reaching approximately to the elbows with moderate forechest, extending beyond the point where the shoulder joins the upper arm. Chest is of moderate width so that it does not interfere with forward motion and extends rearwards to well sprung ribs. *Loins* firm, muscular and of moderate length.

**Forequarters**—Shoulder blades long, wide, sloping well back, fairly close together at the withers. Upper arm and shoulder blades are approximately the same length, and are joined at sufficient angle to bring the elbows rearward along the brisket in line with the top of the withers. The elbows moving freely, incline neither in nor out. *Forelegs* straight and sinewy. Strong, nearly straight pastern. *Feet* rather small, very firm, toes arched and close.

**Hindquarters**—Hindquarters should be wide and powerful with broad, well developed thighs. Hind legs long and muscular from hip to hock; short and perpendicular from hock to ground; well angulated at stifle and hock joints, which, like the elbows, incline neither in nor out. Feet as in front. Angulation of the forequarters and hindquarters should be balanced.

**Coat**—Short and fine on head and forelegs. On all other parts of moderate length and flat. Feathering long and silky on ears; on back of forelegs and thighs long and fine, with a pleasing fringe of hair on belly and brisket extending onto the chest. Fringe on tail moderately long and tapering. All coat and feathering as straight and free as possible from curl or wave. The Irish Setter is trimmed for the show ring to emphasize the lean head and clean neck. The top third of the ears and the throat nearly to the breastbone are trimmed. Excess feathering is removed to show the natural outline of the foot. All trimming is done to preserve the natural appearance of the dog.

**Color**—Mahogany or rich chestnut red with no black. A small amount of white on chest, throat or toes, or a narrow centered streak on skull is not to be penalized.

**Gait**—At the trot the gait is big, very lively, graceful and efficient. At an extended trot the head reaches slightly forward, keeping the dog in balance. The forelegs reach well ahead as if to pull in the ground without giving the appearance of a hackney gait. The hindquarters drive smoothly and with great power. Seen from front or rear, the forelegs, as well as the hind legs below the hock joint, move perpendicularly to the ground, with some tendency towards a single track as speed increases. Structural characteristics which interfere with a straight, true stride are to be penalized.

**Temperament**—The Irish Setter has a rollicking personality. Shyness, hostility or timidity are uncharacteristic of the breed. An outgoing, stable temperament is the essence of the Irish Setter.

Approved August 14, 1990

# Spaniel, American Water

Exactly how, when, and where the American Water Spaniel originated is something of a mystery. Nevertheless, the virtues of the breed have long been appreciated by sportsmen in many parts of the United States. It is principally in the Middle West, however, that the present-day specimen evolved, since the dogs from that section had been known to breed true to type for countless generations. Color, coat and conformation combine to suggest the Irish Water Spaniel and the Curly-Coated Retriever, together with the latter's forebear the old English Water Spaniel, as progenitors, although this cannot be advanced categorically.

Prior to recognition as a breed by the American Kennel Club in 1940, the American Water Spaniel had been purely a working gun dog. He had never been introduced to the show ring since his admirers evidently feared that bench shows might damage his prowess as a hunter. But they were soon to learn that selective breeding along with bench show competition actually enhances the value of a dog no matter how well that dog may have been endowed by nature.

As a retriever the American Water Spaniel leaves little to be desired. He will watch the huntsman drop perhaps four or five birds, then work swiftly and merrily until every one is brought in. Rabbits, chickens, grouse, quail, pheasant, ducks—all he handles with unfailing dispatch and tender care. He swims "like a seal," hence few wounded water fowl escape him; his tail serves as a rudder to aid him, especially in turbulent water.

He is as well an all-around shooting dog possessed of an excellent nose; he works thicket, rough ground, or covert depending on body scent for location of game. His enthusiasm and thoroughness are an inspiration to the huntsman, while his desire to please makes him easily taught. He learns quickly to drop to shot and wing, although occasionally his eagerness may render him over-anxious. He does not point game; instead, he springs it. In addition, he is an efficient watchdog that fits agreeably into the family circle.

## Official Standard for the American Water Spaniel

**General Appearance**—The American Water Spaniel was developed in the United States as an all-around hunting dog, bred to retrieve from skiff or canoes and work ground with relative ease. The American Water Spaniel is an active muscular dog, medium in size with a marcel to curly coat. Emphasis is placed on proper size and a symmetrical relationship of parts, texture of coat and color.

**Size, Proportion, Substance**—15 to 18 inches for either sex. Males weighing 30–45 lbs. Females weighing 25–40 lbs. Females tend to be slightly smaller than the males. There is no preference for size within the given range of either sex providing correct proportion, good substance and balance is maintained. *Proportion* is slightly longer than tall, not too square or compact. However, exact proportion is not as important as the dog being well-balanced and sound, capable of performing the breed's intended function. *Substance,* a solidly built and well-muscled dog full of strength and quality. The breed has as much substance and bone as necessary to carry the muscular structure but not so much as to appear clumsy.

**Head**—The head must be in proportion to the overall dog. Moderate in length. *Expression* is alert, self-confident, attractive and intelligent. Medium size *eyes* set well apart, while slightly rounded, should not appear protruding or bulging. Lids tight, not drooping. Eye color can range from a light yellowish brown to brown, hazel or of dark tone to harmonize with coat. Disqualify yellow eyes. Yellow eyes are a bright color like that of lemon, not to be confused with the light yellowish brown. *Ears* set slightly above the eye line but not too high on the head, lobular, long and wide with leather extending to nose.

*Skull* rather broad and full, *stop* moderately defined, but not too pronounced. *Muzzle* moderate in length, square with good depth. No inclination to snipiness. The lips are clean and tight without excess skin or flews. Nose dark in color, black or dark brown. The nose sufficiently wide and with well-developed nostrils to insure good scenting power. *Bite* either scissor or level.

**Neck, Topline, Body**—*Neck* round and of medium length, strong and muscular, free of throatiness, set to carry head with dignity, but arch not accentuated. *Topline* level or slight, straight slope from withers. *Body* well-developed, sturdily constructed but not too compactly coupled. Well-developed brisket extending to elbow neither too broad nor too narrow. The ribs well-sprung, but not so well-sprung that they interfere with the movement of the front assembly. The loins strong, but not having a tucked-up look. *Tail* is moderate in length, curved in a rocker fashion, can be carried either slightly below or above the level of the back. The tail is tapered, lively and covered with hair with moderate feathering.

**Forequarters**—Shoulders sloping, clean and muscular. Legs medium in length, straight and well-boned but not so short as to handicap for field work or so heavy as to appear clumsy. Pasterns strong with no suggestion of weakness. Toes closely grouped, webbed and well-padded. Size of feet to harmonize with size of dog. Front dewclaws are permissible.

**Hindquarters**—Well-developed hips and thighs with the whole rear assembly showing strength and drive. The hock joint slightly rounded, should not be small and sharp in contour, moderately angulated. Legs from hock joint to foot pad moderate in length, strong and straight with good bone structure. Hocks parallel.

**Coat**—Coat can range from marcel (uniform waves) to closely curled. The amount of waves or curls can vary from one area to another on the dog. It is important to have undercoat to provide sufficient density to be of protection against weather, water or punishing cover, yet not too coarse or too soft. The throat, neck and rear of the dog well-covered with hair. The ear well-covered with hair on both sides with ear canal evident upon inspection. Forehead covered with short smooth hair and without topknot. Tail covered with hair to tip with moderate feathering. Legs have moderate feathering with waves or curls to harmonize with coat of dog. Coat may be trimmed to present a well-groomed appearance; the ears may be shaved; but neither is required.

**Color**—Color either solid liver, brown or dark chocolate. A little white on toes and chest permissible.

**Gait**—The American Water Spaniel moves with well-balanced reach and drive. Watching a dog move towards one, there should be no signs of elbows being out. Upon viewing the dog from the rear, one should get the impression that the hind legs, which should be well-muscled and not cowhocked, move as nearly parallel as possible, with hocks doing their full share of work and flexing well, thus giving the appearance of power and strength.

**Temperament**—Demeanor indicates intelligence, eagerness to please and friendly. Great energy and eagerness for the hunt yet controllable in the field.

**DISQUALIFICATION**

*Yellow eyes.*

Approved March 13, 1990

# Spaniel, Clumber

**B**ecause in type the Clumber Spaniel differs so widely from other members of the spaniel group, his origin probably will always remain in doubt, as is the case for that matter with many another breed. About all we can do is to ponder the statements of many authorities and then, with the conformation and detail of the breed in mind, resolve the whole into a reasonable supposition—which is that the long, low body resulted from Basset Hound crosses, and the heavy head (with noticeable haw) from an infusion of the early Alpine Spaniel.

Even within the same litters, the old land spaniels were called by various names—"cockers," "springers," "cock-flushers," etc.—but we do not find the name "Clumber" ascribed at that time. However, this is not to imply that the Clumber was a later development. Indeed, he is believed to be one of the earliest spaniels; developed for special uses.

The breed is believed to have originated in France. One of the earliest visual records of the breed is "The Return from Shooting," a painting by Frances Wheatley in 1788 depicting the second Duke of Newcastle and three of his Clumbers. Theory has it that at the time of the French Revolution, the Duc de Noailles of France moved his kennel of spaniels—which he had been carefully breeding for generations—to England for sanctuary, housing them at the kennels of the Duke of Newcastle at Clumber Park (hence the breed name) in Nottinghamshire.

The popularity of the breed was rigidly guarded by members of the English aristocracy in the district known as the "Dukeries." The dogs of the Duke of Portland, Lord Arthur Cecil and Earl Spencer probably were descended from the spaniels of Clumber Park. Prince Albert, Queen Victoria's consort, developed an interest in the breed after he had observed these spaniels working on the Duke of Newcastle's estate. And, Edward VII gave his royal Clumbers the prefix of Sandringham after purchasing Sandringham House in 1861.

Clumber Spaniels were first shown in England in 1859. The breed arrived in America relatively early—entering Canada in 1844 with Lt. Venables of Her Majesty's 97th Regiment, who was stationed in Halifax, Nova Scotia. The first Clumber Spaniel registered with the American Kennel Club is recorded for the date of 1878, six years before the establishment of the AKC. (The explanation for this is that the records of breedings of dogs in the United States existed long before the AKC's founding, and three volumes of stud books were accepted by the AKC as the basis for its Stud Book Register, which has been published continuously since 1887.)

When the standard for the breed was being written in England in the early 1900s, controversy arose over the exposed haw. Some felt it rendered the eye more liable to injury in a sporting dog, while others maintained it was one of the most typical characteristics of the best early specimens of the breed. The present AKC standard states: "Some haw may show."

The Clumber is a rather slow worker, moving with a distinctive rolling gait fully described in its standard—a comfortable gait that can be maintained at steady trot for a day of work in the fields without exhaustion. He is particularly adaptable for use in heavy covert; he generally hunts mute and is able to come up very close to the game. He is a sure finder and a splendid retriever when trained.

## Official Standard for the Clumber Spaniel

**General Appearance**—The Clumber is a long, low, heavy dog. His heavy brow, deep chest, straight forelegs, powerful hindquarters, massive bone and good feet all give him the power and endurance to move through dense underbrush in pursuit of game. His white coat enables him to be seen by the hunter as he works within gun range. His stature is dignified, his expression pensive, but at the same time, he shows great enthusiasm for work and play.

**Size, Proportion, Substance**—Males are about 19 to 20 inches at the withers, bitches are about 17 to 19 inches at the withers. Males weigh between 70 and 85 pounds, bitches between 55 and 70 pounds. The Clumber possesses massive bone, and is rectangular in shape. Length to height is approximately 11 to 9 measured from the withers to the base of the tail and from the floor to the withers.

**Head**—The head is massive. The eyes are dark amber in color, large, soft in expression, deep set in either a diamond shaped rim or a rim with a "V" on the bottom and a curve on the top. Some haw may show. Prominent or round shaped eyes are to be penalized. Excessive tearing, evidence of entropion or ectropion are to be penalized. Ears are broad on top, set low and attached to the skull about eye level. They are triangular in shape with a rounded lower edge. They are slightly feathered with straight hair, and ear leather is thick. The top skull is flat with a pronounced occiput. A slight furrow runs between the eyes and up through the center of the skull. Marked stop, heavy brow. The muzzle is broad and deep to facilitate retrieving many species of game. The nose is large, square and colored shades of brown, which includes beige, rose and cherry. The flews of the upper jaw are strongly developed and overlap the lower jaw to give a square look when viewed from the side. A scissors bite is preferred.

**Neck, Topline, Body**—The Clumber should have a long neck, with some slackness of throat or presence of dewlap not to be faulted. The neck is strong and muscular and fits into well laid back shoulders. The back is straight, firm, long and level. The chest is both deep and wide. The brisket is deep. The ribs are well sprung. The loin is only slightly arched.

The tail should be docked in keeping with the overall proportion of the adult dog. The tail is set on just below the line of the back and is normally carried parallel to the ground.

**Forequarters**—The Clumber shoulder is well laid back. The humerus or upper arm is of sufficient length to place the elbow under the highest point of the shoulder. The forelegs are short, straight, heavy in bone with elbows held close to the body. Pasterns are strong and only slightly sloped. The feet are large, compact and have thick pads which act as shock absorbers. Dewclaws may be removed. The hair may be trimmed for neatness and utility in the field.

**Hindquarters**—The thighs are heavily muscled, and when viewed from behind, the rear is round and broad. The stifle shows good functional angulation and hock to heel is short and perpendicular to the ground. Lack of angulation is objectionable. The feet on the rear legs are neither as large, nor as round as on the forelegs, but are compact, have thick pads, and are of substantial size.

**Coat**—The body coat is dense, straight, flat and is of good weather resistant texture; it is soft to the touch, not harsh. Ears are slightly feathered with straight hair. Feathering on the legs and belly is moderate. The Clumber has a good neck frill and on no condition should his throat be shaved. The feet may be trimmed to show the natural outline, as well as the rear legs up to the point of hock. Tail feathering may be tidied. Trimming of whiskers is optional. No other trimming or shaving is to be condoned.

**Color and Markings**—The Clumber is primarily a white dog with lemon or orange markings. Marking around one eye, both eyes or white face are of equal value. Freckles on the muzzle and forelegs are common. The fewer markings on the body, the better, although a spot near the root of the tail is common.

**Gait**—The Clumber moves easily and freely with good reach in front and strong drive from behind, neither crossing over nor elbowing out. The hocks drive in a straight line without rocking or twisting. Because of his wide body and short legs, he tends to roll slightly. The proper Clumber roll occurs when the dog with correct proportion reaches forward with rear legs toward the center line of travel and rotates the hip downward while the back remains level and straight. The gait is comfortable and can be maintained at a steady trot for a day of work in the fields without exhaustion.

**Temperament**—The Clumber is a loyal and affectionate dog; sometimes reserved with strangers, but never hostile or timid.

Approved October 10, 1989

# Spaniel, Cocker

**Cocker Spaniel, Black**

The Spaniel family is a large one, of considerable antiquity. As far back as 1368 we find mention of the *Spanyell*, which came to be divided into two groups, the land spaniel and the water spaniel. A further division separated the land spaniels on a basis of size, when the "cockers" and the very small or toy spaniels were separated from spaniels of larger dimensions. Then, as the cockers and the toys were used for markedly different purposes, these two were once more divided. The toys eventually became the English Toy Spaniels which were maintained principally as pets or comforters, while the Cockers retained their early classification as sporting dogs. That is why the Cocker is called the smallest member of the sporting-dog family.

As a valued helpmeet to the huntsman, this dog was known in his early days by various names, among them "cocker," "cocking spaniel," and finally Cocker Spaniel, the name deriving, according to some authorities, from especial proficiency on woodcock. Not until 1883 were classes provided for him at English bench shows; and not until 1892 was he given breed status in England's Kennel Club stud book.

The Cocker has been exhibited in the United States since the early 1880s. As developed here, however, the American Cocker has evolved somewhat differently in type, size, and coloring from the breed now recognized as the English Cocker Spaniel.

Cocker Spaniel, ASCOB

Cocker Spaniel, Parti-Color

Field trials for the breed in this country were started by the Cocker Spaniel Field Trial Club in 1924. The Cocker's inherent desire to hunt renders him a capable gun dog when judiciously trained. The usual method of hunting is to let him quarter the ground ahead of the gun, covering all territory within gun range. This he should do at a fast snappy pace. Upon flushing the game he should stop or preferably drop to a sitting position so as not to interfere with the shot, after which he should retrieve on command only. He should, of course, be so trained that he will be under control at all times. He is likewise valuable for occasional water retrieving and as a rule takes to water readily.

Many of the qualities that make it a valued hunter have served to make it a highly treasured companion for the home. Almost from the moment it appeared in the show rings, the Cocker achieved great popularity. Energetic, readily trainable, intelligent, affectionate and—as their constantly wagging tails tell us—quite merry, the handsome Cocker is today one of America's favorite pure-breds, No. 2 in AKC registrations.

## Official Standard for the Cocker Spaniel

**General Appearance**—The Cocker Spaniel is the smallest member of the Sporting Group. He has a sturdy, compact body and a cleanly chiseled and refined head, with the overall dog in complete balance and of ideal size. He stands well up at the shoulder on straight forelegs with a topline sloping slightly toward strong, muscular quarters. He is a dog capable of considerable speed, combined with great endurance. Above all he must be free and merry, sound, well balanced throughout, and in action show a keen inclination to work; equable in temperament with no suggestion of timidity.

**Head**—To attain a well-proportioned head, which must be in balance with the rest of the dog, it embodies the following; *Skull*—Rounded but not exaggerated with no tendency toward flatness; the eyebrows are clearly defined with a pronounced stop. The bony structure beneath the eyes is well chiseled with no prominence in the cheeks. *Muzzle*—Broad and deep, with square, even jaws. The upper lip is full and of sufficient depth to cover the lower jaw. To be in correct balance, the distance from the stop to the tip of the nose is one half the distance from the stop up over the crown to the base of the skull. *Teeth*—Strong and sound, not too small, and meet in a scissors bite. *Nose*—Of sufficient size to balance the muzzle and foreface, with well-developed nostrils typical of a sporting dog. It is black in color in the blacks and black and tans. In other colors it may be brown, liver or black, the darker the better. The color of the nose harmonizes with the color of the eye rim. *Eyes*—Eyeballs are round and full and look directly forward. The shape of the eye rims gives a slightly almond-shaped appearance; the eye is not weak or goggled. The color of the iris is dark brown and in general the darker the better. The expression is intelligent, alert, soft and appealing. *Ears*—Lobular, long, of fine leather, well feathered, and placed no higher than a line to the lower part of the eye.

**Neck and Shoulders**—The neck is sufficiently long to allow the nose to reach the ground easily, muscular and free from pendulous "throatiness." It rises strongly from the shoulders and arches slightly as it tapers to join the head. The shoulders are well laid back forming an angle with the upper arm of approximately 90 degrees which permits the dog to move his forelegs in an easy manner with considerable forward reach. Shoulders are clean-cut and sloping without protrusion and so set that the upper points of the withers are at an angle which permits a wide spring of rib.

**Body**—The body is short, compact and firmly knit together, giving an impression of strength. The distance from the highest point of the shoulder blades to the ground is fifteen percent or approximately two inches more than the length from this point to the set-on of the tail. Back is strong and sloping evenly and slightly downward from the shoulders to the set-on of the docked tail. Hips are wide and quarters well rounded and muscular. The chest is deep, its lowest point no higher than the elbows, its front sufficiently wide for adequate heart and lung space, yet not so wide as to interfere with the straightforward movement of the forelegs. Ribs are deep and well sprung. The Cocker Spaniel never appears long and low. *Tail*—The docked tail is set on and carried on a line with the topline of the back, or slightly higher; never straight up like a terrier and never so low as to indicate timidity. When the dog is in motion the tail action is merry. **Legs and Feet**—Forelegs are parallel, straight, strongly boned and muscular and set close to the body well under the scapulae. When viewed from the side with the forelegs vertical, the elbow is directly below the highest point of the shoulder blade. The pasterns are short and strong. The hind legs are strongly boned and muscled with good angulation at the stifle and powerful, clearly defined thighs. The stifle joint is strong and there is no slippage of it in motion or when standing. The hocks are strong, well let down, and when viewed from behind, the hind legs are parallel when in motion and at rest. *Feet*— Compact, large, round and firm with horny pads; they turn neither in nor out. Dewclaws on hind legs and forelegs may be removed.

**Coat**—On the head, short and fine; on the body, medium length, with enough undercoating to give protection. The ears, chest, abdomen and legs are well feathered, but not so excessively as to hide the Cocker Spaniel's true lines and movement or affect his appearance and function as a sporting dog. The *texture* is most important. The coat is silky, flat or slightly wavy, and of a texture which permits easy care. Excessive or curly or cottony textured coat is to be penalized.

**Color and Markings**—*Black Variety*—Solid color black, to include black with tan points. The black should be jet; shadings of brown or liver in the sheen of the coat is not desirable. A small amount of white on the chest and/or throat is allowed, white in any other location shall disqualify. *Any Solid Color Other Than Black*—Any solid color other than black and any such color with tan points. The color shall be of a uniform shade, but lighter coloring of the feather is permissible. A small amount of white on the chest and/or throat is allowed, white in any other location shall disqualify. *Parti-Color Variety*—Two or more definite, well-broken colors, one of which must be white, including those with tan points; it is preferable that the tan markings be located in the same pattern as for the tan points in the Black and ASCOB varieties. Roans are classified as parti-colors, and may be of any of the usual roaning patterns. Primary color which is ninety percent (90%) or more shall disqualify. *Tan Points*—The color of the tan may be from the lightest cream to the darkest red color and should be restricted to ten percent (10%) or less of the color of the specimen; tan markings in excess of that amount shall disqualify.

In the case of tan points in the Black or ASCOB variety, the markings shall be located as follows:

1. A clear tan spot over each eye
2. On the sides of the muzzle and on the cheeks
3. On the undersides of the ears
4. On all feet and/or legs
5. Under the tail
6. On the chest (optional, presence or absence not penalized)

Tan markings which are not readily visible or which amount only to traces, shall be penalized. Tan on the muzzle which extends upward, over and joins shall also be penalized. The absence of tan markings in the Black or ASCOB variety in any of the specified locations in an otherwise tan-pointed dog shall disqualify.

**Movement**—The Cocker Spaniel, though the smallest of the sporting dogs, possesses a typical sporting dog gait. Prerequisite to good movement is balance between the front and rear assemblies. He drives with his strong, powerful rear quarters and is properly constructed in the shoulders and forelegs so that he can reach forward without constriction in a full stride to counterbalance the driving force from the rear. Above all, his gait is coordinated, smooth and effortless. The dog must cover ground with his action and excessive animation should never be mistaken for proper gait.

**Height**—The ideal height at the withers for an adult dog is 15 inches and for an adult bitch 14 inches. Height may vary one-half inch above or below this ideal. A dog whose height exceeds 15½ inches or a bitch whose height exceeds 14½ inches shall be disqualified. An adult dog whose height is less than 14½ inches or an adult bitch whose height is less than 13½ inches shall be penalized.

*Note:* Height is determined by a line perpendicular to the ground from the top of the shoulder blades, the dog standing naturally with its forelegs and the lower hind legs parallel to the line of measurement.

### DISQUALIFICATIONS

*Color and Markings*—

*Black Variety—White markings except on chest and throat.*
*Any Solid Color Other Than Black Variety—White markings except on chest and throat.*
*Parti-Color Variety—Primary color ninety percent (90%) or more.*
*Tan Points—(1) Tan markings in excess of ten percent (10%); (2) Absence of tan markings in black or ASCOB variety in any of the specified locations in an otherwise tan pointed dog.*

**Height**—*Males over 15½ inches; females over 14½ inches*

Approved May 10, 1983.

# Spaniel, English Cocker

One of the oldest types of land spaniel known, the Cocker Spaniel descended from the original spaniels of Spain as one of a family destined to become highly diversified in size, type, coloring, and hunting ability.

Prior to the 17th century all members of the group were designated merely as spaniels, whether they were large or small, long-bodied or short, fast or slow on their feet. Gradually the marked difference in size began to impress those who used the dogs for hunting, with the result that the larger dogs were soon springing game and the smaller ones hunting woodcock. The names springer spaniel and cocker, or woodcock spaniel naturally followed, and in 1892 the Kennel Club (England) finally recognized them as separate breeds. This Cocker Spaniel was the English Cocker Spaniel.

It should be remembered that the Springers and Cockers above described, both before and after the date of their official separation in England, appeared in the same litters. Size alone was the dividing line between them. They enjoyed the same heritage, the same colorings, the same hunting skill and much the same general type. Cocker and Springer developed side by side. In fact, the Springer inheritance, naturally incorporated in the Cocker, was a fortunate directive for the success of the English Cocker, for it enabled him to become one of the finest of the smaller hunting dogs.

Exhaustive research disclosed that during the 19th century there were two other lines of "cocker" development. One involved the dogs known as "Field or Cocker Spaniels," which eventually branched out into Sussex, Field, and Cocker Spaniels, the latter weighing less than 25 pounds and being usually black in color. The other involved the spaniels of the House of Marlborough, of which there were two types—a small, round-headed, short-nosed red-and-white, and a slightly larger dog with shorter ears and longer foreface. The Marlborough "cockers" at long last became the English Toy Spaniels, but before they emerged as a distinct breed, they fused with the smaller cockers of partial Field Spaniel derivation. From these two lines combined came a spaniel approximating the size and type fancied by American importers of that period.

The English Cocker Spaniel Club of America was formed in 1935 to promote the interest of the English Cocker, which had already been recognized as a variety of Cocker Spaniel but not as a breed in its own right. The club's initial specialty show was held the same year on the estate of E.S. Willing near Bryn Mawr, Pennsylvania, while on May 12, 1936, the standard then operative in England was adopted.

The immediate aim of the club was to discourage the interbreeding of the English and American varieties which English Cocker fanciers considered detrimental to the type they sponsored. Separate classes had been provided at the shows for the English variety; nevertheless, English and American interbred Cockers for some time continued to compete side by side with pure English and pure American specimens. Many an American Cocker, in fact, was entered in the show ring as English on a basis of larger size alone. The resultant confusion militated against the best interests of both varieties, but nothing could be done because no one knew which dogs, genetically, were pure English, which were American, and which a combination of two.

Under the direction of Mrs. Geraldine R. Dodge, then president of the club, an extensive pedigree search was made of the Cockers of England, Canada, and the United States back to the beginning of official Cocker history abroad in 1892, in order to separate out the pure English lines of descent entirely devoid of American Cocker admixture. When, finally in 1941, this information was obtained, the English Cocker Spaniel Club was in a position to advise authoritatively on the problems of selection and breeding.

Meantime, in 1940 the Canadian Kennel Club recognized the English Cocker Spaniel as a separate breed, as did the American Kennel Club in September, 1946. Not until January, 1947, however, did breed registrations appear in the *Stud Book* under their own heading, for so much had to be done in the interim to comply with the provisions laid down for the official certification of pedigrees.

# Official Standard for the English Cocker Spaniel

**General Appearance**—The English Cocker Spaniel is an active, merry sporting dog, standing well up at the withers and compactly built. He is alive with energy; his gait is powerful and frictionless, capable both of covering ground effortlessly and penetrating dense cover to flush and retrieve game. His enthusiasm in the field and the incessant action of his tail while at work indicate how much he enjoys the hunting for which he was bred. His head is especially characteristic. He is, above all, a dog of balance, both standing and moving, without exaggeration in any part, the whole worth more than the sum of its parts.

**Size, Proportion, Substance**—*Size*—Height at withers: males 16 to 17 inches; females 15 to 16 inches. Deviations to be penalized. The most desirable weights: males, 28 to 34 pounds; females, 26 to 32 pounds. Proper conformation and substance should be considered more important than weight alone. *Proportion*—Compactly built and short-coupled, with height at withers slightly greater than the distance from withers to set-on of tail. *Substance*—The English Cocker is a solidly built dog with as much bone and substance as is possible without becoming cloddy or coarse.

**Head**—General appearance: strong, yet free from coarseness, softly contoured, without sharp angles. Taken as a whole, the parts combine to produce the expression distinctive of the breed. *Expression*—Soft, melting, yet dignified, alert, and intelligent. *Eyes*—The eyes are essential to the desired expression. They are medium in size, full and slightly oval; set wide apart; lids tight. Haws are inconspicuous; may be pigmented or unpigmented. Eye color dark brown, except in livers and liver parti-colors where hazel is permitted, but the darker the hazel the better. *Ears*—Set low, lying close to the head; leather fine, extending to the nose, well covered with long, silky, straight or slightly wavy hair. *Skull*—Arched and slightly flattened when seen both from the side and from the front. Viewed in profile, the brow appears not appreciably higher than the back-skull. Viewed from above, the sides of the skull are in planes roughly parallel to those of the muzzle. Stop definite, but moderate, and slightly grooved. *Muzzle*—Equal in length to skull; well cushioned; only as much narrower than the skull as is consistent with a full eye placement; cleanly chiselled under the eyes. Jaws strong, capable of carrying game. Nostrils wide for proper development of scenting ability; color black, except in livers and parti-colors of that shade where they will be brown; reds and parti-colors of that shade may be brown, but black is preferred. Lips square, but not pendulous or showing prominent flews. *Bite*—Scissors. A level bite is not preferred. Overshot or undershot to be severely penalized.

**Neck, Topline and Body**—*Neck*—Graceful and muscular, arched toward the head and blending cleanly, without throatiness, into sloping shoulders; moderate in length and in balance with the length and height of the dog. *Topline*—The line of the neck blends into the shoulder and backline in a smooth curve. The backline slopes very slightly toward a gently rounded croup, and is free from sagging or rumpiness. *Body*—Compact and well-knit, giving the impression of strength without heaviness. Chest deep; not so wide as to interfere with action of forelegs, nor so narrow as to allow the front to appear narrow or pinched. Forechest well developed, prosternum projecting moderately beyond shoulder points. Brisket reaches to the elbow and slopes gradually to a moderate tuck-up. Ribs well sprung and springing gradually to mid-body, tapering to back ribs which are of good depth and extend well back. Back short and strong. Loin short, broad and very slightly arched, but not enough to affect the topline appreciably. Croup gently rounded, without any tendency to fall away sharply. *Tail*—Docked. Set on to conform to croup. Ideally, the tail is carried horizontally and is in constant motion while the dog is in action. Under excitement, the dog may carry his tail somewhat higher, but not cocked up.

**Forequarters**—The English Cocker is moderately angulated. Shoulders are sloping, the blade flat and smoothly fitting. Shoulder blade and upper arm are approximately equal in length. Upper arm set well back, joining the shoulder with sufficient angulation to place the elbow beneath the highest point of the shoulder blade when the dog is standing naturally. *Forelegs*—Straight, with bone nearly uniform in size from elbow to heel; elbows set close to the body; pasterns nearly straight, with some flexibility. *Feet*—Proportionate in size to the legs, firm, round and catlike; toes arched and tight; pads thick.

**Hindquarters**—Angulation moderate and, most importantly, in balance with that of the forequarters. Hips relatively broad and well rounded. Upper thighs broad, thick and muscular, providing plenty of propelling power. Second thighs well muscled and approximately equal in length to the upper. Stifle strong and well bent. Hock to pad short. Feet as in front.

**Coat**—On head, short and fine; of medium length on body; flat or slightly wavy; silky in texture. The English Cocker is well-feathered, but not so profusely as to interfere with field work. Trimming is permitted to remove overabundant hair and to enhance the dog's true lines. It should be done so as to appear as natural as possible.

**Color**—Various. Parti-colors are either clearly marked, ticked or roaned, the white appearing in combination with black, liver or shades of red. In parti-colors it is preferable that solid markings be broken on the body and more or less evenly distributed; absence of body markings is acceptable. Solid colors are black, liver or shades of red. White feet on a solid are undesirable; a little white on throat is acceptable; but in neither case do these white markings make the dog a parti-color. Tan markings, clearly defined and of rich shade, may appear in conjunction with black, livers and parti-color combinations of those colors. Black and tans and liver and tans are considered solid colors.

**Gait**—The English Cocker is capable of hunting in dense cover and upland terrain. His gait is accordingly characterized more by drive and the appearance of power than by great speed. He covers ground effortlessly and with extension both in front and in rear, appropriate to his angulation. In the ring, he carries his head proudly and is able to keep much the same topline while in action as when standing for examination. Going and coming, he moves in a straight line without crabbing or rolling, and with width between both front and rear legs appropriate to his build and gait.

**Temperament**—The English Cocker is merry and affectionate, of equable disposition, neither sluggish nor hyperactive, a willing worker and a faithful and engaging companion.

Approved October 11, 1988

# Spaniel, English Springer

The name "springing spaniel" included in one classification the ancestral stock from which many of our present-day land spaniels emanated. In the 1800s, Springers and Cockers were often born within the same litter, size alone being the distinguishing factor. In 1902 the Kennel Club of England recognized the English Springer Spaniel as a distinct breed.

In 1880, the American Spaniel Club was founded and theirs was the task of sorting out the breed by size, with anything over 28 pounds being classified as a Springer. Though several individuals in America had these spaniels for their shooting, it was not until 1924 when the English Springer Spaniel Field Trial Association was formed, that they became better known. Field trials were inaugurated, and three years later (1927) the English Springer Spaniel Field Trial Association became the parent club of the breed.

This association has aimed to further the English Springer Spaniel both on the bench and in the field. Its AKC standard, formed in 1927 and first revised in 1932, was made as nearly as possible to foster the natural ability of the Springer Spaniel, a hunting dog that, with training, could do the work required of him. The association has also conducted field trials every year, and it has endeavored to demonstrate to the public just how good the dogs are as shooting dogs. As competition becomes greater, they must of necessity be able to cover their ground rapidly and, if well trained, to obey signals or orders given them.

Unquestionably the present standard has helped to make the Springer more uniform as a breed, and as a result the dogs as individuals have become much more uniform at bench shows and in field trials. They are admittedly great sporting dogs, hence should not be allowed to lose any of their standard characteristics; that is, they must not become heavy-boned and stocky in type and thus risk any loss of usefulness in the field. Their one purpose is to hunt and find game.

## Official Standard for the English Springer Spaniel

**General Appearance**—The English Springer Spaniel is a medium-size sporting dog with a neat, compact body, and a docked tail. His coat is moderately long and glossy with feathering on his legs, ears, chest and brisket. His pendulous ears, soft gentle expression, sturdy build and friendly wagging tail proclaim him unmistakably a member of the ancient family of Spaniels. He is above all a well proportioned dog, free from exaggeration, nicely balanced in every part. His carriage is proud and upstanding, body deep, legs strong and muscular with enough length to carry him with ease. His short level back, well developed thighs, good shoulders, excellent feet, suggest power, endurance, agility. Taken as a whole he looks the part of a dog that can go and keep going under difficult hunting conditions, and moreover he enjoys what he is doing. At his best he is endowed with style, symmetry, balance, enthusiasm and is every inch a sporting dog of distinct spaniel character, combining beauty and utility. *To be penalized*—Those lacking true English Springer type in conformation, expression, or behavior.

**Size, Proportion, Substance**—The Springer is built to cover rough ground with agility and reasonable speed. He should be kept to medium size—neither too small nor too large and heavy to do the work for which he is intended. The ideal *shoulder height* for dogs is 20 inches; for bitches, 19 inches. *To be penalized*—Oversize or undersize specimens (those more than one inch under or over the breed ideal). Length of topline (the distance from top of the shoulders to the root of the tail) should be approximately equal to the dog's shoulder height—never longer than his height—and not appreciably less. The dog too long in body, especially when long in loin, tires easily and lacks the compact outline characteristic of the breed. Equally undesirable is the dog too short in body for the length of his legs, a condition that destroys his balance and restricts the gait. *Weight* is dependent on the dog's other dimensions: a 20-inch dog, well proportioned, in good condition should weigh about 49–55 pounds. The resulting appearance is a well-knit, sturdy dog with good but not too heavy bone, in no way coarse or ponderous. *To be penalized*—Over-heavy specimens, cloddy in build. Leggy individuals, too tall for their length and substance.

**Head**—The head is impressive without being heavy. Its beauty lies in a combination of strength and refinement. It is important that the size and proportion be in balance with the rest of the dog. Viewed in profile the head should appear approximately the same length as the neck and should blend with the body in substance. The stop, eyebrow and the chiseling of the bony structure around the eye sockets contribute to the Springer's beautiful and characteristic expression. The *expression* to be alert, kindly, trusting. *Eyes*—More than any other feature the eyes contribute to the Springer's appeal. Color, placement, size influence expression and attractiveness. The eyes to be of medium size, neither small, round, full and prominent, nor bold and hard in expression. Set rather well apart and fairly deep in their sockets. The color of the iris to harmonize with the color of the coat, preferably a good dark hazel in the liver dogs and black or deep brown in the black and white specimens. The lids, tight with little or no haw showing. *To be penalized*—Eyes yellow or brassy in color or noticeably lighter than the coat. Sharp expression indicating unfriendly or suspicious nature. Loose droopy lids. Prominent haw (the third eyelid or membrane in the inside corner of the eye). *Ears*—The correct ear set is on a level with the line of the eye; on the side of the skull and not too far back. The flaps to be long and fairly wide, hanging close to the cheeks, with no tendency to stand up or out. The leather, thin, approximately long enough to reach the tip of the nose. *To be penalized*—Short round ears. Ears set too high or too low or too far back on the head. The *skull* (upper head) to be of medium length, fairly broad, flat on top, slightly rounded at the sides and back. The occiput bone inconspicuous, rounded rather than peaked or angular. The foreface (head in front of the eyes) approximately the same length as the skull, and in harmony as to width and general character. Looking down on the head the muzzle to appear to be about one half the width of the skull. As the skull rises from the foreface it makes a brow or "stop," divided by a groove or fluting between the eyes. This groove continues upward and gradually disappears as it reaches the middle of the forehead. The amount of "stop" can best be described as moderate. It must not be a pronounced feature; rather it is a subtle rise where the muzzle blends into the upper head, further emphasized by the groove and by the position and shape of the eyebrows which should be well developed. The *cheeks* to be flat, (not rounded, full or thick) with nice chiseling under the eyes. Viewed in profile the topline of the skull and the *muzzle* lie in two approximately parallel planes. The nasal bone should be straight, with no inclination downward toward the tip of the nose which gives a downfaced look so undesirable in this breed. Neither should the nasal bone be concave resulting in a "dish-faced" profile; nor convex giving the dog a Roman nose. The nostrils, well opened and broad, liver color or black depending on the color of the coat. Flesh-colored ("Dudley noses") or spotted ("butterfly noses") are undesirable. The *jaws* to be of sufficient length to allow the dog to carry game easily; fairly square, lean, strong, and even (neither undershot nor overshot). The upper lip to come down full and rather square to cover the line of the lower jaw, but *lips* not to be pendulous nor exaggerated. *To be penalized*—Oval, pointed or heavy skull. Cheeks prominently rounded, thick and protruding. Too much or too little stop. Over-heavy muzzle. Muzzle too short, too thick, too narrow. Pendulous slobbery lips. Under- or overshot jaws—a very serious fault, to be heavily penalized. The *teeth* should be strong, clean, not too small; and when the mouth is closed the teeth should meet in a close *scissors bite* (the lower incisors touching the inside of the upper incisors). *To be penalized*—Any deviation from the above description. Irregularities due to faulty jaw formation to be severely penalized.

**Neck, Topline, Body**—The *neck* to be moderately long, muscular, slightly arched at the crest, gradually blending into sloping shoulders. Not noticeably upright, nor coming into the body at an abrupt angle. *To be penalized*—Short neck, often the sequence to steep shoulders. Concave neck, sometimes called ewe neck or upside-down neck (the opposite of arched). Excessive throatiness. The **topline** slopes *very gently* from withers to tail—the line from withers to back descending without a sharp drop; the back practically level; arch over hips somewhat lower than the withers. The **body** to be well coupled, strong, compact; the *chest* deep but not so wide or round as to interfere with the action of the front legs; the brisket sufficiently developed to reach to the level of the elbows. The ribs fairly long, springing gradually to the middle of the body, then tapering as they approach the end of the ribbed section. The bottom line, starting on a level with the elbows, to continue backward with almost no up-curve until reaching the end of the ribbed section, then a more noticeable upcurve to the flank, but not enough to make the dog appear small waisted or "tucked up."

The *back* (section between the withers and loin) to be straight and strong, with no tendency to dip or roach. The *loins* to be strong, short; a slight arch over loins and hip bones. Hips nicely rounded, blending smoothly into hind legs. *Croup* sloping gently to base of tail; tail carried to follow the natural line of the body. The Springer's **tail** is an index both to his temperament and his conformation. Merry tail action is characteristic. The proper set is somewhat low following the natural line of the croup. The carriage should be nearly horizontal, slightly elevated when dog is excited. Carried straight is untypical of the breed. The tail should not be docked too short. *To be penalized*—Topline sloping sharply, indicating steep withers (straight shoulder placement) and a too low tail set. Body too shallow, indicating lack of brisket. Ribs too flat sometimes due to immaturity. Ribs too round (barrel shaped), hampering the gait. Sway back (dip in back), indicating weakness or lack of muscular development, particularly to be seen when dog is in action and viewed from the side. Roach back (too much arch over loin and extending forward into middle section). Croup falling away too sharply; or croup too high—unsightly faults, detrimental to outline and good movement. Tail habitually upright. Tail set too high or too low. Clamped down tail (indicating timidity or undependable temperament, even less to be desired than the tail carried too gaily).

**Forequarters**—**Shoulders** (fairly close together at the tips) to lie flat and mold smoothly into the contour of the body. Efficient movement in front calls for proper shoulders, the blades sloping back to form an angle with the upper arm of approximately 90 degrees which permits the dog to swing his forelegs forward in an easy manner. **Elbows** close to the body with free action from the shoulders. The **forelegs** to be straight with the same degree of size to the foot. The bone, strong, slightly flattened, not too heavy or round. The knee, straight, almost flat; the **pasterns** short, strong. *To be penalized*—Shoulders set at a steep angle limiting the stride. Loaded shoulders (the blades standing out from the body by overdevelopment of the muscles). Loose elbows, crooked legs. Bone too light or too coarse and heavy. Weak pasterns that let down the feet at a pronounced angle.

The *feet* to be round, or slightly oval, compact, well arched, medium size with thick pads, well feathered between the toes. Excess hair to be removed to show the natural shape and size of the foot. *To be penalized*—Thin, open or splayed feet (flat with spreading toes). Hare foot (long, rather narrow foot).

**Hindquarters**—The Springer should be shown in hard muscular condition, well developed in hips and thighs and the whole rear assembly should suggest strength and driving power. The **hip joints** to be set rather wide apart and the hips nicely rounded. The **thighs** broad and muscular; the stifle joint strong and moderately bent. The **hock joint** somewhat rounded, not small and sharp in contour, and moderately angulated. Leg from hock joint to foot pad, short and strong with good bone structure. When viewed from the rear the hocks to be parallel whether the dog is standing or in motion. *To be penalized*—Too little or too much angulation. Narrow, undeveloped thighs. Hocks too short or too long (a proportion of ⅓ the distance from hip joint to foot is ideal). Cowhocks—hocks turning in toward each other. Flabby muscles. Weakness of joints. Feet as in front.

**Coat**—On ears, chest, legs and belly the Springer is nicely furnished with a fringe of feathering of moderate length and heaviness. On head, front of forelegs, and below hocks on front of hind legs, the hair is short and fine. The body coat is flat or wavy, of medium length, sufficiently dense to be waterproof, weatherproof and thornproof. The texture fine, and the hair should have the clean, glossy, live appearance indicative of good health. It is legitimate to trim about head, feet, ears; to remove dead hair; to thin and shorten excess feathering, particularly from the hocks to the feet and elsewhere as required to give a smart, clean appearance. Tail should be well fringed with wavy feather. It is legitimate to shape and shorten the feathering but enough should be left to blend with the dog's other furnishings. *To be penalized*—Rough curly coat. Overtrimming, especially of the body coat. Any chopped, barbered or artificial effect. Excessive feathering that destroys the clean outline desirable in a sporting dog.

**Color**—May be black or liver with white markings or predominantly white with black or liver markings; tricolor; black and white or liver and white with tan markings (usually found on eyebrows, cheeks, inside of ears and under tail); blue or liver roan. Any white portions of coat may be flecked with ticking. All preceding combinations of colors and markings to be equally acceptable. *To be penalized*—Off colors such as lemon, red or orange not to place.

**Gait**—In judging the Springer there should be emphasis on proper movement, which is the final test of a dog's conformation and soundness. Prerequisite to good movement is balance of the front and rear assemblies. The two must match in angulation and muscular development if the gait is to be smooth and effortless. Good shoulders laid back at an angle that permit a long stride are just as essential as the excellent rear quarters that provide the driving power. When viewed from the front, the dog's legs should appear to swing forward in a free and easy manner, with no tendency for the feet to cross over or interfere with each other. Viewed from the rear, the hocks should drive well under the body following on a line with the forelegs, neither too widely nor too closely spaced. As speed increases there is a natural tendency for the legs to converge toward the center line of gravity or a single line of travel. Seen from the side, the Springer should exhibit a good, long forward stride, without high-stepping or wasted motion. *To be penalized*—Short choppy stride, mincing steps with up-and-down movement, hopping. Moving with forefeet wide, giving roll or swing to body. Weaving or crossing of fore- or hind feet.

**Temperament**—The typical Springer is friendly, eager to please, quick to learn, willing to obey. In the show ring he should exhibit poise, attentiveness, tractability, and should permit himself to be examined by the judge without resentment or cringing. *To be penalized*—Excessive timidity, with due allowance for puppies or novice exhibits.

**SUMMARY**

In judging the English Springer Spaniel, the overall picture is a primary consideration. It is urged that the judge look for type which includes general appearance, outline and temperament and also for soundness, especially as seen when the dog is in motion. Inasmuch as the dog with a smooth easy gait must be reasonably sound and well balanced he is to be highly regarded in the show ring; however, not to the extent of forgiving him for not looking like an English Springer Spaniel. A quite untypical dog, leggy, foreign in head and expression, may move well. But he should not be placed over a good all-round specimen that has a minor fault in movement. It should be remembered that the English Springer Spaniel is first and foremost a sporting dog of the Spaniel family and he must look and behave and move in character.

Approved June 13, 1978
Reformatted February 14, 1989

# Spaniel, Field

The Field Spaniel, to probably greater extent than any variety within the great spaniel group, has been taken over the hurdles of man's fancy for exaggerations in type, and as a result the breed suffered greatly.

Phineas Bullock of England is credited with perpetuating a dog of tremendous body length and lowness to the ground, together with phenomenal bone which culminated for a time in a grotesque caricature of a spaniel. Apparently the type was established by repeated crosses of the "Welsh Cocker" with the Sussex Spaniel. Later, largely through the efforts of Mortimer Smith, the breed was improved—it took on a type which all who like sporting spaniels can really admire.

Considerable difficulty was encountered in establishing the modern Field Spaniel in the United States due to the necessity for introducing Springer and Cocker crosses in order to eliminate the exaggerations, and this, of course, rendered many individuals ineligible for registration with the American Kennel Club. In fact, in the early 1880s when the Cocker was introduced to America and until 1901 the sole distinction between the Cockers and the Field Spaniels for show purposes was one of size—with any over 25 pounds designated as a Field, and 25 pounds or under as a Cocker.

Usually black in color, the Field Spaniel became a useful and handsome breed, sound, straight in the forelegs, and with a height more nearly in balance to length. When built along these lines, he is a dog possessed of endurance, moderate speed and agility. He is level-headed and intelligent, and a dog of great perseverance.

## Official Standard for the Field Spaniel

**General Appearance**—The Field Spaniel is a combination of beauty and utility. It is a well balanced, substantial hunter-companion of medium size, built for activity and endurance in heavy cover and water. It has a noble carriage; a proud but docile attitude; is sound and free-moving. Symmetry, gait, attitude and purpose are more important than any one part.

**Size, Proportion, Substance**—Balance between these three components is essential. *Size*—Ideal height for mature adults at the withers is 18 inches for dogs and 17 inches for bitches. A one-inch deviation either way is acceptable. *Proportion*—A well balanced dog, somewhat longer than tall. The ratio of length to height is approximately 7:6. (Length is measured on a level from the foremost point of the shoulder to the rearmost point of the buttocks.) *Substance*—Solidly built, with moderate bone, and firm smooth muscles.

**Head**—Conveys the impression of high breeding, character and nobility, and must be in proportion to the size of the dog. *Expression*—Grave, gentle and intelligent. *Eyes*—Almond in shape, open, and of medium size; set moderately wide and deep. Color: Dark hazel to dark brown. The lids are tight and show no haw; rims comparable to nose in color. *Ears*—Moderately long (reaching the end of the muzzle) and wide. Set on slightly below eye level; pendulous, hanging close to the head; rolled and well feathered. Leather is moderately heavy, supple, and rounded at the tip. *Skull*—The crown is slightly wider at the back than at the brow and lightly arched laterally; sides and cheeks are straight and clean. The occiput is distinct and rounded. Brows are slightly raised. The stop is moderate, but well-defined by the brows. The face is chiselled beneath the eyes. *Muzzle*—Strong, long and lean; neither snipy nor squarely cut. The nasal bone is straight and slightly divergent from the plane of the top skull. In profile, the lower plane curves gradually from nose to throat. Jaws are level. *Nose*—Large, fleshy and well developed with open nostrils. Set on as an extension of the muzzle. Color: solid; light to dark brown or black, as befits the color of the coat. *Lips*—Close fitting, clean, and sufficiently deep to cover the lower jaw without being pendulous. *Bite*—Scissor or level, with complete dentition. Scissor preferred.

**Neck, Topline, Body**—*Neck*—Long, strong, muscular, slightly arched, clean, and well set into shoulders. *Topline*—The neck slopes smoothly into the withers; the back is level, well muscled, firm and strong; the croup is short and gently rounded. *Body*—The prosternum is prominent and well fleshed. The depth of chest is roughly equal to the length of the front leg from elbow to ground. The length of rib cage is ⅔ of the body length. Ribs are oval, well sprung, and curve gently into a firm loin. *Loin*—Short, strong and deep, with little or no tuck-up. *Tail*—Set on low, in line with the croup; at rest slanting downward. Should be docked to balance the overall dog.

**Forequarters**—Shoulder blades are oblique and sloping. The upper arm is close-set; elbows are directly below the withers, and turn neither in nor out. Bone is flat. Forelegs are straight and well boned to the feet. Pasterns are moderately sloping but strong. Dewclaws may be removed. Feet face forward and are large, rounded, and webbed, with strong, well arched, relatively tight toes and thick pads.

**Hindquarters**—Strong and driving; stifles and hocks only moderately bent. Hocks well let down; pasterns relatively short, strong and parallel when viewed from the rear. Hips moderately broad and muscular; upper thigh broad and powerful; second thigh well muscled. Bone corresponds to that of forelegs. No dewclaws.

**Coat**—Single; moderately long; flat or slightly wavy; silky and glossy; dense and water-repellent. Setter-like feathering adorns the chest, underbody, backs of the legs, buttocks, and the underside of the tail. Pasterns have clean outlines to the ground. There is short, soft hair between the toes. Overabundance of coat, or cottony texture, impractical for work, are incorrect. Trimming is limited to that which enhances the natural appearance of the dog.

**Color**—Black, liver, golden liver, roan, or any of these with tan points. A small amount of white on the chest and/or throat is allowed.

**Gait**—The head is carried alertly, always above the level of the back. There is good forward reach that begins in the shoulder, coupled with strong drive from the rear, giving the characteristic effortless, long, low and majestic stride. The legs move straight, with a slight convergence at increased speed. In action, the tail is carried inclined downward or level with the back, and with a wagging motion. Side movement is straight and clean, without energy wasting motions. Overreaching and single tracking are incorrect. The Field Spaniel should be shown at its own natural speed in an endurance trot.

**Temperament**—Unusually docile, sensitive, fun-loving, independent and intelligent, with a great affinity for human companionship. They may be somewhat reserved in initial meetings. Any display of shyness, fear or aggression is to be severely penalized.

Approved August 14, 1990

# Spaniel, Irish Water

That the Irish Water Spaniel is a dog of very ancient lineage is supported by the research made by Alan J. Stern, and reported upon in four articles in *Pure-Bred Dogs—American Kennel Gazette*, January–April, 1965.

The articles noted that a Harvard archaeological expedition to Ireland in 1934–36, excavating a lake dwelling of Lagore near Dunshaughlin, unearthed among other dog remains an Irish Water Spaniel type skull—medium-sized, with clearly defined stop and a more pronounced dome—identified to dogs living in the 7th or 8th century, A.D.. The same type of skull was found in the Lake Districts of Central Europe, dating from later Stone and Bronze ages. Old Roman ruins bear carvings which most resemble the Irish Water Spaniel.

In the late 1100s, before the days of King McCarthy II, dogs found in southern Ireland below the River Shannon were called Shannon Spaniels, Irish Water Spaniels, Rat-Tail Spaniels or Whip-Tail Spaniels. Ireland's Sir Robert Cecil is recorded as having sent the King of France an Irish Water Spaniel in 1598. In 1607, Topsell in his *Historie of the four-footed Beastes* tells of the Water Spagnel with his long, rough, curled hair and a tail somewhat bare and naked. Captain Thomas Brown, in the mid-1700s, remarks on the long ears of the Irish Water Spaniel and the crisp, curly texture of the coat.

These evidences indicate that the dog known as the Southern Irish Water

Spaniel was well established centuries before the legendary "Boatswain" (1834–1852), the famous sire of many outstanding gun and show dogs who is often credited as having been the first of the breed as it is known today. Boatswain (pedigree unknown) was bred by Justin McCarthy.

However disputable the breed's development before him, in Boatswain's wake a clear type was bred, exhibited and accepted by kennel club officialdom. In 1849 he sired "Jack," whose name appears in many early pedigrees. The first special class for Irish Water Spaniels was provided in 1859. In 1866, "Doctor"—a great-grandson of Boatswain—won first (Best of Breed) at Birmingham. An oil painting of "Rake," bred in 1864 of Boatswain's bloodlines, shows the contemporary Irish Water Spaniel.

In America, we note that there was an entry of 4 Irish Water Spaniels at the first Westminster Kennel Club show in 1877. One of these was listed as having been imported from Ireland in 1873.

The Irish Water Spaniel is often called the clown of the spaniel family, possibly due to the unique appearance of a characteristic topknot together with a peak of curly hair between the eyes. He is likewise the tallest of our spaniels. Ordinarily he is loyal to those he knows, but forbidding to strangers. He is a grand water dog, not only because he likes water, but because his coat is naturally water-shedding. For this reason he is used in some parts of the country as a duck retriever, although he is not quite as adaptable for upland work because his coat tends to catch on briars.

## Official Standard for the Irish Water Spaniel

**General Appearance**—The Irish Water Spaniel presents a picture of a smart, upstanding strongly built sporting dog. Great intelligence is combined with rugged endurance and a bold, dashing eagerness of temperament. Distinguishing characteristics are a topknot of long, loose curls, a body covered with a dense, crisply curled liver colored coat, contrasted by a smooth face and a smooth "rat" tail.

**Size, Proportion, Substance**—Strongly built and well boned, the Irish Water Spaniel is a dog of medium length, slightly rectangular in appearance. He is well balanced and shows no legginess or coarseness. Dogs 22 to 24 inches, bitches 21 to 23 inches, measured at the highest point of the shoulder. Dogs 55 to 65 pounds, bitches 45 to 58 pounds.

**Head**—The head is cleanly chiseled, not cheeky, and should not present a short, wedge shaped appearance. The skull is rather large and high in the dome, with a prominent occiput and a gradual stop. The muzzle is square and rather long, with a deep mouth opening and lips fine in texture. The nose large and liver in color. Teeth strong and regular with a scissor or level bite. The hair on the face is short and smooth, except for a beard which grows in a narrow line at the back of the jaw. *Topknot*—A characteristic of the breed, consists of long, loose curls growing down into a well-defined peak between the eyes and falling like a shawl over the tops of the ears and occiput. Trimming of this breed characteristic in an exaggerated manner is highly objectionable. *Eyes*—Medium in size, slightly almond shaped with tight eyelids. Eyes are hazel in color, preferably of a dark shade. The expression is keenly alert, intelligent, direct and quizzical. *Ears*—Long, lobular, set low, with leathers reaching about to the end of the nose when extended forward, and abundantly covered with long curls, extending two or more inches below the tips of the leathers.

**Neck, Topline, Body**—The neck is long, arching, strong and muscular; smoothly set into cleanly sloping shoulders. *Topline*—Strong and level, or slightly higher in the rear; never descending, or showing sag or roach. *Body*—The body is of medium length, slightly rectangular. Chest deep, with brisket extending to the elbows. Ribs well sprung and carried well back. Immediately behind the shoulders ribs are flattened enough to allow free movement of the forelegs, becoming rounder behind. Loin short, wide and muscular. The body should not present a tucked-up appearance.

**Forequarters**—The entire front gives the impression of strength without heaviness. Shoulders are sloping and clean. Forelegs well boned, muscular, medium in length; with sufficient length of upper arm to ensure efficient reach. Elbows close set. Forefeet are large, thick and somewhat spreading; well clothed with hair both over and between the toes.

**Hindquarters**—Sound hindquarters are of great importance to provide swimming power and drive. They should be as high or slightly higher than the shoulders, powerful and muscular, with well developed upper and second thighs. Hips wide, stifles moderately bent, hocks low set and moderately bent. Rear angulation is moderate, and balance of front and rear angulation is of paramount importance. Rear feet are large, thick and somewhat spreading; well clothed with hair. Tail should be set on low enough to give a rather rounded appearance to the hindquarters and should be carried nearly level with the back.

**Tail**—The so-called "rat tail" is a striking characteristic of the breed. At the root it is thick and covered for two or three inches with short curls. It tapers to a fine point at the end; and from the root curls is covered with short, smooth hair so as to look as if it had been clipped. The tail should not be long enough to reach the hock joint.

**Coat**—Proper double coat is of vital importance to protect the dog while working. The neck, back, sides, and rear are densely covered with tight, crisp ringlets, with the hair longer underneath the ribs. Forelegs are well covered with abundant curls or waves. The hind legs should also be abundantly covered by hair falling in curls or waves, except that the hair should be short and smooth on the front of the legs below the hocks. The hair on the throat is very short and smooth, forming a V-shaped patch. All curled areas should be clearly defined by curls of sufficient length to form a sharp contrast with the smooth coat on face, throat, tail, and rear legs below the hocks. Fore and hind feet should be well clothed with hair both over and between the toes. Dogs may be shown in natural coat or trimmed. However, no dog should be groomed or trimmed so excessively as to obscure the curl or texture of the coat.

**Color**—Solid liver. With the exception of graying due to age, white hair or markings objectionable.

**Gait**—The Irish Water Spaniel moves with a smooth, free, ground covering action that, when viewed from the side, exhibits balanced reach and drive. True and precise coming and going. When walking or standing, the legs are perpendicular to the ground, toeing neither in nor out.

**Temperament**—Very alert and inquisitive, the Irish Water Spaniel is often reserved with strangers. However, aggressive behavior or excessive shyness should be penalized. A stable temperament is essential in a hunting dog.

### FAULTS

The foregoing description is that of the ideal Irish Water Spaniel in hard working condition. Any deviation from the above described dog must be penalized to the extent of the deviation, keeping in mind the importance of the various features toward the basic original purpose of the breed.

Approved June 12, 1990

Irish Water Spaniel — *Ludwig*

Cocker Spaniel — *Ludwig*

Pointer puppies

English Cocker Spaniels

English Springer Spaniel — *Lud*

Weimaraners — *Cumbers*

Golden Retriever — *Lindemaier*

Irish Setter — *Allen*

Sussex Spaniels — *Cumbers*

Clumber Spaniels - *Cumbers*

English Setters — *Cumbers*

German Shorthaired Pointers — *Cumbers*

Curly-Coated Retriever — *Wesseltoft*

Flat-Coated Retrievers — *Cumbers*

Labrador Retrievers — *Cumbers*

Vizsla — *Lyons*

Field Spaniel — *Roslin-Williams*

Brittany — *Conalde*

German Wirehaired Pointer — *Alberts*

Gordon Setter puppy

Chesapeake Bay Retrievers — *Cumbers*

Afghan Hound — *Anderson*

Smooth Dachshund — *Anderson*

Wirehaired Dachshunds — *Cumbers*

Miniature Longhaired Dachshund — *Cumbers*

Norwegian Elkhounds

Rhodesian Ridgeback — *Megginson*

Basset Hound — *Lindemaier*

Beagle — *Cumbers*

Greyhound — *Thompson*

Whippets — *Roslin-Williams*

Borzoi — *Ashbey*

Basenjis — *Cumbers*

Irish Wolfhounds

Otter Hounds — *Roslin-Williams*

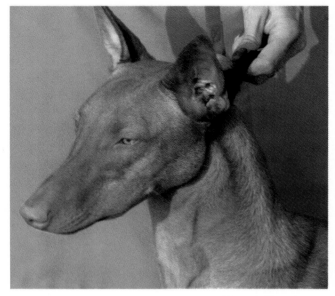

Pharaoh Hound

Saluki — *Cumbers*

Scottish Deerhounds — *Arnold*

Bloodhound
— *Anderson*

Kuvasz
— *Allen*

Komondor — *Ludwig*

Alaskan Malamutes — *Munger*

Siberian Husky — *Anderson*

Bernese Mountain Dog — *Cumbers*

Great Pyrenees — *Wood*

Boxer — *Kubek*

Bullmastiff — *Anderson*

Rottweiler — *Cumbers*

Mastiff — *Thompson*

Great Danes — *Allen*

Doberman Pinschers — *Bergman*

# Spaniel, Sussex

The Sussex Spaniel derives his name from Sussex, England, where the first and most important kennel of these dogs belonged to a Mr. Fuller—it was he who developed the rich golden liver color that has long distinguished the breed. Phineas Bullock, of Field Spaniel fame, also did notable work in furthering the best interests of the Sussex. Specimens of the breed competed in Britain as far back as the Crystal Palace show of 1862.

During his early days the Sussex was used for certain types of rough shooting in England, where an abundance of game, together with the custom of hunting on foot, rendered the dog satisfactory as a sporting companion. He has not been imported to any great extent to this country, however, probably due to the fact that he has not sufficient speed for the average sportsman, who faces conditions far different from those abroad.

Although he lacks the speed of the Springer and the Cocker, the Sussex has an extremely good nose, and he is a determined hunter, valuable for all forms of upland shooting. He is inclined to give tongue on scent. In disposition he is an entirely normal dog, not too difficult to train, and when properly taught becomes an excellent retriever.

# Official Standard for the Sussex Spaniel

**General Appearance**—The Sussex Spaniel was among the first ten breeds to be recognized and admitted to the Stud Book when the American Kennel Club was formed in 1884, but it has existed as a distinct breed for much longer. As its name implies, it derives its origin from the county of Sussex, England, and it was used there since the eighteenth century as a field dog. During the late 1800s the reputation of the Sussex Spaniel as an excellent hunting companion was well known among the estates surrounding Sussex County. Its short legs, massive build, long body, and habit of giving tongue when on scent made the breed ideally suited to penetrating the dense undergrowth and flushing game within range of the gun. Strength, maneuverability, and desire were essential for this purpose. Although it has never gained great popularity in numbers, the Sussex Spaniel continues today essentially unchanged in character and general appearance from those 19th century sporting dogs.

The Sussex Spaniel presents a long and low, rectangular and rather massive appearance coupled with free movements and nice tail action. The breed has a somber and serious expression. The rich golden liver color is unique to the breed.

**Size, Proportion, Substance**—*Size*—The height of the Sussex Spaniel as measured at the withers ranges from 13 to 15 inches. Any deviation from these measurements is a minor fault. The weight of the Sussex Spaniel ranges between 35 and 45 pounds. *Proportion*—The Sussex Spaniel presents a rectangular outline as the breed is longer in body than it is tall. *Substance*—The Sussex Spaniel is muscular and rather massive.

**Head**—Correct head and expression are important features of the breed. *Eyes*—The eyes are hazel in color, fairly large, soft and languishing, but do not show the haw overmuch. *Expression*—The Sussex Spaniel has a somber and serious appearance, and its fairly heavy brows produce a frowning expression. *Ears*—The ears are thick, fairly large, and lobe-shaped and are set moderately low, slightly, above the outside corner of the eye. *Skull and Muzzle*—The skull is moderately long and also wide with an indentation in the middle and with a full stop. The brows are fairly heavy, the occiput is full but not pointed, the whole giving an appearance of heaviness without dullness. The muzzle should be approximately three inches long, broad, and square in profile. The skull as measured from the stop to the occiput is longer than the muzzle. The nostrils are well-developed and liver colored. The lips are somewhat pendulous. *Bite*—A scissors bite is preferred. Any deviation from a scissors bite is a minor fault.

**Neck, Topline, Body**—*Neck*—The neck is rather short, strong, and slightly arched, but does not carry the head much above the level of the back. There should not be much throatiness about the skin. *Topline and Body*—The whole body is characterized as low and long with a level topline. The chest is round, especially behind the shoulders, and is deep and wide which gives a good girth. The back and loin are long and very muscular both in width and depth. For this development, the back ribs must be deep. *Tail*—The tail is docked from 5 to 7 inches and set low. When gaiting the Sussex Spaniel exhibits nice tail action, but does not carry the tail above the level of the back.

**Forequarters**—The shoulders are well laid back and muscular. The upper arm should correspond in length and angle of return to the shoulder blade so that the legs are set well under the dog. The forelegs should be very short, strong, and heavily boned. They may show a slight bow. Both straight and slightly bowed constructions are proper and correct. The pasterns are very short and heavily boned. The feet are large and round with short hair between the toes.

**Hindquarters**—The hindquarters are full and well-rounded, strong, and heavily boned. They should be parallel with each other and also set wide apart—about as wide as the dog at the shoulders. The hind legs are short from the hock to the ground, heavily boned, and should seem neither shorter than the forelegs nor much bent at the hocks. The hindquarters must correspond in angulation to the forequarters. The hocks should turn neither in nor out. The rear feet are like the front feet.

**Coat**—The body coat is abundant, flat or slightly waved, with no tendency to curl. The legs are moderately well-feathered, but clean below the hocks. The ears are furnished with soft, wavy hair. The neck has a well-marked frill in the coat. The tail is thickly covered with moderately long feather. No trimming is acceptable except to shape foot feather, or to remove feather between the pads or between the hock and the feet. The feather between the toes must be left in sufficient length to cover the nails.

**Color**—Rich golden liver is the only acceptable color and is a certain sign of the purity of the breed. Dark liver or puce is a major fault. White on the chest is a minor fault. White on any other part of the body is a major fault.

**Gait**—The round, deep and wide chest of the Sussex Spaniel coupled with its short legs and long body produce a rolling gait. While its movement is deliberate, the Sussex Spaniel is in no sense clumsy. Gait is powerful and true with perfect coordination between the front and hind legs. The front legs do not paddle, wave, or overlap. The head is held low when gaiting. The breed should be shown on a loose lead so that its natural gait is evident.

**Temperament**—Despite its somber and serious expression, the breed is friendly and has a cheerful and tractable disposition.

### FAULTS

The standard ranks features of the breed into three categories. The most important features of the breed are color and general appearance. The features of secondary importance are the head, ears, back and back ribs, legs, and feet. The features of lesser importance are the eyes, nose, neck, chest and shoulders, tail, and coat. Faults also fall into three categories. Major faults are color that is too light or too dark, white on any part of the body other than the chest, and a curled coat. Serious faults are a narrow head, weak muzzle, the presence of a topknot, and a general appearance that is sour and crouching. Minor faults are light eyes, white on chest, the deviation from proper height ranges, lightness of bone, shortness of body or a body that is flat-sided, and a bite other than scissors. There are no disqualifications in the Sussex Spaniel standard.

Approved, April 7, 1992

# Spaniel, Welsh Springer

The history of the Welsh Springer Spaniel begins as far back as 7000 B.C., when the first hunting dogs were employed by man. The likely ancestors of most of today's domestic hunting dogs, these canines accompanied man on his hunting sojourns on the coastlines of Brittany, Cornwall, Wales, Ireland and Scotland during the Mesolithic period.

By approximately 250 B.C., the ancestors of the Welsh Springer had developed into the Agassian hunting dog, belonging to the wild tribes of Roman-occupied Briton. Writings of the time include mention of the dog's "springing" action while on the hunt. Oppian, a Roman poet alive during this time also described the dog in detail.

During the Renaissance, the "Land Spaniel," a Welsh Springer-type dog with red and white markings, was used for retrieving. The dog was used when hunting with the falcon, gun and bow, as these were all means employed at the time. Tapestries woven during the period show the Land Spaniel as having nearly the same colorings and physical characteristics as today's Welsh.

In the 1700s, the British masters included the red and white spaniel in a number of their oil paintings. According to some experts, the stance, color and conformation of the dogs depicted in this art are those of the modern Welsh. This spaniel gained some popularity in England during this period, and was a favorite hunting dog of many well-to-do individuals.

However, by the 1800s, the breed had been primarily replaced by liver and white- or black and white-colored spaniels. During this lapse in the breed's popularity in England, it is thought that the dog was still maintained in the region of South Wales, notably in the Neath Valley.

A trend in selective breeding, spurred on by the newly popularized Darwinian theory, eventually brought the red and white spaniel back to Victorian England. Emphasis was put on breeding dogs for color, and subsequently, the popularity of the breed grew during this time. The Kennel Club was formed in 1873, and the red and white spaniel was shown at the club's first competition, along with other spaniels. Both the Welsh Springer and the English Springer were judged together since their only differences at the time were in color. The breeds were eventually separated in the classes.

Welsh Springer Spaniels apparently gained popularity in the late 1800s in America, since the American Kennel Club officially recognized them in 1906. The first dog, named "Faircroft Bob," was registered in 1914, and was soon followed by five others, all in the same year. However, between the years of 1926 and 1948, there were no Welsh registered by the AKC. Many believe that by the time World War II had ended, no Welsh Springers were alive in the United States. Importing soon changed this situation, and in 1949, 11 dogs were registered with the American Kennel Club. The Welsh Springer Spaniel club of America was formed in 1961.

The Welsh Springer is an excellent water dog; a keen, hard-working dog—no day is too long, no country too rough—and under all circumstances he is a faithful and willing worker for man. He has an excellent nose. He can be used on any kind of game; the well-trained Welshman compares with any gun dog. As a companion, the Welsh Springer is a true pal of handy size, larger and stronger than the Cocker, but smaller than the English Springer. He makes a good guard, too, yet is ordinarily gentle with children and other animals.

## Official Standard for the Welsh Springer Spaniel

**General Appearance**—The Welsh Springer Spaniel is a dog of distinct variety and ancient origin, who derives his name from his hunting style and not his relationship to other breeds. He is an attractive dog of handy size, exhibiting substance without coarseness. He is compact, not leggy, obviously built for hard work and endurance. The Welsh Springer Spaniel gives the impression of length due to obliquely angled forequarters and well developed hindquarters. Being a hunting dog, he should be shown in hard muscled working condition. His coat should not be so excessive as to hinder his work as an active flushing spaniel, but should be thick enough to protect him from heavy cover and weather.

**Size, Proportion, Substance**—A dog is ideally 18–19 inches in height at the withers and a bitch is 17–18 inches at the withers. Any animal above or below the ideal to be proportionately penalized. Weight should be in proportion to height and overall balance. Length of body from the withers to the base of the tail is very slightly greater than the distance from the withers to the ground. This body length may be the same as the height but never shorter, thus preserving the rectangular silhouette of the Welsh Springer Spaniel.

**Head**—The Welsh Springer Spaniel head is unique and should in no way approximate that of other spaniel breeds. Its overall balance is of primary importance.

Head is in proportion to body, never so broad as to appear coarse nor so narrow as to appear racy. The skull is of medium length, slightly domed, with a clearly defined stop. It is well chiseled below the eyes. The top plane of the skull is very slightly divergent from that of the muzzle, but with no tendency toward a down-faced appearance. A short chubby head is most objectionable. *Eyes* should be oval in shape, dark to medium brown in color with a soft expression. Preference is for a darker eye though lighter shades of brown are acceptable. Yellow or mean-looking eyes are to be heavily penalized. Medium in size, they are neither prominent, nor sunken, nor do they show haw. Eye rims are tight and dark pigmentation is preferred. *Ears* are set on approximately at eye level and hang close to the cheeks. Comparatively small, the leather does not reach to the nose. Gradually narrowing towards the tip, they are shaped somewhat like a vine leaf and are lightly feathered. The length of the *muzzle* is approximately equal to, but never longer than that of the skull. It is straight, fairly square, and free from excessive flew. Nostrils are well developed and black or any shade of brown in color. A pink nose is to be severely penalized. A scissors *bite* is preferred. An undershot jaw is to be severely penalized.

**Neck, Topline, Body**—The *neck* is long and slightly arched, clean in throat, and set into long, sloping shoulders. *Topline* is level. The loin is slightly arched, muscular, and close-coupled. The croup is very slightly rounded, never steep nor falling off. The topline in combination with proper angulation fore and aft presents a silhouette that appears rectangular. The *chest* is well developed and muscular with a prominent forechest, the ribs well sprung and the brisket reaching to the elbows. The *tail* is an extension of the topline. Carriage is nearly horizontal or slightly elevated when the dog is excited. The tail is generally docked and displays a lively action.

**Forequarters**—The shoulder blade and upper arms are approximately equal in length. The upper arm is set well back, joining the shoulder blade with sufficient angulation to place the elbow beneath the highest point of the shoulder blade when standing. The forearms are of medium length, straight and moderately feathered. The legs are well boned but not to the extent of coarseness. The Welsh Springer Spaniel's elbows should be close to the body and its pasterns short and slightly sloping. Height to the elbows is approximately equal to the distance from the elbows to the top of the shoulder blades. Dewclaws are generally removed. Feet should be round, tight and well arched with thick pads.

**Hindquarters**—The hindquarters must be strong, muscular, and well boned, but not coarse. When viewed in profile the thighs should be wide and the second thighs well developed. The angulation of the pelvis and femur corresponds to that of the shoulder and upper arm. Bend of stifle is moderate. The bones from the hocks to the pads are short with a well angulated hock joint. When viewed from the side or rear they are perpendicular to the ground. Rear dewclaws are removed. Feet as in front.

**Coat**—The coat is naturally straight flat and soft to the touch, never wiry or wavy. It is sufficiently dense to be waterproof, thornproof, and weatherproof. The back of the forelegs, the hind legs above the hocks, chest and underside of the body are moderately feathered. The ears and tail are lightly feathered. Coat so excessive as to be a hindrance in the field is to be discouraged. Obvious barbering is to be avoided as well.

**Color**—The color is rich red and white only. Any pattern is acceptable and any white area may be flecked with red ticking.

**Gait**—The Welsh Springer moves with a smooth, powerful, ground covering action that displays drive from the rear. Viewed from the side, he exhibits a strong forward stride with a reach that does not waste energy. When viewed from the front, the legs should appear to move forward in an effortless manner with no tendency for the feet to cross over or interfere with each other. Viewed from the rear, the hocks should follow on a line with the forelegs, neither too widely nor too closely spaced. As the speed increases the feet tend to converge towards a center line.

**Temperament**—The Welsh Springer Spaniel is an active dog displaying a loyal and affectionate disposition. Although reserved with strangers, he is not timid, shy nor unfriendly. To this day he remains a devoted family member and hunting companion.

Approved June 13, 1989

# Vizsla

The origin of the Vizsla, or Hungarian Pointer, has been obscured by the centuries, but it is fair to assume that its ancestors were the hunters and companions of the Magyar hordes which swarmed over Central Europe more than a thousand years ago and settled in what is now Hungary. Primitive stone etchings of the 10th century show a Magyar huntsman with his falcon and a dog resembling the Vizsla. As far back as the 14th century, a manuscript of early Hungarian codes carried a chapter on falconry which was illustrated with a picture of a dog reasonably well identified as a Vizsla. Apparently the breed became a favorite of the early barons and warlords who, either deliberately or by accident, preserved its purity through the years.

The reason for the Vizsla's continued existence, even in that far time, lay in the fact that its innate hunting ability was fostered and developed by the terrain in which it grew, namely, the plains of Hungary.

Here was a section of that country almost entirely agricultural and pastoral; where grains were raised in great abundance; where the growing season was long, the summers hot, the winters tempered by the proximity of water. Here wheat and corn, rye and barley attracted the partridge and other game birds, while the Hungarian hare flourished and grew large. Amid such plenty, it was inevitable that a hunting dog suited to the climatic conditions, and the available game, would be developed. What the huntsman needed and what he eventually got was a dog swift of foot, and cautious so as not to alert quarry in an almost totally uncovered territory; a close-working dog of superior nose and generally high-class hunting ability; a dog, in short, that would combine the duties of the specialists as both pointer and retriever.

The great wars interfered markedly with what otherwise would have been normal breed progress. The close of World War I found the Vizsla all but extinct, and preserved in only a small way by a few of its firmest friends. The years between the two wars were difficult ones, but those who loved the breed refused to let it die out. Hungarians who fled before the Russian occupation in 1945 took their dogs with them into Austria, Italy and Germany. Likewise there are some in Czechoslovakia, Turkey, and southern Russia.

Importation into the United States began in the 1950s and the breed was admitted to AKC registry in 1960. Vizslas are giving a good account of themselves as robust and enduring hunters as well as gentle and friendly companions.

Essentially Pointer in type, the Vizsla is a distinguished looking dog of aristocratic bearing. His short coat is an attractive rusty-gold, he is powerfully built, but lithe and well balanced, with a light-footed, smooth, and graceful gait. He is a multiple-purpose dog for work on upland game, on rabbits, and for waterfowl retrieving.

## Official Standard for the Vizsla

**General Appearance**— That of a medium-sized short-coated hunting dog of distinguished appearance and bearing. Robust but rather lightly built; the coat is an attractive solid golden rust. This is a dog of power and drive in the field yet a tractable and affectionate companion in the home. It is strongly emphasized that field conditioned coats, as well as brawny or sinewy muscular condition and honorable scars indicating a working and hunting dog are never to be penalized in this dog. The qualities that make a "dual dog" are always to be appreciated not deprecated.

**Head**—Lean and muscular. Skull moderately wide between the ears with a median line down the forehead. Stop between skull and foreface is moderate, not deep. Foreface or muzzle is of equal length or slightly shorter than skull when viewed in profile, should taper gradually from stop to tip of nose. Muzzle square and deep. It must not turn up as in a "dish" face nor should it turn down. Whiskers serve a functional purpose; their removal is permitted but not preferred. Nostrils slightly open. Nose brown. Any other color is faulty. A *totally black nose is a disqualification.* Ears, thin, silky and proportionately long, with rounded-leather ends, set fairly low and hanging close to cheeks. Jaws are strong with well developed white teeth meeting in a scissors bite. Eyes medium in size and depth of setting, their surrounding tissue covering the whites. Color of the iris should blend with the color of the coat. Yellow or any other color is faulty. Prominent pop-eyes are faulty. Lower eyelids should neither turn in nor out since both conditions allow seeds and dust to irritate the eye. Lips cover the jaws completely but are neither loose nor pendulous.

**Neck and Body**—Neck strong, smooth and muscular, moderately long, arched and devoid of dewlap, broadening nicely into shoulders which are moderately laid back. This is mandatory to maintain balance with the moderately angulated hindquarters. Body is strong and well proportioned. Back short. Withers high and the topline slightly rounded over the loin to the set on of the tail. Chest moderately broad and deep reaching down to the elbows. Ribs well-sprung; underline exhibiting a slight tuck-up beneath the loin. Tail set just below the level of the croup, thicker at the root and docked one-third off. Ideally, it should reach to the back of the stifle joint and be carried at or near the horizontal. An undocked tail is faulty.

**Forequarters**—Shoulder blades proportionately long and wide sloping moderately back and fairly close at the top. Forelegs straight and muscular with elbows close. Feet catlike, round and compact with toes close. Nails brown and short. Pads thick and tough. Dewclaws, if any, to be removed on front and rear feet. Hare feet are faulty.

**Hindquarters**—Hind legs have well developed thighs with moderately angulated stifles and hocks in balance with the moderately laid back shoulders. They must be straight as viewed from behind. Too much angulation at the hocks is as faulty as too little. The hocks are let down and parallel to each other.

**Coat**—Short, smooth, dense and close-lying, without woolly undercoat.

**Color**—Solid golden rust in different shadings. Solid dark mahogany red and pale yellow are faulty. Small white spots on chest are not faulted but massive areas of white on chest or white anywhere else on the body is a disqualification. Occasional white hairs on toes are acceptable but solid white extending above the toes is a disqualification. White due to aging shall not be faulted. Any noticeable area of black in the coat is a serious fault.

**Gait**—Far reaching, light footed, graceful and smooth. When moving at a fast trot, a properly built dog single tracks.

**Size**—The ideal male is 22 to 24 inches at the highest point over the shoulder blades. The ideal female is 21 to 23 inches. Because the Vizsla is meant to be a medium-sized hunter, any dog measuring more than 1½ inches over or under these limits must be disqualified.

**Temperament**—A natural hunter endowed with a good nose and above-average ability to take training. Lively, gentle-mannered, demonstrably affectionate and sensitive though fearless with a well developed protective instinct. Shyness, timidity or nervousness should be penalized.

**DISQUALIFICATIONS**

*Completely black nose.*

*Massive areas of white on chest; white anywhere else on the body. Solid white extending above the toes.*

*Any male over 25½ inches, or under 20½ inches and any female over 24½ inches or under 19½ inches at the highest point over the shoulder blades.*

Approved April 12, 1983

# Weimaraner

## (Vy-mah-rah-ner)

As history is reckoned, the Weimaraner is a young dog, dating back only to the early 19th century. The Bloodhound is believed to be among its ancestors, if not in direct line of descent, then certainly in a collateral way. In their breed investigations, historians stopped when they got as far back as the Red Schweisshund, but it is difficult to imagine that any of the several varieties of Schweisshund did not trace to the Bloodhound, which was well established in Europe at the time of the Crusades. Indeed, the red-tan Schweisshund found in the vicinity of Hanover is described as having "many of the characteristics of the Bloodhound." It was, however, a breed measuring about 21 inches at the shoulder, compared with the Bloodhound's average height of 26 inches and the Weimaraner's top of 27 inches.

The Weimaraner that we know today is the product of selective breeding; of judicious crosses followed by generations of line breeding to fix type and quality. It came from the same general stock which has produced a number of Germany's hunting breeds, one of its cousins being the German Shorthaired Pointer. In fact, in its early days, the Weimaraner was known simply as the Weimar Pointer. Since then height and weight have both been increased, but the distinctive coat color, described as silver grizzle or mouse gray, was approximately the same.

Throughout its early career the Weimaraner was sponsored by the sportsmen nobles in the court of Weimar. Long accustomed to many types of hunting, these men determined to meld into one breed all the qualities they had found worthwhile in their forays against the then abundant game of Germany. In short, the dog had to have good scenting ability, speed, courage, and intelligence.

Formerly the Weimaraner had been a big-game dog used on such quarry as wolves, wildcats, deer, mountain lion, bear, etc. By the time big game in Germany became a rarity, the breed was supported by a club originally started by a few of the men who had drawn up the dog's specifications. They were amateur sportsmen who desired to breed for sport rather than for profit. Accordingly, it was not easy to purchase a Weimaraner in Germany and practically impossible in any foreign country. One had to become a member of the club before purchasing, while gaining admittance to the club meant that the applicant's previous record of sportsmanship must assure proper maintenance of the club's breeding rules. One of these rules demanded that litters resulting from matings deemed unsuitable by a breed survey were not given place in the stud book; another, that specimens, even from approved litters, which did not measure up physically and temperamentally were to be destroyed. Hence there was no chance of a boom in the breed.

America came to know the Weimaraner back in 1929 when an American sportsman and dog breeder, Howard Knight, was made a member of Germany's Weimaraner Club. Permitted to bring back two specimens, he helped found the club in this country and served as its first president. The club has made every effort to carry out the same principles that mapped the career of the breed in its native land.

It should be mentioned in passing that with the demise of big game hunting in Germany, the Weimaraner was trained as a bird dog used on various types of game in upland shooting and as a water retriever noted for its soft mouth. However, both in Germany and in America the dog has been used more as a personal hunting companion than as a field-trial competitor.

Obedience trials incited the first interest in the breed over here, even before recognition was granted in 1943 by the American Kennel Club. A bitch qualified for her C.D. in three straight shows in 1941, and later, another specimen went through all the degrees except the tracking test before reaching his tenth month. Curiously enough, the Weimaraner has seen more actual competition of various kinds in America than it did in all its decades in Germany.

As for temperament, this dog is not happy when relegated to the kennel. He is accustomed to being a member of the family and he accepts the responsibilities which that entails.

# Official Standard for the Weimaraner

**General Appearance**—A medium-sized gray dog, with fine aristocratic features. He should present a picture of grace, speed, stamina, alertness and balance. Above all, the dog's conformation must indicate the ability to work with great speed and endurance in the field.

**Height**—Height at the withers: dogs, 25 to 27 inches; bitches, 23 to 25 inches. One inch over or under the specified height of each sex is allowable but should be penalized. Dogs measuring less than 24 inches or more than 28 inches and bitches measuring less than 22 inches or more than 26 inches shall be disqualified.

**Head**—Moderately long and aristocratic, with moderate stop and slight median line extending back over the forehead. Rather prominent occipital bone and trumpets well set back, beginning at the back of the eye sockets. Measurement from tip of nose to stop equal that from stop to occipital bone. The flews should be straight, delicate at the nostrils. Skin drawn tightly. Nick clean-cut and moderately long. Expression kind, keen and intelligent. *Ears*—Long and lobular, slightly folded and set high. The ear when drawn snugly alongside the jaw should end approximately 2 inches from the point of the nose. *Eyes*—In shades of light amber, gray or blue-gray, set well enough apart to indicate good disposition and intelligence. When dilated under excitement the eyes may appear almost black. *Teeth*—Well set, strong and even; well-developed and proportionate to jaw with correct scissors bite, the upper teeth protruding slightly over the lower teeth but not more than 1/16 of an inch. Complete dentition is greatly to be desired. *Nose*— Gray. *Lips and Gums*—Pinkish flesh shades.

**Body**—The back should be moderate in length, set in a straight line, strong, and should slope slightly from the withers. The chest should be well developed and deep with shoulders well laid back. Ribs well sprung and long. Abdomen firmly held; moderately tucked-up flank. The brisket should extend to the elbow.

**Coat and Color**—Short, smooth and sleek, solid color, in shades of mouse-gray to silver-gray, usually blending to lighter shades on the head and ears. A small white marking on the chest is permitted, but should be penalized on any other portion of the body. White spots resulting from injury should not be penalized. A distinctly long coat is a disqualification. A distinctly blue or black coat is a disqualification.

**Forelegs**—Straight and strong, with the measurement from the elbow to the ground approximately equaling the distance from the elbow to the top of the withers.

**Hindquarters**—Well-angulated stifles and straight hocks. Musculation well developed.

**Feet**—Firm and compact, webbed, toes well arched, pads closed and thick, nails short and gray or amber in color. *Dewclaws*—Should be removed.

**Tail**—Docked. At maturity it should measure approximately 6 inches with a tendency to be light rather than heavy and should be carried in a manner expressing confidence and sound temperament. A non-docked tail shall be penalized.

**Gait**—The gait should be effortless and should indicate smooth coordination. When seen from the rear, the hind feet should be parallel to the front feet. When viewed from the side, the topline should remain strong and level.

**Temperament**—The temperament should be friendly, fearless, alert and obedient.

### FAULTS

*Minor Faults*—Tail too short or too long. Pink nose.

*Major Faults*—Doggy bitches. Bitchy dogs. Improper muscular condition. Badly affected teeth. More than four teeth missing. Back too long or too short. Faulty coat. Neck too short, thick or throaty. Low-set tail. Elbows in or out. Feet east and west. Poor gait. Poor feet. Cowhock. Faulty backs, either roached or sway. Badly overshot, or undershot bite. Snipy muzzle. Short ears.

*Very Serious Faults*—White, other than a spot on the chest. Eyes other than gray, blue-gray or light amber. Black mottled mouth. Non-docked tail. Dogs exhibiting strong fear, shyness or extreme nervousness.

### DISQUALIFICATIONS

*Deviation in height of more than one inch from standard either way.*
*A distinctly long coat. A distinctly blue or black coat.*

Approved December 14, 1971

# Wirehaired Pointing Griffon

The origin of the Wirehaired Pointing Griffon came in the great period of biological awakening—the last quarter of the 19th century. Just a few years before, the Austrian abbot, Mendel, had published his experiments on inheritance, and the youth of Western Europe were anxious to try their skill at breeding.

Thus it was that E. K. Korthals, the son of a wealthy banker at Schooten, near Haarlem, in Holland, began to assemble the dogs from which he was to establish a new sporting breed. His first purchase, in 1874, was Mouche, described as a griffon bitch, about seven years old, gray and brown. It is said of her that she was equally excellent in the woods or in the open.

Korthals acquired five other dogs during the next three years—Janus, Hector, Satan, Junon, and Banco. Janus had woolly hair, Junon was short-haired, and the others were rough-coated.

The first breeding of importance was that of Huzaar, son of the rough-coated Mouche and the woolly-coated Janus, to the short-haired bitch, Junon. From this mating came Trouvee, a bitch with a harder coat than any of the others. Trouvee then was bred to Banco, and she whelped Moustache I, Querida, and

Lina—three specimens from which, it is agreed, springs the best line in the breed.

Although the origin of the Wirehaired Pointing Griffon is undoubtedly Dutch, it is regarded principally as a French breed, for it was in France that the major portion of the development took place. If any single factor can be credited with the spread of interest in the Wirehaired Pointing Griffon, or Korthals griffon as it is known in France, it was the traveling done by the young breeder during the years he spent as the advance agent of the French nobleman, the Duke of Penthievre. Korthals never forgot his hobby, and whenever he found congenial company he extolled the virtues of the new breed. Admitting that it was a deliberate, even slow worker, his enthusiasm over its keen nose and its ability to point and retrieve game was infectious.

Korthals moved from Holland to Biebesheim, Germany, and resumed his breeding activities. In replenishing his stock, his first new brood matron in Germany was Donna, purchased in 1879. She was of the boulet type, which meant that her coat was rather long. Donna was mated twice to Moustache I, and left two daughters, Augot and Clairette, both of which showed the characteristics desired. Six years later, Korthals affected a lease for the bitch Vesta, and the breeding from her provided another successful line. Vesta had rough hair, and all her descendants were typical species that carried the right sort of coat.

While there remains some doubt as to the various crosses in the background of the dogs known as the "Korthals patriarchs," it has been suggested by a wide number of authorities that they carried setter, spaniel, and Otter Hound blood. It is known that certain specimens, described in *Livre des Origines du Griffon a poil dur,* as true griffons, trace their ancestry back to the ancient breed called the griffon hound; and it also is known that at least one cross with a Pointer—no doubt the German Shorthair—was effected.

Korthals was a man of wide acquaintance among the sporting fraternity of Europe, and invariably he was present at any major field activity connected with dogs. Later he followed the bench shows closely, seeking to popularize the type of griffon—for there had been dogs called griffons for several centuries—that he had originated.

The Wirehaired Pointing Griffon was exhibited in England shortly after it was developed, and it attracted considerable attention. Still, classes were not provided until some years later, the first record of these being at the Barn Elms show in 1888. The breed came across the Atlantic twelve years later. The first specimen registered by the American Kennel Club was Zolette, 6773, by Guerre, ex Tambour. The registration appears as a "Russian Setter (Griffon)" in Vol. 4, published in 1887. The sire, Guerre, was a grandson of Donna. So started the American fancy.

The Wirehaired Pointing Griffon is particularly adapted for swampy country, where its harsh coat is a great protection. It also is a strong swimmer and serves as an excellent water retriever, though adherents of the breed claim it can be trained and entered to any game.

# Official Standard for the Wirehaired Pointing Griffon

**General Appearance**—Medium sized, with a noble, square-shaped head, strong of limb, bred to cover all terrain encountered by the walking hunter. Movement showing an easy catlike gracefulness. Excels equally as a pointer in the field, or a retriever in the water. Coat is hard and coarse, never curly or woolly, with a thick undercoat of fine hair, giving an unkempt appearance. His easy trainability, devotion to family, and friendly temperament endear him to all. The nickname of "supreme gundog" is well earned.

**Size, Proportion, Substance**—*Size*—22 to 24 inches for males, 20 to 22 inches for females. Correct size is important. Oversize to be *severely penalized*. *Proportion*— Slightly longer than tall, in a ratio of 10 to 9. Height from withers to ground; length from point of shoulder to point of buttocks. The Griffon must not evolve towards a square conformation. *Substance* medium, reflecting his work as an all-terrain hunting dog.

**Head**—The *head* is to be in proportion to the overall dog. The *skull* is of medium width with equal length from nose to stop and from stop to occiput. The skull is slightly rounded on top, but from the side the *muzzle* and head are square. The *stop* and *occiput* are only slightly pronounced. The required abundant mustache and eyebrows contribute to the friendly *expression*. The *eyes* are large and well open, more rounded than elliptical. They have an alert, friendly, and intelligent expression. Eye color ranges in all shades of yellow and brown. Haws should not show nor should there be protruding eyes. The *ears* should be of medium size, lying flat and close to the head, set high, at the height of the eye line. *Nose*—Well open nostrils are essential. Nose color is always brown. Any other color is a *disqualification*. *Bite* scissor. Overshot or undershot bite is a *serious fault*.

**Neck, Topline, Body**—*Neck* rather long, slightly arched, no dewlap. *Topline*—The *back* is strong and firm, descending in a gentle slope from the slightly higher withers to the base of the tail. *Body*—*Chest*—The *chest* must descend to the level of the elbow, with a moderate spring of rib. The chest must neither be too wide nor too narrow, but of medium width to allow freedom of movement. The *loin* is strong and well developed, being of medium length. The croup and rump are stoutly made with adequate length to favor speed. The *tail* extends from the back in a continuation of the topline. It may be carried straight or raised slightly. It is docked by one-third to one-half length.

**Forequarters**—*Shoulders* are long, with good angulation, and well laid back. The *forelegs* are straight and vertical from the front and set well under the shoulder from the side. *Pasterns* are slightly sloping. Dewclaws should be removed. *Feet* are round, firm, with tightly closed webbed toes. Pads are thick.

**Hindquarters**—The *thighs* are long and well muscled. Angulation in balance with the front. The *legs* are vertical with the hocks turning neither in nor out. The *stifle* and *hock joints* are strong and well angulated. *Feet* as in front.

**Coat**—The coat is one of the distinguishing features of the breed. It is a double coat. The outer coat is medium length, straight and wiry, never curly or woolly. The harsh texture provides protection in rough cover. The obligatory undercoat consists of a fine, thick down, which provides insulation as well as water resistance. The undercoat is more or less abundant, depending upon the season, climate, and hormone cycle of the dog. It is usually lighter in color. The head is furnished with a prominent mustache and eyebrows. These required features are extensions of the undercoat, which gives the Griffon a somewhat untidy appearance. The hair covering the ears is fairly short and soft, mixed with longer harsh hair from the coat. The overall feel is much less wiry than the body. The legs, both front and rear, are covered with denser, shorter, and less coarse hair. The coat on the tail is the same as the body; any type of plume is prohibited. The breed should be exhibited in full body coat, not stripped short in pattern. Trimming and stripping are only allowed around the ears, top of head, cheeks and feet.

**Color**—Preferably steel gray with brown markings, frequently chestnut brown, or roan, white and brown; white and orange also acceptable. A uniformly brown coat, all white coat, or white and orange are less desirable. A black coat *disqualifies.*

**Gait**—Although close working, the Griffon should cover ground in an efficient, tireless manner. He is a medium-speed dog with perfect coordination between front and rear legs. At a trot, both front and rear legs tend to converge toward the center line of gravity. He shows good extension both front and rear. Viewed from the side, the topline is firm and parallel to the line of motion. A smooth, powerful ground-covering ability can be seen.

**Temperament**—The Griffon has a quick and intelligent mind and is easily trained. He is outgoing, shows a tremendous willingness to please and is trustworthy. He makes an excellent family dog as well as a meticulous hunting companion.

### DISQUALIFICATIONS

*Nose any color other than brown.*
*Black coat.*

Approved October 8, 1991

# HOUNDS

## Afghan Hound

The Afghan Hound was discovered by the Western world in Afghanistan and surrounding regions during the 19th century. The first specimens of the breed were brought to England in the latter part of that century, and the earliest known pictorial representation of an unmistakable, full-coated Afghan Hound is a drawing reproduced in some copies of a volume of letters written in India in 1809 and published in London in 1813.

Of the breed's origin and its history prior to then, little is known for certain.

137

A vast amount of research, however, has turned up no basis for the once popular belief that the Afghan Hound existed in Egypt thousands of years ago, or for the theory that the breed evolved on the steppes of Asia and represents the original sight hound.

The basic structure of the dog beneath the coat is that of a relatively sturdy coursing hound of a type which might have evolved or been created from other canine types almost anytime, anywhere. The extremely fine, longhaired coat, however, is of a sort found among animals native to high altitudes, and the desired coat pattern of contrasting short hair on the foreface, back and dorsal surface of the tail may also be related to climate.

A problem in any study of the breed is that, like so many other breeds recognized today, the Afghan Hound, as we know and describe it in the standard, represents a blending of dogs of more than one type. Some sources in Afghanistan divide the breed as found there into a half-dozen or more varieties based on locality, color, etc. Although intermediate variations undoubtedly exist, it has been more common to speak in terms of two extremes in type— the hounds of the southern and western desert regions, which tend to be relatively rangy in build, light in color and sparse in outer coat; and the hounds of the northern mountain regions, which tend to be more compact in structure, darker in color and more heavily coated. These and other variations represent logical adaptations to the wide diversity of climate and terrain in the area of Afghanistan.

Among other things, this diversity in the breed—plus the diversity in the Afghan people, their culture and their country—helps explain the apparent conflicts among accounts of how the breed was utilized in its native land. Some tell of Afghan Hounds serving as guard dogs and herd dogs, which are within the capabilities of the breed as we know it. The major role of these dogs, however, was undoubtedly that of hunting. The kings of Afghanistan maintained a kennel of hunting hounds for many generations.

The breed is primarily a coursing hound, pursuing its quarry by sight and followed by the huntsman on horseback. Because these dogs tended to outdistance the horses, the Afghan Hounds hunted "on their own," without direction by the huntsman, giving rise to the independence of thought and spirit still typical of the breed.

We are variously told of Afghan Hounds being hunted singly, in dog-and-bitch pairs, in packs, and in a combination with specially trained falcons. Undoubtedly the breed was hunted in all of these ways, but the method would vary according to locality and the nature of the quarry, so that not all Afghan Hounds did all things in all places.

The same principle would apply to the extremely wide variety of game on which they reportedly were used. The Afghan Hound could and quite certainly was employed to hunt whatever animals the locality provided and the huntsman wanted to hunt. In the truest coursing-hound sense, they ran down game such as mountain deer, plains antelopes and hares wherever they might be found. They could also be used to bring to bay such predators as wolves, jackals, wild dogs and snow leopards. They were also used, as a spaniel would be, to flush quail and partridge for the falcon or gun. And they are the equal to any terrier for dispatching marmots, greatly prized by the mountain people for their fur and flesh.

As coursing dogs Afghan Hounds excel, not so much in straightaway speed—although they have considerable—as in the ability to traverse rough terrain swiftly and sure-footedly. This requires agility in leaping and quickness in turning, plus the stamina to maintain such a strenuous chase for as long as it may take to close on the quarry.

The first recorded appearance of the Afghan Hound in the West was in the latter part of the 19th century, when British officers and others returning from the Indian-Afghanistan border wars brought dogs from that area back to England, some of which were exhibited at dog shows as "Afghan Hounds." These aroused some interest but no real enthusiasm until 1907, when Captain John Barff brought from Persia via India his dog "Zardin"—a typy, well-coated dog with a dark mask and a great deal of style. This, English dog fanciers decided, was what an Afghan Hound should be! There was some breeding of Afghan Hounds in Great Britain at this time, and some specimens from there or Afghanistan may have reached America prior to World War I.

During that war, however, the breed literally disappeared in the Western world, and the start of the Afghan Hounds we have today dates to 1920, when Major and Mrs. G. Bell Murray and Miss Jean C. Manson brought to Scotland a group of Afghan Hounds they had acquired or bred during an eight year stay in Baluchistan—then an independent state south of Afghanistan, and today a part of Pakistan. Most of these dogs were of the "desert" type— racy, fine headed and light in coat. Breeding from these imports, Miss Manson, the Major and others further developed the "Bell-Murray strain" throughout the 1920s.

In 1925, Mrs. Mary Amps shipped to England the first of a group of Afghan Hounds from the kennel she had maintained in Kabul. These were mainly of the "mountain" type—sturdily built, relatively short-coupled and more or less full-coated. From these imports—the most successful of which as a show dog and sire was the English Champion Sirdar of Ghazni—Mrs. Amps and others developed what is called (from her kennel name) the "Ghazni strain."

During the '20s, a number of "Bell-Murray" Afghan Hounds were exported to the United States, and when the AKC Stud Book was opened to the breed, some of these were registered, beginning in October 1926. From two of them came the first registered American-bred Afghan Hound in 1927.

The real start of the breed in this country, however, dates to the first "Ghazni" imports in 1931, when Zeppo Marx and his wife brought from England a bitch, Asra of Ghazni, and a dog, Westmill Omar. Asra and Omar were later acquired by Q. A. Shaw McKean's "Prides Hill" kennels in Massachusetts. Mr. McKean soon added a young English champion, Badshah of Ainsdart, a bitch of pure "Bell-Murray" breeding. These three—Asra, Omar and Bad-shah—formed the cornerstone of the breed in America.

Most of the American breeders of the 1930s came into Afghan Hounds with a background of success in other breeds. As a rule their kennels were founded on Prides Hill stock bred to one or more of the dozens of imports then coming from Great Britain, and the several from India and Afghanistan. Afghanistan now forbids the exportation of these hounds.

Although the Afghan Hound was admitted to the AKC Stud Book in 1926, there was no parent club for the breed until a group of leading fanciers met at the 1937 Westminster Kennel Club show and organized what, after a reorganization the following year, became the Afghan Hound Club of America. In 1940 the club was admitted to AKC membership and held its first specialty show.

There being no parent club in 1926, the AKC had adopted a standard which was an expanded version of one then in use by an English breed club. This standard, in turn, was little more than a description of Zardin written some 20 years earlier. One of the first tasks assigned to AHCA, therefore, was the drafting of a "clarified standard." After two very different American drafts failed to win approval and an attempt to have a common standard with English was frustrated, a new and quite original standard was drafted and approved by the AHCA membership without dissent in 1948 and adopted by the AKC later that year.

Much of the Afghan Hound's popularity here has been generated by the breed's spectacular qualities as a show dog. The Afghan Hound also excels in lure racing and, although its tendency to think for itself makes for something less than perfect precision in executing set exercises and commands, the breed has also done well in obedience work.

Over and beyond their success in such fields, however, Afghan Hounds are prized and loved by their owners as companions and members of the family. With its highly individual personality and with its coat which requires regular care and grooming, it is not the breed for all would-be dog owners, but where the dog and owner combination is right, there is no animal which can equal the Afghan Hound as a pet.

## Official Standard for the Afghan Hound

**General Appearance**—The Afghan Hound is an aristocrat, his whole appearance one of dignity and aloofness with no trace of plainness or coarseness. He has a straight front, proudly carried head, eyes gazing into the distance as if in memory of ages past. The striking characteristics of the breed—exotic, or "Eastern," expression, long silky top-knot, peculiar coat pattern, very prominent hipbones, large feet, and the impression of a somewhat exaggerated bend in the stifle due to profuse trouserings—stand out clearly, giving the Afghan Hound the appearance of what he is, a king of dogs, that has held true to tradition throughout the ages.

**Head**—The head is of good length, showing much refinement, the skull evenly balanced with the foreface. There is a slight prominence of the nasal bone structure causing a slightly Roman appearance, the center line running up over the foreface with little or no stop, falling away in front of the eyes so there is an absolutely clear outlook with no interference; the underjaw showing great strength, the jaws long and punishing; the mouth level, meaning that the teeth from the upper jaw and lower jaw match evenly, neither overshot nor undershot. This is a difficult mouth to breed. A scissors bite is even more punishing and can be more easily bred into a dog than a level mouth, and a dog having a scissors bite, where the lower teeth slip inside and rest against the teeth of the upper jaw, should not be penalized. The occipital bone is very prominent. The head is surmounted by a topknot of long silky hair. **Ears**—The ears are long, set approximately on level with outer corners of the eyes, the leather of the ear reaching nearly to the end of the dog's nose, and covered with long silky hair. **Eyes**—The eyes are almond-shaped (almost triangular), never full or bulgy, and are dark in color. **Nose**—Nose is of good size, black in color. **Faults**—Coarseness; snipiness; overshot or undershot; eyes round or bulgy or light in color; exaggerated Roman nose; head not surmounted with topknot.

**Neck**—The neck is of good length, strong and arched, running in a curve to the shoulders which are long and sloping and well laid back. **Faults**—Neck too short or too thick; a ewe neck; a goose neck; a neck lacking in substance.

**Body**—The back line appearing practically level from the shoulders to the loin. Strong and powerful loin and slightly arched, falling away toward the stern, with the hipbones very pronounced; well ribbed and tucked up in flanks. The height at the shoulders equals the distance from the chest to the buttocks; the brisket well let down, and of medium width. **Faults**—Roach back, swayback, goose rump, slack loin; lack of prominence of hipbones; too much width of brisket, causing interference with elbows.

**Tail**—Tail set not too high on the body, having a ring, or a curve on the end; should never be curled over, or rest on the back, or be carried sideways; and should never be bushy.

**Legs**—Forelegs are straight and strong with great length between elbow and pastern; elbows well held in; forefeet large in both length and width; toes well arched; feet covered with long thick hair; fine in texture; pasterns long and straight; pads of feet unusually large and well down on the ground. Shoulders have plenty of angulation so that the legs are well set underneath the dog. Too much straightness of shoulder causes the dog to break down in the pasterns, and this is a serious fault. All four feet of the Afghan Hound are in line with the body, turning neither in nor out. The hind feet are broad and of good length; the toes arched, and covered with long thick hair; hindquarters powerful and well muscled, with great length between hip and hock; hocks are well let down; good angulation of both stifle and hock; slightly bowed from hock to crotch. **Faults**—Front or back feet thrown outward or inward; pads of feet not thick enough; or feet too small; or any other evidence of weakness in feet; weak or broken down pasterns; too straight in stifle; too long in hock.

**Coat**—Hindquarters, flanks, ribs, forequarters, and legs well covered with thick, silky hair, very fine in texture; ears and all four feet well feathered; from in front of the shoulders; and also backwards from the shoulders along the saddle from the flanks and the ribs upwards, the hair is short and close, forming a smooth back in mature dogs—this is a traditional characteristic of the Afghan Hound. The Afghan Hound should be shown in its natural state; the coat is not clipped or trimmed; the head is surmounted (in the full sense of the word) with a topknot of long, silky hair—that is also an outstanding characteristic of the Afghan Hound. Showing of short hair on cuffs on either front or back legs is permissible. *Fault*—Lack of shorthaired saddle in mature dogs.

**Height**—Dogs, 27 inches, plus or minus one inch; bitches, 25 inches, plus or minus one inch.

**Weight**—Dogs, about 60 pounds; bitches, about 50 pounds.

**Color**—All colors are permissible, but color or color combinations are pleasing; white markings, especially on the head, are undesirable.

**Gait**—When running free, the Afghan Hound moves at a gallop, showing great elasticity and spring in his smooth, powerful stride. When on a loose lead, the Afghan can trot at a fast pace; stepping along, he has the appearance of placing the hind feet directly in the foot prints of the front feet, both thrown straight ahead. Moving with head and tail high, the whole appearance of the Afghan Hound is one of great style and beauty.

**Temperament**—Aloof and dignified, yet gay.

**Faults**—Sharpness or shyness.

Approved September 14, 1948

# Basenji

## (Buh-sen´jee)

The Basenji, popularly known as the "barkless dog," is one of the oldest breeds. The first specimens were brought from the source of the Nile as presents to the Pharaohs of ancient Egypt. Later, when the civilization of Egypt declined and fell, the Basenji lapsed into obscurity. However, it was still valued and preserved in its native land of Central Africa, where it was highly prized for its intelligence, speed, hunting power, and silence.

Centuries later an English explorer rediscovered the Basenji and a pair were brought to England in 1895. Unfortunately, these little dogs contracted distemper and shortly thereafter died. Aside from that abortive attempt to make the breed known, the "outside" world in general did not hear of the Basenji until 1937, when it was successfully introduced to England. At the same time, a pair were brought to America by Mrs. Byron Rogers of New York City. Unfortunately for America, this pair and a litter of puppies produced from mating these specimens contracted distemper. All died except the older male dog, Bois.

In 1941 a young female Basenji was brought from Africa to Boston; Alexander Phemister of Kingston, Mass., obtained her and shortly afterward also acquired the male dog, Bois, that Mrs. Rogers had brought into the country in 1937. The young female, Congo, and Bois, both African-bred, were mated, resulting in the first litter of Basenji puppies to be raised to maturity in America. Later other Basenjis were imported from the Canadian kennels of Dr. A. R. B. Richmond, and still others were brought over from England.

Dog lovers all over the country became interested in this breed—so old, yet so new in America—and later purchased young specimens as foundation breeding stock. In 1942 the Basenji Club of America was formed and accepted the breed standard as drawn up by the Basenji Club of England. In 1943, the American Kennel Club accepted the breed for registration in the Stud Book, and approved the standard. Within a few months, there were 59 Basenjis registered.

The Basenji is about the size and build of a Fox Terrier. The first impression one gets of a Basenji is that he is a proud little dog, and then one is impressed with his beauty, grace, and intelligence. In fact, he has often been compared to a little deer.

The coat of the Basenji is one of his most beautiful features. Coming from a tropical climate, the mixture is silky and shines like burnished copper in the sun. In colder countries the coat tends to become more course, but it never loses its brilliant luster. Other distinctive features include: the lack of bark; the forehead deeply furrowed with wrinkles; the prick ears, standing straight up from their heads; and the dark, intelligent, far-seeing eyes.

The Basenji's intelligence and courage stands proven by his use in his native habitat. The natives use him for pointing, retrieving, for driving game into nets, and for hunting wounded quarry. He is also used for hunting the reed rats—vicious long-toothed creatures weighing from 12 to 20 pounds—and here his silence is a particularly valuable asset.

Those in America and England who have had the opportunity to know the little Basenji have found him to be all they could hope for in a dog. He is a fascinating, endearing fellow, full of play, yet gentle as a kitten. His fastidious, dainty habits, such as cleaning himself all over as does a cat, make him an ideal dog for the immaculate housekeeper.

The Basenji's distinctive sound of happiness fairly thrills one, yet it's a sound hard to describe. It is somewhere between a chortle and a yodel. However, he is usually very happy when he makes it and one can't help but share the happiness with him.

He is, by nature, an obedient dog—tractable and anxious to please. His sprightly, alert manner in the show and obedience rings, and his beautiful gait (resembling that of a thoroughbred horse), elicits much favorable comment.

# Official Standard for the Basenji

**General Appearance**—The Basenji is a small, short haired hunting dog from Africa. It is short backed and lightly built, appearing high on the leg compared to its length. The wrinkled head is proudly carried on a well arched neck and the tail is set high and curled. Elegant and graceful, the whole demeanor is one of poise and inquiring alertness. The balanced structure and the smooth musculature enables it to move with ease and agility. The Basenji hunts by both sight and scent. **Characteristics**—The Basenji should not bark but is not mute. The wrinkled forehead, tightly curled tail and swift, effortless gait (resembling a racehorse trotting full out) are typical of the breed. **Faults**—Any departure from the following points must be considered a fault, and the seriousness with which the fault is regarded is to be in exact proportion to its degree.

**Size, Proportion, Substance**—Ideal height for dogs is 17 inches and bitches 16 inches. Dogs 17 inches and bitches 16 inches from front of chest to point of buttocks. Approximate weight for dogs, 24 pounds and bitches, 22 pounds. Lightly built within this height to weight ratio.

**Head**—The head is proudly carried. **Eyes**—Dark hazel to dark brown, almond shaped, obliquely set and farseeing, rims dark. **Ears**—Small, erect and slightly hooded, of fine texture and set well forward on top of head. The skull is flat, well chiseled and of medium width, tapering toward the eyes. The foreface tapers from eye to muzzle with a perceptible stop. Muzzle shorter than skull, neither coarse nor snipy, but with rounded cushions. Wrinkles appear upon the forehead when ears are erect, and are fine and profuse. Side wrinkles are desirable, but should never be exaggerated into dewlap. Wrinkles are most noticeable in puppies, and because of lack of shadowing, less noticeable in blacks, tricolors and brindles. **Nose**—Black greatly desired. **Teeth**—Evenly aligned with a scissors bite.

**Neck, Topline, Body**—Neck of good length, well crested and slightly full at base of throat. Well set into shoulders. **Topline**—Back level. **Body**—Balanced with a short back, short coupled and ending in a definite waist. Ribs moderately sprung, deep to elbows and oval. Slight forechest in front of point of shoulder. Chest of medium width. **Tail** is set high on topline, bends acutely forward and lies well curled over to either side.

**Forequarters**—Shoulders moderately laid back. Shoulder blade and upper arm of approximately equal length. Elbows tucked firmly against brisket. Legs straight with clean fine bone, long forearm and well-defined sinews. Pasterns of good length, strong and flexible. **Feet**—Small, oval and compact with thick pads and well arched toes. Dewclaws are usually removed.

**Hindquarters**—Medium width, strong and muscular, hocks well let down and turned neither in nor out, with long second thighs and moderately bent stifles. **Feet**—Same as in "Forequarters."

**Coat and Color**—Coat short and fine. Skin very pliant. **Color**—Chestnut red; pure black; tricolor (pure black and chestnut red); or brindle (black stripes on a background of chestnut red); all with white feet, chest and tail tip. White legs, blaze and collar optional. The amount of white should never predominate over primary color. Color and markings should be rich, clear and well-defined, with a distinct line of demarcation between the black and red of tricolors and the stripes of brindles.

**Gait**—Swift, tireless trot. Stride is long, smooth, effortless and the topline remains level. Coming and going, the straight column of bones from shoulder joint to foot and from hip joint to pad remains unbroken, converging toward the centerline under the body. The faster the trot, the greater the convergence.

**Temperament**—An intelligent, independent, but affectionate and alert breed. Can be aloof with strangers.

Approved May 8, 1990

# Basset Hound

Since the 1950s the Basset Hound has emerged from relative obscurity to become one of the most publicized and characterized breeds. Actually, the Basset Hound is an old, aristocratic breed. Originally of French lineage, it has flourished for centuries in Europe, primarily in France and Belgium, where it was used chiefly for the slow trailing of rabbits, hares, deer and any other game that can be trailed on foot or taken to ground.

The foremost use of the Basset Hound in the United States is for the hunting of rabbits. However, it is possible to train them for hunting other game such as raccoons and for the trailing, flushing and retrieving of wounded pheasants and other game birds. The Basset is a sturdy, accurate trailer; his tongue is loud and distinctive. The shortness of his legs and his tight, close coat make him particularly useful in dense cover. In trailing ability, the accuracy of his nose makes him second only to the Bloodhound. His slow going ways and appealing clownish appearance belie great intelligence.

Gentle in disposition, the Basset is agreeable to hunting in packs as well as singly. Medium as to size, loyal and devoted to his master and family, not requiring extensive coat care or trimming, considered an "easy keeper"—all makes the Basset an ideal family pet and housedog.

The first mention of the word "Basset" as applied to a breed of dog appears to have been in an early text on hunting written by Fouilloux in 1585. This book is illustrated with what is considered the first drawing of a Basset, a woodcut showing a sportsman going out in his *charette de chasse* accompanied by his "badger dogs" and Fouilloux gives advice on training the dogs for the purpose of badger hunting.

It is thought that the friars of the French Abbey of St. Hubert were instrumental in selective breeding from various other strains of French Hounds to produce a lower set, hence slower moving dog which could be followed on foot. The word "Basset," derived from the French adjective *bas*, means a "low thing" or "a dwarf." Since hunting was a classic sport in medieval France, it is not surprising that many of the thoroughly efficient small hounds found their way into the kennels of the aristocracy, only to be dispersed with the changing life style brought on by the Revolution. However, the breed was not lost and we find them mentioned again by M. Blaze in his sporting book *Le Chasseur*, written in 1850. About the same time, in his book *Chiens de Chasse*, M. Robert writes: "The Basset will hunt all animals, even boar and wolf, but he is especially excellent for the *chasse a tir* (shooting with the aid of hounds) of rabbits and hares."

By the mid-19th century, the two largest breeders of Bassets in France were producing dogs of slightly different type, especially in head and eye, the two types being identified by the names of their respective breeders. M. Lane's hounds were broader of skull, shorter of ear and with a rounder and more prominent eye. They were generally lemon and white in marking and had a tendency to knuckling. Count Le Couteulx produced hounds that had more narrow heads, more doming in topskull, a softer, more sunken eye with prominent jaw and a down-faced look that created more facial expression. The more glamorous tricolors of the Le Couteulx hounds made them preferred.

In 1886 Lord Galway imported a pair of French Bassets of the Le Couteulx type to England. The following year a mating of these two produced a litter of five pups, but as there was no public exposure of them, no interest in the breed was stirred. It was not until 1874 when Sir Everett Millais imported from France the hound, Model, that real activity with the breed began in England. For his support of the breed and continued drive on a breeding program within his own kennel as well as cooperation with breeding programs established by Lord Onslow and George Krehl, Sir Everett Millais has to be considered the "father of the breed" in England. He first exhibited a Basset at an English dog show in 1875, but it was not until he helped make up a large entry for the Wolverhampton show in 1880 that a great deal of public attention was drawn to the breed. A few years later further interest was created when Queen Alexandra kept Basset Hounds in the royal kennels.

In the United States it is thought that George Washington was the owner of Basset Hounds presented to him as a gift by Lafayette after the American Revolution. In 1883 and 1884 English importations were made by American fanciers of the breed. In 1884 Westminster Kennel Club held a class for the Basset Hound and the English import, Nemours, made his debut before the American public. After subsequent entries at Eastern shows, he completed his championship at Boston in 1886. The first Basset Hounds were registered with the American Kennel Club in 1885.

Gradually the breed began to find favor. By the 1920s Gerald Livingston was making multiple importations for his Kilsyth Kennels on Long island. About the same time Erastus Tefft brought over to his kennels a number of English Bassets, drawing heavily from the Walhampton Pack. Carl Smith imported two French Bassets, one a French champion. Bassets were beginning to be represented regularly at larger shows.

Further attention was drawn to the breed when the February 27, 1928 issue of *Time* magazine carried the picture of a Basset puppy on the cover. The accompanying cover story was a write-up of the 52nd annual dog show of the Westminster Kennel Club at Madison Square Garden as if it were attended and observed by the puppy.

In 1935 a national parent breed club was organized in the United States, the Basset Hound Club of America. Annual Nationals of the club are held which bring together the various fields of activity for this capable breed: conformation, field trailing, pack hunting, obedience and tracking.

By the 1950s, the Basset Hound was synonymous with TV's "Cleo" for the general public, and in England the cartoonist Graham of the *Daily Mail* had made "Fred Basset" almost human by having him represent Everyman. But the dependable and multi-purpose qualities of the breed can never be completely obscured behind a droll facade.

## Official Standard for the Basset Hound

**General Appearance**—The Basset Hound possesses in marked degree those characteristics which equip it admirably to follow a trail over and through difficult terrain. It is a short-legged dog, heavier in bone, size considered, than any other breed of dog, and while its movement is deliberate, it is in no sense clumsy. In temperament it is mild, never sharp or timid. It is capable of great endurance in the field and is extreme in its devotion.

**Head**—The head is large and well proportioned. Its length from occiput to muzzle is greater than the width at the brow. In over-all appearance the head is of medium width. The **skull** is well domed, showing a pronounced occipital protuberance. A broad flat skull is a fault. The length from nose to stop is approximately the length from stop to occiput. The sides are flat and free from cheek bumps. Viewed in profile the top lines of the muzzle and skull are straight and lie in parallel planes, with a moderately defined stop. The skin over the whole of the head is loose, falling in distinct wrinkles over the brow when the head is lowered. A dry head and tight skin are faults. The **muzzle** is deep, heavy, and free from snipiness. The **nose** is darkly pigmented, preferably black, with large wide-open nostrils. A deep liver-colored nose conforming to the coloring of the head is permissible but not desirable. The **teeth** are large, sound, and regular, meeting in either a scissors or an even bite. A bite either overshot or undershot is a serious fault. The **lips** are darkly pigmented and are pendulous, falling squarely in front and, toward the back, in loose hanging flews. The *dewlap* is very pronounced. The **neck** is powerful, of good length, and well arched. The *eyes* are soft, sad, and slightly sunken, showing a prominent haw, and in color are brown, dark brown preferred. A somewhat lighter-colored eye conforming to the general coloring of the dog is acceptable but not desirable. Very light or protruding eyes are faults. The *ears* are extremely long, low set, and when drawn forward, fold well over the end of the nose. They are velvety in texture, hanging in loose folds with the ends curling slightly inward. They are set far back on the head at the base of the skull and, in repose, appear to be set on the neck. A high set or flat ear is a serious fault.

**Forequarters**—The *chest* is deep and full with prominent sternum showing clearly in front of the legs. The *shoulders* and elbows are set close against the sides of the chest. The distance from the deepest point of the chest to the ground, while it must be adequate to allow free movement when working in the field, is not to be more than one-third the total height at the withers of an adult Basset. The shoulders are well laid back and powerful. Steepness in shoulder, fiddle fronts, and elbows that are out, are serious faults. The *forelegs* are short, powerful, heavy in bone, with wrinkled skin. Knuckling over of the front legs is a disqualification. The *paw* is massive, very heavy with tough heavy pads, well rounded and with both feet inclined equally a trifle outward, balancing the width of the shoulders. Feet down at the pastern are a serious fault. The *toes* are neither pinched together nor splayed, with the weight of the forepart of the body borne evenly on each. The dewclaws may be removed.

**Body**—The rib structure is long, smooth, and extends well back. The ribs are well sprung, allowing adequate room for heart and lungs. Flatsidedness and flanged ribs are faults. The topline is straight, level, and free from any tendency to sag or roach, which are faults.

**Hindquarters**—The hindquarters are very full and well rounded, and are approximately equal to the shoulders in width. They must not appear slack or light in relation to the over-all depth of the body. The dog stands firmly on its hind legs showing a well-let-down stifle with no tendency toward a crouching stance. Viewed from behind, the hind legs are parallel, with the hocks turning neither in nor out. Cowhocks or bowed legs are serious faults. The hind feet point straight ahead. Steep, poorly angulated hindquarters are a serious fault. The dewclaws, if any, may be removed.

**Tail**—The tail is not to be docked, and is set in continuation of the spine with but slight curvature, and carried gaily in hound fashion. The hair on the underside of the tail is coarse.

**Size**—The height should not exceed 14 inches. Height over 15 inches at the highest point of the shoulder blades is a disqualification.

**Gait**—The Basset Hound moves in a smooth, powerful, and effortless manner. Being a scenting dog with short legs, it holds its nose low to the ground. Its gait is absolutely true with perfect coordination between the front and hind legs, and it moves in a straight line with hind feet following in line with the front feet, the hocks well bent with no stiffness of action. The front legs do not paddle, weave, or overlap, and the elbows must lie close to the body. Going away, the hind legs are parallel.

**Coat**—The coat is hard, smooth, and short, with sufficient density to be of use in all weather. The skin is loose and elastic. A distinctly long coat is a disqualification.

**Color**—Any recognized hound color is acceptable and the distribution of color and markings is of no importance.

### DISQUALIFICATIONS

*Height of more than 15 inches at the highest point of the shoulder blades.*
*Knuckled over front legs.*
*Distinctly long coat.*

Approved January 14, 1964

# Beagle

The actual origin of the Beagle is lost in the mists of ancient days and no research, it seems, can ever bring its true history to light. Several well-known Beaglers have written their opinions on the origin of the breed, and the following remarks are by Captain Otho Paget of Melton Mowbray, England, who was, perhaps, the dean of all Beaglers.

According to Xenophon there were hounds that hunted by scent in his day and the Romans acquired many of the sports of ancient Greece. There were, however, in England, packs of hounds before the time of the Romans and it is on record that Pwyll, Prince of Wales, a contemporary of King Arthur, had a special breed of white hounds of great excellence. Wales, to this day is still celebrated for its hounds, generally of a light color. Admirers of shooting dogs, setters, spaniels and other kinds, have asserted that these animals were used in building up the hound. By exercise of a little thought it will seem that this must be wrong and that in fact it is the other way about. The hound was the original progenitor of all sporting dogs, and the two distinct breeds would be the "Gaze" or "Greyhound" that hunted by sight alone, and the hound, probably the Bloodhound, that relied entirely on its nose. By the time of good Queen Bess, nearly every country gentleman in England kept a pack of hounds of some sort and hunted the animal of his choice. The fox was not at that time an honored beast of the chase. Hounds in those days seem to have been divided into two classes, the large and the small. The large sort were called "Buck Hounds" and hunted the deer, and the smaller variety were called "Beagles" from the French "Begle" and were hunted on hare.

Coming down to the middle of the 18th century, we find fox hunting becoming popular with the younger generations, who wanted something quicker and more exhilarating than watching hounds puzzling out the intricate windings of a hare. The Foxhound was undoubtedly evolved from a mixture of buck hound and Beagle. By this time the vagaries of breeders had produced two distinct types of hare-hunting hounds, one of which was called the Southern hound and the other the North Country Beagle. The former was slow and ponderous, with long ears and deep voice, while the other was the exact opposite. According to a writer of that day the "North Country Beagle" was nimble and vigorous and did his business as furiously as Jehu himself could wish him.

In the middle of the 19th century Parson Honeywood got together a good pack and showed some excellent sport in Essex. His pack dates as the beginning of the modern Beagle, and nearly every well-known pack of subsequent date owed its origin to that inheritance. We can accept it as true that the Beagle is one of the oldest breeds in history and, with the Bloodhound and perhaps the Otter Hound, closest to the original breed of hounds.

Previous to about 1870 in the United States, the little hunting hounds of the Southern States, then called Beagles, were more of the type of straight-legged Bassets or Dachshunds with weaker heads than the Bassets and were mostly white with few dark markings. They were said to be snappy, tireless hunters, full of vim and quick at a turn, but not handsome in outline. The importations of General Richard Rowett of Carlinsville, Illinois, in the 1860s marks the turning point in the history of the American strain or strains of Beagle and brought to this country an acquisition of canine beauty little thought of by those who hitherto had hunted with Beagles. From what packs in England General Rowett obtained his hounds is not known.

About 1880 Mr. Arnold of Providence, R.I., imported a pack from the Royal Rock Beagles in the North of England, and this also had a good deal of influence on the development of American Beagles. In 1896 James L. Kernochan imported a pack from England and from then on a great many high-class hounds were brought over.

In 1888 the National Beagle Club was formed and held the first field trial. From that time on field trials carrying championship points sprang up rapidly all over the United States, and as many more clubs were sanctioned to hold informal trials. At all these, packs are run in single classes for hounds 13 to 15 inches in height and classes for those under 13 inches, and at the national trials the pack classes are an important feature. There are single classes for young hounds called "derbies" and all-age classes for large and small dogs and bitches. At the national there are, in addition to these single classes, four pack classes which, of course, cannot be run against each other at the same time, as are the hounds in the single classes. Each pack is hunted separately and scored by the judges.

In addition to the regular all-breed American Kennel Club shows, almost all the field-trial clubs conduct specialty shows in connection with their field trials, and in addition to this again, there are hound shows limited to the various breeds of hounds.

Those who are interested in hunting Beagles as a pack generally enjoy hunting the larger hares, rather than cottontail rabbits. Hares do not go to ground and spoil a hunt, and they give much longer, straighter, and faster runs. The white hare, or snowshoe rabbit, is found in northern swamps and provides excellent sport for a pack, but these hares will not do well when imported to other communities and disappear immediately.

There are thousands of men all over the United States who keep a few Beagles and hunt them individually. In addition, there are many packs recorded with the National Beagle Club. They are all hunted in the legitimate manner with a regular hunt staff, in hunt liveries, with their own distinctive colored collar, etc.

The height limit of a Beagle in the United States is 15 inches and in England 16 inches. Hounds above this height cannot be entered in field trials or shows.

The soft brown eyes of the Beagle betray his warm personality but do not instantly reveal his admirable courage and stamina. The latter qualities are especially important while the Beagle is at work in the field, but in the home no gentler, more trustworthy friend could be found.

## Official Standard for the Beagle

**Head** — The skull should be fairly long, slightly domed at occiput, with cranium broad and full. **Ears**—Ears set on moderately low, long, reaching when drawn out nearly, if not quite, to the end of the nose; fine in texture, fairly broad—with almost entire absence of erectile power—setting close to the head, with the forward edge slightly inturning to the cheek—rounded at tip. **Eyes**—Eyes large, set well apart—soft and houndlike—expression gentle and pleading; of a brown or hazel color. **Muzzle**—Muzzle of medium length—straight and square-cut—the stop moderately defined. **Jaws**—Level. Lips free from flews; nostrils large and open. **Defects**—A very flat skull, narrow across the top; excess of dome, eyes small, sharp and terrierlike, or prominent and protruding muzzle long, snipy or cut away decidedly below the eyes, or very short. Roman-nosed, or up-turned, giving a dish-face expression. Ears short, set on high or with a tendency to rise above the point of origin.

**Body**—**Neck and Throat**—Neck rising free and light from the shoulders strong in substance yet not loaded, of medium length. The throat clean and free from folds of skin; a slight wrinkle below the angle of the jaw, however, may be allowable. **Defects**—A thick, short, cloddy neck carried on a line with the top of the shoulders. Throat showing dewlap and folds of skin to a degree termed "throatiness."

**Shoulders and Chest**—Shoulders sloping—clean, muscular, not heavy or loaded—conveying the idea of freedom of action with activity and strength. Chest deep and broad, but not broad enough to interfere with the free play of the shoulders. *Defects*—Straight, upright shoulders. Chest disproportionately wide or with lack of depth.

**Back, Loin and Ribs**—Back short, muscular and strong. Loin broad and slightly arched, and the ribs well sprung, giving abundance of lung room. *Defects*—Very long or swayed or roached back. Flat, narrow loin. Flat ribs.

**Forelegs and Feet**—*Forelegs*—Straight, with plenty of bone in proportion to size of the hound. Pasterns short and straight. *Feet*—Close, round and firm. Pad full and hard. *Defects*—Out at elbows. Knees knuckled over forward, or bent backward. Forelegs crooked or Dachshundlike. Feet long, open or spreading.

**Hips, Thighs, Hind Legs and Feet**—Hips and thighs strong and well muscled, giving abundance of propelling power. Stifles strong and well let down. Hocks firm, symmetrical and moderately bent. Feet close and firm. *Defects*—Cowhocks, or straight hocks. Lack of muscle and propelling power. Open feet.

**Tail**—Set moderately high; carried gaily, but not turned forward over the back; with slight curve; short as compared with size of the hound; with brush. *Defects*—A long tail. Teapot curve or inclined forward from the root. Rat tail with absence of brush.

**Coat**—A close, hard, hound coat of medium length. *Defects*—A short, thin coat, or of a soft quality.

**Color**—Any true hound color.

**General Appearance**—A miniature Foxhound, solid and big for his inches, with the wear-and-tear look of the hound that can last in the chase and follow his quarry to the death.

### SCALE OF POINTS

| Head | | | Running Gear | | |
|---|---|---|---|---|---|
| Skull | 5 | | Forelegs | 10 | |
| Ears | 10 | | Hips, thighs and hind | | |
| Eyes | 5 | | legs | 10 | |
| Muzzle | 5 | 25 | Feet | 10 | 30 |
| Body | | | | | |
| Neck | 5 | | Coat | 5 | |
| Chest and Shoulders | 15 | | Stern | 5 | 10 |
| Back, loin and ribs | 15 | 35 | TOTAL | | 100 |

**Varieties**—There shall be two varieties:
Thirteen Inch—which shall be for hounds not exceeding 13 inches in height.
Fifteen Inch—which shall be for hounds over 13 but not exceeding 15 inches in height.

## DISQUALIFICATION

*Any hound measuring more than 15 inches shall be disqualified.*

### SCORE OF POINTS FOR JUDGING—PACKS OF BEAGLES

| | | |
|---|---|---|
| *Hounds*—General levelness of pack | 40% | |
| Individual merit of hounds | 30% | |
| | | 70% |
| Manners | | 20% |
| Appointments | | 10% |
| TOTAL | | 100% |

**Levelness of Pack**—The first thing in a pack to be considered is that they present a unified appearance. The hounds must be as near to the same height, weight, conformation and color as possible.

**Individual Merit of the Hounds**—Is the individual bench-show quality of the hounds. A very level and sporty pack can be gotten together and not a single hound be a good Beagle. This is to be avoided.

**Manners**—The hounds must all work gaily and cheerfully, with flags up—obeying all commands cheerfully. They should be broken to heel up, kennel up, follow promptly and stand. Cringing, sulking, lying down to be avoided. Also, a pack must not work as though in terror of master and whips. In Beagle packs it is recommended that the whip be used as little as possible.

**Appointments**—Master and whips should be dressed alike, the master or huntsman to carry horn—the whips and master to carry light thong whips. One whip should carry extra couplings on shoulder strap.

### RECOMMENDATIONS FOR SHOW LIVERY

*Black velvet cap, white stock, green coat, white breeches or knickerbockers, green or black stocking, white spats, black or dark brown shoes. Vest and gloves optional. Ladies should turn out exactly the same except for a white skirt instead of white breeches.*

Approved September 10, 1957

# Black and Tan Coonhound

Although a comparatively recent addition to our roster of pure-breds, the Black and Tan Coonhound is actually an old breed as history is reckoned. In all probability he has descended from the Talbot hound which was known in England during the reign of William I, Duke of Normandy, in the 11th century; thence down through the Bloodhound and the Foxhound via this country's own Virginia Foxhound, frequently referred to as the "black and tan."

Selectively bred on a basis of color (for there were "cooners" of other colors as well) and for proficiency on possum and raccoon, the black-and-tan strain was carefully developed over a period of years and admitted to registry by the American Kennel Club in 1945.

The Black and Tan Coonhound works his trail with consummate skill and determination, albeit not at a particularly fast pace. In fact, he trails Bloodhound fashion, entirely by scent, with nose to the ground, "barking up" or giving voice the moment his quarry is treed. And despite the fact that the dog has been nurtured as a specialist on coon, he can do equally well in hunting deer, mountain lion, bear, and possibly other big game.

# Official Standard for the Black and Tan Coonhound

**General Appearance**—The Black and Tan Coonhound is first and fundamentally a working dog, a trail and tree hound, capable of withstanding the rigors of winter, the heat of summer, and the difficult terrain over which he is called upon to work. Used principally for trailing and treeing raccoon, the Black and Tan Coonhound runs his game entirely by scent. The characteristics and courage of the Coonhound also make him proficient on the hunt for deer, bear, mountain lion and other big game. Judges are asked by the club sponsoring the breed to place great emphasis upon these facts when evaluating the merits of the dog. The general impression is that of power, agility and alertness. He immediately impresses one with his ability to cover the ground with powerful rhythmic strides.

**Size, Proportion, Substance**—*Size* measured at the shoulder—Males 25 to 27 inches; females 23 to 25 inches. Oversized dogs should not be penalized when general soundness and proportion are in favor. *Penalize* undersize. **Proportion**—Measured from the point of shoulder to the buttocks and from withers to ground the length of body is equal to or slightly greater than the height of the dog at the withers. Height is in proportion to general conformation so that dog appears neither leggy nor close to the ground. *Substance*—Considering their job as a hunting dog, the individual should exhibit moderate bone and good muscle tone. Males are heavier in bone and muscle tone than females.

**Head**—The head is cleanly modeled. From the back of the skull to the nose the head measures from 9 to 10 inches in males and from 8 to 9 inches in females. *Expression* is alert, friendly and eager. The skin is devoid of folds. Nostrils well open and always black. The flews are well developed with typical hound appearance. *Penalize* excessive wrinkles. *Eyes* are from hazel to dark brown in color, almost round and not deeply set. *Penalize* yellow or light eyes. *Ears* are low set and well back. They hang in graceful folds, giving the dog a majestic appearance. In length they extend naturally well beyond the tip of the nose and are set at eye level or lower. *Penalize* ears that do not reach the tip of the nose and are set too high on the head. *Skull* tends toward oval outline. Medium stop occurring midway between occiput bone and nose. Viewed from profile the line of the skull is on a practically parallel plane to the foreface or muzzle. *Teeth* fit evenly with scissors bite. *Penalize* excessive deviation from scissors bite.

**Neck, Topline, Body**—The neck is muscular, sloping, medium length. The skin is devoid of excess dewlap. The back is level, powerful and strong. The dog possesses full, round, well sprung ribs, avoiding flatsidedness. Chest reaches at least to the elbows. The *tail* is strong, with base slightly below level of backline, carried free and when in action at approximately right angle to back.

**Forequarters**—Powerfully constructed shoulders. The forelegs are straight, with elbows turning neither in nor out; pasterns strong and erect. *Feet* are compact, with well knuckled, strongly arched toes and thick, strong pads. *Penalize* flat or splayed feet.

**Hindquarters**—Quarters are well boned and muscled. From hip to hock long and sinewy, hock to pad short and strong. Stifles and hocks well bent and not inclining either in or out. When standing on a level surface, the hind feet are set back from under the body and the leg from pad to hock is at right angles to the ground. *Fault*—Rear dewclaws.

**Coat**—The coat is short but dense to withstand rough going.

**Color**—As the name implies, the color is coal black with rich tan markings above eyes, on sides of muzzle, chest, legs and breeching, with black pencil markings on toes. *Penalize* lack of rich tan markings, excessive areas of tan markings, excessive black coloration. *Faults*—White on chest or other parts of body is highly undesirable, and a solid patch of white which extends more than one inch in any direction is a disqualification.

**Gait**—When viewed from the side, the stride of the Black and Tan Coonhound is easy and graceful with plenty of reach in front and drive behind. When viewed from the front the forelegs, which are in line with the width of the body, move forward in an effortless manner, but never cross. Viewed from the rear the hocks follow on a line with the forelegs, being neither too widely nor too closely spaced, and as the speed of the trot increases the feet tend to converge toward a center line or single track indicating soundness, balance and stamina. When in action, his head and tail carriage is proud and alert; the topline remains level.

**Temperament**—Even temperament, outgoing and friendly. As a working scent hound, must be able to work in close contact with other hounds. Some may be reserved but never shy or vicious. Aggression toward people or other dogs is most undesirable.

*Note*—Inasmuch as this is a hunting breed, scars from honorable wounds shall not be considered faults.

### DISQUALIFICATIONS

*A solid patch of white which extends more than one inch in any direction.*

Approved December 11, 1990

# Bloodhound

**W**hen Claudius Aelianus, or "Aelian," wrote his famous *Historia Animalium* in the third century A.D., he mentioned in especially glowing terms a breed of hound that was unrivaled for its scenting powers and which was possessed of such great determination that it would not leave the trail until the quarry was located. Thus the early Italian scholar gives us a picture of the dog that is known today as the Bloodhound, a breed that has improved considerably in appearance but which still retains its peculiarly intensified ability to follow the faintest scent.

There has been little evidence to prove how far back the origin of the Bloodhound extends, but it is believed by many authorities that it was known throughout the Mediterranean countries long before the Christian Era. It is called the modern representative of the oldest race of hounds that hunt by scent, indicating, of course, that selective breeding over many centuries has made it outwardly changed from the breed the ancients extolled. Yet its characteristics are so distinctive that cynologists have traced it throughout the dog history.

The Bloodhound made its appearance in Europe long before the Crusades, the first specimens being brought from Constantinople. There were two

**160**

strains, black and white. The blacks were the famed St. Huberts of the 8th century, while the whites later became known as the Southern hounds. It was from the black stock that importations were made to England. Both varieties have played big parts in the development of other hounds and hound-type dogs.

In the 12th century, when even Bishops rode to hounds, dignitaries of the Church were among the foremost in fostering the development of the Blood-hound. A number of high ecclesiastics maintained packs, and the kennel was an important part of every monastery. To them goes a great deal of the credit for keeping the strain clean. In fact, so much care was taken in the breeding of this hound that it came to be called the "blooded hound," meaning aristo-cratic.

Several centuries later that noted English physician and dog lover, Dr. Johannes Caius, gives a different explanation of the name, but his description of the breed is interesting. It follows:

> . . . The larger class remain to be mentioned; these too have drooping lips and ears, and it is well known that they follow their prey not only while alive but also after death when they have caught the scent of blood. For whether the beasts are wounded alive and slip out of the hunter's hands, or are taken dead out of the warren (but with a profusion of blood in either case), these hounds perceive it at once by smell and follow the trail. For that reason they are properly called Sanguinaraii.
>
> Frequently, however, an animal is stolen, and owing to the cleverness of thieves there is no effusion of blood; but even so they are clever enough to follow dry human footsteps for a huge distance, and can pick a man out of a crowd however large, pressing on through the densest thickets, and they will still go on even though they have to swim across a river. When they arrive at the opposite bank, by a circular movement, they find out which way a man has gone, even if at first they do not hit on the track of the thief. Thus they supplement good luck by artifice and deserve what Aelian says of them in his *Historia Animalium* . . .

Although the Bloodhound reached approximately its modern form in England, the breed has perhaps reached its greatest development in the United States, as far as usefulness is concerned. The breed has been known in America for over a century. Abolitionists once drew touching pictures of poor fugitive slaves pursued by the Bloodhounds, but it is doubted if many of the breed—then fairly numerous in the South—were so employed. Mongrels were frequently called "bloodhounds" and no doubt some of these did harass the slaves.

The pure-bred Bloodhound is one of the most docile of all breeds. His trailing is more for his own sport than for anything else. Unlike the police-trained dog, he does not attack the man he is trailing. The Bloodhound's task ends once he has followed the trail to its termination. But so accurate is he in following a trail that his evidence has been accepted in a court of law.

Some of the great Bloodhounds of the United States have brought about more convictions for police departments than the best human detectives. One dog was credited with more than 600 actual convictions. The famous dog Nick Carter picked up a trail that was 105 hours old and followed it to a subsequent conviction. This record, set in the early 1900s, has since been more than doubled. Owners have proven that a good Bloodhound can be a show champion and a working mantrailer as well; and the lawmen of National Police Bloodhound Association plus the volunteers of Search and Rescue clubs throughout the country increasingly have been putting him back to his traditional work. The breed's stamina and determination are apparent in the great distances it will travel. Several specimens have followed human quarry for more than 50 miles, and one led the detectives 138 miles—all with success.

In obedience, Bloodhounds are quick to learn but may prove obstinate unless taught to enjoy this type of work. In recent years, a growing number have earned their Companion Dog degrees and a few have gone on to get their CDX and Utility degrees.

Bloodhounds have been exhibited in the United States almost from the beginning of organized dog shows in America. The American Bloodhound Club, a national breed organization, has enabled fanciers to conduct Specialty shows from East to West.

## Official Standard for the Bloodhound

**General Character**—The Bloodhound possesses, in a most marked degree, every point and characteristic of those dogs which hunt together by scent (Sagaces). He is very powerful, and stands over more ground than is usual with hounds of other breeds. The skin is thin to the touch and extremely lose, this being more especially noticeable about the head and neck, where it hangs in deep folds.

**Height**—The mean average height of adult dogs is 26 inches, and of adult bitches 24 inches. Dogs usually vary from 25 inches to 27 inches, and bitches from 23 inches to 25 inches; but, in either case, the greater height is to be preferred, provided that character and quality are also combined.

**Weight**—The mean average weight of adult dogs, in fair condition, is 90 pounds, and of adult bitches 80 pounds. Dogs attain the weight of 110 pounds, bitches 100 pounds. The greater weights are to be preferred, provided (as in the case of height) that quality and proportion are also combined.

**Expression**—The expression is noble and dignified, and characterized by solemnity, wisdom, and power.

**Temperament**—In temperament he is extremely affectionate, neither quarrelsome with companions nor with other dogs. His nature is somewhat shy, and equally sensitive to kindness or correction by his master.

**Head**—The head is narrow in proportion to its length, and long in proportion to the body, tapering but slightly from the temples to the end of the muzzle, thus (when viewed from above and in front) having the appearance of being flattened at the sides and of being nearly equal in width throughout its entire length. In profile the upper outline of the skull is nearly in the same plane as that of the foreface. The length from end of nose to stop (midway between the eyes) should be not less than that from stop to back of occipital protuberance (peak). The entire length of head from the posterior part of the occipital protuberance to the end of the muzzle should be 12 inches, or more, in dogs, and 11 inches, or more, in bitches. **Skull**—The skull is long and narrow, with the occipital peak very pronounced. The brows are not prominent, although, owing to the deep-set eyes, they may have that appearance. **Foreface**—The foreface is long, deep, and of even width throughout, with square outline when seen in profile. **Eyes**—The eyes are deeply sunk in the orbits, the lids assuming a lozenge or diamond shape, in consequence of the lower lids being dragged down and everted by the heavy flews. The eyes correspond with the general tone of color of the animal, varying from deep hazel to yellow. The hazel color is, however, to be preferred, although very seldom seen in red-and-tan hounds. **Ears**—The ears are thin and soft to the touch, extremely long, set very low, and fall in graceful folds, the lower parts curling inward and backward. **Wrinkle**—The head is furnished with an amount of loose skin, which in nearly every position appears superabundant, but more particularly so when the head is carried low; the skin then falls into loose, pendulous ridges and folds, especially over the forehead and sides of the face. **Nostrils**—The nostrils are large and open. **Lips, Flews, and Dewlap**—In front the lips fall squarely, making a right angle with the upper line of the foreface, whilst behind they form deep, hanging flews, and, being continued into the pendant folds of loose skin about the neck, constitute the dewlap, which is very pronounced. These characteristics are found, though in a less degree, in the bitch.

**Neck, Shoulders and Chest**—The neck is long, the shoulders muscular and well sloped backwards; the ribs are well sprung; and the chest well let down between the forelegs, forming a deep keel.

**Legs and Feet**—The forelegs are straight and large in bone, with elbows squarely set; the feet strong and well knuckled up; the thighs and second thighs (gaskins) are very muscular; the hocks well bent and let down and squarely set.

**Back and Loin**—The back and loins are strong, the latter deep and slightly arched. **Stern**—The stern is long and tapering, and set on rather high, with a moderate amount of hair underneath.

**Gait**—The gait is elastic, swinging and free, the stern being carried high, but not too much curled over the back.

**Color**—The colors are black and tan, red and tan, and tawny; the darker colors being sometimes interspersed with lighter or badger-colored hair, and sometimes flecked with white. A small amount of white is permissible on chest, feet, and tip of stern.

# Borzoi

## (Bawr-zoy)

The Borzoi, known here prior to 1936 as the Russian Wolfhound, is a sight hound dependent on his extreme speed, agility and courage to pursue, overtake and hold the quarry. Today these beautiful and intelligent dogs are as at home in our living rooms as they are in the field.

With a history clouded by the misty past of Czarist Russia, we know the dogs were bred by the Russian aristocracy for hundreds of years. There are, in fact, accounts of hunting expeditions of several Mongol rulers from the time of the conqueror, Genghis Khan, in the 13th century in which long hounds were mentioned as principal coursing dogs. In Russia, the precursors of the Borzoi were thought to be of several different types including the long-coated, smooth-faced bearhound of early Russia, the Southern coursing hounds of the Tatars, the Owtchar—a tall Russian sheepdog, as well as other ancient sight-hound types. Whatever the Borzoi origin, by 1260 the coursing of hare for sport is mentioned in connection with the Court of the Grand Duke of Novgorod at the time of the First Czar, and in 1650 the first Borzoi standard was written (reportedly it did not differ greatly from the standard of today). From the time of the first Czars to the abolition of serfdom in 1861, hunting with Borzois reached the level of the national sport of the aristocracy.

Great rural estates, thousands of acres in extent, with hundreds of serfs, were given over to the breeding and training of, and hunting with, Borzois. In fact, it is difficult today to even imagine the grand scale and magnificence to which the gentle Borzoi is heir. Prior to 1861, and to a lesser extent after that time up to the Russian Revolution in 1917, the time, effort and money expended on these "hunts," as they were called, is surely unequaled in the development of any breed.

During the season, the hunt might have been conducted near its base or it might have traveled from one locale to another seeking out game. Walzoff, writing in his monograph on the Perchino Hunt, says a special hunting train used to transport the people, horses, dogs, tents, kitchens and carriages, etc. to a hunting ground consisted of 40 freight cars, one first- and one second-class passenger car, with the Grand Duke and guests arriving on another special train. The hunting party itself would consist of over 100 Borzois, as many foxhounds, and as many people to assist. Often all the horses of a hunt were matched, as well as the leashes of the Borzois and the foxhound packs. Once the team arrived at the spot where wolves were known to be, plans were drawn, preparations made and the hunting commenced. The beaters accompanying a pack of foxhounds would dislodge the game, most notably the wolf, from the forest into the open field where awaiting them at a respectable distance were the mounted huntsmen, each with a trio of Borzois consisting of a bitch and two dogs. When game was sighted, the dogs were slipped by the huntsman. With the Borzois in pursuit of the wolf, and the mounted huntsmen in pursuit of the Borzois, a hair-raising ride ensued and, if the wolf did not escape, the Borzois were required to capture, pin and hold the creature until the arrival of the huntsmen. Arriving full tilt on the scene, the approved style was for the huntsmen to leap headlong into the fray, gag and bind the wolf, after which the wolf was often set free—surely wiser and much more wary for the next time. A moving account of such a hunt can be read in Tolstoy's *War and Peace* (Book II, Part 4, Chapter 3).

From after the Napoleonic Wars to the abolition of serfdom in 1861, there was a period of uncertainty which seemed to result in many experimental outcrosses in the breed. By 1873, only a few Borzois of the old type existed, and in that year the Imperial Association was formed to protect and promote this ancient type. This Association is of great interest to the present-day Borzoi fancier as many bloodlines of Borzois in America today, if not most, can be traced back to breeders who were members of this group. Most notable among these was the Grand Duke Nicholas, uncle to the Czar and Field Marshal of the Russian armies. Second in importance was Artem Boldareff, a wealthy landowner. With these two men in the foreground, members of the Association found, bred and protected the old type Borzoi. And it is to their hunts at Perchino and Woronzova that many of today's Borzois owe their heritage.

As far as is known, the first Borzoi that came to America was brought over from England in 1889 by William Wade of Hulton, Pennsylvania, this hound being purchased from Freeman Lloyd. This was a bitch named Elsie, described in *The English Stockkeeper* as, "nothing much to look at, being small, light and weedy, with no bone, straight back, very curly tail and too much bent in stifles."

The first American to visit Russia and import Borzois directly from that country (including two who became AKC champions) was C. Steadman Hanks, who established the Seacroft Kennels in Massachusetts in the 1890s.

Beginning in 1903, Joseph B. Thomas (acting for the Valley Farm Kennels) made three trips to Russia, the importations from which were to play a very important part in the establishment of American Borzoi bloodlines. Included in these importations were Borzois from the Perchino Kennels owned by the Grand Duke Nicholas, and from the Woronzova Kennels owned by Artem Boldareff.

The Borzoi today remains largely unchanged from his Russian ancestors, both in terms of his appearance, his quiet, gentle nature and his abilities. In the West, the dogs are often coursed and throughout the country lure coursing is gaining in popularity. His intelligence and easy training have resulted in many Borzois winning Obedience certificates. While the hunt has been the primary purpose of the Borzoi, his beauty and temperament were also always of prime importance. He was always a companion *par excellence* and the amourment of the salon. Today, this noble breed easily finds its way to the heart of its owner and, while the circumstances of the Borzoi have changed from those of Czarist Russia, they remain true aristocrats.

## Official Standard for the Borzoi

**General Appearance**—The Borzoi was originally bred for the coursing of wild game on more or less open terrain, relying on sight rather than scent. To accomplish this purpose, the Borzoi needed particular structural qualities to chase, catch and hold his quarry. Special emphasis is placed on sound running gear, strong neck and jaws, courage and agility, combined with proper condition. The Borzoi should always possess unmistakable elegance, with flowing lines, graceful in motion or repose. Males, masculine without coarseness; bitches, feminine and refined.

**Head**—Skull slightly domed, long and narrow, with scarcely any perceptible stop, inclined to be Roman-nosed. Jaws long, powerful and deep, somewhat finer in bitches but not snipy. Teeth strong and clean with either an even or a scissors bite. Missing teeth should be penalized. Nose large and black. **Ears**—Small and fine in quality, lying back on the neck when in repose with the tips when thrown back almost touching behind occiput; raised when at attention. **Eyes**—Set somewhat obliquely, dark in color, intelligent but rather soft in expression; never round, full nor staring, nor light in color; eye rims dark; inner corner midway between tip of nose and occiput.

**Neck**—Clean, free from throatiness; slightly arched, very powerful and well set on.

**Shoulders**—Sloping, fine at the withers and free from coarseness or lumber.

**Chest**—Rather narrow, with great depth of brisket.

**Ribs**—Only slightly sprung, but very deep, giving room for heart and lung play.

**Back**—Rising a little at the loins in a graceful curve.

**Loins**—Extremely muscular, but rather tucked up, owing to the great depth of chest and comparative shortness of back and ribs.

**Forelegs**—Bones straight and somewhat flattened like blades, with the narrower edge forward. The elbows have free play and are turned neither in nor out. Pasterns strong.

**Feet**—Hare-shaped, with well-arched knuckles, toes close and well padded.

**Hindquarters**—Long, very muscular and powerful with well bent stifles; somewhat wider than the forequarters; strong first and second thighs; hocks clean and well let down; legs parallel when viewed from the rear.

**Dewclaws**—Dewclaws, if any, on the hind legs are generally removed; dewclaws on the forelegs may be removed.

**Tail**—Long, set on and carried low in a graceful curve.

**Coat**—Long, silky (not woolly), either flat, wavy or rather curly. On the head, ears and front of legs it should be short and smooth; on the neck the frill should be profuse and rather curly. Feather on hindquarters and tail, long and profuse, less so on chest and back of forelegs.

**Color**—Any color, or combination of colors, is acceptable.

**Size**—Mature males should be at least 28 inches at the withers and mature bitches at least 26 inches at the withers. Dogs and bitches below these respective limits should be severely penalized; dogs and bitches above the respective limits should not be penalized as long as extra size is not acquired at the expense of symmetry, speed and staying quality. Range in weight for males from 75 to 105 pounds and for bitches from 15 to 20 pounds less.

**Gait**—Front legs must reach well out in front with pasterns strong and springy. Hackneyed motion with mincing gait is not desired nor is weaving and crossing. However, while the hind legs are wider apart than the front, the feet tend to move closer to the center line when the dog moves at a fast trot. When viewed from the side there should be a noticeable drive with a ground-covering stride from well-angulated stifles and hocks.

The over-all appearance in motion should be that of effortless power, endurance, speed, agility, smoothness and grace.

FAULTS

*The foregoing description is that of the ideal Borzoi. Any deviation from the above described dog must be penalized to the extent of the deviation, keeping in mind the importance of the contribution of the various features toward the basic original purpose of the breed.*

Approved June 13, 1972

# Dachshund

## (Docks-hoond)

The name Dachshund (*dachs*, badgers; *hund*, dog) at once reveals and conceals the origin of the breed. In medieval European books on hunting, dogs similar only in possessing the tracking ability of hounds and the proportions and temperament of terriers, because they were used to follow badger to earth, were called badger-dogs or *dachs-hunds*. A parallel is suggested by the current use of the name "rabbit dog" in various parts of this country for dogs of various breeding, used to hunt rabbits.

Illustrations dating from the 15th, 16th and 17th centuries show badgers hunted by dogs with elongated bodies, short legs, and hound-type ears—some with the bent front legs of the Basset, some with the heads of terriers, and some with indications of smooth and long coats. It is well to consider that these illustrations were made before the days of photography, that artists capable of depicting dogs with anatomical fidelity have always been rare, and that woodcuts do not lend themselves to fine reproductions of coat distinctions. At best, the pictures and descriptive words can be interpreted with certainty only as defining functions of the dogs used on badger.

The preponderance of available evidence indicates that smooth and longhaired coats were separated by selective breeding long prior to recorded registrations; whereas within such recorded history, the wirehaired coat was produced for protection against briar and thorn by crossing in harsh, wiry terrier coats and then breeding out incompatible characteristics of conformation. Early in the 17th century the name Dachshund became the designation of a breed type with smooth and longhaired coat varieties, and since 1890 wirehairs have been registered as the third variety. German breeders early learned that crossing between longhairs and either smooths or wirehairs did more harm than good, and barred such crosses from registration. During the early decades of wirehairs when breeding stock was comparatively rare, crosses with smooths were permitted. Now, with sufficient breeding stock within each of the three varieties to provide any desired characteristics, there is no advantage in coat crossing, with inevitable production of intermediate coats conforming to neither coat standard, and uncertainty of coat texture for several generations.

The badger was a formidable 25 to 40 pound adversary. Strength and stamina, as well as keenness and courage above and below ground, were required of badger dogs. Weights of 30 to 35 pounds were not uncommon. Such Dachshunds in packs also were serviceable against wild boar. With this start the breed was adapted to hunt other game. A smaller 16 to 22 pound Dachshund proved effective against foxes and to trail wounded deer, and this size has become best known in this country. Still smaller 12-pound Dachshunds

**Smooth Dachshund**

**Longhaired Dachshund**

**Wirehaired Dachshund**

were used on stoat and hare. In the first quarter of the 20th century, for bolting cottontail rabbits, miniatures with adult weights under five pounds and chest girths under 12 inches, but with plenty of hunting spirit, were produced.

Before the German Dachshund or *Deutscher Teckelklub* was founded in 1888, "racial characteristics," or a standard for the breed had been set up in 1879, and German registration of Dachshunds was included (not always with complete generation data or systematic coat notations) in a general all-breed stud book, the *Deutscher Hunde-Stammbuch*. Its first volume, in 1840, recorded 54 Dachshunds and the names of several subsequently prominent breeders, and publication continued until it was officially terminated in 1935. The *Gebrauchsteckel-Klubs*, or hunting Dachshund associations, kept separate stud books, in which were recorded only dogs of demonstrated hunting accomplishment, with scant attention to coat or conformation. From early volumes of the *Deutscher Teckelklub* stud book, first published in 1890, despite meager correlation with older records, pedigrees have been extended back as far as 1860 and 1859. Stud books maintained by clubs devoted to wirehairs, longhairs, and miniatures have waxed and waned. Not until 1915 did the coat-identifying initials K for *Kurzhaar* or smooth, R for *Rauhhaar* or wirehair, and L for *Langhaar* or longhair, become integral components of the *Teckelklub* registration numbers. Later Z was added to distinguish *Zwerg* and *Kaninchentechel*, or miniatures, by re-registration after one year on official certification of eligible size. It can be recommended to American Dachshund breeders of longhairs and wirehairs to incorporate the initials L and W, respectively, in names submitted to the AKC for registration of Dachshunds of these coats.

The management of the breed in Germany, as well as the stud books, had been divided. The *Teckelklub* managed the bench shows, while the *Gebrauchsteckel-Klubs* conducted organized hunting activities. In 1935, the nationalized consolidation of all German Dachshund clubs as the *Fachschaft Dachshunde im Reichsverband fur das Deutsche Hundewesen* (FD-RDG) unified the breed stud books and coordinated the conduct of bench shows with natural-hunting field trials.

Since World War II, management of the Dachshund breed in Germany has reverted to the *Deutscher Teckelklub* (whose registrations are accepted by the AKC) and the *Gebrauchsteckelklub*. The balance of breeding for hunting and symmetry which advanced the breed for 25 years before the war was altered after the war to stress hunting, with a more terrier-like conformation, whereas in this country the prewar objectives have continued to direct the breed.

Importation of Dachshunds into this country antedates the earliest American dog shows of stud books; eleven were included in AKC *Stud Book, Volume II* in 1885. Our dogs have found little employment in organized hunting, as we lack the badger and wild boar and do not hunt deer with dogs, nor foxes with pick and shovel. The true character and conformation of the breed have been encouraged by frequent importation of German hunting strains; and to encourage hunting capacity and exemplary conformation and temperament, field trials under AKC rules were instituted in 1935.

The advance of the breed in this country has not been without reverses. Fostered since 1895 by the Dachshund Club of America, by 1913 and 1914 it had gained a place among the ten most numerous breeds at the Westminster Kennel Club shows—to fall in the postwar years to a mere dozen and temporarily translate its name to "badger dog."

After World War I, with replenished breeding stock, there were noteworthy gains. From 1930 to 1940, Dachshunds advanced from 28th to sixth rank among American registrations, and maintained this average rank through World War II by constructive public relations. Since that time, as the all-breed registration totals have continued to increase year by year, the Dachshund has maintained an important place in the proportionate number of dogs registered and exhibited in the ring.

It is unlikely that one American Dachshund in a thousand is used to hunt, but to understand the functional origin and development of the breed helps us to appreciate its elegant, streamlined proportions, and gives significance to the application of the breed standard.

The medium-sized, smooth-haired Dachshund, which predominates in this country is small enough to live in house or apartment, yet large enough for street, suburb, or country. Its short legs insure maximum exercise per mile. Its odorless, sleek, dark, short coat requires no plucking, trimming, brushing, combing, oiling, and no bathing except to remove accidental dirt. Outdoors the Dachshund is hardy, vigorous, and tireless; indoors he is affectionate and responsive, companionable in restful mood, hilarious in play, alert in announcing strangers. The breed offers a range of three coat varieties; standard and miniature sizes; red and black-and-tan and a number of other colors.

## Official Standard for the Dachshund

**General Appearance**—Low to ground, long in body and short of leg with robust muscular development, the skin is elastic and pliable without excessive wrinkling. Appearing neither crippled, awkward, nor cramped in his capacity for movement, the Dachshund is well-balanced with bold and confident head carriage and intelligent, alert facial expression. His hunting spirit, good nose, loud tongue and distinctive build make him well-suited for below-ground work and for beating the bush. His keen nose gives him an advantage over most other breeds for trailing.

Note: Inasmuch as the Dachshund is a hunting dog, scars from honorable wounds shall not be considered a fault.

**Size, Proportion, Substance**—Bred and shown in two sizes, standard and miniature, miniatures are not a separate classification but compete in a class division for "11 pounds and under at 12 months of age and older." Weight of the standard size is usually between 16 and 32 pounds.

**Head**—Viewed from above or from the side, the head tapers uniformly to the tip of the nose. The *eyes* are of medium size, almond-shaped and dark-rimmed, with an energetic, pleasant expression; not piercing; very dark in color. The bridge bones over the eyes are strongly prominent. Wall eyes, except in the case of dappled dogs, are a serious fault. The *ears* are set near the top of the head, not too far forward, of moderate length, rounded, not narrow, pointed or folded. Their carriage, when animated, is with the forward edge just touching the cheek so that the ears frame the face. The *skull* is slightly arched, neither too broad nor too narrow, and slopes gradually with little perceptible stop into the finely-formed, slightly arched muzzle. Black is the preferred color of the nose. *Lips* are tightly stretched, well covering the lower jaw. Nostrils well open. Jaws opening wide and hinged well back of the eyes, with strongly developed bones and teeth. *Teeth*—Powerful canine teeth: teeth fit closely together in a scissors bite. An even bite is a minor fault. Any other deviation is a serious fault.

**Neck**—Long, muscular, clean-cut, without dewlap, slightly arched in the nape, flowing gracefully into the shoulders.

**Trunk**—The trunk is long and fully muscled. When viewed in profile, the back lies in the straightest possible line between the withers and the short very slightly arched loin. A body that hangs loosely between the shoulders is a serious fault. *Abdomen*—slightly drawn up.

**Forequarters**—For effective underground work, the front must be strong, deep, long and cleanly muscled. Forequarters in detail: *Chest*—The breastbone is strongly prominent in front so that on either side a depression or dimple appears. When viewed from the front, the thorax appears oval and extends downward to the mid-point of the forearm. The enclosing structure of well-sprung ribs appears full and oval to allow, by its ample capacity, complete development of heart and lungs. The keel merges gradually into the line of the abdomen and extends well beyond the front legs. Viewed in profile, the lowest point of the breast line is covered by the front leg. *Shoulder Blades*—Long, broad, well-laid back and firmly placed upon the fully developed thorax, closely fitted at the withers, furnished with hard yet pliable muscles. *Upper Arm*—Ideally the same length as the shoulder blade and at right angles to the latter, strong of bone and hard of muscle, lying close to the ribs, with elbows close to the body, yet capable of free movement. *Forearm*—Short; supplied with hard yet pliable muscles on the front and outside, with tightly stretched tendons on the inside and at the back, slightly curved inwards. The joints between the forearms and the feet (wrists) are closer together than the shoulder joints, so that the front does not appear absolutely straight. Knuckling over is a disqualifying fault. *Feet*—Front paws are full, tight, compact, with well-arched toes and tough, thick pads. They may be equally inclined a trifle outward. There are five toes, four in use, close together with a pronounced arch and strong, short nails. Front dewclaws may be removed.

**Hindquarters**—Strong and cleanly muscled. The pelvis, the thigh, the second thigh, and the metatarsus are ideally the same length and form a series of right angles. From the rear, the thighs are strong and powerful. The legs turn neither in nor out. *Metatarsus*— Short and strong, perpendicular to the second thigh bone. When viewed from behind, they are upright and parallel. *Hind Paws*—Smaller than the front paws with four compactly closed and arched toes with tough, thick pads. The entire foot points straight ahead and is balanced equally on the ball and not merely on the toes. Rear dewclaws should be removed. *Croup*—Long, rounded and full, sinking slightly toward the tail. *Tail*—Set in continuation of the spine, extending without kinks, twists, or pronounced curvature, and not carried too gaily.

**Gait**—Fluid and smooth. Forelegs reach well forward, without much lift, in unison with the driving action of hind legs. The correct shoulder assembly and well-fitted elbows allow the long, free stride in front. Viewed from the front, the legs do not move in exact parallel planes, but incline slightly inward to compensate for shortness of leg and width of chest. Hind legs drive on a line with the forelegs, with hocks (metatarsus) turning neither in nor out. The propulsion of the hind leg depends on the dog's ability to carry the hind leg to complete extension. Viewed in profile, the forward reach of the hind leg equals the rear extension. The thrust of correct movement is seen when the rear pads are clearly exposed during rear extension. Feet must travel parallel to the line of motion with no tendency to swing out, cross over, or interfere with each other. Short, choppy movement, rolling or high-stepping gait, close or overly wide coming or going are incorrect. The Dachshund must have agility, freedom of movement, and endurance to do the work for which he was developed.

**Temperament**—The Dachshund is clever, lively and courageous to the point of rashness, persevering in above and below ground work, with all the senses well-developed. Any display of shyness is a serious fault.

### Special Characteristics of the Three Coat Varieties

The Dachshund is bred with three varieties of coat: (1) Smooth; (2) Wirehaired; (3) Longhaired and is shown in two sizes, standard and miniature. All three varieties and both sizes must conform to the characteristics already specified. The following features are applicable for each variety:

#### Smooth Dachshund
*Coat*—Short, smooth and shining. Should be neither too long nor too thick. Ears not leathery. *Tail*—Gradually tapered to a point, well but not too richly haired. Long sleek bristles on the underside are considered a patch of strong-growing hair, not a fault. A brush tail is a fault, as is also a partly or wholly hairless tail.
*Color of Hair*—Although base color is immaterial, certain patterns and basic colors predominate. One-colored Dachshunds include red (with or without a shading of interspersed dark hairs or sable) and cream. A small amount of white on the chest is acceptable, but not desirable. Nose and nails—black.

Two-colored Dachshunds include black, chocolate, wild boar, gray (blue) and fawn (Isabella), each with tan markings over the eyes, on the sides of the jaw and underlip, on the inner edge of the ear, front, breast, inside and behind the front legs, on the paws and around the anus, and from there to about one-third to one-half of the length of the tail on the underside. Undue prominence or extreme lightness of tan markings is undesirable. A small amount of white on the chest is acceptable but not desirable. Nose and nails—in the case of black dogs, black; for chocolate and all other colors, dark brown, but self-colored is acceptable.

Dappled Dachshunds—The "single" dapple pattern is expressed as lighter-colored areas contrasting with the darker base color, which may be any acceptable color. Neither the light nor the dark color should predominate. Nose and nails are the same as for one- and two-colored Dachshunds. Partial or wholly blue (wall) eyes are as acceptable as dark eyes. A large area of white on the chest of a dapple is permissible.

A "double" dapple is one in which varying amounts of white coloring occur over the body in addition to the dapple pattern. Nose and nails: as for one- and two-color Dachshunds; partial or wholly self-colored is permissible. Brindle is a pattern (as opposed to a color) in which black or dark stripes occur over the entire body although in some specimens the pattern may be visible only in the tan points.

### Wirehaired Dachshund

*Coat*—With the exception of jaw, eyebrows, and ears, the whole body is covered with a uniform tight, short, thick, rough, hard, outer coat but with finer, somewhat softer, shorter hairs (undercoat) everywhere distributed between the coarser hairs. The absence of an undercoat is a fault. The distinctive facial furnishings include a beard and eyebrows. On the ears the hair is shorter than on the body, almost smooth. The general arrangement of the hair is such that the wirehaired Dachshund, when viewed from a distance, resembles the smooth. *Any sort of soft hair in the outercoat, wherever found on the body, especially on the top of the head, is a fault.* The same is true of long, curly, or wavy hair, or hair that sticks out irregularly in all directions. *Tail*—Robust, thickly haired, gradually tapering to a point. A flag tail is a fault. *Color of Hair*—While the most common colors are wild boar, black and tan, and various shades of red, all colors are admissible. A small amount of white on the chest, although acceptable, is not desirable. Nose and nails—same as for the smooth variety.

### Longhaired Dachshund

*Coat*—The sleek, glistening, often slightly wavy hair is longer under the neck and on the forechest, the underside of the body, the ears, and behind the legs. The coat gives the dog an elegant appearance. Short hair on the ear is not desirable. Too profuse a coat which masks type, equally long hair over the whole body, a curly coat, or a pronounced parting on the back are faults. *Tail*—Carried gracefully in prolongation of the spine; the hair attains its greatest length here and forms a veritable flag. *Color of Hair*—Same as for the smooth Dachshund. Nose and nails: same as for the smooth.

The foregoing description is that of the ideal Dachshund. Any deviation from the above described dog must be penalized to the extent of the deviation keeping in mind the importance of the contribution of the various features toward the basic original purpose of the breed.

#### DISQUALIFICATION

*Knuckling over of front legs.*

Approved April 7, 1992

# Foxhound, American

According to well-known authorities on the American Hound, the first mention that we have of hound importations to America appears in a diary of one of DeSoto's retainers. It is further mentioned that hounds were utilized to hunt Indians instead of foxes and hare.

From this same good authority we learn that in 1650 Robert Brooke sailed for the Crown Colony in America, taking his pack of hounds with him, which according to this authority were the taproot of several strains of American Hounds and remained in the family for nearly 300 years. Then Mr. Thomas Walker of Albemarle County, Virginia, imported hounds from England in 1742; in 1770 George Washington subscribed to the importation of hounds from England, and in 1785 received some French Hounds from Lafayette, their voices being "like the bells of Moscow." These importations formed the foundation from which have developed some of the strains of the present-day Virginia hounds.

In 1808 the Gloucester Foxhunting Club imported some of the "best English Hounds," and the Baltimore Hunt Club made many importations from England. Then followed the Rosseau importations from France, and the Irish importations of 1830. The latter are the taproot of the Henry-Birdsong and Trigg strains. Around 1857 General Maupin got from east Tennessee the dog,

Tennessee Lead, which, crossed on English importations, produced the "Maupin dog" now known as the Walker hound, another well-known strain of American Hound.

The Foxhound in this country is used for four purposes, all of them quite different from each other, and thus calling for hounds of a different characteristic.

1. The field trial hound which is run competitively at field trials where speed and a rather jealous nature are important.
2. A hound for hunting a fox with a gun. Here a slow-trailing hound with a good voice is needed.
3. "Trail" hounds, or drag hounds, which are raced or hunted on a drag, speed alone counting.
4. Hounds to hunt in large numbers (say fifteen to twenty or more) in a pack. This latter class is, of course, the type used by the hunt clubs and hunting farmers.

The types of American hounds have varied widely in different localities, but in the last few years the American Foxhound Club and the hunts which are members of the Masters of Foxhounds Association have made great strides in developing a more standard type.

## Official Standard for the American Foxhound

**Head—*Skull*—**Should be fairly long, slightly domed at occiput, with cranium broad and full. ***Ears*—**Ears set on moderately low, long, reaching when drawn out nearly, if not quite, to the tip of the nose; fine in texture, fairly broad, with almost entire absence of erectile power—setting close to the head with the forward edge slightly inturning to the cheek—round at tip. ***Eyes*—**Eyes large, set well apart—soft and houndlike—expression gentle and pleading; of a brown or hazel color. ***Muzzle*—**Muzzle of fair length—straight and square-cut—the stop moderately defined. ***Defects*—**A very flat skull, narrow across the top; excess of dome; eyes small, sharp and terrierlike, or prominent and protruding; muzzle long and snipy, cut away decidedly below the eyes, or very short. Roman-nosed, or upturned, giving a dish-faced expression. Ears short, set on high, or with a tendency to rise above the point of origin.

**Body—*Neck and Throat*—**Neck rising free and light from the shoulders, strong in substance yet not loaded, or medium length. The throat clean and free from folds of skin, a slight wrinkle below the angle of the jaw, however, is allowable. ***Defects*—**A thick, short, cloddy neck carried on a line with the top of the shoulders. Throat showing dewlap and folds of skin to a degree termed "throatiness."

**Shoulders, Chest and Ribs—**Shoulders sloping—clean, muscular, not heavy or loaded—conveying the idea of freedom of action with activity and strength. Chest should be deep for lung space, narrower in proportion to depth than the English hound—28 inches (*girth*) in a 23-inch hound being good. Well-sprung ribs—back ribs should extend well back—a three-inch flank allowing springiness. *Back and Loins*—Back moderately long, muscular and strong. Loins broad and slightly arched. *Defects*—Very long or swayed or roached back. Flat, narrow loins.

**Forelegs and Feet**—*Forelegs*—Straight, with fair amount of bone. Pasterns short and straight. *Feet*—Foxlike. Pad full and hard. Well-arched toes. Strong nails. *Defects*—Straight, upright shoulders, chest disproportionately wide or with lack of depth. Flat ribs. Out at elbow. Knees knuckled over forward, or bent backward. Forelegs crooked. Feet long, open or spreading.

**Hips, Thighs, Hind Legs and Feet**—Hips and thighs, strong and muscled, giving abundance of propelling power. Stifles strong and well let down. Hocks firm, symmetrical and moderately bent. Feet close and firm. *Defects*—Cowhocks, or straight hocks. Lack of muscle and propelling power. Open feet.

**Tail**—Set moderately high; carried gaily, but not turned forward over the back; with slight curve; with very slight brush. *Defects*—A long tail, Teapot curve or inclined forward from the root. Rat tail, entire absence of brush.

**Coat**—A close, hard, hound coat of medium length. *Defects*—A short thin coat, or of a soft quality.

**Height**—Dogs should not be under 22 or over 25 inches. Bitches should not be under 21 or over 24 inches measured across the back at the point of the withers, the hound standing in a natural position with his feet well under him.

**Color**—Any color.

### SCALE OF POINTS

| Head | | | Running Gear | | |
|---|---|---|---|---|---|
| Skull | 5 | | Forelegs | 10 | |
| Ears | 5 | | Hips, thighs and hind | | |
| Eyes | 5 | | legs | 10 | |
| Muzzle | 5 | 20 | Feet | 15 | 35 |
| Body | | | Coat and Tail | | |
| Neck | 5 | | Coat | 5 | |
| Chest and shoulders | 15 | | Tail | 5 | 10 |
| Back, loins and ribs | 15 | 35 | TOTAL | | 100 |

# Foxhound, English

Foxhunting in the United States is almost contemporaneous with the sport in Great Britain. The Foxhound with which we are dealing is known in the United States in dog shows and elsewhere as the *English* Foxhound, though why it should be designated by that name any more than a Fox Terrier should be called an *English* Fox Terrier, is hard to understand. The English Foxhound has been bred along careful lines for over 150 years. The stud books published by the Masters of Foxhounds Association (of England) date back before 1800 and it is an easy matter for any owner of any English Foxhound to trace its pedigree back. The breeding of Foxhounds in England has always been in the hands of masters of hounds, who kept the most careful records of their breeding operations.

For the benefit of those who may be interested in knowing how long the English Foxhound in his pure state has been in the United States, we find that there are records which establish that the first Lord Fairfax imported hounds from England in 1738, and there are unauthenticated records of even earlier importations. The *English Foxhound Stud Book of America*, published by the Masters of Foxhounds Association of America, dates its earliest entries back to 1890, but there are earlier records which would incline one to the belief that there were many earlier importations. Certainly the blood of the Genesee Valley pack must date at least twenty years before that time, records having been kept of it with fair accuracy ever since.

In England as in America these hounds have always been used for foxhunting as followed in the English fashion of riding to hounds. There have been over 250 packs of hounds in Great Britain, all of which used English Hounds, while in America we have over a hundred packs, of which not over 10% use hounds which would be eligible for the *English Foxhound Stud Book*, although the blood has been freely mixed with the American Foxhound.

In appearance the English Hound is far stouter than his American cousin, and perhaps no better description of his general appearance can be given than to quote a passage from Cuthbert Bradley's *Reminiscences of Frank Gillard*, in which he describes Belvoir Gambler '85, one of the greatest Foxhounds that was ever bred:

> Although Belvoir Gambler cannot be bred from rule of thumb, the proportions of this remarkable Foxhound are worth preserving as an example of what symmetry should be. Standing twenty-three inches at the shoulder, from the extreme point of his shapely shoulders to the outer curve of his well-turned quarters, he measured twenty-seven and a half inches in length whilst from elbow to ground his height was only twelve inches. Possessing great depth of rib and room round the heart, he girthed thirty-one inches, and his arm below was eight and a quarter inches round. Below the knee he measured eight and a quarter inches of solid bone, while round the thigh he spanned full nine and a quarter inches. The extended neck was ten inches from cranium to shoulder and the head ten inches and a half long. His color was of the richest, displaying all of the beautiful "Belvoir tan," and his head had that brainy appearance expressive of the highest intelligence. Gambler might have inspired that earnest poet, Cannon Kingsley, when he described the modern Foxhound, "The result of nature not limited, but developed by high civilization. Next to an old Greek statue there are few such combinations of grace and strength as in a fine Foxhound."

Although the tendency today is to breed hounds a little bigger, the above description cannot be equaled.

## Official Standard for the English Foxhound

**Head**—Should be of full size, but by no means heavy. Brow pronounced, but not high or sharp. There should be a good length and breadth, sufficient to give in a dog hound a girth in front of the ears of fully 16 inches. The nose should be long (4½ inches) and wide, with open nostrils. Ears set on low and lying close to the cheeks. Most English hounds are "rounded" which means that about 1½ inches is taken off the end of the ear. The teeth must meet squarely, either a *pig-mouth* (overshot) or undershot being a disqualification.

**Neck**—Must be long and clean, without the slightest throatiness, not less than 10 inches from cranium to shoulder. It should taper nicely from shoulders to head, and the upper outline should be slightly convex.

**The Shoulders** should be long and well clothed with muscle, without being heavy, especially at the points. They must be well sloped, and the true arm between the front and the elbow must be long and muscular, but free from fat or lumber. *Chest and Back Ribs*—The chest should girth over 31 inches in a 24-inch hound, and the back ribs must be very deep.

**Back and Loin**—Must both be very muscular, running into each other without any contraction between them. The couples must be wide, even to raggedness, and the topline of the back should be absolutely level, the *Stern* well set on and carried gaily but not in any case curved *over* the back like a squirrel's tail. The end should taper to a point and there should be a fringe of hair below. The *Hindquarters* or propellers are required to be very strong, and as endurance is of even greater consequence than speed, straight stifles are preferred to those much bent as in a Greyhound. *Elbows* set quite straight, and neither turned in nor out are a *sine qua non*. They must be well let down by means of the long true arm above mentioned.

**Legs and Feet**—Every Master of Foxhounds insists on legs as straight as a post, and as strong; size of bone at the ankle being especially regarded as all important. The desire for straightness had a tendency to produce knuckling-over, which at one time was countenanced, but in recent years this defect has been eradicated by careful breeding and intelligent adjudication, and one sees very little of this trouble in the best modern Foxhounds. The bone cannot be too large, and the feet in all cases should be round and catlike, with well-developed knuckles and strong horn, which last is of the greatest of importance.

**Color and Coat**—Not regarded as very important, so long as the former is a good "hound color," and the latter is short, dense, hard, and glossy. Hound colors are black, tan, and white, or any combination of these three, also the various "pies" compounded of white and the color of the hare and badger, or yellow, or tan. The *Symmetry* of the Foxhound is of the greatest importance, and what is known as "quality" is highly regarded by all good judges.

**SCALE OF POINTS**

| | | | |
|---|---|---|---|
| Head | 5 | Elbows | 5 |
| Neck | 10 | Legs and feet | 20 |
| Shoulders | 10 | Color and coat | 5 |
| Chest and back ribs | 10 | Stern | 5 |
| Back and loin | 15 | Symmetry | 5 |
| Hindquarters | 10 | TOTAL | 100 |

**DISQUALIFICATION**

*Pig-mouth (overshot) or undershot.*

Approved 1935

# Greyhound

Swift as a ray of light, graceful as a swallow, and wise as a Solomon, there is some basis for the prediction that the Greyhound is a breed that will never die. His fame, first written in the hot sands of Egypt, can be traced in the varying terrains of almost every country, on every continent on the globe. His was the type the ancients knew, and from time immemorial he has been a symbol of the aristocracy. Yet the Greyhound is a dog that needs no fanfare to herald his approach, no panoply to keep him in the public eye. His innate qualities give him admittance to any circles, high or low.

The first knowledge of the Greyhound comes from the Tomb of Amten, in the Valley of the Nile, regarded by Egyptologists as belonging to the fourth dynasty, which in modern chronology would be between 2900 and 2751 B.C. The carvings in this old tomb show dogs of unmistakable Greyhound type in three separate scenes. In two they are attacking a deer, while in the other an animal with horns, somewhat similar to the American mountain goat. The dogs have ring tails.

The origin of the name "Greyhound" is somewhat open to dispute, and a number of suppositions have been advanced. One is that it is derived from *Graius*, meaning Grecian, because the dog was in high esteem among the ancient Greeks. Another conjecture is that it derives from the old British *grech* or *greg*, meaning a dog. Also, some say that it came to use because gray was once the prevailing color in the breed.

While the old Egyptian scenes establish the Greyhound as a recognizable type at a very early date, it is from a Roman source that there has come the first complete description of the breed. This was written by Ovid, who lived from 43 B.C. to A.D. 17. Reading this, one can have little doubt that the dog of ancient times is the same as the one of today. With certain allowances, it fits perfectly.

The Greyhound always has had a cultural and aristocratic background. He was the favorite of royalty in Egypt, and he was bred and raised in such luxurious surroundings that there was every reason for the oppressed races and the common people of those times to hate this dog. Yet the disposition of the dog was just as lovable and tractable then as it is today. Had the common people been allowed to own specimens of this dog, the story would have been entirely different, but his ownership was restricted to the ruling classes.

The ancient traditions connected with the Greyhound have come down throughout history. He is found in England at a very early date. In fact, a manuscript from the ninth century A.D. is illustrated with a picture of Elfric, Duke of Mercia; and beside this old Saxon chieftain stands his huntsman with a brace of Greyhounds. Just how many centuries before the time of Elfric the Greyhound was known in England is not known, but there is every reason to suppose that the breed had been there a long time.

The famous Canute Laws, written in Danish—for at that time the Danes had conquered much of what is now England—and enacted in a Parliament held at Winchester in 1016, give further evidence as to the status of the Greyhound. No. 31 of these Canute Laws states:

> No meane person may keepe any greihounds, but freemen may keepe greihounds, so that their knees may be cut before the verderons of the forest, and without cutting of their knees also, if he does not abide 10 miles from the bounds of the forest. But if they doe come any nearer to the forest, they shall pay 12 pence for every mile; but if the greihound be found within the forest, the master or owner of the dog shall forfeit the dog and ten shillings to the king.

The Greyhound has been used on practically all kinds of small game from time to time, including deer, stags, foxes, and so forth, but the hare is his natural quarry, and coursing the sport with which he has been associated for centuries. In fact, coursing has been done on an organized basis in England for nearly two centuries.

The Greyhound came to America long before 1776. Laurel Drew, a historian of the breed, has traced Greyhounds that were brought to this country (along with Mastiffs) by Spanish explorers in the early 1500s "to guard, hunt, intimidate and punish their enemies—in this case, the Indians." The reports tell of

Greyhound hunting prowess, of how they "went into the woods that were near and returned bringing hares and rabbits."

The Greyhound figures prominently in the journals of George Cartwright, an English explorer to Labrador in 1770. And Baron Freidrich von Steuben, the German professional soldier who was so helpful to General Washington in the American Revolutionary War, was always accompanied by a huge Greyhound named Azor.

One of the most celebrated of many Greyhound owners in history was General George A. Custer. Custer was especially fond of coursing breeds—Greyhounds and "staghounds"—and traveled with a hound pack that numbered about forty. One book reports that Custer's dogs were about to run a matched race the day before he left on his fatal expedition to Big Horn River in 1876.

Greyhounds were among the earliest at American dog shows, too. The catalog of the first Westminster Kennel Club show in 1877 includes an entry of 18 Greyhounds, and the breed was in the second edition of the AKC stud book (in 1885) with listings of three males and five bitches.

The invention of the mechanical lure by O. P. Smith in 1912, leading to the introduction of track racing for Greyhounds in the 1920s, added another—and sizeable—dimension to interest in the breed. This interest is as strong as ever today.

## Official Standard for the Greyhound

**Head**—Long and narrow, fairly wide between the ears, scarcely perceptible stop, little or no development of nasal sinuses, good length of muzzle, which should be powerful without coarseness. Teeth very strong and even in front. **Ears**—Small and fine in texture, thrown back and folded, except when excited, when they are semipricked. **Eyes**—Dark, bright, intelligent, indicating spirit.

**Neck**—Long, muscular, without throatiness, slightly arched, and widening gradually into the shoulder.

**Shoulders**—Placed as obliquely as possible, muscular without being loaded.

**Forelegs**—Perfectly straight, set well into the shoulders, neither turned in nor out, pasterns strong.

**Chest**—Deep, and as wide as consistent with speed, fairly well-sprung ribs.

**Back**—Muscular and broad.

**Loins**—Good depth of muscle, well arched, well cut up in the flanks.

**Hindquarters**—Long, very muscular and powerful, wide and well let-down, well-bent stifles. Hocks well bent and rather close to ground, wide but straight fore and aft.

**Feet**—Hard and close, rather more hare- than cat-feet, well knuckled up with good strong claws.

**Tail**—Long, fine and tapering with a slight upward curve.

**Coat**—Short, smooth and firm in texture.

**Color**—Immaterial.

**Weight**—Dogs, 65 to 70 pounds; bitches, 60 to 65 pounds.

### SCALE OF POINTS

| | | | |
|---|---|---|---|
| General symmetry and quality | 10 | Back | 10 |
| Head and neck | 20 | Quarters | 20 |
| Chest and shoulders | 20 | Legs and feet | 20 |
| | | TOTAL | 100 |

# Harrier

$P$robably the oldest work on hare hunting is the famous essay penned by the ancient Greek historian Xenophon about 400 B.C., and with that as a basis, hare hunting has been a favorite subject of the greatest authorities on the dog for the past 2300 years. Regardless of that, there is a striking unanimity of doubt concerning the direct ancestors of this old breed of scent hound.

The Harrier, as he exists today, was unknown in Xenophon's time, although he describes two types of hounds that were used with equal success in the early hunting of the hare. One he calls "the Castorean," which was reputed to be the favorite of the demi-god Castor. The other is designated as "the fox-breed," which is explained as a product of the fox and the dog. On the other hand, Xenophon has listed the qualities of a hound suitable for the purposes, and they bear amazing similarity to the desirable points of modern times.

This early treatise on hunting is no fragmentary remnant of a scholarly mind, but one of the most definite and minute portrayals of a sport that ever has been written. Perhaps the only real difference between the way the Greeks hunted the hare and the manner accepted in England and other countries is that in 400 B.C. the hares were driven into nets. This practice would bring great censure on hunters of today. Still, sportsmanship was given some consideration in ancient times, for Xenophon says: "In tracking the hare, no delay should be made, for it is sportsmanlike, as well as a proof of fondness for exertion, to use every means to capture the animals speedily."

Even the great English authority on all breeds, Stonehenge, was a little mystified by the origin of the Harrier. The theory he advances rather cautiously is that it springs from the old Southern hound, with an infusion of a little Greyhound blood.

Undoubtedly the Southern hound has played a great part in the development of all scent hound breeds in the British Isles, yet there is little or no mention of the origin of this basic breed. The most logical supposition appears to be that it was brought to England by the Normans, for hunting is of great antiquity on the Continent.

The first pack of Harriers in England was the Penistone, which was established by Sir Elias de Midhope in 1260. These Harriers were held together for at least five centuries, and it is recorded that in the 14th, 17th, and the 18th centuries, the masters were supplied by the Wilsons of Broomhead Hall. Hunting the hare has always had great popularity throughout the British Isles, and in some ways enjoyed greater favor than foxhunting. One great cause of its popularity was that a pack of Harriers could be followed on foot. This enlisted the interest of many, and among the hundred odd packs that hunted regularly in England half a century ago, many were scratch packs. A scratch pack was made up of hounds owned by various individuals—thus bringing the sport down to the level of the poorer man. However, horses are used in most cases today.

In support of the Norman origin of this and other hound breeds, there has been an interesting bit of information supplied by Wynn in regard to the name *harrier*. He shows that this may have come from the Norman word *harier*, denoting Saxon raches, or hounds. Further, *harier* was used down to 1750 for all hounds, not necessarily hare-hounds. And back in 1570, Dr. Caius mentioned stag- and fox-harriers.

Despite all stories of the ancient origin of Harriers, it is the general belief that the dog of today is merely a smaller edition of the Foxhound, and that he has been bred down from the larger hound by selective breeding. Save in size, the Harrier is the external replica of the Foxhound. Some specimens of the Harrier bear a unique, blue mottle color, which is not recognized in English Foxhounds, but in the majority of cases their colors are the same. It also is said that some Harriers are somewhat heavier in the head, in proportion, than is the Foxhound.

Harriers have been known in the United States as long as any of the scent-hound breeds, and they have been used for hunting since Colonial times. In later times, the Harrier proved a great favorite of the drag hunt, in which his slower pace is no detriment.

## Official Standard for the Harrier

**General Appearance**—Developed in England to hunt hare in packs, Harriers must have all the attributes of a scenting pack hound. They are very sturdily built with large bone for their size. They must be active, well balanced, full of strength and quality, in all ways appearing able to work tirelessly, no matter the terrain, for long periods. Running gear and scenting ability are particularly important features. The Harrier should, in fact, be a smaller version of the English Foxhound.

**Size, Proportion, Substance**—*Size*—19 to 21 inches for dogs and bitches, variation of one inch in either direction is acceptable. *Proportion* is off-square. The Harrier is slightly longer from point of shoulder to rump than from withers to ground. *Substance*—Solidly built, full of strength and quality. The breed has as much substance and bone as possible without being heavy or coarse.

**Head**—The head is in proportion to the overall dog. No part of the head should stand out relative to the other parts. The expression is gentle when relaxed, sensible yet alert when aroused. *Eyes* are medium size, set well apart, brown or hazel color in darker dogs, lighter hazel to yellow in lighter dogs, though darker colors are always desired. *Ears* are set on low and lie close to the cheeks, rounded at the tips.

The *skull* is in proportion to the entire animal, with good length and breadth and a bold forehead. The *stop* is moderately defined. The *muzzle* from stop to tip of nose is approximately the same length as the skull from stop to occiput. The muzzle is substantial with good depth, and the *lips* complete the square, clean look of the muzzle, without excess skin or flews. A good *nose* is essential. It must be wide, with well opened nostrils. Teeth meet in a scissors *bite* or they may be level. Overshot or undershot bites faulted to the degree of severity of the misalignment.

**Neck, Topline, Body**—The *Neck* is long and strong with no excess skin or throatiness, sweeping smoothly into the muscling of the forequarters. The *topline* is level. Back muscular with no dip behind the withers or roach over the loin. *Body*—Chest deep, extending to the elbows, with well sprung ribs that extend well back, providing plenty of heart and lung room. The ribs should not be so well sprung that they interfere with the free, efficient movement of the front assembly. The loin is short, wide and well muscled.

The *tail* is long, set on high and carried up from 12 o'clock to 3 o'clock, depending on attitude. It tapers to a point with a brush of hair. The tail should not be curled over the back.

**Forequarters**—Moderate angulation, with long shoulders sloping into the muscles of the back, clean at the withers. The shoulders are well clothed with muscle without being excessively heavy or loaded, giving the impression of free, strong action. Elbows are set well away from the ribs, running parallel with the body and not turning outwards. Good straight legs with plenty of bone running well down to the toes, but not overburdened, inclined to knuckle over very slightly but not exaggerated in the slightest degree. *Feet* are round and catlike, with toes set close together turning slightly inwards. The pads are thick, well developed and strong.

**Hindquarters**—Angulation in balance with the front assembly, so that rear drive is in harmony with front reach. Well developed muscles, providing strength for long hours of work, are important. Endurance is more important than pure speed, and as such, the stifles are only moderately angulated. *Feet* point straight ahead, are round and catlike with toes set close together, and thick, well developed pads.

**Coat**—Short, dense, hard and glossy. Coat texture on the ears is finer than on the body. There is a brush of hair on the underside of the tail.

**Color**—Any color, not regarded as very important.

**Gait**—Perfect coordination between the front and hind legs. Reach and drive are consistent with the desired moderate angulation. Coming and going, the dog moves in a straight line, evidencing no sign of crabbing. A slight toeing-in of the front feet is acceptable. Clean movement coming and going is important, but not nearly as important as side gait, which is smooth, efficient and ground-covering.

**Temperament**—Outgoing and friendly, as a working pack breed, Harriers must be able to work in close contact with other hounds. Therefore, aggressiveness towards other dogs cannot be tolerated.

Approved December 13, 1988

# Ibizan Hound

Ibizan Hound history is traceable back to approximately 3400 B.C. The glory that was ancient Egypt was a most fitting setting for this regal hound, which was owned and hunted by the Pharaohs.

Numerous artifacts found in the tombs of the Pharaohs now reinforce the existence of such a dog in those long past times. Hemako, who reigned in the period of the 1st Dynasty (3100 to 2700 B.C.) was buried in a tomb near Saggara. When this site was unearthed many artifacts were uncovered, one of which was a carved dish bearing the image of the Ibizan. These dogs, which are also referred to as Galgo Hounds, are quite distinct in their appearance; therefore, no other could be mistaken as being represented. Nevermat, of the 4th Dynasty, who lived at approximately 2600 B.C., Tutankhamen of the 14th century B.C. and the Ptolemies of the 30th and final Dynasty, all have tombs which have yielded further proof of the hound's ancient and proud heritage. Cleopatra was an ardent devotee of the Galgo, and her reign was the twilight of the Pharaohs' time in Egypt.

The tomb of Tutankhamen proved a treasure trove when discovered in 1922. Anubis, "The Watchdog of the Dead," a long honored deity, was well represented by a full sized true to life statue, which is the identical duplicate of the

Ibizan Hound of today. This marvelously preserved piece of carved statuary was coated with resins and varnishes. The eyes are of obsidian (a volcanic variety of rock which has a very glassy look and is deep black) and are rimmed with gold leaf, as are the insides of the ears. Anubis also bears a beautiful collar of gold, but time had not deteriorated his beauty nor the fact that the original model could only have been the greyhound-type, prick eared, sickle tailed dog now known as the Ibizan. It was originally thought that the jackal had been the original model, this miscalculation due to the fact that the Ibizan was extinct in its land of origin at the time of these numerous discoveries.

We can but surmise the movement of the breed from Egypt to the island from which it now derives its name. The hardy sea-traders of Phoenicia were well traveled in those days and had entree to many lands. It is thought that they are basically responsible for the survival of this breed. It was the Phoenicians who discovered the island now known as Ibiza in the 8th or 9th century B.C. Now belonging to Spain, Ibiza has been ruled and conquered by many—Egyptians, Chaldeans, Carthaginians, Romans, Vandals and Arabs. Roman coins bear the head of an Ibizan Hound, and Hasdrubal once ruled this land. Conejera, a member of this Balearic grouping, was a small off island also which claims historical fame by being the birthplace of the famed Hannibal. It is said that the Ibizan Hound was the dog which accompanied him with his mighty elephants on that long trek across the Alps.

This breed has survived even the hard life that the Ibizan group of islands has imposed on it. Only the fittest could survive, as food is scarce, and the natives used these dogs to assist in providing the necessary food to sustain their lives. As a result these dogs have learned to hunt with great skill, tenacity, and patience. The owners of these hounds also culled their litters diligently, for only the strongest and most perfect specimens could survive the hardships. We must give our thanks to those early owners and breeders, for through their dedication we have seen a breed travel through centuries unmarked by numerous problems evident in many other breeds. These animals are as strong, fit and vigorous today as they were in the days of the Pharaohs.

The first Ibizans reached the United States in mid-1956, imported by Colonel and Mrs. Seoane of Rhode Island. Hannibal (Stop) and Certera (Tanit) created quite a stir and soon it was known that the first litter would arrive in the fall. Eight pups were the result of the first breeding and the 4 males and 4 females (Asuncion, Malchus V, Denia, Heulalia, Granada, Mago, Gisco and Sertorius), along with several other imports and their parents, form the foundations of the breed here.

Over the years the breed has flourished in this country and they are respected by all who have come into intimate contact with them as lively companions, pets, watchdogs, hunters, and friends. They lend themselves well to family life and the ever-changing American lifestyles. Their temperament is excellent, and their health has proven superior. Structurally they are extremely strong and resilient. The Ibizan Hound Club of the United States has been most stringent in impressing upon the owners and breeders of this hound the importance of fully retaining the fine qualities of this dog first and foremost, and has kept its pledge to preserve it true to form.

The Ibizan Hound was admitted to AKC stud book registration effective October 1, 1978, and became eligible for show competition January 1, 1979.

# Official Standard for the Ibizan Hound

**General Appearance**—The Ibizan's clean-cut lines, large prick ears and light pigment give it a unique appearance. A hunting dog whose quarry is primarily rabbits, this ancient hound was bred for thousands of years with function being of prime importance. Lithe and racy, the Ibizan possesses a deerlike elegance combined with the power of a hunter. Strong, without appearing heavily muscled, the Ibizan is a hound of moderation. With the exception of the ears, he should not appear extreme or exaggerated. In the field the Ibizan is as fast as top coursing breeds and without equal in agility, high jumping and broad jumping ability. He is able to spring to great heights from a standstill.

**Size, Proportion, Substance**—*Size*—The height of dogs is 23½ inches to 27½ inches at the withers. Bitches are 22½ to 26 inches at the withers. There is no preference for size within this range. Sizes slightly over or under the norms are not to be regarded as demerits when other qualities are good. *Weight*—Average weight of dogs is 50 pounds; bitches, 45 pounds. *Proportion*—Slightly longer than tall. *Substance*—The Ibizan possesses clean, fine bone. The muscling is strong, yet flat, with no sign of heaviness.

**Head**—Long and narrow in the form of a sharp cone truncated at its base. Finely chiseled and extremely dry fleshed. *Expression*—The Ibizan has an elegant, deer-like look. The *eyes* are oblique and small, ranging in color from clear amber to caramel. The rims are the color of the nose and are fully or partially pigmented. The appearance of the eye is intelligent, alert and inquisitive. The *ears* are large, pointed, and natural. On alert the ear should never droop, bend or crease. Highly mobile, the ear can point forward, sideways, or be folded backward, according to mood. On alert, the lowest point of the base is at level of the eye. On frontal examination, the height of the ear is approximately 2½ times that of the widest point of the base. *Skull*—Long and flat, prominent occipital bone, little defined *stop;* narrow brow. The *muzzle* is elongated, fine, and slender with a very slight Roman convex. The length from the eyes to point of nose is equal to the distance from eyes to occiput. The muzzle and skull are on parallel *planes.* The *nose* is prominent, extending beyond the lower jaw. It is of a rosy flesh color, never black or liver, and tends to harmonize with the coat. Pigment is solid or butterfly. Nostrils are open. *Lips* are thin and tight and the color of the nose. Flews are tight and dry fleshed. *Bite*—The teeth are perfectly opposed in a scissors bite; strong and well set.

**Neck, Topline, Body**—The *neck* is long, slender, slightly arched and strong, yet flat muscled. The *topline*, from ears to tail, is smooth and flowing. The *back* is level and straight. *Body*—The chest is deep and long with the breastbone sharply angled and prominent. The ribs are slightly sprung. The brisket is approximately 2½ inches above the elbow. The deepest part of the chest, behind the elbow, is nearly to or to the elbow. The abdomen is well tucked up, but not exaggerated. The *loin* is very slightly arched, of medium breadth and well muscled. The *croup* is very slightly sloping. The *tail* is set low, highly mobile, and reaches at least to the hock. It is carried in a sickle, ring, or saber position, according to the mood and individual specimen.

**Forequarters—Angulation** is moderate. The **shoulders** are elastic but never loose with moderate breadth at the withers. The shoulder blades are well laid back. At the *point of the shoulder* they join to a rather upright **upper arm.** The *elbow* is positioned in front of the deepest part of the chest. It is well held in but not so much as to restrict movement. *Legs*—The forearms are very long, strong, straight, and close, lying flat on the chest and continuing in a straight line to the ground. Bone is clean and fine. The *pasterns* are strong and flexible, slightly sloping, with well developed tendons. *Dewclaw* removal is optional. *Feet:* hare-foot. The toes are long, closed and very strong. Interdigital spaces are well protected by hair. Pads are durable. Nails are white.

**Hindquarters—Angulation** is moderate with the hindquarters being set under the body. *Legs*—The thighs are very strong with flat muscling. The hocks are straight when viewed from the rear. Bone is clean and fine. There are no rear dewclaws. The *feet* are as in front.

**Coat**—There are two types of coat; both untrimmed. *Short*—shortest on head and ears and longest at back of the thighs and under the tail. *Wire-haired* can be from one to three inches in length with a possible generous moustache. There is more hair on the back, back of thighs, and tail. Both types of coat are hard in texture and neither coat is preferable to the other.

**Color**—White or red (from light, yellowish-red called "lion" to deep red), solid or in any combination. No color or pattern is preferable to the other. *Disqualify* any color other than white or red.

**Gait**—An efficient, light and graceful single-tracking movement. A suspended trot with joint flexion when viewed from the side. The Ibizan exhibits smooth reach in front with balanced rear drive, giving the appearance of skimming over the ground.

**Temperament**—The Ibizan Hound is even-tempered, affectionate and loyal. Extremely versatile and trainable, he makes an excellent family pet, and is well suited to the breed ring, obedience, tracking and lure-coursing. He exhibits a keen, natural hunting instinct with much determination and stamina in the field.

### DISQUALIFICATION

*Any color other than white or red.*

Approved September 11, 1989

# Irish Wolfhound

Early Irish literature abounds in references to these large dogs which are called, interchangeably, "Irish dogs," "Big Dogs of Ireland," "Greyhounds (or Grehounds) of Ireland," "Wolfdogs of Ireland," "Great Hounds of Ireland." Irish Wolfhound is the more modern name.

By the year 391 A.D., the breed was known in Rome, when the first authentic mention of it was written by the Roman Consul Quintus Aurelius, who had received seven of them as a gift which "all Rome viewed with wonder." Through the ensuing centuries the Irish Wolfhound has inspired poets and authors. In 1790 it was written, "The Irish Greyhound is the largest of dogkind and its appearance the most beautiful. He is about 3 feet high, somewhat like a Greyhound but more robust. His aspect is mild, his disposition is peaceable, yet his strength so great that in combat the Mastiff or Bulldog is far from being equal to him."

In the following century another wrote of the Irish Wolfhound, "This noble animal is similar in shape to the Greyhound, larger than the Mastiff, tractable as the Spaniel."

He was coveted for his hunting prowess, particularly in the pursuit of the gigantic Irish elk which stood six feet at the shoulders, and the wolf. With the disappearance from Ireland of these animals, and the excessive exportation of the dwindling ranks of Wolfhounds, the breed was allowed to become almost extinct.

It was at this point that Captain George A. Graham, a Scot in the British Army, gathered the remaining specimens and restored the breed. His work began in 1862 and 23 years later, under his supervision, the first breed standard was set forth. To meet the requirements of this standard remains the goal which every bona fide breeder strives to attain.

The Irish Wolfhound is a large rough-coated, shaggy-browed hound, built on galloping lines. Even as he lies by a modern hearth or romps about an enclosed lawn, gallops in a meadow or along a beach, it is easy to imagine him as the prominent figure he once was in the feudal life of the Middle Ages.

Because of his great size and the amount of exercise essential to his well-being, the Irish Wolfhound is not a dog to be acquired without serious forethought. His ideal home is one which provides fenced property of sufficient size to accommodate the galloping natural to this athletic sight hound. Hunting by sight and chase is what he was bred and historically used for; the length of leg and back, the deep chest, the power of his limbs and body attest to the heritage and needs of the Irish Wolfhound.

His ideal owner is one who has the capacity to respond to the gentle nature which dwells within his great frame; who discerns the intelligence which manifests itself in his response to everyday situations as they occur. The Irish Wolfhound does best when human companionship is the core of his daily life. At maturity, despite his space-eating size, he is a calm presence within a family circle, dignified and responsive, providing no harshness of attitude or deed is directed his way. A sensitive dog, the Irish Wolfhound's development is thwarted when his environment is ungiving.

His nature and temperament make him totally unsuitable as guard dog, watch dog, or patrol dog, in country, town or city. Though alert he is not suspicious; though courageous he is not aggressive.

City dwellers and those in closely populated suburbs frequently are seeking guard or watch dogs, and frequently today, these are working couples who want a dog to be on solitary duty in an apartment or house from morning to night. Emphatically, the Irish Wolfhound is not a satisfactory choice. As an incidental function, by his very appearance, he is a formidable deterrent to intruders, but he is more likely to serenade the moon than bark at noises and people. To confine a mature dog of this size as his way of life is foolhardy; subjecting a puppy to such circumstances should be unthinkable. Wolfhound puppyhood lasts a year or more and left alone a puppy can demolish a room per hour and injure himself in the process. A six-month-old Irish Wolfhound puppy weighs about 100 pounds, is not yet through teething; nor are his body functions ready for prolonged containment.

An occasional Irish Wolfhound is raised and kept successfully under less than ideal conditions by owners who have not only the wish, but the will and the stamina to provide very extensive leash walking and to cope with sidewalks and traffic, close neighbors and pedestrians. The hygienic responsibility incumbent upon owners of giant breeds of dogs is awesome.

Irish Wolfhounds have only the kindest intentions toward children. Common sense, however, precludes the mingling of a small child with a young Wolfhound; the child is no match for an affectionate, playful puppy weighing 50 to 100 pounds, a toss of whose head or a running sideswipe of whose body can have bruising consequences.

A completely natural breed, the Wolfhound's ears are uncropped, his tail undocked. Clippers and trimmers are enemies to his coat; no part of him, particularly his head, should appear styled.

Irish Wolfhounds compete in dog shows from coast to coast, though he is seen in greater number at those held outdoors, which better suit him. No stranger to obedience competition and coursing trials, he has won degrees and titles in both.

The habitat of most Irish Wolfhounds bred in this century has been the private home where his quiet manners, gentle nature and comfortable sense of companionship have made it a natural one. Although the chase is not his preoccupation, we must never forget it is his natural sport and the sight of him in characteristic gallop, swiftly covering the ground beneath him, is exhilarating and leaves no doubt of his need to exercise this birthright.

## Official Standard for the Irish Wolfhound

**General Appearance**—Of great size and commanding appearance, the Irish Wolfhound is remarkable in combining power and swiftness with keen sight. The largest and tallest of the galloping hounds, in general type he is a rough-coated, Greyhoundlike breed; very muscular, strong though gracefully built; movements easy and active; head and neck carried high, the tail carried with an upward sweep with a slight curve towards the extremity. The minimum height and weight of dogs should be 32 inches and 120 pounds; of bitches, 30 inches and 105 pounds; these to apply only to hounds over 18 months of age. Anything below this should be debarred from competition. Great size, including height at shoulder and proportionate length of body, is the desideratum to be aimed at, and it is desired to firmly establish a race that shall average from 32 to 34 inches in dogs, showing the requisite power, activity, courage and symmetry.

**Head**—Long, the frontal bones of the forehead very slightly raised and very little indentation between the eyes. Skull, not too broad. Muzzle, long and moderately pointed. Ears, small and Greyhoundlike in carriage.

**Neck**—Rather long, very strong and muscular, well arched, without dewlap or loose skin about the throat.

**Chest**—Very deep. Breast, wide.

**Back**—Rather long than short. Loins arched.

**Tail**—Long and slightly curved, of moderate thickness, and well covered with hair.

**Belly**—Well drawn up.

**Forequarters**—Shoulders, muscular, giving breadth of chest, set sloping. Elbows well under, neither turned inwards nor outwards.

**Leg**—Forearm muscular, and the whole leg strong and quite straight.

**Hindquarters**—Muscular thighs and second thigh long and strong as in the Greyhound, and hocks well let down and turning neither in nor out.

**Feet**—Moderately large and round, neither turned inwards nor outwards. Toes, well arched and closed. Nails, very strong and curved.

**Hair**—Rough and hard on body, legs and head; especially wiry and long over eyes and underjaw.

**Color and Markings**—The recognized colors are gray, brindle, red, black, pure white, fawn, or any other color that appears in the Deerhound.

### FAULTS

Too light or heavy a head, too highly arched frontal bone; large ears and hanging flat to the face; short neck; full dewlap; too narrow or too broad a chest; sunken or hollow or quite straight back; bent forelegs; overbent fetlocks; twisted feet; spreading toes; too curly a tail; weak hindquarters and a general want of muscle; too short in body. Lips or nose liver-colored or lacking pigmentation.

### LIST OF POINTS IN ORDER OF MERIT

1. *Typical.* The Irish Wolfhound is a rough-coated Greyhoundlike breed, the tallest of the coursing hounds and remarkable in combining power and swiftness.
2. *Great size* and commanding appearance.
3. Movements easy and active.
4. Head, long and level, carried high.
5. Forelegs, heavily boned, quite straight; elbows well set under.
6. Thighs long and muscular; second thighs, well muscled, stifles nicely bent.
7. Coat, rough and hard, specially wiry and long over eyes and under jaw.
8. Body, long, well-ribbed up, with ribs well sprung, and great breadth across hips.

9. Loins arched, belly well drawn up.
10. Ears, small, with Greyhoundlike carriage.
11. Feet, moderately large and round; toes, close, well arched.
12. Neck, long, well arched and very strong.
13. Chest, very deep, moderately broad.
14. Shoulders, muscular, set sloping.
15. Tail, long and slightly curved.
16. Eyes, dark.

*Note*—The above in no way alters the "Standard of Excellence," which must in all cases be rigidly adhered to; they simply give the various points in order of merit. If in any case they appear at variance with Standard of Excellence, it is the latter which is correct.

Approved September 12, 1950

# Norwegian Elkhound

Comrade to the Vikings, guardian of lonely farms and *saeters*, herder of flocks and defender from wolves and bear, a hunter always and roamer with hardy men, the Norwegian Elkhound comes down to us through more than six millennia with all his Nordic traits untainted, a fearless dog and friendly, devoted to man and the chase. We read of him in sagas, we find his remains by the side of his Viking-master along with the Viking's weapons—sure proof of the esteem in which he was held; and in the Viste Cave at Jaeren, in western Norway, his skeleton was uncovered among the stone implements in a stratum dating from 4000 to 5000 B.C.

Selected and bred for his ability to accomplish a definite purpose, the Elkhound achieved his distinctive type by natural methods. No form was imposed upon him; he was not squeezed into a preconceived standard; his structure and rare beauty, like those of the thoroughbred horse, were evolved from the tests of performance. Every physical characteristic is the expression of a need. His compactness, his muscled robustness, his squareness, his width and depth are true expressions of nature's requirements for a dog that would hunt day after day, all day long, in rugged country, where stamina rather than extreme speed is called for.

For, though the Elkhound in foreign countries has become known and loved chiefly, perhaps, for his engaging and sensitive qualities as a comrade of man

**199**

and his reliability and quickness to learn and adapt himself to any circumstances and conditions, it should never be forgotten that from first to last he has been at all times the peerless hunter of big game.

Many years ago, bear were still common in Norway, but today they are almost extinct, and the native dog's main use is the hunting of elk. (*Elk* is incorrectly used in the United States for the Wapiti, *Cervus Canadensis*, and our *moose* is a true elk.) A century ago, Captain Lloyd, an English sportsman, a mighty hunter and a fascinating writer, devoted his leisure to the description of bear hunting in Norway; and from that time on, everyone that has seen the Elkhound work in the forests of his native land has added to his praise.

The Elkhound's highly developed senses amount almost to intuition. It is common to read of, or—if one is fortunate—experience such incidents as seeing a seasoned dog take body scent at from two to three miles or to hear him indicating to his master by a slight whimpering that the elk has become alarmed and has begun to run, at a time when no human senses can apprehend any sign by which the hound ascertains this fact.

Equally subtle is his method of engaging a bull. Knowing well that an elk can outfoot him, he holds the animal by just enough barking to attract his attention. Even with a skillful dog, however, the elk often moves on before the hunter can get up over the steep countryside; and in that case, the dog, aware that the bull, if not excited by sound or scent, will soon pause, works silently and very carefully up wind until he is once more with his quarry. After a while, the bull, becoming angry at the small beast annoying him, begins to attack with a wide sweeping movement of the great antlers and by striking with his deadly forefeet. But now, the Elkhound, short-backed so that he can, to use Herr Aarflot's apt expression "bounce like a rubber ball" jumps nimbly in and out, while giving full and furious tongue so that his high-pitched voice will reach his master.

The Elkhound is well adapted to the hunting of any other four-footed game and soon becomes expert on lynx, mountain lion, and raccoon. Sir Henry Pottinger declares that he is also an excellent tracker of fox. The same authority states: "There is no more deadly way of approaching capercailzie, black game, and other forest birds than with a dog of the breed under discussion, held or fastened to the belt by a long leash and allowed to precede the hunter."

The Elkhound, then, is an exceedingly versatile dog developed through constant contact with man in pursuit of game. It was not until 1877 that he began to be considered from an exhibition point of view. In that year the Norwegian Hunters' Association held its first show, and shortly thereafter pedigrees, which had been handed down, were checked and traced as far back as feasible, a stud book (*Norsk Hundestambok*) was published, and a standard drawn up. Before that time, there had been some confusion of type owing to different developments in different parts of the country; but if we study the photograph of such a grand dog as that pillar of the stud book, known to fame as Gamle Bamse Gram (Old Bamse that belonged to Consul Gram), we shall see that all the essential elements of the modern show dog were already there, needing only a little refinement, a little emphasis.

At any rate, by the turn of the century, the breed was making very rapid progress, and, though there were few or no really large kennels, there were many expert breeders devoted to the Elkhound's improvement, and when the Norwegian Kennel Club (*Norsk Kennelklub*) inaugurated its annual shows at Oslo, the Elkhound came into his own as Norway's great contribution to dogdom. Since then he has been exported in ever-increasing numbers; and his friendly disposition, his intelligence, his staunchness, his absolute dependability and trustworthiness, his eagerness to please, his sensitivity and his fearless confidence have gained for him everywhere a popularity based even more on his comradely character than on his unsurpassed abilities as a hunting dog.

## Official Standard for the Norwegian Elkhound

**General Appearance**—The Norwegian Elkhound is a hardy gray hunting dog. In appearance, a typical northern dog of medium size and substance, square in profile, close coupled and balanced in proportions. The head is broad with prick ears, and the tail is tightly curled and carried over the back. The distinctive gray coat is dense and smooth lying. As a hunter, the Norwegian Elkhound has the courage, agility and stamina to hold moose and other big game at bay by barking and dodging attack, and the endurance to track for long hours in all weather over rough and varied terrain.

**Size, Proportion, Substance**—*Height* at the withers for dogs is 20½ inches, for bitches 19½ inches. *Weight* for dogs about 55 pounds, for bitches about 48 pounds. Square in profile and close coupled. Distance from brisket to ground appears to be half the height at the withers. Distance from forechest to rump equals the height at the withers. Bone is substantial, without being coarse.

**Head**—*Head* broad at the ears, wedge shaped, strong and dry (without loose skin). *Expression* keen, alert, indicating a dog with great courage. *Eyes* very dark brown, medium in size, oval, not protruding. *Ears* set high, firm and erect, yet very mobile. Comparatively small; slightly taller than their width at the base with pointed (not rounded) tips. When the dog is alert, the orifices turn forward and the outer edges are vertical. When relaxed or showing affection, the ears go back, and the dog should not be penalized for doing this during the judge's examination. Viewed from the side, the forehead and back of the *skull* are only slightly arched; the *stop* not large, yet clearly defined. The *muzzle* is thickest at the base and, seen from above or from the side, tapers evenly without being pointed. The bridge of the *nose* is straight, parallel to and about the same length as the skull. *Lips* are tightly closed and *teeth* meet in a scissors bite.

**Neck, Topline, Body**—*Neck* of medium length, muscular, well set up with a slight arch and with no loose skin on the throat. *Topline*—The back is straight and strong from its high point at the withers to the root of the tail. The *body* is short and close-coupled with the rib cage accounting for most of its length. *Chest* deep and moderately broad; brisket level with points of elbows; and ribs well sprung. **Loin** short and wide with very little tuck-up. **Tail** set high, tightly curled, and carried over the centerline of the back. It is thickly and closely haired, without brush, natural and untrimmed.

**Forequarters**—Shoulders sloping with elbows closely set on. **Legs** well under body and medium in length; substantial, but not coarse, in bone. Seen from the front, the legs appear straight and parallel. Single dewclaws are normally present. **Feet**—Paws comparatively small, slightly oval with tightly closed toes and thick pads. Pasterns are strong and only slightly bent. Feet turn neither in nor out.

**Hindquarters**—Moderate angulation at stifle and hock. **Thighs** are broad and well muscled. Seen from behind, legs are straight, strong and without dewclaws. **Feet** as in front.

**Coat**—Thick, hard, weather resisting and smooth lying; made up of soft, dense, woolly undercoat and coarse, straight covering hairs. Short and even on head, ears, and front of legs; longest on back of neck, buttocks and underside of tail. The coat is not altered by trimming, clipping or artificial treatment. Trimming of whiskers is optional. In the show ring, presentation in a natural, unaltered condition is essential.

**Color**—Gray, medium preferred, variations in shade determined by the length of black tips and quantity of guard hairs. Undercoat is clear light silver as are legs, stomach, buttocks, and underside of tail. The gray body color is darkest on the saddle, lighter on the chest, mane and distinctive harness mark (a band of longer guard hairs from shoulder to elbow). The muzzle, ears and tail tip are black. The black of the muzzle shades to lighter gray over the forehead and skull. Yellow or brown shading, white patches, indistinct or irregular markings, "sooty" coloring on the lower legs and light circles around the eyes are undesirable. Any overall color other than gray as described above, such as red, brown, solid black, white or other solid color, disqualifies.

**Gait**—Normal for an active dog constructed for agility and endurance. At a trot the stride is even and effortless; the back remains level. As the speed of the trot increases, front and rear legs converge equally in straight lines toward a center line beneath the body, so that the pads appear to follow in the same tracks (single track). Front and rear quarters are well balanced in angulation and muscular development.

**Temperament**—In temperament, the Norwegian Elkhound is bold and energetic, an effective guardian yet normally friendly, with great dignity and independence of character.

**Summary**—The Norwegian Elkhound is a square and athletic member of the northern dog family. His unique coloring, weather resistant coat and stable disposition make him an ideal multipurpose dog at work or at play.

### DISQUALIFICATION

*An overall color other than gray.*

Approved December 13, 1988

# Otterhound

**W**hile there are allusions to otter hunting and Otterhounds in the time of King John, who reigned in England from 1199 to 1216, it is not until Edward II (1307–1327) that there is any sort of a description of the kind of dogs that made up a pack of Otterhounds. This record has been left, fortunately, by William Twici, the huntsman. He makes mention of them as a "rough sort of dog, between a hound and a terrier."

The hunting of the otter never was a so-called major sport in England, but it appears to have existed from very early times. It first was practiced because the otters were preying on the fish in the rivers and streams to an annoying extent. Later it enjoyed a considerable vogue because it was the only kind of hunting possible from April to September.

The undoubted heyday of the Otterhound in England extended from the middle to the end of the 19th century. During many of those years there were 18 to 20 packs hunting regularly through the season. Most famous, for its record of killing otters, was the Hawkstone pack of the Hon. Geoffrey Hill. From 1870 to 1890 this pack disposed of 704 otters.

Still, all authorities agree that the best trained pack of Otterhounds ever hunted in England was that of Squire Lomax of Clitheroe. This was at the peak of its perfection about 1868. The Squire was a stickler for the fine points of the game, and, while results interested him, his major concern was the manner in which his pack worked. It is said that they were trained so well that his signals could be given with the most casual wave of the hand.

The origin of the Otterhound is shrouded in mystery, but the earliest writers advance a number of logical opinions as to its origin. According to Stonehenge, its ancestors are the Southern hound and the Welsh Harrier. This is supported by the fact that there were large numbers of Otterhounds to be found in Devonshire, the chief stronghold of the Southern hound, and in Wales.

A somewhat less acceptable opinion is that of E. Buckley, who ascribes the coat of the Otterhound to the Water Spaniel—a somewhat different type from the breed known today—and credits the hardiness to the Bulldog. Other writers mention the Bloodhound, supporting this by the domed shape of the skull, and the length of the ears. In fact, writing as early as 1575, Turberville makes no distinction between the Bloodhound and the Otterhound in describing the hunting of the otter.

The French origin of the Otterhound appears to be one of the most reasonable. This is the opinion of Marples, who, describing the Otterhound, says it is the almost exact duplicate of the old Vendee hound of France. The two breeds are alike in both coat and body formation.

The Otterhound is a big dog, ranging from 24 to 27 inches, and weighing from 75 to 115 pounds. He has a hard, crisp and close coat of an oily nature that can stand any amount of immersion in water. The most desired combination of colors always has been the blue and white, but the breed ranges through many shades to black and tan. It is a peer among swimmers, its progress through the water being aided greatly by its webbed feet.

The working qualities of the Otterhound always have been emphasized to such an extent that it never has been popularly known as a bench-show specimen in England. Still, it usually was the custom for some of the great packs to send a few to the major shows. The Carlisle and Kendal packs were noted for their show dogs.

Otterhounds first made their appearance in the United States about the year 1900. They made their bench-show debut in 1907 in Claremont, Oklahoma, and registrations are recorded. These are of Hartland Moss-trooper and Hartland Statesman, both owned by H. S. Wardner of New York City. Incidentally, Mr. Wardner was one of the two exhibitors of 1907, and he undoubtedly was America's first breeder.

While the Otterhound never has grown to wide popularity in the United States, its sagacity and character have retained for it many steadfast friends. What it lacks in smartness of appearance is compensated by its working qualities and its unfailing devotion to its master.

# Official Standard for the Otterhound

**General Appearance**—The Otterhound is a large, rough-coated hound with an imposing head showing great strength and dignity, and the strong body and long striding action fit for a long day's work. It has an extremely sensitive nose, and is inquisitive and perseverant in investigating scents. The Otterhound hunts its quarry on land and water and requires a combination of characteristics unique among hounds—most notably a rough, double coat; and substantial webbed feet. Otterhounds should not be penalized for being shown in working condition (lean, well muscled, with a naturally stripped coat). Any departure from the following points should be considered a fault; its seriousness should be regarded in exact proportion to its degree.

**Size, Proportion, Substance**—Males are 24 to 27 inches at the withers and weigh 75 to 115 lbs. Bitches are 23 to 26 inches at the withers and weigh 65 to 100 lbs. The Otterhound is *slightly* rectangular in body; the length from point of shoulder to buttocks is slightly greater than the height at the withers. The Otterhound has good substance with strongly boned legs and broad muscles, without being coarse. Balance, soundness, and type are of greater importance than size.

**Head**—The head is large, fairly narrow, and well covered with hair. The head should measure 11 to 12 inches from tip of nose to occiput in a hound 26″ at the withers, with the muzzle and skull approximately equal in length. This proportion should be maintained in larger and smaller hounds. The *expression* is open and amiable. The *eyes* are deeply set. The haw shows only slightly. The eyes are dark, but eye color and eye rim pigment will complement the color of the hound. Dogs with black pigmented noses and eye rims should have darker eyes, while those with liver or slate pigment may have hazel eyes. The *ears*, an essential feature of this breed, are long, pendulous, and folded (the leading edge folds or rolls to give a draped appearance). They are set low, at or below eye level, and hang close to the head, with the leather reaching at least to the tip of the nose. They are well covered with hair. The *skull* (cranium) is long, fairly narrow under the hair, and only slightly domed. The *stop* is not pronounced. The *muzzle* is square, with no hint of snipiness; the jaws are powerful with deep flews. From the side, the planes of the muzzle and skull should be parallel. The *nose* is large, dark, and completely pigmented, with wide nostrils. The *jaws* are powerful and capable of a crushing grip. A *scissors bite* is preferred.

**Neck, Topline, Body**—The *neck* is powerful and blends smoothly into well laid back, clean shoulders, and should be of sufficient length to allow the dog to follow a trail. It has an abundance of hair; a slight dewlap is permissible. The *topline* is level from the withers to the base of the tail. The *chest* is deep rather than wide, reaching to the elbows in the mature hound. The well sprung, oval *rib cage* extends well towards the rear of the body. The *loin* is short, broad, and strong. The *tail* is set high on a slightly sloping *croup*. The tail is long, reaching at least to the hock. It is thicker at the base, tapers to a point, and is feathered (covered and fringed with hair). It is carried saber fashion (not forward over the back) when a dog is moving or alert, but may droop when the dog is at rest.

**Forequarters**—*Shoulders* are clean, powerful, and well sloped with moderate angulation at shoulders and elbows. *Legs* are strongly boned and straight, with strong, slightly sprung *pasterns*. Dewclaws on the forelegs may be removed. *Feet*—Both front and rear feet are large, broad, compact when standing, but capable of spreading. They have thick, deep pads, with arched toes; they are web-footed (membranes connecting the toes allow the foot to spread).

**Hindquarters**—*Thighs and second thighs* are large, broad, and well muscled. *Legs* have moderately bent stifles with well-defined hocks. *Hocks* are well let down, turning neither in nor out. Legs on a standing hound are parallel when viewed from the rear. Angulation front and rear must be balanced and adequate to give forward reach and rear drive. Dewclaws, if any, on the hind legs are generally removed. Feet are as previously described.

**Coat**—The coat is an essential feature of the Otterhound. Coat texture and quality are more important than the length. The *outer coat* is dense, rough, coarse and crisp, of broken appearance. Softer hair on the head and lower legs is natural. The outer coat is two to four inches long on the back and shorter on the extremities. A water-resistant *undercoat* of short, woolly, slightly oily hair is essential, but in summer months may be hard to find except on thighs and shoulders. The ears are well covered with hair, and the tail is feathered (covered and fringed with hair). A naturally stripped coat lacking length and fringes is correct for an Otterhound that is being worked. A proper hunting coat will show the hard outer coat and woolly undercoat. The Otterhound is shown in a natural coat that should be free of dead hair, with no sculpturing or shaping of the coat. *Faults*—A soft outer coat is a *very* serious fault as is a woolly textured outer coat. Lack of undercoat is a serious fault. An outer coat much longer than six inches becomes heavy when wet and is a fault.

**Color**—Any color or combination of colors is acceptable. There should be no discrimination on the basis of color. The nose should be dark and fully pigmented, black, liver, or slate, depending on the color of the hound. Eye rim pigment should match the nose.

**Gait**—The Otterhound moves freely with forward reach and rear drive. The gait is smooth, effortless, and capable of being maintained for many miles. Characteristic of the Otterhound gait is a very loose, shambling walk, which springs immediately into a loose and very long striding, sound, active trot with natural extension of the head. The gallop is smooth and exceptionally long striding. Otterhounds single track at slow speeds. Otterhounds do not lift their feet high off the ground and may shuffle when they walk or move at a slow trot. The Otterhound should be shown on a loose lead.

**Temperament**—The Otterhound is amiable, boisterous and even-tempered.

Approved May 9, 1989

# Petit Basset Griffon Vendéen

The Petit Basset Griffon Vendéen, one of many small varieties of the French hounds, is of ancient origin. The breed can be traced to the sixteenth century and to the Griffon Vendéen, his larger, more powerful ancestor. His name in French reveals much about him: *Petit*—small; *Basset*—low to the ground; *Griffon*—rough or wire coated; and *Vendéen*—the area of France in which he originated. In the United States the breed is referred to as "Petits," in England as "Griffs" or "Roughies," and in Denmark as "Griffs" or "Petits."

This small hunting dog has an intriguing and charming appearance and personality. But it is important to remember that the Petit Basset Griffon Vendéen is, first and foremost, a hound developed to hunt game by scent. Furthermore, his physical evolution is directly related to the environment and terrain on the western coast of France—the Vendée, characterized by thick underbrush, rocks, thorns, and brambles. This difficult terrain demanded a hardy, alert, bold, determined, intelligent hunter with both mental and physical stamina.

The Petit Basset Griffon Vendéen is a proud member of some 28 hound breeds which are bred in France, even today, to serve their original purpose. They are used to hunt small game, especially hare and rabbit, in France and other European countries, and in the United States and Canada.

Most French hound breeds came in large and small versions and were used for different prey. The *Grand* Basset Griffon Vendéen was used for such large game as roedeer and wolf, while the *Petit* Basset Griffon Vendéen was used to trail and drive smaller quarry such as rabbit, hare and sometimes even feathered game.

The attempt to standardize the breed type was not undertaken seriously until the latter half of the nineteenth century. Until 1898, when the first official standard for the Basset Griffon Français was adopted, judges made their placements without an official standard. The Dezamy family, headed by Paul Dezamy—the first president of the newly founded Club du Basset Vendéen (1907), is known for having devised the first standard. The same standard described the Petit and Grand, both of which came from the same litters at that time. In 1909, a standard for the Basset Griffon Vendéen recognized two types—one standing 34 to 38 cm (or approximately 13 to 15 inches) at the shoulder, and the other 38 to 42 cm (15 to 17 inches). The Petit was distinguished by his smaller size only, with sometimes semi-crooked legs. The taller, or Grand, always had straight legs.

It was not until the 1950s that the Societé de Venerie published a new book of standards in which the Petit Basset Griffon Vendéen was given an official standard of its own and considered a separate breed. But with the earlier practice of interbreeding the Petit and the Grand, it was common at that time for offspring from the same litter to be entered—some as Petit and some as Grand—at the French Exhibition. Paul Dezamy himself did not breed Petits but became famous for his 42 cm Grands, referred to as "42 Dezamys," though he was responsible for the standards.

Finally, in 1975, through the efforts of Hubert Dezamy, third president of the club, the interbreeding of the Grand and Petit was disallowed. However, as a result of the longtime practice of interbreeding, when Petits are bred today both Grand and Petit characteristics manifest themselves and are likely to do so for generations to come. For this reason, heavy emphasis is placed on type and size, and it is hoped that breeders and judges will learn the features unique to a Petit so that the right characteristics will be encouraged.

The Petit Basset Griffon Vendéen Club of America was founded at the AKC Centennial Show in 1984 to protect and promote the breed in this country. The breed was admitted to AKC registration effective December 1, 1990 and became eligible to compete at AKC-licensed shows effective February 1, 1991.

## Official Standard for the Petit Basset Griffon Vendéen

**General Appearance**—The Petit Basset Griffon Vendéen is a scent hound developed to hunt small game over the rough and difficult terrain of the Vendéen region. To function efficiently, he must be equipped with certain characteristics. He is bold and vivacious in character; compact, tough and robust in construction. He has an alert outlook, lively bearing and a good voice freely used.

The most distinguishing characteristics of this bold hunter are his rough, unrefined outline; his proudly carried head, displaying definitive long eyebrows, beard, and moustache; his strong, tapered tail carried like a sabre, alert and in readiness. Important to the breed type is the compact, casual, rather tousled appearance, with no feature exaggerated and his parts in balance.

Any deviation from the ideal described in the standard should be penalized to the extent of the deviation. Structural faults common to all breeds are as undesirable in the PBGV as in any other breed, regardless of whether they are specifically mentioned.

**Size, Proportion, Substance**—*Size*—Both sexes should measure between 13 and 15 inches at the withers, with a ½ inch tolerance in either direction being acceptable. Height over 15½ inches at the withers is a disqualification. *Proportion*—Somewhat longer than tall. A correctly proportioned dog will be approximately 50% longer than tall when the entire body is measured from sternum to buttocks as compared to withers to ground. *Substance*—Strong bone with substance in proportion to overall dog.

**Head**—The head is carried proudly and, in size, must be in balance with the overall dog. It is longer than its width in a ratio of approximately two to one. A coarse or overly large head is to be penalized. *Expression* alert, friendly and intelligent. *Eyes* large and dark, showing no white. The red of the lower eyelid should not show. They are surmounted by long eyebrows, standing forward, but not obscuring the eyes. *Ears* supple, narrow and fine, covered with long hair, folding inward and ending in an oval shape. The leathers reach almost to the end of the nose. They are set on low, not above the line of the eyes. An overly long or high-set ear should be penalized. *Skull* domed, oval in shape when viewed from the front. It is well cut away under the eyes and has a well developed occipital protuberance. *Stop* clearly defined. *Muzzle*—The length of the muzzle is slightly shorter than the length from stop to occiput. The underjaw is strong and well developed. *Nose* black and large, with wide nostrils. A somewhat lighter shading is acceptable in lighter colored dogs. *Lips*—The lips are covered by long hair forming a beard and moustache. *Bite*—It is preferable that the teeth meet in a scissors bite, but a level bite is acceptable.

**Neck, Topline, Body**—*Neck*—The neck is long and strong, without throatiness, and flows smoothly into the shoulders. *Topline*—The back is level with a slight arch over a strong loin. Viewed in profile, the withers and the croup should be equidistant from the ground. *Body* muscular, somewhat longer than tall. *Chest* deep, with prominent sternum. *Ribs* moderately rounded, extending well back. *Loin* strong; muscular and rounded about the lateral axis of the dog. *Tail* of medium length, set on high, it is strong at the base and tapers regularly. It is well furnished with hair, has but a slight curve and is carried proudly like the blade of a sabre; normally about 20 degrees to the aft of vertical. In a curved downward position the tip of the tail bone should reach approximately to the hock joint.

**Forequarters**—*Shoulders* clean and well laid back. *Upper arm* approximately equal in length to the shoulder blade. *Elbows* close to the body. *Legs*—The length of leg from elbow to ground should be slightly less than ½ the length from withers to ground. Viewed from the front, it is desirable that the forelegs be straight, but a slight crook is acceptable. The leg is strong and well boned. *Pasterns* strong and slightly sloping. Any tendency to knuckle over is a serious fault. *Dewclaws* may, or may not, be removed. *Feet* not too long, with hard, tight pads. Slight turnout of the feet is acceptable. The nails are strong and short.

**Hindquarters**—Strong and muscular with good bend of stifle. A well-defined second thigh. Hocks are short and well angulated, perpendicular from hock to ground. Feet are as in front except that they must point straight ahead.

**Coat**—The coat is rough, long without exaggeration and harsh to the touch, with a thick shorter undercoat. It is never silky or woolly. The eyes are surmounted by long eyebrows, standing forward, but not obscuring the eyes. The ears are covered by long hair. The lips are covered by long hair forming a beard and moustache. The tail is well furnished with hair. The overall appearance is casual and tousled. *Hounds are to be shown untrimmed.* Indications of scissoring for the purposes of shaping or sculpturing are to be severely penalized.

**Color**—White with any combination of lemon, orange, black, tricolor or grizzle markings.

**Gait**—The movement should be free at all speeds. Front action is straight and reaching well forward. Going away, the hind legs are parallel and have great drive. Convergence of the front and rear legs towards his center of gravity is proportional to the speed of his movement. Gives the appearance of an active hound, capable of a full day's hunting.

**Temperament**—Happy, extroverted, independent, yet willing to please.

### DISQUALIFICATION

*Height of more than 15½ inches at the withers.*

Approved August 14, 1990

# Pharaoh Hound

The Pharaoh Hound, one of the oldest domesticated dogs in recorded history, traces his lineage to roughly 3,000 B.C. Fortunately, the history of Egyptian civilization was well documented and preserved through paintings and hieroglyphics and from these we learn that this unique dog was treasured for his great hunting ability and his affinity for close family relationships.

King Tutankhamen, legendary ruler of upper and lower Egypt, so loved to watch his graceful hound, Abuwitiyuw, leap with joy at the sight of a gazelle and to have him as a companion at the hunt, that when the hound died, he commanded the dog to be buried as would be fitting of a nobleman; he was laid in a coffin with fine linen, perfumed ointment and incense so that he might be honored before the God, Anubis. A striking model of a dog was found at the entrance to Tutankhamen's tomb during the excavations.

Reliefs of these hounds hunting can be found in the tomb chapel of Mereruwka and in the tomb chapel of Senbi. Both the Pharaoh Hound Club of England the Pharaoh Hound Club of America, Inc., use as their emblem the dog depicted on the tomb of Antefa II, XI Dynasty, about 2,000 B.C. The dogs are described in a translation of a letter of the XIX Dynasty: "The red, long-tailed dog goes at night into the stalls of the hills, he is better than the long faced dog. He makes no delay in hunting, his face glows like a God and he delights to do his work." This "blushing" trait has not been lost through the ages. It is beautiful to see a Pharaoh Hound glow with excitement or happiness—the nose and ears turning a deep rose color, and the lovely amber eyes further enriched with a deep rose hue.

It seems reasonably certain that the origins of this dog lie in Egypt and they were carried by Phoenician traders to the island of Malta well before the birth of Christ. The breeders of Malta maintained a purity of breed type over a period of 2,000 years, for the dog today still closely resembles his Egyptian forebears.

In Malta, the Pharaoh Hound was bred to hunt rabbit and only the best hunters were used in selective breeding programs. The high esteem in which these dogs have been held was evidenced in 1979, when a silver coin bearing the likeness of a standing Pharaoh Hound was minted to commemorate the occasion of the dog being declared the National Dog of Malta.

Pharaoh Hounds were apparently first imported into England in the early 1930s, but records are inconclusive. In 1963, author Pauline Block, who had become an admirer of the breed while living in Malta, returned home to England with Bahri of Twinley. This Pharaoh Hound was the first to be shown in England at the Hound Show at Alexandria Palace in London.

The first Pharaoh Hound was brought to the United States in 1967 by Mrs. Ruth Taft Harper, a bitch secured with the help of Pauline Block and her husband, General Adam Block. The first litter of Pharaoh Hounds was whelped in the United States in 1970.

In January 1979, the American Kennel Club admitted the Pharaoh Hounds into the Miscellaneous Class. Then, effective August 1, 1983, the breed was recognized for registration in AKC's Stud Book, and effective January 1, 1984, became eligible to compete in the Hound Group at AKC licensed events.

The Pharaoh Hound gives a striking impression of elegance, power and grace. He is intelligent, friendly and affectionate. His great speed combined with his alertness and agility give him a marked keenness for hunting both by sight and by scent.

An outstanding feature of the breed is their haunting beautiful amber eyes. Their nose, eye rims and lips are flesh colored, blending with the coat. Many Pharaoh Hounds display a marvelous trait of smiling, showing their pearly white scissors bite. They are particularly fond of children and never lose their fondness for romping and playing as they crave human attention. Their short glossy coats tend to make them most enjoyable as house dogs and another desirable feature is that they have no doggie odor, even when wet. Their willingness to please allows them to be trained swiftly which makes them excellent candidates for hunting, obedience and coursing.

# Official Standard for the Pharaoh Hound

**General Appearance**—General Appearance is one of grace, power and speed. The Pharaoh Hound is medium sized, of noble bearing with hard clean-cut lines—graceful, well balanced, very fast with free easy movement and alert expression.

The following description is that of the ideal Pharaoh Hound. Any deviation from the below described dog must be penalized to the extent of the deviation.

**Size, Proportion, Substance**—**Height**—Dogs 23 inches–25 inches. Bitches 21 inches–24 inches. Allover balance must be maintained. Length of body from breast to haunch bone slightly longer than height of withers to ground. Lithe.

**Head**—Alert **expression.** **Eyes** amber colored, blending with coat; oval, moderately deep set with keen intelligent expression. **Ears** medium high set, carried erect when alert, but very mobile, broad at the base, fine and large. **Skull** long, lean and chiseled. Only slight stop. Foreface slightly longer than the skull. Top of the skull parallel with the foreface representing a blunt wedge. **Nose** flesh colored, blending with the coat. No other color. Powerful jaws with strong teeth. Scissors **bite.**

**Neck, Topline, Body**—**Neck** long, lean and muscular with a slight arch to carry the head on high. Clean throat line. Almost straight **topline.** Slight slope from croup to root of tail. **Body** lithe. Deep brisket almost down to point of elbow. Ribs well sprung. Moderate tuck-up. **Tail** medium set—fairly thick at the base and tapering whiplike, reaching below the point of hock in repose. Well carried and curved when in action. The tail should not be tucked between the legs. A screw tail is a fault.

**Forequarters**—**Shoulders** long and sloping and well laid back. Strong without being loaded. **Elbows** well tucked in. **Forelegs** straight and parallel. Pasterns strong. Dewclaws may be removed. **Feet** neither cat nor hare but strong, well knuckled and firm, turning neither in nor out. Paws well padded.

**Hindquarters**—Strong and muscular. Limbs parallel. Moderate sweep of stifle. Well developed second thigh. Dewclaws may be removed. **Feet** as in front.

**Coat**—Short and glossy, ranging from fine and close to slightly harsh with no feathering. Accident blemishes should not be considered as faults.

**Color**—Ranging from tan/rich tan/chestnut with white markings allowed as follows: White tip on tail strongly desired. White on chest (called "the Star"). White on toes and slim white snip on center line of face permissible. Flecking or other white undesirable, except for any solid white spot on the back of neck, shoulder, or any part of the back or sides of the dog, which is a *disqualification.*

**Gait**—Free and flowing; the head should be held fairly high and the dog should cover the ground well without any apparent effort. The legs and feet should move in line with the body; any tendency to throw the feet sideways, or a high stepping "hackney" action is a definite fault.

**Temperament**—Intelligent, friendly, affectionate and playful. Alert and active. Very fast with a marked keenness for hunting, both by sight and scent.

### DISQUALIFICATION

*Any solid white spot on the back of neck, shoulder, or any part of the back or sides of the dog.*

Approved May 10, 1983
Reformatted April 3, 1989

# Rhodesian Ridgeback

$\text{T}$he Rhodesian Ridgeback, sometimes referred to as the African Lion Hound, is a native of South Africa having been bred by the Boer farmers to fill their specific need for a serviceable hunting dog in the wilds.

The Dutch, Germans, and Huguenots who emigrated to South Africa in the 16th and 17th centuries brought with them Danes, Mastiffs, Greyhounds, Bloodhounds, Terriers, and other breeds. For one hundred years from 1707, European immigration was closed, and the native dogs played an important part in the development and ultimate character of the Ridgeback.

The Hottentots, a native race living within range of these early settlers, had a hunting dog that was half wild with a ridge on his back formed by the hair growing forward. There was interbreeding between these dogs and those of the settlers, and this crossbreeding, in due course, established the foundation stock of our present-day Ridgeback.

Good hunting dogs were hard to come by in those days and their value was high. The Boer settler needed a dog that could flush a few partridge, pull down a wounded buck, guard the farm from marauding animals and prowlers at night. He also needed a dog that could withstand the rigors of the African Bush, hold up under the drastic changes in temperature from the heat of the day to nights below freezing, and go a full 24 hours or more without water. He required a shorthaired dog that would not be eaten by ticks. In addition, he needed a companion that would stay by him while he slept in the Bush and that would be devoted to his wife and children. Of necessity, then, the Boer farmer developed, by selective breeding, a distinct breed of the African Veldt—the Ridgeback.

In 1877, the Reverend Helm introduced two Ridgebacks into Rhodesia where the big game hunters, Selons, Upcher, Van Rooyen, and others, found them outstanding in the sport of hunting lions on horseback. They raised and bred these dogs with an appreciation of their exceptional hunting qualities, the ridge on their back becoming a unique trademark. In 1922, a group of Rhodesian breeders set up a standard for Ridgebacks which has remained virtually unchanged ever since.

Some outstanding specimens were imported to the United States in 1950, and the breed was admitted to registry by the AKC in 1955.

The Ridgeback, in a comparatively short space of time, has won himself many admirers in the United States for his innate qualities. He is clean, an easy keeper and never noisy or quarrelsome. Because of his heritage, obedience training comes readily to him and his desire to please his master, coupled with his general good nature and liking for children, is making him new friends each year.

## Official Standard for the Rhodesian Ridgeback

The peculiarity of this breed is the *ridge* on the back, which is formed by the hair growing in the opposite direction to the rest of the coat. The ridge must be regarded as the characteristic feature of the breed. The ridge should be clearly defined, tapering and symmetrical. It should start immediately behind the shoulders and continue to a point between the prominence of the hips, and should contain two identical crowns opposite each other. The lower edges of the crown should not extend further down the ridge than one third of the ridge.

**General Appearance**—The Ridgeback should represent a strong muscular and active dog, symmetrical in outline, and capable of great endurance with a fair amount of speed.

**Head**—Should be of a fair length, the skull flat and rather broad between the ears and should be free from wrinkles when in repose. The stop should be reasonably well defined. *Muzzle*—Should be long, deep and powerful, jaws level and strong with well-developed teeth, especially the canines or holders. The lips clean, closely fitting the jaws. *Eyes*—Should be moderately well apart, and should be round, bright and sparkling, with intelligent expression, their color harmonizing with the color of the dog. *Ears*—Should be set rather high, of medium size, rather wide at base, and tapering to a rounded point. They should be carried close to the head. *Nose*—Should be black, or brown, in keeping with the color of the dog. No other colored nose is permissible. A black nose should be accompanied by dark eyes, a brown nose by amber eyes.

**Neck and Shoulders**—The neck should be fairly strong and free from throatiness. The shoulders should be sloping, clean and muscular, denoting speed.

**Body, Back, Chest and Loins**—The chest should not be too wide, but very deep and capacious; ribs moderately well sprung, never rounded like barrel hoops (which would indicate want of speed), the back powerful, the loins strong, muscular and slightly arched.

**Legs and Feet**—The forelegs should be perfectly straight, strong and heavy in bone; elbows close to the body. The feet should be compact, with well-arched toes, round, tough, elastic pads, protected by hair between the toes and pads. In the hind legs the muscles should be clean, well defined, and hocks well down.

**Tail**—Should be strong at the insertion, and generally tapering towards the end, free from coarseness. It should not be inserted too high or too low, and should be carried with a slight curve upwards, never curled.

**Coat**—Should be short and dense, sleek and glossy in appearance, but neither woolly nor silky.

**Color**—Light wheaten to red wheaten. A little white on the chest and toes permissible but excessive white there and any white on the belly or above the toes is undesirable.

**Size**—A mature Ridgeback should be a handsome, upstanding dog; dogs should be of a height of 25 to 27 inches, and bitches 24 to 26 inches.

**Weight**—(Desirable) dogs 75 pounds, bitches 65 pounds.

### SCALE OF POINTS

| | | | |
|---|---|---|---|
| Ridge | 20 | Coat | 5 |
| Head | 15 | Tail | 5 |
| Neck and shoulders | 10 | Size, symmetry, general | |
| Body, back, chest, loins | 10 | appearance | 20 |
| Legs and feet | 15 | TOTAL | 100 |

Approved November, 1955

# Saluki

The Saluki, royal dog of Egypt, is perhaps the oldest known breed of domesticated dog, identified by some historians as "a distinct breed and type as long ago as 329 B.C. when Alexander the Great invaded India." He is said to be as old as the earliest known civilization, the claim being based on the fact that the hounds shown on the earliest carvings look more like Salukis than any other breed: they have a Greyhound body with feathered ears, tail, and legs. Exactly the same hound appears on the Egyptian tombs of 2100 B.C. and more recent excavations of the still older Sumerian empire, estimated at 7000–6000 B.C., have produced carvings of striking resemblance to the Saluki.

Claim has been made that "Whenever one sees the word 'dog' in the Bible it means the Saluki." Though the Mohammedan religion classes the dog as unclean, the Moslems declared the Saluki sacred and called him "the noble one" given them by Allah for their amusement and benefit. This permitted them to eat of the meat brought down in the chase. The Saluki was the only dog of the time allowed to sleep on the carpet of the Sheikh's tent. So great was the esteem in which the dog was held that his body was often mummified like the bodies of the Pharaohs themselves. The remains of numerous specimens have thus been found in the ancient tombs of the Upper Nile region.

As the desert tribes are nomadic, the habitat of the Saluki comprised all the region stretching from the Caspian Sea to the Sahara, including Egypt, Arabia, Palestine, Syria, Mesopotamia, Anatholia, and Persia. Naturally the types varied somewhat in this widely scattered area—mostly in size and coat. Thus we find the Arabian-bred Saluki of a smaller type with less feathering on the legs and ears than the Persian variety.

Salukis were first brought into England in 1840: a bitch owned by Sir Hamilton Smith, a dog in Regents Park Zoological Gardens, and one owned by the Duke of Devonshire at Chatsworth. They were then known as Persian Greyhounds, since these three came from Persia. There was no real interest, however, until the Hon. Florence Amherst imported the first Arabian Salukis in 1895, from the kennels of Prince Abdulla in Transjordania.

England later learned more about the Saluki from her army officers stationed in the East during World War I. Other specimens, either prizes of war or the gifts of friendly tribes, were brought home.

Having tremendous speed, the Saluki was used by the Arabs principally in bringing down the gazelle, that fastest of antelopes. It is recorded that the Pharaohs rode to the chase with their hawks on their wrists and Salukis on the lead. We also believe the Saluki was used on jackals, foxes, and hares. A cut published in 1852 shows a wild boar hunt in Algeria with Salukis tackling the boar. In England, the dog is used largely on hares, and regular coursing meets are held, with the judging based on ability to turn quickly and overtake the hare in the best possible time. The Saluki hunts largely by sight, although he has a fair nose. The sport of racing Salukis is much enjoyed in England and on the Continent, where a special track with a mechanical rabbit and hurdles at intervals is used.

The Saluki's sight is remarkable, and his hereditary traits often crop out—he loves to lie on the sand and watch an eagle soaring for his prey while paying no attention to the gull. Sarona Dhole, soon after his arrival in America, chased a fox and registered a kill within a few seconds after sighting the quarry.

On his native heath the Saluki gets no pampering. He lives hard, and it is a case of survival of the fittest—one reason for his strong constitution and sturdy frame, enabling him to stand any climate in unheated kennels. His feet are hard and firm, and the hair between the toes is a great protection. In all his running and dodging over the roughest kind of ground and rocky country, he never damages pads or toes.

His beauty is that of the thoroughbred horse: grace and symmetry of form; clean-cut and graceful; short silky hair except on the ears, legs, and tail; slender, well-muscled neck, shoulders, and thighs; arched loins; long tail carried naturally in a curve with silky hair hanging from the underside; the arched toes; the rather long head with deep, far-seeing eyes—an expression of dignity mixed with gentleness.

Salukis come in a wide variety of colors, including white, cream, fawn, golden, red, grizzle and tan, tri-color (white, black and tan), and black and tan.

In disposition he shows great attachment to his master. He is affectionate without being demonstrative, a good watchdog but not aggressive.

The Saluki was a well-established breed in England for a number of years before he began to come into his own in this country. It was not until November 1927, that the breed was officially recognized by the American Kennel Club.

## Official Standard for the Saluki

**Head**—Long and narrow, skull moderately wide between the ears, not domed, stop not pronounced, the whole showing great quality. Nose black or liver. *Ears*—Long and covered with long silky hair hanging close to the skull and mobile. *Eyes*—Dark to hazel and bright; large and oval, but not prominent. *Teeth*—Strong and level.

**Neck**—Long, supple and well muscled.

**Chest**—Deep and moderately narrow.

**Forequarters**—Shoulders sloping and set well back, well muscled without being coarse. *Forelegs*—Straight and long from the elbow to the knee.

**Hindquarters**—Strong, hipbones set well apart and stifle moderately bent, hocks low to the ground, showing galloping and jumping power.

**Loin and Back**—Back fairly broad, muscles slightly arched over loin.

**Feet**—Of moderate length, toes long and well arched, not splayed out, but at the same time not cat-footed; the whole being strong and supple and well feathered between the toes.

**Tail**—Long, set on low and carried naturally in a curve, well feathered on the underside with long silky hair, not bushy.

**Coat**—Smooth and of a soft silky texture, slight feather on the legs, feather at the back of the thighs and sometimes with slight woolly feather on the thigh and shoulder.

**Colors**—White, cream, fawn, golden, red, grizzle and tan, tricolor (white, black and tan) and black and tan.

**General Appearance**—The whole appearance of this breed should give an impression of grace and symmetry and of great speed and endurance coupled with strength and activity to enable it to kill gazelle or other quarry over deep sand or rocky mountains. The expression should be dignified and gentle with deep, faithful, far-seeing eyes. Dogs should average in height from 23 to 28 inches and bitches may be considerably smaller, this being very typical of the breed.

***The Smooth Variety***—In this variety the points should be the same with the exception of the coat, which has no feathering.

# Scottish Deerhound

The origin of the breed is of such antiquity, and the earliest descriptive names bestowed on it so inextricably mixed, that no sound conclusion can be arrived at as to whether the Deerhound was at one time identical with the ancient Irish Wolfdog and, in the course of centuries, bred to a type better suited to hunt deer, or whether, as some writers claim, he is the descendant of the hounds of the Picts. Very early descriptive names were used to identify the purpose of the dog rather than to identify species. We find such names as "Irish Wolf Dog," "Scotch Greyhound," "Rough Greyhound," "Highland Deerhound." Dr. Caius, in his book *Of Englishe Dogges* (1576) speaking of Greyhounds, relates: "Some are of a greater sorte, some of a lesser; some are smoothe skynned and some curled, the bigger therefore are appointed to hunt the bigger beastes, the duck, the hart, the doe."

All this is relatively unimportant when we can definitely identify the breed as Deerhounds as early as the 16th and 17th centuries. From there on the term Deerhound has been applied to the breed, which of all dogs has been found best suited for the pursuit and killing of the deer.

At all times great value has been set on the Deerhound. The history of the breed teems with romance increasing in splendor right down through the Age of Chivalry when no one of rank lower than an earl might possess these dogs. A leash of Deerhounds was held the fine whereby a noble lord condemned to death might purchase his reprieve. Records of the Middle Ages allude repeatedly to the delightful attributes of this charming hound, his tremendous courage in the chase, his gentle dignity in the home.

So highly has the Deerhound been esteemed that the desire for exclusive ownership has at many times endangered the continuance of the breed. As the larger beasts of the chase became extinct or rare in England and southern Scotland, the more delicate, smooth Greyhound took the place of the larger Deerhound. The Highlands of Scotland, last territory wherein the stag remained numerous in a wild state, became the last stronghold of this breed. Here again the highland Chieftains assumed exclusive proprietorship to such an extent that it was rare to find a good specimen south of the River Forth. So severely was this policy pursued that in 1769 the breed physically and numerically ran very low. This, of course, must be attributed in great measure to the collapse of the clan system after Culloden 1745. It was not until about 1825, when the restoration of the breed was undertaken very successfully by Archibald and Duncan McNeill (the latter afterwards Lord Colonsay), that the Deerhound regained his place of pre-eminence and former perfection. World War I had considerable effect on the breed when so many of the large estates in Scotland and England were broken up. Although this "Royal Dog of Scotland" is represented at English shows in good numbers and to an extent at shows in this country, the Deerhound remains a rare dog of such historical interest and character that ownership should give anyone great pride of possession.

The high valuation of the Deerhound is not the result of rarity so much as the fact that as a hunter he is preeminent, with a high aggregate of desirable characteristics. He has a keen scent, which may be used in tracking, but it is that combination of strength and speed necessary to cope with the large Scottish deer (often weighing 250 pounds) that is most valued. The hounds are usually hunted singly or in pairs. Centuries of hunting as the companions and guards of Highland Chieftains have given the Deerhound an insatiable desire for human companionship. For this reason the best Deerhounds are seldom raised as kennel dogs. In character the Deerhound is quiet and dignified, keen and alert, and although not aggressive, has great persistence and indomitable courage when necessary. While it might savor of boasting to claim that the Deerhound of today is identical with the dog of early history, descriptions of which are mostly legendary, it is nevertheless a well-established fact that in type, size, and character he closely conforms to authentic records of the 18th and 19th centuries.

The hunting of antlered game with dogs is not permitted in the United States, but the Deerhound has been used very successfully on wolves, coyotes, and rabbits, and is keen to match his speed with anything that runs. As a companion the Deerhound is ideal, being tractable and easy to train and possessing the most dependable loyalty and utmost devotion to his master. The best descriptions of the breed are found in 19th century British dog books.

The grace, dignity and beauty of the Deerhound have been faithfully depicted in many of Landseer's paintings and drawings, and Sir Walter Scott, who owned the famous Deerhound Maida, penned many enthusiastic allusions to the breed, which he described as "the most perfect creature of Heaven."

## Official Standard for the Scottish Deerhound

**Head**—Should be broader at the ears, narrowing slightly to the eyes, with the muzzle tapering more decidedly to the nose. The muzzle should be pointed, but the teeth and lips level. The head should be long, the skull flat rather than round with a very slight rise over the eyes but nothing approaching a stop. The hair on the skull should be moderately long and softer than the rest of the coat. The nose should be black (in some blue fawns—blue) and slightly aquiline. In lighter colored dogs the black muzzle is preferable. There should be a good mustache of rather silky hair and a fair beard.

**Ears**—Should be set on high; in repose, folded back like a Greyhound's, though raised above the head in excitement without losing the fold, and even in some cases semierect. A prick ear is bad. Big thick ears hanging flat to the head or heavily coated with long hair are bad faults. The ears should be soft, glossy, like a mouse's coat to the touch and the smaller the better. There should be no long coat or long fringe, but there is sometimes a silky, silvery coat on the body of the ear and the tip. On all Deerhounds, irrespective of color of coat, the ears should be black or dark colored.

**Neck and Shoulders**—The neck should be long—of a length befitting the Greyhound character of the dog. Extreme length is neither necessary nor desirable. Deerhounds do not stoop to their work like the Greyhounds. The mane, which every good specimen should have, sometimes detracts from the apparent length of the neck. The neck, however, must be strong as is necessary to hold a stag. The nape of the neck should be very prominent where the head is set on, and the throat clean cut at the angle and prominent. Shoulders should be well sloped; blades well back and not too much width between them. Loaded and straight shoulders are very bad faults.

**Tail**—Should be tolerably long, tapering and reaching to within 1½ inches of the ground and about 1½ inches below the hocks. Dropped perfectly down or curved when the Deerhound is still, when in motion or excited, curved, but in no instance lifted out of line of the back. It should be well covered with hair, on the inside, thick and wiry, underside longer and towards the end a slight fringe is not objectionable. A curl or ring tail is undesirable.

**Eyes**—Should be dark—generally dark brown, brown or hazel. A very light eye is not liked. The eye should be moderately full, with a soft look in repose, but a keen, far-away look when the Deerhound is roused. Rims of eyelids should be black.

**Body**—General conformation is that of a Greyhound of larger size and bone. Chest deep rather than broad but not too narrow or slab-sided. Good girth of chest is indicative of great lung power. The loin well arched and drooping to the tail. A straight back is not desirable, this formation being unsuited for uphill work, and very unsightly.

**Legs and Feet**—Legs should be broad and flat, and good broad forearms and elbows are desirable. Forelegs must, of course, be as straight as possible. Feet close and compact, with well-arranged toes. The hindquarters drooping, and as broad and powerful as possible, the hips being set wide apart. A narrow rear denotes lack of power. The stifles should be well bent, with great length from hip to hock, which should be broad and flat. Cowhocks, weak pasterns, straight stifles and splay feet are very bad faults.

**Coat**—The hair on the body, neck and quarters should be harsh and wiry, about 3 or 4 inches long; that on the head, breast and belly much softer. There should be a slight fringe on the inside of the forelegs and hind legs but nothing approaching the "feather" of a Collie. A woolly coat is bad. Some good strains have a mixture of silky coat with the hard which is preferable to a woolly coat. The climate of the United States tends to produce the mixed coat. The ideal coat is a thick, close-lying ragged coat, harsh or crisp to the touch.

**Color**—is a matter of fancy, but the dark blue-gray is most preferred. Next come the darker and lighter grays or brindles, the darkest being generally preferred. Yellow and sandy red or red fawn, especially with black ears and muzzles, are equally high in estimation. This was the color of the oldest known strains—the McNeil and Chesthill Menzies. White is condemned by all authorities, but a white chest and white toes, occurring as they do in many of the darkest-colored dogs, are not objected to, although the less the better, for the Deerhound is a self-colored dog. A white blaze on the head, or a white collar, should entirely disqualify. The less white the better but a slight white tip to the stern occurs in some of the best strains.

**Height**—*Height of Dogs*—From 30 to 32 inches, or even more if there be symmetry without coarseness, which is rare. *Height of Bitches*—From 28 inches upwards. There is no objection to a bitch being large, unless too coarse, as even at her greatest height she does not approach that of the dog, and therefore could not be too big for work as overbig dogs are.

**Weight**—From 85 to 110 pounds in dogs, and from 75 to 95 pounds in bitches.

### POINTS OF THE DEERHOUND ARRANGED IN ORDER OF IMPORTANCE

1. *Typical*—A Deerhound should resemble a rough-coated Greyhound of larger size and bone.
2. *Movements*—Easy, active and true.
3. As tall as possible consistent with quality.
4. *Head*—Long, level, well balanced, carried high.
5. *Body*—Long, very deep in brisket, well-sprung ribs and great breadth across hips.
6. *Forelegs*—Strong and quite straight, with elbows neither in nor out.

7. *Thighs*—Long and muscular, second thighs well muscled, stifles well bent.
8. *Loins*—Well arched, and belly well drawn up.
9. *Coat*—Rough and hard, with softer beard and brows.
10. *Feet*—Close, compact, with well-knuckled toes.
11. *Ears*—Small (dark) with Greyhoundlike carriage.
12. *Eyes*—Dark, moderately full.
13. *Neck*—Long, well arched, very strong with prominent nape.
14. *Shoulders*—Clean, set sloping.
15. *Chest*—Very deep but not too narrow.
16. *Tail*—Long and curved slightly, carried low.
17. *Teeth*—Strong and level.
18. *Nails*—Strong and curved.

### DISQUALIFICATION

*White blaze on the head, or a white collar.*

Approved March, 1935

# Whippet

The Whippet, an English Greyhound in miniature, is a sporting dog of the first flight as well as a very charming, affectionate, and intelligent pet. He is the fastest domesticated animal of his weight, capable of speeds up to 35 miles per hour. Though his main forte is as a racedog, he is a rabbit courser of great ability. His rat-killing feats, too, are nearly equal to those of the most hard-bitten terriers. As an animal of beauty, grace of outline, and smoothness of action, he stands near the top in the realm of dogdom.

He is extraordinarily keen when racing or on game, though in the living room he is quiet, dignified, unobtrusive, and above all, highly decorative. His intelligence, when treated as a member of the family, compares favorably with most terriers. He is never snappy or "barky," though as a watchdog he is excellent. Contrary to external appearances, he is by no means delicate and difficult to care for. All in all, he makes an ideal dual-purpose small dog for an owner of discrimination.

As a breed the Whippet is not one of our oldest, having been evolved in England a hundred and some years ago, though it was not until 1891 that official recognition was given by the English Kennel Club.

It is said that when such barbaric pastimes as bull- and bearbaiting and dogfighting began to lose favor, the sporting gentry of that period originated the Whippet for the milder (to them) entertainment of coursing rabbits in an enclosure. The early specimens differed a great deal from our best present-day dogs. These were crosses of small English Greyhounds and various terriers, both smooth and rough-coated. It was not until a much later date that fanciers added an infusion of Italian Greyhound blood which aided so materially in improving type.

At first the breed was known as "snap-dog," and the so-called sport was termed "snap-dog coursing." This was because the dog that caught or snapped-up the greatest number of rabbits during a match was declared winner. It will be noted that this ignoble pastime, in which the rabbit had absolutely no chance of escape, differed greatly from legitimate coursing in the open with Greyhounds and was purely a gambling proposition. Later the Whippet was used primarily for straight racing. This sport had its inception, and still flourishes for that matter, in Lancashire and Yorkshire. Here the colliers nicknamed the Whippet, "the poor man's race horse."

The standard course is 200 yards straightaway, and the method of racing unique. Each dog has two attendants—a slipper and a handler. All dogs are held on their handicap marks by their slippers while their handlers trot up the track and across the finish line, all the while yelling encouragement and frantically waving towels or rags (which the Whippets are trained from puppyhood to run to) to their charges. At the "Get set!" command of the starter, each slipper picks his dog up by the tail and the skin of the neck and when the pistol cracks the animals are literally thrown into their stride. They then race at top speed up the track and grab the waving rags of their handlers, who are some twenty yards behind the actual finish. Different-colored wool collars are worn to distinguish the entries.

As Whippets vary in weight, from 10 to 28 pounds, a rather elaborate system of handicapping was evolved. This is based upon the fact that the heavier the dog, everything else being equal, the faster he should be. Times as fast as eleven and one-half seconds have been recorded, but any dog that can do twelve flat from his handicap mark is considered excellent. Generally speaking, bitches are slightly faster and are usually handicapped accordingly.

Whippets appear first to have been brought to America by English mill operatives of Massachusetts. Lawrence and Lowell, for many years, were the center of Whippet racing in this country. Later, however, the sport moved South when Maryland, particularly in the neighborhood of Baltimore, held the spotlight. Many refinements have been made that have improved racing immensely. Electric starting boxes are used, steeplechases have been inaugurated, and the entire establishments patterned after the best of horse tracks.

From the standpoint of the fancier, Whippets make an ideal exhibition dog. With their small size (around 20 pounds) and smooth coat they are neither difficult to transport nor keep in condition. Their quiet deportment in the ring makes them comparatively easy to show, as is attested by the winnings of numerous novices who handle their own entries.

# Official Standard for the Whippet

**General Appearance**—A medium size sighthound giving the appearance of elegance and fitness, denoting great speed, power and balance without coarseness. A true sporting hound that covers a maximum of distance with a minimum of lost motion. Should convey an impression of beautifully balanced muscular power and strength, combined with great elegance and grace of outline. Symmetry of outline, muscular development and powerful gait are the main considerations; the dog being built for speed and work, all forms of exaggeration should be avoided.

**Size, Proportion, Substance**—Ideal height for dogs, 19 to 22 inches; for bitches, 18 to 21 inches, measured at the highest point of the withers. One-half inch above or below the stated limits will disqualify. Length from forechest to buttocks equal to or slightly greater than height at the withers. Moderate bone throughout.

**Head**—Keen intelligent alert expression. *Eyes* large and dark. Both eyes must be of the same color. Yellow or light eyes should be strictly penalized. Blue or wall eyes shall disqualify. Fully pigmented eyelids are desirable. Rose *ears*, small, fine in texture; in repose, thrown back and folded along neck. Fold should be maintained when at attention. Erect ears should be severely penalized. *Skull* long and lean, fairly wide between the ears, scarcely perceptible stop. *Muzzle* should be long and powerful, denoting great strength of bite, without coarseness. Lack of underjaw should be strictly penalized. *Nose* entirely black. *Teeth* of upper jaw should fit closely over teeth of lower jaw creating a scissors bite. Teeth should be white and strong. Undershot shall disqualify. Overshot one-quarter inch or more shall disqualify.

**Neck, Topline, Body**—Neck long, clean and muscular, well arched with no suggestion of throatiness, widening gracefully into the top of the shoulder. A short thick neck, or a ewe neck, should be penalized. The *back* is broad, firm and well muscled, having length over the loin. The backline runs smoothly from the withers with a graceful natural arch, not too accentuated, beginning over the loin and carrying through over the croup; the arch is continuous without flatness. A dip behind shoulder blades, wheelback, flat back, or a steep or flat croup should be penalized. *Brisket* very deep, reaching as nearly as possible to the point of the elbow. *Ribs* well sprung but with no suggestion of barrel shape. The space between the forelegs is filled in so that there is no appearance of a hollow between them. There is a definite tucking of the underline. The *tail* long and tapering, reaching to the hipbone when drawn through between the hind legs. When the dog is in motion, the tail is carried low with only a gentle upward curve; tail should not be carried higher than top of back.

**Forequarters**—*Shoulder blade* long, well laid back, with flat muscles, allowing for moderate space between shoulder blades at peak of withers. Upper arm of equal length, placed so that the elbow falls directly under the withers. The points of the elbows should point neither in nor out, but straight back. A steep shoulder, short upper arm, a heavily muscled or loaded shoulder, or a very narrow shoulder, all of which restrict low free movement, should be strictly penalized. *Forelegs* straight, giving appearance of strength and substance of bone. Pasterns strong, slightly bent and flexible. Bowed legs, tied-in elbows, legs lacking substance, legs set far under the body so as to create an exaggerated forechest, weak or upright pasterns should be strictly penalized. Both front and rear feet must be well formed with hard, thick pads. Feet more hare than cat, but both are acceptable. Flat, splayed or soft feet without thick hard pads should be strictly penalized. Toes should be long, close and well arched. Nails strong and naturally short or of moderate length. Dewclaws may be removed.

**Hindquarters**—Long and powerful. The thighs are broad and muscular, stifles well bent; muscles are long and flat and carry well down toward the hock. The hocks are well let down and close to the ground. Sickle or cow hocks should be strictly penalized.

**Coat**—Short, close, smooth and firm in texture. Any other coat shall be a disqualification. Old scars and injuries, the result of work or accident, should not be allowed to prejudice the dog's chance in the show ring.

**Color**—Color immaterial.

**Gait**—Low, free moving and smooth, with reach in the forequarters and strong drive in the hindquarters. The dog has great freedom of action when viewed from the side; the forelegs move forward close to the ground to give a long low reach; the hind legs have strong propelling power. When moving and viewed from front or rear, legs should turn neither in nor out, nor should feet cross or interfere with each other. Lack of front reach or rear drive, or a short, hackney gait with high wrist action, should be strictly penalized. Crossing in front or moving too close should be strictly penalized.

**Temperament**—Amiable, friendly, gentle, but capable of great intensity during sporting pursuits.

### DISQUALIFICATIONS

*One-half inch above or below stated height limits.*
*Blue or wall eyes.*
*Undershot, overshot one-quarter inch or more.*
*Any coat other than short, close, smooth and firm in texture.*

Approved December 11, 1989

# WORKING DOGS

## Akita

### (A-keé-ta)

The Akita is one of seven breeds designated as a national monument in his native country of Japan. Bred as a versatile hunting dog in the rugged mountains of Northern Japan, the breed is a wonderful combination of dignity with good nature, alert courage and docility.

There is a spiritual significance attached to the Akita. In Japan they are affectionately regarded as loyal companions and pets, protectors of the home and a symbol of good health. When a child is born, the proud family will usually receive a small statue of an Akita signifying health, happiness and a long life. If a person is ill, friends will send a small statue of an Akita to express their wish for a speedy recovery.

The Akita is very affectionate with family members and friends and thrives

**231**

on human companionship. Since times long past, Japanese mothers have left their children in the trusted care of the family Akita. Typically reserved in demeanor, he will stand to the defense of his family whenever a threatening stranger or animal arouses his protective instinct.

The Akita today is the modern-day, large-sized descendant of the ancient Japanese dog whose likeness has been found carved in the tombs of the early Japanese people. The upright ears and tail curled over the back are unmistakable.

Historical records cite the breed's development early in the 17th century. A famous nobleman was exiled to Akita Prefecture, the northernmost province of the island of Honshu, Japan, and ordered to live out his days as a provincial ruler. The nobleman had an ardent interest in dogs and encouraged the land barons in his domain to compete in the breeding of a large, versatile, intelligent hunting dog. Through generations of selective breeding there evolved the Akita, of superior size and frame, with keen hunting abilities, powerful working attributes and a fearless spirit.

An ancient Japanese word *matagi* means esteemed hunter, an honor applied to the men of a village having the best hunting skills. The northern Akita is a rugged mountainous area with cold snowy winters. There the Akita was known as *Matagiinu*, esteemed dog hunter, and used to hunt bear, deer and wild boar. The Yezo, largest and fiercest of old world bears, was held at bay by a team of Akitas, a male and a female, awaiting the arrival of the hunter with arrow or spear.

The Akita's hunting abilities include great strength, keen eye and nose, silence and speed in a resoundingly durable, sturdy body, suitable for hunting in deep snows. His hard, intelligent, never-give-in attitude in the field was prized by his masters. His soft mouth enabled him to retrieve waterfowl after they had been brought down by the hunter's arrow. The breed is said to have been used to drive fish at sea into the fisherman's nets.

Once ownership was restricted to the Imperial family and the ruling aristocracy. Care and feeding of the Akita were detailed in elaborate ceremony and special leashes were used to denote the Akita's rank and the standing of his owner. A special vocabulary was used to address the Akita and in speaking about them. Each Akita became the charge of a specially appointed caretaker who wore an ornate costume commensurate with the esteem in which the individual Akita was held.

Several times during the next 300 years the breed suffered near extinction, as interest in the continuity of selective breeding surged and waned, depending on the inclination of the current ruling class. Fortunately periodic favor managed to perpetuate the breed through the Meiji and Taisho eras. As the 20th century drew near and Japan was exposed to other societies, being a dog-devotee became very fashionable in emulation of the European culture.

In 1927, the Akitainu Hozankai society of Japan was established to preserve the purity of the breed. In July 1931, the government of Japan designated the Akita breed as a national monument and as one of Japan's national treasures.

So highly regarded is the breed that the Japanese government will subsidize the care and feeding of an Akita champion if the owner is unable to do so.

Each year at a solemn ceremony in Tokyo's Shibuya railroad station hundreds of dog lovers do homage to the loyalty and devotion of an Akita dog, Hachiko, faithful pet of Dr. Eisaburo Ueno, a professor at Tokyo University.

It was the daily habit of Hachiko to accompany his master to the train station to see him off. Every afternoon Hachiko would return to the station to greet his master. On a May evening in 1925, Professor Ueno did not return; he had died that afternoon at the university. Hachiko, the loyal Akita, waited at the station until midnight. The next day and for the next nine years Hachiko returned to the station and waited for his beloved master before walking home, alone. Nothing and no one could discourage Hachiko from maintaining his nightly vigil. It was not until he followed his master in death, in March 1934, that Hachiko failed to appear in his place at the railroad station.

The fidelity of Hachiko was known throughout Japan. Upon his death, newspaper stories led to the suggestion that a statue be erected in the station. Contributions from the United States and other countries were received. Today the statue of the Akita, Hachiko, pays silent tribute to the breed's faithfulness and loyalty.

The renowned Helen Keller is credited with bringing the first Akitas into the United States. While visiting the Prefecture of Akita in June 1937, she was presented with a two month old puppy by the Ministry of Education. Later, after the death of the puppy, the Ministry forwarded a second Akita to Miss Keller.

The breed's popularity in the United States following World War II may be attributed to American servicemen of the occupational forces, who so admired the noble dogs that they took them home to their families. They were attracted to the Akita because of the breed's intelligence and adaptability to different situations.

The Akita Club of America was founded in 1956. The breed was admitted to registration in the American Kennel Club Stud Book in October, 1972, and to regular show classification in the Working Group at AKC shows beginning April 4, 1973.

## Official Standard for the Akita

**General Appearance**—Large, powerful, alert, with much substance and heavy bone. The broad head, forming a blunt triangle, with deep muzzle, small eyes and erect ears carried forward in line with back of neck, is characteristic of the breed. The large, curled tail, balancing the broad head, is also characteristic of the breed.

**Head**—Massive but in balance with body; free of wrinkle when at ease. Skull flat between ears and broad; jaws square and powerful with minimal dewlap. Head forms a blunt triangle when viewed from above. *Fault*—Narrow or snipy head. **Muzzle**—Broad and full. Distance from nose to stop is to distance from stop to occiput as 2 is to 3. **Stop**—Well defined, but not too abrupt. A shallow furrow extends well up forehead. **Nose**—Broad and black. Liver permitted on white Akitas, but black always preferred. *Disqualification*—Butterfly nose or total lack of pigmentation on nose. **Ears**—The ears of the Akita are characteristic of the breed. They are strongly erect and small in relation to rest of head. If ear is folded forward for measuring length, tip will touch upper eye rim. Ears are triangular, slightly rounded at tip, wide at base, set wide on head but not too low, and carried slightly forward over eyes in line with back of neck. *Disqualification*— Drop or broken ears. **Eyes**—Dark brown, small, deep-set and triangular in shape. Eye rims black and tight. **Lips and Tongue**—Lips black and not pendulous; tongue pink. **Teeth**—Strong with scissors bite preferred, but level bite acceptable. *Disqualification*— Noticeably undershot or overshot.

**Neck and Body**—*Neck*—Thick and muscular; comparatively short, widening gradually toward shoulders. A pronounced crest blends in with base of skull. **Body**—Longer than high, as 10 is to 9 in males; 11 to 9 in bitches. Chest wide and deep; depth of chest is one-half height of dog at shoulder. Ribs well sprung, brisket well developed. Level back with firmly-muscled loin and moderate tuck-up. Skin pliant but not loose. *Serious Faults*—Light bone, rangy body.

**Tail**—Large and full, set high and carried over back or against flank in a three-quarter, full, or double curl, always dipping to or below level of back. On a three-quarter curl, tip drops well down flank. Root large and strong. Tail bone reaches hock when let down. Hair coarse, straight and full, with no appearance of a plume. *Disqualification*—Sickle or uncurled tail.

**Forequarters and Hindquarters**—*Forequarters*—Shoulders strong and powerful with moderate layback. Forelegs heavy-boned and straight as viewed from front. Angle of pastern 15 degrees forward from vertical. *Faults*—Elbows in or out, loose shoulders. **Hindquarters**—Width, muscular development and bone comparable to forequarters. Upper thighs well developed. Stifle moderately bent and hocks well let down, turning neither in nor out. **Dewclaws**—On front legs generally not removed; dewclaws on hind legs generally removed. **Feet**—Cat feet, well knuckled up with thick pads. Feet straight ahead.

**Coat**—Double-coated. Undercoat thick, soft, dense and shorter than outer coat. Outer coat straight, harsh and standing somewhat off body. Hair on head, legs and ears short. Length of hair at withers and rump approximately two inches, which is slightly longer than on rest of body, except tail, where coat is longest and most profuse. *Fault*—Any indication of ruff or feathering.

**Color**—Any color including white; brindle; or pinto. Colors are brilliant and clear and markings are well balanced, with or without mask or blaze. White Akitas have no mask. Pinto has a white background with large, evenly placed patches covering head and more than one-third of body. Undercoat may be a different color from outer coat.

**Gait**—Brisk and powerful with strides of moderate length. Back remains strong, firm and level. Rear legs move in line with front legs.

**Size**—Males 26 to 28 inches at the withers; bitches 24 to 26 inches. *Disqualification*— Dogs under 25 inches; bitches under 23 inches.

**Temperament**—Alert and responsive, dignified and courageous. Aggressive toward other dogs.

### DISQUALIFICATIONS

*Butterfly nose or total lack of pigmentation on nose.*
*Drop or broken ears.*
*Noticeably undershot or overshot.*
*Sickle or uncurled tail.*
*Dogs under 25 inches; bitches under 23 inches.*

Approved December 12, 1972

# Alaskan Malamute

## (Mahla-myoot)

The Alaskan Malamute, one of the oldest Arctic sled dogs, was named after the native Innuit tribe called Mahlemuts, who settled along the shores of Kotzebue Sound in the upper western part of Alaska. Long before Alaska became a possession of the United States, this Arctic region was called "Alashak" or "Alyeska," (meaning "vast country") by the Russians, who were its discoverers. Native people were already living in Alyeska land when these Asiatic sailors visited the shores, having been forced by storms when whaling in Bering Strait to land in this North country opposite Siberia. Returned to their homeland, they told stories about seeing "native people using dogs to haul sledges."

The origin of these people and of the dogs has never been ascertained. We do know that they had been in Alaska for generations, but where they came from is as indefinite as it is with any of the other Arctic natives.

Well-informed Arctic writers who have made a study of Arctic formations seem to disagree about the origin of the Arctic peoples. Some believe that during the Glacier Age there was land connecting Asia and Alaska, and also Greenland and Labrador. Perhaps our Alaskan natives and Labrador Eskimos came into these countries by dog power. Others claim immigration spread from the Hudson Bay country, east and west; others that Greenland was originated by Norwegians who went "native" and likewise, Alaska by Asiatic people. This happened many generations ago—all we know today is that Arctic breeds were found and that the Alaskan Arctic sledge dog native to that country is the breed now called the Malamute.

The tribe of Mahlemuts, now spelled Malamutes, were called "high-type" Innuits. Translations from Russian explorers and records left by Englishmen who traveled the Alaskan coast, give agreeing accounts of these fine Innuits. *Innuit* means "people" in the Orarian language. Never are the Mahlemuts mentioned without reference to their dogs. One writer, who went to Alaska in the early days of exploration after it had become a possession of the United States, reported:

> Upon arriving at Unalakleet, I found that a party of Mahlemuts had arrived the day before by dog teams. They had carried mail from Point Barrow down along the coast wherever White Men were living. They had also been runners for the Russian Muscovy Whaling Company when they had landed in this Arctic region. These Mahlemuts were wonderful looking natives . . . taller than their Greenland cousins. They were industrious, skilled in hunting and fishing, made perfect sledges, and had dogs of . . . beauty and endurance. These dogs had traveled . . . hundreds of miles and being better cared for by their drivers than is the usual lot of Arctic dogs . . . [they] were affectionate and seemed tireless . . .

This description differs from tales told by people who have seen other native dogs in the Arctic, whose dispositions perhaps resulted from the environment in which they lived. The usual treatment of sledge dogs in the North has been harsh, owing to the uncivilized tribes who wandered from place to place until white men invaded their villages.

Another Alaskan traveler, a missionary who journeyed thousands of miles by dog team, writes:

> These Malamutes, now spelled *Malamute,* a corruption of the original word Mahlemut (Mahle meaning name of the Innuit tribe and Mut meaning Village in Orarian vocabulary of the Mahlemut dialect), are a high type people. They are peaceful, happy, hard workers, believe in one wife, are able guides and have wonderful dogs. Even though uncivilized, they have realized that it is important to have fine animals to pull sledges; that without them, means of travel in this sort of country would be impossible at times. The dogs are powerful looking, have thick dense double coats (outer coat of thick coarse fur and inner coat of fuzzy down lying close to skin) called weather coats, erect ears, magnificently bushy tails carried over their backs like waving plumes, tough feet, colors varying but mostly wolf grey or black and white. The dogs have remarkable endurance and fortitude. The Malamute people and their dogs are much respected among other Innuits.

A Russian translation gives another reference about the "Mahlemuts found over the sea in the Vast Land" called the "stopping-off" place by the Russian sailors. This writer referred to the workmanship of the Mahlemuts and the sledges, and admitted the "Mahlemut dogs and sledges are better than those of the Russians for interior travel."

It is confirmed that these Alaskan Malamute sledge dogs were used as draught animals and they have never lost their identity. When Alaska became settled by white men, it is true that the Arctic breed was mingled with that of outside dogs, just as they had been in Greenland, Labrador, Siberia, and the other Arctic countries. During the Alaskan Sweepstakes, the lure of racing became so popular that many drivers tried all sorts of experiments in mixing the Arctic breed with some outside strain, and this period from 1909 to 1918 was the age of "decay of the Arctic sledge dog." Fortunately, the sport of sled-dog racing became popular in the United States, and interest in developing the pure strain of the native Alaskan Malamute started in 1926 after a careful study of all types of Northern breeds had been made. Malamutes still hold many racing records.

The Alaskan Malamute is the native Alaskan Arctic breed, cousin to the Samoyed of Russia, Siberian Husky (Kolyma River Region), and the Eskimo dogs of Greenland and Labrador.

The Alaskan Malamute was recognized for AKC registration in 1935. As pets they have become popular sled dogs among sportspeople who enjoy this winter recreation. They are very fond of people and especially children, who enjoy driving them to sleds.

## Official Standard for the Alaskan Malamute

**General Appearance and Characteristics**—The Alaskan Malamute is a powerful and substantially built dog with a deep chest and strong, compact body, not too short coupled, with a thick, coarse guard coat of sufficient length to protect a dense, woolly undercoat, from 1 to 2 inches in depth when dog is in full coat. Stands well over pads, and this stance gives the appearance of much activity, showing interest and curiosity. The head is broad, ears wedge-shaped and erect when alerted. The muzzle is bulky with only slight diminishing in width and depth from root to nose, not pointed or long, but not stubby. The Malamute moves with a proud carriage, head erect and eyes alert. Face markings are a distinguishing feature. These consist of either cap over head and rest of face solid color, usually grayish white, or face marked with the appearance of a mask. Combinations of cap and mask are not unusual. The tail is plumed and carried over the back, not like a fox brush, or tightly curled, more like a plume waving.

Malamutes are of various colors, but are usually wolfish gray or black and white. Their feet are of the "snowshoe" type, tight and deep, with well-cushioned pads, giving a firm and compact appearance. Front legs are straight with big bone. Hind legs are broad and powerful, moderately bent at stifles, and without cowhocks. The back is straight, gently sloping from shoulders to hips. The loin should not be so short or tight as to interfere with easy, tireless movement. Endurance and intelligence are shown in body and expression. The eyes have a "wolf-like" appearance by their position, but the expression is soft and indicates an affectionate disposition.

**Temperament**—The Alaskan Malamute is an affectionate, friendly dog, not a "one-man" dog. He is a loyal, devoted companion, playful on invitation, but generally impressive by his dignity after maturity.

**Head**—The head should indicate a high degree of intelligence, and is broad and powerful as compared with other "natural" breeds, but should be in proportion to the size of the dog so as not to make the dog appear clumsy or coarse. **Skull**—The skull should be broad between the ears, gradually narrowing to eyes, moderately rounded between ears, flattening on top as it approaches the eyes, rounding off to cheeks, which should be moderately flat. There should be a slight furrow between the eyes, the topline of skull and topline of the muzzle showing but little break downward from a straight line as they join. **Muzzle**—The muzzle should be large and bulky in proportion to size of skull, diminishing but little in width and depth from junction with skull to nose; lips close fitting; nose black; upper and lower jaws broad with large teeth, front teeth meeting with a scissors grip but never overshot or undershot. **Eyes**—Brown, almond shaped, moderately large for this shape of eye, set obliquely in skull. Dark eyes preferred. Blue eyes are a disqualifying fault. **Ears**—The ears should be of medium size, but small in proportion to head. The upper halves of the ears are triangular in shape, slightly rounded at tips, set wide apart on outside back edges of the skull with the lower part of the ear joining the skull on a line with the upper corner of the eye, giving the tips of the ears the appearance, when erect, of standing off from the skull. When erect, the ears point slightly forward, but when the dog is at work the ears are sometimes folded against the skull. High-set ears are a fault.

**Neck**—The neck should be strong and moderately arched.

**Body**—The chest should be strong and deep; body should be strong and compactly built but not short coupled. The back should be straight and gently sloping to the hips. The loins should be well muscled and not so short as to interfere with easy, rhythmic movement with powerful drive from the hindquarters. A long loin which weakens the back is also a fault. No excess weight.

**Shoulders, Legs and Feet**—Shoulders should be moderately sloping; forelegs heavily boned and muscled, straight to pasterns, which should be short and strong and almost vertical as viewed from the side. The feet should be large and compact, toes, tight-fitting and well-arched, pads thick and tough, toenails short and strong. There should be a protective growth of hair between toes. Hind legs must be broad and powerfully muscled through thighs; stifles moderately bent, hock joints broad and strong, moderately bent and well let down. As viewed from behind, the hind legs should not appear bowed in bone, but stand and move true in line with movement of the front legs, and not too close or too wide. The legs of the Malamute must indicate unusual strength and tremendous propelling power. Any indication of unsoundness in legs or feet, standing or moving, is to be considered a serious fault. Dewclaws on the hind legs are undesirable and should be removed shortly after pups are whelped.

**Tail**—Moderately set and following the line of the spine at the start, well furred and carried over the back when not working—not tightly curled to rest on back—or short furred and carried like a fox brush, a waving plume appearance instead.

**Coat**—The Malamute should have a thick, coarse guard coat, not long and soft. The undercoat is dense, from 1 to 2 inches in depth, oily and woolly. The coarse guard coat stands out, and there is thick fur around the neck. The guard coat varies in length, as does the undercoat; however, in general, the coat is moderately short to medium along the sides of the body with the length of the coat increasing somewhat around the shoulders and neck, down the back and over the rump, as well as in the breeching and plume. Malamutes usually have shorter and less dense coats when shed out during the summer months.

**Color and Markings**—The usual colors range from light gray through the intermediate shadings to black, always with white on underbodies, parts of legs, feet, and part of mask markings. Markings should be either caplike and/or mask-like on face. A white blaze on forehead and/or collar or spot on nape is attractive and acceptable, but broken color extending over the body in spots or uneven splashings is undesirable. One should distinguish between mantled dogs and splash-coated dogs. The only solid color allowable is the all-white.

**Size**—There is a natural range in size in the breed. The desirable freighting sizes are: **Males**—25 inches at the shoulders—85 pounds. **Females**—23 inches at the shoulders—75 pounds.

However, size consideration should not outweigh that of type, proportion, and functional attributes, such as shoulders, chest, legs, feet, and movement. When dogs are judged equal in type, proportion, and functional attributes, the dog nearest the desirable freighting size is to be preferred.

*Important*—In judging Malamutes their function as a sledge dog for heavy freighting must be given consideration above all else. The judge must bear in mind that this breed is designed primarily as the working sledge dog of the North for hauling heavy freight, and therefore he should be a heavy-boned, powerfully built, compact dog with sound legs, good feet, deep chest, powerful shoulders, steady, balanced, tireless gait, and the other physical equipment necessary for the efficient performance of his job. He isn't intended as a racing sled dog designed to compete in speed trials with the smaller Northern breeds.

The Malamute as a sledge dog for heavy freighting is designed for strength and endurance and any characteristic of the individual specimen, including temperament, which interferes with the accomplishment of this purpose is to be considered the most serious of faults. Faults under this provision would be splayfootedness, any indication of unsoundness or weakness in legs, cowhocks, bad pasterns, straight shoulders, lack of angulation, stilted gait or any gait which isn't balanced, strong, and steady, ranginess, shallowness, ponderousness, lightness of bone, poor over-all proportion, and similar characteristics.

### SCALE OF POINTS

| | | | | |
|---|---|---|---|---|
| General Appearance | 20 | | Feet | 10 |
| Head | 15 | | Coat and Color | 10 |
| Body | 20 | | Tail | 5 |
| Legs and Movement | 20 | | TOTAL | 100 |

### DISQUALIFICATION

*Blue eyes.*

Approved August 10, 1982

# Bernese Mountain Dog

Aristocratic in appearance, ancient in lineage, the Bernese Mountain Dog has long been at home on the farms in the middle land of Switzerland. One of the four varieties of Swiss Mountain Dogs, the Bernese—known in his native land as the Berner Sennenhund—shares similar distinctive coloring with the other varieties, but is the only one of the four to have a long, silky coat. The other three are the Appenzeller Sennenhund, the Entlebucher Sennenhund, and the Greater Swiss Mountain Dog. These dogs worked as drovers and draft dogs as well as watch dogs in the farmyards mainly in the Canton of Berne.

The ancestors of these dogs were brought into Switzerland over two thousand years ago by the invading Roman soldiers. But until a few years before World War I, they had been almost forgotten by all save the oldest inhabitants of Berne. They were still found in the area of Duerrbach, but the breed had degenerated to such an extent as to be practically unrecognizable. When in 1982 the Swiss fancier Franz Schertenleib attempted to find good specimens to be used as breeding stock, his search was a long one. However, he was successful, and several other fanciers became interested as well. The rehabilitation was started, and succeeded under the knowledgeable leadership of the great geologist, canine researcher and judge, Professor Albert Heim. In 1907, a specialty club was formed and the breed found favor with many Swiss, who developed them as house pets and companions, although their old role on farms still continued.

A handsome, long haired, sturdily built dog, the Bernese is jet black in color, with rich russet markings on his legs, cheeks, spots over each eye, and on either side of the snowy white chest markings. A white blaze adorns its muzzle and forehead, and it is highly desirable that the dogs have white feet, white tail tip and that the white chest marking forms a Swiss cross. The coat is thick and moderately long with a slight wave. His broad and firm back, deep chest, well-sprung ribs and strong loins show that he is well suited to hard work.

The Bernese is an extremely hardy dog, thriving in cold weather. He needs only a small amount of daily grooming to look well kept. For his emotional development and well being he needs human companionship, and he is a willing and quick learner. He is self-confident and exceptionally faithful.

First brought to the United States in 1926, the breed acquired AKC recognition in 1937.

## Official Standard for the Bernese Mountain Dog

**General Appearance**—The Bernese Mountain Dog is a striking, tri-colored, large dog. He is sturdy and balanced. He is intelligent, strong and agile enough to do the draft and droving work for which he was used in the mountainous regions of his origin. Dogs appear masculine, while bitches are distinctly feminine.

**Size, Proportion, Substance**—Measured at the withers, dogs are 25 to 27½ inches; bitches are 23 to 26 inches. Though appearing square, Bernese Mountain Dogs are slightly longer in body than they are tall. Sturdy bone is of great importance. The body is full.

**Head**—*Expression* is intelligent, animated, and gentle. The *eyes* are dark brown and slightly oval in shape with close-fitting eyelids. Inverted or everted eyelids are serious faults. Blue eye color is a disqualification. The *ears* are medium sized, set high, triangular in shape, gently rounded at the tip, and hang close to the head when in repose. When the Bernese Mountain Dog is alert, the ears are brought forward and raised at the base; the top of the ear is level with the top of the skull. The *skull* is flat on top and broad, with a slight furrow and a well-defined, but not exaggerated stop. The *muzzle* is strong and straight. The *nose* is always black. The *lips* are clean and, as the Bernese Mountain Dog is a dry-mouthed breed, the flews are only slightly developed. The *teeth* meet in a scissors bite. An overshot or undershot bite is a serious fault. Dentition is complete.

**Neck, Topline, Body**—The *neck* is strong, muscular and of medium length. The *topline* is level from the withers to the croup. The *chest* is deep and capacious with well-sprung, but not barrel-shaped, ribs and brisket reaching at least to the elbows. The back is broad and firm. The *loin* is strong. The *croup* is broad and smoothly rounded to the tail insertion. The *tail* is bushy. It should be carried low when in repose. An upward swirl is permissible when the dog is alert, but the tail may never curl or be carried over the back. The bones in the tail should feel straight and should reach to the hock joint or below. A kink in the tail is a fault.

**Forequarters**—The shoulders are moderately laid back, flat-lying, well-muscled and never loose. The *legs* are straight and strong and the *elbows* are well under the shoulder when the dog is standing. The *pasterns* slope very slightly, but are never weak. *Dewclaws* may be removed. The *feet* are round and compact with well-arched toes.

**Hindquarters**—The *thighs* are broad, strong and muscular. The *stifles* are moderately bent and taper smoothly into the hocks. The *hocks* are well let down and straight as viewed from the rear. *Dewclaws* should be removed. *Feet* are compact and turned neither in nor out.

**Coat**—The *coat* is thick, moderately long and slightly wavy or straight. It has a bright natural sheen. Extremely curly or extremely dull-looking coats are undesirable. The Bernese Mountain Dog is shown in natural coat and undue trimming is to be discouraged.

**Color and Markings**—The Bernese Mountain Dog is tri-colored. The ground color is jet black. The markings are rich rust and clear white. Symmetry of markings is desired. Rust appears over each eye, on the cheeks reaching to at least the corner of the mouth, on each side of the chest, on all four legs, and under the tail. There is a white blaze and muzzle band. A white marking on the chest typically forms an inverted cross. The tip of the tail is white. White on the feet is desired but must not extend higher than the pasterns. Markings other than described are to be faulted in direct relationship to the extent of the deviation. White legs or a white color are serious faults. Any ground color other than black is a disqualification.

**Gait**—The natural working gait of the Bernese Mountain Dog is a slow trot. However, in keeping with his use in draft and droving work, he is capable of speed and agility. There is good reach in front. Powerful drive from the rear is transmitted through a level back. There is no wasted action. Front and rear legs on each side follow through in the same plane. At increased speed, legs tend to converge toward the center line.

**Temperament**—The *temperament* is self-confident, alert and good-natured, never sharp or shy. The Bernese Mountain Dog should stand steady, though may remain aloof to the attentions of strangers.

### DISQUALIFICATIONS

*Blue eye color.*
*Any ground color other than black.*

Approved February 10, 1990

# Boxer

Although it has reached its greatest perfection in Germany during the past hundred years, the Boxer springs from a line of dogs known throughout the whole of Europe since the 16th century. Prior to that time, ancestors of the breed would hardly be recognized as Boxers could they be placed beside modern specimens. Still, evidence points to the Boxer as one of the many descendants of the old fighting dog of the high valleys of Tibet.

The Boxer is cousin to practically all recognized breeds of the Bulldog type, and these all go back to basic Molossus blood. Few other strains can claim such courage and stamina; and from this line emanates the attractive fawn color that has recurred throughout the centuries.

Flemish tapestries of the 16th and 17th centuries show scenes of stag and boar hunting; the dogs are the same as the Spanish Alano, found in great numbers in Andalusia and Estramadura, and the Matin de Terceira or Perro do Presa, from the Azores. The Alano and the Matin have been regarded as the same breed—they are either ancestors of the Boxer or they trace back to a common ancestor.

In France, there is a breed known as the Dogue de Bordeaux that is very close, both in appearance and size to the old Tibetan Mastiff, and it is from this massive dog that the Bouldogue de Mida was developed. The Bouldogue du Mida, found principally in the south of France, possesses many of the points of the Boxer.

While all the European breeds mentioned are related to the Boxer, this favorite of Germany has been developed along scientific lines that not only have succeeded in retaining all his old qualities, but have resulted in a much more attractive appearance. Besides Bulldog blood, the Boxer carries a certain heritage from a terrier strain. There is also some reason to believe that English Bulldogs were at one time imported into Germany. Indeed, Reinagle's noted Bulldog, done in 1803, is not unlike the Boxer, and pictures of some English specimens of 1850 are almost identical with the German dog.

Until dogfighting and bullbaiting were outlawed by most civilized peoples in the middle of the 19th century, the Boxer, like all dogs of his type, was used for this purpose. Today he has become an accredited member of society, but he still has the same degree of courage and the ability to defend, as well as aggressiveness when needed. Withal, he is devoted to his master.

The quality of the Boxer is best emphasized, perhaps, when we remember that he was one of the first selected in Germany for police training. This work demands intelligence, fearlessness, agility, and strength.

Considering that the entire modern history of the Boxer is wrapped up with Germany, it seems rather curious that he bears a name obviously English. Yet the name fits him. It arises from his manner of fighting, for invariably he begins a fight with his front paws, somewhat like a man boxing.

The first AKC registration of a Boxer was in 1904, and the first championship was finished in 1915, but it was not until about 1940 that the United States public began to take a real interest in the breed. This came about because of the consistent Group and Best in Show wins scored by some outstanding Boxers.

## Official Standard for the Boxer

**General Appearance—**The *ideal* Boxer is a medium-sized, square built dog of good substance with short back, strong limbs, and short, tight-fitting coat. His well developed muscles are clean, hard and appear smooth under taut skin. His movements denote energy. The gait is firm, yet elastic, the stride free and ground-covering, the carriage proud. Developed to serve as guard, working and companion dog, he combines strength and agility with elegance and style. His expression is alert and temperament steadfast and tractable.

The chiseled head imparts to the Boxer a unique individual stamp. It must be in correct proportion to the body. The broad, blunt muzzle is the distinctive feature, and great value is placed upon its being of proper form and balance with the skull.

In judging the Boxer, first consideration is given to general appearance to which attractive color and arresting style contribute. Next is overall balance with special attention devoted to the head, after which the individual body components are examined for their correct construction, and efficiency of gait is evaluated.

**Size, Proportion, Substance**—*Height*—Adult males 22½ to 25 inches; females 21 to 23½ inches at the withers. Preferably, males should not be under the minimum nor females over the maximum; however, proper balance and quality in the individual should be of primary importance since there is no size disqualification. *Proportion*—The body in profile is of square proportion in that a horizontal line from the front of the forechest to the rear projection of the upper thigh should equal the length of a vertical line dropped from the top of the withers to the ground. *Substance*—Sturdy with balanced musculature. Males larger boned than their female counterparts.

**Head**—The beauty of the head depends upon harmonious proportion of muzzle to skull. The blunt muzzle is ⅓rd the length of the head from the occiput to the tip of the nose, and ⅔rds the width of the skull. The head should be clean, not showing deep wrinkles (wet). Wrinkles typically appear upon the forehead when ears are erect, and folds are always present from the lower edge of the stop running downward on both sides of the muzzle. *Expression*—Intelligent and alert. *Eyes*—Dark brown in color, not too small, too protruding or too deep-set. Their mood-mirroring character combined with the wrinkling of the forehead, gives the Boxer head its unique quality of expressiveness. *Ears*—Set at the highest points of the sides of the skull are cropped, cut rather long and tapering, raised when alert. *Skull*—The top of the skull is slightly arched, not rounded, flat nor noticeably broad, with the occiput not overly pronounced. The forehead shows a slight indentation between the eyes and forms a distinct stop with the topline of the muzzle. The cheeks should be relatively flat and not bulge (cheekiness), maintaining the clean lines of the skull, and should taper into the muzzle in a slight, graceful curve. *Muzzle*—The muzzle, proportionately developed in length, width and depth, has a shape influenced first through the formation of both jawbones, second through the placement of the teeth, and third through the texture of the lips. The top of the muzzle should not slant down (downfaced), nor should it be concave (dishfaced); however, the tip of the nose should lie slightly higher than the root of the muzzle.

The nose should be broad and black.

The upper jaw is broad where attached to the skull and maintains this breadth except for a very slight tapering to the front. The lips, which complete the formation of the muzzle, should meet evenly in front. The upper lip is thick and padded, filling out the frontal space created by the projection of the lower jaw, and laterally is supported by the canines of the lower jaw. Therefore, these canines must stand far apart and be of good length so that the front surface of the muzzle is broad and squarish and, when viewed from the side, shows moderate layback. The chin should be perceptible from the side as well as from the front. *Bite*—The Boxer bite is undershot; the lower jaw protrudes beyond the upper and curves slightly upward. The incisor teeth of the lower jaw are in a straight line, with the canines preferably up front in the same line to give the jaw the greatest possible width. The upper line of incisors is slightly convex with the corner upper incisors fitting snugly back of the lower canine teeth on each side. *Faults*—Skull too broad. Cheekiness. Wrinkling too deep (wet) or lacking (dry). Excessive flews. Muzzle too light for skull. Too pointed a bite (snipy), too undershot, teeth or tongue showing when mouth closed. Eyes noticeably lighter than ground color of coat.

**Neck, Topline, Body**—*Neck*—Round, of ample length, muscular and clean without excessive hanging skin (dewlap). The neck has a distinctly marked nape with an elegant arch blending smoothly into the withers. *Topline*—Smooth, firm and slightly sloping.

*Body*—The chest is of fair width, and the forechest well defined and visible from the side. The brisket is deep, reaching down to the elbows; the depth of the body at the lowest point of the brisket equals half the height of the dog at the withers. The ribs, extending far to the rear, are well arched but not barrel shaped. The back is short, straight and muscular and firmly connects the withers to the hindquarters. The loins are short and muscular. The lower stomach line is slightly tucked up, blending into a graceful curve to the rear. The croup is slightly sloped, flat and broad. Tail is set high, docked and carried upward. Pelvis long and in females especially broad. *Faults*—Short heavy neck. Chest too broad, too narrow or hanging between shoulders. Lack of forechest. Hanging stomach. Slab-sided rib cage. Long or narrow loin, weak union with croup. Falling off of croup. Higher in rear than in front.

*Forequarters*—The shoulders are long and sloping, close-lying, and not excessively covered with muscle (loaded). The upper arm is long, approaching a right angle to the shoulder blade. The elbows should not press too closely to the chest wall nor stand off visibly from it. The forelegs are long, straight and firmly muscled and when viewed from the front, stand parallel to each other. The pastern is strong and distinct, slightly slanting, but standing almost perpendicular to the ground. The dewclaws may be removed. Feet should be compact, turning neither in nor out, with well arched toes. *Faults*—Loose or loaded shoulders. Tied in or bowed out elbows.

*Hindquarters*—The hindquarters are strongly muscled with angulation in balance with that of the forequarters. The thighs are broad and curved, the breech musculature hard and strongly developed. Upper and lower thigh long. Leg well angulated at the stifle with a clearly defined, well "let down" hock joint. Viewed from behind, the hind legs should be straight with hock joints leaning neither in nor out. From the side, the leg below the hock (metatarsus) should be almost perpendicular to the ground, with a slight slope to the rear permissible. The metatarsus should be short, clean and strong. The Boxer has no rear dewclaws. *Faults*—Steep or over-angulated hindquarters. Light thighs or overdeveloped hams. Over-angulated (sickle) hocks. Hindquarters too far under or too far behind.

*Coat*—Short, shiny, lying smooth and tight to the body.

*Color*—The colors are fawn and brindle. Fawn shades vary from light tan to mahogany. The brindle ranges from sparse, but clearly defined black stripes on a fawn background, to such a heavy concentration of black striping that the essential fawn background color barely, although clearly, shows through (which may create the appearance of "reverse brindling"). White markings should be of such distribution as to enhance the dog's appearance, but may not exceed one-third of the entire coat. They are not desirable on the flanks or on the back of the torso proper. On the face, white may replace part of the otherwise essential black mask and may extend in an upward path between the eyes, but it must not be excessive, so as to detract from true Boxer expression. *Faults*—Unattractive or misplaced white markings. *Disqualifications*—Boxers that are any color other than fawn or brindle. Boxers with a total of white markings exceeding one-third of the entire coat.

*Gait*—Viewed from the side, proper front and rear angulation is manifested in a smoothly efficient, level-backed, ground covering stride with powerful drive emanating from a freely operating rear. Although the front legs do not contribute impelling power, adequate "reach" should be evident to prevent interference, overlap or "sidewinding" (crabbing). Viewed from the front, the shoulders should remain trim and the elbows not flare out. The legs are parallel until gaiting narrows the track in proportion to increasing speed, then the legs come in under the body but should never cross. The line from the shoulder down through the leg should remain straight although not necessarily perpendicular to the ground. Viewed from the rear, a Boxer's rump should not roll. The hind feet should "dig in" and track relatively true with the front. Again, as speed increases, the normally broad rear track will become narrower. *Faults*— Stilted or inefficient gait. Lack of smoothness.

**Character and Temperament**— These are of paramount importance in the Boxer. Instinctively a "hearing" guard dog, his bearing is alert, dignified and self-assured. In the show ring, his behavior should exhibit constrained animation. With family and friends, his temperament is fundamentally playful, yet patient and stoical with children. Deliberate and wary with strangers, he will exhibit curiosity but, most importantly, fearless courage if threatened. However, he responds promptly to friendly overtures honestly rendered. His intelligence, loyal affection and tractability to discipline make him a highly desirable companion. *Faults*— Lack of dignity and alertness. Shyness.

### DISQUALIFICATIONS

*Boxers that are any color other than fawn or brindle. Boxers with a total of white markings exceeding one-third of the entire coat.*

Approved March 14, 1989

# Bullmastiff

The known history of the Bullmastiff begins about the year 1860 in England. It is probable that the story of the breed is really centuries old, but proof is difficult.

Toward the end of the 19th century in England, the problem of keeping large estates and game preserves free from the depredations of poachers was an acute one. Penalties were severe, yet poaching seemed impossible to eradicate by mere laws. Accordingly, the gamekeeper's life was anything but safe. Poachers would often prefer to shoot it out with the keeper on the chance of escape rather than accept the penalties which they would incur upon apprehension.

It is not surprising, therefore, that the gamekeepers decided to enlist the aid of the greatest protector nature has given to man—the dog. These men cared nothing for the looks of a dog as long as he served them well. Numerous breeds were therefore tried. The Mastiff, while courageous and powerful, was not fast enough and not sufficiently aggressive. The Bulldog, big, strong and active in those days, was a trifle too ferocious and not large enough for their needs. These men wanted dogs that would remain silent at the approach of poachers. They needed fearless dogs that would attack on command. They wanted the poachers thrown and held, but not mauled. For these needs, they crossed Mastiff and Bulldog, and from this utilitarian birth, the Bullmastiff was founded.

Inevitably, came the rivalry between keepers as to the quality of their dogs. Inevitably, also, came the breeding to and from outstanding performers of their time—a true survival of the fittest. For many years, then, after the birth of the breed, its history was wholly a utilitarian one. The only contests in which the Bullmastiffs engaged were against man, either on the moor or in demonstrations. In those days the Bullmastiff was known sometimes by his present name, but more often as the "Gamekeeper's Night-Dog."

During the breed's early years, we find interesting references by contemporary writers. One appears in the book *Dog Breaking*, published in 1885: "Bulldogs have good noses. I have known of the cross between them and the Mastiff being taught to follow the scent of a man almost as truly as a Bloodhound."

In *The Field*, August 20, 1901, we find the following:

> Mr. Burton of Thorneywood Kennels brought to the show one Night-Dog (not for competition) and offered any person one pound who could escape from it while securely muzzled. One of the spectators who had had experience with dogs volunteered and amused a large assembly of sportsmen and keepers who had gathered there. The man was given a long start and the muzzled dog slipped after him. The animal caught him immediately and knocked down this man the first spring. The latter bravely tried to hold his own, but was floored every time he got on his feet, ultimately being kept to the ground until the owner of the dog released him. The man had three rounds with the powerful canine, but was beaten each time and was unable to escape.

For this type of work, dogs of a dark brindle color were preferred owing to their lack of visibility. It was inevitable, however, that as the breed gained in popularity and true Mastiff blood was used, a large number of light fawns should appear. With the gradual disappearance of poaching and the continued demand for Bullmastiffs as guards and watchdogs, this color became popular. The black mask and densely colored ears were often inherited from the Mastiff.

Finally, owing to the increasing popularity of the breed, a number of pioneers started, on a scientific basis, to breed to type in an effort to set a goal which pure-bred dog breeders might seek. This type finally became sufficiently distinct for the English Kennel Club to grant recognition of the Bullmastiff as a pure-bred dog in 1924. At this time the Kennel Club differentiated between the Bullmastiff, crossbred, and the Bullmastiff, pure-bred, the latter being, of necessity, the descendant of three generations of dogs which were neither pure Mastiff nor pure Bulldog. Classes were then provided at a few shows and the dogs were finally awarded Challenge Certificates in 1928. In time the breed became known in many countries, having been exported from England to Siam, India, the Federated Malay States, Africa, and America. The short coat has proved convenient in warm climates, and yet the dog can live in the open in inclement weather.

The American Kennel Club granted recognition to the Bullmastiff in October, 1933 and since that time the breed has made numerous friends in this country.

## Official Standard for the Bullmastiff

**General Appearance**—That of a symmetrical animal, showing great strength, endurance, and alertness; powerfully built but active. The foundation breeding was 60% Mastiff and 40% Bulldog. The breed was developed in England by gamekeepers for protection against poachers.

**Size, Proportion, Substance**—*Size*—Dogs, 25 to 27 inches at the withers, and 110 to 130 pounds weight. Bitches, 24 to 26 inches at the withers, and 100 to 120 pounds weight. Other things being equal, the more substantial dog within these limits is favored. *Proportion*—The length from tip of breastbone to rear of thigh exceeds the height from withers to ground only slightly, resulting in a nearly square appearance.

**Head**—*Expression*—Keen, alert, and intelligent. *Eyes*—Dark and of medium size. *Ears*—V-shaped and carried close to the cheeks, set on wide and high, level with occiput and cheeks, giving a square appearance to the skull; darker in color than the body and medium in size. *Skull*—Large, with a fair amount of wrinkle when alert; broad, with cheeks well developed. Forehead flat. *Stop*—Moderate. *Muzzle*—Broad and deep; its length, in comparison with that of the entire head, approximately as 1 is to 3. Lack of foreface with nostrils set on top of muzzle is a reversion to the Bulldog and is very undesirable. A dark muzzle is preferable. *Nose*—Black, with nostrils large and broad. *Flews*— Not too pendulous. *Bite*—Preferably level or slightly undershot. Canine teeth large and set wide apart.

**Neck, Topline, Body**—*Neck*—Slightly arched, of moderate length, very muscular, and almost equal in circumference to the skull. *Topline*—Straight and level between withers and loin. *Body*—Compact. Chest wide and deep, with ribs well sprung and well set down between the forelegs. *Back*—Short, giving the impression of a well balanced dog. *Loin*—Wide, muscular, and slightly arched, with fair depth of flank. *Tail*—Set on high, strong at the root, and tapering to the hocks. It may be straight or curved, but never carried hound fashion.

**Forequarters**—Shoulders muscular but not loaded, and slightly sloping. Forelegs straight, well boned, and set well apart; elbows turned neither in nor out. Pasterns straight, feet of medium size, with round toes well arched. Pads thick and tough, nails black.

**Hindquarters**—Broad and muscular, with well developed second thigh denoting power, but not cumbersome. Moderate angulation at hocks. Cowhocks and splay feet are serious faults.

**Coat**—Short and dense, giving good weather protection.

**Color**—Red, fawn, or brindle. Except for a very small white spot on the chest, white marking is considered a fault.

**Gait**—Free, smooth, and powerful. When viewed from the side, reach and drive indicate maximum use of the dog's moderate angulation. Back remains level and firm. Coming and Going, the dog moves in a straight line. Feet tend to converge under the body, without crossing over, as speed increases. There is not twisting in or out at the joints.

**Temperament**—Fearless and confident yet docile. The dog combines the reliability, intelligence, and willingness to please required in a dependable family companion and protector.

Approved February 8, 1992

# Doberman Pinscher

With its racial roots somewhat obscure, the Doberman Pinscher became within a comparatively short time a dog of fixed type, whose characteristics of both body and spirit have extended its popularity in many lands. Originating in Apolda, in Thueringen, Germany, around 1890, the breed was officially recognized in 1900. It takes its name from Louis Dobermann of Apolda.

Of medium size and clean-cut appearance, the dog at first glance does not give evidence of its great muscular power. So compact is its structure, so dense the laying on of muscle under the short coat, and so elegant and well chiseled the outline, that the novice would probably underestimate the weight by 15 to 20 pounds. Weight is the only particular, however, in which the Doberman is deceptive. Its qualities of alertness, agility, muscular and temperamental fire stand patent for any eye to see. It is an honest dog, uncamouflaged by superfluous coat or the wiles of the artful conditioner. One gains at once the impression of sinewy nimbleness, of the quick coordination of the well-trained athlete.

There is also an air of nobility about the Doberman Pinscher which is part of its birthright. More than most other breeds, it gives the impression of a blue-blooded animal, or aristocrat. From the strong muzzle and wedge-shaped head to the clearly defined stifle, the outline is definite and sharply etched. The fearless and inquisitive expression of the dark eye is in harmony with the bodily characteristics. The Doberman looks upon the stranger boldly and judges him with unerring instinct. He is ready, if need be, to give prompt alarm and to back his warning with defense of his master and his master's goods. Yet, he is affectionate, obedient, and loyal.

Traditionally compounded of the old shorthaired shepherd-dog stock, with admixtures of Rottweiler, Black and Tan Terrier, and smooth-haired German Pinscher, the Doberman has been fortunate, with the aid of selective breeding, to have absorbed the good qualities of the breeds which have contributed to its heritage. It has been from the beginning a working dog devoted to the service of mankind.

The properly bred and trained Doberman has proved itself as friend and guardian. As it developed, its qualities of intelligence and ability to absorb and retain training brought it into demand as police and war dog. In this service its agility and courage make it highly prized. An excellent nose adapted the dog to criminal trailing; it has also led to its use as a hunting dog.

In the United States the breed's popularity has been fostered by the Doberman Pinscher Club of America, which was founded in February 1921. Through the efforts of this organization, the Doberman is currently near the top of all breeds in registrations.

## Official Standard for the Doberman Pinscher

**General Appearance**—The appearance is that of a dog of medium size, with a body that is square. Compactly built, muscular and powerful, for great endurance and speed. Elegant in appearance, of proud carriage, reflecting great nobility and temperament. Energetic, watchful, determined, alert, fearless, loyal and obedient.

**Size, Proportion, Substance**—*Height* at the withers: *Dogs* 26 to 28 inches, ideal about 27½ inches; *Bitches* 24 to 26 inches, ideal about 25½ inches. The height, measured vertically from the ground to the highest point of the withers, equalling the length measured horizontally from the forechest to the rear projection of the upper thigh. Length of head, neck and legs in proportion to length and depth of body.

**Head**—Long and dry, resembling a blunt wedge in both frontal and profile views. When seen from the front, the head widens gradually toward the base of the ears in a practically unbroken line. *Eyes* almond shaped, moderately deep set, with vigorous, energetic expression. Iris, of uniform color, ranging from medium to darkest brown in black dogs; in reds, blues, and fawns the color of the iris blends with that of the markings, the darkest shade being preferable in every case. *Ears* normally cropped and carried erect. The upper attachment of the ear, when held erect, is on a level with the top of the skull. Top of *skull* flat, turning with slight stop to bridge of muzzle, with muzzle line extending parallel to top line of skull. Cheeks flat and muscular. *Nose* solid black on black dogs, dark brown on red ones, dark gray on blue ones, dark tan on fawns. Lips lying close to jaws. Jaws full and powerful, well filled under the eyes. **Teeth** strongly developed and white. Lower incisors upright and touching inside of upper incisors—a true scissors bite. 42 *correctly placed teeth*, 22 in the lower, 20 in the upper jaw. Distemper teeth shall not be penalized. *Disqualifying Faults:* Overshot more than ³⁄₁₆ of an inch. Undershot more than ⅛ of an inch. Four or more missing teeth.

**Neck, Topline, Body**—*Neck* proudly carried, well muscled and dry. Well arched, with nape of neck widening gradually toward body. Length of neck proportioned to body and head. **Withers** pronounced and forming the highest point of the body. Back short, firm, of sufficient width, and muscular at the loins, extending in a straight line from withers to the slightly rounded croup. **Chest** broad with forechest well defined. **Ribs** well sprung from the spine, but flattened in lower end to permit elbow clearance. **Brisket** reaching deep to the elbow. **Belly** well tucked up, extending in a curved line from the brisket. **Loins** wide and muscled. **Hips** broad and in proportion to body, breadth of hips being approximately equal to breadth of body at rib cage and shoulders. **Tail** docked at approximately second joint, appears to be a continuation of the spine, and is carried only slightly above the horizontal when the dog is alert.

**Forequarters**—**Shoulder Blade** sloping forward and downward at a 45-degree angle to the ground meets the upper arm at an angle of 90 degrees. Length of shoulder blade and upper arm are equal. Height from elbow to withers approximately equals height from ground to elbow. **Legs** seen from front and side, perfectly straight and parallel to each other from elbow to pastern; muscled and sinewy, with heavy bone. In normal pose and when gaiting, the elbows lie close to the brisket. **Pasterns** firm and almost perpendicular to the ground. Dewclaws may be removed. **Feet** well arched, compact, and catlike, turning neither in nor out.

**Hindquarters**—The angulation of the hindquarters balances that of the forequarters. **Hip Bone** falls away from spinal column at an angle of about 30 degrees, producing a slightly rounded, well filled-out croup. **Upper Shanks** at right angles to the hip bones, are long, wide, and well muscled on both sides of thigh, with clearly defined stifles. Upper and lower shanks are of equal length. While the dog is at rest, hock to heel is perpendicular to the ground. Viewed from the rear, the legs are straight, parallel to each other, and wide enough apart to fit in with a properly built body. Dewclaws, if any, are generally removed. **Cat feet** as on front legs, turning neither in nor out.

**Coat**—Smooth-haired, short, hard, thick and close lying. Invisible gray undercoat on neck permissible.

**Color and Markings**—*Allowed Colors:* Black, red, blue and fawn (Isabella). *Markings:* Rust, sharply defined, appearing above each eye and on muzzle, throat and forechest, on all legs and feet, and below tail. White patch on chest, not exceeding ½ square inch, permissible. *Disqualifying Fault:* Dogs not of an allowed color.

**Gait**—Free, balanced, and vigorous, with good reach in the forequarters and good driving power in the hindquarters. When trotting, there is strong rear-action drive. Each rear leg moves in line with the foreleg on the same side. Rear and front legs are thrown neither in nor out. Back remains strong and firm. When moving at a fast trot, a properly built dog will single-track.

**Temperament**—Energetic, watchful, determined, alert, fearless, loyal and obedient. *The judge shall dismiss from the ring any shy or vicious Doberman. Shyness:* A dog shall be judged fundamentally shy if, refusing to stand for examination, it shrinks away from the judge; if it fears an approach from the rear; if it shies at sudden and unusual noises to a marked degree. *Viciousness:* A dog that attacks or attempts to attack either the judge or its handler, is definitely vicious. An aggressive or belligerent attitude toward other dogs shall not be deemed viciousness.

### FAULTS

The foregoing description is that of the ideal Doberman Pinscher. Any deviation from the above described dog must be penalized to the extent of the deviation.

### DISQUALIFICATIONS

Overshot more than 3/16 of an inch. Undershot more than 1/8 of an inch. Four or more missing teeth. Dogs not of an allowed color.

Approved February 6, 1982
Reformatted November 6, 1990

# Giant Schnauzer

$F$ew races have been more prolific in their development of new breeds of dog than the Germanic peoples. Not only have they evinced rare patience in tracing ancestries, but they have proved their ability to fix type. One of the most notable examples of their breeding skill is the Schnauzer, for here is a dog not only brought to splendid physical conformation and keen mental development, but reproduced in three distinct sizes. The one under consideration here is the *Riesenschnauzer*—the Giant.

It is important to realize that the Miniature, the Standard, and the Giant Schnauzers are three separate and distinct breeds. Schnauzer breeding has been remarkable in that it has produced, from various sources that intermingled only in rare instances, if at all, three breeds which have developed toward one comparable standard of perfection.

Of the three, the dog now known in America as the Standard Schnauzer, which is the medium-sized specimen, is without doubt the oldest. He is the one apparently portrayed in paintings by Durer, dating from 1492, and he is also the one of the *"Nachtwächter-Brunnen"* the statue of a night watchman and his dog erected in a square in Stuttgart, Wurttemberg, in 1620. These instances are important only as they indicate the antiquity of the type of dog perfected at those dates and still retained today.

**257**

In unearthing the history of this breed it must be remembered that occupations of men had a great deal to do with all development in dogs. There were no bench shows in those days, and when a new breed was produced, it was aimed at a specific work. Also, its characteristics were governed to large extent by weather and living conditions.

All Schnauzers had their origin in the neighboring kingdoms of Wurttemberg and Bavaria. These are agricultural sections where the raising of sheep, cattle, and other livestock has been a major occupation for years. Since railroads were not known, sheep and cattle had to be driven to market, which meant that dogs were necessary to help the shepherds.

There is little doubt that when Bavarian cattlemen went to Stuttgart they came across the medium-sized Schnauzer. Here was a dog to catch anyone's attention, for even then it was sound, while it showed power throughout its trim lines. The Bavarians liked the dog, but they were not satisfied with its size. The sheepmen could use this size of dog, but the drovers needed a larger specimen for cattle.

The first attempts to produce a drover's dog on terrier lines, with a wiry coat, were no doubt by crossings between the medium-sized Schnauzer and some of the smooth-coated driving and dairymen's dogs then in existence. Later there were crossings with the rough-haired sheep dogs, and much later, with the black Great Dane. There is also reason to believe that the Giant Schnauzer is closely related to the Bouvier des Flandres, which was the driving dog of Flanders.

For many years the Giant Schnauzer was called the *Münchener*, and it was widely known as a great cattle and driving dog. Von Stephanitz places its origin as Swabia—in the south of Bavaria, and it was found in a state of perfection in the region between Munich and Augsburg.

The Giant Schnauzer was practically unknown outside of Bavaria until nearly the end of the first decade of this century. Cattle-driving was then a thing of the past, but the breed was still found in the hands of butchers, at stockyards, and at breweries. The breweries maintained the dogs as guards, at which duty they were preeminently successful.

Not until just before World War I did the Giant Schnauzer begin to come to nationwide attention in Germany as a suitable subject to receive police training at the schools in Berlin and other principal cities. He proved such an intelligent pupil that police work has been his main occupation since that time. His progress in this capacity in the United States has been very slow. Making his appearance here at the time when the German Shepherd was reaching its peak, the Bavarian dog had little chance to make headway against such well-established, direct competition.

# Official Standard for the Giant Schnauzer

**General Description**—The Giant Schnauzer should resemble, as nearly as possible, in general appearance, a larger and more powerful version of the Standard Schnauzer, on the whole a bold and valiant figure of a dog. Robust, strongly built, nearly square in proportion of body length to height at withers, active, sturdy, and well muscled. Temperament which combines spirit and alertness with intelligence and reliability. Composed, watchful, courageous, easily trained, deeply loyal to family, playful, amiable in repose, and a commanding figure when aroused. The sound, reliable temperament, rugged build, and dense weather-resistant wiry coat make for one of the most useful, powerful, and enduring working breeds.

**Head**—Strong, rectangular in appearance, and elongated; narrowing slightly from the ears to the eyes, and again from the eyes to the tip of the nose. The total length of the head is about one-half the length of the back (withers to set-on of tail). The head matches the sex and substance of the dog. The top line of the muzzle is parallel to the top line of the skull; there is a slight stop which is accentuated by the eyebrows. **Skull**—(Occiput to Stop). Moderately broad between the ears; occiput not too prominent. Top of skull flat; skin unwrinkled. **Cheeks**—Flat, but with well-developed chewing muscles; there is no "cheekiness" to disturb the rectangular head appearance (with beard). **Muzzle**— Strong and well filled under the eyes; both parallel and equal in length to the topskull; ending in a moderately blunt wedge. The nose is large, black, and full. The lips are tight, and not overlapping, black in color. **Bite**—A full complement of sound white teeth (6/6 incisors, 2/2 canines, 8/8 premolars, 4/6 molars) with a scissors bite. The upper and lower jaws are powerful and well formed. **Disqualifying Fault**—Overshot or undershot. **Ears**—When cropped, identical in shape and length with pointed tips. They are in balance with the head and are not exaggerated in length. They are set high on the skull and carried perpendicularly at the inner edges with as little bell as possible along the other edges. When uncropped, the ears are V-shaped button ears of medium length and thickness, set high and carried rather high and close to the head. **Eyes**—Medium size, dark brown, and deep-set. They are oval in appearance and keen in expression with lids fitting tightly. Vision is not impaired nor eyes hidden by too long eyebrows.

**Neck**—Strong and well arched, of moderate length, blending cleanly into the shoulders, and with the skin fitting tightly at the throat; in harmony with the dog's weight and build.

**Body**—Compact, substantial, short-coupled, and strong, with great power and agility. The height at the highest point of the withers equals the body length from breastbone to point of rump. The loin section is well developed, as short as possible for compact build.

**Forequarters**—The forequarters have flat, somewhat sloping shoulders and high withers. Forelegs are straight and vertical when viewed from all sides with strong pasterns and good bone. They are separated by a fairly deep brisket which precludes a pinched front. The elbows are set close to the body and point directly backwards.

**Chest**—Medium in width, ribs well sprung but with no tendency toward a barrel chest; oval in cross section; deep through the brisket. The breastbone is plainly discernible, with strong forechest; the brisket descends at least to the elbows, and ascends gradually toward the rear with the belly moderately drawn up. The ribs spread gradually from the first rib so as to allow space for the elbows to move close to the body.

**Shoulders**—The sloping shoulder blades (scapulae) are strongly muscled, yet flat. They are well laid back so that from the side the rounded upper ends are in a nearly vertical line above the elbows. They slope well forward to the point where they join the upper arm (humerus), forming as nearly as possible a right angle. Such an angulation permits the maximum forward extension of the forelegs without binding or effort. Both shoulder blades and upper arm are long, permitting depth of chest at the brisket.

**Back**—Short, straight, strong, and firm.

**Tail**—The tail is set moderately high and carried high in excitement. It should be docked to the second or not more than the third joint (approximately one and one-half to about three inches long at maturity).

**Hindquarters**—The hindquarters are strongly muscled, in balance with the forequarters; upper thighs are slanting and well bent at the stifles, with the second thighs (tibiae) approximately parallel to an extension of the upper neckline. The legs from the hock joint to the feet are short, perpendicular to the ground while the dog is standing naturally, and from the rear parallel to each other. The hindquarters do not appear over-built or higher than the shoulders. Croup full and slightly rounded.

**Feet**—Well-arched, compact and catlike, turning neither in nor out, with thick tough pads and dark nails. *Dewclaws*— Dewclaws, if any, on hind legs should be removed; on the forelegs, may be removed.

**Gait**—The trot is the gait at which movement is judged. Free, balanced and vigorous, with good reach in the forequarters and good driving power in the hindquarters. Rear and front legs are thrown neither in nor out. When moving at a fast trot, a properly built dog will single-track. Back remains strong, firm, and flat.

**Coat**—Hard, wiry, very dense; composed of a soft undercoat and a harsh outer coat which, when seen against the grain, stands slightly up off the back, lying neither smooth nor flat. Coarse hair on top of head; harsh beard and eyebrows, the Schnauzer hallmark.

**Color**—Solid black or pepper and salt.

***Black***—A truly pure black. A small white spot on the breast is permitted; any other markings are disqualifying faults.

***Pepper and Salt***—Outer coat of a combination of banded hairs (white with black and black with white) and some black and white hairs, appearing gray from a short distance. *Ideally:* an intensely pigmented medium gray shade with "peppering" evenly distributed throughout the coat, and a gray undercoat. *Acceptable:* all shades of pepper and salt from dark iron-gray to silver-gray. Every shade of coat has a dark facial mask to emphasize the expression; the color of the mask harmonizes with the shade of the body coat. Eyebrows, whiskers, cheeks, throat, chest, legs, and under tail are lighter in color but include "peppering." Markings are disqualifying faults.

**Height**—The height of the withers of the male is 25½ to 27½ inches, and of the female, 23½ to 25½ inches, with the mediums being desired. Size alone should never take precedence over type, balance, soundness, and temperament. It should be noted that too small dogs generally lack the power and too large dogs, the agility and maneuverability, desired in a working dog.

### FAULTS

The foregoing description is that of the ideal Giant Schnauzer. Any deviation from the above described dog must be penalized to the extent of the deviation.

*The judge shall dismiss from the ring any shy or vicious Giant Schnauzer.*

**Shyness**—A dog shall be judged fundamentally shy if, refusing to stand for examination, it repeatedly shrinks away from the judge; if it fears unduly any approach from the rear; if it shies to a marked degree at sudden and unusual noises.

**Viciousness**—A dog that attacks or attempts to attack either the judge or its handler, is definitely vicious. An aggressive or belligerent attitude towards other dogs shall not be deemed viciousness.

### DISQUALIFICATIONS

*Overshot or undershot.*
*Markings other than specified.*

Approved October 11, 1983

# Great Dane

In appearance and nature the Great Dane is one of the most elegant and distinguished varieties of giant-type dog.

The name of the breed (in the English language) is a translation of an old French designation, *grand Danois*, meaning "big Danish." This was only one of half a dozen names which had been used for centuries in France. Why the English adopted the name "Great Dane" from the French is a mystery. At the same time the French were also calling it *dogue allemand* or "German Mastiff." "Mastiff" in English, *dogge* in the Germanic, *dogue* or *dogo* in the Latin languages, all meant the same thing: a giant dog with heavy head for fighting or hunting purposes. It was one of the dozen varieties of dog recognized as distinctive enough at that time to have a name of its own.

There is no known reason for connecting Denmark with either the origin or the development of the breed. It was "made in Germany," and it was German fanciers who led the world in breeding most of the finest specimens.

If the reader is susceptible to the charms of antiquity, he will be interested in Cassel's claim that on Egyptian monuments of about 3000 B.C. there are drawings of dogs much like the Great Dane. Also, the earliest written description of a dog resembling the breed may be found in Chinese literature of 1121 B.C. (an article by Dr. G. Ciaburri, Great Dane Club of Italy publication, 1929).

Eminent zoologists believe that the Mastiff breeds originated in Asia. They think the modern Tibetan Mastiff, occasionally shown in England, is the most direct descendant of the prototype.

The great naturalist Buffon (1707–1788) claimed the Irish Wolfhound as the principal ancestor of our Great Dane. The comparative anatomist Cuvier (1769-1832) found more evidence in favor of the old English Mastiff as the root from which it sprang. Both Irish and English breeds are known to have been carefully bred for 1300 years and more. Today most students favor the idea that the Great Dane, or Deutsche Dogge, resulted from a mixture of both these ancient types.

This is not to say that the German Mastiff or Great Dane is a new breed. It is, indeed, a very old one which has been cultivated as a distinct type for probably 400 years, if not longer. Like all old varieties of dog, it was developed for a useful purpose. The Germans used the Great Dane as a boar hound. Europe's erstwhile boar was one of the most savage, swift, powerful, and well-armed of all big game on the Continent. To tackle the wild boar required a superdog, and that is precisely what the Germans developed. We who fancy him speak of him as the king of dogs.

In common with all other breeds, the Great Dane's history of and development to a modern standard type began in the latter 19th century. In 1880 at Berlin, Dr. Bodinus called a meeting of Great Dane judges who declared that the breed should be known as *Deutsche dogge* and that all other designations, especially the term "Great Dane," should be abolished thereafter. So far as the German people are concerned this declaration has been observed, but English-speaking people have paid no heed. The Italians, who have a large Great Dane fancy, have also failed to give Germany credit for the name selected: *alano*. This word means "a mastiff," consequently the name of their organization means "Mastiff Club of Italy." This, however, has not prevented close cooperation between fanciers of the two countries. The leading Italian breeders have based their operation on nothing but German imported stock or its descendants.

In 1891 the Great Dane Club of Germany adopted a precise standard, or official description of the ideal specimen. In 1885, there was a Great Dane Club in England, and in 1889 at Chicago the German Mastiff or Great Dane Club of America was founded with G. Muss-Arnoldt as first delegate. Two years later the club reorganized as the Great Dane Club of America. At that time, its membership was mostly of Eastern fanciers.

The Great Dane has developed steadily in popularity all over the world. Breeders have kept before them the image of the boar hound and the special qualities it called for. A merely "pretty" dog has not been enough. He must have size and weight, nobility and courage, speed and endurance. What more can one ask for in a dog?

# Official Standard for the Great Dane

**General Appearance**—The Great Dane combines, in its regal appearance, dignity, strength and elegance with great size and a powerful, well-formed, smoothly muscled body. It is one of the giant working breeds, but is unique in that its general conformation must be so well balanced that it never appears clumsy, and shall move with a long reach and powerful drive. it is always a unit—the Apollo of dogs. A Great Dane must be spirited, courageous, never timid; always friendly and dependable. This physical and mental combination is the characteristic which gives the Great Dane the majesty possessed by no other breed. It is particularly true of this breed that there is an impression of great masculinity in dogs, as compared to an impression of femininity in bitches. Lack of true Dane breed type, as defined in this standard, is a serious fault.

**Size, Proportion, Substance**—The male should appear more massive throughout than the bitch, with larger frame and heavier bone. In the ratio between length and height, the Great Dane should be square. In bitches, a somewhat longer body is permissible, providing she is well proportioned to her height. Coarseness or lack of substance are equally undesirable. The male shall not be less than 30 inches at the shoulders, but it is preferable that he be 32 inches or more, providing he is well proportioned to his height. The female shall not be less than 28 inches at the shoulders, but it is preferable that she be 30 inches or more, providing she is well proportioned to her height. Danes under minimum height must be disqualified.

**Head**—The head shall be rectangular, long, distinguished, expressive, finely chiseled, especially below the eyes. Seen from the side, the Dane's forehead must be sharply set off from the bridge of the nose (a strongly pronounced stop). The plane of the skull and the plane of the muzzle must be straight and parallel to one another. The skull plane under and to the inner point of the eyes must slope without any bony protuberance in a smooth line to a full square jaw with a deep muzzle (fluttering lips are undesirable). The masculinity of the male is very pronounced in structural appearance of the head. The bitch's head is more delicately formed. Seen from the top, the skull should have parallel sides and the bridge of the nose should be as broad as possible. The cheek muscles should not be prominent. The length from the tip of the nose to the center of the stop should be equal to the length from the center of the stop to the rear of the slightly developed occiput. The head should be angular from all sides and should have flat planes with dimensions in proportion to the size of the Dane. Whiskers may be trimmed or left natural. *Eyes* shall be medium size, deep set, and dark, with a lively intelligent expression. The eyelids are almond-shaped and relatively tight, with well developed brows. Haws and mongolian eyes are serious faults. In harlequins, the eyes should be dark; light colored eyes, eyes of different colors and walleyes are permitted but not desirable. *Ears* shall be high set, medium in size and of moderate thickness, folded forward close to the cheek. The top line of the folded ear should be level with the skull. If cropped, the ear length is in proportion to the size of the head and the ears are carried uniformly erect. *Nose* shall be black, except in the blue Dane, where it is a dark blue-black. A black spotted nose is permitted on the harlequin; a pink colored nose is not desirable. A split nose is a disqualification. *Teeth* shall be strong, well developed, clean and with full dentition. The incisors of the lower jaw touch very lightly the bottoms of the inner surface of the upper incisors (scissors bite). An undershot jaw is a very serious fault. Overshot or wry bites are serious faults. Even bites, misaligned or crowded incisors are minor faults.

**Neck, Topline, Body**—The neck shall be firm, high set, well arched, long and muscular. From the nape, it should gradually broaden and flow smoothly into the withers. The neck underline should be clean. Withers shall slope smoothly into a short level back with a broad loin. The chest shall be broad, deep and well muscled. The forechest should be well developed without a pronounced sternum. The brisket extends to the elbow, with well sprung ribs. The body underline should be tightly muscled with a well-defined tuck-up. The croup should be broad and very slightly sloping. The tail should be set high and smoothly into the croup, but not quite level with the back, a continuation of the spine. The tail should be broad at the base, tapering uniformly down to the hock joint. At rest, the tail should fall straight. When excited or running, it may curve slightly, but never above the level of the back. A ring or hooked tail is a serious fault. A docked tail is a disqualification.

**Forequarters**—The forequarters, viewed from the side, shall be strong and muscular. The shoulder blade must be strong and sloping, forming, as near as possible, a right angle in its articulation with the upper arm. A line from the upper tip of the shoulder to the back of the elbow joint should be perpendicular. The ligaments and muscles holding the shoulder blade to the rib cage must be well developed, firm and securely attached to prevent loose shoulders. The shoulder blade and the upper arm should be the same length. The elbow should be one-half the distance from the withers to the ground. The strong pasterns should slope slightly. The feet should be round and compact with well-arched toes, neither toeing in, toeing out, nor rolling to the inside or outside. The nails should be short, strong and as dark as possible, except that they may be lighter in harlequins. Dewclaws may or may not be removed.

**Hindquarters**—The hindquarters shall be strong, broad, muscular and well angulated, with well let down hocks. Seen from the rear, the hock joints appear to be perfectly straight, turned neither toward the inside nor toward the outside. The rear feet should be round and compact, with well-arched toes, neither toeing in nor out. The nails should be short, strong and as dark as possible, except they may be lighter in harlequins. Wolf claws are a serious fault.

**Coat**—The coat shall be short, thick and clean with a smooth glossy appearance.

**Color, Markings and Patterns**—*Brindle*—The base color shall be yellow gold and always brindled with strong black cross stripes in a chevron pattern. A black mask is preferred. Black should appear on the eye rims and eyebrows, and may appear on the ears and tail tip. The more intensive the base color and the more distinct and even the brindling, the more preferred will be the color. Too much or too little brindling are equally undesirable. White markings at the chest and toes, black-fronted, dirty colored brindles are not desirable. *Fawn*—The color shall be yellow gold with a black mask. Black should appear on the eye rims and eyebrows, and may appear on the ears and tail tip. The deep yellow gold must always be given the preference. White markings at the chest and toes, black-fronted dirty colored fawns are not desirable. *Blue*—The color shall be a pure steel blue. White markings at the chest and toes are not desirable. **Black**—The color shall be a glossy black. White markings at the chest and toes are not desirable. **Harlequin**—Base color shall be pure white with black torn patches irregularly and well distributed over the entire body; a pure white neck is preferred. The black patches should never be large enough to give the appearance of a blanket, nor so small as to give a stippled or dappled effect. Eligible, but less desirable, are a few small gray patches, or a white base with single black hairs showing through, which tend to give a salt and pepper or dirty effect. *Any variance in color or markings as described above shall be faulted to the extent of the deviation. Any Great Dane which does not fall within the above color classifications must be disqualified.*

**Gait**—The gait denotes strength and power with long, easy strides resulting in no tossing, rolling or bouncing of the topline or body. The backline shall appear level and parallel to the ground. The long reach should strike the ground below the nose while the head is carried forward. The powerful rear drive should be balanced to the reach. As speed increases, there is a natural tendency for the legs to converge toward the centerline of balance beneath the body. There should be no twisting in or out at the elbow or hock joints.

**Temperament**—The Great Dane must be spirited, courageous, always friendly and dependable, and never timid or aggressive.

**DISQUALIFICATIONS**

*Danes under minimum height.*
*Split nose.*
*Docked Tail.*
*Any color other than those described under "Color, Markings and Patterns."*

Approved September 11, 1990

# Great Pyrenees

$P$erhaps no other breed can boast such a colorful history of association with, and service to, mankind through as many centuries as can the Great Pyrenees, *Le Grande Chien des Montagnes, Le Chien des Pyrenees,* or, as he is known in England and on the Continent, the Pyrenean Mountain Dog, the dog of French royalty and nobility and working associate of the peasant shepherds high on the slopes of the Pyrenees Mountains. His remains are found in the fossil deposits of the Bronze Age, which roughly dates his appearance in Europe between 1800 and 1000 B.C., although it is believed that he came originally from Central Asia or Siberia and followed the Aryan migration into Europe. It is also generally accepted that he is a descendant of the mastiff type whose remains are found in the kitchen-middens of the Baltic and North Sea coasts in the oldest strata containing evidence of the domestic dog, and which appear in Babylonian art about the close of the third millennium B.C. in the size and general appearance resembling the Great Pyrenees.

Once in Europe, the Great Dog of the Mountains developed under climatic conditions similar to those of his habitat and there remained isolated in the high mountainous areas until medieval times, when we find him gracing bas-reliefs at Carcassone, bearing the royal arms of France approximately some five hundred years before his adoption as the court dog in the 17th century. As early as 1407 the historian Mons. Bourdet describes the regular guard of Pyrenees dogs owned by the Chateau of Lordes. These dogs were given a special place in the sentry boxes along with the armed guards; they also accompanied the gaolers on their daily rounds. Their use for these purposes became very general and each large chateau boasted its band of Great Pyrenees. It was not until the young Dauphin, accompanied by Mme. de Maintenon in 1675 on a visit to Barreges, fell in love with a beautiful *Patou* (a generic name for the breed meaning "shepherd") and insisted on taking it back to the Louvre with him, and not until the Marquis de Louvois also succumbed to their charm, that the dog of the shepherd of the Pyrenees became the companion and pet of nobility. Once accepted at court, every noble wanted one, and the breed gained prominence.

It was, however, in the isolation of the lonely mountain pastures that the Pyrenean Mountain Dog developed his inherent traits of devotion, fidelity, sense of guardianship, and intelligent understanding of mankind. Here, in the days when packs of wild animals roamed the mountain slopes freely, he was the official guardian of the flocks. Having a precocious sense of smell and keen sight, he was an invaluable companion of the shepherd, his worth being counted equal to that of two men. Armed by nature with a long, heavy coat which rendered him invulnerable against attack except for the point of the chin and the base of the brain, and armed by his masters with a broad iron collar from which protruded spikes an inch and a half long, the Pyrenees dog was an almost unbeatable foe which won such glory and fame as a vanquisher of wolves and bears that he became known as the Pyrenean wolf dog or hound, and the Pyrenean bearhound.

By disposition and profession, no better dog could have been chosen to assume the role of protector and friend of the early settlements of the Biscay fisherfolk on Newfoundland Island. By 1662, when their first permanent colony at Rougnoust was made, it was the Great Pyrenees dog which had become the companion of the people. Here he was crossed with the black English Retriever, brought over by the English settlers, and from this cross resulted the Newfoundland. The old Landseer type, with its black and white coat, showed the cross far more markedly because of his coloring than the black Newfoundland, although the resemblance in general type is quite noticeable in both.

With the diminution of the wild beasts in the Pyrenees, the breed seemed destined to extinction for a while. Moreover, it was eagerly sought after by breeders in continental Europe and great numbers were exported from France. However, thanks to the efforts of some gentlemen sportsmen, as well as to the fact that dogs were of use about the peasants' farms in winter (when their services were not required on the mountain slopes), they were bred in increasing numbers until today the breed is well established in its habitat once again. The dogs are not infrequently referred to as "mat-dogs" because of their habit of lying outside the cottage doors when not busying themselves with menial chores such as pulling carts.

The Great Pyrenees has come into general prominence only since its recognition by the American Kennel Club in February, 1933. It seems hard to realize that the first pair were brought over by General Lafayette for his friend, J. S. Skinner, in 1824, being "recommended by him from personal experience as of inestimable value to wool-growers in all regions exposed to the depredations of wolves and sheepkilling dogs." Thus writes Mr. Skinner in his book *The Dog and the Sportsman.* Following this a few scattered specimens were imported, but not until 1933 was the actual breeding of the dogs launched in America. Today, he ranks in the top half of the AKC annual breed registrations.

The nearer his appearance approaches that of the brown bear, except for the color and the drooping ears, the closer he is to the perfect type. Certainly no more picturesque animal could be found; he has been aptly called "an animated snowdrift of the Pyrenees Mountains." Preeminently a watchdog and companion, the Great Pyrenees holds promise also as a dog suited for the sportsman. His love of pulling carts makes him amenable to sled work in winter, and his instinct for feeling out soft places in the snow makes him ideal for pack and guide work on ski trips. He was used during World War I for pack service and for many years for running contraband goods over the Franco-Spanish border by similar methods. Taking dangerous byways impossible for man to travel, he ran the circuit regularly, successfully avoiding the customs officials. His beauty also recommends him for use in the moving picture industry, especially as he has already been used with success for this purpose in France.

## Official Standard for the Great Pyrenees

**General Appearance**—The Great Pyrenees dog conveys the distinct impression of elegance and unsurpassed beauty combined with great overall size and majesty. He has a white or principally white coat that may contain markings of badger, gray, or varying shades of tan. He possesses a keen intelligence and a kindly, while regal, expression. Exhibiting a unique elegance of bearing and movement, his soundness and coordination show unmistakably the purpose for which he has been bred, the strenuous work of guarding the flocks in all kinds of weather on the steep mountain slopes of the Pyrenees.

**Size, Proportion, Substance**—*Size*—The height at the withers ranges from 27 inches to 32 inches for dogs and from 25 inches to 29 inches for bitches. A 27 inch dog weighs about 100 pounds and a 25 inch bitch weighs about 85 pounds. Weight is in proportion to the overall size and structure. ***Proportion***—The Great Pyrenees is a balanced dog with the height measured at the withers being somewhat less than the length of the body measured from the point of the shoulder to the rearmost projection of the upper thigh (buttocks). These proportions create a somewhat rectangular dog, slightly longer than it is tall. Front and rear angulation are balanced. *Substance*—The Great Pyrenees is a dog of medium substance whose coat deceives those who do not feel the bone and muscle. Commensurate with his size and impression of elegance there is sufficient bone and muscle to provide a balance with the frame. *Faults*—Size—Dogs and bitches under minimum size or over maximum size. Substance—Dogs too heavily boned or too lightly boned to be in balance with their frame.

**Head**—Correct head and expression are essential to the breed. The head is not heavy in proportion to the size of the dog. It is wedge shaped with a slightly rounded crown. *Expression*—The expression is elegant, intelligent and contemplative. *Eyes*—Medium sized, almond shaped, set slightly obliquely, rich dark brown. Eyelids are close fitting with black rims. *Ears*—Small to medium in size, V-shaped with rounded tips, set on at eye level, normally carried low, flat, and close to the head. There is a characteristic meeting of the hair of the upper and lower face which forms a line from the outer corner of the eye to the base of the ear. *Skull and Muzzle*—The muzzle is approximately equal in length to the back skull. The width and length of the skull are approximately equal. The muzzle blends smoothly with the skull. The cheeks are flat. There is sufficient fill under the eyes. A slight furrow exists between the eyes. There is no apparent stop. The boney eyebrow ridges are only slightly developed. Lips are tight fitting with the upper lip just covering the lower lip. There is a strong lower jaw. The nose and lips are black. *Teeth*—A scissor bite is preferred, but a level bite is acceptable. It is not unusual to see dropped (receding) lower central incisor teeth. *Faults*—Too heavy head (St. Bernard or Newfoundland-like). Too narrow or small skull. Foxy appearance. Presence of an apparent stop. Missing pigmentation on nose, eye rims, or lips. Eyelids round, triangular, loose or small. Overshot, undershot, wry mouth.

**Neck, Topline, Body**—*Neck*—Strongly muscled and of medium length, with minimal dewlap. *Topline*—The backline is level. *Body*—The chest is moderately broad. The rib cage is well sprung, oval in shape, and of sufficient depth to reach the elbows. Back and loin are broad and strongly coupled with some tuck-up. The croup is gently sloping with the tail set on just below the level of the back. *Tail*—The tailbones are of sufficient length to reach the hock. The tail is well plumed, carried low in repose and may be carried over the back, "making the wheel," when aroused. When present, a "shepherd's crook" at the end of the tail accentuates the plume. When gaiting, the tail may be carried either over the back or low. Both carriages are equally correct. *Fault*—Barrel ribs.

**Forequarters**—*Shoulders*—The shoulders are well laid back, well muscled, and lie close to the body. The upper arm meets the shoulder blade at approximately a right angle. The upper arm angles backward from the point of the shoulder to the elbow and is never perpendicular to the ground. The length of the shoulder blade and the upper arm is approximately equal. The height from the ground to the elbow appears approximately equal to the height from the elbow to the withers. *Forelegs*—The legs are of sufficient bone and muscle to provide a balance with the frame. The elbows are close to the body and point directly to the rear when standing and gaiting. The forelegs, when viewed from the side, are located directly under the withers and are straight and vertical to the ground. The elbows, when viewed from the front, are set in a straight line from the point of shoulder to the wrist. Front pasterns are strong and flexible. Each foreleg carries a single dewclaw. *Front Feet*—Rounded, close-cupped, well padded, toes well arched.

**Hindquarters**—The angulation of the hindquarters is similar in degree to that of the forequarters. **Thighs**—Strongly muscular upper thighs extend from the pelvis at right angles. The upper thigh is the same length as the lower thigh, creating moderate stifle joint angulation when viewed in profile. The rear pastern (metatarsus) is of medium length and perpendicular to the ground as the dog stands naturally. This produces a moderate degree of angulation in the hock joint, when viewed from the side. The hindquarters from the hip to the rear pastern are straight and parallel, as viewed from the rear. The rear legs are of sufficient bone and muscle to provide a balance with the frame. Double dewclaws are located on each rear leg. **Rear Feet**—The rear feet have a structural tendency to toe out slightly. This breed characteristic is not to be confused with cowhocks. The rear feet, like the forefeet, are rounded, close-cupped, well padded with toes well arched. **Fault**—Absence of double dewclaws on each rear leg.

**Coat**—The weather resistant double coat consists of a long, flat, thick, outer coat of coarse hair, straight or slightly undulating, and lying over a dense, fine, woolly undercoat. The coat is more profuse about the neck and shoulders where it forms a ruff or mane which is more pronounced in males. Longer hair on the tail forms a plume. There is feathering along the back of the front legs and along the back of the thighs, giving a "pantaloon" effect. The hair on the face and ears is shorter and of finer texture. Correctness of coat is more important than abundance of coat. **Faults**—Curly coat. Stand-off coat (Samoyed type).

**Color**—White or white with markings of gray, badger, reddish brown, or varying shades of tan. Markings of varying size may appear on the ears, head (including a full face mask), tail, and as a few body spots. The undercoat may be white or shaded. All of the above described colorings and locations are characteristic of the breed and equally correct. **Fault**—Outer coat markings covering more than one third of the body.

**Gait**—The Great Pyrenees moves smoothly and elegantly, true and straight ahead, exhibiting both power and agility. The stride is well balanced with good reach and strong drive. The legs tend to move toward the center line as speed increases. Ease and efficiency of movement are more important than speed.

**Temperament**—Character and temperament are of utmost importance. In nature, the Great Pyrenees is confident, gentle, and affectionate. While territorial and protective of his flock or family when necessary, his general demeanor is one of quiet composure, both patient and tolerant. He is strong willed, independent and somewhat reserved, yet attentive, fearless and loyal to his charges both human and animal.

*Although the Great Pyrenees may appear reserved in the show ring, any sign of excessive shyness, nervousness, or aggression to humans is unacceptable and must be considered an extremely serious fault.*

Approved June 12, 1990

# Komondor

Of the three breeds of working dog native for ten centuries to the sheep and cattle countries of Hungary, there seems little doubt that the king of them all is the Komondor. This heavily coated dog is an almost direct descendant of the *Aftscharka*, which the Huns found on the southern steppes when they passed through Russia. Many of today's Komondorok (plural) bear striking resemblance to the massive, long-legged Russian herdsman's dog, but the breed generally has become more compact.

The Komondor is a mighty fellow. His head is impressive in its generous formation, and his general appearance is commanding. At first sight he is likely to create fear. Strangers of evil intent have reason to be fearful, but he is a devoted companion to his master and readily mingles with friends of the master.

One often sees pictures of the Komondor that show him with a heavily matted coat and with his head covered all over with long hair. The dog thus seems unkempt, and this is the way he is found in his habitat, where he lives in the open practically all the time. Under such circumstances, it would be impossible for the Komondor to have a well-groomed appearance, but he responds readily to care. When reared in kennels and prepared for shows, he is a handsome dog.

The Komondor is the chief of the herdsman's dogs, but he is not often utilized for rounding up the herds. He merely accompanies the flocks and herds in exceptional cases, and then more in the capacity of protector than as herder. His vigilance and courage have earned him a rather enviable position of trust, and much of the routine work is left to the smaller dogs.

The Magyars who have bred the Komondor for more than a thousand years attend principally to their herds and flocks and do not concern themselves with keeping pedigrees of their dogs. However, there is no need of pedigrees for them, as the dogs are not permitted to mate outside their own breed.

It is doubtful if any dogs with pedigrees could be found in the so-called *Puszta*, for the shepherds and herdsmen do not look upon dog breeding either as a commercial venture or as a hobby. Still, the crossing of a Komondor and a Kuvasz would be unimaginable, and also practically impossible. The Komondor still resides in the Puszta, while the Kuvasz has become, in recent times, more the watchdog of the village.

The history of pure-bred dog breeding in Hungary is not unlike that of any other country in the world. Definite records go back hardly a century, but those in existence are soundly attested by reliable parties. The Hungarian Kennel Club and the Hungarian Komondor Club maintain a strong control over the interests of the Komondor, these organizations having accepted the Standard of the breed as drawn up by a committee made up of members of the two clubs. The American Kennel Club's standard of the breed is a translation of the Hungarian.

In reading the standard, it should be noted that its salient points denote the strength and protective features that have been bred into the Komondor for centuries, and these should be maintained. Today there is not perhaps as pressing a need for such a self-reliant dog as there was in the past. In times of old he had to be ready at any moment to fight all manner of beasts of prey, many of which were his superior in size and weight. When the odds were against him, he could depend to some extent on that heavy coat to cover his most vulnerable points, and could call, too, upon an intelligence far superior to that of his wild adversaries.

## Official Standard for the Komondor

**General Appearance**—The Komondor is characterized by imposing strength, courageous demeanor, and pleasing conformation. In general, it is a big, muscular dog with plenty of bone and substance, covered with an unusual, heavy, white coat.

**Size, Proportion, Substance**—Dogs, 25½ inches and upward at the withers; bitches, 23½ inches and upward at the withers. While size is important, type, character, symmetry, movement and ruggedness are of the greatest importance and are on no account to be sacrificed for size alone. The body is rectangular, only slightly longer than the height at the withers. Plenty of bone and substance. *Fault*—Size below limit.

**Head**—The **head** looks somewhat short in comparison to the seemingly wide forehead. *Eyes* medium sized and almond shaped, not too deeply set. The edges of the eyelids are gray. The iris of the eyes is dark brown; light color is not desirable. The outlines of eyelids are dark or gray. *Fault*—Light-colored eyes. Blue-white eyes are *disqualifying*. *Ears* medium set, hanging, and V-shaped. *Faults*—Erect ears or ears that move toward an erect position. The *skull* is somewhat arched when viewed from the side. *Stop* is moderate. The *muzzle* is somewhat shorter than the length of the skull. The muzzle is powerful. The top of the muzzle is straight and about parallel with the line of the top of the skull. In comparison to the length of the head, the muzzle is wide, coarse, and not pointed. *Nose*—Nostrils are wide. Color of the nose is black. A dark gray or dark brown nose is not desirable but is acceptable. Nose and lips are dark or gray. It is good if the gums and palate are also dark. Flesh-colored noses are *disqualifying*. *Bite* is scissors, level bite is acceptable. Any missing teeth is a *serious fault*. Distinctly undershot or overshot bite is a *serious fault*.

**Neck, Topline, Body**—*Neck* muscular, of medium length, moderately arched. The head erect. Any dewlap is a *fault*. *Topline*—The back is level. *Body* characterized chiefly by the powerful, deep chest which is muscular and proportionately wide. The belly is somewhat drawn up at the rear. Rump is wide, muscular, slightly sloping towards the root of the tail. *Fault*—Looseness or slackness.

**Tail**—A straight continuation of the rumpline, and reaches down to the hocks. Slightly curved upwards at its end. When the dog is excited the tail is raised up to the level of the back. The tail is not to be docked. A short or curly tail is a *fault*. Bobtails are *disqualifying*.

**Forequarters**—Shoulders are moderately sloping. Forelegs straight, well boned, and muscular. Viewed from any side, the legs are like vertical columns. The upper arms join the body closely, without loose elbows.

**Feet**—Strong, rather large and with close, well arched toes. Nails are black or gray. Pads are hard, elastic and dark or gray.

**Hindquarters**—The steely, strong bone structure is covered with highly developed muscles. The legs are straight as viewed from the rear. Stifles well bent. Rear dewclaws must be removed. Feet as in the front.

**Coat**—Characteristic of the breed is the dense, weather-resisting double coat. The puppy coat is relatively soft, but it shows a tendency to fall into cords. In the mature dog the coat consists of a dense, soft, woolly undercoat, much like the puppy coat, and a coarser outer coat that is wavy or curly. The coarser hairs of the outer coat trap the softer undercoat, forming permanent, strong cords that are felty to the touch. A grown dog is covered with a heavy coat of these tassel-like cords, which form themselves naturally, and once formed, require no care other than washing. The coat is longest at the rump, loins, and tail. It is of medium length on the back, shoulders, and chest. Shorter on the cheeks, around the eyes, ears, neck, and on the extremities. It is shortest around the mouth and the lower part of the legs up to the hocks. Short and too curly coat is a *fault*. Straight or silky coat is a *serious fault*. Short, smooth hair on head and legs is a *disqualification*. Failure of the coat to cord by two years of age is a *disqualification*.

**Color**—Color of the coat is white. Any color other than white is *disqualifying*. In the ideal specimen the skin is gray. Pink skin is less desirable but is acceptable if no evidence of albinism.

**Gait**—Light, leisurely, and balanced. Takes long strides.

**Temperament**—An excellent houseguard. It is wary of strangers. As a guardian of herds, it is, when grown, an earnest, courageous, and very faithful dog. The young dog, however, is as playful as any other puppy. It is devoted to its master and will defend him against attack by any stranger. Because of this trait, it is not used for driving the herds, but only for guarding them. The Komondor's special task is to protect the animals. It lives during the greater part of the year in the open, without protection against strange dogs and beasts of prey.

### DISQUALIFICATIONS

> *Blue-white eyes.*
> *Flesh-colored nose.*
> *Bobtails.*
> *Short, smooth hair on head and legs.*
> *Failure of the coat to cord by two years of age.*
> *Color other than white.*

Approved February 13, 1973
Reformatted July 26, 1989

# Kuvasz

From Tibet, that strange high-flung domain of the lamas, came the ancestors of the breed that today is known as the Kuvasz (plural, Kuvaszok). Yet this is not a new name for the breed. It is merely a corrupted spelling of Turkish and Arabian words that signified the unexcelled guarding instincts of this big dog.

The Turkish word is *kawasz*, which means "armed guard of the nobility." In the Arabian this appears as *kawwasz*, which signifies "archer," an expression that probably was a mere figure of speech to denote the high esteem in which the dog was held, since many centuries ago an archer was regarded with great respect. Words with nearly the same spelling and meaning are found throughout all the countries whose languages originate in Tibet.

There is little doubt of the part that the Kuvasz played in the history of the kingdoms and empires which flourished throughout Europe five to eight centuries ago. Dogs of this breed were the constant companions of many a ruler of a turbulent country; indeed, none but those within the favor of the royal circles were permitted to own specimens of the Kuvasz.

Known in many countries, it was in Hungary that the Kuvasz developed into the form in which he is seen today. He still is a big dog, but he is not the giant of ancient times. At present he measures 28 to 30 inches at the withers, but there is every reason to believe that the dog which issued from Tibet stood considerably higher. He was a dog of which the common people stood in awe; his appearance alone was enough to discourage attacks on noblemen by the populace.

The first great period in the Hungarian history of the Kuvasz seemed to reach a climax during the second half of the 15th century. His renown reached far and wide. There were numerous big estates that bred the dog and kept their own stud books. Many were trained for hunting, and they proved very successful on the big game of those times.

King Matthias I, who reigned from 1458 to 1490, had at least one Kuvasz with him whenever he traveled, and there were numerous specimens about his palace and the surrounding grounds. Few other rulers have had to strive so hard to hold his domains together. Plots and political intrigue were the rule rather than the exception, while assassinations were not uncommon. It is said that King Matthias was reluctant to place any great trust in even the members of his own household, and his court was filled with ambitious noblemen.

It is no wonder that King Matthias relied more upon his dogs than upon his human guards. He knew that in this big, sturdy fellow he had, perhaps, the only true security that was possible. Often, when the tumultuous day was over—and he waged wars almost continually—the king would spend half the night poring over his books and his maps, preparing his orders for the following day, and while he worked, a big white Kuvasz sprawled just inside the door.

King Matthias became so impressed with the Kuvasz that he developed a large pack to be used for hunting purposes. His kennels on his large estates in Siebenbuergen were among the most impressive in Europe, and the scope of his breeding did a great deal toward perpetuating a splendid strain of the breed. Surplus puppies were presented only to the noblemen and to visiting dignitaries.

Eventually, many specimens got into the hands of the commoners, but this was long after the time of King Matthias I, when herders found them suitable for work with sheep and cattle. It was in this later period that the name of the breed was corrupted to its present spelling. Incidentally, this spelling is rather unfortunate, because it changes the meaning rather ridiculously to that of "mongrel."

According to von Stephanitz, the great German authority on all Central European breeds, the Kuvasz is related to the Komondor, which had been brought from the Russian steppes by the Huns. He ventured the opinion that the *kawasz* or *kawwasz* was crossed with the indigenous country dog of Hungary. While this is something of a conjecture, there is strong evidence that points to truth. At any rate, the original type has proved dominant, and the

Kuvasz of today—perhaps a little smaller—is very similar to his earliest progenitors.

## Official Standard for the Kuvasz

**General Appearance**—A working dog of larger size, sturdily built, well balanced, neither lanky nor cobby. White in color with no markings. Medium boned, well muscled, without the slightest hint of bulkiness or lethargy. Impresses the eye with strength and activity combined with light-footedness, moves freely on strong legs. The following description is that of the ideal Kuvasz. Any deviation must be penalized to the extent of the deviation.

**Size, Proportion, Substance**—*Height* measured at the withers: Dogs, 28 to 30 inches; bitches, 26 to 28 inches. *Disqualifications*—Dogs smaller than 26 inches. Bitches smaller than 24 inches. *Weight*—Dogs approximately 100 to 115 pounds, bitches approximately 70 to 90 pounds. Trunk and limbs form a horizontal rectangle slightly deviated from the square. *Bone* in proportion to size of body. Medium, hard. Never heavy or coarse. Any tendency to weakness or lack of substance is a decided fault.

**Head**—Proportions are of great importance as the head is considered to be the most beautiful part of the Kuvasz. Length of head measured from tip of nose to occiput is slightly less than half the height of the dog at the withers. Width is half the length of the head. *Eyes* almond-shaped, set well apart, somewhat slanted. In profile, the eyes are set slightly below the plane of the muzzle. Lids tight, haws should not show. Dark brown, the darker the better. *Ears* V-shaped, tip is slightly rounded. Rather thick, they are well set back between the level of the eye and the top of the head. When pulled forward the tip of the ear should cover the eye. Looking at the dog face to face, the widest part of the ear is about level to the eye. The inner edge of the ear lies close to the cheek, the outer edge slightly away from the head forming a V. In the relaxed position, the ears should hold their set and not cast backward. The ears should not protrude above the head. The *skull* is elongated but not pointed. The stop is defined, never abrupt, raising the forehead gently above the plane of the muzzle. The longitudinal midline of the forehead is pronounced, widening as it slopes to the muzzle. Cheeks flat, bony arches above the eyes. The skin is dry. *Muzzle*: length in proportion to the length of the head, top straight, not pointed, underjaw well developed. Inside of the mouth preferably black. *Nose* large, black nostrils well opened. *Lips* black, closely covering the teeth. The upper lip covers tightly the upper jaw only; no excess flews. Lower lip tight and not pendulous. *Bite*—dentition full, scissors bite preferred. Level bite acceptable. *Disqualifications*—overshot bite; undershot bite.

**Neck, Topline, Body**—*Neck* muscular, without dewlap, medium length, arched at the crest. *Back* is of medium length, straight, firm and quite broad. The loin is short, muscular and tight. The croup well muscled, slightly sloping. Forechest is well developed. When viewed from the side, the forechest protrudes slightly in front of the shoulders. Chest deep with long, well-sprung ribs reaching almost to the elbows. The brisket is deep, well developed and runs parallel to the ground. The stomach is well tucked up. *Tail* carried low, natural length reaching at least to the hocks. In repose it hangs down resting on the body, the end but slightly lifted. In state of excitement, the tail may be elevated to the level of the loin, the tip slightly curved up. Ideally there should not be much difference in the carriage of the tail in state of excitement or in repose.

**Forequarters**—Shoulders muscular and long. Topline—withers are higher than the back. The scapula and humerus form a right angle, are long and of equal length. Elbows neither in nor out. Legs are medium boned, straight and well muscled. The joints are dry, hard. Dewclaws on the forelegs should not be removed. *Feet* well padded. Pads resilient, black. Feet are closed tight, forming round "cat feet." Some hair between the toes, the less the better. Dark nails are preferred.

**Hindquarters**—The portion behind the hip joint is moderately long, producing wide, long and strong muscles of the upper thigh. The femur is long, creating well-bent stifles. Lower thigh is long, dry, well muscled. Metatarsus is short, broad and of great strength. Dewclaws, if any, are removed. Feet as in front, except the rear paws somewhat longer.

**Coat**—The Kuvasz has a double coat, formed by guard hair and fine undercoat. The texture of the coat is medium coarse. The coat ranges from quite wavy to straight. Distribution follows a definite pattern over the body regardless of coat type. The head, muzzle, ears and paws are covered with short, smooth hair. The neck has a mane that extends to and covers the chest. Coat on the front of the forelegs up to the elbows and the hind legs below the thighs is short and smooth. The backs of the forelegs are feathered to the pastern with hair 2 to 3 inches long. The body and sides of the thighs are covered with a medium length coat. The back of the thighs and the entire tail are covered with hair 4 to 6 inches long. It is natural for the Kuvasz to lose most of the long coat during hot weather. Full luxuriant coat comes in seasonally, depending on climate. Summer coat should not be penalized.

**Color**—White. The skin is heavily pigmented. The more slate gray or black pigmentation the better. *Disqualification:* any color other than white.

**Gait**—Easy, free and elastic. Feet travel close to the ground. Hind legs reach far under, meeting or even passing the imprints of the front legs. Moving toward an observer, the front legs do not travel parallel to each other, but rather close together at the ground. When viewed from the rear, the hind legs (from the hip joint down) also move close to the ground. As speed increases, the legs gradually angle more inward until the pads are almost single-tracking. Unless excited, the head is carried rather low at the level of the shoulders. Desired movement cannot be maintained without sufficient angulation and firm slimness of body.

**Temperament**—A spirited dog of keen intelligence, determination, courage and curiosity. Very sensitive to praise and blame. Primarily a one-family dog. Devoted, gentle and patient without being overly demonstrative. Always ready to protect loved ones even to the point of self-sacrifice. Extremely strong instinct to protect children. Polite to accepted strangers, but rather suspicious and very discriminating in making new friends. Unexcelled guard, possessing ability to act on his own initiative at just the right moment without instruction. Bold, courageous and fearless. Untiring ability to work and cover rough terrain for long periods of time. Has good scent and has been used to hunt game.

DISQUALIFICATIONS

*Overshot bite. Undershot bite.*
*Dogs smaller than 26 inches. Bitches smaller than 24 inches.*
*Any color other than white.*

Approved July 9, 1974
Reformatted March 28, 1991

# Mastiff

The breed commonly called "Mastiff" in English speaking countries is more properly described as the *Old English* Mastiff. It is a giant short-haired dog, with heavy head and short muzzle, which has been bred in England for over two thousand years as a watchdog. The term "mastiff" describes a group of giant varieties of dog rather than a single breed. They are supposed to have originated in Asia.

So little is known about dogs of any sort prior to a century ago that almost all theories of ancestry are of small importance. Every partisan would like to claim the greatest antiquity for his particular sort of Mastiff as well as to say that the other sorts sprang from it. There is very little proof one way or the other.

Cassel finds drawings on Egyptian monuments of typical Mastiffs dating about 3000 B.C. In literature, the earliest reference is in Chinese about 1121 B.C. So much for the undoubted antiquity of the Mastiff group's ancestry.

So far as the Mastiff is concerned, it has a longer history than most. Caesar describes them in his account of invading Britain in 55 B.C., when they fought beside their masters against the Roman legions with such courage and power as to make a great impression. Soon afterward we find several different accounts of the huge British fighting dogs brought back to Rome where they defeated all other varieties in combat at the Circus. They were also matched against human gladiators as well as against bulls, bears, lions, and tigers.

Today we are likely to think of such cruel spectacles as belonging only to the dim ages of the past, but this is not true. Dog fights, bullbaiting, and bearbaiting were respectable and popular forms of amusement in England and America little more than a century ago. Such brutalizing events were patronized by nobility and clergy in England, while public-spirited citizens left legacies so that the common folk might be entertained in this way on holidays.

Dogfighting and animal-baiting were made illegal in England in 1835, but for twenty years longer the law was little obeyed. American dog fanciers are interested in the word *fancier*, which was synonymous with *bettor*—meaning especially a bettor on a dog or prize fight—and are interested also in the name of one of the most fashionable sporting establishments in London, over a hundred years ago, called the "Westminster Pit," with 300 seats. *Westminster* meant "dogs" even then—but fighting dogs!

While the Mastiff was always in front rank as a fighting dog, this does not account for his popularity in England for two thousand years. It was as bandogs, or tiedogs (tied by day but loose at night) that they were found everywhere. In fact, long ago, keeping of these Mastiffs was compulsory for the peasants. During Anglo-Saxon times there had to be kept at least one Mastiff for each two villeins. By this means wolves and other savage game were kept under control. They were also used in hunting packs by the nobility. It was as protectors of the home, however, that they were most used, and probably as a result of centuries of such service the Mastiff has acquired unique traits as a family dog.

That the Mastiff has long been numerous is indicated by the development of the English language itself. The ancient word in Anglo-Saxon and in over a score of kindred languages for a member of the canine race is *hound* or something very similar. A rather modern word coming from the Latin languages is like *dog*, but in all but English it means a *Mastiff* sort. So we can believe that when the Normans conquered the Anglo-Saxons in 1066 and made Norman-French the official language of England, *dogues* (or Mastiffs) were so plentiful that people forgot eventually there was any other name for a canine creature. This is the only explanation a dog man can offer for such a peculiar change in a language.

Anecdotes extolling the power and agility of Mastiffs as well as their devotion to their masters would fill a large volume of marvels. Herodotus tells of Cyrus the Great, founder of the Persian Empire about 550 B.C., who received a Mastiff as a gift from the King of Albania. Cyrus matched the dog against another and also set it against a bull. But the Mastiff was meek, so Cyrus in disgust had it killed. News of this reception of his gift came back to the King of Albania. He sent messengers with another Mastiff—a bitch—to Cyrus, telling him that a Mastiff was no ordinary cur and that it scorned to notice such common creatures as a Persian dog or a bull. He urged him to select a worthy opponent such as a lion or even an elephant. The King of Albania concluded by saying Mastiffs were rare and royal gifts and that he would not send Cyrus another. Whereupon, says Herodotus, the Mastiff bitch was set to attack an elephant and did so with such fury and efficiency that she worried the elephant down to the ground and would have killed it.

That is probably the tallest Mastiff tale on record! However, it gives proof of the reputation of Mastiffs as powerful, agile, and courageous dogs. It is even more interesting to know that Albania was the land of the people known as Alani, an Asiatic race. Also that similar names stand for "mastiffs," *e.g. Alano, Alan,* and *Alaunt.*

The story of Sir Peers Legh, Knight of Lyme Hall (near Stockport, Cheshire) at the Battle of Agincourt, October 25, 1415, is well-known. He had brought his favorite Mastiff—also a bitch—to France, and when he fell, she stood over him and defended him many hours until he was picked up by English soldiers and carried to Paris, where he died of his wounds. The faithful Mastiff was returned to England and from her is descended the famous Lyme Hall strain which the family has bred over a period of over five centuries. In the drawing room of the castle is still to be seen an old stained-glass window portraying the gallant Sir Peers and his devoted Mastiff.

The present-day English Mastiff is based on the strains of Lyme Hall and that of the Duke of Devonshire's Kennels at Chatsworth. Chaucer writing in Middle English (a language resulting from a cross between old Anglo-Saxon and Norman-French) 300 years after the Norman Conquest, described the Old English Mastiff in his "Knight's Tale." He tried to use the Italian-French word for Mastiff, *Alan,* which is still used in English heraldry to describe the figure of "a Mastiff with cropped ears" on a coat of arms:

> Aboute his char ther wenten white *Alaunts*
> Twenty and mo, as gret as any stere
> To hunten at the leon or the dere.

So here is proof that 600 years ago Mastiffs were hunted in packs in England on such different game as lion or deer. Chaucer says they were as large as steer! Even though cattle were much smaller in those days, this is hard to credit. The white color is authentic. We have plenty of pictures and descriptions of white and piebald Mastiffs, often with long coats, of about a century ago.

The American Mastiff Club was formed in 1879, and some time thereafter disbanded. In 1920, the first Mastiff Club of America was founded and the present Club was established in 1929.

# Official Standard for the Mastiff

**General Appearance**—The Mastiff is a large, massive, symmetrical dog with a well-knit frame. The impression is one of grandeur and dignity. Dogs are more massive throughout. Bitches should not be faulted for being somewhat smaller in all dimensions while maintaining a proportionally powerful structure. A good evaluation considers positive qualities of type and soundness with equal weight.

**Size, Proportion, Substance**—*Size*—Dogs, minimum, 30 inches at the shoulder. Bitches, minimum, 27½ inches at the shoulder. *Fault*—Dogs or bitches below the minimum standard. The farther below standard, the greater the fault. **Proportion**—Rectangular, the length of the dog from forechest to rump is somewhat longer than the height at the withers. The height of the dog should come from depth of body rather than from length of leg. **Substance**—Massive, heavy boned, with a powerful muscle structure. Great depth and breadth desirable. *Fault*—Lack of substance or slab sided.

**Head**—In general, outline giving a massive appearance when viewed from any angle. Breadth greatly desired. **Eyes** set wide apart, medium in size, never too prominent. **Expression** alert but kindly. Color of eyes brown, the darker the better, and showing no haw. Light eyes or a predatory expression is undesirable. **Ears** small in proportion to the skull, V-shaped, rounded at the tips. Leather moderately thin, set widely apart at the highest points on the sides of the skull continuing the outline across the summit. They should lie close to the cheeks when in repose. Ears dark in color, the blacker the better, conforming to the color of the muzzle. **Skull** broad and somewhat flattened between the ears, forehead slightly curved, showing marked wrinkles which are particularly distinctive when at attention. Brows (superciliary ridges) moderately raised. Muscles of the temples well developed, those of the cheeks extremely powerful. Arch across the skull a flattened curve with a furrow up the center of the forehead. This extends from between the eyes to halfway up the skull. The **stop** between the eyes well marked but not too abrupt. Muzzle should be half the length of the skull, thus dividing the head into three parts—one for the foreface and two for the skull. In other words, the distance from the tip of the nose to stop is equal to one-half the distance between the stop and the occiput. Circumference of the muzzle (measured midway between the eyes and nose) to that of the head (measured before the ears) is as 3 is to 5. **Muzzle** short, broad under the eyes and running nearly equal in width to the end of the nose. Truncated, i.e. blunt and cut off square, thus forming a right angle with the upper line of the face. Of great depth from the point of the nose to the underjaw. Underjaw broad to the end and slightly rounded. Muzzle dark in color, the blacker the better. *Fault*—Snipiness of the muzzle. **Nose** broad and always dark in color, the blacker the better, with spread flat nostrils (not pointed or turned up) in profile. **Lips** diverging at obtuse angles with the septum and sufficiently pendulous so as to show a modified square profile. **Canine Teeth** healthy and wide apart. Jaws powerful. **Scissors bite** preferred, but a moderately undershot jaw should not be faulted providing the teeth are not visible when the mouth is closed.

**Neck, Topline, Body**—*Neck* powerful, very muscular, slightly arched, and of medium length. The neck gradually increases in circumference as it approaches the shoulder. Neck moderately "dry" (not showing an excess of loose skin). *Topline*—In profile the topline should be straight, level, and firm, not swaybacked, roached, or dropping off sharply behind the high point of the rump. *Chest* wide, deep, rounded, and well let down between the forelegs, extending at least to the elbow. Forechest should be deep and well defined with the breastbone extending in front of the foremost point of the shoulders. Ribs well rounded. False ribs deep and well set back. *Underline*—There should be a reasonable, but not exaggerated, tuck-up. *Back* muscular, powerful, and straight. When viewed from the rear, there should be a slight rounding over the rump. *Loins* wide and muscular. *Tail* set on moderately high and reaching to the hocks or a little below. Wide at the root, tapering to the end, hanging straight in repose, forming a slight curve, but never over the back when the dog is in motion.

**Forequarters**—*Shoulders* moderately sloping, powerful and muscular, with no tendency to looseness. Degree of front angulation to match correct rear angulation. *Legs* straight, strong and set wide apart, heavy boned. *Elbows* parallel to body. *Pasterns* strong and bent only slightly. *Feet* large, round, and compact with well arched toes. Black nails preferred.

**Hindquarters**—*Hindquarters* broad, wide and muscular. *Second thighs* well developed, leading to a strong hock joint. *Stifle joint* is moderately angulated matching the front. *Rear legs* are wide apart and parallel when viewed from the rear. When the portion of the leg below the hock is correctly "set back" and stands perpendicular to the ground, a plumb line dropped from the rearmost point of the hindquarters will pass in front of the foot. This rules out straight hocks, and since stifle angulation varies with hock angulation, it also rules out insufficiently angulated stifles. *Fault*—Straight stifles.

**Coat**—Outer coat straight, coarse, and of moderately short length. Undercoat dense, short, and close lying. Coat should not be so long as to produce "fringe" on the belly, tail, or hind legs. *Fault*—Long or wavy coat.

**Color**—Fawn, apricot, or brindle. Brindle should have fawn or apricot as a background color which should be completely covered with very dark stripes. Muzzle, ears, and nose must be dark in color, the blacker the better, with similar color tone around the eye orbits and extending upward between them. A small patch of white on the chest is permitted. *Faults*—Excessive white on the chest or white on any other part of the body. Mask, ears, or nose lacking dark pigment.

**Gait**—The gait denotes power and strength. The rear legs should have drive, while the forelegs should track smoothly with good reach. In motion, the legs move straight forward; as the dog's speed increases from a walk to a trot, the feet move in toward the center line of the body to maintain balance.

**Temperament**—A combination of grandeur and good nature, courage and docility. Dignity, rather than gaiety, is the Mastiff's correct demeanor. Judges should not condone shyness or viciousness. Conversely, judges should also beware of putting a premium on showiness.

Approved November 12, 1991

# Newfoundland

There is much uncertainty about the origin of the Newfoundland. Some say that his ancestors are the white Great Pyrenees, dogs brought to the coast of Newfoundland by the Basque fishermen; others that he descended from a "French hound" (probably the Boarhound); but all agree that he originated in Newfoundland and that his ancestors were undoubtedly brought there by fishermen from the European continent. Many old prints of Newfoundlands show apparent evidence of a Husky ancestor, while other traits can be traced to other breeds. At any rate, a dog evolved which was particularly suited to the island of his origin.

He was a large dog, with size and strength to perform the tasks required of him. He had a heavy coat to protect him from the long winters and the icy waters surrounding his native island. His feet were large, strong, and webbed so that he might travel easily over marshes and shores. Admired for his physical powers and attractive disposition, he was taken to England where he was extensively bred. Today, most Newfoundlands of pedigree, even in Newfoundland, are descended from forebears born in England.

At the present time, the Newfoundland is admired and bred in many different countries including, besides his native land, England, France, Holland, Germany, Switzerland, Italy, Canada, and the United States.

The breed standard was written for a working dog, essentially a dog as much at home in the water as on dry land. Canine literature gives us stories of brave Newfoundlands which have rescued men and women from watery graves; stories of shipwrecks made less terrible by dogs which carried life lines to stricken vessels; of children who have fallen into deep water and have been brought safely ashore by Newfoundlands; and of dogs whose work was less spectacular but equally valuable as they helped their fishermen owners with their heavy nets and performed other tasks necessary to their occupations. Although he is a superior water dog, the Newfoundland has been used and is still used in Newfoundland and Labrador as a true working dog, dragging carts, or more often carrying burdens as a pack horse.

In order to perform these duties the Newfoundland must be a large dog—large enough to bring ashore a drowning man. He must have powerful hindquarters and a lung capacity which enables him to swim for great distances. He must have the heavy coat which protects him from the icy waters. In short, he must be strong, muscular, and sound so that he may do the work for which he has become justly famous. Above all things, the Newfoundland must have the intelligence, the loyalty, and the sweetness which are his best-known traits. He must be able and willing to help his master perform his necessary tasks at command, and also have the intelligence to act on his own responsibility when rescue work demands it.

In this country, where the Newfoundland is kept, not as an active worker, but as a companion, guard, and friend, we appreciate particularly the sterling traits of the true Newfoundland disposition. Here we have the great size and strength which makes him an effective guard and watchdog combined with the gentleness which makes him a safe companion. For generations he has been the traditional children's protector and playmate. He is not easily hurt by small tugging fingers (as is a smaller dog) and he seems to undertake the duties of nursemaid of his own accord without training. We know of no better description of the character of the Newfoundland dog than the famous epitaph on the monument at Lord Byron's estate, at Newstead Abbey in England:

> Near this spot
> are deposited the Remains of one
> who possessed Beauty without Vanity,
> Strength without Insolence,
> Courage without Ferocity,
> and all the Virtues of Man without his Vices.

This Praise, which would be unmeaning Flattery
if inscribed over human Ashes,
is but a just tribute to the Memory of
BOATSWAIN, a DOG,
who was born in Newfoundland May 1803
and died at Newstead Nov. 18th, 1808.

## Official Standard for the Newfoundland

**General Appearance**—The Newfoundland is a sweet-dispositioned dog that acts neither dull nor ill-tempered. He is a devoted companion. A multi-purpose dog, at home on land and in water, the Newfoundland is capable of draft work and possesses natural lifesaving abilities.

The Newfoundland is a large, heavily coated, well balanced dog that is deep-bodied, heavily boned, muscular, and strong. A good specimen of the breed has dignity and proud head carriage.

The following description is that of the ideal Newfoundland. Any deviation from this ideal is to be penalized to the extent of the deviation. Structural and movement faults common to all working dogs are as undesirable in the Newfoundland as in any other breed, even though they are not specifically mentioned herein.

**Size, Proportion, Substance**—Average height for adult dogs is 28 inches, for adult bitches, 26 inches. Approximate weight of adult dogs ranges from 130 to 150 pounds, adult bitches from 100 to 120 pounds. The dog's appearance is more massive throughout than the bitch's. Large size is desirable, but never at the expense of balance, structure, and correct gait. The Newfoundland is slightly longer than tall when measured from the point of shoulder to point of buttocks and from withers to ground. He is a dog of considerable substance which is determined by spring of rib, strong muscle, and heavy bone.

**Head**—The head is massive, with a broad *skull,* slightly arched crown, and strongly developed occipital bone. Cheeks are well developed. *Eyes* are dark brown. (Browns and Grays may have lighter eyes and should be penalized only to the extent that color affects expression.) They are relatively small, deepset, and spaced wide apart. Eyelids fit closely with no inversion. *Ears* are relatively small and triangular with rounded tips. They are set on the skull level with, or slightly above, the brow and lie close to the head. When the ear is brought forward, it reaches to the inner corner of the eye on the same side. *Expression* is soft and reflects the characteristics of the breed: benevolence, intelligence, and dignity.

Forehead and face are smooth and free of wrinkles. Slope of the stop is moderate but, because of the well developed brow, it may appear abrupt in profile. The *muzzle* is clean-cut, broad throughout its length, and deep. Depth and length are approximately equal, the length from tip of nose to stop being less than that from stop to occiput. The top of the muzzle is rounded, and the bridge, in profile, is straight or only slightly arched. Teeth meet in a scissors or level *bite.* Dropped lower incisors, in an otherwise normal bite, are not indicative of a skeletal malocclusion and should be considered only a minor deviation.

**Neck, Topline, Body**—The *neck* is strong and well set on the shoulders and is long enough for proud head carriage. The *back* is strong, broad, and muscular and is level from just behind the withers to the croup. The chest is full and deep with the brisket reaching at least down to the elbows. Ribs are well sprung, with the anterior third of the rib cage tapered to allow elbow clearance. The flank is deep. The croup is broad and slopes slightly. *Tail*—Tail set follows the natural lines of the croup. The tail is broad at the base and strong. It has no kinks, and the distal bone reaches to the hock. When the dog is standing relaxed, its tail hangs straight or with a slight curve at the end. When the dog is in motion or excited, the tail is carried out, but it does not curl over the back.

**Forequarters**—Shoulders are muscular and well laid back. Elbows lie directly below the highest point of the withers. Forelegs are muscular, heavily boned, straight, and parallel to each other, and the elbows point directly to the rear. The distance from elbow to ground equals about half the dog's height. Pasterns are strong and slightly sloping. Feet are proportionate to the body in size, webbed, and cat foot in type. Dewclaws may be removed.

**Hindquarters**—The rear assembly is powerful, muscular, and heavily boned. Viewed from the rear, the legs are straight and parallel. Viewed from the side, the thighs are broad and fairly long. Stifles and hocks are well bent and the line from hock to ground is perpendicular. Hocks are well let down. Hind feet are similar to the front feet. Dewclaws should be removed.

**Coat**—The adult Newfoundland has a flat, water-resistant, double coat that tends to fall back into place when rubbed against the nap. The outer coat is coarse, moderately long, and full, either straight or with a wave. The undercoat is soft and dense, although it is often less dense during the summer months or in warmer climates. Hair on the face and muzzle is short and fine. The backs of the legs are feathered all the way down. The tail is covered with long dense hair. Excess hair may be trimmed for neatness. Whiskers need not be trimmed.

**Color**—Color is secondary to type, structure, and soundness. Recognized Newfoundland colors are black, brown, gray, and white and black.

**Solid Colors**—Blacks, Browns, and Grays may appear as solid colors or solid colors with white at any, some, or all, of the following locations: chin, chest, toes, and tip of tail. Any amount of white found at these locations is typical and is not penalized. Also typical are a tinge of bronze on a black or gray coat and lighter furnishings on a brown or gray coat.

**Landseer**—White base coat with black markings. Typically, the head is solid black, or black with white on the muzzle, with or without a blaze. There is a separate black saddle and black on the rump extending onto a white tail.

Markings, on either Solid Colors or Landseers, might deviate considerably from those described and should be penalized only to the extent of the deviation. Clear white or white with minimal ticking is preferred.

Beauty of markings should be considered only when comparing dogs of otherwise comparable quality and never at the expense of type, structure and soundness.

**Disqualifications**—Any colors or combinations of colors not specifically described are disqualified.

**Gait**—The Newfoundland in motion has good reach, strong drive, and gives the impression of effortless power. His gait is smooth and rhythmic, covering the maximum amount of ground with the minimum number of steps. Forelegs and hind legs travel straight forward. As the dog's speed increases, the legs tend toward single tracking. When moving, a slight roll of the skin is characteristic of the breed. Essential to good movement is the balance of correct front and rear assemblies.

**Temperament**—Sweetness of temperament is the hallmark of the Newfoundland; this is the most important single characteristic of the breed.

### DISQUALIFICATIONS

*Any colors or combinations of colors not specifically described are disqualified.*

Approved May 8, 1990

# The Portuguese Water Dog

The Portuguese Water Dog once existed all along Portugal's coast, where it was taught to herd fish into the nets, to retrieve lost tackle or broken nets, and to act as a courier from ship to ship, or ship to shore. Portuguese Water Dogs rode in bobbing trawlers as they worked their way from the warm Atlantic waters of Portugal to the frigid fishing waters off the coats of Iceland where the fleets caught saltwater codfish to bring home.

In Portugal, the breed is called *Cao de Agua* (pronounced Kown-d'Ahgwa). *Cao* means dog, *de Agua* means of water. In his native land, the dog is also known as the Portuguese Fishing Dog. *Cao de Agua de Pelo Ondulado* is the name given the long-haired variety, and *Cao de Ague de Pelo Encaradolado* is the name for the curly-coat variety.

A calm intelligent breed of fine temperament, rugged and robust, with a profuse non-allergenic, non-shedding, waterproof coat and webbed feet, he is an ideal outdoor dog, capable of limitless work. He stands 20 to 23 inches (17 to 21 for bitches) and weighs between 42 and 60 pounds (35 and 50 for bitches) —a variation explained for by the fact that small dogs were more practical for small boats, and larger dogs for the larger boats.

He is shown in either of two clips—the lion clip, with the middle, hind-quarters and muzzle clipped short and the rest of the coat left long, and in the working-retriever clip. Adherents of the lion clip say it shows off a good rear and displays the muscles better, while advocates of the working-retriever clip like the fact that it is easy to care for, and prepares the dog for all sorts of outdoor adventure.

Some belief exists that the breed traces as far back as 700 B.C. to the wild central-Asian steppes, near the Chinese-Russian border, terrains and waters guaranteed to nourish ruggedness. The early people who lived here raised cattle, sheep, camels or horses, dependent upon where they lived. They also raised dogs to herd them. Isolated from the rest of the world, these dogs developed into a definite type, very much like the heavier long-coated Portuguese Water Dog.

One theory of these long-perished times is that some of the rugged Asian herding dogs were captured by the fierce Berbers. The Berbers spread slowly across the face of North Africa to Morocco. Their descendants, the Moors, arrived in Portugal in the 8th century, bringing the water dogs with them.

Another theory purports that some of the dogs left the Asian steppes with the Goths, a confederation of German tribes. Some (the Ostrogoths) went West and their dogs became the German *pudel*. Others (the Visigoths) went south to fight the Romans, and their dogs became the Lion Dog. In A.D. 400, the Visigoths invaded Spain and Portugal (then known only as Iberia) and the dogs found their homeland.

Portuguese Water Dog (lion clip)

Portuguese Water Dog (working-retriever clip)

These theories explain how the Poodle and the Portuguese Water Dog may have developed from the same ancient genetic pool. At one time the Poodle was a longer-coated dog, as is one variety of the Portuguese Water Dog. The possibility also exists that some of the long-coated water dogs grew up with the ancient Iberians. In early times, Celtiberians migrated from lands which now belong to southwestern Germany. Swarming over the Pyrenees, circulating over the whole of western Europe, they established bases in Iberia, as well as in Ireland, Wales and Brittany. The Irish Water Spaniel is believed to be a descendant of the Portuguese Water Dog.

Cloistered along remote cliffs of the rugged coast of southern Portugal, the breed remained in its rough form for centuries. But early in the 20th century, as the now agricultural country experienced social upheaval, the dog shared the fate of the Portuguese fishermen who were quickly vanishing from the coastline.

In the 1930s a wealthy Portuguese shipping magnate and dog fancier, Dr. Vasco Bensuade, took it upon himself to save the breed. The *Clube dos Cacadores Portuguese* was reorganized, the breed was exhibited in shows, a standard was written, and the breed was classified as a Working Dog by the *Clube Portuguese de Caniculture.*

In 1954, a few Portuguese Water Dogs were exported from Portugal to England. The Kennel Club (England) recognized the breed as a Working Dog. Though accepted, the breed languished in the British Isles, and there were no registrations after 1957.

Interest in the United States first began in 1958 when Mr. and Mrs. Harrington of New York received a pair from England as part of a trade of rare breeds. Among those taking an early interest in the breed were Mr. and Mrs. Herbert Miller of Connecticut, who acquired the first direct import to this country from Portugal—a puppy bitch purchased from Senhora Branco, a former lady bullfighter who had inherited Dr. Bensuade's kennels in Portugal.

On August 13, 1972, 16 people involved with the breed met at the Millers' home to form the Portuguese Water Dog Club of America. At the time there were only 12 known dogs of the breed in America, but the breeders worked dedicatedly, and by September 1982 the number of dogs had grown to over 650, located in 41 states, and there were over 50 serious breeders. The Portuguese Water Dog was admitted to the Miscellaneous class on June 3, 1981. Three months later, the breed had its first Obedience champion, Spindrift Kedge. The Portuguese Water Dog was accepted for registration in AKC stud books effective August 1, 1983, and became eligible to compete in the show rings as a member of the Working Group, effective January 1, 1984.

# Official Standard for the Portuguese Water Dog

**General Appearance**—Known for centuries along Portugal's coast, this seafaring breed was prized by fishermen for a spirited, yet obedient nature, and a robust, medium build that allowed for a full day's work in and out of the water. The Portuguese Water Dog is a swimmer and diver of exceptional ability and stamina, who aided his master at sea by retrieving broken nets, herding schools of fish, and carrying messages between boats and to shore. He is a loyal companion and alert guard. This highly intelligent utilitarian breed is distinguished by two coat types, either curly or wavy; an impressive head of considerable breadth and well proportioned mass; a ruggedly built, well-knit body; and a powerful, thickly based tail, carried gallantly or used purposefully as a rudder. The Portuguese Water Dog provides an indelible impression of strength, spirit, and soundness.

**Size, Proportion, Substance**—*Size*—Height at the withers—Males, 20 to 23 inches. The ideal is 22 inches. Females 17 to 21 inches. The ideal is 19 inches. Weight for males, 42 to 60 pounds; for females, 35 to 50 pounds. *Proportion*—Off square; slightly longer than tall when measured from posternum to rearmost point of the buttocks, and from withers to ground. *Substance*—Strong, substantial bone; well developed, neither refined nor coarse, and a solidly built, muscular body.

**Head**—An essential characteristic; distinctively large, well proportioned and with exceptional breadth of topskull. *Expression*—Steady, penetrating, and attentive. *Eyes*—Medium in size; set well apart, and a bit obliquely. Roundish and neither prominent nor sunken. Black or various tones of brown in color. Darker eyes are preferred. Eye rims fully pigmented with black edges in black, black and white, or white dogs; brown edges in brown dogs. Haws are dark and not apparent. *Ears*—Set well above the line of the eye. Leather is heart shaped and thin. Except for a small opening at the back, ears are held nicely against the head. Tips should not reach below the lower jaw. *Skull*—In profile, it is slightly longer than the muzzle, its curvature more accentuated at the back than in the front. When viewed head-on, the top of the skull is very broad and appears domed, with a slight depression in the middle. The forehead is prominent, and has a central furrow, extending two-thirds of the distance from stop to occiput. The occiput is well defined. *Stop*—Well defined. *Muzzle*—Substantial; wider at the base than at the nose. *Jaws*—Strong and neither over nor undershot. *Nose*—Broad, well flared nostrils. Fully pigmented; black in dogs with black, black and white, or white coats; various tones of brown in dogs with brown coats. *Lips*—Thick, especially in front; no flew. Lips and mucous membranes of the roof of the mouth, under tongue, and gums are quite black, or well ticked with black in dogs with black, black and white, or white coats; various tones of brown in dogs with brown coats. *Bite*—Scissors or level. *Teeth*—Not visible when the mouth is closed. Canines strongly developed.

**Neck, Topline, Body**—*Neck*—Straight, short, round, and held high. Strongly muscled. No dewlap. *Topline*—Level and firm. *Body*—*Chest* is broad and deep, reaching down to the elbow. *Ribs* are long and well-sprung to provide optimum lung capacity. *Abdomen* well held up in a graceful line. *Back* is broad and well muscled. *Loin* is short and meets the croup smoothly. *Croup* is well formed and only slightly inclined with hip bones hardly apparent. *Tail*—Not docked; thick at the base and tapering; set on slightly below the line of the back; should not reach below the hock. When the dog is attentive the tail is held in a ring, the front of which should not reach forward of the loin. The tail is of great help when swimming and diving.

**Forequarters**—*Shoulders* are well inclined and very strongly muscled. *Upper arms* are strong. *Forelegs* are strong and straight with long, well muscled forearms. *Carpus* is heavy-boned, wider in front than at the side. *Pasterns* are long and strong. Dewclaws may be removed. *Feet* are round and rather flat. Toes neither knuckled up nor too long. Webbing between the toes is of soft skin, well covered with hair, and reaches the toe tips. Central pad is very thick, others normal. Nails held up slightly off the ground. Black, brown, white, and striped nails are allowed.

**Hindquarters**—Powerful; well balanced with the front assembly. *Legs,* viewed from the rear, are parallel to each other, straight and very strongly muscled in upper and lower thighs. *Buttocks* are well developed. *Tendons* and hocks are strong. *Metatarsus* long, no dewclaws. *Feet* similar in all respects to forefeet.

**Coat**—A profuse, thickly planted coat of strong, healthy hair, covering the whole body evenly, except where the forearm meets the brisket and in the groin area, where it is thinner. No undercoat, mane or ruff. There are *two varieties of coat: **Curly***—Compact, cylindrical curls, somewhat lusterless. The hair on the ears is sometimes wavy. **Wavy**— Falling gently in waves, not curls, and with a slight sheen. *No preference will be given to coat type, either curly or wavy.*

**Clip**—Two clips are acceptable: *Lion Clip*—As soon as the coat grows long, the middle part and hindquarters, as well as the muzzle, are clipped. The hair at the end of the tail is left at full length. *Retriever Clip*—In order to give a natural appearance and a smooth unbroken line, the entire coat is scissored or clipped to follow the outline of the dog, leaving a short blanket of coat no longer than one inch in length. The hair at the end of the tail is left at full length. *No discrimination will be made against the correct presentation of a dog in either Lion Clip or Retriever Clip.*

**Color**—Black, white, and various tones of brown; also combinations of black or brown with white. A white coat does not imply albinism provided nose, mouth, and eyelids are black. In animals with black, white, or black and white coats, the skin is decidedly bluish.

**Gait**—Short, lively steps when walking. The trot is a forward striding, well balanced movement.

**Temperament**—An animal of spirited disposition, self-willed, brave, and very resistant to fatigue. A dog of exceptional intelligence and a loyal companion, it obeys its master with facility and apparent pleasure. It is obedient with those who look after it or with those for whom it works.

**Summary Statement**—The Portuguese Water Dog is spirited yet obedient, robust, and of unexaggerated, functional conformation; sure, substantially boned and muscled, and able to do a full day's work in and out of the water.

### FAULTS

Any deviation from the described ideal is a fault. However, those inherent characteristics that are imperative for the maintenance of proper type, and therefore cannot be overlooked, are listed as Major Faults.

### MAJOR FAULTS

1. *Temperament*—Shy, vicious, or unsound behavior.
2. *Head*—Unimpressive; small in overall size; narrow in topskull; snipy in muzzle.
3. *Substance*—Light or refined in bone; lacking in muscle.
4. *Coat*—Sparse; naturally short, close-lying hair, partially or overall; wispy or wiry in texture; brittle; double-coated.
5. *Tail*—Other than as described. Extremely low set. Heavy or droopy in action.
6. *Pigment*—Any deviation from described pigmentation; other than black or various tones of brown eye color; pink or partial pigmentation in nose, lips, eyes, or eye rims.
7. *Bite*—Overshot or undershot.

Approved January 15, 1991

# Rottweiler

The origin of the Rottweiler is not a documented record. Once this is recognized, actual history tempered by reasonable supposition indicates the likelihood he is descended from one of the drover dogs indigenous to ancient Rome. This drover dog has been described by various accredited sources as having been of the Mastiff type—a dependable, rugged, willing worker, possessed of great intelligence and a strong guarding instinct.

The transition from Roman herding dog to the dog we know today as the Rottweiler can be attributed to the ambitions of the Roman Emperors to conquer Europe. Very large armies were required for these expeditions and the logistics of feeding that number of men became a major consideration. No means of refrigeration existed which meant that the meat for the soldiers had to accompany the troops "on the hoof." The services of a dog capable of keeping the herd intact during the long march were needed. The above described "Mastiff type" was admirably suited to both that job and the additional responsibility of guarding the supply dumps at night.

Campaigns of the Roman Army varied in scope, but the one of concern to us took place approximately A.D. 74. Its route was across the Alps terminating in what is now southern Germany. Arae Flaviae, as the new territory was called, had natural advantages of climate, soil and central location. There is much evidence pointing to the vital role of the fearless Roman drover dog on this trek from Rome to the banks of the Neckar River.

We have no reason to doubt that descendants of the original Roman drover dogs continued to guard the herds through the next two centuries. Circa A.D. 260 the Swabians ousted the Romans from Arae Flaviae, taking over the city. Agriculture and the trading of cattle remained their prime occupations, insuring the further need for the dogs.

About A.D. 700 the local Duke ordered a Christian church built on the site of the former Roman Baths. Excavations unearthed the red tiles of Roman villas. To distinguish the town from others, it was then named "das Rote Wil" (the red tile), which of course is recognizable as the derivation of the present Rottweil.

Rottweil's dominance as a cultural and trade center increased unabated and in the middle of the 12th Century further fame and fortune came to it. An all new town with elaborate fortifications was built on the heights above the river. The security thus provided attracted yet increased commerce in cattle. Butchers concentrated in the area and inevitably more dogs were needed to drive the cattle to and from the markets.

The descendants of the Roman drover dog plied their trade without interruption until the middle of the 19th Century at which time the driving of cattle was outlawed; in addition the donkey and the railroad replaced the dog cart.

The Rottweiler Metzgerhund (butcher dog), as he came to be called, then fell on hard times. His function had been severely curtailed and in those days, dogs earned their keep or there was no reason for their existence. The number of Rottweilers declined so radically that in 1882 the dog show in Heilbronn, Germany reported just one poor example of the breed present.

The annals of cynology make no further mention of the breed until 1901 when a combined Rottweiler and Leonberger Club was formed. This Club was short lived but notable because the first Rottweiler standard appeared under its auspices. It is of value for us to know that the general type advocated has not changed substantially and the character called for, not at all.

In these years (1901–1907) the Rottweiler again found favor as a police dog. Several clubs were organized as dissension was most common until 1921 when it was agreed to form the *Allegmeiner Deutscher Rottweiler Klub* (ADRK). By that time 3400 Rottweilers had been registered by three or four clubs. Duplications and confusion ended when the ADRK published its first stud book in 1924.

Since its inception, despite the difficulties encountered during and in the aftermath of World War II, the ADRK has remained intact and through its leadership enlightened, purposeful breeding programs have been promoted both in Germany and abroad.

The first Rottweiler was admitted to the American Kennel Club Stud Book in 1931. The standard was adopted in 1935. The first obedience title awarded an American Rottweiler was achieved in 1939 and the first championship nine years later in 1948. Parent club of the breed is the American Rottweiler Club, organized in 1971, and approved for its first Specialty Show in 1981.

Perhaps he has departed physically from his Roman ancestor, but assuredly the characteristics for which he was so admired in Roman times have been preserved and are the very attributes for which the Rottweiler is held in such high esteem today.

## Official Standard for the Rottweiler

**General Appearance**—The ideal Rottweiler is a medium large, robust and powerful dog, black with clearly defined rust markings. His compact and substantial build denotes great strength, agility and endurance. Dogs are characteristically more massive throughout with larger frame and heavier bone than bitches. Bitches are distinctly feminine, but without weakness of substance or structure.

**Size, Proportion, Substance**—Dogs—24 inches to 27 inches. Bitches—22 inches to 25 inches, with preferred size being mid-range of each sex. Correct proportion is of primary importance, as long as size is within the standard's range. The length of body, from prosternum to the rearmost projection of the rump, is slightly longer than the height of the dog at the withers, the most desirable proportion of the height to length being 9 to 10. The Rottweiler is neither coarse nor shelly. Depth of chest is approximately fifty percent (50%) of the height of the dog. His bone and muscle mass must be sufficient to balance his frame, giving a compact and very powerful appearance. *Serious Faults*—Lack of proportion, undersized, oversized, reversal of sex characteristics (bitchy dogs, doggy bitches).

**Head**—Of medium length, broad between the ears; forehead line seen in profile is moderately arched; zygomatic arch and stop well developed with strong broad upper and lower jaws. The desired ratio of backskull to muzzle is 3 to 2. Forehead is preferred dry, however some wrinkling may occur when dog is alert. *Expression* is noble, alert, and self-assured. *Eyes* of medium size, almond shaped with well fitting lids, moderately deep-set, neither protruding nor receding. The desired color is a uniform dark brown. *Serious Faults*—Yellow (bird of prey), eyes, eyes of different color or size, hairless eye rim. *Disqualification*—Entropion. Ectropion. *Ears* of medium size, pendant, triangular in shape; when carried alertly the ears are level with the top of the skull and appear to broaden it. Ears are to be set well apart, hanging forward with the inner edge lying tightly against the head and terminating at approximately mid-cheek. *Serious Faults*—Improper carriage (creased, folded or held away from cheek/head). *Muzzle*—Bridge is straight, broad at base and slight tapering toward tip. The end of the muzzle is broad with well developed chin. Nose is broad rather than round and always black. Lips—Always black; corners closed; inner mouth pigment is preferred dark. *Serious Faults*—Total lack of mouth pigment (pink mouth). *Bite and Dentition*—Teeth 42 in number (20 upper, 22 lower), strong, correctly placed, meeting in a scissors bite—lower incisors touching inside of upper incisors. *Serious Faults*—Level bite; any missing tooth. *Disqualifications*—Overshot, undershot (when incisors do not touch or mesh); wry mouth; two or more missing teeth.

**Neck, Topline, Body**—*Neck*—Powerful, well muscled, moderately long, slightly arched and without loose skin. *Topline*—The back is firm and level, extending in a straight line from behind the withers to the croup. The back remains horizontal to the ground while the dog is moving or standing. *Body*—The chest is roomy, broad and deep, reaching to elbow, with well pronounced forechest and well sprung, oval ribs. Back is straight and strong. Loin is short, deep and well muscled. Croup is broad, of medium length and only slightly sloping. Underline of a mature Rottweiler has a slight tuck-up. Males must have two normal testicles properly descended into the scrotum. *Disqualification*—Unilateral cryptorchid or cryptorchid males. *Tail*—Tail docked short, close to body, leaving one or two tail vertebrae. The set of the tail is more important than length. Properly set, it gives an impression of elongation of topline; carried slightly above horizontal when the dog is excited or moving.

**Forequarters**—Shoulder blade is long and well laid back. Upper arm equal in length to shoulder blade, set so elbows are well under body. Distance from withers to elbow and elbow to ground is equal. Legs are strongly developed with straight, heavy bone, not set close together. Pasterns are strong, springy and almost perpendicular to the ground. Feet are round, compact with well arched toes, turning neither in nor out. Pads are thick and hard. Nails short, strong and black. Dewclaws may be removed.

**Hindquarters**—Angulation of hindquarters balances that of forequarters. Upper thigh is fairly long, very broad and well muscled. Stifle joint is well turned. Lower thigh is long, broad and powerful, with extensive muscling leading into a strong hock joint. Rear pasterns are nearly perpendicular to the ground. Viewed from the rear, hind legs are straight, strong and wide enough apart to fit with a properly built body. Feet are somewhat longer than the front feet, turning neither in nor out, equally compact with well arched toes. Pads are thick and hard. Nails short, strong, and black. Dewclaws must be removed.

**Coat**—Outer coat is straight, coarse, dense, of medium length and lying flat. Undercoat should be present on neck and thighs, but the amount is influenced by climatic conditions. Undercoat should not show through outer coat. The coat is shortest on head, ears and legs, longest on breeching. The Rottweiler is to be exhibited in the natural condition with no trimming. *Fault*—Wavy coat. *Serious Faults*—Open, excessively short, or curly coat; total lack of undercoat; any trimming that alters the length of the natural coat. *Disqualification*—Long coat.

**Color**—Always black with rust to mahogany markings. The demarcation between black and rust is to be clearly defined. The markings should be located as follows: a spot over each eye; on cheeks; as a strip around each side of muzzle, but not on the bridge of the nose; on throat; triangular mark on both sides of prosternum; on forelegs from carpus downward to the toes; on inside of rear legs showing down the front of the stifle and broadening out to front of rear legs from hocks to toes, but not completely eliminating black from rear of pasterns; under tail; black penciling on toes. The undercoat is gray, tan, or black. Quantity and location of rust markings is important and should not exceed ten percent of body color. *Serious Faults*—Straw-colored, excessive, insufficient or sooty markings; rust marking other than described above; white marking any place on dog (a few rust or white hairs do not constitute a marking). *Disqualifications*—Any base color other than black; absence of all markings.

**Gait**—The Rottweiler is a trotter. His movement should be balanced, harmonious, sure, powerful and unhindered, with strong forereach and a powerful rear drive. The motion is effortless, efficient, and ground-covering. Front and rear legs are thrown neither in nor out, as the imprint of hind feet should touch that of forefeet. In a trot the forequarters and hindquarters are mutually coordinated while the back remains level, firm and relatively motionless. As speed increases the legs will converge under body towards a center line.

**Temperament**—The Rottweiler is basically a calm, confident and courageous dog with a self-assured aloofness that does not lend itself to immediate and indiscriminate friendships. A Rottweiler is self-confident and responds quietly and with a wait-and-see attitude to influences in his environment. He has an inherent desire to protect home and family, and is an intelligent dog of extreme hardness and adaptability with a strong willingness to work, making him especially suited as a companion, guardian and general all-purpose dog.

The behavior of the Rottweiler in the show ring should be controlled, willing and adaptable, trained to submit to examination of mouth, testicles, etc. An aloof or reserved dog should not be penalized, as this reflects the accepted character of the breed. An aggressive or belligerent attitude towards other dogs should not be faulted.

A judge shall excuse from the ring any shy Rottweiler. A dog shall be judged fundamentally shy if, refusing to stand for examination, it shrinks away from the judge.

A dog that in the opinion of the judge menaces or threatens him/her, or exhibits any sign that it may not be safely approached or examined by the judge in the normal manner, shall be excused from the ring. A dog that in the opinion of the judge attacks any person in the ring shall be disqualified.

### SUMMARY

**Faults**—The foregoing is a description of the ideal Rottweiler. Any structural fault that detracts from the above described working dog must be penalized to the extend of the deviation.

### DISQUALIFICATIONS

*Entropion, ectropion. Overshot, undershot (when incisors do not touch or mesh); wry mouth; two or more missing teeth. Unilateral cryptorchid or cryptorchid males. Long coat. Any base color other than black; absence of all markings. A dog that in the opinion of the judge attacks any person in the ring.*

Approved May 8, 1990

**Saint Bernard (Longhaired)**

**Saint Bernard (Shorthaired)**

# Saint Bernard

Shrouded in legend and the mists of time, the origin of the Saint Bernard is subject to many theories.

It seems most probable that the Saint Bernard developed from stock that resulted from the breeding of heavy Asian "Molosser" (*Canis molossus*), brought to Helvetia (Switzerland) by Roman armies during the first two centuries A.D., with native dogs which undoubtedly existed in the region at the time of the Roman invasions.

During the following centuries, these dogs were widely used in the valley farms and Alpine dairies for a variety of guarding, herding, and drafting duties. Referred to as *Talhund* (Valley Dog) or *Bauernhund* (Farm Dog), they were apparently well established by A.D. 1050, when Archdeacon Bernard de Menthon founded the famous Hospice in the Swiss Alps as a refuge for travelers crossing the treacherous passes between Switzerland and Italy.

Just when dogs were first brought to the Hospice is debatable, since the Hospice was destroyed by fire in the late 16th century, and, soon after, a large part of the Hospice archives were lost. The first notation concerning the dogs was not until 1707. This, however, was merely a casual reference to dogs at the Hospice and carried the implication that their rescue work at the St. Bernard Pass was a fact well known at the time. From a digest of early references, it appears that the dogs were first brought to the Hospice sometime between 1660 and 1670. It is likely that large dogs were recruited from the valley areas below to serve as watchdogs for the Hospice and companions for the Monks during the long winter months when the Hospice was almost completely isolated.

This isolation of the Hospice no doubt resulted in inbreeding of the original stock which soon produced the distinctive strain of "Hospice Dog." It also follows that only those animals with the strongest instincts for survival in the extremely adverse conditions at the Hospice were to leave their genetic imprint upon the breed during those early years.

The lonely Monks, who took the dogs along on their trips of mercy, soon discovered the animals were excellent pathfinders in the drifting snow, and the dogs' highly developed sense of smell made them invaluable in locating helpless persons overcome during storms. Thus began this working together of Monk and dog which made many of the world's most romantic pages of canine history.

During the three centuries that Saint Bernards have been used in rescue work at the Hospice, it is estimated that they have been responsible for the saving of well over 2,000 human lives. Although the building of railroad tunnels through the Alps has lessened foot and vehicular travel across the St. Bernard Pass, the Monks have continued to maintain these fine dogs for companionship and in the honor of the Hospice tradition.

We are told that Saint Bernards required no training for their work since generations of service in this capacity seemed to have stamped the rescuing instinct indelibly upon their character. It would be more accurate to say that the dogs' rescue instincts were used as the basis for training by the Monks. In the company of the Monks, young dogs were taken on patrols with a pack of older dogs in search of possible traveler casualties. When the dogs came upon a victim, they would lie down beside him to provide warmth for their bodies, and lick the person's face to restore consciousness. In the meantime, one of the patrol dogs would be on his way back to the Hospice to give the alarm and guide a rescue party to the scene.

In addition to their pathfinding capabilities and keen sense of smell which enables them to locate human beings buried under the snow, the dogs are reputed to possess an uncanny sixth sense which warns them of approaching avalanches. Instances have been reported where a dog would suddenly change position for no apparent reason a few seconds before an avalanche came hurtling down across the spot where he had stood, burying it under tons of snow and ice.

Although it was well known that a special type of dog did rescue work at the Hospice by 1800, the breed at that time had been given no name other than "Hospice Dogs." Between 1800 and 1810, Barry, perhaps the most celebrated dog in history, lived at the Hospice. For fully half a century after his death, the Hospice dogs in certain parts of Switzerland were called "Barryhund" (Barry dog) in his honor.

Barry is credited with saving forty lives. Although legend has it that he was killed by the forty-first person he attempted to rescue, who mistook his bulk for that of a wolf, this tale is only an interesting story. As a matter of fact, Barry was given a painless death in Bern, Switzerland, in 1814, after he had attained a ripe old age. His likeness in mounted form is now preserved in the Natural History Museum in Bern.

The years 1816 to 1818 were seasons of uncommonly severe weather at the Hospice, and, as a result, many of the leading Hospice strains perished. It was easy at that time, however, to get good animals of like breeding from the lower valleys, and within a few years, the dog situation at the Hospice was again satisfactory. Confronted by a similar situation in 1830, coupled with the fact that their breed was considerably weakened by inbreeding and disease, the Monks resorted to an outcross to give added size and new vigor to their dogs. The Newfoundland, which at that time was larger than the Saint Bernard and shared strong rescuing instincts, was the breed decided upon to give the new blood. Results of this cross showed all of the desired objectives and, at the same time, did not destroy the Saint Bernard type and characteristics. Due to this crossing, however, the first longhaired Saint Bernards appeared—prior to 1830 all the Saint Bernards were shorthaired dogs.

At first it was believed that the longhaired variety might have an advantage in the snow and icy conditions existing at the Hospice. Unfortunately, ice clung to the coat and made the longhaired dogs unsuited to the tasks of the rescue dogs. After this was determined, the Monks gave the longhaired dogs as gifts to friends and benefactors in the valley areas, and only the shorthaired dogs were kept at the Hospice.

The English, who as early as 1810, imported some of the Hospice dogs to replenish their Mastiff blood, referred to the breed for a number of years as "Sacred Dogs." In Germany, around 1828, the name of "Alpendog" was proposed. In 1833, a writer, Daniel Wilson, first spoke of the so-called Saint Bernard dog, but it was not until 1865 that this name definitely appeared, and only since 1880 has it been recognized as the official designation for the breed.

During the last half of the 1800s, breeding of both the longhaired and shorthaired Saint Bernards continued in the valleys of Switzerland, and eventually the breed spread across Germany and other continental European countries and England.

In 1887, an International Congress was held in Zurich which was guided by Swiss authorities on the breed. At this Congress, an International Standard for the perfection of the breed was developed.

The Saint Bernard Club of America was organized in 1888, the year following the Zurich Congress, and the International Standard was adopted by it. This club continues to function for the interests of the Saint Bernard and is one of the oldest specialty clubs in the United States.

## Official Standard for the Saint Bernard

### SHORTHAIRED

**General**—Powerful, proportionately tall figure, strong and muscular in every part, with powerful head and most intelligent expression. In dogs with a dark mask the expression appears more stern, but never ill-natured.

**Head**—Like the whole body, very powerful and imposing. The massive skull is wide, slightly arched and the sides slope in a gentle curve into the very strongly developed, high cheek bones. Occiput only moderately developed. The supraorbital ridge is very strongly developed and forms nearly a right angle with the horizontal axis of the head. Deeply imbedded between the eyes and starting at the root of the muzzle, a furrow runs over the whole skull. It is strongly marked in the first half, gradually disappearing toward the base of the occiput. The lines at the sides of the head diverge considerably from the outer corner of the eyes toward the back of the head. The skin of the forehead, above the eyes, forms rather noticeable wrinkles, more or less pronounced, which converge toward the furrow. Especially when the dog is in action, the wrinkles are more visible without in the least giving the impression of morosity. Too strongly developed wrinkles are not desired. The slope from the skull to the muzzle is sudden and rather steep. The muzzle is short, does not taper, and the vertical depth at the root of the muzzle must be greater than the length of the muzzle. The bridge of the muzzle is not arched, but straight; in some dogs, occasionally, slightly broken. A rather wide, well-marked, shallow furrow runs from the root of the muzzle over the entire bridge of the muzzle to the nose. The flews of the upper jaw are strongly developed, not sharply cut, but turning in a beautiful curve into the lower edge, and slightly overhanging. The flews of the lower jaw must not be deeply pendant. The teeth should be sound and strong and should meet in either a scissors or an even bite; the scissors bite being preferable. The undershot bite, although sometimes found with good specimens, is not desirable. The overshot bite is a fault. A black roof to the mouth is desirable. *Nose* (Schwamm)—Very substantial, broad, with wide open nostrils, and, like the lips, always black. *Ears*—Of medium size, rather high set, with very strongly developed burr (Muschel) at the base. They stand slightly away from the head at the base, then drop with a sharp bend to the side and cling to the head without a turn. The flap is tender and forms a rounded triangle, slightly elongated toward the point, the front edge lying firmly to the head, whereas the back edge may stand somewhat away from the head, especially when the dog is at attention. Lightly set ears, which at the base immediately cling to the head, give it an oval and too little marked exterior, whereas a strongly developed base gives the skull a squarer, broader and much more expressive appearance. *Eyes*—Set more to the front than the sides, are of medium size, dark brown, with intelligent, friendly expression, set moderately deep. The lower eyelids, as a rule, do not close completely and, if that is the case, form an angular wrinkle toward the inner corner of the eye. Eyelids which are too deeply pendant and show conspicuously the lachrymal glands, or a very red, thick haw, and eyes that are too light, are objectionable.

**Neck**—Set high, very strong and in action is carried erect. Otherwise horizontally or slightly downward. The junction of head and neck is distinctly marked by an indentation. The nape of the neck is very muscular and rounded at the sides which makes the neck appear rather short. The dewlap of throat and neck is well pronounced: too strong development, however, is not desirable.

**Shoulders**—Sloping and broad, very muscular and powerful. The withers are strongly pronounced.

**Chest**—Very well arched, moderately deep, not reaching below the elbows.

**Back**—Very broad, perfectly straight as far as the haunches, from there gently sloping to the rump, and merging imperceptibly into the root of the tail.

**Hindquarters**—Well-developed. Legs very muscular.

**Belly**—Distinctly set off from the very powerful loin section, only little drawn up.

**Tail**—Starting broad and powerful directly from the rump is long, very heavy, ending in a powerful tip. In repose it hangs straight down, turning gently upward in the lower third only, which is not considered a fault. In a great many specimens the tail is carried with the end slightly bent and therefore hangs down in the shape of an "*f.*" In action all dogs carry the tail more or less turned upward. However it may not be carried too erect or by any means rolled over the back. A slight curling of the tip is sooner admissible.

**Forearms**—Very powerful and extraordinarily muscular.

**Forelegs**—Straight, strong.

**Hind Legs**—Hocks of moderate angulation. Dewclaws are not desired; if present, they must not obstruct gait.

**Feet**—Broad, with strong toes, moderately closed, and with rather high knuckles. The so-called dewclaws which sometimes occur on the inside of the hind legs are imperfectly developed toes. They are of no use to the dog and are not taken into consideration in judging. They may be removed by surgery.

**Coat**—Very dense, short-haired (stockhaarig), lying smooth, tough, without however feeling rough to the touch. The thighs are slightly bushy. The tail at the root has longer and denser hair which gradually becomes shorter toward the tip. The tail appears bushy, not forming a flag.

**Color**—White with red or red with white, the red in its various shades; brindle patches with white markings. The colors red and brown-yellow are of entirely equal value. Necessary markings are: white chest, feet and tip of tail, noseband, collar or spot on the nape; the latter and blaze are very desirable. Never of one color or without white. Faulty are all other colors, except the favorite dark shadings on the head (mask) and ears. One distinguishes between mantle dogs and splash-coated dogs.

**Height at Shoulder**—Of the dog should be 27½ inches minimum, of the bitch 25 inches. Female animals are of finer and more delicate build.

**Considered as faults**—are all deviations from the Standard, as for instance a swayback and a disproportionately long back, hocks too much bent, straight hindquarters, upward growing hair in spaces between the toes, out at elbows, cowhocks and weak pasterns.

### LONGHAIRED

The longhaired type completely resembles the shorthaired type except for the coat which is not shorthaired (stockhaarig) but of medium length plain to slightly wavy, never rolled or curly and not shaggy either. Usually, on the back, especially from the region of the haunches to the rump, the hair is more wavy, a condition, by the way, that is slightly indicated in the shorthaired dogs. The tail is bushy with dense hair of moderate length. Rolled or curly hair on the tail is not desirable. A tail with parted hair, or a flag tail, is faulty. Face and ears are covered with short and soft hair; long hair at the base of the ear is permissible. Forelegs are only slightly feathered; thighs very bushy.

Approved May 12, 1959

# Samoyed

Dog of the ages, with a history and tradition as fascinating as the breed itself! The legend runs that, from the plateau of Iran, man's first earthly habitat, as the sons of man multiplied, the mightier tribes drove the lesser ones, with their families, their herds, and their dogs, farther and farther away in order that the natural food found there might be ample for those remaining. Onward and still farther northward through Mongolia, then the center of the world's culture, on and on, went the less tribes, until eventually the Samoyed peoples, primitives of the family of Sayantsi, reliably described as a race in the "transition stages between the Mongol pure and the Finn," found themselves safely entrenched behind bulwarks of snow and ice in the vast sketches of tundra reaching from the White Sea to the Yenisei River. Here for generations they have lived a nomadic life, dependent upon their reindeer herds and upon their dogs as reindeer shepherds, sledge dogs, and household companions.

Here, through the centuries, the Samoyed has bred true. Of all modern breeds, the Samoyed is most nearly akin to the primitive dog—no admixture of wolf or fox runs in the Samoyed strain. The Arctic suns and snows have bleached the harsh stand-off coat and tipped the hairs with an icy sheen. The constant companionship with man through the years has given an almost uncanny "human" understanding, while generations of guarding reindeer, requiring always a protector, never a killer, has developed through the ages in a breed a disposition unique in the canine world. Something of the happy child-like air of these primitive peoples is found as well in every Samoyed.

Nor has the long human association made the stalwart Samoyed a pampered pet. As work dogs Samoyeds of the great Arctic and Antarctic expeditions have a record of achievement unexcelled in the canine world. The sledge dogs of early polar explorer Fridtjof Nansen (19 males, averaging 58.7 pounds each, and 9 bitches averaging 50.5 pounds), working day after day under conditions of utmost hardship, drew one and a half times their own weight of supplies, and worked with the joyous abandon and carefree air typical of the breed. Each new expedition—Jackson-Harmsworth, the Duc d'Abruzzi, Borchgrevink, Shackleton, Scott, and most notably, Roald Amundsen in his successful reach of the South Pole in 1911—added new luster to the breed's history.

Introduced in England less than a hundred years ago, practically every show sees the Samoyeds in the forefront. Queen Alexandra was an ardent fancier, and the descendants of her dogs are found today in many English and American kennels. The dog is found in every region—Samoyeds born in northern Siberia have safely crossed the equator and remained in healthy condition to work in Antarctic snows. Dogs from Antarctic expeditions have survived the suns of Australia to return to England and start great kennels there.

Excitingly eye-arresting, the big white dog with the "smiling face" and dark, intelligent eyes, with a strong, sturdy, muscular body on legs built for speed—the Samoyed is for many the most beautiful breed in existence. An excellent watchdog, yet gentle and companionable. Never a troublemaker, yet able to hold his own when forced into a fight. With an independence born of unusual intelligence, yet marked with a loyalty to a loved owner that wins hearts.

His noble characteristics evidence themselves even in puppies—the "little white teddy bears." Dependable guardian, gentle, kind, sturdy, adaptable, the Samoyed carries in its face and heart the spirit of Christmas the whole year through.

## Official Standard for the Samoyed

**GENERAL CONFORMATION:**

**(a) General Appearance**—The Samoyed, being essentially a working dog, should present a picture of beauty, alertness and strength, with agility, dignity and grace. As his work lies in cold climates, his coat should be heavy and weather-resistant, well groomed, and of good quality rather than quantity. The male carries more of a "ruff" than the female. He should not be long in the back as a weak back would make him practically useless for his legitimate work, but at the same time, a close-coupled body would also place him at a great disadvantage as a draft dog. Breeders should aim for the happy medium, a body not long but muscular, allowing liberty, with a deep chest and well-sprung ribs, strong neck, straight front and especially strong loins. Males should be masculine in appearance and deportment without unwarranted aggressiveness; bitches feminine without weakness of structure or apparent softness of temperament. Bitches may be slightly longer in back than males. They should both give the appearance of being capable of great endurance but be free from coarseness. Because of the depth of chest required, the legs should be moderately long. A very short-legged dog is to be deprecated. Hindquarters should be particularly well developed, stifles well bent and any suggestion of unsound stifles or cowhocks severely penalized. General appearance should include movement and general conformation, indicating balance and good substance.

**(b) Substance**—Substance is that sufficiency of bone and muscle which rounds out a balance with the frame. The bone is heavier than would be expected in a dog of this size but not so massive as to prevent the speed and agility most desirable in a Samoyed. In all builds, bone should be in proportion to body size. The Samoyed should never be so heavy as to appear clumsy nor so light as to appear racy. The weight should be in proportion to the height.

**(c) Height**—Males—21 to 23½ inches; females—19 to 21 inches at the withers. An oversized or undersized Samoyed is to be penalized according to the extent of the deviation.

**(d) Coat (Texture & Condition)**—The Samoyed is a double coated dog. The body should be well covered with an undercoat of soft, short, thick, close wool with longer and harsh hair growing through it to form the outer coat, which stands straight out from the body and should be free from curl. The coat should form a ruff around the neck and shoulders, framing the head (more on males than on females). Quality of coat should be weather resistant and considered more than quantity. A droopy coat is undesirable. The coat should glisten with a silver sheen. The female does not usually carry as long a coat as most males and it is softer in texture.

**(e) Color**—Samoyeds should be pure white, white and biscuit, cream, or all biscuit. Any other colors disqualify.

**MOVEMENT:**

**(a) Gait**—The Samoyed should trot, not pace. He should move with a quick agile stride that is well timed. The gait should be free, balanced and vigorous, with good reach in the forequarters and good driving power in the hindquarters. When trotting, there should be a strong rear action drive. Moving at a slow walk or trot, they will not single-track, but as speed increases the legs gradually angle inward until the pads are finally falling on a line directly under the longitudinal center of the body. As the pad marks converge the forelegs and hind legs are carried straight forward in traveling, the stifles not turned in nor out. The back should remain strong, firm and level. A choppy or stilted gait should be penalized.

**(b) Rear End**—Upper thighs should be well developed. Stifles well bent—approximately 45 degrees to the ground. Hocks should be well developed, sharply defined and set at approximately 30 per cent of hip height. The hind legs should be parallel when viewed from the rear in a natural stance, strong, well developed, turning neither in nor out. Straight stifles are objectionable. Double-jointedness or cowhocks are a fault. Cowhocks should only be determined if the dog has had an opportunity to move properly.

**(c) Front End**—Legs should be parallel and straight to the pasterns. The pasterns should be strong, sturdy and straight, but flexible with some spring for proper let-down of feet.

Because of depth of chest, legs should be moderately long. Length of leg from the ground to the elbow should be approximately 55 per cent of the total height at the withers—a very short-legged dog is to be deprecated. Shoulders should be long and sloping, with a layback of 45 degrees and be firmly set. Out at the shoulders or out at the elbows should be penalized. The withers separation should be approximately 1–1½ inches.

**(d) Feet**—Large, long, flattish—a hare-foot, slightly spread but not splayed; toes arched; pads thick and tough, with protective growth of hair between the toes. Feet should turn neither in nor out in a natural stance but may turn in slightly in the act of pulling. Turning out, pigeon-toed, round or cat-footed or splayed are faults. Feathers on feet are not too essential but are more profuse on females than on males.

## HEAD:

**(a) Conformation**—Skull is wedge-shaped, broad, slightly crowned, not round or apple-headed, and should form an equilateral triangle on lines between the inner base of the ears and the central point of the stop. *Muzzle*—Muzzle of medium length and medium width, neither coarse nor snipy; should taper toward the nose and be in proportion to the size of the dog and the width of skull. The muzzle must have depth. *Stop*—Not too abrupt, nevertheless well defined. *Lips*—Should be black for preference and slightly curved up at the corners of the mouth, giving the "Samoyed smile." Lip lines should not have the appearance of being coarse nor should the flews drop predominately at corners of the mouth. *Ears*—Strong and thick, erect, triangular and slightly rounded at the tips; should not be large or pointed, nor should they be small and "bear-eared." Ears should conform to head size and the size of the dog; they should be set well apart but be within the border of the outer edge of the head; they should be mobile and well covered inside with hair; hair full and stand-off before the ears. Length of ear should be the same measurement at the distance from inner base of ear to outer corner of eye. *Eyes*—Should be dark for preference; should be placed well apart and deep-set; almond shaped with lower lid slanting toward an imaginary point approximately the base of ears. Dark eye rims for preference. Round or protruding eyes penalized. Blue eyes disqualifying. *Nose*—Black for preference but brown, liver, or Dudley nose not penalized. Color of nose sometimes changes with age and weather. *Jaws and Teeth*—Strong, well-set teeth, snugly overlapping with scissors bite. Undershot or overshot should be penalized.

**(b) Expression**—The expression, referred to as "Samoyed expression," is very important and is indicated by sparkle of the eyes, animation and lighting up of the face when alert or intent on anything. Expression is made up of a combination of eyes, ears and mouth. The ears should be erect when alert; the mouth should be slightly curved up at the corners to form the "Samoyed smile."

## TORSO:

**(a) Neck**—Strong, well muscled, carried proudly erect, set on sloping shoulders to carry head with dignity when at attention. Neck should blend into shoulders with a graceful arch.

**(b) Chest**—Should be deep, with ribs well sprung out from the spine and flattened at the sides to allow proper movement of the shoulders and freedom for the front legs. Should not be barrel-chested. Perfect depth of chest approximates the point of elbows, and the deepest part of the chest should be back of the forelegs—near the ninth rib. Heart and lung room are secured more by body depth than width.

**(c) Loin and Back**—The withers forms the highest part of the back. Loins strong and slightly arched. The back should be straight to the loin, medium in length, very muscular and neither long nor short-coupled. The dog should be "just off square"—the length being approximately 5 per cent more than the height. Females allowed to be slightly longer than males. The belly should be well shaped and tightly muscled and, with the rear of the thorax, should swing up in a pleasing curve (tuck-up). Croup must be full, slightly sloping, and must continue imperceptibly to the tail root.

**Tail**—The tail should be moderately long with the tail bone terminating approximately at the hock when down. It should be profusely covered with long hair and carried forward over the back or side when alert, but sometimes dropped when at rest. It should not be high or low set and should be mobile and loose—not tight over the back. A double hook is a fault. A judge should see the tail over the back over when judging.

**Disposition**—Intelligent, gentle, loyal, adaptable, alert, full of action, eager to serve, friendly but conservative, not distrustful or shy, not overly aggressive. Unprovoked aggressiveness to be severely penalized.

### DISQUALIFICATIONS

*Any color other than pure white, cream, biscuit, or white and biscuit.*
*Blue eyes.*

Approved April 9, 1963

# Siberian Husky

The Siberian Husky was originated by the Chukchi people of northeastern Asia as an endurance sled dog. When changing conditions forced these semi-nomadic natives to expand their hunting grounds, they responded by developing a unique breed of sled dog, which met their special requirements and upon which their very survival depended. The Chukchis needed a sled dog capable of traveling great distances at a moderate speed, carrying a light load in low temperatures with a minimum expenditure of energy. Research indicates that the Chukchis maintained the purity of their sled dogs through the 19th century and that these dogs were the sole and direct ancestors of the breed known in the United States today as the Siberian Husky.

Shortly after 1900 Americans in Alaska began to hear accounts of this superior strain of sled dog in Siberia. The first team of Siberian Huskies made its appearance in the All Alaska Sweepstakes Race of 1909. The same year a large number of them were imported to Alaska by Charles Fox Maule Ramsay, and his team, driven by John "Iron Man" Johnson, won the grueling 400-mile race in 1910. For the next decade Siberian Huskies, particularly those bred and raced by Leonhard Seppala, captured most of the racing titles in Alaska, where the rugged terrain was ideally suited to the endurance capabilities of the breed.

In 1925 the city of Nome, Alaska was stricken by a diphtheria epidemic

**313**

and supplies of anti-toxin were urgently needed. Many sled dog drivers, including Mr. Seppala, were called upon to relay the life-saving serum to Nome by dog team. This heroic Serum Run focused attention upon Siberian Huskies, and Seppala brought his dogs to the United States on a personal appearance tour. While here, he was invited to compete in sled dog races in New England, where the sport had already been introduced. The superior racing ability and delightful temperament of Seppala's Siberian Huskies won the respect and the hearts of sportsmen from Alaska to New England. It was through the efforts of these pioneer fanciers that the breed was established in the United States and that AKC recognition was granted in 1930. Many Siberian Huskies were assembled and trained at Chinook Kennels in New Hampshire for use on the Byrd Antarctic Expeditions. Dogs of the breed also served valiantly in the Army's Arctic Search and Rescue Unit of the Air Transport Command during World War II.

The Siberian Husky is naturally friendly and gentle in temperament. He possesses at times an independent nature, and although very alert, in many cases he lacks the aggressive or protective tendencies of a watch dog. He is by nature fastidiously clean and free from the body odors that many dense-coated breeds have. Although remarkable for his adaptability to all kinds of living conditions, his natural desire to roam makes a measure of control necessary at all times. The understanding owner will find the Siberian Husky an enjoyable companion in country or city. He has endeared himself to dog fanciers everywhere by his versatility, striking beauty, and amiable disposition.

## Official Standard for the Siberian Husky

**General Appearance**—The Siberian Husky is a medium-size working dog, quick and light on his feet and free and graceful in action. His moderately compact and well furred body, erect ears and brush tail suggest his Northern heritage. His characteristic gait is smooth and seemingly effortless. He performs his original function in harness most capably, carrying a light load at a moderate speed over great distances. His body proportions and form reflect this basic balance of power, speed and endurance. The males of the Siberian Husky breed are masculine but never coarse; the bitches are feminine but without weakness of structure. In proper condition, with muscle firm and well developed, the Siberian Husky does not carry excess weight.

**Size, Proportion, Substance**—Height—Dogs, 21 to 23½ inches at the withers. Bitches, 20 to 22 inches at the withers. Weight—Dogs, 45 to 60 pounds. Bitches, 35 to 50 pounds. Weight is in proportion to height. The measurements mentioned above represent the extreme height and weight limits with no preference given to either extreme. Any appearance of excessive bone or weight should be penalized. In profile, the length of the body from the point of the shoulder to the rear point of the croup is slightly longer than the height of the body from the ground to the top of the withers. *Disqualification*—Dogs over 23½ inches and bitches over 22 inches.

**Head**—*Expression* is keen, but friendly; interested and even mischievous. *Eyes*—almond shaped, moderately spaced and set a trifle obliquely. Eyes may be brown or blue in color; one of each or parti-colored are acceptable. *Faults*—Eyes set too obliquely; set too close together. *Ears* of medium size, triangular in shape, close fitting and set high on the head. They are thick, well furred, and slightly arched at the back and strongly erect, with slightly rounded tips pointing straight up. *Faults*—Ears too large in proportion to the head; too wide set; not strongly erect. *Skull* of medium size and in proportion to the body; slightly rounded on top and tapering from the widest point of the eyes. *Faults*—Head clumsy or heavy; head too finely chiseled. *Stop*—The stop is well-defined and the bridge of the nose is straight from the stop to the tip. *Fault*—Insufficient stop. *Muzzle* of medium length; that is, the distance from the tip of the nose to the stop is equal to the distance from the stop to the occiput. The muzzle is of medium width, tapering gradually to the nose, with the tip neither pointed nor square. *Faults*—Muzzle either too snipy or too coarse; muzzle too short or too long. *Nose* black in gray, tan or black dogs; liver in copper dogs; may be flesh-colored in pure white dogs. The pink-streaked "snow nose" is acceptable. *Lips* are well pigmented and close fitting. *Teeth* closing in a scissors bite. *Fault*—Any bite other than scissors.

**Neck, Topline, Body**—*Neck* medium in length, arched and carried proudly erect when dog is standing. When moving at a trot, the neck is extended so that the head is carried slightly forward. *Faults*—Neck too short and thick; neck too long. *Chest* deep and strong, but not too broad, with the deepest point being just behind and level with the elbows. The ribs are well sprung from the spine but flattened on the sides to allow for freedom of action. *Faults*—Chest too broad; "barrel ribs"; ribs too flat or weak. *Back*—The back is straight and strong, with a level topline from withers to croup. It is of medium length, neither cobby nor slack from excessive length. The loin is taut and lean, narrower than the rib cage, and with a slight tuck-up. The croup slopes away from the spine at an angle, but never so steeply as to restrict the rearward thrust of the hind legs. *Faults*—Weak or slack back; roached back; sloping topline.

**Tail**—The well furred tail of fox-brush shape is set on just below the level of the topline, and is usually carried over the back in a graceful sickle curve when the dog is at attention. When carried up, the tail does not curl to either side of the body, nor does it snap flat against the back. A trailing tail is normal for the dog when in repose. Hair on the tail is of medium length and approximately the same length on tip, sides and bottom, giving the appearance of a round brush. *Faults*—A snapped or tightly curled tail; highly plumed tail; tail set too low or too high.

**Forequarters**—*Shoulders*—The shoulder blade is well laid back. The upper arm angles slightly backward from point of shoulder to elbow, and is never perpendicular to the ground. The muscles and ligaments holding the shoulder to the rib cage are firm and well developed. *Faults*—Straight shoulders; loose shoulders. *Forelegs*—When standing and viewed from the front, the legs are moderately spaced, parallel and straight, with the elbows close to the body and turned neither in nor out. Viewed from the side, pasterns are slightly slanted, with the pastern joint strong, but flexible. Bone is substantial but never heavy. Length of the leg from elbow to ground is slightly more than the distance from the elbow to the top of withers. Dewclaws on forelegs may be removed. *Faults*— Weak pasterns; too heavy bone; too narrow or too wide in the front; out at the elbows. *Feet* oval in shape but not long. The paws are medium in size, compact and well furred between the toes and pads. The pads are tough and thickly cushioned. The paws neither turn in nor out when the dog is in natural stance. *Faults*—Soft or splayed toes; paws too large and clumsy; paws too small and delicate; toeing in or out.

**Hindquarters**—When standing and viewed from the rear, the hind legs are moderately spaced and parallel. The upper thighs are well muscled and powerful, the stifles well bent, the hock joint well-defined and set low to the ground. Dewclaws, if any, are to be removed. *Faults*—Straight stifles, cowhocks, too narrow or too wide in the rear.

**Coat**—The coat of the Siberian Husky is double and medium in length, giving a well furred appearance, but is never so long as to obscure the cleancut outline of the dog. The undercoat is soft and dense and of sufficient length to support the outer coat. The guard hairs of the outer coat are straight and somewhat smooth lying, never harsh nor standing straight off from the body. It should be noted that the absence of the undercoat during the shedding season is normal. Trimming of whiskers and fur between the toes and around the feet to present a neater appearance is permissible. Trimming the fur on any other part of the dog is not to be condoned and should be severely penalized. *Faults*—Long, rough, or shaggy coat; texture too harsh or too silky; trimming of the coat, except as permitted above.

**Color**—All colors from black to pure white are allowed. A variety of markings on the head is common, including many striking patterns not found in other breeds.

**Gait**—The Siberian Husky's characteristic gait is smooth and seemingly effortless. He is quick and light on his feet, and when in the show ring should be gaited on a loose lead at a moderately fast trot, exhibiting good reach in the forequarters and good drive in the hindquarters. When viewed from the front to rear while moving at a walk the Siberian Husky does not single-track, but as the speed increases the legs gradually angle inward until the pads are falling on a line directly under the longitudinal center of the body. As the pad marks converge, the forelegs and hind legs are carried straightforward, with neither elbows not stifles turned in or out. Each hind leg moves in the path of the foreleg on the same side. While the dog is gaiting, the topline remains firm and level. *Faults*— Short, prancing or choppy gait, lumbering or rolling gait; crossing or crabbing.

**Temperament**—The characteristic temperament of the Siberian Husky is friendly and gentle, but also alert and outgoing. He does not display the possessive qualities of the guard dog, nor is he overly suspicious of strangers or aggressive with other dogs. Some measure of reserve and dignity may be expected in the mature dog. His intelligence, tractability, and eager disposition make him an agreeable companion and willing worker.

**Summary**—The most important breed characteristics of the Siberian Husky are medium size, moderate bone, well balanced proportions, ease and freedom of movement, proper coat, pleasing head and ears, correct tail, and good disposition. Any appearance of excessive bone or weight, constricted or clumsy gait, or long, rough coat should be penalized. The Siberian Husky never appears so heavy or coarse as to suggest a freighting animal; nor is he so light and fragile as to suggest a sprint-racing animal. In both sexes the Siberian Husky gives the appearance of being capable of great endurance. In addition to the faults already noted, the obvious structural faults common to all breeds are as undesirable in the Siberian Husky as in any other breed, even though they are not specifically mentioned herein.

### DISQUALIFICATIONS

*Dogs over 23½ inches and bitches over 22 inches.*

Approved October 9, 1990

# Standard Schnauzer

Of the three Schnauzers: Miniature, Standard, and Giant, all of which are bred and registered as distinct breeds, the medium, or Standard, is the prototype. He is a German breed of great antiquity, which in the 15th and 16th centuries must have been in high favor as a household companion, for his portrait appears in many paintings of the period. Albrecht Durer is known to have owned one for at least 12 years, as the portrait of the same dog occurs several times in works of that artist between the years 1492 and 1504. Rembrandt painted several Schnauzers, Lucas Cranach the Elder shows one in a tapestry dated 1501, and in the 18th century one appears in a canvas of the English painter Sir Joshua Reynolds. At Mechlinburg, Germany, in the market place there is a statue of a hunter dating from the 14th century, with a Schnauzer crouching at his feet which conforms very closely to the present-day show Standard.

The general impression of the Schnauzer is that of a compact, sinewy, square-built dog, sturdy and alert, with stiff wiry coat and bristling eyebrows and whiskers. His nature combines high-spirited temperament with unusual intelligence and reliability. He occupies the midway position between the large breeds and the Toys.

As far as can be determined, the Schnauzer originated in the crossing of black German Poodle and gray wolf spitz upon wirehaired Pinscher stock. From the Pinscher element derives the tendency to fawn-colored undercoat, and from the wolf spitz is inherited the typical pepper and salt coat color and its harsh wiry character. Solid black specimens of the breed, while fairly common in Germany, are still rather unusual in this country.

The breed in America was originally classed as a terrier, whereas German breeders have always regarded the Schnauzer principally as a working dog. His principal vocation was that of rat catcher, yard dog, and guard. Before World War I in Germany, fully 90% of the dogs used to guard the carts of farm produce in the market places while the farmers rested themselves and their teams at the inns, were of strong Schnauzer blood. Breeders in the land of their origin hold the Schnauzer second to none for sagacity and fearlessness. Owing to these characteristics, the "dogs with the human brain" (as their owners proudly call them) were much used by the army during the war as dispatch carriers and Red Cross aides; they were also employed in Germany in police work.

In this country and in England, they were used mainly as personal guards and companions, for which purpose their devotion and bravery, coupled with an uncanny perception of approaching danger, renders them most suitable. They are good water dogs and are easily taught to retrieve; and, on at least one western sheep ranch, Schnauzers have proved themselves the most efficient of various breeds tried as protection for the flocks against marauding coyotes.

Schnauzers were first exhibited in Germany as Wire-Haired Pinschers in 1879 at the Third German International Show at Hanover. A standard was published in 1880 and the breed made rapid progress as a show dog. The first specialty show was held at Stuttgart in 1890 with the remarkable entry of 93 dogs. The Pinscher Club was founded at Cologne in 1895 and the Bavarian Schnauzer Club at Munich in 1907. In 1918 the Pinscher and Schnauzer Clubs united to become the official representative of the breed in the German Kennel Club—it is known as the Pinscher-Schnauzer Club. Today there are clubs devoted to the breed in Holland, Austria, Switzerland, Czechoslovakia, England, and America.

From a breeding point of view, there are two major male lines of descent, tracing back to two unregistered dogs, one the above-mentioned Schnauzer and the other called Seppel, while the two most famous basic bitches are Settchen and Jette von Enz. Settchen traces back to Schnauzer and was bred to a dog of the Seppel line called Prinz Harttmuth; by this mating she became the dam of Sieger Rex von Den Gunthersburg. Rex in turn became the sire of Sieger Rigo Schnauzerlust, and these two dogs, Rex and Rigo, had a greater influence on the breed than any others in the stud book. Jette von Enz was the dam of Rigo, and her line traces back to Seppel. A litter-brother of Rigo, named Rex von Egelsee, also figures prominently in the early breeding records; both these dogs were used extensively and with excellent results for inbreeding. Demonstrative of the stamina and virility of Schnauzers is the fact that both Rigo and Rex were successfully serving as studs when they were twelve years old.

Schnauzers became widely known in this country only after World War I, but one is said to have been shown at the Westminster Kennel Club show in the Miscellaneous Class in 1899. The first recorded importation was Fingal, brought over by Mr. Leisching of Rochester, N.Y., in 1905. The Schnauzer Club of America was formed in 1925. The first Schnauzer to become an American champion was the Swiss bitch, Resy Patricia, imported by Mrs. Maurice Newton, who bred from her the first American-bred champion, Fracas Franconia. The first dog to make the American title was Holm von Egelsee, which was also the first Sieger to come to this country. He was imported by William D. Goff.

All Schnauzers in Germany have their ears cropped, but since cropping in this country is governed by the separate laws of the different states, the AKC standard permits both the cropped and the natural ear.

## Official Standard for the Standard Schnauzer

**General Appearance**—The Standard Schnauzer is a robust, heavy-set dog, sturdily built with good muscle and plenty of bone; square-built in proportion of body length to height. His rugged build and dense harsh coat are accentuated by the hallmark of the breed, the arched eyebrows and the bristly mustache and whiskers. *Faults*—Any deviation that detracts from the Standard Schnauzer's desired general appearance of a robust, active, square-built, wire-coated dog. Any deviation from the specifications in the Standard is to be considered a fault and should be penalized in proportion to the extent of the deviation.

**Size, Proportion, Substance**—Ideal height at the highest point of the shoulder blades, 18½ to 19½ inches for males and 17½ inches to 18½ inches for females. Dogs measuring over or under these limits must be faulted in proportion to the extent of the deviation. Dogs measuring more than one half inch over or under these limits must be disqualified. The height at the highest point of the withers equals the length from breastbone to point of rump.

**Head**—*Head* strong, rectangular, and elongated; narrowing slightly from the ears to the eyes and again to the tip of the nose. The total length of the head is about one half the length of the back measured from the withers to the set-on of the tail. The head matches the sex and substance of the dog. *Expression* alert, highly intelligent, spirited. *Eyes* medium size; dark brown; oval in shape and turned forward; neither round nor protruding. The brow is arched and wiry, but vision is not impaired nor eyes hidden by too long an eyebrow. *Ears* set high, evenly shaped with moderate thickness of leather and carried erect when cropped. If uncropped, they are of medium size, V-shaped and mobile so that they break at skull level and are carried forward with the inner edge close to the cheek. *Faults*—Prick, or hound ears. *Skull* (*Occiput to Stop*) moderately broad between the ears with the width of the skull not exceeding two thirds the length of the skull. The skull must be flat; neither domed nor bumpy; skin unwrinkled. There is a slight stop which is accentuated by the wiry brows. *Muzzle* strong, and both parallel and equal in length to the topskull; it ends in a moderately blunt wedge with wiry whiskers accenting the rectangular shape of the head. The topline of the muzzle is parallel with the topline of the skull. *Nose* is large, black and full. The lips should be black, tight and not overlapping. *Cheeks*—Well developed chewing muscles, but not so much that "cheekiness" disturbs the rectangular head form.

*Bite*—A full complement of white teeth, with a strong, sound scissors bite. The canine teeth are strong and well developed with the upper incisors slightly overlapping and engaging the lower. The upper and lower jaws are powerful and neither overshot nor undershot. *Faults*—A level bite is considered undesirable but a lesser fault than an overshot or undershot mouth.

**Neck, Topline, Body**—*Neck* strong, of moderate thickness and length, elegantly arched and blending cleanly into the shoulders. The skin is tight, fitting closely to the dry throat with no wrinkles or dewlaps. The *topline* of the back should not be absolutely horizontal, but should have a slightly descending slope from the first vertebra of the withers to the faintly curved croup and set-on of the tail. *Back* strong, firm, straight and short. Loin well developed, with the distance from the last rib to the hips as short as possible. *Body* compact, strong, short-coupled and substantial so as to permit great flexibility and agility. *Faults*—Too slender or shelly; too bulky or coarse. *Chest* of medium width with well sprung ribs, and if it could be seen in cross section would be oval. The breastbone is plainly discernible. The brisket must descend at least to the elbows and ascend gradually to the rear with the belly moderately drawn up. *Fault*—Excessive tuck-up. Croup full and slightly rounded. *Tail* set moderately high and carried erect. It is docked to not less than one inch nor more than two inches. *Fault*—Squirrel tail.

**Forequarters**—*Shoulders*—The sloping shoulder blades are strongly muscled, yet flat and well laid back so that the rounded upper ends are in a nearly vertical line above the elbows. They slope well forward to the point where they join the upper arm, forming as nearly as possible a right angle when seen from the side. Such an angulation permits the maximum forward extension of the forelegs without binding or effort. *Forelegs* straight, vertical, and without any curvature when seen from all sides; set moderately far apart; with heavy bone; elbows set close to the body and pointing directly to the rear. Dewclaws on the forelegs may be removed. *Feet* small and compact, round with thick pads and strong black nails. The toes are well closed and arched (cat's paws) and pointing straight ahead.

**Hindquarters**—Strongly muscled, in balance with the forequarters, never appearing higher than the shoulders. Thighs broad with well bent stifles. The second thigh, from knee to hock, is approximately parallel with an extension of the upper neck line. The legs, from the clearly defined hock joint to the feet, are short and perpendicular to the ground and, when viewed from the rear, are parallel to each other. Dewclaws, if any, on the hind legs are generally removed. Feet as in front.

**Coat**—Tight, hard, wiry and as thick as possible, composed of a soft, close undercoat and a harsh outer coat which, when seen against the grain, stands up off the back, lying neither smooth nor flat. The outer coat (body coat) is trimmed (by plucking) only to accent the body outline.

As coat texture is of the greatest importance, a dog may be considered in show coat with back hair measuring from ¾ to 2 inches in length. Coat on the ears, head, neck, chest, belly and under the tail may be closely trimmed to give the desired typical appearance of the breed. On the muzzle and over the eyes the coat lengthens to form the beard and eyebrows; the hair on the legs is longer than that on the body. These "furnishings" should be of harsh texture and should not be so profuse as to detract from the neat appearance or working capabilities of the dog. *Faults* —Soft, smooth, curly, wavy or shaggy; too long or too short; too sparse or lacking undercoat; excessive furnishings; lack of furnishings.

**Color**—Pepper and salt or pure black. *Pepper and Salt*—The typical pepper and salt color of the topcoat results from the combination of black and white hairs, and white hairs banded with black. Acceptable are all shades of pepper and salt and dark iron gray to silver gray. Ideally, pepper and salt Standard Schnauzers have a gray undercoat, but a tan or fawn undercoat is not to be penalized. It is desirable to have a darker facial mask that harmonizes with the particular shade of coat color. Also, in pepper and salt dogs, the pepper and salt mixture may fade out to light gray or silver white in the eyebrows, whiskers, cheeks, under throat, across chest, under tail, leg furnishings, under body and inside legs. *Black*—Ideally the black Standard Schnauzer should be a true rich color, free from any fading or discoloration or any admixture of gray or tan hairs. The undercoat should also be solid black. However, increased age or continued exposure to the sun may cause a certain amount of fading and burning. A small white smudge on the chest is not a fault. Loss of color as a result of scars from cuts and bites is not a fault. *Faults* —Any colors other than specified, and any shadings or mixtures thereof in the topcoat such as rust, brown, red, yellow or tan; absence of peppering; spotting or striping; a black streak down the back; or a black saddle without typical salt and pepper coloring—and gray hairs in the coat of a black; in blacks, any undercoat color other than black.

**Gait**—Sound, strong, quick, free, true and level gait with powerful, well angulated hindquarters that reach out and cover ground. The forelegs reach out in a stride balancing that of the hindquarters. At a trot, the back remains firm and level, without swaying, rolling or roaching. When viewed from the rear, the feet, though they may appear to travel close when trotting, must not cross or strike. Increased speed causes feet to converge toward the center line of gravity. *Faults* —Crabbing or weaving; paddling, rolling, swaying; short, choppy, stiff, stilted rear action; front legs that throw out or in (East and West movers); hackney gait, crossing over, or striking in front or rear.

**Temperament**—The Standard Schnauzer has highly developed senses, intelligence, aptitude for training, fearlessness, endurance and resistance against weather and illness. His nature combines high-spirited temperament with extreme reliability. *Faults* —In weighing the seriousness of a fault, greatest consideration should be given to deviation from the desired alert, highly intelligent, spirited, reliable character of the Standard Schnauzer. Dogs that are shy or appear to be highly nervous should be seriously faulted and dismissed from the ring. Vicious dogs shall be disqualified.

## DISQUALIFICATIONS

*Males under 18 inches or over 20 inches in height. Females under 17 inches or over 19 inches in height. Vicious dogs.*

Approved February 9, 1991

# TERRIERS

## Airedale Terrier

The origin of the Airedale Terrier is enveloped in the same veil of theory and conjecture that shrouds the origin of all species in man's attempt to retrace the stages in evolution. Antique art records the existence of English dogs having a distinct resemblance to the terriers of later days and from which undoubtedly sprang the Broken-haired or Old English Terrier.

This extinct black and tan type is thought by some authorities to have been the common progenitor of the Irish, Fox, Welsh, and Airedale Terrier. At all events, an admixture of his varying types and sizes from 17 to 30 pounds in weight formed the roots, so to speak, of the genealogical tree of the breed fostered by sporting Yorkshiremen for hunting the fox, badger, weasel, foumart,

**325**

otter, water rat, and small game in the valleys of the rivers Colne, Calder, Warfe, and Aire. These constant companions and guardians, while excelling in agility, eyesight, hearing, and untiring courage, lacked the keen nose and swimming ability of the rough-coated Otter Hound, with which they competed in the chase, and was the wise reason for crossing the two breeds in the constructive attempt to embody the virtues of both in a better breed of larger and stronger terriers.

From 1864 on, the earlier whelps were called Working, Waterside, and Bingley Terriers. They were shown in increasing numbers at local agricultural shows at the time dog shows were in their early growth.

In 1879 classes were first provided for Airedale Terriers at the Airedale Agricultural Society's show held at Bingley, Yorkshire. The towns of Skipton, Bradford, Keighley, and Otley followed Bingley with classifications, and some years later the competition for the Otley gold medal became the premier win in the breed.

Champion Master Briar (1897–1906) is conceded to be the patriarch of the breed. He may be likened to the trunk of the family tree whose branches grew in many directions. His great sons, Ch. Clonmel Monarch and Crompton Marvel, carried on his prepotency. The former was exported to Philadelphia, where ardent fanciers molded the breed in this hemisphere.

Very influential in the leading position the Airedale held at pre-World War II dog shows, was Eng. Ch. Warland Ditto (1919–1927). Warland Ditto, his sire Cragsman Dictator, his dam Ch. Warland Strategy, and her sire Ch. Rhosddu Royalist were all exported to the U.S.A.

The degree of perfection of type attained in the breed by those who have carried on the idea of their standard is attested by the frequency with which Airedales have been judged best of all breeds in the most important all-breed shows of England and America. They shine, however, greatest in the minds of their many fond owners who value the faithful attachment, companionship, and protection of their families as a priceless possession.

Airedale Terriers are used on great game in Africa, India, Canada, and our game lands. They were among the first breeds used for police duty in Germany and Great Britain. They have also been used in several wars as dependable dispatch bearers due to their ability to suffer wounds without faltering at the next order for duty. Their sweet disposition, possibly inherited from the hound blood, has endeared them to many of the best breeders and owners of leading kennels, many of whom are women who take a pride in showing their own stock. The correct temperament in puppyhood is one of discretion, and when mature, a certain dignified aloofness both with strangers and their kind. Their disposition can be molded by the patience of their masters in any environment, but when trained for defense and attack they are usually unbeatable for their weight.

# Official Standard for the Airedale Terrier

**Head**—Should be well balanced with little apparent difference between the length of skull and foreface. *Skull* should be long and flat, not too broad between the ears and narrowing very slightly to the eyes. Scalp should be free from wrinkles, stop hardly visible and cheeks level and free from fullness. *Ears* should be V-shaped with carriage rather to the side of the head, not pointing to the eyes, small but not out of proportion to the size of the dog. The topline of the folded ear should be above the level of the skull. *Foreface* should be deep, powerful, strong and muscular. Should be well filled up before the eyes. *Eyes* should be dark, small, not prominent, full of terrier expression, keenness and intelligence. *Lips* should be tight. *Nose* should be black and not so small. *Teeth* should be strong and white, free from discoloration or defect. Bite either level or vise-like. A slightly overlapping or scissors bite is permissible without preference.

**Neck**—Should be of moderate length and thickness gradually widening towards the shoulders. Skin tight, not loose.

**Shoulders and Chest**—Shoulders long and sloping well into the back. Shoulder blades flat. From the front, chest deep but not broad. The depth of the chest should be approximately on a level with the elbows.

**Body**—Back should be short, strong and level. Ribs well sprung. Loins muscular and of good width. There should be but little space between the last rib and the hip joint.

**Hindquarters**—Should be strong and muscular with no droop.

**Tail**—The root of the tail should be set well up on the back. It should be carried gaily but not curled over the back. It should be of good strength and substance and of fair length.

**Legs**—*Forelegs* should be perfectly straight, with plenty of muscle and bone. *Elbows* should be perpendicular to the body, working free of sides. *Thighs* should be long and powerful with muscular second thigh, stifles well bent, not turned either in or out, hocks well let down parallel with each other when viewed from behind. *Feet* should be small, round and compact with a good depth of pad, well cushioned; the toes moderately arched, not turned either in or out.

**Coat**—Should be hard, dense and wiry, lying straight and close, covering the dog well over the body and legs. Some of the hardest are crinkling or just slightly waved. At the base of the hard very stiff hair should be a shorter growth of softer hair termed the undercoat.

**Color**—The head and ears should be tan, the ears being of a darker shade than the rest. Dark markings on either side of the skull are permissible. The legs up to the thighs and elbows and the under-part of the body and chest are also tan and the tan frequently runs into the shoulder. The sides and upper parts of the body should be black or dark grizzle.

A red mixture is often found in the black and is not to be considered objectionable. A small white blaze on the chest is a characteristic of certain strains of the breed.

**Size**—Dogs should measure approximately 23 inches in height at the shoulder; bitches, slightly less. Both sexes should be sturdy, well muscled and boned.

**Movement**—Movement or action is the crucial test of conformation. Movement should be free. As seen from the front the forelegs should swing perpendicular from the body free from the sides, the feet the same distance apart as the elbows. As seen from the rear the hind legs should be parallel with each other, neither too close nor too far apart, but so placed as to give a strong well-balanced stance and movement. The toes should not be turned either in or out.

### FAULTS

Yellow eyes, hound ears, white feet, soft coat, being much over or under the size limit, being undershot or overshot, having poor movement, are faults which should be severely penalized.

### SCALE OF POINTS

| | | | |
|---|---|---|---|
| Head | 10 | Color | 5 |
| Neck, shoulders and chest | 10 | Size | 10 |
| Body | 10 | Movement | 10 |
| Hindquarters and tail | 10 | General characteristics | |
| Legs and feet | 10 | expression | 15 |
| Coat | 10 | TOTAL | 100 |

Approved July 14, 1959

# American Staffordshire Terrier

To give correctly the origin and history of the American Staffordshire Terrier, it is necessary to comment briefly on two other dogs, namely the Bulldog and the terrier.

Until the early part of the 19th century, the Bulldog was bred with great care in England for the purpose of baiting bulls. The Bulldog of that day was vastly different from our present-day "sourmug." Pictures from as late as 1870 represent the Bulldog as agile and as standing straight on his legs—his front legs in particular. In some cases he was even possessed of a muzzle, and long rat tails were not uncommon. The Bulldog of that day, with the exception of the head, looked more like the present-day American Staffordshire Terrier than like the present-day Bulldog.

Some writers contend it was the white English Terrier, or the Black-and-Tan Terrier, that was used as a cross with the Bulldog to perfect the Staffordshire Terrier. It seems easier to believe that any game terrier, such as the Fox Terrier of the early 1800s, was used in this cross, since some of the foremost authorities on dogs of that time state that the Black-and Tan and the white English Terrier were none too game, but these same authorities go on to stress the gameness of the Fox Terrier. It is reasonable to believe that breeders who were attempting to perfect a dog that would combine the spirit and agility of the terrier with the courage and tenacity of the Bulldog, would not use a terrier that was not game. In analyzing the three above-mentioned terriers at that time, we find that there was not a great deal of difference in body conformation, the greatest differences being in color, aggressiveness, and spirit.

In any event, it was the cross between the Bulldog and the terrier that resulted in the Staffordshire Terrier, which was originally called the Bull-and-Terrier Dog, Half and Half, and at times Pit Dog or Pit Bullterrier. Later, it assumed the name in England of Staffordshire Bull Terrier.

These dogs began to find their way into America as early as 1870, where they became known as Pit Dog, Pit Bull Terrier, later American Bull Terrier, and still later as Yankee Terrier.

In 1936, they were accepted for registration in the American Kennel Club stud book as Staffordshire Terriers. The name of the breed was revised effective January 1, 1972 to American Staffordshire Terrier. Breeders in this country had developed a type which is heavier in weight than the Staffordshire Bull Terrier of England and the name change was to distinguish them as separate breeds.

The American Staffordshire Terrier's standard allows a variance in weight, but it should be in proportion to size. The dog's chief requisites should be strength unusual for his size, soundness, balance, a strong powerful head, a well-muscled body, and courage that is proverbial.

To clarify the confusion that may exist, even in the minds of dog fanciers, as to the difference between the American Staffordshire Terrier and the Bull Terrier, a comment on the latter may be helpful. The Bull Terrier was introduced by James Hinks of Birmingham, who had been experimenting for several years with the old bull-and-terrier dog, now known as Staffordshire. It is generally conceded that he used the Staffordshire, crossed with the white English Terrier, and some writers contend that a dash of Pointer and Dalmatian blood was also used to help perfect the all-white Bull Terrier.

In mentioning the gameness of the Staffordshire, it is not the intention to tag him as a fighting machine, or to praise this characteristic. These points are discussed because they are necessary in giving the correct origin and history of the breed. The good qualities of the dogs are many, and it would be difficult for anyone to overstress them. In appearance, they are flashy-looking and they attract much attention on the show bench. As to character, they exceed being dead game; nevertheless, they should not be held in ill repute merely because man has been taking advantage of this rare courage to use them in the pit as gambling tools. These dogs are docile, and with a little training are even tractable around other dogs. They are intelligent, excellent guardians, and they protect their masters' property with an air of authority that counts; they easily discriminate between strangers who mean well and those who do not. They have another characteristic that is unusual: when they are sold, or change hands, they accept their new master in a comparatively short time.

# Official Standard for the American Staffordshire Terrier

**General Appearance**—The American Staffordshire Terrier should give the impression of great strength for his size, a well-put-together dog, muscular, but agile and graceful, keenly alive to his surroundings. He should be stocky, not long-legged or racy in outline. His courage is proverbial.

**Head**—Medium length, deep through, broad skull, very pronounced cheek muscles, distinct stop; and ears are set high. *Ears*—Cropped or uncropped, the latter preferred. Uncropped ears should be short and held half rose or prick. Full drop to be penalized. *Eyes*—Dark and round, low down in skull and set far apart. No pink eyelids. *Muzzle*—Medium length, rounded on upper side to fall away abruptly below eyes. Jaws well defined. Underjaw to be strong and have biting power. Lips close and even, no looseness. Upper teeth to meet tightly outside lower teeth in front. Nose definitely black.

**Neck**—Heavy, slightly arched, tapering from shoulders to back of skull. No looseness of skin. Medium length.

**Shoulders**—Strong and muscular with blades wide and sloping.

**Back**—Fairly short. Slight sloping from withers to rump with gentle short slope at rump to base of tail. Loins slightly tucked.

**Body**—Well-sprung ribs, deep in rear. All ribs close together. Forelegs set rather wide apart to permit chest development. Chest deep and broad.

**Tail**—Short in comparison to size, low set, tapering to a fine point; not curled or held over back. Not docked.

**Legs**—The front legs should be straight, large or round bones, pastern upright. No resemblance of bend in front. Hindquarters well-muscled, let down at hocks, turning neither in nor out. Feet of moderate size, well-arched and compact. Gait must be springy but without roll or pace.

**Coat**—Short, close, stiff to the touch, and glossy.

**Color**—any color, solid, parti, or patched is permissible, but all white, more than 80 percent white, black and tan, and liver not to be encouraged.

**Size**—Height and weight should be in proportion. A height of about 18 to 19 inches at shoulders for the male and 17 to 18 inches for the female is to be considered preferable.

**Faults**—Faults to be penalized are: Dudley nose, light or pink eyes, tail too long or badly carried, undershot or overshot mouths.

Approved June 10, 1936

# Australian Terrier

The Australian Terrier was the first Australian breed to be recognized and shown in its native land, and was also the first Australian breed to be accepted officially in other countries. An Australian native-bred, broken-coated terrier made its first appearance on the show bench in Melbourne in 1868. In 1899 the breed was exhibited specifically as "Australian Terriers, Rough-Coated," and both sandy/red and blue/tan colors are noted in show records of that year. An Australian Rough-Coated Terrier Club, founded in Melborne in 1887, made the first attempt at standardizing the breed, and by 1896 a Standard for the breed had been established. Exports to England and the United States soon followed, and in 1933 breed status was granted in England. The American Kennel Club admitted the breed to registry in 1960, its first terrier addition in 24 years and the 114th breed entered in the AKC Stud Book.

In 1977, the Australian Terrier Club of America became a member club of the AKC. Today the breed is officially recognized and shown in many countries world-wide.

This dog, one of the smallest of the working terriers, was bred to be both helper and companion in rough times and terrain. A native dog known as the Rough-Coated Terrier, a close relative of the old Scotch dog of Great Britain (not the present-day Scottish Terrier), had been in Tasmania since the early 1880s. These terriers are believed to have been cross-bred with a number of other breeds of British terrier stock to produce the fast, sturdy, rough, weather-proof, fearless little dog which the settlers needed as they expanded the frontiers of their country—helping to control rodents and snakes on the waterfronts, farms, sheep and cattle stations in the outback, sometimes tending sheep, sounding an alarm when intruders appeared, and being a companion. The breeds chosen for cross breeding were selected to promote specific desired traits. Although there are differences among writers of the histories of the Australian Terrier breed, there is consensus of opinion that the breeds used included the precursors of the Dandie Dinmont, Skye, Yorkshire, and the old Black-and-Tan Terriers (today's Manchester) with perhaps the Irish and Cairn Terriers. Fortunately, the various cross breedings produced a handsome dog which the prosperous settlers were proud to show at home or in public.

The Australian Terrier is an excellent choice for show, city home or farmland. He is very spirited, with an air of self-assurance and inquiry into all that goes on about him. His excellent hearing and good eyesight make him a fine watch-alert dog to warn of any kind of disturbance. He is generally adaptable to any climate and terrain, and his weatherproof double coat, which sheds little, keeps him comfortable year-round.

He continues to be a natural and tireless ratter and sporting terrier. Perhaps because he was developed in close association with man under often stressful conditions, he has a very strong sense of devotion and affection for his humans, and accepts full responsibility for his household. He is a good family dog and also a fine companion for the person alone. He indeed seems to have fulfilled the dream of early breeders to produce a dog who was tough, smart and able to withstand a full day's work outdoors and yet small and biddable enough to come into the home at night.

## Official Standard for the Australian Terrier

**General Appearance**—A small, sturdy, medium-boned working terrier, rather long in proportion to height with pricked ears and docked tail. Blue and tan, solid sandy or solid red in color, with harsh-textured outer coat, a distinctive ruff and apron, and a soft, silky topknot. As befits their heritage as versatile workers, Australian Terriers are sound and free moving with good reach and drive. Their expression keen and intelligent; their manner spirited and self-assured.

The following description is that of the ideal Australian Terrier. Any deviation from this description must be penalized to the extent of the deviation.

**Size, Proportion, Substance**—*Size*—Height 10–11 inches at the withers. Deviation in either direction is to be discouraged. ***Proportion***—The body is long in proportion to the height of the dog. The length of back from withers to the front of the tail is approximately 1–1½ inches longer than from withers to the ground.

**Substance**—Good working condition, medium bone, correct body proportions, symmetry and balance determine proper weight.

**Head**—*Head*—The head is long and strong. The length of the muzzle is equal to the length of the skull. *Expression*—Keen and intelligent. *Eyes*—Small, dark brown to black (the darker the better), keen in expression, set well apart. Rims are black, oval in shape. *Faults:* Light-colored or protruding eyes. *Ears*—Small, erect and pointed; set high on the skull yet well apart, carried erect without any tendency to flare obliquely off the skull. *Skull*—Viewed from the front or side is long and flat, slightly longer than it is wide and full between the eyes, with slight but definite stop. *Muzzle*—Strong and powerful with slight fill under the eyes. The jaws are powerful. *Nose*—Black. A desirable breed characteristic is an inverted V-shaped area free of hair extending from the nose up the bridge of the muzzle, varying in length in the mature dog. *Lips*—Tight and dark brown- or black-rimmed. *Bite*—Scissors with teeth of good size.

**Neck, Topline, Body**—*Neck*—Long, slightly arched and strong, blending smoothly into well laid back shoulders. *Topline*—Level and firm. *Body*—The body is of sturdy structure with ribs well-sprung but not rounded, forming a chest reaching slightly below the elbows with a distinct keel. The loin is strong and fairly short with slight tuck-up. *Faults:* Cobbiness, too long in loin. *Tail*—Set on high and carried erect at a twelve to one o'clock position, docked in balance with the overall dog leaving slightly less than one half, a good hand-hold when mature.

**Forequarters**—*Shoulders*—Long blades, well laid back with only slight space between the shoulder blades at the withers. The length of the upper arm is comparable to the length of the shoulder blade. The angle between the shoulder and the upper arm is 90 degrees. *Faults:* Straight, loose and loaded shoulders. *Elbows*—Close to the chest. *Forelegs*—Straight, parallel when viewed from the front; the bone is round and medium in size. They should be set well under the body, with definite body overhang (keel) before them when viewed from the side. *Pasterns*—Strong, with only slight slope. *Fault:* Down on pasterns. *Dewclaws*—Removed. *Feet*—Small, clean, catlike; toes arched and compact, nicely padded turning neither inward nor outward. *Nails*—Short, black and strong.

**Hindquarters**—Strong; legs well angulated at the stifles and hocks, short and perpendicular from the hocks to the ground. Upper and lower thighs are well muscled. Viewed from behind the rear legs are straight from the hip joints to the ground and in the same plane as the forelegs. *Faults:* Lack of muscular development or excessive muscularity. *Feet*—(See under Forequarters.)

**Coat**—*Outer Coat*—Harsh and straight; 2½ inches all over the body except the tail, pasterns, rear legs from the hocks down, and the feet which are kept free of long hair. Hair on the ears is kept very short. *Undercoat*—Short and soft. *Furnishings*—Softer than body coat. The neck is well furnished with hair, which forms a protective ruff blending into the apron. The forelegs are slightly feathered to the pasterns. *Topknot*—Covering only the top of the skull; of finer and softer texture than the rest of the coat.

**Color and Markings**—Colors: Blue and tan, solid sandy and solid red. *Blue and tan*—Blue: dark blue, steel-blue, dark gray-blue, or silver-blue. In silver-blues, each hair carries blue and silver alternating with the darker color at the tips. Tan markings (not sandy or red), as rich as possible, on face, ears, underbody, lower legs and feet, and around vent.

The richer the color and more clearly defined the better. **Topknot**—Silver or a lighter shade than head color. **Sandy or Red**—Any shade of solid sandy or solid red, the clearer the better. **Topknot**—Silver or a lighter shade of body coat. **Faults:** All black body coat in the adult dog. Tan smut in the blue portion of the coat, or dark smut in sandy/red coated dogs. In any color, white markings on chest or feet are to be penalized.

**Gait**—As seen from the front and from the rear, the legs are straight from the shoulder and hip joints to the pads, and move in planes parallel to the centerline of travel. The rear legs move in the same planes as the front legs. As the dog moves at a faster trot, the front and rear legs and feet may tend to converge toward the centerline of travel, but the legs remain straight even as they flex or extend. Viewed from the side, the legs move in a ground-covering stride. The rear feet should meet the ground in the same prints as left by the front feet, with no gap between them. Topline remains firm and level, without bounce.

**Temperament**—The Australian Terrier is spirited, alert, courageous, and self-confident, with the natural aggressiveness of a ratter and hedge hunter; as a companion, friendly and affectionate. **Faults:** Shyness or aggressiveness toward people.

Approved August 9, 1988

# Bedlington Terrier

The Bedlington Terrier takes his name from the mining shire of that name, in the County of Northumberland, England. Purely a Northumbrian production, he first came to be known as the Rothbury Terrier, having originated in the Hannys hills, where the sporting squires loved a game terrier.

The origin of the breed remains a mystery. However, going back to 1820, we find that a Joseph Ainsley of Bedlington acquired a bitch, Coates Phoebe. In 1825 Phoebe was mated to a Rothbury dog, Anderson's Piper, also acquired by Ainsley, and the fruit of this union was a dog referred to as Ainsley's Piper—the first dog known to have been called a Bedlington Terrier.

About this time there flourished in Bedlington a colony of nailers who took to the breed and became noted for their plucky terriers. Of this dog's gameness there was not the slightest doubt—he never shirked at any kind of vermin and could more than hold his own at drawing a badger or at ratting in or out of Wales.

Both Piper and his mother, Phoebe, were considerably lighter in weight and small in stature than the dogs of the present day. But it is on record that Piper was set on a badger at eight months old and was constantly at work, more or less on badgers, foxes, otters and other vermin. He drew a badger after he was 14 years old, when toothless and nearly blind, after several other terriers had failed.

Although any crosses were introduced, there was always a band of enthusiastic admirers who kept to the original breed. In 1877 the National Bedlington Terrier Club (England) was formed by a few influential fanciers who made themselves responsible for bringing him to the notice of the public by exhibiting him on the show bench. Since then the Bedlington has made vast improvement in type.

Many tales have been told by the older generation of matches made by the miners and nailers of that period, where large sums were at stake on the result of a fight between terriers of their respective fancies. The Bedlington was never a mischief seeker, but once he started fighting, it was to the death.

As time went on, he was taken into the home of the elite, who found him a tractable and first-class companion. He was not long in developing into a pet, his great heart and lovable nature endearing him to all fortunate enough to own him.

There are two distinct colors, liver and blue, and it is only a question of fancy as to which is preferred. In the early days the liver was much in evidence, and some great dogs were of that color; in fact, the liver dog was preferred to the blue which is now so fashionable. Whether the former shade has become rarer from a change of tastes on the part of Bedlington breeders, or whether it is merely a coincidence that so few good liver-colored specimens happen to be shown at the present time, we are unable to say, but the fact remains that of late high-class blue Bedlingtons far outnumber good liver specimens. While there have been many good specimens of both colors, it is noticeable that the mother of the celebrated Piper was a blue-black bitch, possessing a light-colored topknot, a characteristic which has been meticulously preserved.

One reason there were fewer Bedlingtons at one time than their desirability warranted was the trimming necessary for exhibition in the show ring. Known only to a few so-called experts, this trimming seemed difficult. Gradually, however, the knack was mastered so that now most owners trim their own dogs and find it quite easy. It is only necessary to see it done by someone who knows how, after which, with a little practice, the novice becomes expert. The dog is hardy and not difficult to raise, and his feeding is the same as that required for other terriers of like weight.

## Official Standard for the Bedlington Terrier

**General Appearance**—A graceful, lithe, well-balanced dog with no sign of coarseness, weakness or shelliness. In repose the expression is mild and gentle, not shy or nervous. Aroused, the dog is particularly alert and full of immense energy and courage. Noteworthy for endurance, Bedlingtons also gallop at great speed, as their body outline clearly shows.

**Head**—Narrow, but deep and rounded. Shorter in skull and longer in jaw. Covered with a profuse topknot which is lighter than the color of the body, highest at the crown, and tapering gradually to just back of the nose. There must be no stop and the unbroken line from crown to nose end reveals a slender head without cheekiness or snipiness. Lips are black in the blue and tans and brown in all other solid and bi-colors. *Eyes*—Almond-shaped, small, bright and well sunk with no tendency to tear or water. Set is oblique and fairly high on the head. Blues have dark eyes; blues and tans, less dark with amber lights; sandies, sandies and tans, light hazel; liver, livers and tans, slightly darker. Eye rims are black in the blue and blue and tans, and brown in all other solid and bi-colors. *Ears*—Triangular with rounded tips. Set on low and hanging flat to the cheek in front with a slight projection at the base. Point of greatest width approximately 3 inches. Ear tips reach the corners of the mouth. Thin and velvety in texture, covered with fine hair forming a small silky tassel at the tip. *Nose*—Nostrils large and well defined. Blues and blues and tans have black noses. Livers, livers and tans, sandies, sandies and tans have brown noses. *Jaws*—Long and tapering. Strong muzzle sell filled up with bone beneath the eye. Close-fitting lips, no flews. *Teeth*—Large, strong and white. Level or scissors bite. Lower canines clasp the outer surface of the upper gum just in front of the upper canines. Upper premolars and molars lie outside those of the lower jaw.

**Neck and Shoulders**—Long, tapering neck with no throatiness, deep at the base and rising well up from the shoulders which are flat and sloping with no excessive muscu-lature. The head is carried high.

**Body**—Muscular and markedly flexible. Chest deep. Flat-ribbed and deep through the brisket, which reaches to the elbows. Back has a good natural arch over the loin, creating a definite tuck-up of the underline. Body slightly greater in length than height. Well-muscled quarters are also fine and graceful.

**Legs and Feet**—Lithe and muscular. The hind legs are longer than the forelegs, which are straight and wider apart at the chest than at the feet. Slight bend to pasterns which are long and sloping without weakness. Stifles well angulated. Hocks strong and well let down, turning neither in nor out. Long hare feet with thick, well-closed-up, smooth pads. Dewclaws should be removed.

**Coat**—A very distinctive mixture of hard and soft hair standing well out from the skin. Crisp to the touch but not wiry, having a tendency to curl, especially on the head and face. When in show trim must not exceed 1 inch on body; hair on legs is slightly longer.

**Tail**—Set low, scimitar-shaped, thick at the root and tapering to a point which reaches the hock. Not carried over the back or right to the underbody.

**Color**—Blue, sandy, liver, blue and tan, sandy and tan, liver and tan. In bi-colors the tan markings are found on the legs, chest, and under the tail, inside the hindquarters and over each eye. The topknots of all adults should be lighter than the body color. Patches of darker hair from an injury are not objectionable, as these are only temporary. Darker body pigmentation of all colors is to be encouraged.

**Height**—The preferred Bedlington Terrier dog measures 16½ inches at the withers, the bitch 15½ inches. Under 16 inches or over 17½ inches for dogs and under 15 inches or over 16½ inches for bitches are serious faults. Only where comparative superiority of a specimen outside these ranges clearly justifies it, should greater latitude be taken.

**Weight**—To be proportionate to height within the range of 17 to 23 pounds.

**Gait**—Unique lightness of movement. Springy in the slower paces, not stilted or hackneyed. Must not cross, weave or paddle.

Approved September 12, 1967

# Border Terrier

As the name suggests, the Border Terrier has its origin on either side of the Cheviot Hills which form the Border country, and may be regarded as one of the oldest kinds of terriers in Great Britain. As a purely "working terrier," Border farmers, shepherds, and sportsmen for generations carefully preserved a particular strain of this dog which could be found in almost every Border homestead.

With the hills at their disposal and miles from habitation, stock was subjected to the ravages of the powerful hill foxes, and to hunt and kill them the Border farmer and shepherd required a game terrier with length of leg sufficient to follow a horse, yet small enough to follow a fox to ground. The dogs had to be active, strong, and tireless; they had to have weather-resisting coats in order to withstand prolonged exposure to drenching rains and mists in the hills.

The Border Terrier is a tireless, hard worker for his size, and he is full of pluck. There is no wall he cannot get over or wire entanglement he cannot scramble through. Should the fox run to earth, he will bolt him every time, or stay the night in the earth until the matter is settled from his point of view. It may therefore be gathered that in order to meet these requirements the Border Terrier, as now known, was evolved by a process of judicious selection from the native hill terriers.

Until the English Kennel Club recognition was given, the Border Terrier was unknown to the great majority, but he was always exhibited in considerable numbers at most of the Agricultural Societies' shows in the Border country. Following recognition by the English Kennel Club and the formation of the Border Terrier Club in 1920, the breed has been catered to at many of the important shows in the British Isles. The first registration of the breed in the United States was in 1930.

## Official Standard for the Border Terrier

**General Appearance**—He is an active terrier of medium bone, strongly put together, suggesting endurance and agility, but rather narrow in shoulder, body and quarter. The body is covered with a somewhat broken though close-fitting and intensely wiry jacket. the characteristic "otter" head with its keen eye, combined with a body poise which is "at the alert," gives a look of fearless and implacable determination characteristic of the breed.

Since the Border Terrier is a working terrier of a size to go to ground and able, within reason, to follow a horse, his conformation should be such that he be ideally built to do his job. No deviations from this ideal conformation should be permitted, which would impair his usefulness in running his quarry to earth and in bolting it therefrom. For this work he must be alert, active and agile, and capable of squeezing through narrow apertures and rapidly traversing any kind of terrain. His head, "like that of an otter," is distinctive, and his temperament ideally exemplifies that of a terrier. By nature he is good-tempered, affectionate, obedient, and easily trained. In the field he is hard as nails, "game as they come" and driving in attack. It should be the aim of Border Terrier breeders to avoid such overemphasis of any point in the Standard as might lead to unbalanced exaggeration.

**Size, Proportion, Substance**—*Weight*—Dogs, 13–15½ pounds, bitches, 11½–14 pounds, are appropriate weight for Border Terriers in hardworking condition. The ***proportions*** should be that the height at the withers is slightly greater than the distance from the withers to the tail, *i.e.* by possibly 1–1½ inches in a 14-pound dog. Of medium bone, strongly put together, suggesting endurance and agility, but rather narrow in shoulder, body and quarter.

**Head**—Similar to that of an otter. *Eyes* dark hazel and full of fire and intelligence. Moderate in size, neither prominent nor small and beady. *Ears* small, V-shaped and of moderate thickness, dark preferred. Not set high on the head but somewhat on the side, and dropping forward close to the cheeks. They should not break above the level of the skull. Moderately broad and flat in *skull* with plenty of width between the eyes and between the ears. A slight, moderately broad curve at the stop rather than a pronounced indentation. Cheeks slightly full. *Muzzle* short and "well filled." A dark muzzle is characteristic and desirable. A few short whiskers are natural to the breed. *Nose* black, and of a good size. *Teeth* strong, with a scissors bite, large in proportion to size of dog.

**Neck, Topline, Body**—*Neck* clean, muscular and only long enough to give a well-balanced appearance. It should gradually widen into the shoulder. *Back* strong but laterally supple, with no suspicion of a dip behind the shoulder. *Loin* strong. *Body* deep, fairly narrow and of sufficient length to avoid any suggestions of lack of range and agility. The body should be capable of being spanned by a man's hands behind the shoulders. Brisket not excessively deep or narrow. Deep ribs carried well back and not oversprung in view of the desired depth and narrowness of the body. The *underline* fairly straight. *Tail* moderately short, thick at the base, then tapering. Not set on too high. Carried gaily when at the alert, but not over the back. When at ease, a Border may drop his stern.

**Forequarters**—*Shoulders* well laid back and of good length, the blades converging to the withers gradually from a brisket not excessively deep or narrow. *Forelegs* straight and not too heavy in bone and placed slightly wider than in a Fox Terrier. *Feet* small and compact. Toes should point forward and be moderately arched with thick pads.

**Hindquarters**—Muscular and racy, with *thighs* long and nicely molded. *Stifles* well bent and *hocks* well let down. *Feet* as in front.

**Coat**—A short and dense undercoat covered with a very wiry and somewhat broken topcoat which should lie closely, but it must not show any tendency to curl or wave. With such a coat a Border should be able to be exhibited almost in his natural state, nothing more in the way of trimming being needed than a tidying up of the head, neck and feet. *Hide* very thick and loose fitting.

**Color**—Red, grizzle and tan, blue and tan, or wheaten. A small amount of white may be allowed on the chest but white on the feet should be penalized. A dark muzzle is characteristic and desirable.

**Gait**—Straight and rhythmical before and behind, with good length of stride and flexing of stifle and hock. The dog should respond to his handler with a gait which is free, agile and quick.

**Temperament**—His temperament ideally exemplifies that of a terrier. By nature he is good-tempered, affectionate, obedient, and easily trained. In the field he is hard as nails, "game as they come" and driving in attack.

### SCALE OF POINTS

| | | | |
|---|---|---|---|
| Head, ears, neck and teeth | 20 | Back and loin | 10 |
| Legs and feet | 15 | Hindquarters | 10 |
| Coat and skin | 10 | Tail | 5 |
| Shoulders and chest | 10 | General Appearance | 10 |
| Eyes and expression | 10 | TOTAL | 100 |

Approved March 14, 1950
Reformatted July 13, 1990

# Bull Terrier

There are two varieties of the Bull Terrier breed, the white and the colored. The breed dates back to about 1835. It is almost unanimously believed that it was established by mating a Bulldog to the now extinct white English Terrier. The results were known as the "bull and terrier." Some few years later, to gain size, this dog was crossed with the Spanish Pointer, and even to this day evidence of Pointer inheritance is seen occasionally.

Then about the year 1860 fanciers decided that an entirely white dog would be more attractive, so James Hinks produced an all white one which was taken up enthusiastically by young bloods of the day as the most fashionable dog.

It was a dog for sportsmen in times when life in general was more strenuous and of rougher, coarser fiber—when dog fights were allowed and well attended. As fighting dog or "gladiator" of the canine world, such a dog had to be of great strength, agility, and courage. Withal, he was bred by gentlemen for gentlemen, for those who had a great sense of fair play, and who scorned the liar and the deceiver in any game. The dog was taught to defend himself and his master courageously, yet he was not to seek or provoke a fight—and so the white variety became known as "the white cavalier," a title which he bears with distinction to this day.

Contrary to the opinion of those who do not know him, the Bull Terrier is an exceedingly friendly dog; he thrives on affection, yet is always ready for a fight and a frolic. The preference in this country is for a well-balanced animal, not freaky in any particular, but well-put-together, active and agile—a gladiator of perfect form.

There is also the Colored Bull Terrier which, in accordance with its standard, must be any color other than white, or any color with white just so long as the white does not predominate. The "Colored" was voted a separate variety of Bull Terrier in 1936.

## Official Standard for the Bull Terrier

**WHITE**

The Bull Terrier must be strongly built, muscular, symmetrical and active, with a keen determined and intelligent expression, full of fire but of sweet disposition and amenable to discipline.

**Head** — Should be long, strong and deep right to the end of the muzzle, but not coarse. Full face it should be oval in outline and be filled completely up giving the impression

**White Bull Terrier**

**Colored Bull Terrier**

of fullness with a surface devoid of hollows or indentations, *i.e.*, egg shaped. In profile it should curve gently downwards from the top of the skull to the tip of the nose. The forehead should be flat across from ear to ear. The distance from the tip of the nose to the eyes should be perceptibly greater than that from the eyes to the top of the skull. The underjaw should be deep and well defined. The **Lips** should be clean and tight. The **Teeth** should meet in either a level or in a scissors bite. In the scissors bite the upper teeth should fit in front of and closely against the lower teeth, and they should be sound, strong and perfectly regular. The **Ears** should be small, thin and placed close together. They should be capable of being held stiffly erect, when they should point upwards. The **Eyes** should be well sunken and as dark as possible, with a piercing glint and they should be small, triangular and obliquely placed; set near together and high up on the dog's head. Blue eyes are a disqualification. The **Nose** should be black, with well-developed nostrils bent downward at the tip.

**Neck** — Should be very muscular, long, arched and clean, tapering from the shoulders to the head and it should be free from loose skin. The **Chest** should be broad when viewed from in front, and there should be great depth from withers to brisket, so that the latter is nearer the ground than the belly.

**Body** — Should be well rounded with marked spring of rib, the back should be short and strong. The back ribs deep. Slightly arched over the loin. The shoulders should be strong and muscular but without heaviness. The shoulder blades should be wide and flat and there should be a very pronounced backward slope from the bottom edge of the blade to the top edge. Behind the shoulders there should be no slackness or dip at the withers. The underline from the brisket to the belly should form a graceful upward curve.

**Legs** — Should be big boned but not to the point of coarseness; the forelegs should be of moderate length, perfectly straight, and the dog must stand firmly upon them. The elbows must turn neither in nor out, and the pasterns should be strong and upright. The hind legs should be parallel viewed from behind. The thighs very muscular with hocks well let down. Hind pasterns short and upright. The stifle joint should be well bent with a well-developed second thigh. The **Feet** round and compact with well-arched toes like a cat.

**Tail** — Should be short, set on low, fine, and ideally should be carried horizontally. It should be thick where it joins the body, and should taper to a fine point.

**Coat** — Should be short, flat, harsh to the touch and with a fine gloss. The dog's skin should fit tightly. The **Color** is white though markings on the head are permissible. Any markings elsewhere on the coat are to be severely faulted. Skin pigmentation is not to be penalized.

**Movement**—The dog shall move smoothly, covering the ground with free, easy strides, fore and hind legs should move parallel each to each when viewed from in front or behind. The forelegs reaching out well and hind legs moving smoothly at the hip and flexing well at the stifle and hock. The dog should move compactly and in one piece but with a typical jaunty air that suggests agility and power.

### FAULTS

Any departure from the foregoing points shall be considered a fault, and the seriousness of the fault shall be in exact proportion to its degree, *i.e.* a very crooked front is a very bad fault; a rather crooked front is a rather bad fault; and a slightly crooked front is a slight fault.

### DISQUALIFICATION

*Blue eyes.*

### COLORED

The Standard for the Colored Variety is the same as for the White except for the sub-head "Color" which reads: *Color.* Any color other than white, or any color with white markings. Other things being equal, the preferred color is brindle. A dog which is predominantly white shall be disqualified.

### DISQUALIFICATIONS

*Blue eyes.*
*Any dog which is predominantly white.*

Approved July 9, 1974

# Cairn Terrier

The history of the Cairn Terrier is enhanced by the fact that the modern Cairn is an attempt to preserve in typical form the old-time working terrier of the Isle of Skye.

From Martin's *History of the Dog* in 1845, Capt. McDonald's description and measurements of the ideal Cairn in 1876, from Ross's *Cairn Terrier*, Darley Matheson's *Terriers*, and from many other writers, it is plain that these were working terriers, with courage for the bolting of otter, foxes, and other vermin from among rocks, cliffs, and ledges on the wild shores of their misty isle.

Scotland's terriers had been grouped together as Scotch Terriers until 1873, when they were separated into two classifications—Dandie Dinmont Terriers and Skye Terriers. The breeds we now know as the Scottish Terrier, the West Highland White Terrier, and the Cairn Terrier, were included in classes for Skye Terriers. The Scottish, West Highland and Cairn had developed from the same stock, originating in the islands and highlands of western Scotland. The three often were found in the same litter, distinguished only by color. A club for Hard-Haired Scotch Terriers embracing the three was formed in 1881, and a standard was approved in 1882. White markings were considered a fault, though an all-white dog was valued.

Toward the end of the 19th century, fanciers of the Scottish Terrier type (who were in the majority) began to breed along separate lines. The Kennel

Club was petitioned by a group known as The White Scottish Terrier club for separate classes for whites in 1899. The request originally had been denied, but at Crufts in 1907 separate classes were available for white terriers. The stud books were opened to West Highland White Terriers as a separate breed, with the first registrations listed as 1908.

In 1909, the show at Inverness offered classes for Short-Haired Skyes. At a meeting of the Skye Terrier Club, fanciers protested the use of the name. The confusion over the classification of these "Short-Haired Skyes" was once again apparent when they were entered in classes for Skye Terriers at Crufts in 1910, even though classes for Short-Haired Skyes were provided. The judge refused to judge these dogs as entered and marked her book "wrong class." A change of name to the "Cairn Terrier of Skye" was suggested for the Short-Haired Skye. (Cairns were piles of stones which served as landmarks or memorials. Common throughout much of Scotland, cairns were frequent hiding places for small mammals. Farmers used small terriers to bolt the animals from their rocky lairs.) The shortened name, Cairn Terrier, was agreed upon and in 1912 the breed was permitted to compete for challenge certificates.

The Cairn Terrier standard in England permitted white as a color until 1923. The interbreeding of Cairns and West Highland White Terriers had occurred in both England and the United States. However, the AKC (who had given the breed official recognition in 1913) in 1917 barred any Cairn from registration if it was a product of "such a mixed breeding practice."

The modern Cairn should have the hardiness to meet the performance of his old-time prototype. Utility should be the aim of the fancier, since the expressed object of the Cairn Terrier clubs is to preserve the breed in its best old-working type.

The height of the Cairn, which differs from that of other terriers, is important in giving the breed the distinctive conformation that has been called "Cairnishess." He is not so low to ground, in proportion to his size, as the Sealyham and the Scottish Terrier. There is one, and only one, correct size for the Cairn Terrier—14 pounds for dogs, 13 pounds for bitches, and the dogs should be in proper proportion to those weights.

If the breed is to resist passing fads and the inroads of modernization, the first consideration in judging should be given to those qualities which are unique in the Cairn.

## Official Standard for the Cairn Terrier

**General Appearance**—That of an active, game, hardy, small working terrier of the short-legged class; very free in its movements, strongly but not heavily built, standing well forward on its forelegs, deep in the ribs, well coupled with strong hindquarters and presenting a well-proportioned build with a medium length of back, having a hard, weather-resisting coat; head shorter and wider than any other terrier and well furnished with hair giving a general foxy expression.

**Head**—*Skull*—Broad in proportion to length with a decided stop and well furnished with hair on the top of the head, which may be somewhat softer than the body coat. *Muzzle*—Strong but not too long or heavy. *Teeth*—Large, mouth neither overshot nor undershot. *Nose*—Black. *Eyes*—Set wide apart, rather sunken, with shaggy eyebrows, medium in size, hazel or dark hazel in color, depending on body color, with a keen terrier expression. *Ears*—Small, pointed, well carried erectly, set wide apart on the side of the head. Free from long hairs.

**Tail**—In proportion to head, well furnished with hair but not feathery. Carried gaily but must not curl over back. Set on at back level.

**Body**—Well-muscled, strong, active body with well-sprung, deep ribs, coupled to strong hindquarters, with a level back of medium length, giving an impression of strength and activity without heaviness.

**Shoulders, Legs and Feet**—A sloping shoulder, medium length of leg, good but not too heavy bone; forelegs should not be out at elbows, and be perfectly straight, but forefeet may be slightly turned out. Forefeet larger than hind feet. Legs must be covered with hard hair. Pad should be thick and strong and dog should stand well up on its feet.

**Coat**—Hard and weather-resistant. Must be double-coated with profuse harsh outer coat and short, soft, close furry undercoat.

**Color**—May be of any color except white. Dark ears, muzzle and tail tip are desirable.

**Ideal Size**—Involves the weight, the height at the withers and the length of body. Weight for bitches, 13 pounds; for dogs, 14 pounds. Height at the withers—bitches, 9½ inches; dogs, 10 inches. Length of body from 14¼ to 15 inches form the front of the chest to back of hindquarters. The dog must be of balanced proportions and appear neither leggy nor too low to ground; and neither too short nor too long in body. Weight and measurements are for matured dogs at two years of age. Older dogs may weigh slightly in excess and growing dogs may be under these weights and measurements.

**Condition**—Dogs should be shown in good hard flesh, well muscled and neither too fat or thin. Should be full good coat with plenty of head furnishings, be clean, combed, brushed and tidied up on ears, tail, feet and general outline. Should move freely and easily on a loose lead, should not cringe on being handled, should stand up on their toes and show with marked terrier characteristics.

### FAULTS

1. *Skull*—Too narrow in skull.
2. *Muzzle*—Too long and heavy a foreface; mouth overshot or undershot.
3. *Eyes*—Too large, prominent, yellow, and ringed are all objectionable.

4. *Ears*—Too large, round at points, set too close together, set too high on the head; heavily covered with hair.

5. *Legs and Feet*—Too light or too heavy bone. Crooked forelegs or out at elbow. Thin, ferrety feet; feet let down on the heel or too open and spread. Too high or too low on the leg.

6. *Body*—Too short back and compact a body, hampering quickness of movement and turning ability. Too long, weedy and snaky a body, giving an impression of weakness. Tail set too low. Back not level.

7. *Coat*—Open coats, blousy coats, too short or dead coats, lack of sufficient undercoat, lack of head furnishings, lack of hard hair on the legs. Silkiness or curliness. A slight wave permissible.

8. *Nose*—Flesh or light-colored nose.

9. *Color*—White on chest, feet or other parts of body.

Approved May 10, 1938

# Dandie Dinmont Terrier

The Dandie Dinmont Terrier was bred from selected specimens of the rough native terrier of the Border hunters in the Cheviot Hills between England and Scotland and was first recorded as a distinct type of breed about 1700. He was distinguished by his preeminence in hunting the otter and the badger. A direct line of these dogs descended to the farmers in the Teviotdale Hills, where Sir Walter Scott in his travels chanced upon them and made them famous in his *Guy Mannering*, published in 1814. His character Dandie Dinmont, a farmer (believed to have been a Mr. James Davidson of Hindlee, near Hawick) kept the immortal six: Auld Pepper, Auld Mustard, Young Pepper, Young Mustard, Little Pepper and Little Mustard. Sir Walter gives an excellent description of their pluck: "I have them a' regularly entered, first wi' rottens, then wi' stots or weasels, and then wi' the tods and brocks, and now they fear naething that ever cam' wi' a hairy skin on't." From the time of the popularity of *Guy Mannering* to the present day, the breed has been known as "Dandie Dinmont's Terriers."

Terriers recognizable as Dandies appear in paintings by Ansdell and Landseer made before 1850. King Louis Philippe of France owned a pair of the breed in 1845.

Today the hunting qualities of the Dandie are not so often required, but his other qualities make him an excellent house dog. He is intelligent, fond of children, and an excellent guard. He has a will of his own and will sometimes obey a command reluctantly, with a look of "I'll do it, but please don't make me."

The points of a Dandie are quite the opposite of the average terrier—there are no straight lines. Head, large with a full doomed skull; eyes, large, full of a very deep hazel and luminous, the darker the better; jaw, strong, deep and punishing; body, long, back rather low at the shoulder with a corresponding arch over the loins and slight drop to the root of the tail, combined with a broad, deep, and powerful chest; front legs, short, with paws slightly outcurved for digging; hind legs, longer and not so heavy; tail, set low, slightly curved and carried at an angle of about 45 degrees—it should come up like a scimitar. There are two distinct colors: pepper—blue gray to light silver with light tan or silver points and very light gray or white topknot; and mustard—dark ocher color to cream with white points and topknot. The intermediate shades in each color are the more desirable. The Dandie has a rough double coat, made up of hard and soft hair in the proportion of about double the amount of hard hair to that of soft. This forms a thorough watershed which feels crisp to the touch, but does not have the harsh feel of the wire-coated dog. The head is covered with soft, silky hair, which should not be confined to a mere topknot. When groomed and properly shaped, this forms one of the characteristic features of the "show" Dandie.

Regular coat care is necessary for a Dandie. Frequent plucking will improve the texture and color of the coat. Only the longest hairs should be removed to keep the double coat and penciled appearance. If the coat is neglected for a long period, it may be necessary to strip it down close to the skin. This will leave only undercoat and the Dandie may appear white. It can take months for the coat to grow in to proper length and texture after stripping.

Dandies fit in anywhere, either in a rough-and-tumble out-of-doors life or in the confines of a city apartment. They are in ideal size, between 18 and 24 pounds, small enough to fit a small apartment and yet a dog big in character.

## Official Standard for the Dandie Dinmont Terrier

**General Appearance**—Originally bred to go to ground, the Dandie Dinmont Terrier is a long, low-stationed working terrier with a curved outline. The distinctive head with silken topknot is large but in proportion to the size of the dog. The dark eyes are large and round with a soft, wise expression. The sturdy, flexible body and scimitar shaped tail are covered with a rather crisp double coat, either mustard or pepper in color.

**Size, Proportion, Substance**—*Height* is from 8 to 11 inches at the top of the shoulders. *Length* from top of shoulders to root of tail is one to two inches less than twice the height. For a dog in good working condition, the preferred *weight* is from 18 to 24 pounds. Sturdily built with ample bone and well developed muscle, but without coarseness. The overall balance is more important than any single specification.

**Head**—The *head* is strongly made and large, but in proportion to the dog's size. Muscles are well developed, especially those covering the foreface. The **expression** shows great determination, intelligence and dignity. The *eyes* are large, round, bright and full, but not protruding. They are set wide apart and low, and directly forward. Color, a rich dark hazel. Eye rims dark. The *ears* are set well back, wide apart and low on the skull, hanging close to the cheek, with a very slight projection at the fold. The shape is broad at the base, coming almost to a point. The front edge comes almost straight down from base to tip; the tapering is primarily on the back edge. The cartilage and skin of the ear are rather thin. The ear's length is from three to four inches. The **skull** is broad between the ears, gradually tapering toward the eyes, and measures about the same from stop to occiput as it does from ear to ear. Forehead (brow) well domed. Stop well defined. The **cheeks** gradually taper from the ears toward the muzzle in the same proportion as the taper of the skull. The **muzzle** is deep and strong. In length, the proportions are a ratio of three (muzzle) to five (skull). The nose is moderately large and black or dark colored. The lips and inside of the mouth are black or dark colored. The **teeth** meet in a tight scissors bite. The teeth are very strong, especially the canines, which are an extraordinary size for a small dog. The canines mesh well with each other to give great holding and punishing power. The incisors in each jaw are evenly spaced and six in number.

**Neck, Topline, Body**—The **neck** is very muscular, well developed and strong, showing great power of resistance. It is well set into the shoulders and moderate in length. The **topline** is rather low at the shoulder, having a slight downward curve and a corresponding arch over the loins, with a very slight gradual drop from the top of the loins to the root of the tail. Both sides of the backbone well muscled. The outline is a continuous flow from the crest of the neck to the tip of the tail. The **body** is long, strong and flexible. *Ribs* are well sprung and well rounded. The *chest* is well developed and well let down between the forelegs. The underline reflects the curves of the topline. The **tail** is 8 to 10 inches in length, rather thick at the root, getting thicker for about four inches, then tapering off to a point. The set-on of the tail is a continuation of the very slight gradual drop over the croup. The tail is carried a little above the level of the body in a curve like a scimitar. Only when the dog is excited may the tip of the tail be aligned perpendicular to its root.

**Forequarters**—There should be sufficient layback of **shoulder** to allow good reach in front; angulation in balance with hindquarters. *Upper arms* nearly equal in length to the shoulder blades, elbows lying close to the ribs and capable of moving freely. The **forelegs** are short with good muscular development and ample bone, set wide apart. Feet point forward or very slightly outward. Pasterns nearly straight when viewed from the side. Bandy legs and fiddle front are objectionable.

**Hindquarters**—The **hind legs** are a little longer than the forelegs and are set rather wide apart, but not spread out in an unnatural manner. The upper and lower thighs are rounded and muscular and approximately the same length; stifles angulated, in balance with forequarters. The hocks are well let down and rear pasterns perpendicular to the ground.

**Feet**—The *feet* are round and well cushioned. Dewclaws preferably removed on forelegs. Rear feet are much smaller than the front feet and have no dewclaws. Nails strong and dark; nail color may very according to the color of the dog. White nails are permissible. Flat feet are objectionable.

**Coat**—This is a very important point: The hair should be about two inches long; the body coat is a mixture of about ⅔ hardish hair with about ⅓ soft hair, giving a sort of crisp texture. The hard is not wiry. The body coat is shortened by plucking. The coat is termed pily or pencilled, the effect of the natural intermingling of the two types of hair. The hair on the underpart of the body is softer than on the top. The head is covered with very soft, silky hair, the silkier the better. It should not be confined to a mere topknot but extends to cover the upper portion of the ears, including the fold, and frames the eyes. Starting about two inches from the tip, the ear has a thin feather of hair of nearly the same color and texture as the topknot, giving the ear the appearance of ending in a distinct point. The body of the ear is covered with short, soft, velvety hair. The hair on the muzzle is of the same texture as the foreleg feather. For presentation, the hair on the top of the muzzle is shortened. The hair behind the nose is naturally more sparse for about an inch. The forelegs have a feather about two inches long, the same texture as the muzzle. The hind leg hair is of the same texture but has considerably less feather. The upper side of the tail is covered with crisper hair than that on the body. The underside has a softer feather about two inches long, gradually shorter as it nears the tip, shaped like a scimitar. Trimming for presentation is to appear entirely natural; exaggerated styling is objectionable.

**Color**—The color is pepper or mustard. *Pepper* ranges from dark bluish black to a light silvery gray, the intermediate shades preferred. The topknot and ear feather are silvery white, the lighter the color the better. The hair on the legs and feet should be tan, varying according to the body color from a rich tan to a very pale fawn. **Mustard** varies from a reddish brown to a pale fawn. The topknot and ear feather are a creamy white. The hair on the legs and feet should be a darker shade than the topknot. In both colors the body color comes well down the shoulders and hips, gradually merging into the leg color. Hair on the underpart of the body is lighter in color than on the top. The hair on the muzzle (beard) is a little darker shade than the topknot. Ear color harmonizes with the body color. The upper side of the tail is a darker shade than the body color, while the underside of the tail is lighter, as the legs. Some white hair on the chest is common.

**Gait**—Proper movement requires a free and easy stride, reaching forward with the front legs and driving with evident force form the rear. The legs move in a straight plane from shoulder to pad and hip to pad. A stiff, stilted, hopping or weaving gait and lack of drive in the rear quarters are faults to be penalized.

**Temperament**—Independent, determined, reserved and intelligent. The Dandie Dinmont Terrier combines an affectionate and dignified nature with, in a working situation, tenacity and boldness.

Approved February 9, 1991

# Fox Terriers

For close to 100 years, the Fox Terrier had been registered and shown in the United States as one breed of two varieties, Smooth and Wire. On December 11, 1984, the Board of Directors of the AKC approved separate breed standards for the Smooth Fox Terrier and the Wire Fox Terrier, which became effective on June 1, 1985.

One of the best known and most widely distributed of pure-bred dogs, the Fox Terrier is an ancient breed of English origin. As early as 1790, a smooth-coated white terrier with markings (Colonel Thornton's Pitch) was recorded both in print and on canvas.

It is probable that the Smooth and the Wire sprang from widely different sources. A profound student of the related breeds claims that the ancestor of the Wire was the old rough-coated black-and-tan working terrier of Wales, Derbyshire, and Durham, and that the more important ancestors of the Smooth were the smooth-coated black-and tan, the Bull Terrier, the Greyhound, and the Beagle.

The Smooth antedated the Wire by some 15 or 20 years in the show ring, and at first was classified among the sporting breeds. This was a tribute to his keen nose, remarkable eyesight, and staying powers in accomplishing his work of driving the fox from his hole or the drain in which he had taken refuge when too closely pursued by the hounds.

Wires were liberally crossed with Smooths in the earlier days of breeding in order to give the Wire the predominating white pigmentation, cleaner-cut head, and more classical outline of the Smooth. The practice of interbreeding the Smooth with the Wire (and vice versa) has been almost universally discontinued for many years.

The original breed standard was so well drawn by the Fox Terrier Club (England) in 1876 that, with the exception of reducing the weight of a male dog in show condition from 20 pounds to 18 pounds, no change was found necessary for many decades. The American Fox Terrier Club, parent club of the breed in this country, adopted this standard when the club was founded in 1885.

## Official Standard for the Smooth Fox Terrier

**General Appearance**—The dog must present a generally gay, lively and active appearance; bone and strength in a small compass are essentials; but this must not be taken to mean that a Fox Terrier should be cloddy, or in any way coarse—speed and endurance must be looked to as well as power, and the symmetry of the Foxhound taken as a model.

**355**

Smooth Fox Terrier

Wire Fox Terrier

The Terrier, like the Hound, must on no account be leggy, nor must he be too short in the leg. He should stand like a cleverly made hunter, covering a lot of ground, yet with a short back, as stated below. He will then attain the highest degree of propelling power, together with the greatest length of stride that is compatible with the length of his body. Weight is not a certain criterion of a Terrier's fitness for his work—general shape, size and contour are the main points; and if a dog can gallop and stay, and follow his fox up a drain, it matters little what his weight is to a pound or so. **N.B.** Old scars or injuries, the result of work or accident, should not be allowed to prejudice a Terrier's chance in the show ring, unless they interfere with its movement or with its utility for work or stud.

**Size, Proportion, Substance**—According to present-day requirements a full-sized well balanced dog should not exceed 15½ inches at the withers—the bitch being proportionately lower—nor should the length of back withers to root of tail exceed 12 inches, while to maintain the relative proportions, the head should not exceed 7¼ inches or be less than 7 inches. A dog with these measurements should scale 18 pounds in show condition—a bitch weighing some two pounds less—with a margin of one pound either way. *Balance*—This may be defined as the correct proportions of a certain point, or points, when considered in relation to a certain other point or points. It is the keystone of the Terrier's anatomy. The chief points for consideration are the relative proportions of skull and foreface; head and back; height at withers and length of body from shoulder point to buttock—the ideal of proportion being reached when the last two measurements are the same. It should be added that, although the head measurements can be taken with absolute accuracy, the height at withers and length of back and coat are approximate, and are inserted for the information of breeders and exhibitors rather than as a hard-and-fast rule.

**Head**—*Eyes* and *rims* should be dark in color, moderately small and rather deep set, full of fire, life and intelligence and as nearly possible circular in shape. Anything approaching a yellow eye is most objectionable. *Ears* should be V-shaped and small, of moderate thickness, and dropping forward close to the cheek, not hanging by the side of the head like a Foxhound. The topline of the folded ear should be well above the level of the skull. *Disqualifications*—Ears prick, tulip or rose. The **skull** should be flat and moderately narrow, gradually decreasing in width to the eyes. Not much "stop" should be apparent, but there should be more dip in the profile between the forehead and the top jaw than is seen in the case of a Greyhound. It should be noticed that although the foreface should gradually taper from eye to muzzle and should tip slightly at its junction with the forehead, it should not "dish" or fall away quickly below the eyes, where it should be full and well made up, but relieved from "wedginess" by a little delicate chiseling. There should be apparent little difference in length between the skull and foreface of a well balanced head. *Cheeks* must not be full. *Jaws*, upper and lower, should be strong and muscular and of fair punishing strength, but not so as in any way to resemble the Greyhound or modern English Terrier. There should not be much falling away below the eyes. This part of the head should, however, be moderately chiseled out, so as not to go down in a straight slope like a wedge. The **nose**, towards which the muzzle must gradually taper, should be black. *Disqualifications*— Nose white, cherry or spotted to a considerable extent with either of these colors. The **teeth** should be as nearly as possible together, i.e., the points of the upper (incisors) teeth on the outside of or slightly overlapping the lower teeth. *Disqualifications*—much undershot, or much overshot.

**Neck, Topline, Body**—*Neck* should be clean and muscular, without throatiness, of fair length, and gradually widening to the shoulders. *Back* should be short, straight (i.e., level), and strong, with no appearance of slackness. *Chest* deep and not broad. *Brisket* should be deep, yet not exaggerated. The foreribs should be moderately arched, the back ribs deep and well sprung, and the dog should be well ribbed up. *Loin* should be very powerful, muscular and very slightly arched. *Stern* should be set on rather high, and carried gaily, but not over the back or curled. It should be of good strength, anything approaching a "Pipestopper" tail being especially objectionable.

**Forequarters**—*Shoulders* should be long and sloping, well laid back, fine at the points, and clearly cut at the withers. The elbows should hang perpendicular to the body, working free of the sides. The forelegs viewed from any direction must be straight with bone strong right down to the feet, showing little or no appearance of ankle in front, and being short and straight in pastern. Both fore and hind legs should be carried straight forward in traveling. *Feet* should be round, compact, and not large; the soles hard and tough; the toes moderately arched, and turned neither in nor out.

**Hindquarters**—Should be strong and muscular, quite free from droop or crouch; the thighs long and powerful, stifles well curved and turned neither in nor out; hocks well bent and near the ground should be perfectly upright and parallel each with the other when viewed from behind, the dog standing well up on them like a Foxhound, and not straight in the stifle. The worst possible form of hindquarters consists of a short second thigh and a straight stifle. Both fore and hind legs should be carried straight forward in traveling, the stifles not turning outward. Feet as in front.

**Coat**—Should be smooth, flat, but hard, dense and abundant. The belly and underside of the thighs should not be bare.

**Color**—White should predominate; brindle, red or liver markings are objectionable. Otherwise this point is of little or no importance.

**Gait**—Movement, or action, is the crucial test of conformation. The Terrier's legs should be carried straight forward while traveling, the forelegs hanging perpendicular and swinging parallel with the sides, like the pendulum of a clock. The principal propulsive power is furnished by the hind legs, perfection of action being found in the Terrier possessing long thighs and muscular second thighs well bent at the stifles, which admit of a strong forward thrust or "snatch" of the hocks. When approaching, the forelegs should form a continuation of the straight line of the front, the feet being the same distance apart as the elbows. When stationary it is often difficult to determine whether a dog is slightly out at shoulder, but, directly he moves, the defect—if it exists—becomes more apparent, the forefeet having a tendency to cross, "weave," or "dish." When, on the contrary, the dog is tied at the shoulder, the tendency of the feet is to move wider apart, with a sort of paddling action. When the hocks are turned in—cow-hocks—the stifles and feet are turned outwards, resulting in a serious loss of propulsive power. When the hocks are turned outwards the tendency of the hind feet is to cross, resulting in an ungainly waddle.

**Temperament**—The dog must present a generally gay, lively and active appearance.

### DISQUALIFICATIONS

*Ears prick, tulip or rose.*
*Nose white, cherry or spotted to a considerable extent*
*with either of these colors.*
*Mouth much undershot, or much overshot.*

Approved February 9, 1991

## Official Standard for the Wire Fox Terrier

**General Appearance**—The Terrier should be alert, quick of movement, keen of expression, on the tip-toe of expectation at the slightest provocation. Character is imparted by the expression of the eyes and by the carriage of ears and tail. Bone and strength in a small compass are essential, but this must not be taken to mean that a Terrier should be "cloddy," or in any way coarse—speed and endurance being requisite as well as power. The Terrier must on no account be leggy, nor must he be too short on the leg. He should stand like a cleverly made, short-backed hunter, covering a lot of ground. **N.B.** Old scars or injuries, the result of work or accident, should not be allowed to prejudice a Terrier's chance in the show ring, unless they interfere with its movement or with its utility for work or stud.

**Size, Proportion, Substance**—According to present-day requirements, a full-sized, well balanced dog should not exceed 15½ inches at the withers—the bitch being proportionately lower—nor should the length of back from withers to root of tail exceed 12 inches, while to maintain the relative proportions, the head—as mentioned below—should not exceed 7¼ inches or be less than 7 inches. A dog with these measurements should scale 18 pounds in show condition—a bitch weighing some two pounds less—with a margin of one pound either way. The dog should be balanced and this may be defined as the correct proportions of a certain point or points, when considered in relation to a certain other point or points. It is the keystone of the Terrier's anatomy. The chief points for consideration are the relative proportions of skull and foreface; head and back; height at withers; and length of body from shoulder point to buttock—the ideal of proportion being reached when the last two measurements are the same. It should be added that, although the head measurements can be taken with absolute accuracy, the height at withers and length of back are approximate, and are inserted for the information of breeders and exhibitors rather than as a hard-and-fast rule.

**Head**—The length of the *head* of a full-grown well developed dog of correct size—measured with calipers—from the back of the occipital bone to the nostrils—should be from 7 to 7¼ inches, the bitch's head being proportionately shorter. Any measurement in excess of this usually indicates an oversized or long-backed specimen, although occasionally—so rarely as to partake of the nature of a freak—a Terrier of correct size may boast a head 7½ inches in length. In a well balanced head there should be little apparent difference in length between skull and foreface. If, however, the foreface is noticeably shorter, it amounts to a fault, the head looking weak and "unfinished." On the other hand, when the eyes are set too high up in the skull and too near the ears, it also amounts to a fault, the head being said to have a "foreign appearance." Keen of *expression. Eyes* should be dark in color, moderately small, rather deep-set, not prominent, and full of fire, life, and intelligence; as nearly as possible circular in shape, and not too far apart. Anything approaching a yellow eye is most objectionable. *Ears* should be small and V-shaped and of moderate thickness, the flaps neatly folded over and dropping forward close to the cheeks. The topline of the folded ear should be well above the level of the skull. A pendulous ear, hanging dead by the side of the head like a Hound's, is uncharacteristic of the Terrier, while an ear which is semierect is still more undesirable. *Disqualifications*—Ears prick, tulip or rose. The topline of the *skull* should be almost flat, sloping slightly and gradually decreasing in width towards the eyes, and should not exceed 3½ inches in diameter at the widest part—measuring with the calipers—in the full-grown dog of correct size, the bitch's skull being proportionately narrower. If this measurement is exceeded, the skull is termed "coarse," while a full-grown dog with a much narrower skull is termed "bitchy" in head. Although the *foreface* should gradually taper from eye to muzzle and should dip slightly at its juncture with the forehead, it should not "dish" or fall away quickly below the eyes, where it should be full and well made up, but relieved from "wedginess" by a little delicate chiseling. While well developed *jaw bones,* armed with a set of strong, white teeth, impart that appearance of strength to the foreface which is so desirable, an excessive bony or muscular development of jaws is both unnecessary and unsightly, as it is partly responsible for the full and rounded contour of the cheeks to which the term "cheeky" is applied. *Nose* should be black. *Disqualifications*—Nose white, cherry or spotted to a considerable extent with either of these colors. *Mouth*—Both upper and lower jaws should be strong and muscular, the *teeth* as nearly as possible level and capable of closing together like a vise—the lower canines locking in front of the upper and the points of the upper incisors slightly overlapping the lower. *Disqualifications*—Much undershot, or much overshot.

**Neck, Topline, Body**—*Neck* should be clean, muscular, of fair length, free from throatiness and presenting a graceful curve when viewed from the side. The *back* should be short and level with no appearance of slackness—the *loins* muscular and very slightly arched. The term "slackness" is applied both to the portion of the back immediately behind the withers when it shows any tendency to dip, and also the flanks when there is too much space between the back ribs and hipbone. When there is little space between the ribs and hips, the dog is said to be "short in couplings," "short-coupled," or "well ribbed up." A Terrier can scarcely be too short in back, provided he has sufficient length of neck and liberty of movement. The bitch may be slightly longer in couplings than the dog. *Chest* deep and not broad, a too narrow chest being almost as undesirable as a very broad one. Excessive depth of chest and brisket is an impediment to a Terrier when going to ground. The *brisket* should be deep, the front ribs moderately arched, and the back ribs deep and well sprung. *Tail* should be set on rather high and carried gaily but not curled. It should be of good strength and substance and of fair length—a three-quarters dock is about right—since it affords the only safe grip when handling working Terriers. A very short tail is suitable neither for work nor show.

**Forequarters—*Shoulders*** when viewed from the front should slope steeply downwards from their juncture, with the neck towards the points, which should be fine. When viewed form the side they should be long, well laid back, and should slope obliquely backwards from points to withers, which should always be clean-cut. A shoulder well laid back gives the long forehand which, in combination with a short back, is so desirable in Terrier or Hunter. The elbows should hang perpendicular to the body, working free of the sides, carried straight through in traveling. Viewed from any direction the legs should be straight, the bone of the forelegs strong right down to the feet. *Feet* should be round, compact, and not large—the pads tough and well cushioned, and the toes moderately arched and turned neither in nor out. A Terrier with good-shaped forelegs and feet will wear his nails down short by contact with the road surface, the weight of the body being evenly distributed between the toe pads and the heels.

**Hindquarters—**Should be strong and muscular, quite free from droop or crouch; the thighs long and powerful; the stifles well curved and turned neither in nor out; the hock joints well bent and near the ground; the hocks perfectly upright and parallel with each other when viewed from behind. The worst possible form of hindquarters consists of a short second thigh and a straight stifle, a combination which causes the hind legs to act as props rather than instruments of propulsion. The hind legs should be carried straight through in traveling. Feet as in front.

**Coat—**The best coats appear to be broken, the hairs having a tendency to twist, and are of dense, wiry texture—like coconut matting—the hairs growing so closely and strongly together that, when parted with the fingers, the skin cannot be seen. At the base of these stiff hairs is a shorter growth of finer and softer hair—termed the undercoat. The coat on the sides is never quite so hard as that on the back and quarters. Some of the hardest coats are "crinkly" or slightly waved, but a curly coat is very objectionable. The hair on the upper and lower jaws should be crisp and only sufficiently long to impart an appearance of strength to the foreface. The hair on the forelegs should also be dense and crisp. The coat should average in length from ¾ to one inch on shoulders and neck, lengthening to 1½ inches on withers, back, ribs, and quarters. These measurements are given rather as a guide to exhibitors than as an infallible rule, since the length of coat depends on the climate, seasons, and individual animal. The judge must form his own opinion as to what constitutes a "sufficient" coat on the day.

**Color—**White should predominate; brindle, red, liver or slaty blue are objectionable. Otherwise, color is of little or no importance.

**Gait—**The movement or action is the crucial test of conformation. The Terrier's legs should be carried straight forward while traveling, the forelegs hanging perpendicular and swinging parallel to the sides, like the pendulum of a clock. The principal propulsive power is furnished by the hind legs, perfection of action being found in the Terrier possessing long thighs and muscular second thighs well bent at the stifles, which admit of a strong forward thrust or "snatch" of the hocks. When approaching, the forelegs should form a continuation of the straight of the front, the feet being the same distance apart as the elbows. When stationary it is often difficult to determine whether a dog is slightly out at shoulder but, directly he moves, the defect—if it exists—becomes more apparent, the forefeet having a tendency to cross, "weave," or "dish." When, on the contrary, the dog is tied at the shoulder, the tendency of the feet is to move wider apart, with a sort of paddling action. When the hocks are turned in—cow-hocks—the stifles and feet are turned outwards, resulting in a serious loss of propulsive power. When the hocks are turned outwards the tendency of the hind feet is to cross, resulting in an ungainly waddle.

**Temperament**—The Terrier should be alert, quick of movement, keen of expression, on the tiptoe of expectation at the slightest provocation.

**DISQUALIFICATIONS**

*Ears prick, tulip or rose.*
*Nose white, cherry or spotted to a considerable extent*
*    with either of these colors.*
*Mouth much undershot, or much overshot.*

Approved February 9, 1991

# Irish Terrier

The Irish Terrier had been established in his native country and elsewhere and truly bred long before entering the show ring. His origin has been much debated, but there is indisputable evidence that he is one of the oldest of the terrier breeds. In his beautiful red jacket, alert and trim, his piercing eyes reflecting a rare intelligence, he is a gallant picture of authentic terrier type and character.

The first record of an Irish Terrier being shown as a recognized breed dates back to 1875 when a class was held for it at a show in Glasgow. In 1879, Champion "Erin" and "Killney Boy" appeared. They were bred and their progeny included a remarkable number of champions, establishing their place in Irish Terrier history as the "mother and father" of the breed. In the 1880s, the Irish Terrier was the fourth most popular breed in England.

In 1889, the Irish Terrier Club (of England) ruled that any Irish Terrier born after a certain date of that year and exhibiting in any shows under British Kennel Club rules, must be uncropped. This ruling instigated the debate which eventually led to the abolition of cropped ears in any breed exhibited in the U.K.

The Irish Terrier's popularity quickly extended to the United States. Westminster held its first class for the breed in 1881; the Irish Terrier Club of

America was founded in 1896, adopting the British standard for the breed; and by 1929 the breed ranked 13th among the 79 then recognized by AKC.

The outline and conformation of this terrier of Erin are peculiar to the breed and differ markedly from those of any other in the terrier group. The body is longer (proportionately) than the Fox Terrier's, for example, with a much more decided trend racy lines, but with no lack of substance or sturdiness of bone structure. Another comparison may be helpful: the similarity in outline of the Irish Terrier to the grand old Irish Wolfhound is unmistakable; the drawing of one is almost a miniature of the other, and there are equally striking similarities of character.

The Irish Terrier is an incomparable pal, and the loyal, unyielding protector of those he loves. None is hardier or more adaptable. He is equally at home on the country estate, in the city apartment, or in camp; he thrives in the northland or in the tropics. He is the interested playmate and protector of children, eager to join in their fun and frolic. In their service, as in his master's, he challenges whatever may menace. He is a born guardsman.

The Irish Terrier is an accomplished sportsman. In this country he will catch and kill woodchucks and other small game, and rates with any dog in hunting rabbits. He is death on vermin. A natural water dog, and not apt to be gun-shy, he may be trained to retrieve in water as well as on land. Indeed, the Irish Terrier has many of the sporting gifts and talents of the Chesapeake Bay Retriever, the Beagle, and the Spaniel. He has hunted big game successfully in the far north and in the tropics.

The Irish Terrier scored as a war dog in World War I. As messenger and sentinel he did his bit with that incomparable spirit and disregard of danger for which he has always been justly famed. The following is a brief excerpt from an article written by Lt. Col. E. H. Richardson, later Commandant of the British War-Dog School, reviewing the Irish Terrier's services:

I can say with decided emphasis that the Irish Terriers of the service more than did their part. Many a soldier is alive today through the effort of one of these very Terriers. Isolated with his unit in some advanced position, entirely cut off from the main body by a wall of shells, and thus prevented communicating his position or circumstance by telephone or runner so that help might follow, this messenger dog was often the only means his officers had of carrying the dispatch which eventually would bring relief. My opinion of this breed is indeed a high one. They are highly sensitive, spirited dogs of fine mettle, and those of us who respect and admire the finer qualities of mind will find them amply reflected in these terriers. They are extraordinarily intelligent, faithful, and honest, and a man who has one of them as a companion will never lack a true friend.

As a show dog, the Irish Terrier's style and deportment are peculiarly his own. In competition he is an impressive picture of intrepid terrier character. He has been styled "the D'Artagnan of the show ring."

# Official Standard for the Irish Terrier

**General Appearance**—The over-all appearance of the Irish Terrier is important. In conformation he must be more than a sum of his parts. He must be all-of-a-piece, a balanced vital picture of symmetry, proportion and harmony. Furthermore, he must convey character. This terrier must be active, lithe and wiry in movement, with great animation; sturdy and strong in substance and bone structure, but at the same time free from clumsiness, for speed, power and endurance are most essential. The Irish Terrier must be neither "cobby" nor "cloddy," but should be built on lines of speed with a graceful, racing outline.

**Head**—Long, but in nice proportion to the rest of the body; the skull flat, rather narrow between the ears, and narrowing slightly toward the eyes; free from wrinkle, with the stop hardly noticeable except in profile. The jaws must be strong and muscular, but not too full in the cheek, and of good punishing length. The foreface must not fall away appreciably between or below the eyes; instead, the modeling should be delicate. An exaggerated foreface, or a noticeably short foreface, disturbs the proper balance of the head and is not desirable. The foreface and the skull from occiput to stop should be approximately equal in length. Excessive muscular development of the cheeks, or bony development of the temples, conditions which are described by the fancier as "cheeky," or "strong in head," or "thick in skull" are objectionable. The "bumpy" head, in which the skull presents two lumps of bony structure above the eyes, is to be faulted. The hair on the upper and lower jaws should be similar in quality and texture to that on the body, and of sufficient length to present an appearance of additional strength and finish to the foreface. Either the profuse, goat-like beard, or the absence of beard, is unsightly and undesirable. *Teeth*—Should be strong and even, white and sound; and neither overshot nor undershot. *Lips*—Should be close and well-fitting, almost black in color. *Nose*—Must be black. *Eyes*—Dark brown in color; small, not prominent; full of life, fire and intelligence, showing an intense expression. The light or yellow eye is most objectionable, and is a bad fault. *Ears*—Small and V-shaped; of moderate thickness; set well on the head, and dropping forward closely toward the outside corner of the eye. The top of the folded ear should be well above the level of the skull. A "dead" ear, hound-like in appearance, must be severely penalized. It is not characteristic of the Irish Terrier. The hair should be much shorter and somewhat darker in color than that on the body.

**Neck**—Should be of fair length and gradually widening toward the shoulders; well and proudly carried, and free from throatiness. Generally there is a slight frill in the hair at each side of the neck, extending almost to the corner of the ear.

**Shoulders and Chest**—Shoulders must be fine, long, and sloping well into the back. The chest should be deep and muscular, but neither full nor wide.

**Body**—The body should be moderately long. The short back is not characteristic of the Irish Terrier, and is extremely objectionable. The back must be strong and straight, and free from an appearance of slackness or "dip" behind the shoulders. The loin should be strong and muscular, and slightly arched, the ribs fairly sprung, deep rather than round, reaching to the level of the elbow. The bitch may be slightly longer than the dog.

**Hindquarters**—Should be strong and muscular; thighs powerful; hocks near the ground; stifles moderately bent.

**Stern**—Should be docked, taking off about one quarter. It should be set on rather high, but not curled. It should be of good strength and substance; of fair length and well covered with harsh, rough hair.

**Feet and Legs**—The feet should be strong, tolerably round, and moderately small; toes arched and turned neither out nor in, with dark toenails. The pads should be deep, and must be perfectly sound and free from corns. Cracks alone do not necessarily indicate unsound feet. In fact, all breeds have cracked pads occasionally, from various causes.

Legs moderately long, well set from the shoulders, perfectly straight, with plenty of bone and muscle; the elbows working clear of the sides; pasterns short, straight, and hardly noticeable. Both fore and hind legs should move straight forward when traveling; the stifles should not turn outwards. "Cowhocks"—that is, the hocks turned in and the feet turned out—are intolerable. The legs should be free from feather and covered with hair of similar texture to that on the body to give proper finish to the dog.

**Coat**—Should be dense and wiry in texture, rich in quality, having a broken appearance, but still lying fairly close to the body, the hairs growing so closely and strongly together that when parted with the fingers the skin is hardly visible; free of softness or silkiness, and not so long as to alter the outline of the body, particularly in the hindquarters. On the sides of the body the coat is never as harsh as on the back and quarters, but it should be plentiful and of good texture. At the base of the stiff outer coat there should be a growth of finer and softer hair, lighter in color, termed the undercoat. Single coats, which are without any undercoat, and wavy coats are undesirable; the curly and the kinky coats are most objectionable.

**Color**—Should be whole-colored: bright red, golden red, red wheaten, or wheaten. A small patch of white on the chest, frequently encountered in all whole-colored breeds, is permissible but not desirable. White on any other part of the body is most objectionable. Puppies sometimes have black hair at birth, which should disappear before they are full grown.

**Size**—The most desirable weight in show condition is 27 pounds for the dog and 25 pounds for the bitch. The height at the shoulder should be approximately 18 inches. These figures serve as a guide to both breeder and judge. In the show ring, however, the informed judge readily identifies the oversized or undersized Irish Terrier by its conformation and general appearance. Weight is not the last word in judgment. It is of the greatest importance to select, insofar as possible, terriers of moderate and generally accepted size, possessing the other various characteristics.

**Temperament**—The temperament of the Irish Terrier reflects his early background: he was family pet, guard dog, and hunter. He is good tempered, spirited and game. It is of the utmost importance that the Irish Terrier show fire and animation. There is a heedless, reckless pluck about the Irish Terrier which is characteristic, and which, coupled with the headlong dash, blind to all consequences, with which he rushes at his adversary, has earned for the breed the proud epithet of "Daredevil." He is of good temper, most affectionate, and absolutely loyal to mankind. Tender and forebearing with those he loves, this rugged, stouthearted terrier will guard his master, his mistress and children with utter contempt for danger or hurt. His life is one continuous and eager offering of loyal and faithful companionship and devotion. He is ever on guard, and stands between his home and all that threatens.

Approved December 10, 1968

# Kerry Blue Terrier

The Kerry Blue Terrier originated in Ireland, having been noticed first in the mountainous regions of County Kerry, hence the name. The dogs had been pure-bred in that section for over a hundred years.

Gentle, lovable, and intelligent, the Kerry is an all-round working and utility terrier, used in Ireland and England for hunting small game and birds, and for retrieving from land and water. He is used quite successfully, too, for herding sheep and cattle.

These dogs were always considered as working and sporting terriers, no thought being given to them as a bench-show dog. However, after the formation of the Republic, they began to appear on the bench and met with quick favor. The first few came out at the Dublin show. English fanciers were quick to realize their possibilities if properly groomed, and the Kennel Club there provided regular classification for them. Their rise to popularity was almost instant, and each show brought out increasing numbers of entries.

The Kerry in Ireland is fostered by the Irish Blue Terrier Club of Dublin, organized by H. G. Fotterell. The principal variance in standard is that the Irish will not permit the trimming of coat. Dogs must be shown in the rough.

The Blue Terrier Club of England, organized by Captain Watts Williams, is the supporting organization back of the Blues for England. The English standard is with a few minor exceptions identical with the American standard in that coats must be trimmed.

There is more or less conjecture as to who imported the first Kerry and where it was first shown in this country. However, it appears that the first important show at which Kerries appeared was at Westminster in 1922. For two years following their initial exhibition at Madison Square Garden they were relegated to the Miscellaneous Class, but in 1924 they were officially recognized by the American Kennel Club as a breed and given championship rating.

During the Westminster show of 1926, a group of fanciers met at the Waldorf-Astoria in New York City and organized the Kerry Blue Terrier Club of America. Their stated purpose was to encourage the breeding of Kerries, assist its fanciers, adopt a standard, and foster both the utilitarian and sporting qualities of the dog (with aim toward field trials as well as dog shows).

The Kerry is a dog of many-sided accomplishment. He is an instinctive trailer and retrieves well. He is adaptable to all manner of farmwork, for which he is easily trained. He is an indomitable foe and cannot be surpassed as a watchdog and companion. In some instances in England he has even been used for police work. With proper treatment, food, and exercise, the Kerry Blue Terrier is very long-lived and will usually retain his activeness until the end; in fact, Kerries at six and eight years of age might be taken for young dogs.

## Official Standard for the Kerry Blue Terrier

**Head**—Long, but not exaggerated and in good proportion to the rest of the body. Well-balanced, with little apparent difference between the length of the skull and foreface. (*20 points*) *Skull*—Flat, with very slight stop, of but moderate breadth between the ears, and narrowing very slightly to the eyes. *Cheeks*—Clean and level, free from bumpiness. *Ears*—V-shaped, small but not out of proportion to the size of the dog, of moderate thickness, carried forward close to the cheeks with the top of the folded ear slightly above the level of the skull. A "dead" ear, houndlike in appearance, is very undesirable. *Foreface*—Jaws deep, strong and muscular. Foreface full and well made up, not falling away appreciably below the eyes but moderately chiseled out to relieve the foreface from wedginess. *Nose*—Black, nostrils large and wide. *Teeth*—Strong, white and either level or with the upper (incisors) teeth slightly overlapping the lower teeth. An undershot mouth should be strictly penalized. *Eyes*—Dark, small, not prominent, well placed and with a keen terrier expression. Anything approaching a yellow eye is very undesirable.

**Neck**—Clean and moderately long, gradually widening to the shoulders upon which it should be well set and carried proudly. (*5 points*)

**Shoulders and Chest**—Shoulders fine, long and sloping, well laid back and well knit. Chest deep and of but moderate breadth. (*10 points*)

**Legs and Feet**—Legs moderately long with plenty of bone and muscle. The forelegs should be straight from both front and side view, with the elbows hanging perpendicularly to the body and working clear of the sides in movement, the pasterns short, straight and hardly noticeable. Both forelegs and hind legs should move straight forward when traveling, the stifles turning neither in nor out. (*10 points*) Feet should be strong, compact, fairly round and moderately small, with good depth of pad free from cracks, the toes arched, turned neither in nor out, with black toenails.

**Body**—Back short, strong and straight (*i.e.* level), with no appearance of slackness. Loin short and powerful with a slight tuck-up, the ribs fairly well sprung, deep rather than round. (*10 points*)

**Hindquarters and Stern**—Hindquarters strong and muscular with full freedom of action, free from droop or crouch, the thighs long and powerful, stifles well bent and turned neither in nor out, hocks near the ground and, when viewed from behind, upright and parallel with each other, the dog standing well up on them. Tail should be set on high, of moderate length and carried gaily erect, the straighter the tail the better. (*10 points*)

**Color**—The correct mature color is any shade of blue gray or gray blue from deep slate to light blue gray, of a fairly uniform color throughout except that distinctly darker to black parts may appear on the muzzle, head, ears, tail and feet. (*10 points*) Kerry color, in its process of "clearing" from an apparent black at birth to the mature gray blue or blue gray, passes through one or more transitions—involving a very dark blue (darker than deep slate), shades or tinges of brown, and mixtures of these, together with a progressive infiltration of the correct mature color. Up to 18 months such deviations from the correct mature color are permissible without preference and without regard for uniformity. Thereafter, deviation from it to any significant extent must be severely penalized. Solid black is never permissible in the show ring. Up to 18 months any doubt as to whether a dog is black or a very dark blue should be resolved in favor of the dog, particularly in the case of a puppy. Black on the muzzle, head, ears, tail and feet is permissible at any age.

**Coat**—Soft, dense and wavy. A harsh, wire or bristle coat should be severely penalized. In show trim the body should be well covered but tidy, with the head (except for the whiskers) and the ears and cheeks clear. (*15 points*)

**General Conformation and Character**—The typical Kerry Blue Terrier should be upstanding, well knit and in good balance, showing a well developed and muscular body with definite terrier style and character throughout. A low-slung Kerry is not typical. (*10 points*)

**Height**—The ideal Kerry should be 18½ inches at the withers for a dog, slightly less for a bitch. In judging Kerries, a height of 18–19½ inches for a dog, and 17½–19 inches for a bitch should be given primary preference. Only where the comparative superiority of a specimen outside of the ranges noted clearly justifies it, should greater latitude be taken. In no case should it extend to a dog over 20 inches or under 17½ inches, or to a bitch over 19½ inches or under 17 inches. The minimum limits do not apply to puppies.

**Weight**—The most desirable weight for a fully developed dog is from 33–40 pounds, bitches weighing proportionately less.

### DISQUALIFICATIONS

*Solid black.*
*Dewclaws on hind legs.*

Approved September 15, 1959

# Lakeland Terrier

The Lakeland Terrier is one of the oldest working terrier breeds still known today. It was bred, raised, and worked in the lake districts of England long before there was a kennel club or an official stud book. The fact that it has been outstripped by many younger terrier breeds is not so much a reflection on its quality as a tribute to the scope of its working ability. The name "Lakeland," indeed, is a modern acquisition. In olden times the breed was known as the Patterdale Terrier.

It is related that long before the days of the great John Peel, or before any packs of hounds were formed, the Lakeland was kept by the farmers in the mountain districts, who, at that time, would form a hunt with a couple of hounds and these terriers. Their work was to destroy the foxes found raiding the sheepfolds. There was sport, but it was not sport for sport's sake alone. It was a very practical matter.

The color of these dogs did not matter to their owners; they bred principally for gameness at first. The color was quite secondary as long as the dogs were game enough to withstand the punishment meted out by the foxes in their rocky mountain lairs. Later came the packs of hounds, but there was not a single pack in the lake district that did not have one or two game old terriers that had continually shown their courage with fox or otter. These were coveted as breeding material. None of their puppies were ever destroyed. They were given out among various friends and followers of the hunt, later to be tried and the best workers retained to carry on the traditions of the older dogs.

So great was the courage of the native Lakeland Terriers that they would follow underground for tremendous distances. It is told that, in 1871, Lord Lonsdale had one which crawled 23 feet under rock after an otter. In order to extricate the dog it was necessary to undertake extensive blasting operations. Finally, after three days' work, they reached the dog, and he was gotten out, none the worse for his experience. Still other dogs have been known to be locked underground for ten or twelve days and have been taken out alive. Others have paid the penalty.

Classes for the likeliest-looking terrier, suitable for fox or otter, were judged in connection with agricultural shows throughout the lake district about 1896, when more interest was evinced in this game old breed. They were judged by masters of hounds or other experienced hunting men. At that time, the color ranged from grizzle to blue and tan, red or wheaten, with a sprinkling of white terriers. Later these classes were divided in color; for white working terriers and for colored working terriers. Always working ability was taken into consideration.

Usually the white terriers were found working with the Otter Hounds, as in many cases a dark terrier got severely mauled in the muddy waters due to the excitement of the younger hounds when the otter had been dislodged from under tree roots and drains.

It is believed by experienced terrier men that the somewhat remote ancestors of the Lakeland Terrier are similar to the progenitor of the Border Terrier. In fact, there is sound evidence that the Lakeland is an offshoot of the breed that became known later as the Bedlington, which was closely related to the Dandie Dinmont.

In 1830 or thereabouts, these northern counties of England, Northumberland, Cumberland, and Westmoreland, had many varieties of terrier, each named after the small locality in which it was found in greatest numbers. Many of the old names have been lost since the breeds have gained recognition. This changing of names usually took place when specialist clubs were formed, with breeders unwilling to agree on any of the older names; and, of course, there were cases where the same dog might have been known by half a dozen different names.

Cumberland was the birthplace of the Lakeland Terrier. This is a particularly beautiful country, richly studded with lakes, particularly in the southern part. The Bedlington is attributed to neighboring Northumberland county, but it is not difficult to suppose that there was certain traffic in dogs at that time.

The first organized effort to promote the interest of this Cumberland County breed came at the Kersurck show in 1912, when a terrier club was formed. The new club made considerable headway for two years, and then came the outbreak of World War I. Naturally, all civilian activities were under a damper, and little or nothing was heard of the Lakeland Terrier again until 1921. That year fanciers met at Whitehaven, in Cumberland. According to Thomas Hosking, who later came to the United States and who was one of the nine fanciers who attended, the name Lakeland Terrier was chosen at that meeting. The standard was drawn up at that time, and shortly afterward the breed was made eligible for registration in the stud book of the Kennel Club (England). The Lakeland Terrier was accepted for registration in the AKC stud book in 1934.

Although a worker for generations, the Lakeland makes a very good appearance in the ring. He has a dense, weather-resisting coat, strong jaws of moderate length, powerful hindquarters, and good legs and feet on a short, strong back. Despite his gameness and courage, he has an attractive, quiet disposition.

## Official Standard for the Lakeland Terrier

**General Appearance**—The Lakeland Terrier was bred to hunt vermin in the rugged shale mountains of the Lake District of northern England. He is a small, workmanlike dog of square, sturdy build. His body is deep and relatively narrow, which allows him to squeeze into rocky dens. He has sufficient length of leg under him to cover rough ground easily. His neck is long, leading smoothly into high withers and a short topline ending in a high tail set. His attitude is gay, friendly, and self-confident, but not overly aggressive. He is alert and ready to go. His movement is lithe and graceful, with a straight-ahead, free stride of good length. His head is rectangular, jaws are powerful, and ears are V-shaped. A dense, wiry coat is finished off with longer furnishings on muzzle and legs.

**Size, Proportion, Substance**—The ideal height of the mature dog is 14½ inches from the withers to the ground, with up to one-half inch deviation either way permissible. Bitches may measure as much as one inch less than dogs. The weight of the well balanced, mature male in hard show condition averages approximately 17 pounds. Dogs of other heights will be proportionately more or less. The dog is squarely built, and bitches may be slightly longer than dogs. Balance and proportion are of primary importance. Short-legged, heavy-bodied dogs or overly refined, racy specimens are atypical and should be penalized. The dog should have sufficient bone and substance, so as to appear sturdy and workmanlike without any suggestion of coarseness.

**Head**—The *expression* depends on the dog's mood of the moment: although typically alert, it may be intense and determined, or gay and even impish. The *eyes,* moderately small and somewhat oval in outline, are set squarely in the skull, fairly wide apart. In liver or liver and tan dogs, the eyes are dark hazel to warm brown and eye rims are brown. In all other colors, the eyes are warm brown to black and eye rims are dark. The *ears* are small, V-shaped, their fold just above the top of the skull, the inner edge close to the side of the head, and the flap pointed toward the outside corner of the eye. The *skull* is flat on top and moderately broad, the cheeks flat and smooth as possible. The *stop* is barely perceptible. The *muzzle* is strong with straight nose bridge and good fill-in beneath the eyes. The head is well balanced, rectangular, the length of skull equaling the length of the muzzle when measured from occiput to stop, and from stop to nose tip. The proportions of the head are critical to correct type. An overlong foreface or short, wedge shaped head are atypical and should be penalized.

The **nose** is black. A "winter" nose with faded pigment is permitted, but not desired. Liver colored noses and lips are permissible on liver coated dogs only. A pink or distinctly spotted nose is very undesirable. The lips are dark. Jaws are powerful. The **teeth,** which are comparatively large, may meet in either a level, edge to edge bite, or a slightly overlapping scissors bite. Specimens with teeth overshot or undershot are to be disqualified.

**Neck, Topline, Body**—The **neck** is long; refined but strong; clean at the throat; slightly arched, and widening gradually and smoothly into the shoulders. The withers, that point at the back of the neck where neck and body meet, are noticeably higher than the level of the back. The **topline,** measured from the withers to the tail, is short and level. The **body** is strong and supple. The moderately narrow oval *chest* is deep, extending to the elbows. The *ribs* are well sprung and moderately rounded off the vertebrae. The Lakeland Terrier is a breed of moderation. A barrel-chested, big-bodied dog or one which is slab-sided and lacking substance is atypical and should be penalized. The *loins* are taut and short, although they may be slightly longer in bitches. There is moderate *tuck-up.* The **tail** is set high on the back. It is customarily docked so that when the dog is set up in show position, the tip of the tail is level with the occiput. In carriage, it is upright and a slight curve toward the head is desirable. Behind the tail is a well-defined, broad pelvic shelf. It is more developed in dogs than in bitches. The tail tightly curled over the back is a fault.

**Forequarters**—The *shoulders* are well angulated. An imaginary line drawn from the top of the shoulder blade should pass through the elbow. The shoulder blade is long in proportion to the upper arm, which allows for reasonable angulation while maintaining the more upright "terrier front." The musculature of the shoulders is flat and smooth. The *elbows* are held close to the body, standing or moving. The *forelegs* are strong, clean and straight when viewed from the front or side. There is no appreciable bend at the pasterns. The *feet* are round and point forward, the toes compact and strong. The pads are thick and black or dark gray, except in liver colored dogs when they are brown. The nails are strong and may be black or self-colored. Dewclaws are removed.

**Hindquarters**—The *thighs* are powerful and well muscled. The *hind legs* are well angulated, but not so much as to affect the balance between front and rear, which allows for smooth efficient movement. The *stifles* turn neither in nor out. The distance from the *hock* to the ground is relatively short and the line from the hock to toes is straight when viewed from the side. From the rear the hocks are parallel to each other. *Feet* same as front. Dewclaws, if any, are removed.

**Coat**—Two-ply or double, the *outer coat* is hard and wiry in texture, the *undercoat* is close to the skin and soft and should never overpower the wiry outer coat. The Lakeland is hand stripped to show his outline. (Clipping is inappropriate for the show ring.) The appearance should be neat and workmanlike. The coat on the skull, ears, forechest, shoulders and behind the tail is trimmed short and smooth. The coat on the body is longer (about one-half to one inch) and may be slightly wavy or straight. The furnishings on the legs and foreface are plentiful as opposed to profuse and should be tidy. They are crisp in texture. The legs should appear cylindrical. The face is traditionally trimmed, with the hair left longer over the eyes to give the head a rectangular appearance from all angles, with the eyes covered from above. From the front, the eyes are quite apparent, giving the Lakeland his own unique mischievous expression.

**Color**—The Lakeland Terrier comes in a variety of colors, all of which are equally acceptable. Solid colors include blue, black, liver, red, and wheaten. In saddle marked dogs, the saddle covers the back of the neck, back, sides and up the tail. A saddle may be blue, black, liver, or varying shades of grizzle. The remainder of the dog (head, throat, shoulders, and legs) is a wheaten or golden tan. Grizzle is a blend of red or wheaten intermixed in varying proportions with black, blue or liver.

**Gait**—Movement is straightforward and free, with good reach in front and drive behind. It should be smooth, efficient and ground-covering. Coming and going, the legs should be straight with feet turning neither in nor out; elbows close to the sides in front and hocks straight behind. As the dog moves faster he will tend to converge toward his center of gravity. This should not be confused with close movement.

**Temperament**—The typical Lakeland Terrier is bold, gay and friendly, with a confident, cock-of-the-walk attitude. Shyness, especially shy-sharpness, in the mature specimen is to be heavily penalized. Conversely, the overly aggressive, argumentative dog is not typical and should be strongly discouraged.

### DISQUALIFICATIONS

*Teeth overshot or undershot.*

Approved January 15, 1991

# Manchester Terrier

Generations ago, before the days of dog shows, there was in England a Black-and-Tan Terrier, less graceful in outline and coarser in type than those of today. Those early dogs did not have penciled toes and dotted brows, and their tan was smutty; nevertheless they were sound, game, and useful. They were accomplished rat killers, whether in the pits or along the watercourses. In fact their value was reckoned not at all upon any consideration of make and shape but solely upon the number of rats they had killed.

The Black-and-Tan Terrier was one of the breeds mentioned by Dr. Caius in the famous letter concerning the dogs of England that was sent to Gesner for inclusion in his encyclopedic work on the dogs of all nations. Dr. Caius completed his survey in 1570. He described the breed as carrying the essential colors and characteristics, but as being rougher in coat and shorter on the leg.

The Manchester district of England was a noted center for two "poor men's sports," rat killing and rabbit coursing. A fancier by the name of John Hulme, with the idea of producing a dog that could be used at both contests, mated a Whippet bitch with a celebrated rat-killing dog, a crossbred terrier dark brown in color. On this basis the roached back, seldom found in a terrier, is explained. The dogs proved useful, other fanciers took to breeding them, and the Manchester school of terriers was launched.

The name Manchester, however, was regarded as somewhat misleading, for similar dogs were known in many parts of England. Designation of the new breed did not take place until 1860 or thereabouts, at which time the city for which the dog was named had become a breed center. Manchesters soon spread over the British isles and eventually came to this country in considerable numbers, but years were to pass before the name was stabilized. Actually it was dropped for a time as being too restricted in designation, and the dog was once again known as the Black-and-Tan Terrier. In 1923, however, the newly formed Manchester Terrier Club of America changed the name back to Manchester Terrier, and there it has remained.

Whippet, Greyhound, and Italian Greyhound have all been mentioned (with how much accuracy none can say) as partners of more or less importance in the creation of the Manchester. But supposition regarding heritage does not end there. That extensive investigator, Ash, surmised a bit regarding a Dachshund ancestor. He said it would be interesting to know not whether the Dachshund is related, but how closely it is related to the Manchester Terrier. In substantiation of the conjecture is the description by Whitaker in 1771 of the dog of Manchester as a "short-legged, crooked-legged dog." Such a relationship seems fantastic; even so it is not an impossibility, since the Dachshund's forebears were not so exaggerated as are the dogs of this day.

As a sagacious, intelligent house pet and companion, no breed is superior to the well-bred Manchester. There is a sleek, breedy look about him that no other dog presents. His long, clean head, keen expression, glossy coat, whip tail, and smart, wide-awake appearance always command attention, while his clean habits and short coat admit him to homes which might shut out his rough-haired brothers. Moreover his weight leaves nothing to be desired, for there is a medium-sized type weighing over 12 and not exceeding 22 pounds, and a toy weighing 12 pounds or under.

Up until 1959 the Manchester Terrier and the Toy Manchester Terrier were registered as two separate breeds, although interbreeding between the two breeds was permitted. Since that date they have been registered as a single breed, the Manchester Terrier, with two varieties, the Toy and the Standard, for dog-show purposes.

Development of the Toy from the larger dog was first a matter of chance and later a matter of selective breeding. It came about in this manner: two of the larger specimens would produce a litter in which all but one puppy attained the same size as the parents. As has happened again and again in the breeding of dogs, the tiny prototype attracted attention to such a degree as to create a demand for more. So naturally the breeders tried to produce more puppies of the smaller size. It had been claimed that the Toy was so highly prized as to prompt surreptitious matings with Italian Greyhounds in order to keep the dog small. Fortunately these crosses were not perpetuated.

At this point excessive inbreeding took its toll. As can be readily understood, there are few toy-size dogs to breed from, so inbreeding became the order of the day. In Victorian times size diminished alarmingly to around two and one-half pounds, and the tiny ones were admittedly delicate. Realizing their mistake, breeders endeavored to correct their technique; they aimed for, and got, more normal toy weight together with renewed vigor.

When the anti-cropping edict was passed in England, many of the older fanciers grew discouraged after trying for a time to produce an attractive-looking dog with small button ears, and consequently many ceased breeding. A few staunch devotees, however, kept the breed alive. They loved the game little fellow, whether his ears were up or down, trimmed or untrimmed, and they stayed with him through lean times and good.

No longer are extremes of any sort favored or fostered within the breed, for "the gentleman's terrier," as he was known long ago, has come into his own. He exhibits that true Manchester type, with its flat skull, triangular eyes, accented kiss marks, and sleek ebony coat with clearly delineated markings. The sole difference between the larger dog and the Toy is concerned with the ears. Both varieties have moderately small, thin ears, narrow at the base and pointed at the tips. They are set high on the skull and quite close together. In the Standard variety, ears may be erect or button; if cropped, they are long and carried straight up. In the Toy variety, however, cropping disqualifies. The Toy ear is carried naturally erect, without sidewise flare.

## Official Standard for the Manchester Terrier

**General Appearance**—A small, black, short-coated dog with distinctive rich mahogany markings and a taper style tail. In structure the Manchester presents a sleek, sturdy, yet elegant look, and has a wedge-shaped, long and clean head with a keen, bright, alert expression. The smooth, compact, muscular body expresses great power and agility, enabling the Manchester to kill vermin and course small game. Except for size and ear options, there are no differences between the Standard and Toy varieties of the Manchester Terrier. The Toy is a diminutive version of the Standard variety.

**Size, Proportion, Substance**—The *Toy variety* shall not exceed 12 pounds. It is suggested that clubs consider dividing the American-bred and Open classes by weight as follows: 7 pounds and under, over 7 pounds and not exceeding 12 pounds. The *Standard variety* shall be over 12 pounds and not exceeding 22 pounds. Dogs weighing over 22 pounds shall be disqualified. It is suggested that clubs consider dividing the American-bred and Open classes by weight as follows: over 12 pounds and not exceeding 16 pounds, over 16 pounds and not exceeding 22 pounds. The Manchester Terrier, overall, is slightly longer than tall. The height, measured vertically from the ground to the highest point of the withers, is slightly less than the length, measured horizontally from the point of the shoulders to the rear projection of the upper thigh.

The bone and muscle of the Manchester Terrier is of sufficient mass to ensure agility and endurance.

**Head**—The Manchester Terrier has a keen and alert *expression*. The nearly black, almond shaped *eyes* are small, bright, and sparkling. They are set moderately close together, slanting upwards on the outside. The eyes neither protrude nor sink in the skull. Pigmentation must be black. Correct **ears** for the *Standard variety* are either the naturally erect ear, the cropped ear, or the button ear. No preference is given to any of the ear types. The naturally erect ear, and the button ear, should be wider at the base tapering to pointed tips, and carried well up on the skull. Wide, flaring, blunt tipped, or "bell" ears are a serious fault. Cropped ears should be long, pointed and carried erect. The only correct **ear** for the *Toy variety* is the naturally erect ear. They should be wider at the base tapering to pointed tips, and carried well up on the skull. Wide, flaring, blunt tipped, or "bell" ears are a serious fault. Cropped, or cut ears are a disqualification in the Toy variety. The **head** is long, narrow, tight skinned, and almost flat with a slight indentation up the forehead. It resembles a blunted wedge in frontal and profile views. There is a visual effect of a slight *stop* as viewed in profile.

The **muzzle** and **skull** are equal in length. The *muzzle* is well filled under the eyes with no visible cheek muscles. The underjaw is full and well defined and the **nose** is black. Tight black *lips* lie close to the jaw. The jaws should be full and powerful with full and proper **dentition.** The teeth are white and strongly developed with a true scissors bite. Level bite is acceptable.

**Neck, Topline, Body**—The slightly arched **neck** should be slim and graceful, and of moderate length. It gradually becomes larger as it approaches, and blends smoothly with the sloping shoulders. Throatiness is undesirable. The **topline** shows a slight arch over the robust loins falling slightly to the tail set. A flat back or roached back is to be severely penalized. The **chest** is narrow between the legs and deep in the brisket. The forechest is moderately defined. The **ribs** are well sprung, but flattened in the lower end to permit clearance of the forelegs. The **abdomen** should be tucked up extending in an arched line from the deep brisket. The taper style **tail** is moderately short reaching no further than the hock joint. It is set on at the end of the croup. Being thicker where it joins the body, the tail tapers to a point. The tail is carried in a slight upward curve, but never over the back.

**Forequarters**—The **shoulder blades** and **upper arm** should be relatively the same length. The distance form the elbow to the withers should be approximately the same as the distance form the elbow to the ground. The **elbows** should lie close to the brisket. The **shoulders** are well laid back. The **forelegs** are straight, or proportionate length, and placed well under the brisket. The pasterns should be almost perpendicular. The **front feet** are compact and well arched. The two middle toes should be slightly longer than the others. The pads should be thick and the toenails should be jet black.

**Hindquarters**—The **thigh** should be muscular with the length of the upper and lower thighs being approximately equal. The stifle is well turned. The well let down hocks should not turn in nor out as viewed from the rear. The hind legs are carried well back. The **hind feet** are shaped like those of a cat with thick pads and jet black nails.

**Coat**—The coat should be smooth, short, dense, tight, and glossy; not soft.

**Color**—The coat color should be jet black and rich mahogany tan, which should not run or blend into each other, but abruptly form clear, well defined lines of color. There shall be a very small tan spot over each eye, and a very small tan spot on each cheek. On the head, the muzzle is tanned to the nose. The nose and nasal bone are jet black. The tan extends under the throat, ending in the shape of the letter V. The inside of the ears are partly tan. There shall be tan spots, called "rosettes," on each side of the chest above the front legs. These are more pronounced in puppies than in adults. There should be a black "thumbprint" patch on the front of each foreleg at the pastern. The remainder of the foreleg shall be tan to the carpus joint. There should be a distinct black "pencil mark" line running lengthwise on the top of each toe on all four feet. Tan on the hind leg should continue from the pencilling on the toes up the inside of the legs to a little below the stifle joint. The outside of the hind legs should be black. There should be tan under the tail, and on the vent, but only of such size as to be covered by the tail. White on any part of the coat is a serious fault, and shall disqualify whenever the white shall form a patch or stripe measuring as much as one half inch at its longest dimension.

Any color other than black and tan shall be disqualified. Color and/or markings should never take precedence over soundness and type.

**Gait**—The gait should be free and effortless with good reach of the forequarters, showing no indication of hackney gait. Rear quarters should have strong, driving power to match the front reach. Hocks should fully extend. Each rear leg should move in line with the foreleg of the same side, neither thrown in nor out. When moving at a trot, the legs tend to converge towards the center of gravity line beneath the dog.

**Temperament**—The Manchester Terrier is neither aggressive nor shy. He is keenly observant, devoted, but discerning. Not being a sparring breed, the Manchester is generally friendly with other dogs. Excessive shyness or aggressiveness should be considered a serious fault.

### DISQUALIFICATIONS

*Standard variety—Weight over 22 pounds.*
*Toy variety—Cropped or cut ears.*
*Both varieties—White on any part of the coat whenever the white shall form a patch or stripe measuring as much as one half inch at its longest dimension.*
*Any color other than black and tan.*

Approved June 10, 1991

# Miniature Bull Terrier

The Miniature Bull Terrier is no newcomer to the world of pure-bred dogs. As a matter of fact, for over eighty years he has been highly prized as a distinctive small dog noted among other things for tenacity and remarkable courage. He is a sturdy chap, muscular, active and full of fire but withal good tempered and amenable to discipline.

Miniature beginnings date back to the early 19th century when the Bulldog and the now extinct White English Terrier were interbred to produce the "Bull and Terrier" later known as the Bull Terrier. There are some who say, too, that the Black and Tan played a part in the dog's creation. The original offshoot of the cross was a rather small dog that was crossed again, this time with the Spanish Pointer to increase the size.

Possessed of such a heritage it is small wonder that the earliest specimens came in a wide range of sizes. There were Toys that weighed from four to seven pounds, medium sized ones of some fifteen and sixteen pounds, as well as the more usual sort resembling the full-sized Bull Terrier of this day. The small dog came in various colors; some black-patched, a few blue and others pure white. Incidentally, the tiny white ones were known for a while as Coverwood Terriers after England's kennel of that name.

The Toys were exhibited abroad up to about 1914 but they elicited scant response from the fanciers because their type was poor. Dogs of medium or miniature size fared better since particularly in eyes and foreface they more closely approximated the type desired. This has been exactly what the fanciers have been aiming for, namely a down-faced smaller dog weighing around sixteen pounds and identical in make and shape and every single feature with the full-sized Bull Terrier.

The Miniature Bull Terrier became eligible to be shown in the Miscellaneous Class in 1963, and was accepted as a breed in 1991.

## Official Standard for the Miniature Bull Terrier

**General Appearance**—The Miniature Bull Terrier must be strongly built, symmetrical and active, with a keen, determined and intelligent expression. He should be full of fire, having a courageous, even temperament and be amenable to discipline.

**Size, Proportion, Substance**—*Height* 10 inches to 14 inches. Dogs outside these limits should be faulted. *Weight* in proportion to height. In *proportion*, the Miniature Bull Terrier should give the appearance of being square.

**Head**—The *head* should be long, strong and deep, right to the end of the muzzle, but not coarse. The *full face* should be oval in outline and be filled completely up, giving the impression of fullness with a surface devoid of hollows or indentations, i.e., *egg* shaped. The *profile* should curve gently downwards from the top of the skull to the tip of the nose. The *forehead* should be flat across from ear to ear. The distance from the tip of the nose to the eyes should be perceptibly greater than that from the eyes to the top of the skull. The *underjaw* should be deep and well defined. To achieve a keen, determined and intelligent *expression*, the *eyes* should be well sunken and as dark as possible with a piercing glint. They should be small, triangular and obliquely placed, set near together and high up on the dog's head. The *ears* should be small, thin and placed close together, capable of being held stiffly erect when they point upwards. The *nose* should be black, with well developed nostrils bent downwards at the tip. The *lips* should be clean and tight. The *teeth* should meet in either a *level* or *scissors bite*. In the scissors bite, the top teeth should fit in front of and closely against the lower teeth. The teeth should be sound, strong and perfectly regular.

**Neck, Topline, Body**—The *neck* should be very muscular, long, and arched: tapering from the shoulders to the head, it should be free from loose skin. The *back* should be short and strong with a slight arch over the loin. Behind the shoulders there should be no slackness or dip at the withers. The *body* should be well rounded with marked spring of rib. The back ribs deep. The *chest* should be broad when viewed from in front. There should be great depth from withers to brisket, so that the latter is nearer to the ground than the belly. The *underline,* from the brisket to the belly, should form a graceful upward curve. The *tail* should be short, set on low, fine, and should be carried horizontally. It should be thick where it joins the body, and should taper to a fine point.

**Forequarters**—The *shoulders* should be strong and muscular, but without heaviness. The shoulder blades should be wide and flat and there should be a very pronounced backward slope from the bottom edge of the blade to the top edge. The *legs* should be big boned but not to the point of coarseness. The *forelegs* should be of moderate length, perfectly straight, and the dog must stand firmly up on them. The *elbows* must turn neither in nor out, and the *pasterns* should be strong and upright.

**Hindquarters**—The *hind legs* should be parallel when viewed from behind. The *thighs* are very muscular with *hocks* well let down. The stifle joint is well bent with a well developed second thigh. The *hind pasterns* should be short and upright.

**Feet**—The *feet* are round and compact with well arched toes like a cat.

**Coat**—The *coat* should be short, flat and harsh to the touch with a fine gloss. The dog's skin should fit tightly.

**Color**—For white, pure white coat. Markings on head and skin pigmentation are not to be penalized. For colored, any color to predominate.

**Gait**—The dog shall move smoothly, covering the ground with free, easy strides. Fore and hind legs should move parallel to each other when viewed from in front or behind, with the forelegs reaching out well and the hind legs moving smoothly at the hip and flexing well at the stifle and hock. The dog should move compactly and in one piece but with a typical jaunty air that suggests agility and power.

**Temperament**—The temperament should be full of fire and courageous, but even and amenable to discipline.

**Faults**—Any departure from the foregoing points shall be considered a fault, and the seriousness of the fault shall be in exact proportion to its degree.

Approved May 14, 1991

# Miniature Schnauzer

The Schnauzer is of German origin, said to be recognizable in pictures of the 15th century. The Miniature Schnauzer is derived from the Standard Schnauzer and is said to have come from mixing of Affenpinschers and Poodles with small Standards. The Miniature Schnauzer was exhibited as a distinct breed as early as 1899.

Today's Miniature Schnauzer in the United States is an elegant dog of the Terrier Group. While the breed resembles other dogs in this group, almost all of which were bred in the British Isles to "go to ground" to attack vermin of all kinds, his origin and blood are quite different, giving the Miniature Schnauzer a naturally happy temperament.

The breed is characterized by its stocky build, wiry coat and abundant whiskers and leg furnishings. A Miniature Schnauzer may be of several colors with salt and pepper (gray) being the most common, although blacks and black and silvers are now seen in increasing numbers. The salt and pepper color is the result of unique light and dark banding of each hair instead of mixing of light and dark hairs. The correct coat can be retained only by stripping and is lost when the coat is clipped. The breed has a soft undercoat which can range from black and dark gray to very light gray or beige. If the animal is clipped, in time only the undercoat will remain.

The breed is hardy, healthy, intelligent and fond of children. It was developed as a small farm dog, used as a ratter. His size (12–14 inches at the withers) has permitted him to adapt easily to small city quarters. On the other hand, he is still at home in the country and can cover a substantial amount of ground without tiring. As a rule a Miniature Schnauzer is not a fighter, although he will stand up for himself if necessary.

There is no standard weight for the breed, but a grown bitch of about 13 inches should weigh about 14 pounds, with a dog weighing somewhat more. The weight depends, to a great extent, on the amount of bone.

The Miniature Schnauzer is now viewed primarily as a charming and attractive companion. He is seldom addicted to wandering. He is devoted to his home and family and functions very well as a guard dog in that he can give an alarm as well as a larger dog. His good health, good temperament and attractive appearance combine to fit him admirably for his role as family pet.

Miniature Schnauzers have been bred in the United States since 1925 and have gained steadily in popular favor. The American Miniature Schnauzer Club began its independent operation in August 1933.

## Official Standard for the Miniature Schnauzer

**General Appearance**—The Miniature Schnauzer is a robust, active dog of terrier type, resembling his larger cousin, the Standard Schnauzer, in general appearance, and of an alert, active disposition. *Faults—Type*—Toyishness, raciness or coarseness.

**Size, Proportion, Substance**—*Size*—From 12 to 14 inches. He is sturdily built, nearly square in **proportion** of body length to height with plenty of bone, and without any suggestion of toyishness. *Disqualifications*—Dogs or bitches under 12 inches or over 14 inches.

**Head**—*Eyes* small, dark brown and deep-set. They are oval in appearance and keen in *expression. Faults*—Eyes light and/or large and prominent in appearance. *Ears*—When cropped, the ears are identical in shape and length, with pointed tips. They are in balance with the head and not exaggerated in length. They are set high on the skull and carried perpendicularly at the inner edges, with as little bell as possible along the outer edges. When uncropped, the ears are small and V-shaped, folding close to the skull. *Head* strong and rectangular, its width diminishing slightly from ears to eyes, and again to the tip of the nose. The forehead is unwrinkled. The *topskull* is flat and fairly long. The foreface is parallel to the topskull, with a slight stop, and it is at least as long as the topskull. The *muzzle* is strong in proportion to the skull: it ends in a moderately blunt manner, with thick whiskers which accentuate the rectangular shape of the head. *Faults*—Head coarse and cheeky. The *teeth* meet in a *scissors bite.* That is, the upper front teeth overlap the lower front teeth in such a manner that the inner surface of the upper incisors barely touch the outer surface of the lower incisors when the mouth is closed. *Faults*—Bite— Undershot or overshot jaw. Level bite.

**Neck, Topline, Body**—*Neck* strong and well arched, blending into the shoulders, and with the skin fitting tightly at the throat. *Body* short and deep, with the brisket extending at least to the elbows. Ribs are well sprung and deep, extending well back to a short loin. The underbody does not present a tucked up appearance at the flank. The *backline* is straight; it declines slightly from the withers to the base of the tail. The withers form the highest point of the body. The overall length from chest to buttocks appears to equal the height at the withers. *Faults*—Chest too broad or shallow in brisket. Hollow or roach back. *Tail* set high and carried erect. It is docked only long enough to be clearly visible over the backline of the body when the dog is in proper length of coat. *Fault*— Tail set too low.

**Forequarters**—Forelegs are straight and parallel when viewed from all sides. They have strong pasterns and good bone. They are separated by a fairly deep brisket which precludes a pinched front. The elbows are close, and the ribs spread gradually from the first rib so as to allow space for the elbows to move close to the body. *Fault*—Loose elbows. The sloping *shoulders* are muscled, yet flat and clean. They are well laid back, so that from the side the tips of the shoulder blades are in a nearly vertical line above the elbow. The tips of the blades are placed closely together. They slope forward and downward at an angulation which permits the maximum forward extension of the forelegs without binding or effort. Both the shoulder blades and upper arms are long, permitting depth of chest at the brisket. *Feet* short and round (cat feet) with thick, black pads. The toes are arched and compact.

**Hindquarters**—The hindquarters have strong-muscled, slanting thighs. They are well bent at the stifles. There is sufficient angulation so that, in stance, the hocks extend beyond the tail. The hindquarters never appear overbuilt or higher than the shoulders. The rear pasterns are short and, in stance, perpendicular to the ground and, when viewed from the rear, are parallel to each other. *Faults*—Sickle hocks, cow hocks, open hocks or bowed hindquarters.

**Coat**—Double, with hard, wiry, outer coat and close undercoat. The head, neck, ears, chest, tail, and body coat must be plucked. When in show condition, the body coat should be of sufficient length to determine texture. Close covering on neck, ears and skull. Furnishings are fairly thick but not silky. *Faults*—Coat too soft or too smooth and slick in appearance.

**Color**—The recognized colors are salt and pepper, black and silver and solid black. All colors have uniform skin pigmentation, i.e. no white or pink skin patches shall appear anywhere on the dog. *Salt and Pepper*—The typical salt and pepper color of the topcoat results from the combination of black and white banded hairs and solid black and white unbanded hairs, with the banded hairs predominating. Acceptable are all shades of salt and pepper, from light to dark mixtures with tan shadings permissible in the banded or unbanded hair of the topcoat. In salt and pepper dogs, the salt and pepper mixture fades out to light gray or silver white in the eyebrows, whiskers, cheeks, under throat, inside ears, across chest, under tail, leg furnishings, and inside hind legs. It may or may not also fade out on the underbody. However, if so, the lighter underbody hair is not to rise higher on the sides of the body than the front elbows. *Black and Silver*—The black and silver generally follows the same pattern as the salt and pepper. The entire salt and pepper section must be black. The black color in the topcoat of the black and silver is a true rich color with black undercoat. The stripped portion is free from any fading or brown tinge and the underbody should be dark. ***Black***—Black is the only solid color allowed. Ideally, the black color in the topcoat is a true rich glossy solid color with the undercoat being less intense, a soft matting shade of black. This is natural and should not be penalized in any way. The stripped portion is free from any fading or brown tinge. The scissored and clippered areas have lighter shades of black. A small white spot on the chest is permitted, as is an occasional single white hair elsewhere on the body. ***Disqualifications***—Color solid white or white striping, patching, or spotting on the colored areas of the dog, except for the small white spot permitted on the chest of the black.

The body coat color in salt and pepper and black and silver dogs fades out to light gray or silver white under the throat and across the chest. Between them there exists a natural body coat color. Any irregular or connecting blaze or white mark in this section is considered a white patch on the body, which is also a disqualification.

**Gait**—The trot is the gait at which movement is judged. When approaching, the forelegs, with elbows close to the body, move straight forward, neither too close nor too far part. Going away, the hind legs are straight and travel in the same planes as the forelegs. ***Note***—*It is generally accepted that when a full trot is achieved, the rear legs continue to move in the same planes as the forelegs, but a very slight inward inclination will occur. It begins at the point of the shoulder in front and at the hip joint in the rear. Viewed from the front or rear, the legs are straight from these points to the pads. The degree of inward inclination is almost imperceptible in a Miniature Schnauzer that has correct movement. It does not justify moving close, toeing in, crossing, or moving out at the elbows.*

Viewed from the side, the forelegs have good reach, while the hind legs have strong drive, with good pickup of hocks. The feet turn neither inward nor outward. ***Faults***— Single tracking, sidegaiting, paddling in front, or hackney action. Weak rear action.

**Temperament**—The typical Miniature Schnauzer is alert and spirited, yet obedient to command. He is friendly, intelligent and willing to please. He should never be over-aggressive or timid.

### DISQUALIFICATIONS

*Dogs or bitches under 12 inches or over 14 inches.*

*Color solid white or white striping, patching, or spotting on the colored areas of the dog, except for the small white spot permitted on the chest of the black. The body coat color in salt and pepper and black and silver dogs fades out to light gray or silver white under the throat and across the chest. Between them there exists a natural body coat color. Any irregular or connecting blaze or white mark in this section is considered a white patch on the body, which is also a disqualification.*

Approved January 15, 1991

# Norfolk Terrier

$T$he Norfolk Terrier is small and sturdy, alert and fearless, with sporting instincts and an even temperament. Good natured and gregarious, the Norfolk has proved adaptable under a wide variety of conditions.

In England at the turn of the century working terriers from stables in Cambridge, Market Harborough, and Norwich, were used by Frank "Roughrider" Jones to develop a breed recognized by the English Kennel Club in 1932 as the Norwich Terrier. In the early days there was a diversity in type, size, color, coat and ear carriage. Correct color and ear carriage were constantly argued. When the Norwich breed standard was drawn up the drop ear and the prick ear terriers remained one breed. The English Kennel Club, in 1964, recognized them as two breeds—the drop ear variety as the Norfolk and the prick ear as the Norwich.

The year that the breed divided in England an article in *The Field* stated: "Actually there is nothing new about the Norfolk Terrier, but simply the name under which it is registered. The Eastern Counties have always produced these principally wheaten, red and otherwise black and tan or grizzle good-ribbed short-legged terriers, built on the generally accepted lines of a hunt terrier. They go to ground readily and are famous ratters."

In the United States those who remember the "Roaring Twenties" still refer to the Norwich as a "Jones Terrier" after Frank Jones, from whom many American sportsmen traveling abroad bought their first little red terriers. In 1936, thanks to the efforts of Gordon Massey (who registered the first Norwich Terrier in this country) and Henry Bixby, then Executive Vice President of the American Kennel Club, the Norwich Terrier was accepted as a breed by the AKC. It remained one breed until 1979 when division by ear carriage became official. The drop ears are now recognized as the Norfolk, while the prick ears remain Norwich.

Visually there appears to be a distinct difference between the two breeds, resulting in two slightly different breed standards. Each breed has developed with success since separation.

Today, although as many live in cities as in foxhunting country, the Norfolk should still conform to the standard. The characteristic coat requires regular grooming but trimming is heavily penalized. The ears should be neatly dropped, slightly rounded at the tip, carried close to the cheek and not falling lower than the outer corner of the eye.

The Norfolk Terrier is essentially a sporting terrier—not a Toy. His chief attributes are gameness, hardiness, loyalty to his master, and great charm. He is affectionate and reasonably obedient. He must be kept small enough to conform with the standard. Above all, the outstanding personality, characteristic of the breed, must never be subordinated for the sake of appearance and conformation.

## Official Standard for the Norfolk Terrier

**General Appearance**—The Norfolk Terrier, game and hardy, with expressive dropped ears, is one of the smallest of the working terriers. It is active and compact, free-moving, with good substance and bone. With its natural, weather-resistant coat and short legs, it is a "perfect demon" in the field. This versatile, agreeable breed can go to ground, bolt a fox and tackle or dispatch other small vermin, working alone or with a pack. Honorable scars from wear and tear are acceptable in the ring.

**Size, Proportion, Substance**—*Height* at the withers 9 to 10 inches at maturity: Bitches tend to be smaller than dogs. Length of back from point of withers to base of tail should be slightly longer than the height at the withers. Good *substance* and bone. **Weight** 11 to 12 pounds or that which is suitable for each individual dog's structure and balance. Fit working condition is a prime consideration.

**Head**—*Eyes* small, dark and oval, with black rims. Placed well apart with a sparkling, keen and intelligent *expression.* *Ears* neatly dropped, small, with a break at the skull line, carried close to the cheek and not falling lower than the outer corner of the eye. V-shaped, slightly rounded at the tip, smooth and velvety to the touch. *Skull* wide, slightly rounded, with good width between the ears. *Muzzle* is strong and wedge shaped. Its length is one-third less than a measurement from the occiput to the well-defined *stop.* Jaw clean and strong. Tight-lipped with a scissor *bite* and large teeth.

**Neck, Topline, Body**—*Neck* of medium length, strong and blending into well laid back shoulders. Level *topline.* Good width of *chest.* *Ribs* well sprung, chest moderately deep. Strong *loins. Tail* medium docked, of sufficient length to ensure a balanced outline. Straight, set on high, the base level with the topline. Not a squirrel tail.

**Forequarters**—Well laid back *shoulders. Elbows* close to the ribs. Short, powerful *legs,* as straight as is consistent with the digging terrier. Pasterns firm. *Feet* round, pads thick, with strong, black nails.

**Hindquarters**—Broad with strong, muscular *thighs.* Good turn of *stifle. Hocks* well let down and straight when viewed from the rear. *Feet* as in front.

**Coat**—The protective coat is hard, wiry and straight, about 1½ to 2 inches long, lying close to the body, with a definite undercoat. The mane on neck and shoulders is longer and also forms a ruff at the base of the ears and the throat. Moderate furnishings of harsh texture on legs. Hair on the head and ears is short and smooth, except for slight eyebrows and whiskers. Some tidying is necessary to keep the dog neat, but shaping should be heavily penalized.

**Color**—All shades of red, wheaten, black and tan, or grizzle. Dark points permissible. White marks are not desirable.

**Gait**—Should be true, low and driving. In front, the legs extend forward from the shoulder. Good rear angulation showing great powers of propulsion. Viewed from the side, hind legs follow in the track of the forelegs, moving smoothly from the hip and flexing well at the stifle and hock. Topline remains level.

**Temperament**—Alert, gregarious, fearless and loyal. Never aggressive.

Approved October 13, 1981
Reformatted March 23,1990

# Norwich Terrier

The roots of the Norwich were firmly planted in East Anglia, England. By the 1880s owning a small ratting terrier was a fad among the sporting undergraduates of Cambridge University. A popular strain developed of very small red and black and tan working crossbreeds from native, Yorkshire, and Irish den stock.

By the turn of the century one of these Trumpington Terriers moved to a stable near the city of Norwich. "Rags" was sandy colored, short of leg, stocky, with cropped ears. A notorious ratter and dominant sire, he is the modern breed's progenitor. For the next two decades various horsemen bred other game terrier types to "Rags" and his descendants, including a half-sized brindle Staffordshire. So from companions and barnyard ratters there gradually developed a line of excellent fox bolters, and one of these introduced the breed to America in 1914.

Bred in Market Harborough by the noted "Roughrider" Frank Jones, "Willum" became the inseparable companion of a Philadelphia sportsman, Robert Strawbridge. This Jones' terrier was also low legged, cropped and docked but his very hard coat had black shadings and his head showed a marked resemblance to a Bull Terrier. "Willum" proved a charming muscular 12 pound ambassador, and a prolific sire of M.F.H. Hunt Terriers in Vermont, New York,

Pennsylvania and Virginia. He died at 14 years of age defending his hearth from a vicious canine intruder, just a few years before the breed was recognized in England in 1932. Though the AKC made Norwich Terriers official in 1936, there are still some Americans who associate Norwich with "Willum's" breeder and steadfastly call them Jones' Terriers.

In 1964 England recognized the drop ear Norwich as a separate breed, terming them the Norfolk Terrier. The American Kennel Club took the same step effective January 1, 1979. The recognition of the two varieties as separate breeds is now the rule in all English speaking countries and in Europe and Scandinavia.

Norwich are hardy, happy-go-lucky, weatherproof companions. Though game on vermin, they are usually gregarious with children, adults and other domestic animals. Today they still weigh about 12 pounds, are short legged, sturdy and can be any shade from wheaten to dark red, black and tan or grizzle. They are very loyal, alert and have a sensitive intelligence.

Their body lengths and breadths vary, but their docked tails should be long enough to firmly grasp. Smooth coated and wedge shaped, their heads should have plenty of brain room with ears spaced well apart. A delineated stop between the wide set eyes should be just nearer the muzzle than the top of the skull. The small dark almond eyes coupled with a slightly foxy muzzle give Norwich their typical impish expression.

Most Norwich owners prefer a terrier of sagacious character with a harsh carefree coat, large close fitting teeth and tolerate the variations of color and conformation which befit its heritage. Its unique standard employs horsemens' terms and the breed's characteristic mane calls for coarser, longer protective hair on neck and shoulders. Breeders must remain watchful and guard against show fads, exaggerations, excessive coats or fancy trimming. To keep personality a priority factor, the parent club rewards working abilities, obedience and racing competitions along with show ring events.

## Official Standard for the Norwich Terrier

**General Appearance**—The Norwich Terrier, spirited and stocky with sensitive prick ears and a slightly foxy expression, is one of the smallest working terriers. This sturdy descendent of ratting companions, eager to dispatch small vermin alone or in a pack, has good bone and substance and an almost weatherproof coat. A hardy hunt terrier— honorable scars from fair wear and tear are accepted.

**Size, Proportion, Substance**—One of the smallest of the terriers, the ideal **height** should not exceed 10 inches at the withers. Distance from the top of the withers to the ground and from the withers to base of tail is approximately equal. Good bone and **substance**. **Weight** approximately 12 pounds. It should be in proportion to the individual dog's structure and balance. Fit working condition is a prime consideration.

**Head**—A slightly foxy *expression.* *Eyes* small, dark and oval shaped with black rims. Placed well apart with a bright and keen expression. *Ears* medium size and erect. Set well apart with pointed tips. Upright when alert.

The *skull* is broad and slightly rounded with good width between the ears. The *muzzle* is wedge shaped and strong. Its length is about one-third less than the measurement from the occiput to the well-defined *stop.* The jaw is clean and strong. Nose and lip pigment black. Tight-lipped with large teeth. A scissor *bite.*

**Neck, Topline, Body**—*Neck* of medium length, strong and blending into well laid back shoulders. Level *topline.* *Body* moderately short. Compact and deep. Good width of *chest.* Well-sprung *ribs* and short *loins.* *Tail* medium docked. The terrier's working origin requires that the tail be of sufficient length to grasp. Base level with topline; carried erect.

**Forequarters**—Well laid back *shoulders.* Elbows close to ribs. short, powerful *legs,* as straight as is consistent with the digging terrier. Pasterns firm. *Feet* round with thick pads. Nails black. The feet point forward when standing or moving.

**Hindquarters**—Broad, strong and muscular with well-turned *stifles.* *Hocks* low set and straight when viewed form the rear. *Feet* as in front.

**Coat**—Hard, wiry and straight, lying close to the body with a definite undercoat. The coat on neck and shoulders forms a protective mane. The hair on head, ears and muzzle, except for slight eyebrows and whiskers, is short and smooth. This breed should be shown with as natural a coat as possible. A minimum of tidying is permissible but shaping should be heavily penalized.

**Color**—All shades of red, wheaten, black and tan or grizzle. White marks are not desirable.

**Gait**—The legs moving parallel, extending forward, showing great powers of propulsion. Good rear angulation with a true, yet driving movement. The forelegs move freely with feet and elbows the same distance apart, converging slightly with increased pace. Hind legs follow in the track of the forelegs, flexing well at the stifle and hock. The topline remains level.

**Temperament**—Gay, fearless, loyal and affectionate. Adaptable and sporting, they make ideal companions.

Approved October 13, 1981
Reformatted March 23, 1990

# Scottish Terrier

Most lovers of the Scottish Terrier have a deep and abiding belief that this breed is the most ancient of any of the Highland terriers; that the other breeds are only offshoots from this, the parent stem, and that the Scottie is the original, dyed-in-the-wool, simon-pure Highland terrier. They will tell you that the Skye Terrier mentioned in early histories and chronicles was not the Skye as we know it today, but the forerunner of our favorite and similar in type to it. They will refer you to such early writers as Jacques du Fouilloux, who published *La Venerie* in 1561, Turberville and Dr. Stevens, whose books *The Noble Art of Venerie* and *The Maison Rustique* appeared in 1575 and 1572, respectively. All of these works described an "earth dog used in hunting the fox and the brocke," and these descriptions fit closely to what might have been the forerunner of our present-day Scottie.

In the 17th century, when King James VI of Scotland became James I of England, he wrote to Edinburgh to have a half dozen terriers sent to France as a present and addressed the letter to the Laird of Caldwell, naming the Earl of Montieth as having good ones. Later, the great English authority, Rawdon B. Lee, wrote as follows:

> The Scottie is the oldest variety of the canine race indigenous to Britain. . . . For generations he had been a popular dog in the Highlands where, strangely enough, he

was always known as the Skye Terrier, although he is different from the long-coated, unsporting-like creature with which that name is now associated.

While all this is very interesting and quite possibly true, the fact remains that it is neither definite nor conclusive.

Leaving the realm of speculation and inference and coming down to history and known facts, we do know that the Scottish Terrier as we find it today has been bred in purity for many years. The first show to have a class for Scottish Terriers was at Birmingham in England, in 1860. Later, a number of other shows carried this classification, but the dogs shown in these classes were not Scottish Terriers, but Skyes, Dandie Dinmonts, and Yorkshires.

All the while, however, Scotchmen who saw these dogs winning as Scottish Terriers were indignant, and about 1877 they broke into print in the *Live Stock Journal* with a series of letters protesting the situation and discussing the points and character of the true Scottish Terrier. The discussion waxed so furious that the editors finally called a halt with the statement, "We see no use in prolonging this discussion unless each correspondent described the dog which he holds to be the true type." This challenge was taken up by Captain Gordon Murray, who in a letter to the *Stock Keeper* under the *nom de plume* of "Strathbogie," described in detail his conception of a proper Scottish Terrier. This quieted the warring factions and about 1880 J. B. Morrison was persuaded to draw up a standard. This was accepted by all parties.

The essentials of this standard have been retained in all the later standards, only minor changes having been introduced. In 1882 the Scottish Terrier Club was organized with joint officers for England and Scotland. Later, as interest in the breed grew, the two countries organized separate clubs, although they have always worked harmoniously together.

John Naylor is credited with being the first to introduce the Scottish Terrier to this country; his initial importation in 1883 was of a dog and a bitch, Tam Glen and Bonnie Belle. He showed extensively and continued importing, among his later importations being his famous dogs Glenlyon and Whinstone. The first Scottish Terrier registered in America was Dake (3688), a brindle dog whelped September 15, 1884, bred by O. P. Chandler of Kokomo, Indiana. His sire was Naylor's Glenlyon. This was in the *American Kennel Register*, published by *Forest and Stream*, at about the time the American Kennel Club was being organized. In December, 1887, a bitch Lassie was registered, bred by W. H. Todd of Vermillion, Ohio. Her sire was Glencoe, by Imp. Whinstone *ex.* Imp. Roxie. Here we find Whinstone figuring as a sire. Now Whinstone was by Allister, which together with Dundee formed the two great fountainheads of the breed. Whinstone sired Ch. Bellingham Baliff which was acquired by J. J. Little, founder of the famous Newcastle Kennels. Whinstone therefore was the forerunner and progenitor of the Scottish Terrier in this country today.

Since those days there have been thousands of importations and many notable breeders have carried on the work. Probably none of the early blood is to be found today. Nevertheless, these early dogs must take their place in history; and to that pioneer breeder and missionary of the breed, John Naylor, the great popularity of this staunch little breed today stands as an enduring monument.

## Official Standard for the Scottish Terrier

**General Appearance**—The face should wear a keen, sharp and active expression. Both head and tail should be carried well up. The dog should look very compact, well muscled and powerful, giving the impression of immense power in a small size.

**Skull**—Long, of medium width, slightly domed and covered with short, hard hair. It should not be quite flat, as there should be a slight stop or drop between the eyes.

**Muzzle**—In proportion to the length of skull, with not too much taper toward the nose. Nose should be black and of good size. The jaws should be level and square. The nose projects somewhat over the mouth, giving the impression that the upper jaw is longer than the lower. The teeth should be evenly placed, having a scissors or level bite, with the former being preferable.

**Eyes**—Set wide apart, small and of almond shape, not round. Color to be dark brown or nearly black. To be bright, piercing and set well under the brow.

**Ears**—Small, prick, set well up on the skull, rather pointed but not cut. The hair on them should be short and velvety.

**Neck**—Moderately short, thick and muscular, strongly set on sloping shoulders, but not so short as to appear clumsy.

**Chest**—Broad and very deep, well let down between the forelegs.

**Body**—Moderately short and well ribbed up with strong loin, deep flanks and very muscular hindquarters.

**Legs and Feet**—Both forelegs and hind legs should be short and very heavy in bone in proportion to the size of the dog. Forelegs straight or slightly bent with elbows close to the body. Scottish Terriers should not be out at the elbows. Stifles should be well bent and legs straight from hock to heel. Thighs very muscular. Feet round and thick with strong nails, forefeet larger than the hind feet. *Note*—The gait of the Scottish Terrier is peculiarly its own and is very characteristic of the breed. It is not the square trot or walk that is desirable in the long-legged breeds. The forelegs do not move in exact parallel planes—rather in reaching out incline slightly inward. This is due to the shortness of leg and width of chest. The action of the rear legs should be square and true and at the trot both the hocks and stifles should be flexed with a vigorous motion.

**Tail**—Never cut and about 7 inches long, carried with a slight curve but not over the back.

**Coat**—Rather short, about 2 inches, dense undercoat with outer coat intensely hard and wiry.

**Size and Weight**—Equal consideration must be given to height, length of back and weight. Height at shoulder for either sex should be about 10 inches. Generally, a well-balanced Scottish Terrier dog of correct size should weigh from 19 to 22 pounds and a bitch, from 18 to 21 pounds. The principal objective must be symmetry and balance.

**Color**—Steel or iron gray, brindled or grizzled, black, sandy or wheaten. White markings are objectionable and can be allowed only on the chest and that to a slight extent only.

**Penalties**—Soft coat, round, or very light eye, overshot or undershot jaw, obviously oversize or undersize, shyness, timidity or failure to show with head and tail up are faults to be penalized. No judge should put to Winners or Best of Breed any Scottish Terrier not showing real terrier character in the ring.

### SCALE OF POINTS

| | | | |
|---|---|---|---|
| Skull | 5 | Legs and feet | 10 |
| Muzzle | 5 | Tail | 2½ |
| Eyes | 5 | Coat | 15 |
| Ears | 10 | Size | 10 |
| Neck | 5 | Color | 2½ |
| Chest | 5 | General Appearance | 10 |
| Body | 15 | TOTAL | 100 |

Approved June 10, 1947

# Sealyham Terrier

The Sealyham Terrier derives its name from Sealyham, Haverfordwest, Wales, the estate of Captain John Edwardes who, between 1850 and 1891, developed from obscure ancestry a strain of dogs noted for prowess in quarrying badger, otter, and fox. The requisite qualities were extreme gameness and endurance with as much substance as could be encompassed in a dog small and quick enough to dig and battle underground.

As the working ability of Sealyham Terriers drew public interest, they began to take their places with other terrier breeds in prominent homes and on the show bench. Their first recorded appearance at a dog show was at Haverfordwest, Wales, in October, 1903. In January, 1908, a group of Welsh fanciers founded the Sealyham Terrier Club of Haverfordwest and at their first meeting drew up the original standard for the breed. The first championship show at which Sealyhams appeared was at the English Kennel Show in October, 1910. The breed was recognized on March 8, 1911, by The Kennel Club, which offered the first Challenge Certificates for Sealyham Terriers at the Great Joint Terrier Show, London, June 10, 1911.

The breed was recognized by the American Kennel Club in 1911, shortly after its original importation into the United States. Since its American show debut at San Mateo, California, in September 1911, its popularity as a show dog has remained fairly constant. Among many honors, the breed has won Best in Show at Westminster four times.

The American Sealyham Terrier Club was founded on May 15, 1913, to

**399**

promote the interests of the breed in the United States and to encourage exhibition and working trials. The latter have succumbed to a suburban sprawl and a more humane feeling among Sealyham owners. However, a new interest is rising in the more controlled All-Terrier trials. The club offers, for club members, annual trophies for the most Bests in Show, most Group firsts, and most Bests of Breed won during the year. Annual specialty shows are held in an Eastern state during the winter, in the Midwest in late spring, and as part of the Montgomery County Kennel Club Terrier show in Pennsylvania in the fall.

The Sealyham of today is chiefly a companion, but when given the opportunity makes a very good working terrier. He is very outgoing, friendly yet a good house watchdog whose big-dog bark discourages intruders. He is easily trained but more often than not will add his own personal touch to the exercise or trick being taught. With proper care, food, and training, a Sealyham is very long-lived, 12 to 16 years not being uncommon, and active to the end.

Sealyhams require coat care at regular intervals. They do not shed which means that the dead hair must be pulled or combed out to prevent the formation of hair mats. Regular plucking of the dead hair, trimming of the head, neck, tail, and feet, will keep a smart looking, clean terrier which is a joy to own.

## Official Standard for the Sealyham Terrier

The Sealyham should be the embodiment of power and determination, ever keen and alert, of extraordinary substance, yet free from clumsiness.

**Height**—At withers about 10½ inches.

**Weight**—23–24 pounds for dogs; bitches slightly less. It should be borne in mind that size is more important than weight.

**Head**—Long, broad and powerful, without coarseness. It should, however, be in perfect balance with the body, joining neck smoothly. Length of head roughly, three-quarters height at withers, or about an inch longer than neck. Breadth between ears a little less than one-half length of head. *Skull*—Very slightly domed, with a shallow indentation running down between the brows, and joining the muzzle with a moderate stop. *Cheeks*—Smoothly formed and flat, without heavy jowls. *Jaws*—Powerful and square. Bite level or scissors. Overshot or undershot bad faults. *Teeth*—Sound, strong and white, with canines fitting closely together. *Nose*—Black, with large nostrils. White, cherry or butterfly bad faults. *Eyes*—Very dark, deeply set and fairly wide apart, of medium size, oval in shape with keen terrier expression. Light, large or protruding eye bad faults. Lack of eye rim pigmentation not a fault. *Ears*—Folded level with top of head, with forward edge close to cheek. Well rounded at tip, and of length to reach outer corner of eye. Thin, not leathery, and of sufficient thickness to avoid creases. Prick, tulip, rose or hound ears bad faults.

**Neck**—Length slightly less than two-thirds of height of dog at withers. Muscular without coarseness, with good reach, refinement at throat, and set firmly on shoulders.

**Shoulders**—Well laid back and powerful, but not over-muscled. Sufficiently wide to permit freedom of action. Upright or straight shoulder placement highly undesirable.

**Legs**—Forelegs strong, with good bone; and as straight as is consistent with chest being well let down between them. Down on pasterns, knuckled over, bowed, and out at elbow, bad faults. Hind legs longer than forelegs and not so heavily boned. *Feet*—Large but compact, round with thick pads, strong nails. Toes well arched and pointing straight ahead. Forefeet larger, though not quite so long as hind feet. Thin, spread or flat feet bad faults.

**Body**—Strong, short-coupled and substantial, so as to permit great flexibility. Brisket deep and well let down between forelegs. Ribs well sprung. *Back*—Length from withers to set-on of tail should approximate height at withers, or 10½ inches. Topline level, neither roached nor swayed. Any deviations from these measurements undesirable. *Hindquarters*—Very powerful, and protruding well behind the set-on of tail. Strong second thighs, stifles well bent, and hocks well let down. Cowhocks bad fault. *Tail*—Docked and carried upright. Set on far enough forward to that spine does not slope down to it.

**Coat**—Weather-resisting, comprised of soft, dense undercoat and hard, wiry top coat. Silky or curly coat bad fault.

**Color**—All white, or with lemon, tan or badger markings on head and ears. Heavy body markings and excessive ticking should be discouraged.

**Action**—Sound, strong, quick, free, true and level.

### SCALE OF POINTS

| | | | | |
|---|---|---|---|---|
| General character, balance and size | | 15 | Shoulders and brisket | 10 |
| Head | 5 | | Body, ribs & loin | 10 |
| Eyes | 5 | | Hindquarters | 10 |
| Mouth | 5 | | Legs and feet | 10 |
| Ears | 5 | | Coat | 10 | 50 |
| Neck | 5 | 25 | Tail | 5 |
| | | | Color (body marking & ticking) | 5 | 10 |
| | | | TOTAL | | 100 |

Approved February 9, 1974

# Skye Terrier

The majority of terriers have attained something of their present-day form within the last century but the Skye Terrier of nearly four centuries ago was like the specimens of today.

One may find mention of the Skye Terrier in that historic volume, *Of Englishe Dogges,* By John Caius, master of Gonville and Caius College, Cambridge University, and court physician to Edward VI, Queen Mary, and Queen Elizabeth. He was a man of broad education aside from the sciences, and also a great traveler and sportsman. Referring to the breed, he says it was "brought out of barbarous borders fro' the uttermost countryes northward. . . . which, by reason of the length of heare, makes showe neither of face nor of body."

Thus we find the Skye Terrier of today. His flowing coat is the same as the one that proved such a grand protection in the days when his only occupation was to challenge vicious animals that otherwise might have crippled him at a single bite. Perhaps this long coat has been a handicap, for all followers of this game old working terrier have witnessed him surpassed in popularity by one after another of the newer breeds. Still they are reluctant to change him in any manner. Indeed, they stand by the motto of the Skye Club of Scotland—"Wha daur meddle wi' me."

The breed takes its name from the chief of those northwestern islands of Scotland that, as far back as he can be traced, formed his native home, and in which he was found in greatest perfection. He is the only terrier distinctively belonging to the northwestern islands that is not common to the whole of Scotland. Those who have the best practical knowledge of the Skye maintain that he is without rival in his own peculiar domain, and that wherever there are rocks, dens, burrows, cairns, or covers to explore, or waters to take to, his services should be called.

From the nature of Dr. Caius' allusion to him, it is evident that the Skye Terrier had become known in the cities of England, especially in the royal palace. The kings and queens of England have always set the styles in that country, and as soon as the Skye had been accepted in court—evidently in the middle of the 16th century when Dr. Caius penned the historic work—he was soon the fashionable pet of all degrees of nobility, and after that of the commoners.

The Skye was the most widely known of all the terriers down to the end of the 19th century. Queen Victoria's early interest and Sir Edwin Landseer's paintings featuring the breed helped attract attention. He was kept in all the English-speaking countries. Since then he has slipped quietly into the background, yet his admirers in England and Scotland—where he has maintained his greatest foothold—are happy to point to the time when "a duchess would almost be ashamed to be seen in the park unaccompanied by her long-coated Skye."

The Skye Terrier was first registered with AKC in 1887 and was one of the most important breeds at American bench shows before the turn of the century. The rivalry among the leading kennels was exceptionally keen. Although the frontiers of his activities have been somewhat curtailed, the true value of the Skye Terrier is evinced by the tenacious grasp which he has on those who have come in contact with him. Thus, entries may sometimes be small at bench shows today, but seldom does one find a major show without some specimens of this old terrier breed.

## Official Standard for the Skye Terrier

**General Appearance**—The Skye Terrier is a dog of style, elegance and dignity: agile and strong with sturdy bone and hard muscle. Long, low and level—he is twice as long as he is high—he is covered with a profuse coat that falls straight down either side of the body over oval-shaped ribs. The hair well feathered on the head veils forehead and eyes to serve as protection from brush and briar as well as amid serious encounters with other animals. He stands with head high and long tail hanging and moves with a seemingly effortless gait. He is strong in body, quarters and jaw.

**Size, Proportion, Substance**—*Size*—The ideal shoulder height for dogs is 10 inches and bitches 9½ inches. Based on these heights a 10 inch dog measured from chest bone over tail at rump should be 20 inches. A slightly higher or lower dog of either sex is acceptable. Dogs 9 inches or less and bitches 8½ inches or less at the withers are to be penalized. ***Proportion***—The ideal ratio of body length to shoulder height is 2 to 1, which is considered the correct proportion. ***Substance***—Solidly built, full of strength and quality without being coarse. Bone is substantial.

**Head**—Long and powerful, strength being deemed more important than extreme length. ***Eyes*** brown, preferably dark brown, medium in size, close-set and alight with life and intelligence. ***Ears*** symmetrical and gracefully feathered. They may be carried prick or drop. If prick, they are medium in size, placed high on the skull, erect at their outer edges, and slightly wider apart at the peak than at the skull. Drop ears, somewhat larger in size and set lower, hang flat against the skull. Moderate width at the back of the skull tapers gradually to a strong muzzle. The stop is slight. The dark muzzle is just moderately full as opposed to snipy. Powerful and absolutely true jaws. The nose is always black. A Dudley, flesh-colored or brown nose shall disqualify. Mouth with the incisor teeth closing level, or with upper teeth slightly overlapping the lower.

**Neck, Topline, Body**—***Neck***—Long and gracefully arched, carried high and proudly. The backline is level. ***Body*** pre-eminently long and low, the chest deep, with oval-shaped ribs. The sides appear flattish due to the straight falling and profuse coat. ***Tail*** long and well feathered. When hanging, its upper section is pendulous, following the line of the rump, its lower section thrown back in a moderate arc without twist or curl. When raised, its height makes it appear a prolongation of the backline. Though not to be preferred, the tail is sometimes carried high when the dog is excited or angry. When such carriage arises from emotion only, it is permissible. But the tail should not be constantly carried above the level of the back or hang limp.

**Forequarters**—Shoulders well laid back, with tight placement of shoulder blades at the withers and elbows should fit closely to the sides and be neither loose nor tied. Forearm should curve slightly around the chest. Legs short, muscular and straight as possible. "Straight as possible" means straight as soundness and chest will permit, it does not mean "Terrier straight." ***Feet***—Large hare-feet preferably pointing forward, the pads thick and nails strong and preferably black.

**Hindquarters**—Strong, full, well developed and well angulated. Legs short, muscular and straight when viewed from behind. Feet as in front.

**Coat**—Double. Undercoat short, close, soft and wooly. Outer coat hard, straight and flat. 5½ inches long without extra credit granted for greater length. The body coat hangs straight down each side, parting from head to tail. The head hair, which may be shorter, veils forehead and eyes and forms a moderate beard and apron. The long feathering on the ears falls straight down from the tips and outer edges, surrounding the ears like a fringe and outlining their shape. The ends of the hair should mingle with the coat of the neck. Tail well feathered.

**Color**—The coat must be of one over-all color at the skin but may be of varying shades of the same color in the full coat, which may be black, blue, dark or light grey, silver platinum, fawn or cream. The dog must have no distinctive markings except for the desirable black points of ears, muzzle and tip of tail, all of which points are preferably dark even to black. The shade of head and legs should approximate that of the body. There must be no trace of pattern, design or clear-cut color variations, with the exception of the breed's only permissible white which occasionally exists on the chest not exceeding 2 inches in diameter.

The puppy coat may be very different in color from the adult coat. Therefore, as it is growing and clearing, wide variations of color may occur; consequently, this is permissible in dogs under 18 months of age. However, even in puppies there must be no trace of pattern, design, or clear-cut variations with the exception of the black band encircling the body coat of the creme colored dog, and the only permissible white which, as in the adult dog, occasionally exists on the chest not exceeding 2 inches in diameter.

**Gait**—The legs proceed straight forward when traveling. When approaching, the forelegs form a continuation of the straight line of the front. The feet being the same distance apart as the elbows. The principal propelling power is furnished by the back legs which travel straight forward. Forelegs should move well forward, without too much lift. The whole movement may be termed free, active and effortless and give a more or less fluid picture.

**Temperament**—That of the typical working terrier capable of overtaking game and going to ground, displaying stamina, courage, strength and agility. Fearless, good-tempered, loyal and canny, he is friendly and gay with those he knows and reserved and cautious with strangers.

### DISQUALIFICATION

*A Dudley, flesh-colored or brown nose shall disqualify.*

Approved February 10, 1990

# Soft Coated Wheaten Terrier

The actual origin of the Soft Coated Wheaten Terrier cannot be found in printed record. Recurring reference to a terrier soft in coat, wheaten in color, and of a size to fit the Wheaten of today, lends credence to the belief that the history of the Soft Coated Wheaten began long before records were kept and when the challenge of "best dog" was most often settled in a "fists up" confrontation between the owners.

Known for more than 200 years in Ireland, the Soft Coated Wheaten Terrier is believed by some to be an important ancestor of the Kerry Blue. Legend tells us that when the Spanish Armada was sunk off the shores of Ireland, the blue dogs who swam ashore found terriers with a soft wheaten coat waiting to welcome them.

Bits of information show us a hardy dog who hunted small game cleverly and silently, guarded stock and garden with courage and tenacity, and was both companion and protector to his owners.

Of necessity these early dogs were bred for their working qualities, with shade of coat or exact measurements of small consideration and no record. As only the brave, strong and proficient survived and reproduced, Nature really set the standard for the original stock of the Soft Coated Wheaten Terrier.

Thus has evolved a very attractive, well-made dog of medium size, quick-witted and responsive. The demands of his function required steadiness and discrimination, which have been retained, while preserving the joy in living and the stamina associated with a terrier.

It has produced a dog whose natural attributes have been maintained and whose appearance has not been artificially altered. It has provided a dog whose mature coat is abundant throughout, giving protection from the elements and the enemy. This coat is very soft, wheaten in color, and from it the breed takes its name. The coat goes through a natural progression of change from puppyhood to maturity, but should be clear wheaten by 18 to 24 months of age.

In the standard for the breed, the quality of moderation is emphasized; in fact, lack of exaggeration anywhere has seemed to be the hallmark of the breed.

Sponsored by Dr. G. J. Pierse, the Soft Coated Wheaten Terrier was campaigned to registration with the Irish Kennel Club and on March 17th, 1937, a most fitting day for Irish dogs, made its debut in the Irish Kennel Club Championship Show. For many years this breed was required to qualify in both major and minor field trials over rat, rabbit and badger before attaining championship. Registration with The Kennel Club (England) came in 1943.

The history of the Soft Coated Wheaten in the United States must begin with a quote from the *Boston Globe Post*, November 24, 1946:

"With a cargo which included several hundred tons of choice Scotch and Irish whiskey, seven pedigreed pups (one was lost over the side on the trip) and 18 homing pigeons, the freighter *Norman J. Colman* arrived yesterday after a 12-day voyage from Manchester, Liverpool and Belfast."

Two of the fortunate dogs who survived the passage were consigned to Miss Lydia Vogel of Springfield, Mass., and were, as far as we know, the first Wheatens to come to our side of the Atlantic. They were shown at Westminster in February 1947, and 17 puppies were whelped. However, American Kennel Club registration was not achieved at that time.

Ten years later in March of 1957, the O'Connors of Brooklyn imported Holmenocks Gramachree. Shown in the Miscellaneous Class in Staten Island in 1961, she took her first ribbon. Encouraged by the enthusiasm of exhibitors and spectators, a search was initiated for other Wheaten owners, but only the Arnolds of Connecticut were interested in actively promoting the breed at that time.

In 1962, on St. Patrick's Day—again that most appropriate date—the Soft Coated Wheaten Terrier Club of America was founded when a small group of interested fanciers met in Brooklyn and agreed on a common goal, namely to preserve and protect the Wheaten in the United States and to promote the breed to public interest and American Kennel Club registration. First officers were elected—Margaret O'Connor, Eileen Jackson, Ida Mallory and Charles Arnold.

Also present at that meeting were three Wheatens destined to pioneer the breed in the show rings—Holmenocks Gramachree, Gads Hill and Holmenocks Hallmark, better known as "Irish" (O'Connor), "Liam" and "Maud" (Arnold). Since then, each year has seen substantial gains in registrations, in Club memberships, and in public interest. And each year showing has increased in breed competition and in obedience exhibition.

The Soft Coated Wheaten Terrier was admitted to registration in the American Kennel Club Stud Book on May 1, 1973, and to classification in the Terrier Group at AKC shows October 3, 1973.

## Official Standard for the Soft Coated Wheaten Terrier

**General Appearance**—The Soft Wheaten Terrier is a medium-sized, hardy, well balanced sporting terrier, square in outline. He is distinguished by his soft, silky, gently waving coat of warm wheaten color and his particularly steady disposition. The breed requires moderation both in structure and presentation, and any exaggerations are to be shunned. He should present the overall appearance of an alert and happy animal, graceful, strong and well coordinated.

**Size, Proportion, Substance**—A dog shall be 18 to 19 inches at the withers, the ideal being 18½. A bitch shall be 17 to 18 inches at the withers, the ideal being 17½. *Major Faults*— Dogs under 18 inches or over 19 inches: bitches under 17 inches or over 18 inches. Any deviation must be penalized according to the degree of its severity. Square in outline. Hardy, well balanced. Dogs should weigh 35–40 pounds; bitches 30–35 pounds.

**Head**—Well balanced and in proportion to the body. Rectangular in appearance: moderately long. Powerful with no suggestion of coarseness. *Eyes* dark reddish brown or brown, medium in size, slightly almond shaped and set fairly wide apart. Eye rims black, *Major Fault*—Anything approaching a yellow eye. *Ears* small to medium in size, breaking level with the skull and dropping slightly forward, the inside edge of the ear lying next to the cheek and pointing to the ground rather than to the eye. A hound ear or a high-breaking ear is not typical and should be *severely penalized*. *Skull* flat and clean between ears. Cheekbones not prominent. Defined *stop*. *Muzzle* powerful and strong, well filled below the eyes. No suggestion of snipiness. Skull and foreface of equal length. *Nose* black and large for size of dog. *Major Fault*—Any nose color other than solid black. *Lips* tight and black. *Teeth* large, clean and white: scissors or level *bite*. *Major Fault*— Undershot or overshot.

**Neck, Topline, Body**—*Neck* medium in length, clean and strong, not throaty. Carried proudly, it gradually widens, blending smoothly into the body. *Back* strong and level. *Body* compact; relatively short coupled. *Chest* is deep. *Ribs* are well sprung but without roundness. *Tail* is docked and well set on, carried gaily but never over the back.

**Forequarters**—*Shoulders* well laid back, clean and smooth; well knit. *Forelegs* straight and well boned. All *dewclaws* should be removed. *Feet* are round and compact with good depth of pad. *Pads* black. *Nails* dark.

**Hindquarters**—*Hindlegs* well developed with well bent *stifles* turning neither in nor out; *hocks* well let down and parallel to each other. All *dewclaws* should be removed. The presence of dewclaws on the hind legs should be *penalized*. *Feet* are round and compact with good depth of pad. *Pads* black. *Nails* dark.

**Coat**—A distinguishing characteristic of the breed which sets the dog apart from all other terriers. An abundant single coat covering the entire body, legs and head; coat on the latter falls forward to shade the eyes. Texture soft and silky with a gentle wave. In both puppies and adolescents, the mature wavy coat is generally not yet evident. *Major faults*—Woolly or harsh, crisp or cottony, curly or standaway coat: in the adult, a straight coat is also objectionable. *Presentation*—For show purposes, the Wheaten is presented to show a terrier outline, but coat must be of sufficient length to flow when the dog is in motion. The coat must never be clipped or plucked. Sharp contrasts or stylizations must be avoided. Head coat should be blended to present a rectangular outline. Eyes should be indicated but never fully exposed. Ears should be relieved of fringe, but not taken down to the leather. Sufficient coat must be left on skull, cheeks, neck and tail to balance the proper length of body coat. *Dogs that are overly trimmed shall be severely penalized.*

**Color**—Any shade of wheaten. Upon close examination, occasional red, white or black guard hairs may be found. However, the overall coloring must be clearly wheaten with no evidence of any other color except on ears and muzzle where blue-gray shading is sometimes present. *Major Fault*—Any color save wheaten. *Puppies and Adolescents*—Puppies under a year may carry deeper coloring and occasional black tipping. The adolescent, under two years, is often quite light in color, but must never be white or carry gray other than on ears and muzzle. However, by two years of age, the *proper* wheaten color should be obvious.

**Gait**—Gait is free, graceful and lively with good reach in front and strong drive behind. Front and rear feet turn neither in or out. Dogs who fail to keep their tails erect when moving should be *severely penalized.*

**Temperament**—The Wheaten is a happy, steady dog and shows himself gaily with an air of self-confidence. He is alert and exhibits interest in his surroundings; exhibits less aggressiveness than is sometimes encouraged in other terriers. *Major Fault*—Timid or overly aggressive dogs.

Approved February 12, 1983
Reformatted July 20, 1989

# Staffordshire Bull Terrier

$\text{T}$he Staffordshire Bull Terrier had its beginnings in England many centuries ago when the Bulldog and Mastiff were closely linked. Bull baiting and bear baiting in the Elizabethan era produced large dogs for these sports and later on the 100–120 pound animal gave way to a small, more agile breed of up to 90 pounds.

Early in the 19th century the sport of dog fighting gained popularity and a smaller, faster dog was developed. It was called by names such as "Bulldog Terrier" and "Bull and Terrier." The Bulldog bred then was a larger dog than we know today and weighed about 60 pounds. This dog was crossed with a small native terrier which appears in the history of the present-day Manchester Terrier. The dog which this produced, averaging between 30 and 45 pounds, became the Staffordshire Bull Terrier.

James Hinks, in about 1860, crossed the Old Pit Bull Terrier, now known as the Staffordshire Bull Terrier, and produced the all-white English Bull Terrier. The Bull Terrier obtained recognition by The Kennel Club in England in the last quarter of the 19th century, but the Staffordshire Bull Terrier, due to its reputation as a fighting dog, did not receive this blessing.

In 1935 the Staffordshire Bull Terrier was recognized by the Kennel Club in England and enthusiasts were able to conduct conformation matches. The sport of dog fighting had long been made illegal and the Staffordshire Bull Terrier had evolved into a dog of such temperament as to make him a fine pet and companion and a worthy show dog.

Bull and Terrier breeds were believed to have arrived in North America sometime in the mid-1880s. Here they developed along different lines with a heavier, taller dog being the end result. Today's American Staffordshire Terrier represents that breeding.

The Staffordshire Bull Terrier was admitted to registration in the American Kennel Club Stud Book effective October 1, 1974, with regular show classification in the Terrier Group at AKC shows available on and after March 5, 1975.

## Official Standard for the Staffordshire Bull Terrier

**General Appearance**—The Staffordshire Bull Terrier is a smooth-coated dog. It should be of great strength for its size and, although muscular, should be active and agile.

**Size, Proportion, Substance**—Height at shoulder: 14 to 16 inches. Weight: Dogs, 28 to 38 pounds; bitches, 24 to 34 pounds, these heights being related to weights. Non-conformity with these limits is a fault. In proportion, the length of back, from withers to tailset, is equal to the distance from withers to ground.

**Head**—Short, deep through, broad skull, very pronounced cheek muscles, distinct stop, short foreface, black nose. Pink (Dudley) nose to be considered a serious fault. *Eyes*—Dark preferable, but may bear some relation to coat color. Round, of medium size, and set to look straight ahead. Light eyes or pink eye rims to be considered a fault, except that where the coat surrounding the eye is white the eye rim may be pink. *Ears*—Rose or half-pricked and not large. Full drop or full prick to be considered a serious fault. *Mouth*—A bite in which the outer side of the lower incisors touches the inner side of the upper incisors. The lips should be tight and clean. The badly undershot or overshot bite is a serious fault.

**Neck, Topline, Body**—The neck is muscular, rather short, clean in outline and gradually widening toward the shoulders. The body is close coupled, with a level topline, wide front, deep brisket and well sprung ribs being rather light in the loins. The tail is undocked, of medium length, low set, tapering to a point and carried rather low. It should not curl much and may be likened to an old-fashioned pump handle. A tail that is too long or badly curled is a fault.

**Forequarters**—Legs straight and well boned, set rather far apart, without looseness at the shoulders and showing no weakness at the pasterns, from which point the feet turn out a little. Dewclaws on the forelegs may be removed. The feet should be well padded, strong and of medium size.

**Hindquarters**—The hindquarters should be well muscled, hocks let down with stifles well bent. Legs should be parallel when viewed from behind. Dewclaws, if any, on the hind legs are generally removed. Feet as in front.

**Coat**—Smooth, short and close to the skin, not to be trimmed or de-whiskered.

**Color**—Red, fawn, white, black or blue, or any of these colors with white. Any shade of brindle or any shade of brindle with white. Black-and-tan or liver color to be disqualified.

**Gait**—Free, powerful and agile with economy of effort. Legs moving parallel when viewed from front or rear. Discernible drive from hind legs.

**Temperament**—From the past history of the Staffordshire Bull Terrier, the modern dog draws its character of indomitable courage, high intelligence, and tenacity. This, coupled with its affection for its friends, and children in particular, its off-duty quietness and trustworthy stability, makes it a foremost all-purpose dog.

### DISQUALIFICATION

*Black-and-tan or liver color.*

Approved November 14, 1989

# Welsh Terrier

Judging from the old paintings and prints of the first known terriers, the Welsh Terrier is a very old breed, for these prints show us a rough-haired black-and-tan terrier.

In old times this dog was more commonly known as the Old English Terrier or Black-and-Tan Wire Haired Terrier, and as late as 1886 the English Kennel Club allotted one class for "Welsh or Old English Wire Haired Black and Tan Terriers." Even to this day the color of the Welsh is as it was over a hundred years ago.

In other respects, also, the Welsh Terrier has changed very slightly. He is, as he was then, a sporting dog extensively used in his native home, Wales, for hunting the otter, fox, and badger, and he possesses the characteristic gameness that one naturally looks for in such a dog. Although game, he is not quarrelsome; in fact, he is well mannered and easy to handle.

The first record of Welsh Terriers having a classification of their own in England was in 1884–85 at Carnavon where there were 21 entries, but even at this time it was not uncommon for dogs to be shown as Old English Terriers and also as Welsh Terriers. As late as 1893 Dick Turpin, a well-known show dog of those days, continued in this dual role.

Welsh Terriers were first brought to this country by Prescott Lawrence in 1888, when he imported a dog and a bitch and showed them at the old Madison Square Garden in the Miscellaneous Class. No other Welsh, however, were imported for some time. But about 1901 classification was offered for Welsh at

Westminster, and four or five dogs were shown; from then on their popularity has steadily increased.

## Official Standard for the Welsh Terrier

**General Appearance**—The Welsh Terrier is a sturdy, compact, rugged dog of medium size with a coarse wire-textured coat. The legs, underbody and head are tan; the jacket black (or occasionally grizzle). The tail is docked to length meant to complete the image of a "square dog" approximately as high as he is long. The movement is a terrier trot typical of the long-legged terrier. It is effortless, with good reach and drive. The Welsh Terrier is friendly, outgoing to people and other dogs, showing spirit and courage. Intelligence and desire to please are evident in the attitude. The "Welsh Terrier expression" comes from the set, color and position of the eyes combined with the use of the ears.

**Head**—The entire head is rectangular. The foreface is strong with powerful, punishing jaws. It is only slightly narrower than the back skull. There is a slight stop. The backskull is of equal length to the foreface. They are on parallel planes in profile. The back skull is smooth and flat (not domed) between the ears. There are no wrinkles between the ears. The cheeks are flat and clean (not bulging). *Muzzle*—The muzzle is one-half the length of the entire head from tip of nose to occiput. The foreface in front of the eyes is well made up. The furnishings on the foreface are trimmed to complete—without exaggeration—the total rectangular outline. The muzzle is strong and squared off, never snipy. The lips are black and tight. *Nose*—The nose is black and squared off. *Teeth*—A scissors bite is preferred, but a level bite is acceptable. Either one has complete dentition. The teeth are large and strong, set in powerful, vice-like jaws. *Eyes*—The eyes are small, dark brown and almond-shaped, well set in the skull. They are placed fairly far apart. The size, shape, color and position of the eyes give the steady, confident but alert expression that is typical of the Welsh Terrier. *Ears*—The ears are V-shaped, small, but not too thin. The fold is just above the topline of the skull. The ears are carried forward close to the cheek with the tips falling to, or toward, the outside corners of the eyes when the dog is at rest. The ears move slightly up and forward when at attention.

**Neck**—The neck is of moderate length and thickness, slightly arched and sloping gracefully into the shoulders. The throat is clean with no excess of skin.

**Body**—The body shows good substance, is well ribbed up with a level topline. The loin is strong and moderately short. There is good depth of brisket and moderate width of chest. The front is straight. The shoulders are long, sloping and well laid back.

**Forelegs and Feet**—The legs are straight and muscular with upright and powerful pasterns. The feet are small, round, cat-like. The pads are thick and black. The nails are strong and black. Dewclaws (front and back) are removed.

**Hindquarters**—The hindquarters are strong and muscular with well-developed second thighs and the stifles well bent. The hocks are moderately straight, parallel and short from joint to ground.

**Tail**—The tail is docked to a length approximately level (on an imaginary line) with the occiput, to complete the square image of the whole dog. The root of the tail is set well up on the back. It is carried upright.

**Movement**—The movement is straight, free and effortless, with good reach in front, strong drive behind, with the feet naturally tending to converge toward a median line of travel as speed increases.

**Coat**—The coat is hard, wiry and dense with a close-fitting, thick jacket. There is a short, soft undercoat. Furnishings on muzzle, legs and quarters are dense and wiry.

**Color**—The jacket is black, spreading up onto the neck, down onto the tail and into the upper thighs. The legs, quarters and head are clear tan. The tan is deep reddish brown with slightly lighter shades acceptable. A grizzle jacket is also acceptable.

**Size**—Males are about 15 inches at withers, with an acceptable range between 15 and 15½. Bitches may be proportionally smaller. Twenty pounds is considered an average weight, varying a few pounds depending on the height of the dog, and the density of bone. Both dog and bitch appear solid and of good substance.

**Temperament**—The Welsh Terrier is a game dog—alert, aware, spirited—but at the same time, is friendly and shows self-control. A specimen exhibiting an overly aggressive attitude, or shyness, should be penalized.

**Faults**—Any deviation from the foregoing should be considered a fault, the seriousness of the fault depending upon the extent of the deviation.

Approved June 12, 1984

# West Highland White Terrier

It is probable that the West Highland White Terrier and all the terriers of Scotland came from the same stock; the Scotties, Cairns, Dandie Dinmonts, and West Highland Whites are branches from the same tree and its roots.

The West Highland White Terrier, according to notable authors originated at Poltalloch, Scotland, where they had been bred and maintained for more than 100 years prior to their appearance at dog shows. In 1916 Colonel Malcolm of Poltalloch said that his father and grandfather both kept them. It is probable that the lineage of the Malcolm dogs goes back to the time of King James I, who asked for some "earth-dogges" out of Argyleshire.

Years ago the breed was known as the Roseneath Terrier, also as the Poltalloch Terrier. The name Roseneath was taken from the Duke of Argyll's place in Dumbartonshire, Scotland.

The first show held for the breed was at Crufts in London in 1907. The first AKC registration was in 1908. Originally registered as the Roseneath Terrier, the name was officially changed to West Highland White Terrier on May 31, 1909.

The West Highland is all terrier—a large amount of Scotch spunk, determination, and devotion crammed into a small body. Outdoors they are truly sporty, good hunters, speedy and cunning, with great intelligence. In the house they are all that can be desired of a pet; faithful, understanding, and devoted, yet gay and light-hearted.

**416**

One of the reasons West Highland White Terriers are such delightful little dogs to own is their hardiness. They need no pampering. They love to romp and play in the snow and will follow skaters or walkers for miles across frozen lakes and harbors. They are also easy to show and handle as they require very little trimming and, indeed, look better and more characteristic when in their natural state. Of course, there are always a few hairs which should be pulled out just to smarten the dog up a bit, but there is no prettier sight than a well-kept West Highland White Terrier shown in full coat. The West Highland's outer coat is hard and stiff and should be kept so by proper grooming and dry-cleaning rather than by washing. There are people who think a white dog hard to keep clean, but this is not so. A little time spent each day with a brush and comb keeps him always in the pink of condition.

## Official Standard for the West Highland White Terrier

**General Appearance**—The West Highland White Terrier is a small, game, well-balanced, hardy looking terrier, exhibiting good showmanship, possessed with no small amount of self-esteem, strongly built, deep in chest and back ribs, with a straight back and powerful hindquarters on muscular legs, and exhibiting in marked degree a great combination of strength and activity. The coat is about two inches long, white in color, hard, with plenty of soft undercoat. The dog should be neatly presented, the longer coat on the back and sides trimmed to blend into the shorter neck and shoulder coat. Considerable hair is left around the head to act as a frame for the face to yield a typical Westie expression.

**Size, Proportion, Substance**—The ideal size is eleven inches at the withers for dogs and ten inches for bitches. A slight deviation is acceptable. The Westie is a compact dog, with good balance and substance. The body between the withers and the root of the tail is slightly shorter than the height at the withers. Short-coupled and well boned. *Faults*— Over or under height limits. Fine boned.

**Head**—Shaped to present a round appearance from the front. Should be in proportion to the body. *Expression*—Piercing, inquisitive, pert. *Eyes*—Widely set apart, medium in size, almond shaped, dark brown in color, deep set, sharp and intelligent. Looking from under heavy eyebrows, they give a piercing look. Eye rims are black. *Faults*—Small, full or light colored eyes. *Ears*—Small, carried tightly erect, set wide apart, on the top outer edge of the skull. They terminate in a sharp point, and must never be cropped. The hair on the ears is trimmed short and is smooth and velvety, free of fringe at the tips. Black skin pigmentation is preferred. *Faults*—Round-pointed, broad, large ears set closely together, not held tightly erect, or placed too low on the side of the head. *Skull*—Broad, slightly longer than the muzzle, not flat on top but slightly domed between the ears. It gradually tapers to the eyes. There is a defined stop, eyebrows are heavy. *Faults*—Long or narrow skull. *Muzzle*—Blunt, slightly shorter than the skull, powerful and gradually tapering to the nose, which is large and black. The jaws are level and powerful. Lip pigment is black. *Faults*—Muzzle longer than skull. Nose color other than black. *Bite*— The teeth are large for the size of the dog. There must be six incisor teeth between the canines of both lower and upper jaws. An occasional missing premolar is acceptable. A tight scissors bite with upper incisors slightly overlapping the lower incisors or level mouth is equally acceptable. *Faults*—Teeth defective or misaligned. Any incisors missing or several premolars missing. Teeth overshot or undershot.

**Neck, Topline, Body**—*Neck*—Muscular and well set on sloping shoulders. The length of neck should be in proportion to the remainder of the dog. *Faults*—Neck too long or too short. *Topline*—Flat and level, both standing and moving. *Faults*—High rear, any deviation from above. *Body*—Compact and of good substance. Ribs deep and well arched in the upper half or rib, extending at least to the elbows, and presenting a flattish side appearance. Back ribs of considerable depth, and distance from last rib to upper thigh as short as compatible with free movement of the body. Chest very deep and extending to the elbows, with breadth in proportion to the size of the dog. Loin short, broad and strong. *Faults*—Back weak, either too long or too short. Barrel ribs, ribs above elbows. *Tail*—Relatively short, with good substance, and shaped like a carrot. When standing erect it is never extended above the top of the skull. It is covered with hard hair without feather, as straight as possible, carried gaily but not curled over the back. The tail is set on high enough to that the spine does not slope down to it. The tail is never docked. *Faults*—Set too low, long, thin, carried at half-mast, or curled over back.

**Forequarters**—*Angulation, Shoulders*—Shoulder blades are well laid back and well knit at the backbone. The shoulder blade should attach to an upper arm of moderate length, and sufficient angle to allow for definite body overhang. *Faults*—Steep or loaded shoulders. Upper arm too short or too straight. *Legs*—Forelegs are muscular and well boned, relatively short, but with sufficient length to set the dog up so as not to be too close to the ground. The legs are reasonably straight, and thickly covered with short hard hair. They are set in under the shoulder blades with definite body overhang before them. Height from elbow to withers and elbow to ground should be approximately the same. *Faults*—Out at elbows, light bone, fiddle-front. *Feet*—Forefeet are larger than the hind ones, are round, proportionate in size, strong, thickly padded; they may properly be turned out slightly. Dewclaws may be removed. Black pigmentation is most desirable on pads of all feet and nails, although nails may lose coloration in older dogs.

**Hindquarters**—*Angulation*—Thighs are very muscular, well angulated, not set wide apart, with hock well bent, short, and parallel when viewed from the rear. *Legs*—Rear legs are muscular and relatively short and sinewy. *Faults*—Weak hocks, long hocks, lack of angulation. Cowhocks. *Feet*—Hind feet are smaller than front feet, and are thickly padded. Dewclaws may be removed.

**Coat**—Very important and seldom seen to perfection. Must be double-coated. The head is shaped by plucking the hair, to present the round appearance. The outer coat consists of straight hard white hair, about two inches long, with shorter coat on neck and shoulders, properly blended and trimmed to blend shorter areas into furnishings, which are longer on stomach and legs. The ideal coat is hard, straight and white, but a hard straight coat which may have some wheaten tipping is preferable to a white fluffy or soft coat. Furnishings may be somewhat softer and longer but should never give the appearance of fluff. *Faults*—Soft coat. Any silkiness or tendency to curl. Any open or single coat, or one which is too short.

**Color**—The color is white, as defined by the breed's name. *Faults*—Any coat color other than white. Heavy wheaten color.

**Gait**—Free, straight and easy all around. It is a distinctive gait, not stilted, but powerful, with reach and drive. In front the leg is freely extended forward by the shoulder. When seen from the front the legs do not move square, but tend to move toward the center of gravity. The hind movement is free, strong and fairly close. The hocks are freely flexed and drawn close under the body, so that when moving off the foot the body is thrown or pushed forward with some force. Overall ability to move is usually best evaluated from the side, and topline remains level. *Faults*—Lack of reach in front, and/or drive behind. Stiff, stilted or too wide movement.

**Temperament**—Alert, gay, courageous and self-reliant, but friendly. *Faults*—Excess timidity or excess pugnacity.

Approved December 13, 1988

# GROUP V

# TOYS

## Affenpinscher

One of the most ancient of Toy dogs, the Affenpinscher (translated from German as Monkey-Terrier) originated in central Europe. During the 17th century small terriers frequently were kept around stables on farms or in stores where they served as ratters. Bred down to size, these small terriers became companions in the home and kept mice from overrunning their mistresses' boudoirs.

A game, alert, intelligent, and sturdy little "terrier type," the Affenpinscher is characterized by his "monkeyish" expression, derived from a prominent chin with hair-tuft and mustache. This expression is further accentuated by his bushy eyebrows, shadowing black-bordered eyelids and large, piercing dark eyes. The entire coat is stiff and wiry in texture, and with his cropped ears and docked tail he is every inch a real dog, despite his small size.

The Affenpinscher is believed to have been a major influence in the development of many of the smaller rough-coated breeds of continental Europe, including the Brussels Griffon and the Miniature Schnauzer.

The area around Munich, Germany eventually became the heart of Affen-

**421**

pinscher breeding in Europe. The Pinscher Klub was founded in 1895 in Cologne, and the Bayerischer Schnauzer Klub was formed in 1907. In 1923 these two clubs joined forces as the Pinscher-Schnauzer Klub, which attracted many new breeders.

The breed was admitted to the American Kennel Club's *Stud Book* in 1936. This quaint little dog's popularity has been overshadowed by that of his descendant, the Brussels Griffon, but more recently he is enjoying a return to favor.

## Official Standard for the Affenpinscher

**General Appearance**—The Affenpinscher is a balanced, little, wiry-haired terrier-like toy dog whose intelligence and demeanor make it a good house pet. Originating in Germany, where the name Affenpinscher means "monkey-like terrier," the breed was developed to rid the kitchens, granaries and stables of rodents. In France the breed is described as the *diablotin moustachu* or the moustached little devil. Both these names help to describe the appearance and attitude of this delightful breed. When evaluating the breed, the total overall appearance of the Affenpinscher is more important than any individual characteristic.

**Size, Proportion, Substance**—The Affenpinscher is a sturdy, compact little dog with medium bone and is not delicate in any way. The *height* at the withers is between 9" and 11½", with 10¼" being the ideal. The height at the withers is approximately the same as the length of the body from the point of the shoulder to the point of the buttocks giving a square appearance. The female may be slightly longer.

**Head**—The head is in proportion to the body, carried confidently upright with monkey-like facial expression. *Eyes* full, round, dark, brilliant, and of medium size in proportion to the head but not bulging or protruding. The eye rims are black. *Ears* either cropped to a point, set high and standing erect; or natural, standing erect, semi-erect or dropped. All types of ears if symmetrical are acceptable as long as the monkey-like expression is maintained. *Skull* round and domed but not coarse. *Stop* well defined. *Muzzle* short and narrowing slightly to a blunt nose. The length of the muzzle is approximately the same as the distance between the eyes. *Nose* not obviously turned up or down, with black pigmentation. *Lips* black in color with the lower lip more prominent. *Bite* undershot with the lower teeth closing closely in front of the upper teeth. A level bite is acceptable if the monkey-like expression is maintained. The teeth and tongue do not show when the mouth is closed. The lower jaw is broad enough for the lower teeth to be straight and even.

**Neck, Topline, Body**—*Neck* short and straight with upright carriage. *Topline* straight and level. *Body*—The *chest* is rather broad and deep; the *ribs* are moderately sprung. The *underline* is slightly tucked up at the loin. The *back* is short and straight. The *loin* is short and only slightly tucked. The *croup* has just a perceptible curve before the tail. The *tail* is either docked or left natural. When docked the tail is generally between 1" and

3" long; set high and carried erect. When natural the tail is carried curved gently up over the back while moving. The type of tail is not a major consideration.

**Forequarters**—The front angulation is moderate. *Shoulders* with moderate layback and flexible enough to allow free front action. The length of the upper arm and the forearm are about equal. *Elbows* close to the body. *Front legs* straight when viewed from the front. *Front pasterns* relatively short and straight. *Dewclaws* generally removed. *Feet* small, round and compact with black pads and nails.

**Hindquarters**—The rear angulation is moderate. *Hind legs* straight when viewed from behind. When viewed from the side they are set under the body to maintain a square appearance. The length of the upper thigh and the second thigh are about equal. *Stifle* moderate angulation. *Hock joint* moderate angulation; straight when viewed from behind. *Rear pasterns* short and straight. *Dewclaws* generally removed. *Feet* small, round and compact with black pads and nails.

**Coat**—The hair is dense, rough, harsh textured and approximately 1" in length on the shoulders, body and back, but may be shorter on the rear and tail in contrast to the longer, shaggier and less harsh hair on the head, neck, chest, stomach and legs. At maturity the neck and chest coat may grow longer to form a cape. The longer hair on the head, eyebrows and beard stands off and frames the face to emphasize the monkey-like expression. The hair on the ears is usually cut very short. The correct coat needs little grooming to blend the shorter hair into the longer hair to maintain a neat but shaggy appearance.

**Color**—Black, gray, silver, or black and tan, with symmetrical markings, or red, varying from a brownish red to an orangey tan. Some blacks may have a rusty cast or have white or silver hairs mixed in the coat and furnishings. Some reds have black, brown, and/or white hairs mixed in the coat with tan furnishings. With the various colors, the furnishings may be a bit lighter and some may have black masks. A small white spot or fine line of white hairs on the chest is not penalized, but large white patches are undesirable. Color is not a major consideration.

**Gait**—The Affenpinscher has a light, sound, balanced, confident gait and tends to carry itself with comic seriousness. When viewed from the front or rear while walking, the legs move parallel to each other. While trotting the feet will converge toward a midline depending on the speed.

**Temperament**—The general demeanor of the Affenpinscher is game, alert and inquisitive with great loyalty and affection toward its master and friends. The breed is generally quiet but can become vehemently excited when threatened or attacked and is fearless toward any aggressor.

Approved April 10, 1990

# Brussels Griffon

The Brussels Griffon is not a dog of beauty as measured by accepted standards, but one teeming with personality, hence it is not surprising that he makes lasting friends wherever he is known. He comes of neither exalted nor ancient lineage, yet is one of the most distinctive and unusual of all dogs. Although classified as a Toy, there is nothing of the pampered pet in this bundle of jaunty good nature whose keynote is insouciance from his very turned up nose to the tip of his gaily carried tail. No matter what change of fortune the years may bring, he promises to remain the delightful little Belgian street urchin to the end of time.

The German Affenpinscher and the Belgian street dog, combined, were the true foundation from which our Griffons emanated, and there is only meager data available on both of these 17th-century breeds. To all accounts, in Belgium there was a strong conformity to a distinct type in the peasants' dogs of that epoch. These dogs were nearly as large as our Fox Terriers, but heavily built, as are most Belgian animals. Covered with a shaggy, rough, muddy-colored coat and unlovely of feature, but intelligent and interesting in disposition, they were popularly termed *Griffons D'Ecurie,* Stable Griffons, and they paid for their keep by killing the stable vermin. It is not uncommon to run across mention of these loyal companions as *"chiens barbus"* in the old folk songs and tales of the period, for they were to be found in nearly every household.

On the other hand, the Affenpinscher may be said to resemble the Yorkshire Terrier in many particulars, the likeness being particularly noticeable in head properties as well as in the length of body and leg. Doubtless it was felt that the injection of Affenpinscher into the then Griffons would serve to further increase the ratting ability of the Belgian dogs, although for lack of definite proof, this last must remain a conjecture.

At some later date, the smooth-coated Pug, already established in neighboring Holland, was used as a cross with the Griffon. This cross-breeding was responsible for the two types of coat which we have even in our present-day litters.

Whether there was any definite reason for adding the Ruby Spaniel to this combination, we cannot say. At any rate this breed was also brought into the picture and is largely responsible for the facial characteristics and impression which are so much a part of our present-day dog, but which have made it impossible for him to do the work to which he was once well suited.

And so we come to the 20th-century Brussels Griffon, a small compact dog with a harsh coat similar to that of the Irish Terrier or else a smooth coat traceable to the Pug and termed Brabancon, with a short upturned face best described as a "speaking countenance" and a gay carriage.

The Griffon's super intelligence causes him to be sensitive, and it is not uncommon for a young dog, when in the presence of strangers, to display the same self-consciousness as a child in its awkward teens. Although obedient and easily managed, Griffons are sometimes difficult to break to the leash, hence this training should always be started at a very early age. Strange as it may seem, the Brabancons display a marked stubbornness when on leash, although in all other respects they are every bit as tractable as their rough brothers.

As a young puppy, the Griffon must be given the same intelligent care necessary for a puppy of any of the smaller breeds. The average sized Griffon becomes very sturdy as he matures, and he develops into a real comrade, capable of holding his own on hikes and in swimming.

## Official Standard for the Brussels Griffon

**General Appearance**—A toy dog, intelligent, alert, sturdy, with a thickset, short body, a smart carriage and set-up, attracting attention by an almost human expression. There are two distinct types of coat: rough or smooth. Except for coat, there is no difference between the two.

**Size, Proportion, Substance**—*Size*—Weight usually 8 to 10 pounds, and should not exceed 12 pounds. Type and quality are of greater importance than weight, and a smaller dog that is sturdy and well proportioned should not be penalized. *Proportion*—Square, as measured from point of shoulder to rearmost projection of upper thigh and from withers to ground. *Substance*—Thickset, compact with good balance. Well boned.

**Head**—A very important feature. An almost human *expression*. *Eyes* set well apart, very large, black, prominent, and well open. The eyelashes long and black. Eyelids edged with black. *Ears* small and set rather high on the head. May be shown cropped or natural. If natural they are carried semi-erect. **Skull** large and round, with a domed forehead. The stop deep. **Nose** very black, extremely short, its tip being set back deeply between the eyes so as to form a lay-back. The nostrils large. **Disqualifications**—Dudley or butterfly nose. **Lips** edged with black, not pendulous but well brought together, giving a clean finish to the mouth. **Jaws** must be undershot. The incisors of the lower jaw should protrude over the upper incisors. The lower jaw is prominent, rather broad with an upward sweep. Neither teeth nor tongue should show when the mouth is closed. A wry mouth is a serious fault. **Disqualifications**—Bite overshot. Hanging tongue.

**Neck, Topline, Body**—*Neck* medium length, gracefully arched. **Topline**—Back level and short. **Body**—A thickset, short body. Brisket should be broad and deep, ribs well sprung. Short-coupled. **Tail**—Set and held high, docked to about one-third.

**Forequarters**—*Forelegs* medium length, straight in bone, well muscled, set moderately wide apart and straight from the point of the shoulders as viewed from the front. **Pasterns** short and strong. **Feet** round, small, and compact, turned neither in nor out. Toes well arched. Black pads and toenails preferred.

**Hindquarters**—*Hind legs* set true, thighs strong and well muscled, stifles bent, hocks well let down, turning neither in nor out.

**Coat**—The **rough coat** is wiry and dense, the harder and more wiry the better. On no account should the dog look or feel woolly, and there should be no silky hair anywhere. The coat should not be so long as to give a shaggy appearance, but should be distinctly different all over from the smooth coat. The head should be covered with wiry hair, slightly longer around the eyes, nose, cheeks, and chin, thus forming a fringe. The rough coat is hand-stripped and should never appear unkempt. Body coat of sufficient length to determine texture. The coat may be tidied for neatness of appearance, but coats prepared with scissors and/or clippers should be severely penalized. The **smooth coat** is straight, short, tight and glossy, with no trace of wiry hair.

**Color**—Either 1) **Red:** reddish brown with a little black at the whiskers and chin allowable; 2) **Beige:** black and reddish brown mixed, usually with black mask and whiskers; 3) **Black and Tan:** black with uniform reddish brown markings, appearing under the chin, on the legs, above each eye, around the edges of the ears and around the vent; or 4) **Black:** solid black. Any white hairs are a serious fault, except for "frost" on the muzzle of a mature dog, which is natural. **Disqualification**—White spot or blaze anywhere on coat.

**Gait**—Movement is a straightforward, purposeful trot, showing moderate reach and drive, and maintaining a steady topline.

**Temperament**—Intelligent, alert and sensitive. Full of self-importance.

**SCALE OF POINTS**

| *Head* | | | | *Body and General Conformation* | | |
|---|---|---|---|---|---|---|
| Skull | 5 | | | Body (Brisket and Rib) | 15 | |
| Nose and Stop | 10 | | | Gait | 10 | |
| Eyes | 5 | | | Legs and Feet | 5 | |
| Bite, Chin and Jaws | 10 | | | General Appearance (Neck, | | |
| Ears | 5 | 35 | | Topline and Tail carriage) | 10 | 40 |
| *Coat* | | | | | | |
| Color | 12 | | | | | |
| Texture | 13 | 25 | TOTAL | | | 100 |

**DISQUALIFICATIONS**

*Dudley or butterfly nose.*
*Bite overshot.*
*Hanging tongue.*
*White spot or blaze anywhere on coat.*

Approved September 11, 1990

# Chihuahua

## (Chih-wah-wah)

Long Coat Chihuahua

Smooth Coat Chihuahua

**W**hile little or nothing is known of the previous history of the Toltecs, it has been established that they existed in what is now Mexico as early as the 9th century A.D., and that during their several centuries of occupancy they had a breed of dog called the Techichi. This dog was small, although not tiny, and of heavy-boned structure. His coat was long, while his most distinctive feature was muteness.

The Techichi, regarded as indigenous to Central America, is the progenitor of the Chihuahua that now enjoys popularity throughout the United States, where he has been bred to his greatest perfection. No records of the Techichi are, so far, available prior to the 9th century, but it seems probable that his ancestors were in the locality prior to the advent of the Maya tribes about the 5th century.

The evidence firmly establishing the Techichi to the Toltec period is found in pictures carved on stones—they may be found today in the Monastery of Huejotzingo, on the highway from Mexico City to Puebla. This monastery was constructed by the Franciscan Monks around 1530 from materials of the existing Pyramids of Cholula, built by the Toltecs. The carvings give a full-head view and a picture of an entire dog that closely approximates the Chihuahua of modern times. There also are remains of pyramid constructions and some pointers to the early existence of the Techichi at Chichen Itza in distant Yucatan.

Toltec civilization was centered principally around Tula, which is close to the present Mexico City, and there one finds the most abundant relics of this ancient breed. For that reason, there always has been speculation regarding the discovery of the earliest specimens of the modern breed in the State of Chihuahua. The dogs were found, about 1850, in some old ruins close to Casas

428

Grandes, said to be the remains of a palace built by Emperor Montezuma I.

The conclusions of K. de Blinde, a Mexican breeder and authority who spent years traversing sections of the country on horseback, were that the present form of Chihuahua evolved from crossing the Techichi with the small hairless dog brought from Asia to Alaska over the land bridge where the Bering Strait now runs. This hairless dog, similar to the one found in China, was responsible for the reduction in size.

The Aztec conquerors of the Toltecs flourished for several centuries, and just prior to the coming of Hernando Cortés civilization was at a high state and the wealth prodigious. Dogs of the rich were highly regarded, and the blue-colored ones were held as sacred. Paradoxical as it seems, the common people found little use for this same breed, and there are even tales that they were eaten.

The stormlike career of Cortés in Mexico during 1519–20 left little of either Aztec wealth of civilization. Practically all Montezuma's possessions were wrung from his dying hands, and it is only natural that his dogs became lost for several centuries.

While the Techichi's principal home was Mexico, there is a historic letter written by Christopher Columbus to the King of Spain that adds a curious note to knowledge of the breed. Reporting on the seizure of the present island of Cuba, Columbus stated that he found: "A small kind of dogs, which were mute and did not bark, as usual, but were domesticated." These dogs could not have been taken to Cuba by the Aztecs, who were not a seafaring people.

Legend and history are rich in tales of the ancestors of the present Chihuahua. He is described as a popular pet, as well as a religious necessity, among the ancient Toltec tribes and later among the Aztecs. Archaeologists have discovered remains of this breed in human graves in Mexico and in parts of the United States.

The phenomenon is believed due to the part the dog played in the religious and mythological life of the Aztecs. He was employed in connection with the worship of deities, with the voyage of the soul in the underworld, and in relation to the human body. With the sacrifice of a dog with a red skin, burning it to ashes with the corpse of the deceased, the sins of the human were supposed to be transferred to the dog, and the indignation of the deity thus averted. The dog also was credited with guiding the human soul through the dark regions of the underworld, fighting off evil spirits and leading the soul of the deceased safely to its ultimate destination.

The modern Chihuahua is quite different from his early ancestors, with his variegated colors ranging from snow white to jet black. Mexico favors the jet black with tan markings, and the black and white spotted. The United States prefers the solid colors.

American breeders have produced a diminutive dog that has few comparisons, even among other breeds, in size, symmetry, and conformation, as well as intelligence and alertness. Curiously, the Chihuahua is clannish, recognizing and preferring his own kind, and, as a rule, not liking dogs of other breeds. The smooth-coated are the most numerous in the United States, and the most clannish, but the long-coated Chihuahua is rapidly increasing. It has all the characteristics of the smooth.

## Official Standard for the Chihuahua

**General Appearance**—A graceful, alert, swift-moving little dog with saucy expression, compact, and with terrier-like qualities of temperament.

**Size, Proportion, Substance**—*Weight*—A well balanced little dog not to exceed 6 pounds. *Proportion*—The body is off-square; hence, slightly longer when measured from point of shoulder to point of buttocks, than height at the withers. Somewhat shorter bodies are preferred in males. *Disqualification*—Any dog over 6 pounds in weight.

**Head**—A well rounded "apple-dome" skull, with or without molera. *Expression*—Saucy. *Eyes*—Full, but not protruding, balanced, set well apart—luminous dark or luminous ruby. (Light eyes in blond or white-colored dogs permissible.) *Ears*—Large, erect type ears, held more upright when alert, but flaring to the sides at a 45 degree angle when in repose, giving breadth between the ears. *Muzzle*—Moderately short, slightly pointed. Cheeks and jaws lean. *Nose*—Self-colored in blond types, or black. In moles, blues, and chocolates, they are self-colored. In blond types, pink nose permissible. *Bite*—Level or scissors. Overshot or undershot bite, or any distortion of the bite or jaw, should be penalized as a serious fault. *Disqualifications*—Broken down or cropped ears.

**Neck, Topline, Body**—*Neck*—Slightly arched, gracefully sloping into lean shoulders. *Topline*—Level. *Body*—Ribs rounded and well sprung (but not too much "barrel-shaped"). *Tail*—Moderately long, carried sickle either up or out, or in a loop over the back, with tip just touching the back. (Never tucked between legs.) *Disqualifications*—Cropped tail, bobtail.

**Forequarters**—*Shoulders*—Lean, sloping into a slightly broadening support above straight forelegs that set well under, giving a free play at the elbows. Shoulders should be well up, giving balance and soundness, sloping into a level back. (Never down or low.) This gives a chestiness, and strength of forequarters, yet not of the "Bulldog" chest. *Feet*—A small, dainty foot with toes well split up but not spread, pads cushioned. (Neither the hare nor the cat foot.) *Pasterns*—Fine.

**Hindquarters**—Muscular, with hocks well apart, neither out nor in, well let down, firm and sturdy. The feet are as in front.

**Coat**—In the *Smooth Coats*, the coat should be of soft texture, close and glossy. (Heavier coats with undercoats permissible.) Coat placed well over body with ruff on neck preferred, and more scanty on head and ears. Hair on tail preferred furry. In **Long Coats**, the coat should be of a soft texture, either flat or slightly curly, with undercoat preferred. *Ears*—Fringed. (Heavily fringed ears may be tipped slightly if due to the fringes and not to weak ear leather, never down.) *Tail*—Full and long (as a plume). Feathering on feet and legs, pants on hind legs and large ruff on the neck desired and preferred. *Disqualification*—In Long Coats, too thin coat that resembles bareness.

**Color**—Any color—Solid, marked or splashed.

**Gait**—The Chihuahua should move swiftly with a firm, sturdy action, with good reach in front equal to the drive from the rear. From the rear, the hocks remain parallel to each other, and the foot fall of the rear legs follows directly behind that of the forelegs. The legs, both front and rear, will tend to converge slightly toward a central line of gravity as speed increases. The side view shows good, strong drive in the rear and plenty of reach in the front, with head carried high. The topline should remain firm and the backline level as the dog moves.

**Temperament**—Alert, with terrier-like qualities.

### DISQUALIFICATIONS

*Any dog over 6 pounds in weight.*
*Broken down or cropped ears.*
*Cropped tail, bobtail.*
*In* Long Coats, *too thin coat that resembles bareness.*

Approved September 11, 1990

# Chinese Crested

Chinese Crested (Hairless)

Chinese Crested (Powderpuff)

Although the exact origin of the Chinese Crested is unknown, it is believed to have evolved from African hairless dogs which were reduced in size by the Chinese, who seemed to like smaller Toy breeds. The breed in earlier times was known by several different names including the Chinese Hairless, the Chinese Edible Dog, the Chinese Ship Dog, and the Chinese Royal Hairless. It also took on local nicknames depending on where it was found. Thus, in Egypt it was called a Pyramid or Giza Hairless, in southern Africa it was the South African Hairless, and in Turkey a larger version was known as the Turkish Hairless.

It is believed that for centuries Chinese sailors sailed the high seas with the breed on board, and that puppies were frequently traded with local merchants at port cities. It is known that during the time of the plagues that originated in China, hairless dogs were stowed on board ships to hunt vermin which were heavily infested with fleas carrying the disease. Today the breed can still be found in ancient port cities around the world.

Spanish explorers found Chinese Crested dogs in Mexico and other parts of Central and South America as early as the 1500s. British, French and Portuguese explorers likewise found the breed in various parts of Africa and Asia during the 1700s and 1800s. The diaries of early missionaries, who frequently traveled with the explorers, describe finding the breed in many of these countries.

By the mid-19th century, Cresteds began to appear in numerous European paintings and prints. During the 1850s and 1860s, some dogs of the breed were exhibited at a local zoological show in England, and photos of them were published, but no breeding program was established.

Entries of the breed at American dog shows began in the late 1800s. In the 1800s, Ida Garrett, a young, New York newspaperwoman, became interested in Cresteds and other hairless breeds. Over the course of 60 years Mrs. Garrett bred, exhibited, and wrote extensively about dogs—hairless breeds in particular. She traveled widely and imported several prized Crested. In the 1920s she assisted Debra Woods of Homestead, Florida in obtaining Chinese Cresteds and other hairless breeds, and the two women became close associates. For nearly 40 years they jointly promoted the Chinese Crested—Mrs. Garrett through her prolific writing, speaking, and dog club activities, and Mrs. Woods through her extensive breeding, advertising, and registration service.

Mrs. Woods began keeping a log of all of her dogs in the 1930s and by the 1950s it had become a registration service for all hairless breeds, and eventually the American Hairless Dog Club. She took great pride in maintaining these stud books and closely guarded them until her death in 1969. They were then maintained for nearly 12 years by Jo Ann Orlik and then became the property of the American Chinese Crested Club, founded in 1979.

Gypsy Rose Lee, the famous stage personality, acquired a Crested from her sister, June Havoc, in the early 1950s and became an ardent breeder and helped considerably in publicizing the breed.

The Chinese Crested was admitted to AKC Miscellaneous classification in September 1985. It became eligible for AKC registration effective February 1, 1991, and eligible to show at AKC licensed events on April 1, 1991.

At first sight the two types of Chinese Crested—Hairless and Powderpuff— may appear to be different breeds. However, as one becomes more familiar with the breed it is easy to see that they are almost exactly the same, except that the coated have more hair. The Hairless should have hair on its head, feet and tail—the Powderpuff is born fully coated. Breeding a Hairless to a Hairless, or a Hairless to a Powderpuff, can produce either type. However, breeding a Powderpuff to a Powderpuff, will always produce the Powderpuff type.

A unique feature of hairless dogs is that they have sweat glands. Rather than panting to release body heat as coated dogs do, they simply sweat. Properly cared for, the skin of the Hairless remains soft to the touch, yet it is thicker and tougher than that of a coated dog and it heals very quickly if scratched or cut.

## Official Standard for the Chinese Crested

**General Appearance**—A Toy dog, fine-boned, elegant and graceful. The distinct varieties are born in the same litter. The Hairless with hair only on the head, tail and feet and the Powderpuff, completely covered with hair. The breed serves as a loving companion, playful and entertaining.

**Size, Proportion, Substance**—*Size*—Ideally 11 to 13 inches. However, dogs that are slightly larger or smaller may be given full consideration. ***Proportion*** rectangular—

proportioned to allow for freedom of movement. Body length from withers to base of tail is slightly longer than the height at the withers. *Substance*—Fine-boned and slender but not so refined as to appear breakable or alternatively, not a robust, heavy structure.

**Head**—*Expression*—Alert and intense. *Eyes* almond-shaped, set wide apart. Dark-colored dogs have dark-colored eyes, and lighter-colored dogs may have lighter-colored eyes. Eye rims match the coloring of the dog. *Ears*—Uncropped, large and erect, placed so that the base of the ear is level with the outside corner of the eye. *Skull* is arched gently over the occiput from ear to ear. Distance from occiput to stop equal to distance from stop to tip of nose. The head is wedge-shaped viewed from above and the side. *Stop*—Slight but distinct. *Muzzle*—Cheeks taper cleanly into the muzzle. *Nose*—Dark in dark-colored dogs; may be lighter in lighter-colored dogs. Pigment is solid. *Lips* are clean and tight. *Bite*—Scissors or level in both varieties. Missing teeth in the Powderpuff are to be faulted. The Hairless variety is not to be penalized for absence of full dentition.

**Neck, Topline, Body**—*Neck* is lean and clean, slightly arched from the withers to the base of the skull and carried high. *Topline* level to slightly sloping croup. *Body*—Brisket extends to the elbow. Breastbone is not prominent. Ribs are well developed. The depth of the chest tapers to a moderate tuck-up at the flanks. Light in loin. *Tail* is slender and tapers to a curve. It is long enough to reach the hock. When dog is in motion, the tail is carried gaily and may be carried slightly forward over the back. At rest the tail is down with a slight curve upward at the end resembling a sickle. In the Hairless variety, two-thirds of the end of the tail is covered by long, flowing feathering referred to as a plume. The Powderpuff variety's tail is completely covered with hair.

**Forequarters**—*Angulation*—Layback of shoulders is 45 degrees to point of shoulder allowing for good reach. *Shoulders*—Clean and narrow. *Elbows*—Close to body. *Legs*—Long, slender and straight. *Pasterns*—Upright, fine and strong. Dewclaws may be removed. *Feet*—Hare foot, narrow with elongated toes. Nails are trimmed to moderate length.

**Hindquarters**—*Angulation*—Stifle moderately angulated. From hock joint to ground perpendicular. Dewclaws may be removed. *Feet*—Same as forequarters.

**Coat**—The Hairless variety has hair on certain portions of the body: the head (called a crest), the tail (called a plume) and the feet from the toes to the front pasterns and rear hock joints (called socks). The texture of all hair is soft and silky, flowing to any length. Placement of hair is not as important as overall type. Areas that have hair usually taper off slightly. Wherever the body is hairless, the skin is soft and smooth. Head Crest begins at the stop and tapers off between the base of the skull and the back of the neck. Hair on the ears and face is permitted on the Hairless and may be trimmed for neatness in both varieties. Tail Plume is described under Tail. The Powderpuff variety is completely covered with a double soft and silky coat. Close examination reveals long thin guard hairs over the short silky undercoat. The coat is straight, of moderate density and length. Excessively heavy, kinky or curly coat is to be penalized. Grooming is minimal—consisting of presenting a clean and neat appearance.

**Color**—Any color or combination of colors.

**Gait**—Lively, agile and smooth without being stilted or hackneyed. Comes and goes at a trot moving in a straight line.

**Temperament**—Gay and alert.

Approved June 12, 1990

# English Toy Spaniel

Since the spread of civilization has been from East to West, it is only natural that most of our oldest breeds of dog should trace their origin to the eastern countries. Such is the case of the English Toy Spaniel, an affectionate, intelligent little dog that captivated royalty, aristocrats, and the wealthy for at least three centuries.

It has been a widespread fallacy that the Toy Spaniel made its first appearance in England during the reign of King Charles II, in the 17th century, for it was in honor of this sovereign that the black-and-tan variety took its name. Yet the Toy Spaniel had been known in England and in Scotland more than a hundred years before.

Just how long the Toy Spaniel had been known in Europe, particularly the south of Europe, before it was carried to England, must remain a matter of doubt. Yet most authorities are agreed that it goes back to Japan, and possibly China, of very ancient times.

According to Leighton, the English Toy Spaniel had its origin in Japan, was taken from there to Spain, and thence to England. Yet the extremely short nose of the breed might constitute evidence that it went from Spain to Japan, where it developed its present characteristics. There is a story, also, that specimens of this Toy breed were brought from Japan by Captain Saris, a British naval officer, in 1613. They were presents from the Emperor of Japan—every Japanese royal present always included dogs—to King James I.

The tale of Captain Saris seems a logical one, but it cannot be accepted as marking the debut of the Toy Spaniel into England and Scotland. The breed was known in England long before that, for Dr. Johannes Caius, celebrated professor and the physician to Queen Elizabeth, included it in his work *Of English Dogges*. He refers to it as the "Spaniell Gentle, otherwise called the Comforter." His other references stamp it as almost the identical dog of today.

It is difficult to associate the Toy Spaniel with the austere Elizabeth; evidence that the breed was the favorite of the warmer-hearted Mary, Queen of Scots, in the same century is much more acceptable. The early years of Mary, during the first third of the 16th century, were spent in France. When she returned to Scotland as Queen, she brought specimens of the breed with her, and these dogs remained her favorites up to the time of her execution. In fact, her especial pet refused to leave her, even on the scaffold.

All Toy Spaniels up to the time of King Charles II appear to have been of the black-and-tan variety, later called the King Charles. This king's favorites were brought over from France by Henrietta of Orleans, and one is described as a black and white.

The development of the other varieties—the Prince Charles, which is a tricolor of white, black, and tan; the Ruby, which is chestnut red; and the Blenheim, which is white and chestnut red—occurred at later times. All are identical in their characteristics, with the exception of color. For a long time they were bred without any reference to color. Often the same litter would produce dogs of several varieties. It is only in modern times that the science of color breeding set the different varieties apart.

The history of the Blenheim variety seems more definite than that of the King Charles, although in some ways incompatible with other data. The development of the Blenheim, or red and white, is credited to John Churchill, the first Duke of Marlborough. Churchill, famous soldier and diplomat, was made an Earl in 1689, and became a Duke in 1702. At that time he acquired Blenheim, which has been the family seat of the Marlboroughs ever since.

It is said by Ash that the first Duke received as a present from China a pair of red-and-white Cocker Spaniels, and that these dogs were the basis of his subsequent breeding. The Chinese origin of the breed is mentioned also by Lady de Gex, who claims that during the 15th and 16th centuries there were carried from China to Italy numerous specimens of both red-and-white and black-and-white spaniels. These dogs subsequently were crossed with Cockers and Springers, intensifying the sporting instincts which the Toy still retains.

The Dukes of Marlborough bred the Blenheim variety for many generations, and apparently they did so without the infusion of much outside blood— unless it were that of the Cocker and other varieties of spaniel. It was said by Scott in 1800 that the Duke of Marlborough's Blenheims were the smallest and best Cockers in England. They were used very successfully for woodcock shooting. And writers of a still later period describe the dogs found at Blenheim as larger than other specimens of the red and white. Also, the Marlborough strain did not have such exaggerated short noses.

Regardless of the early history of the English Toy Spaniel, it seems certain that many specimens of modern times trace their origin back to various small spaniels of England. Selective breeding has reduced them down to the limits of nine to twelve pounds, but it has not altogether erased their natural hunting instincts.

## Official Standard for the English Toy Spaniel

**General Appearance**—The English Toy Spaniel is a compact, cobby and essentially square toy dog possessed of a short-nosed, domed head, a merry and affectionate demeanor and a silky, flowing coat. His compact, sturdy body and charming temperament, together with his rounded head, lustrous dark eye, and well cushioned face, proclaim him a dog of distinction and character. *The important characteristics of the breed are exemplified by the head.*

**Size, Proportion, Substance**—*Size*—The most desirable weight of an adult is eight to fourteen pounds. General symmetry and substance are more important than the actual weight; however, all other things being equal, the smaller sized dog is to be preferred. *Proportion*—Compact and essentially square in shape, built on cobby lines. *Substance*—Sturdy of frame, solidly constructed.

**Head**—Head large in comparison to size, with a plush, chubby look, albeit with a degree of refinement which prevents it from being coarse. *Expression*—Soft and appealing, indicating an intelligent nature. *Eyes*—Large and very dark brown or black, set squarely on line with the nose, with little or no white showing. The eye rims should be black. *Ears*—Very long and set low and close to the head, fringed with heavy feathering. *Skull*—High and well domed; from the side, curves as far out over the eyes as possible. *Stop*—Deep and well-defined. *Muzzle*—Very short, with the nose well laid back and with well developed cushioning under the eyes. *Jaw*—Square, broad, and deep, and well turned up, with lips properly meeting to give a finished appearance. *Nose*—Large and jet black in color, with large, wide open nostrils. *Bite*—Slightly undershot; teeth not to show. A wry mouth should be penalized; a hanging tongue is extremely objectionable.

**Neck, Topline, Body**—*Neck*—Moderate in length; nicely arched. *Topline*—Level. *Body*—Short, compact, square and deep, on cobby lines, with a broad back. Sturdy of frame, with good rib and deep brisket. *Tail*—The tail is docked to two to four inches in length and carried at or just slightly above the level of the back. The set of the tail is at the back's level. Many are born with a shorter or screw tail which is acceptable. The feather on the tail should be silky and from three to four inches in length, constituting a marked "flag" of a square shape. The tail and its carriage is an index of the breed's attitude and character.

**Forequarters**—Shoulders well laid back; legs well boned and strong, dropping straight down from the elbow; strong in pastern. Feet, front and rear, are neat and compact; fused toes are often seen and are acceptable.

**Hindquarters**—Rear legs are well muscled and nicely angulated to indicate strength, and parallel of hock.

**Coat**—Profusely coated, heavy fringing on the ears, body, and on the chest, and with flowing feathering on both the front and hind legs, and feathering on the feet. The coat is straight or only slightly wavy, with a silken, glossy texture. Although the Blenheim and the Ruby rarely gain the length of coat and ears of the Prince Charles and King Charles, good coats and long ear fringes are a desired and prized attribute. Overtrimming of the body, feet or tail fringings should be penalized.

**Color**—The Blenheim (red and white) consists of a pearly white ground with deep red or chestnut markings evenly distributed in large patches. The ears and the cheeks are red, with a blaze of white extending from the nose up the forehead and ending between the ears in a crescentic curve. It is preferable that there be red markings around both eyes. The Blenheim often carries a thumb mark or "Blenheim Spot" placed on the top and the center of the skull. The Prince Charles (tricolor) consists of a pearly white ground, with evenly distributed black patches, solid black ears and black face markings. It is preferable that there be black markings around both eyes. The tan markings are of a rich color, and on the face, over the eyes, in the lining of the ears, and under the tail. The King Charles (black and tan) is a rich, glossy black with bright mahogany tan markings appearing on the cheeks, lining of the ears, over the eyes, on the legs and underneath the tail. The presence of a small white chest patch about the size of a quarter, or a few white hairs on the chest of a King Charles Spaniel are not to be penalized; other white markings are an extremely serious fault. The Ruby is a self-colored, rich mahogany red. The presence of a small white chest patch about the size of a quarter, or a few white hairs on the chest of a Ruby Spaniel are not to be penalized. Other white markings are an extremely serious fault.

**Gait**—Elegant with good reach in the front, and sound, driving rear action. The gait as a whole is free and lively, evidencing stable character and correct construction. In profile, the movement exhibits a good length of stride, and viewed from front and rear it is straight and true, resulting from straight-boned fronts and properly made and muscled hindquarters.

**Temperament**—The English Toy Spaniel is a bright and interested little dog, affectionate and willing to please.

Approved June 13, 1989

# Italian Greyhound

The Italian Greyhound is the smallest of the family of gazehounds (dogs that hunt by sight). The breed is believed to have originated more than 2,000 years ago in the Mediterranean basin, possibly in the countries now known as Greece and Turkey. This belief is based on the depiction of miniature Greyhounds in the early decorative arts of these countries and on the archaeological discoveries of small Greyhound skeletons. Though never excessively popular, by the Middle Ages the breed had become distributed throughout Southern Europe and was a favorite of the Italians of the 16th century with whom miniature dogs were much in demand. Thus they became known as "Italian Greyhounds." As a breed it has survived many centuries, prized for its beauty, small size and sweet disposition. They were frequently included in the Renaissance paintings of such artists as Giotto, Carpaccio, Memling, Van der Weyden, Gerard David, Hieronymus Bosch and others.

The breed was a favorite of various royal families of Europe including the consort of England's James I, Anne of Denmark; Mary Beatrice d'Este of Modena, the Italian consort of James II; Frederick the Great of Prussia; Catherine the Great of Russia and Queen Victoria.

The first volume of the English Kennel Club's stud book listed 40 of the breed. Volume III of the American Kennel Club's Stud Book (1886) contains the first Italian Greyhound registration in this country. However, it was not until 1950 that as many as 50 were registered in the United States in a single year and 1957 before an equal number were registered in Great Britain.

Following both World Wars, when the breed was in danger of extinction, fresh stock was imported into England from the United States, giving evidence of the high quality to be found in America. The last twenty years have seen the breed enjoying its greatest recorded popularity ever. Italian Greyhounds have competed successfully in all parts of the country in dog shows and obedience trials with a number of Best-in-Show awards to its credit.

The Italian Greyhound is a true Greyhound in miniature. There is some difference of opinion as to whether he was originally bred for hunting small game or was meant to be simply a pet and companion. It seems most likely that he filled both roles, and for this reason he is very adaptable to both city and country living. He is rather luxury loving and enjoys the comforts of an apartment; at the same time being a true hound, he likes exercise and outdoor activities.

The Italian Greyhound can weigh as little as 5 lbs. or as much as 14 or 15 lbs., but the average weight is about 8 lbs. His coat is short and smooth and requires little grooming. He is odorless and sheds little. Though he gives the impression of fragility, the breed is hardy, seldom ill, and thrives in such northern countries as Sweden and Scotland. The bitches are easy whelpers and good mothers.

Perhaps the most outstanding characteristic of the Italian Greyhound is his affectionate disposition. He thrives best when this affection is returned, and is happiest with his owner and immediate family though he may sometimes seem a trifle aloof with strangers. He is sensitive, alert and intelligent and remains playful until long past puppyhood. He adapts to most households and gets along well with children and with other pets.

While very similar in appearance to the Greyhound, the Italian Greyhound is considerably smaller and more slender in all proportions. He differs also from his larger relative in his characteristic and elegant gait, high stepping and free. His coat should be fine, smooth and glossy, and any color and markings are acceptable except that a dog with brindle markings or a dog with the tan markings normally found on black and tan dogs of other breeds will be disqualified in the show rings.

## Official Standard for the Italian Greyhound

**Description**—The Italian Greyhound is very similar to the Greyhound, but much smaller and more slender in all proportions and of ideal elegance and grace.

**Head**—Narrow and long, tapering to nose, with a slight suggestion of stop. *Skull*—Rather long, almost flat. *Muzzle*—Long and fine. *Nose*—Dark. It may be black or brown or in keeping with the color of the dog. A light or partly pigmented nose is a fault. *Teeth*—Scissors bite. A badly undershot or overshot mouth is a fault. *Eyes*—Dark, bright, intelligent, medium in size. Very light eyes are a fault. *Ears*—Small, fine in texture; thrown back and folded except when alerted, then carried folded at right angles to the head. Erect or button ears severely penalized.

**Neck**—Long, slender and gracefully arched.

**Body**—Of medium length, short coupled; high at withers, back curved and drooping at hindquarters, the highest point of curve at start of loin, creating a definite tuck-up at flanks.

**Shoulders**—Long and sloping.

**Chest**—Deep and narrow.

**Forelegs**—Long, straight, set well under shoulder; strong pasterns, fine bone.

**Hindquarters**—Long, well-muscled thigh; hind legs parallel when viewed from behind, hocks well let down, well-bent stifle.

**Feet**—Harefoot with well-arched toes. Removal of dewclaws optional.

**Tail**—Slender and tapering to a curved end, long enough to reach the hock; set low, carried low. Ring tail a serious fault, gay tail a fault.

**Coat**—Skin fine and supple, hair short, glossy like satin and soft to the touch.

**Color**—Any color and markings are acceptable except that a dog with brindle markings and a dog with the tan markings normally found on black and tan dogs of other breeds must be disqualified.

**Action**—High stepping and free, front and hind legs to move forward in a straight line.

**Size**—Height at withers ideally 13 inches to 15 inches.

### DISQUALIFICATION

*A dog with brindle markings. A dog with the tan markings normally found on black and tan dogs of other breeds.*

Approved December 14, 1976

# Japanese Chin

In Japan, there are *Inu* (dogs) and there are Chin. To the Japanese the distinction needs no clarification. Chin are royalty. They are descendants of dogs that warmed the laps of Chinese aristocracy and kept court with the ladies of the Imperial Palace.

That the Japanese Chin is a very old Toy breed is attested to by the fact that dogs closely resembling them have been noted on the old Chinese temples as well as on ancient pottery and embroideries. Presumably these dogs originated in China, centuries ago, since it is reported that one of the Chinese emperors gave a pair to the emperor of Japan. They were kept in the hands of the nobility and frequently used as gifts of esteem to diplomats and to foreigners who had rendered some outstanding service to Japan.

When in 1853 Commodore Perry steamed into the harbor of Wraga and opened the country's trade to the world, he was presented with some of these dogs; then he in turn gave a pair to Queen Victoria. In time, specimens came to America, but there remains no record as to their final destination here. Others gravitated to this country as a result of thieving among Japanese kennels, when ships took the dogs all over the world. Every ship from the Orient carried several to ready buyers. Unfortunately, the dogs were not long-lived; World War I cut off the supply to America to such an extent that we had to use what we had to maintain and improve the breed. Japan, too, suffered losses among her prized Chin when earthquakes played havoc among her breeders. Since then Japanese fanciers have taken up other breeds and the supply of Chin has diminished. However, Japanese Chin are widely distributed, with breeders in England, France, Switzerland, Austria and Germany, where the high quality of the dogs has been maintained.

From its introduction until August 9, 1977, the breed was known and registered by the AKC as the Japanese Spaniel. Effective with that date, its name officially became the Japanese Chin.

There are different types of Japanese Chin. Essentially, though, the characteristic specimen must look Oriental; must be aristocratic in appearance, stylish in carriage. The larger dog is apt to lack these features, therefore only the small dog is considered of show type. Some specimens carry profuse coats, others shorter and coarser-textured coats; either is correct, but a woolly coat is not favored.

The majority of dogs are black-and-white, although there are whites with lemon or red markings, including all shades from pale lemon to deep red as well as brindle. In each case the nose color must match the markings, with dark eyes regardless. Colors may be mixed within the litter in cases where the sire or dam is of other than pure black-and-white inheritance. Frequently a lemon-and-white produces only black-and-white offspring, and it may require several generations before the colors revert. Years ago, when a black-and-white dog had too much black on the body, a lemon-and-white mate was used in the hope of breaking the color in the next generation. The lemon-and-whites often had more profuse coats, so these were used to improve hair quantity as well as texture. It seems more difficult to produce a good lemon-and-white than a good black-and-white.

A Japanese Chin is a good companion, bright and alert. Naturally clean and game, too, he makes an ideal pet that can thrive in almost any climate. He is sensitive, though, with definite likes and dislikes, but rarely, if ever, does he forget friend or foe.

## Official Standard for the Japanese Chin

**General Appearance**—That of a lively, high-bred little dog with dainty appearance, smart, compact carriage and profuse coat. These dogs should be essentially stylish in movement, lifting the feet high when in action, carrying the tail (which is heavily feathered, proudly curved or plumed) over the back. In size they vary considerably, but the smaller they are the better, provided type and quality are not sacrificed. When divided by weight, classes should be under and over 7 pounds.

**Head**—Should be large for the size of the dog, with broad skull, rounded in front. *Eyes*—Large, dark, lustrous, rather prominent and set wide apart. *Ears*—Small and V-shaped, nicely feathered, set wide apart and high on the head and carried slightly forward. *Nose*—Very short in the muzzle part. The end or nose proper should be wide, with open nostrils, and must be the color of the dog's markings, *i.e.* black in black-marked dogs, and red or deep flesh color in red or lemon-marked dogs. It shall be a disqualification for a black and white Japanese Chin to have a nose any other color than black.

**Neck**—Should be short and moderately thick.

**Body**—Should be squarely and compactly built, wide in chest, "cobby" in shape. The length of the dog's body should be about its height.

**Tail**—Must be well twisted to either right or left from root and carried up over back and flow on opposite side; it should be profusely covered with long hair (ring tails not desirable).

**Legs**—The bones of the legs should be small, giving them a slender appearance, and they should be well feathered.

**Feet**—Small and shaped somewhat long; the dog stands up on its toes somewhat. If feathered, the tufts should never increase in width of the foot, but only its length a trifle.

**Coat**—Profuse, long, straight, rather silky. It should be absolutely free from wave or curl, and not lie too flat, but have a tendency to stand out, especially at the neck, so as to give a thick mane or ruff, which with profuse feathering on thighs and tail gives a very showy appearance.

**Color**—The dogs should be either black and white or red and white, *i.e.* parti-colored. The term red includes all shades of sable, brindle, lemon and orange, but the brighter and clearer the red the better. The white should be clear white, and the color, whether black or red, should be evenly distributed patches over the body, cheek and ears.

### SCALE OF POINTS

| | | | |
|---|---|---|---|
| Head and neck | 10 | Tail | 10 |
| Eyes | 10 | Feet and legs | 5 |
| Ears | 5 | Coat and markings | 15 |
| Muzzle | 10 | Action | 5 |
| Nose | 5 | Size | 10 |
| Body | 15 | TOTAL | 100 |

### DISQUALIFICATION

*In black and whites, a nose any other color than black.*

# Maltese

The Maltese is known as "ye ancient dogge of Malta," which for more than 28 centuries has been an aristocrat of the canine world.

Malta has been prominent in history from earliest times. Though settled by the Phoenicians about 1500 B.C., we know that other Mediterranean races lived there as far back as 3500 B.C. Many writers of old have spoken in glowing terms of the fame and opulence of Malta, justly celebrated for proficiency in the arts and crafts of peace and war as well as for the high state of civilization of its people. Amid these surroundings, among these people, the tiny Maltese lived.

At the time of the Apostle Paul, Publius, the Roman governor of Malta, had a Maltese named Issa of which he was very fond. In this connection the poet Marcus Valerius Martialis (Martial), born in A.D. 38 at Bilbilis in Spain, made this attachment famous in one of his celebrated epigrams:

> Issa is more frolicsome than Catulla's sparrow. Issa is purer than a dove's kiss. Issa is gentler than a maiden. Issa is more precious than Indian gems . . . Lest the last days that she sees light should snatch her from him forever, Publius has had her picture painted.

This last referred to a painting of Issa said to have been so lifelike that it was difficult to tell the picture from the living dog.

Besides Martial, other ancient authors discoursed on the beauty, intelligence, and lovable qualities of Maltese dogs, among them Callimachus the Elder (384–322 B.C.); Strabo (c. B.C.–A.D. 24); Pliny the Elder (A.D. 23–79); Saint Clement of Alexandria in the 2nd century; and others equally celebrated.

The Greeks erected tombs to their Maltese, and from the 5th century on, Greek ceramic art shows innumerable paintings of these dogs. A fine model of one was dug up in the Fayum in Egypt—it is not unlikely that this was the kind of dog worshipped by the Egyptians. And it is said that queens of old served the choicest foods out of golden vases to their Maltese.

Dr. Caius (1570), physician to Queen Elizabeth, wrote in Latin:

There is among us another kind of highbred dogs, but outside the common run those which Callimachus called Melitei from the Island of Melita . . . That kind is very small indeed and chiefly sought after for the pleasure and amusement of women. The smaller the kind, the more pleasing it is; so that they may carry them in their bosoms, in their beds and in their arms while in their carriages.

Aldrovanus, who died in 1607 and who also wrote in Latin, says he saw one of these dogs sold for the equivalent of $2000. Considering the value of the dollar in the time of Queen Elizabeth, the price paid would be equal to a five-figure sum in this day. Since the time of Good Queen Bess the Maltese has often been mentioned, writers invariably drawing attention to its small size. In 1607 E. Topsell said they were "not bigger than common ferrets." Almost 200 years later, in 1792, Linnaeus referred to them as being "about the size of squirrels," while Danberton in his *History Naturelle* writes that "ladies carried them in their sleeves."

The first Maltese exhibited in the United States was white and listed as a Maltese Lion Dog at Westminster's first show in 1877. At the 1879 Westminster a colored Maltese was exhibited as a Maltese Skye Terrier. The American Kennel Club accepted the Maltese for registration in 1888.

The fact that for so many centuries Maltese have been the household pets of people of culture, wealth, and fastidious taste may account for their refinement, fidelity, and cleanliness. It should be remembered that they are spaniels, not terriers, and that, as history has long recorded them, they are healthy and spirited even though tiny.

## Official Standard for the Maltese

**General Appearance**—The Maltese is a toy dog covered from head to foot with a mantle of long, silky, white hair. He is a gentle-mannered and affectionate, eager and sprightly in action, and, despite his size, possessed of the vigor needed for the satisfactory companion.

**Head**—Of medium length and in proportion to the size of the dog. *The skull* is slightly rounded on top, the stop moderate. *The drop ears* are rather low set and heavily feathered with long hair that hangs close to the head. *Eyes* are set not too far apart; they are very dark and round, their black rims enhancing the gentle yet alert expression. *The muzzle* is of medium length, fine and tapered but not snipy. *The nose* is black. *The teeth* meet in an even, edge-to-edge bite, or in a scissors bite.

**Neck**—Sufficient length of neck is desirable as promoting a high carriage of the head.

**Body**—Compact, the height from the withers to the ground equaling the length from the withers to the root of the tail. Shoulder blades are sloping, the elbows well knit and held close to the body. The back is level in topline, the ribs well sprung. The chest is fairly deep, the loins taut, strong, and just slightly tucked up underneath.

**Tail**—A long-haired plume carried gracefully over the back, its tip lying to the side over the quarter.

**Legs and Feet**—Legs are fine-boned and nicely feathered. Forelegs are straight, their pastern joints well knit and devoid of appreciable bend. Hind legs are strong and moderately angulated at stifles and hocks. The feet are small and round, with toe pads black. Scraggly hairs on the feet may be trimmed to give a neater appearance.

**Coat and Color**—The coat is single, that is, without undercoat. It hangs long, flat, and silky over the sides of the body almost, if not quite, to the ground. The long head-hair may be tied up in a topknot or it may be left hanging. Any suggestion of kinkiness, curliness, or woolly texture is objectionable. Color, pure white. Light tan or lemon on the ears is permissible, but not desirable.

**Size**—Weight under 7 pounds, with from 4 to 6 pounds preferred. Over-all quality is to be favored over size.

**Gait**—The Maltese moves with a jaunty, smooth, flowing gait. Viewed from the side, he gives an impression of rapid movement, size considered. In the stride, the forelegs reach straight and free from the shoulders, with elbows close. Hind legs to move in a straight line. Cowhocks or any suggestion of hind leg toeing in or out are faults.

**Temperament**—For all his diminutive size, the Maltese seems to be without fear. His trust and affectionate responsiveness are very appealing. He is among the gentlest mannered of all little dogs, yet he is lively and playful as well as vigorous.

Approved March 10, 1964

# Official Standard for the Manchester Terrier (Toy)

The Standard for the Manchester Terrier (Toy Variety) is the same as for the Manchester Terrier except as regards weight and ears. (*See P. 379.*)

# Miniature Pinscher

The Miniature Pinscher has existed for several centuries. Germany, of course, is its native land, but it has been bred as well in the Scandinavian countries for a long time. Real development of the breed abroad began in 1895 when Germany's Pinscher Klub was formed. This club, now called the Pinscher-Schnauzer Klub, gave the breed its initial standard.

From the time of the Pinscher Klub's formation, the breed improved both in type and popularity, but more rapid headway was evident from 1905 up until World War I. That war of course handicapped progress in almost everything. Following it, or in about 1919, fanciers abroad once more started to advance the Miniature Pinscher, and as a result of importations to the United States, breeding was undertaken here to a limited extent.

There were few Miniature Pinschers seen at American dog shows prior to 1928, the impetus to breed advancement dating from 1929 when the Miniature Pinscher Club of America, Inc., was formed. Previously the breed had been shown in the Miscellaneous Class. The little dog's popularity has increased steadily.

Although the Miniature Pinscher is similar to a Doberman on a smaller scale, it has a nature and way about it suggestive of a much larger dog. It is especially valuable as a watchdog, sometimes keener even than a dog twice its size. It is a born show dog, too, noted for its lively temperament and intelligence, while it is often used on the stage because of its style, smartness, and pep. The close, slick coat requires scant attention, hence always looks neat and clean. And last but not least, the "Minpin's" fondness for home and master is exceptional.

# Official Standard for the Miniature Pinscher

**General Appearance**—The Miniature Pinscher is structurally a well balanced, sturdy, compact, short-coupled, smooth-coated dog. He naturally is well groomed, proud, vigorous and alert. Characteristic traits are his hackney-like action, fearless animation, complete self-possession, and his spirited presence.

**Size, Proportion, Substance**—*Size*—10 inches to 12½ inches in height allowed, with desired height 11 inches to 11½ inches measured at highest point of the shoulder blades. *Disqualification*—Under 10 inches or over 12½ inches in height. Length of males equals height at withers. Females may be slightly longer.

**Head**—In correct proportion to the body. Tapering, narrow with well fitted but not too prominent foreface which balances with the skull. No indication of coarseness. *Eyes* full, slightly oval, clear, bright and dark even to a true black, including eye rims, with the exception of chocolates, whose eye rims should be self-colored. *Ears* set high, standing erect from base to tip. May be cropped or uncropped. *Skull* appears flat, tapering forward toward the muzzle. *Muzzle* strong rather than fine and delicate, and in proportion to the head as a whole. Head well balanced with only a slight drop to the muzzle, which is parallel to the top of the skull. *Nose* black only, with the exception of chocolates which should have a self-colored nose. *Lips* and *Cheeks* small, taut and closely adherent to each other. *Teeth* meet in a scissors bite.

**Neck, Topline, Body**—*Neck* proportioned to head and body, slightly arched, gracefully curved, blending into shoulders, muscular and free from suggestion of dewlap or throatiness. *Topline*—Back level or slightly sloping toward the rear both when standing and gaiting. *Body* compact, slightly wedge-shaped, muscular. *Forechest* well developed. Well-sprung *ribs*. Depth of brisket, the base line of which is level with points of the elbows. Belly moderately tucked up to denote grace of structural form. Short and strong in *loin*. *Croup* level with topline. *Tail* set high, held erect, docked in proportion to size of dog.

**Forequarters**—*Shoulders* clean and sloping with moderate angulation coordinated to permit the hackney-like action. Elbows close to the body. *Legs*—Strong bone development and small clean joints. As viewed from the front, straight and upstanding. *Pasterns* strong, perpendicular. *Dewclaws* should be removed. *Feet* small, catlike, toes strong, well arched and closely knit with deep pads. *Nails* thick, blunt.

**Hindquarters**—Well muscled quarters set wide enough apart to fit into a properly balanced body. As viewed from the rear, the *legs* are straight and parallel. From the side, well angulated. *Thighs* well muscled. *Stifles* well defined. *Hocks* short, set well apart. *Dewclaws* should be removed. *Feet* small, catlike, toes strong, well arched and closely knit with deep pads. *Nails* thick, blunt.

**Coat**—Smooth, hard and short, straight and lustrous, closely adhering to and uniformly covering the body.

**Color**—Solid clear red. Stag red (red with intermingling of black hairs). Black with sharply defined rust-red markings on cheeks, lips, lower jaw, throat, twin spots above eyes and chest, lower half of forelegs, inside of hind legs and vent region, lower portion of hocks and feet. Black pencil stripes on toes. Chocolate with rust-red markings the same as specified for blacks, except brown pencil stripes on toes. In the solid red and stag red a rich vibrant medium to dark shade is preferred.

*Disqualifications*—Any color other than listed. Thumb mark (patch of black hair surrounded by rust on the front of the foreleg between the foot and the wrist; on chocolates, the patch is chocolate hair). White on any part of dog which exceeds one-half inch in its longest dimension.

**Gait**—The forelegs and hind legs move parallel, with feet turning neither in nor out. The hackney-like action is a high-stepping, reaching, free and easy gait in which the front leg moves straight forward and in front of the body and the foot bends at the wrist. The dog drives smoothly and strongly from the rear. The head and tail are carried high.

**Temperament**—Fearless animation, complete self-possession, and spirited presence.

### DISQUALIFICATIONS

*Under 10 inches or over 12½ inches in height.*
*Any color other than listed.*
*Thumb mark (patch of black hair surrounded by rust on the front of the foreleg between the foot and the wrist; on chocolates, the patch is chocolate hair).*
*White on any part of dog which exceeds one-half (½) inch in its longest dimension.*

Approved July 8, 1980
Reformatted February 21, 1990

# Papillon

The Papillon, known in the 16th century as the dwarf spaniel, is the modern development of those little dogs often seen pictured in rare old paintings and tapestries. Rubens, Watteau, Fragonard, and Boucher all depicted them, and their popularity was so great that noble ladies of the day did not consider their portraits complete unless one of these elegant little dogs was pictured with them. Madame de Pompadour was the proud possessor of two, Inez and Mimi by name. Marie Antoinette was another ardent admirer, while as early as 1545 there is record of one having been sold to a lady who later ascended the throne of Poland.

It is Spain that we have to thank for the Papillon's primary rise to fame, though Italy, particularly Bologna, probably developed the largest trade. Many were sold to the court of Louis XIV, who had his choice among those brought into France. Prices ran high, and the chief trader, a Bolognese named Filipponi, developed a large business with the court of France and elsewhere. Most of the dogs were transferred from one country to the other upon the backs of mules.

As time went on, a change developed in the dwarf spaniel which gave rise to the present-day name, Papillon. During the days of Louis the Great, the dwarf spaniel possessed large, drooping ears, but gradually there came into being an erect-eared type, the ears being set obliquely on the head and so fringed as to resemble the wings of a butterfly. (*Papillon* is the French word for butterfly.) The causes of this change remain largely theoretical, but whatever they may be, we now have a Toy dog whose type of body and coat is about the same as that of the original dwarf spaniel of Spain and Italy, but whose ears may be either erect or drooping. Both types may, and often do, appear in the same litter. In continental Europe, as well as Great Britain, the drop-eared

**453**

variety is called *Epagneul Nain,* although the breed as a whole carries the nomenclature of *Papillon,* as it does in this country. Here both types are judged together and with equality. Another change concerns color. Originally, almost all were of solid color. Today white predominates as a ground color, with patches of other colors, and solid-colored dogs are disqualified.

Papillons are hardy dogs. It is unnecessary to coddle them in winter; and they do not suffer particularly in severe hot weather. They delight in country activities and are equally contented in apartments. As ratters, they are extremely useful. Too small to kill a rat outright, they will worry it until it is exhausted, then dispatch it quickly. As a rule the bitches whelp easily and give little trouble when rearing puppies.

Although they have been exhibited for many years in the United States, it was not until 1935 that Papillons were represented in the American Kennel Club by their own breed club, the Papillon Club of America.

## Official Standard for the Papillon

**General Appearance**—The Papillon is a small, friendly, elegant Toy dog of fine-boned structure, light, dainty and of lively action; distinguished from other breeds by its beautiful butterfly-like ears.

**Size, Proportion, Substance**—*Size*—Height at withers, 8 to 11 inches. *Fault*—Over 11 inches. *Disqualification*—Over 12 inches. **Proportion**—Body must be slightly longer than the height at withers. It is not a cobby dog. Weight is in proportion to height. **Substance**—Of fine-boned structure.

**Head**—*Eyes* dark, round, not bulging, of medium size and alert in *expression.* The inner corners of the eyes are on line with the stop. Eye rims black. **Ears**—The ears of either the erect or drop type should be large with rounded tips, and set on the sides and toward the back of the head. (1) Ears of the erect type are carried obliquely and move like the spread wings of a butterfly. When alert, each ear forms an angle of approximately 45 degrees to the head. The leather should be of sufficient strength to maintain the erect position. (2) Ears of the drop type, known as the Phalene, are similar to the erect type, but are carried drooping and must be completely down. *Faults*—Ears small, pointed, set too high; one ear up, or ears partly down. **Skull**—The head is small. The skull is of medium width and slightly rounded between the ears. A well-defined stop is formed where the muzzle joins the skull. **Muzzle**—The muzzle is fine, abruptly thinner than the head, tapering to the nose. The length of the muzzle from the tip of the nose to stop is approximately one-third the length of the head from tip of nose to occiput. **Nose** black, small, rounded and slightly flat on top. *The following fault shall be severely penalized*—Nose not black. **Lips** tight, thin and black. Tongue must not be visible when jaws are closed. **Bite**—Teeth must meet in a scissors bite. *Faults*—Overshot or undershot.

**Neck, Topline, Body**—*Neck* of medium length. **Topline**—The backline is straight and level. **Body**—The chest is of medium depth with ribs well sprung. The belly is tucked up. *Tail* long, set high and carried well arched over the body. The tail is covered with a long, flowing plume. The plume may hang to either side of the body. *Faults*—Low-set tail; one not arched over the back, or too short.

**Forequarters**—Shoulders well developed and laid back to allow freedom of movement. Forelegs slender, fine-boned and must be straight. Removal of dewclaws on forelegs optional. Front feet thin and elongated (hare-like), pointing neither in nor out.

**Hindquarters**—Well developed and well angulated. The hind legs are slender, fine-boned, and parallel when viewed from behind. Hocks inclined neither in nor out. Dewclaws, if any, must be removed from hind legs. Hind feet thin and elongated (hare-like), pointing neither in nor out.

**Coat**—Abundant, long, fine, silky, flowing, straight with resilient quality, flat on back and sides of body. A profuse frill on chest. There is no undercoat. Hair short and close on skull, muzzle, front of forelegs, and from hind feet to hocks. Ears well fringed, with the inside covered with silken hair of medium length. Backs of the forelegs are covered with feathers diminishing to the pasterns. Hind legs are covered to the hocks with abundant breeches (culottes). Tail is covered with a long, flowing plume. Hair on feet is short, but fine tufts may appear over toes and grow beyond them, forming a point.

**Color**—Always parti-color or white with patches of any color(s). On the head, color(s) other than white must cover both ears, back and front, and extend without interruption from the ears over both eyes. A clearly defined white blaze and noseband are preferred to a solidly marked head. Symmetry of facial markings is desirable. The size, shape, placement, and presence or absence of patches of color on the body are without importance. Among the colors there is no preference, provided nose, eye rims and lips are well pigmented black.

*The following faults shall be severely penalized*—Color other than white not covering both ears, back and front, or not extending from the ears over both eyes. A slight extension of the white collar onto the base of the ears, or a few white hairs interspersed among the color, shall not be penalized, provided the butterfly appearance is not sacrificed.

**Gait**—Free, quick, easy, graceful, not paddle-footed, or stiff in hip movements.

**Temperament**—Happy, alert and friendly. Neither shy nor aggressive.

### DISQUALIFICATIONS

*Height over 12 inches.*
*An all white dog or a dog with no white.*

Approved June 10, 1991

# Pekingese

$F$ascinating by reason of its Oriental background and distinctive personality, the Pekingese holds an honored place in the dog world. In ancient times it was held sacred in China, the land of its origin, and intricately carved Foo Dog idols of varying sizes, ranging in materials from ivory to bronze and jewel-studded wood, have been handed down.

The exact date of origin is debatable, the earliest known record of its existence being traceable to the Tang Dynasty of the 8th century. However, the very oldest strains (held only by the imperial family) were kept pure, and the theft of one of the sacred dogs was punishable by death.

The characteristics we seek to retain and perfect today were in evidence in the earliest Pekingese as shown by three of the names by which they were designated in ancient China. Some were called Lion Dogs, evidently because of their massive fronts, heavy manes and tapering hindquarters. We find a second group termed Sun Dogs because of their strikingly beautiful golden red coats. Since those early days as many other darker red shades have become identified with certain strains, but even today we see numerous Sun Dogs at our shows. A third name was Sleeve Dog, this being given only to those diminutive specimens which were carried about in the voluminous sleeves of the members of the imperial household.

Introduction of Pekingese into the western world occurred as a result of the looting of the Imperial Palace at Peking by the British in 1860. It is a matter of history that five were found behind some draperies in the apartments of the aunt of the Chinese emperor. Apparently they were her particular pets—she committed suicide on the approach of the British troops. It is said that throughout the palace the bodies of many of these dogs were found, the Chinese having killed them rather than have them fall into the hands of the Caucasians. The five Pekingese found by the English were of different colors; a fawn and white parti-color was the one presented to Queen Victoria on the return to Great Britain.

Pekingese were not exhibited in England until 1893, when Mrs. Loftus Allen exhibited one at Chester. However, the undeniable beauty and interesting history of the breed placed it in the foreground where it has since remained. The three dogs which were outstanding in the breed's earliest development in the Occident were Ah Cum and Mimosa, termed the "pillars of the stud book" in England, followed by a large black-and-tan specimen named Boxer, so-called because he was obtained by Major Gwayne during the Boxer uprising in 1900. Curiously enough, Boxer had a docked tail and so was never exhibited. He undoubtedly did more for the breed in the early part of the century than any other Pekingese.

The Pekingese was first registered by AKC in 1906. That the Oriental dog took quick hold of the American fancy is evidenced by the age of the Pekingese Club of America, which became a member of the American Kennel Club in 1909.

The transplanting of the Pekingese into Western soil has in no way changed his personality. He combines marked dignity with an exasperating stubbornness which serves only to endear him the more to his owners. He is independent and regal in every gesture; it would be a great indignity to attempt to make a lap dog out of him. Calm and good-tempered, the Pekingese employs a condescending cordiality toward the world in general, but in the privacy of his family enjoys nothing better than a good romp. Although never aggressive, he fears not the devil himself and has never been known to turn tail and run. He has plenty of stamina, much more in fact than have a number of the larger breeds, and he is very easy to care for.

Since he has been brought down from his pedestal in Chinese temples, the Pekingese has but one purpose in life, to give understanding companionship and loyalty to his owners. It may be truly said that the Pekingese fulfills his mission to perfection.

## Official Standard for the Pekingese

**Expression**—Must suggest the Chinese origin of the Pekingese in its quaintness and individuality, resemblance to the lion in directions and independence and should imply courage, boldness, self-esteem and combativeness rather than prettiness, daintiness or delicacy.

**Skull**—Massive, broad, wide and flat between the ears (not dome-shaped), wide between the eyes. *Nose*—Black, broad, very short and flat. *Eyes*—Large, dark, prominent, round, lustrous. *Stop*—Deep. *Ears*—Heart-shaped, not set too high, leather never long enough to come below the muzzle, nor carried erect, but rather drooping, long feather. *Muzzle*—Wrinkled, very short and broad, not overshot nor pointed. Strong, broad underjaw, teeth not to show.

**Shape of Body**—Heavy in front, well-sprung ribs, broad chest, falling away lighter behind, lionlike. Back level. Not too long in body; allowance made for longer body in bitch. *Legs*—Short forelegs, bones of forearm bowed, firm at shoulder; hind legs lighter but firm and well shaped. *Feet*—Flat, toes turned out, not round, should stand well up on feet, not on ankles.

**Action**—Fearless, free and strong, with slight roll.

**Coat, Feather and Condition**—Long, with thick undercoat, straight and flat, not curly nor wavy, rather coarse, but soft; feather on thighs, legs, tail and toes long and profuse. *Mane*—Profuse, extending beyond the shoulder blades, forming ruff or frill round the neck.

**Color**—All colors are allowable. Red, fawn, black, black and tan, sable, brindle, white and parti-color well defined: black masks and spectacles around the eyes, with lines to ears are desirable. *Definition of a Parti-Color Pekingese*—The coloring of a parti-colored dog must be broken on the body. No large portion of any one color should exist. White should be shown on the saddle. A dog of any solid color with white feet and chest is not a parti-color.

**Tail**—Set high; lying well over back to either side; long, profuse, straight feather.

**Size**—Being a toy dog, medium size preferred, providing type and points are not sacrificed; extreme limit 14 pounds.

### SCALE OF POINTS

| | | | |
|---|---|---|---|
| Expression | 5 | Shape of body | 15 |
| Skull | 10 | Legs and feet | 15 |
| Nose | 5 | Coat, feather and condition | 15 |
| Eyes | 5 | Tail | 5 |
| Stop | 5 | Action | 10 |
| Ears | 5 | | |
| Muzzle | 5 | TOTAL | 100 |

### FAULTS

Protruding tongue, badly blemished eye, overshot, wry mouth.

### DISQUALIFICATIONS

*Weight—over 14 pounds.*
*Dudley nose.*

Approved April 10, 1956

# Pomeranian

$A$ member of the family of dogs known unofficially as "the Spitz group," the Pomeranian has descended from the sled dogs of Iceland and Lapland, if we are to consider type as indicative of heritage. The name, of course, traces to Pomerania, not, however, as a point of origin, but possibly because the breed may have been in process of being bred down to size there. At any rate, in its larger form the dog served as an able herder of sheep. In fact, when it first came into notice in Britain about the middle of the 19th century, some specimens are said to have weighed as much as thirty pounds and to have resembled the German wolf spitz in size, coat, and color.

The Pomeranian was not well known until 1870, when the Kennel Club (England) recognized the so-called spitzdog. In 1888 Queen Victoria fell in love with a Pomeranian in Florence, Italy, and brought the dog, "Marco," back to England. Since the Queen was very popular and her activities well chronicled and copied, the breed's popularity grew. Queen Victoria is credited for advocating and publicizing the trend toward smaller Poms. On her dying day, in 1901, the Queen requested that her favorite pet, a Pomeranian named "Turi," be brought to her bedside. "Turi" was lying beside her when the Queen died.

Specimens of the breed were shown in the United States in the Miscellaneous Class as far back as 1892, but regular classification was not provided until 1900 at New York. In 1911 the American Pomeranian Club held its first speciality show.

The majority of early American winners were heavier in bone, larger in ear, and they usually weighed under six pounds. Generally speaking, they had type and good coat texture, although they lacked the profuseness of coat in evidence today. American-breds show marked improvement over those early winners, as the patient efforts of fanciers have brought them closer to the standard. Indeed, American-breds have held their own with the best from anywhere; for instance Ch. Pall Mall His Majesty went to Europe and on several occasions defeated all Toys for the coveted Best in Show. Over here as well, home-bred Pomeranians have contended successfully for highest honors at all-breed fixtures.

Diminutive size, docile temper, and a vivacious spirit plus sturdiness have made Pomeranians great pets and companions.

## Official Standard for the Pomeranian

**General Appearance**—The Pomeranian in build and appearance is a cobby, balanced, short-coupled dog. He exhibits great intelligence in his expression, and is alert in character and deportment.

**Size, Proportion, Substance**—*Size*—The weight of the Pomeranian for exhibition is from three to seven pounds. The ideal size for show specimens is four to five pounds. *Proportion*—The Pomeranian in build and appearance is a cobby, balanced, short-coupled dog. The legs are of medium length in proportion to a well balanced frame. *Substance*—The body is well ribbed and rounded. The brisket is fairly deep and not too wide.

**Head**—*Head* well proportioned to the body, wedge-shaped, with a fox-like expression. *Eyes* bright, dark in color, and medium in size, almond-shaped and not set too wide apart nor close together. Pigmentation around eye rims must be black, except self-colored in brown and blue. *Ears* small, carried erect and mounted high on the head and placed not too far apart. *Skull* not domed in outline. A round, domey skull is a *major fault*. *Muzzle*—There is a pronounced *stop* with a rather fine but not snipy muzzle. Pigment around lips must be black, except self-colored in brown and blue. *Nose*—Pigmentation on the nose must be black, except self-colored in brown and blue. *Bite*—The teeth meet in a scissors bite, in which part of the inner surface of the upper teeth meets and engages part of the outer surface of the lower teeth. One tooth out of line does not mean an undershot or overshot mouth. An undershot mouth is a *major fault*.

**Neck, Topline, Body**—*Neck*—The neck is rather short, its base set well back on the shoulders. *Topline* is level. *Body*—The body is cobby, being well ribbed and rounded. *Chest*—The brisket is fairly deep and not too wide. *Tail*—The tail is characteristic of the breed. It turns over the back and is carried flat, set high.

**Forequarters**—*Shoulders*—The Pom is not straight in shoulder, but has sufficient layback of shoulders to carry the neck proudly and high. *Forelegs*—The forelegs are straight and parallel, of medium length in proportion to a well balanced frame. *Pasterns*—The

Pomeranian stands well up on toes. Down in pasterns is a *major fault*. Dewclaws on the forelegs may be removed. **Feet**—The Pomeranian stands well up on toes.

**Hindquarters**—**Legs**—The hocks are perpendicular to the ground, parallel to each other from hock to heel, and turning neither in nor out. Cow-hocks or lack of soundness in hind legs or stifles are *major faults*. Dewclaws, if any, on the hind legs are generally removed. **Feet**—The Pomeranian stands well up on toes.

**Coat**—**Body Coat**—Double-coated; a short, soft, thick undercoat with longer, coarse, glistening outercoat consisting of guard hairs which must be harsh to the touch in order to give the proper texture for the coat to form a frill of profuse, standing-off straight hair. A soft, flat or open coat is a *major fault*. **Tail Coat**—It is profusely covered with hair. **Leg Coat**—The front legs are well feathered and the hindquarters are clad with long hair or feathering from the top of the rump to the hocks. **Trimming**—Trimming for neatness is permissible around the feet and up the back of the legs to the first joint; trimming of unruly hairs on the edges of the ears and around the anus is also permitted. Overtrimming (beyond the location and amount described in the breed standard) should be *heavily penalized*.

**Color**—**Classifications**—The Open Classes at Specialty shows may be divided by color as follows: Open Red, Orange, Cream & Sable; Open Black, Brown & Blue; Open Any Other Allowed Color.

Acceptable colors to be judged on an equal basis. Any solid color, any solid color with lighter or darker shadings of the same color, any solid color with sable or black shadings, parti-color, sable and black & tan. Black & tan is black with tan or rust, sharply defined, appearing above each eye and on the muzzle, throat, and forechest, on all legs and feet and below the tail. Parti-color is white with any other color distributed in even patches on the body and a white blaze on the head. A white chest, foot, or leg on a whole-colored dog (except white) is a *major fault*.

**Gait**—The Pomeranian moves with a smooth, free, but not loose action. He does not elbow out in front nor move excessively wide nor cow-hocked behind. He is sound in action.

**Temperament**—He exhibits great intelligence in his expression, and is alert in character and deportment.

Approved June 10, 1991

# Official Standard for the Poodle (Toy)

The official standard for the Poodle (Toy variety) is the same as for the Standard and Miniature varieties except as regards height. (See P. 524.)

# Pug

The Pug, one of the oldest breeds, has flourished true to his breed down through the ages from before 400 B.C. He has always been domesticated and has endeared himself to mankind.

The truth of how the Pug came into existence is shrouded in mystery, but authorities are agreed that he is of Oriental origin with some basic similarities to the Pekingese. China, where the breed was the pet of the Buddhist monasteries in Tibet, is its earliest known source. It next appeared in Japan, and then in Europe, where it became the favorite for various royal courts.

In Holland the Pug became the official dog of the House of Orange after one of the breed saved the life of William, Prince of Orange, by giving alarm at the approach of the Spaniards at Hermingny in 1572. An effigy of the monarch with his Pug at his feet is carved over William's tomb in Delft Cathedral. Later, when William II landed at Torbay to be crowned King of England, his retinue included his beloved Pugs and they became the fashionable breed for generations.

By 1790 the Pug's popularity had spread to France where Josephine, wife of Napoleon, depended on her Pug "Fortune" to carry secret messages under his collar to her husband while she was imprisoned at Les Carmes. "Fortune" must have had a possessive nature, for it is said that he bit the future Emperor when he entered the bedchamber on his wedding night.

Called the "Mopshond" (from the Dutch word "to grumble") in Holland, "Mops" in Germany and "Carlin" in France, the origin of the name "Pug Dog" has a variety of explanations. The most likely is that which likens the dog's facial expression to that of the marmoset monkeys that were popular pets of the early 1700s and were known as Pugs; hence "Pug Dog" to distinguish dog from monkey. The appellation of "Pug Dog" has endured to this day.

In 1860, British soldiers sacked the Imperial Palace in Peking, and dogs of the Pug and Pekingese type were brought back to England. This was the first time since the early 16th century that dogs in any great number had been brought out of China. Black Pugs were imported from China and exhibited for the first time in England in 1886.

The Pug was accepted for registration with the American Kennel Club in 1885.

This lovable and staunch little dog is well described by the motto *Multum in Parvo*—"a lot of dog in a small space." His appearance is always that of being well-groomed and ready for the show ring. He is small but requires no coddling and his roguish face soon wiggles its way into the hearts of men, women and especially children—for whom this dog seems to have a special affinity. His great reason for living is to be near his "folks" and to please them. The Pug is at home in a small apartment or country home alike, easily adaptable to all situations.

## Official Standard for the Pug

**General Appearance**—Symmetry and general appearance are decidedly square and cobby. A lean, leggy Pug and a dog with short legs and a long body are equally objectionable.

**Size, Proportion, Substance**—The Pug should be *multum in parvo*, and this condensation (if the word may be used) is shown by compactness of form, well knit proportions, and hardness of developed muscle. **Weight** from 14 to 18 pounds (dog or bitch) desirable. **Proportion** square.

**Head**—The **head** is large, massive, round—not apple-headed, with no indentation of the **skull.** The **eyes** are dark in color, very large, bold and prominent, globular in shape, soft and solicitous in **expression**, very lustrous, and, when excited, full of fire. The **ears** are thin, small, soft, like black velvet. There are two kinds—the "rose" and the "button." Preference is given to the latter. The **wrinkles** are large and deep. The **muzzle** is short, blunt, square, but not upfaced. **Bite**—A Pug's bite should be very slightly undershot.

**Neck, Topline, Body**—The **neck** is slightly arched. It is strong, thick, and with enough length to carry the head proudly. The short **back** is level from the withers to the high tail set. The **body** is short and cobby, wide in chest and well ribbed up. The **tail** is curled as tightly as possible over the hip. The double curl is perfection.

**Forequarters**—The **legs** are very strong, straight, of moderate length, and are set well under. The **elbows** should be directly under the withers when viewed from the side. The *shoulders* are moderately laid back. The *pasterns* are strong, neither steep nor down. The *feet* are neither so long as the foot of the hare, nor so round as that of the cat; well split-up toes, and the nails black. Dewclaws are generally removed.

**Hindquarters**—The strong, powerful hindquarters have moderate bend of *stifle* and short *hocks* perpendicular to the ground. The *legs* are parallel when viewed from behind. The hindquarters are in balance with the forequarters. The *thighs* and *buttocks* are full and muscular. *Feet* as in front.

**Coat**—The coat is fine, smooth, soft, short and glossy, neither hard nor woolly.

**Color**—The colors are silver, apricot-fawn, or black. The silver or apricot-fawn colors should be decided so as to make the contrast complete between the color and the trace and the mask.

**Markings**—The *markings* are clearly defined. The muzzle or mask, ears, moles on cheeks, thumb mark or diamond on forehead, and the back trace should be as black as possible. The mask should be black. The more intense and well defined it is, the better. The trace is a black line extending from the occiput to the tail.

**Gait**—Viewed from the front, the forelegs should be carried well forward, showing no weakness in the pasterns, the paws landing squarely with the central toes straight ahead. The rear action should be strong and free through hocks and stifles, with no twisting or turning in or out at the joints. The hind legs should follow in line with the front. There is a slight natural convergence of the limbs both fore and aft. A slight roll of the hindquarters typifies the gait which should be free, self-assured, and jaunty.

**Temperament**—This is an even-tempered breed, exhibiting stability, playfulness, great charm, dignity, and an outgoing, loving disposition.

Approved October 8, 1991

# Shih Tzu

## (Sheed-zoo)

The legend of the Shih Tzu has come to us from documents, paintings, and objets d'art dating from A.D. 624. During the Tang Dynasty, K'iu T'ai, King of Viqur, gave the Chinese court a pair of dogs, said to have come from the Fu Lin (assumed to be the Byzantine Empire). Mention of these dogs was again made in A.D. 990–994 when people of the Ho Chou sent dogs as tribute.

Another theory of their introduction to China was recorded in the mid-17th century when dogs were brought from Tibet to the Chinese court. These dogs were bred in the Forbidden City of Peking. Many pictures of them were kept in *The Imperial Dog Book*. The smallest of these dogs resembled a lion, as represented in Oriental art. In Buddhist belief there is an association between the lion and their Deity. Shih Tzu means Lion. The dogs for court breeding were selected with great care. From these the Shih Tzu known today developed. They were often called "the chrysanthemum-faced dog" because the hair grows about the face in all directions.

These dogs were small, intelligent, and extremely docile. It is known that the breeding of the Shih Tzu was delegated to certain court eunuchs who vied with each other to produce specimens which would take the Emperor's fancy. Those which were selected had their pictures painted on hangings or tapestries, and the eunuchs responsible for the dogs were given gifts by the Emperor.

It is known that the Shih Tzu was a house pet during most of the Ming

Dynasty and that they were highly favored by the royal family. At the time of the Revolution a large number of dogs were destroyed and only a few escaped the invader's knives.

In 1934, the Peking Kennel Club was formed and by 1938 a standard for the Shih Tzu was developed with the help of Madame de Breuil, a Russian refugee.

Breeding of the Shih Tzu began in England after Miss Madelaine Hutchins brought one pair of her own and another of General and Mrs. Douglas Brownrigg's from China in 1930. The breed was first classified as "Apsos," but after a ruling by the Kennel Club that Lhasa Apsos and Shih Tzu were separate breeds, the Shih Tzu Club of England was formed in 1935.

From England, dogs of this breed were sent to the Scandinavian countries, to other countries in Europe, and to Australia. During World War II, members of the American Armed Forces stationed in England became acquainted with the breed and on their return brought some back to the United States, thus introducing them to this country. Since then many have been imported.

The Shih Tzu was admitted to registration in the American Kennel Club Stud Book in March 1969, and to regular show classification in the Toy Group at AKC shows beginning September 1, 1969.

## Official Standard for the Shih Tzu

**General Appearance**—The Shih Tzu is a sturdy, lively, alert Toy dog with long flowing double coat. Befitting his noble Chinese ancestry as a highly valued, prized companion and palace pet, the Shih Tzu is proud of bearing, has a distinctively arrogant carriage with head well up and tail curved over the back. Although there has always been considerable size variation, the Shih Tzu must be compact, solid, carrying good weight and substance. Even though a Toy dog, the Shih Tzu must be subject to the same requirements of soundness and structure prescribed for all breeds, and any deviation from the ideal described in the standard should be penalized to the extent of the deviation. Structural faults common to all breeds are as undesirable in the Shih Tzu as in any other breed, regardless of whether or not such faults are specifically mentioned in the standard.

**Size, Proportion, Substance**—*Size*—Ideally, height at withers is 9 to 10½ inches; but, not less than 8 inches nor more than 11 inches. Ideally, weight of mature dogs, 9 to 16 pounds. *Proportion*—Length between withers and root of tail is slightly longer than height at withers. *The Shih Tzu must never be so high stationed as to appear leggy, nor so low stationed as to appear dumpy or squatty.* **Substance**—Regardless of size, the Shih Tzu is *always* compact, solid and carries good weight and substance.

**Head**—*Head*—Round, broad, wide between eyes, its size *in balance* with the overall size of dog being neither too large nor too small. *Fault:* Narrow head, close-set eyes. *Expression*—Warm, sweet, wide-eyed, friendly and trusting. An overall well-balanced and pleasant expression supercedes the importance of individual parts. *Care should be taken to look and examine well beyond the hair to determine if what is seen is the*

*actual head and expression rather than an image created by grooming technique.*
**Eyes**—Large, round, not prominent, placed well apart, looking straight ahead. *Very dark.*
Lighter on liver pigmented dogs and blue pigmented dogs. *Fault:* Small, close-set or light
eyes; excessive eye white. **Ears**—Large, set slightly below crown of skull; heavily coated.
**Skull**—Domed. **Stop**—There is a *definite stop.* **Muzzle**—Square, short, unwrinkled,
with good cushioning, set no lower than bottom eye rim; never downturned. Ideally, no
longer than 1 inch from tip of nose to stop, although length may vary slightly in relation
to overall size of dog. Front of muzzle should be flat; lower lip and chin not protruding
and definitely never receding. *Fault:* Snipiness, lack of definite stop. **Nose**—Nostrils are
broad, wide, and open. **Pigmentation**—Nose, lips, eye rims are black on all colors, except
liver on liver pigmented dogs and blue on blue pigmented dogs. *Fault:* Pink on nose, lips,
or eye rims. **Bite**—Undershot. Jaw is broad and wide. A missing tooth or slightly misaligned teeth should not be too severely penalized. Teeth and tongue should not show
when mouth is closed. *Fault:* Overshot bite.

**Neck, Topline, Body**—*Of utmost importance is an overall well-balanced dog with no
exaggerated features.* **Neck**—Well set-on flowing smoothly into shoulders; of sufficient
length to permit natural high head carriage and in balance with height and length of dog.
**Topline**—Level. **Body**—Short-coupled and sturdy with no waist or tuck-up. The Shih
Tzu is slightly longer than tall. *Fault:* Legginess. **Chest**—Broad and deep with good
spring-of-rib, however, not barrel-chested. Depth of ribcage should extend to just below
elbow. Distance from elbow to withers is a little greater than from elbow to ground.
**Croup**—Flat. **Tail**—Set on high, heavily plumed, carried in curve well over back. Too
loose, too tight, too flat, or too low set a tail is undesirable and should be penalized to
extent of deviation.

**Forequarters**—**Shoulders**—Well-angulated, well laid-back, well laid-in, fitting smoothly
into body. **Legs**—Straight, well-boned, muscular, set well-apart and under chest, with
elbows set close to body. **Pasterns**—Strong, perpendicular. **Dewclaws**—May be removed. **Feet**—Firm, well-padded, point straight ahead.

**Hindquarters**—*Angulation of hindquarters should be in balance with forequarters.*
**Legs**—Well-boned, muscular, and straight when viewed from rear with well-bent stifles,
not close set but in line with forequarters. **Hocks**—Well let down, perpendicular. *Fault:*
Hyperextension of hocks. **Dewclaws**—May be removed. **Feet**—Firm, well-padded, point
straight ahead.

**Coat**—Luxurious, double-coated, dense, long, and flowing. Slight wave permissible.
Hair on top of head is tied up. *Fault:* Sparse coat, single coat, curly coat. **Trimming**—
Feet, bottom of coat, and anus may be done for neatness and to facilitate movement.
*Fault:* Excessive trimming.

**Color and Markings**—*All* are permissible and to be considered *equally.*

**Gait**—The Shih Tzu moves straight and must be shown at its own natural speed, *neither
raced nor strung-up,* to evaluate its smooth, flowing, effortless movement with good

front reach and equally strong rear drive, level topline, naturally high head carriage, and tail carried in gentle curve over back.

**Temperament**—As the sole purpose of the Shih Tzu is that of a companion and house pet, it is essential that its temperament be outgoing, happy, affectionate, friendly and trusting towards all.

Approved May 9, 1989

# Silky Terrier

Developed around the turn of the century in Australia from crossings of native Australian Terriers and imported Yorkshire Terriers, the Silky Terrier encompasses many of the best qualities of both.

A number of Yorkshire Terriers from England were brought into the Australian states of Victoria and New South Wales at the end of the 1800s. In an attempt to improve coat color in the blue and tan Australian Terrier, fanciers bred a few of the larger Yorkie dogs with some of their Australian Terrier bitches. The resulting litters produced individuals, some of which were exhibited as Australian Terriers, some as Yorkies and some as Silkys. The Silkys were then bred together until a recognized type was fixed.

In 1906, a standard was developed for the Silky in Sydney, New South Wales and in 1909, a separate standard for the new breed was drawn up in Victoria. Some discrepancies were apparent between the two standards. The New South Wales standard stated that weights should be over six pounds and under twelve pounds, while the standard in Victoria described two classes, one for weights of under six pounds, and the other for six pounds to under twelve pounds. Also, while the New South Wales standard only permitted prick ears, the Victoria standard allowed for both drop and prick ears.

A revised standard was published in 1926 while efforts were being made to stabilize weights. In order to protect the three breeds from further crossings, the Kennel Control Council of Victoria introduced canine legislation in 1932.

Originally known as the Sydney Silky Terrier, in 1955 the official name for the breed in Australia became the Australian Silky Terrier.

The Australian National Kennel Council was formed in 1958, and aware that the American Kennel Club planned to recognize the breed, one of their first acts was to recommend the development of a national standard for the Australian Silky Terrier. In March 1959, a national standard was approved in which weights were narrowed to *"ideally* from eight to ten pounds."

The first official meeting of the Sydney Silky Terrier Club of America was held on March 25, 1955, and in July of that year, the name was changed by a vote of its members to Silky Terrier Club of America.

## Official Standard for the Silky Terrier

**General Appearance**—The Silky Terrier is a true "toy terrier." He is moderately low set, slightly longer than tall, of refined bone structure, but of sufficient substance to suggest the ability to hunt and kill domestic rodents. His coat is silky in texture, parted from the stop to the tail and presents a well groomed but not sculptured appearance. His inquisitive nature and joy of life make him an ideal companion.

**Size, Proportion, Substance**—*Size*—Shoulder height from nine to ten inches. Deviation in either direction is undesirable. *Proportion*—The body is about one fifth longer than the dog's height at the withers. *Substance*—Lightly built with strong but rather fine bone.

**Head**—The head is strong, wedge-shaped, and moderately long. *Expression* piercingly keen, *eyes* small, dark, almond shaped with dark rims. Light eyes are a serious fault. *Ears* are small, V-shaped, set high and carried erect without any tendency to flare obliquely off the skull. *Skull* flat, and not too wide between the ears. The skull is slightly longer than the muzzle. *Stop* shallow. The *nose* is black. *Teeth* strong and well aligned, scissors bite. An undershot or overshot bite is a serious fault.

**Neck, Topline, Body**—The *neck* fits gracefully into sloping shoulders. It is medium long, fine, and to some degree crested. The *topline* is level. A topline showing a roach or dip is a serious fault. *Chest* medium wide and deep enough to extend down to the elbows. The *body* is moderately low set and about one fifth longer than the dog's height at the withers. The body is measured from the point of the shoulder (or forechest) to the rearmost projection of the upper thigh (or point of the buttocks). A body which is too short is a fault, as is a body which is too long. The *tail* is docked, set high and carried at twelve to two o'clock position.

**Forequarters**—Well laid back shoulders, together with proper angulation at the upper arm, set the forelegs nicely under the body. Forelegs are strong, straight and rather fine-boned. *Feet* small, catlike, round, compact. Pads are thick and springy while nails are strong and dark colored. White or flesh-colored nails are a fault. The feet point straight ahead, with no turning in or out. Dewclaws, if any, are removed.

**Hindquarters**—Thighs well muscled and strong, but not so developed as to appear heavy. Well angulated stifles with low hocks which are parallel when viewed from behind. *Feet* as in front.

**Coat**—Straight, single, glossy, silky in texture. On matured specimens the coat falls below and follows the body outline. It should not approach floor length. On the top of the head, the hair is so profuse as to form a topknot, but long hair on the face and ears is objectionable. The hair is parted on the head and down over the back to the root of the tail. The tail is well coated but devoid of plume. Legs should have short hair from the pastern and hock joints to the feet. The feet should not be obscured by the leg furnishings.

**Color**—Blue and tan. The blue may be silver blue, pigeon blue or slate blue, the tan deep and rich. The blue extends from the base of the skull to the tip of the tail, down the forelegs to the elbows, and half way down the outside of the thighs. On the tail the blue should be very dark. Tan appears on muzzle and cheeks, around the base of the ears, on the legs and feet and around the vent. The topknot should be silver or fawn which is lighter than the tan points.

**Gait**—Should be free, light-footed, lively and straightforward. Hindquarters should have strong propelling power. Toeing in or out is to be faulted.

**Temperament**—The keenly alert air of the terrier is characteristic, with shyness or excessive nervousness to be faulted. The manner is quick, friendly, responsive.

Approved October 10, 1989

# Yorkshire Terrier

The Yorkshire Terrier became a fashionable pet in the late Victorian era and even before. But in its beginnings it belonged to the working class, especially the weavers. In fact, it was so closely linked to them that many facetious comments were made regarding the fine texture of its extremely long, silky coat, terming it in the ultimate product of the looms.

The Yorkshire Terrier made its first appearance at a bench show in England in 1861 as a "broken-haired Scotch Terrier." It became known as a Yorkshire Terrier in 1870 when, after the Westmoreland show, Angus Sutherland—the reporter for *The Field*—stated, "They ought no longer to be called Scotch Terriers, but Yorkshire Terriers for having been so improved there." For a number of years thereafter classes were offered for the breed as Yorkshire Terriers, as well as Broken-haired Scotch Terriers. Often members of the same litter were shown in classes of both designations.

The Yorkshire Terrier traces to the Waterside Terrier, a small longish-coated dog, bluish-gray in color, weighing between 6 and 20 pounds (most commonly 10 pounds). A breed common in Yorkshire since early times, the Waterside Terrier—crossed with the old rough-coated Black and Tan English Terrier (common in the Manchester area) and with the Paisley and Clydesdale Terriers—was brought to Yorkshire by the Scotch weavers who migrated from Scotland to England in the middle of the 19th century. All these breeds were bred together to make what is now known as the Yorkshire Terrier.

The earliest record of a Yorkshire Terrier born in the United States dates to

1872. Classes for the breed have been offered at all shows since 1878. At early shows, these classes were divided by weight—under 5 lbs., and 5 lbs. and over. However, the size soon settled down to an average of between 3 and 7 lbs. Only one class was offered when it became apparent from records that the class for larger dogs was rarely filled as well as the one for similar dogs.

Modern specimens of the Yorkshire Terrier breed true to type and their characteristics are well fixed. Coloring is distinctive, with their metallic colors being a dark steel-blue from the occiput to the root of the tail, and a rich golden tan on head, legs, chest and breeches. Puppies that will develop to correct adult colors are always born black with tan markings.

While a Toy, and at various times a greatly pampered one, the Yorkshire is a spirited dog that definitely shows its terrier strain. Although the length of the show dog's coat makes constant care necessary to protect it from damage, the breed is glad to engage in all the roistering activities of the larger terrier breeds.

## Official Standard for the Yorkshire Terrier

**General Appearance**—That of a long-haired toy terrier whose blue and tan coat is parted on the face and from the base of the skull to the end of the tail and hangs evenly and quite straight down each side of body. The body is neat, compact and well proportioned. The dog's high head carriage and confident manner should give the appearance of vigor and self-importance.

**Head**—Small and rather flat on top, the *skull* not too prominent or round, the *muzzle* not too long, with the *bite* neither undershot nor overshot and teeth sound. Either scissors bite or level bite is acceptable. The *nose* is black. *Eyes* are medium in size and not too prominent; dark in color and sparkling with a sharp, intelligent expression. Eye rims are dark. *Ears* are small, V-shaped, carried erect and set not too far apart.

**Body**—Well proportioned and very compact. The back is rather short, the back line level, with height at shoulder the same as at the rump.

**Legs and Feet**—*Forelegs* should be straight, elbows neither in nor out. *Hind legs* straight when viewed from behind, but stifles are moderately bent when viewed from the sides. *Feet* are round with black toenails. Dewclaws, if any, are generally removed from the hind legs. Dewclaws on the forelegs may be removed.

**Tail**—Docked to a medium length and carried slightly higher than the level of the back.

**Coat**—Quality, texture and quantity of coat are of prime importance. Hair is glossy, fine and silky in texture. Coat on the body is moderately long and perfectly straight (not wavy). It may be trimmed to floor length to give ease of movement and a neater appearance, if desired. The fall on the head is long, tied with one bow in center of head or parted in the middle and tied with two bows. Hair on muzzle is very long. Hair should be trimmed short on tips of ears and may be trimmed on feet to give them a neat appearance.

**Colors**—Puppies are born black and tan and are normally darker in body color, showing an intermingling of black hair in the tan until they are matured. Color of hair on body and richness of tan on head and legs are of prime importance in *adult dogs*, to which the following color requirements apply:

BLUE: Is a dark steel-blue, not a silver-blue and not mingled with fawn, bronzy or black hairs.

TAN: All tan hair is darker at the roots than in the middle, shading to still lighter tan at the tips. There should be no sooty or black hair intermingled with any of the tan.

**Color on Body**—The blue extends over the body from back of neck to root of tail. Hair on tail is a darker blue, especially at end of tail.

**Headfall**—A rich golden tan, deeper in color at sides of head, at ear roots and on the muzzle, with ears a deep rich tan. Tan color should not extend down on back of neck.

**Chest and Legs**—A bright, rich tan, not extending above the elbow on the forelegs nor above the stifle on the hind legs.

**Weight**—Must not exceed seven pounds.

Approved April 12, 1966

# NON-SPORTING DOGS

## Bichon Frise

### (Bee-shahn-Free-zay)

The Bichon, like his cousin the Caniche, descended from the Barbet or Water-Spaniel, from which came the name "Barbichon," later contracted to "Bichon." The Bichons were divided into four categories: the Bichon Maltais, the Bichon Bolognais, the Bichon Havanais and the Bichon Teneriffe. All originated in the Mediterranean area.

Appreciated for their dispositions, the dogs traveled much through antiquity. Frequently offered as items of barter, they were transported by sailors from continent to continent. The dogs found early success in Spain and it is generally felt that Spanish seamen introduced the breed to the Canary Island of Teneriffe. Most sources agree that in this period the name "Teneriffe" was retained mainly because of its slightly exotic nature and the enhanced commercial value the name gave the common Bichon.

In the 1300s, Italian sailors rediscovered the little dogs on their voyages and are credited with returning them to the Continent, where they became great favorites with Italian nobility, and as with other dogs of that era, were often cut "lion style."

The "Teneriffe" or "Bichon" made its appearance in France under Francis I, the patron of the Renaissance (1515–1547). However, its greatest success was in the court of Henry III (1574–1589), where it was pampered, perfumed, and beribboned. The breed also enjoyed considerable success in Spain as a favorite of the Infantas, and painters of the Spanish school often included them in their works. One finds such a dog in several of the paintings of Goya.

After a brief renewal of interest under Napoleon III, the fate of this aristocratic dog took a new turn. In the late 1800s, it became the "common dog," running the streets, accompanying the organ grinders of Barbary, leading the blind and doing tricks in circuses and fairs.

At the end of World War I, a few fanciers recognized the potential of the dogs and in France four breeders began establishing their lines through controlled breeding programs. On March 5, 1933, the official standard of the breed (as written by the then President of the Toy Club of France, in conjunction with the Friends of the Belgian Breeds) was adopted by the *Societe Centrale Canine* of France. As the breed was known by two names, "Teneriffe" and "Bichon," the president of the International Canine Federation, Madame Nizet de Leemans, proposed a name based on the characteristics that the dogs presented and the name "Bichon Frise" (plural: Bichons Frises) was adopted. "Frise" refers to the dog's soft, curly hair. On October 18, 1934, the Bichon was admitted to the stud book of the French Kennel Club. The International Canine Federation recognizes the Bichon Frise as "a French-Belgian breed having the right to registration in the Book of Origins from all countries." The breed is recognized in France, Belgium and Italy.

In 1956, Mr. and Mrs. Francois Picault moved to the United States and settled in the Midwest where Etoile de Steren Vor whelped the first Bichon litter born in this country (sired by Eddie White de Steren Vor). In 1959 and 1960, two breeders in different parts of the United States acquired Bichons, thus providing the origins for breed development in this country.

Accepted for entry in the Miscellaneous Class, September 1, 1971, the Bichon Frise was admitted to registration in the American Kennel Club Stud Book in October, 1972, and to regular show classification in the Non-Sporting Group at AKC shows April 4, 1973.

## Official Standard for the Bichon Frise

**General Appearance**—The Bichon Frise is a small, sturdy, white powder puff of a dog whose merry temperament is evidenced by his plumed tail carried jauntily over the back and his dark-eyed inquisitive expression. This is a breed that has no gross or incapacitating exaggerations and therefore there is no inherent reason for lack of balance or unsound movement. Any deviation from the ideal described in the standard should be penalized to the extent of the deviation. Structural faults common to all breeds are as undesirable in the Bichon Frise as in any other breed, even though such faults may not be specifically mentioned in the standard.

**Size, Proportion, Substance**—*Size*—Dogs and bitches 9½ to 11½ inches are to be given primary preference. Only where the comparative superiority of a specimen outside this range clearly justifies it should greater latitude be taken. In no case, however, should this latitude ever extend over 12 inches or under 9 inches. The minimum limits do not apply to puppies. *Proportion*—The body from the forward-most point of the chest to the point of rump is ¼ longer than the height at the withers. The body from the withers to lowest point of chest represents ½ the distance from withers to ground. *Substance*—Compact and of medium bone throughout; neither coarse nor fine.

**Head**—*Expression*—Soft, dark-eyed, inquisitive, alert. *Eyes* are round, black or dark brown and are set in the skull to look directly forward. An overly large or bulging eye is a fault as is an almond shaped, obliquely set eye. Halos, the black or very dark brown skin surrounding the eyes, are necessary as they accentuate the eye and enhance expression. The eye rims themselves must be black. Broken pigment, or total absence of pigment on the eye rims produce a blank and staring expression, which is a definite fault. Eyes of any color other than black or dark brown are a very serious fault and must be severely penalized. *Ears* are drop and are covered with long flowing hair. When extended toward the nose, the leathers reach approximately halfway the length of the muzzle. They are set on slightly higher than eye level and rather forward on the skull, so that when the dog is alert they serve to frame the face. The *skull* is slightly rounded, allowing for a round and forward looking eye. The *stop* is slightly accentuated. *Muzzle*—A properly balanced head is three parts muzzle to five parts skull, measured from the nose to the stop and from the stop to the occiput. A line drawn between the outside corners of the eyes and to the nose will create a near equilateral triangle. There is a slight degree of chiseling under the eyes, but not so much as to result in a weak or snipy foreface. The lower jaw is strong. The *nose* is prominent and always black. *Lips* are black, fine, never drooping. *Bite* is scissors. A bite which is undershot or overshot should be severely penalized. A crooked or out of line tooth is permissible, however, missing teeth are to be severely faulted.

**Neck, Topline and Body**—The arched *neck* is long and carried proudly behind an erect head. It blends smoothly into the shoulders. The length of neck from occiput to withers is approximately ⅓ the distance from forechest to buttocks. The *topline* is level except for a slight, muscular arch over the loin. *Body*—The chest is well developed and wide enough to allow free and unrestricted movement of the front legs. The lowest point of the chest extends at least to the elbow. The rib cage is moderately sprung and extends back to a short and muscular loin. The forechest is well pronounced and protrudes slightly forward of the point of shoulder. The underline has a moderate tuck-up. *Tail* is well plumed, set on level with the topline and curved gracefully over the back so that the hair of the tail rests on the back. When the tail is extended toward the head it reaches at least halfway to the withers. A low tail set, a tail carried perpendicularly to the back, or a tail which droops behind is to be severely penalized. A corkscrew tail is a very serious fault.

**Forequarters**—*Shoulders*—The shoulder blade, upper arm and forearm are approximately equal in length. The shoulders are laid back to somewhat near a forty-five degree angle. The upper arm extends well back so the elbow is placed directly below the withers when viewed from the side. *Legs* are of medium bone; straight, with no bow or curve in the forearm or wrist. The elbows are held close to the body. The *pasterns* slope slightly from the vertical. The dewclaws may be removed. The *feet* are tight and round, resembling those of a cat and point directly forward, turning neither in nor out. *Pads* are black. *Nails* are kept short.

**Hindquarters**—The hindquarters are of medium bone, well angulated with muscular thighs and spaced moderately wide. The upper and lower thigh are nearly equal in length meeting at a well bent stifle joint. The leg from hock joint to foot pad is perpendicular to the ground. Dewclaws may be removed. Paws are tight and round with black pads.

**Coat**—The texture of the coat is of utmost importance. The undercoat is soft and dense, the outercoat of a coarser and curlier texture. The combination of the two gives a soft but substantial feel to the touch which is similar to plush or velvet and when patted springs back. When bathed and brushed, it stands off the body, creating an overall powder puff appearance. A wiry coat is not desirable. A limp, silky coat, a coat that lies down, or a lack of undercoat are very serious faults. *Trimming*—The coat is trimmed to reveal the natural outline of the body. It is rounded off from any direction and never cut so short as to create an overly trimmed or squared off appearance. The furnishings of the head, beard, moustache, ears and tail are left longer. The longer head hair is trimmed to create an overall rounded impression. The topline is trimmed to appear level. The coat is long enough to maintain the powder puff look which is characteristic of the breed.

**Color**—Color is white, may have shadings of buff, cream or apricot around the ears or on the body. Any color in excess of 10% of the entire coat of a mature specimen is a fault and should be penalized, but color of the accepted shadings should not be faulted in puppies.

**Gait**—Movement at a trot is free, precise and effortless. In profile the forelegs and hind legs extend equally with an easy reach and drive that maintain a steady topline. When moving, the head and neck remain somewhat erect and as speed increases there is a very slight convergence of legs toward the center line. Moving away, the hindquarters travel with moderate width between them and the foot pads can be seen. Coming and going, his movement is precise and true.

**Temperament**—Gentle mannered, sensitive, playful and affectionate. A cheerful attitude is the hallmark of the breed and one should settle for nothing less.

Approved October 11, 1988

# Boston Terrier

**O**ne of our very native American breeds, the Boston Terrier was the result of a cross between an English Bulldog and a white English Terrier, later considerably inbred. Incidental peculiarities of the first dogs used as sires are partly responsible for the present type.

About the year 1870 Robert C. Hooper of Boston came into the possession of an imported dog named Judge, which he purchased from William O'Brien of the same city. Judge, commonly known as Hooper's Judge and destined to be the ancestor of almost all true modern Bostons, was a cross between a Bulldog and an English Terrier, and in type he resembled the former. He was a well-built, high-stationed dog of about 32 pounds, of dark brindle color with white blaze. His head was square and blocky and his mouth nearly even. Judge was mated to "Gyp or Kate," as the name appears on old-time pedigrees. This white bitch, owned by Edward Burnett of Southboro, Massachusetts, weighed around 20 pounds; she was low and square.

From the mating of Judge and Gyp descended Wells' Eph, a dog of strong build and, like his dam, low-stationed. He was dark brindle with even white markings and a nearly even mouth. Eph was bred to Tobin's Kate, a comparatively small 20-pound female with fairly short head and straight three-quarter tail. She was golden brindle in color. From these dogs in the main evolved the Boston Terrier breed.

In the year 1889 about thirty fanciers in and around Boston organized what was known as the American Bull Terrier Club, and they exhibited the dogs as Round Heads or Bull Terriers. As time went on, these fanciers met with considerable opposition from Bull Terrier and Bulldog fanciers who objected to the similarity of breed name, pointing out that this new breed was so unlike their own. The AKC was also not convinced that these dogs would breed true to their type, having been established over such a short time. The Boston Terrier fanciers, however, refused to be discouraged, and in 1891 formed the Boston Terrier Club of America. As their dog was bred in Boston, they changed the name to Boston Terrier. After two years of sustained effort to have the Boston recognized as a pure-bred, they succeeded in persuading the American Kennel Club to admit the breed to the stud book in 1893 and the club to membership.

Up to this time, of course, the Boston Terrier was only in its infancy. There was hard work ahead to standardize the breed and to make the Bostons of that day into a more even lot. Great progress has been made, however, since 1900 in developing different strains by careful, selective breeding which included a certain amount of inbreeding. The result is a clean-cut dog, with short head, snow-white markings, dark, soft eyes, and a body approximately the conformation of the terrier rather than the Bulldog.

The Boston, while not a fighter, is well able to take care of himself. He has a characteristically gentle disposition that has won him the name of the American gentleman among dogs. As a companion and house pet, he is eminently suitable.

## Official Standard for the Boston Terrier

**General Appearance**—The Boston Terrier is a lively, highly intelligent, smooth coated, short-headed, compactly built, short-tailed, well balanced dog, brindle, seal or black in color and evenly marked with white. The head is in proportion to the size of the dog and the expression indicates a high degree of intelligence. The body is rather short and well knit, the limbs strong and neatly turned, the tail is short and no feature is so prominent that the dog appears badly proportioned. The dog conveys an impression of determination, strength and activity, with style of a high order; carriage easy and graceful. A proportionate combination of "Color and White Markings" is a particularly distinctive feature of a representative specimen. "Balance, Expression, Color and White Markings" should be given particular consideration in determining the relative value of GENERAL APPEARANCE to other points.

**Size, Proportion, Substance**—Weight is divided by classes as follows: Under 15 pounds; 15 pounds and under 20 pounds; 20 pounds and not to exceed 25 pounds. The length of leg must balance with the length of body to give the Boston Terrier its striking square appearance. The Boston Terrier is a sturdy dog and must not appear to be either spindly or coarse. The bone and muscle must be in proportion as well as an enhancement to the dog's weight and structure. *Fault:* Blocky or chunky in appearance. *Influence of Sex.* In a comparison of specimens of each sex, the only evident difference is a slight refinement in the bitch's conformation.

**Head**—The *skull* is square, flat on top, free from wrinkles, cheeks flat, brow abrupt and the stop well defined. The ideal Boston Terrier *expression* is alert and kind, indicating a high degree of intelligence. This is a most important characteristic of the breed. The *eyes* are wide apart, large and round and dark in color. The eyes are set square in the skull and the outside corners are on a line with the cheeks as viewed from the front. *Disqualify:* Eyes blue in color or any trace of blue. The *ears* are small, carried erect, either natural or cropped to conform to the shape of the head and situated as near to the corners of the skull as possible. The *muzzle* is short, square, wide and deep and in proportion to the skull. It is free from wrinkles, shorter in length than in width or depth; not exceeding in length approximately one-third of the length of the skull. The muzzle from stop to end of the nose is parallel to the top of the skull. The *nose* is black and wide, with a well defined line between the nostrils. *Disqualify:* Dudley nose. The *jaw* is broad and square with short regular teeth. The bite is even or sufficiently undershot to square the muzzle. The chops are of good depth, but not pendulous, completely covering the teeth when the mouth is closed. *Serious Fault:* Wry mouth. *Head Faults:* Eyes showing too much white or haw. Pinched or wide nostrils. Size of ears out of proportion to the size of the head. *Serious Head Faults:* Any showing of the tongue or teeth when the mouth is closed.

**Neck, Topline and Body**—The length of *neck* must display an image of balance to the total dog. It is slightly arched, carrying the head gracefully and setting neatly into the shoulders. The *back* is just short enough to square the body. The *topline* is level and the rump curves slightly to the set-on of the tail. The *chest* is deep with good width, ribs well sprung and carried well back to the loins. The body should appear short. The *tail* is set on low, short, fine and tapering, straight or screw and must not be carried above the horizontal. (Note: The preferred tail does not exceed in length more than one-quarter the distance from set-on to hock.) *Disqualify:* Docked tail. *Body Faults:* Gaily carried tail. *Serious Body Faults:* Roach back, sway back, slab-sided.

**Forequarters**—The *shoulders* are sloping and well laid back, which allows for the Boston Terrier's stylish movement. The *elbows* stand neither in nor out. The *forelegs* are set moderately wide apart and on a line with the upper tip of the shoulder blades. The forelegs are straight in bone with short, strong pasterns. The dewclaws may be removed. The *feet* are small, round and compact, turned neither in nor out, with well arched toes and short nails. *Faults:* Legs lacking in substance; splay feet.

**Hindquarters**—The *thighs* are strong and well muscled, bent at the stifles and set true. The *hocks* are short to the feet, turning neither in nor out, with a well-defined hock joint. The *feet* are small and compact with short nails. *Fault:* Straight in stifle.

**Gait**—The gait of the Boston Terrier is that of a sure footed, straight gaited dog, forelegs and hind legs moving straight ahead in line with perfect rhythm, each step indicating grace and power. *Gait Faults:* There will be no rolling, paddling, or weaving, when gaited. Hackney gait. *Serious Gait Faults:* Any crossing movement, either front or rear.

**Coat**—The coat is short, smooth, bright and fine in texture.

**Color and Markings**—Brindle, seal, or black with white markings. Brindle is preferred ONLY if all other qualities are equal. (Note: SEAL DEFINED. Seal appears black except it has a red cast when viewed in the sun or bright light.) **Disqualify:** Solid black, solid brindle or solid seal without required white markings. Gray or liver colors. **Required Markings:** White muzzle band, white blaze between the eyes, white forechest. **Desired Markings:** White muzzle band, even white blaze between the eyes and over the head, white collar, white forechest, white on part or whole of forelegs and hind legs below the hocks. (Note: A representative specimen should not be penalized for not possessing "Desired Markings.") A dog with a preponderance of white on the head or body must possess sufficient merit otherwise to counteract its deficiencies.

**Temperament**—The Boston Terrier is a friendly and lively dog. The breed has an excellent disposition and a high degree of intelligence, which makes the Boston Terrier an incomparable companion.

**Summary**—The clean-cut short backed body of the Boston Terrier coupled with the unique characteristics of his square head and jaw, and his striking markings have resulted in a most dapper and charming American original: The Boston Terrier.

### SCALE OF POINTS

| | | | |
|---|---|---|---|
| General Appearance | 10 | Forequarters | 10 |
| Expression | 10 | Hindquarters | 10 |
| Head (Muzzle, Jaw, Bite, Skull & Stop) | 15 | Feet | 5 |
| Eyes | 5 | Color, Coat & Markings | 5 |
| Ears | 5 | Gait | 10 |
| Neck, Topline, Body & Tail | 15 | TOTAL | 100 |

### DISQUALIFICATIONS

*Eyes blue in color or any trace of blue.*
*Dudley nose.*
*Docked tail.*
*Solid black, solid brindle, or solid seal without required white markings.*
*Gray or liver colors.*

Approved January 9, 1990

# Bulldog

To the best of our knowledge the Bulldog had its origin in the British Isles, the name bull being applied because of the dog's use in connection with bullbaiting.

Exactly when this old English sport first started is hardly possible to say, but in *The Survey of Stamford* the following reference is made to its probable origin:

> William Earl Warren, Lord of this town in the reign of King John (1209), standing upon the walls of his castle at Stamford, saw two bulls fighting for a cow in the castle meadow, till all the butchers' dogs pursued one of the bulls, which was maddened by the noise and multitude, through the town. This so pleased the Earl that he gave the castle meadow where the bulls combat began, for a common to the butchers of the town after the first grass was mowed, on condition that they should find a "mad bull" on a day six weeks before Christmas for the continuance of that sport forever.

Anyone who has read about the sport of bullbaiting must have been conscious of its extreme cruelty. From this we can gather that the original Bulldog had to be a very ferocious animal. Beauty and symmetry of form were in no way desirable, the appearance of the dog counting for nothing. The extraordinary courage possessed by these dogs is hardly believable. Bred from a long line of fighting ancestors, they grew to be so savage, so courageous as to be almost insensitive to pain. Such was the Bulldog of British sporting days.

Then came the year 1835, when dogfighting as a sport became illegal in England. To all intents and purposes, therefore, the English Bulldog had outlived his usefulness; his days were numbered. However, there were dog lovers who felt a deep disappointment at the passing of so fine a breed, so forthwith they set themselves the task of preserving it. Though ferocity was no longer necessary or desirable, they wished to retain all the dog's other splendid qualities. With this in mind, they proceeded to eliminate the undesirable characteristics and to preserve and accentuate the finer qualities. Scientific breeding brought results, so that within a few generations the English Bulldog became one of the finest physical specimens, minus its original viciousness.

This is the Bulldog we know today; a breed of dog of which we may be justly proud. At the same time we must express our gratitude to our British cousins who realized the value of the English Bull sufficiently to preserve him for posterity.

## Official Standard for the Bulldog

**General Appearance**—The perfect Bulldog must be of medium size and smooth coat; with heavy, thick-set, low-swung body, massive short-faced head, wide shoulders and sturdy limbs. The general appearance and attitude should suggest great stability, vigor and strength. The disposition should be equable and kind, resolute and courageous (not vicious or aggressive), and demeanor should be pacific and dignified. These attributes should be countenanced by the expression and behavior.

**Size, Proportion, Symmetry**—*Size*—The size for mature dogs is about 50 pounds; for mature bitches about 40 pounds. *Proportion*—The circumference of the skull in front of the ears should measure at least the height of the dog at the shoulders. *Symmetry*—The "points" should be well distributed and bear good relation one to the other, no feature being in such prominence from either excess or lack of quality that the animal appears deformed or ill-proportioned. *Influence of Sex*—In comparison of specimens of different sex, due allowance should be made in favor of the bitches, which do not bear the characteristics of the breed to the same degree of perfection and grandeur as do the dogs.

**Head**—*Eyes and Eyelids*—The eyes, seen from the front, should be situated low down in the skull, as far from the ears as possible, and their corners should be in a straight line at right angles with the stop. They should be quite in front of the head, as wide apart as possible, provided their outer corners are within the outline of the cheeks when viewed from the front. They should be quite round in form, of moderate size, neither sunken nor bulging, and in color should be very dark. The lids should cover the white of the eyeball, when the dog is looking directly forward, and the lid should show no "haw." *Ears*—The ears should be set high in the head, the front inner edge of each ear joining the outline of the skull at the top back corner of skull, so as to place them as wide apart, and as high, and as far from the eyes as possible. In size they should be small and thin. The shape termed "rose ear" is the most desirable. The rose ear folds inward at its back lower edge, the upper front edge curving over, outward and backward, showing part of the inside of the burr. (The ears should not be carried erect or prick-eared or buttoned and should never be cropped.) *Skull*—The skull should be very large, and in circumference, in front of the ears, should measure at least the height of the dog at the shoulders. Viewed from the front, it should appear very high from the corner of the lower jaw to the apex of the skull, and also very broad and square. Viewed at the side, the head should appear very high, and very short from the point of the nose to occiput. The forehead should be flat (not rounded or domed), neither too prominent nor overhanging the face. *Cheeks*—The cheeks should be well rounded, protruding sideways and outward beyond the eyes. *Stop*—The temples or frontal bones should be very well defined, broad, square and high, causing a hollow or groove between the eyes. This indentation, or stop, should be both broad and deep and extend up the middle of the forehead, dividing the head vertically, being traceable to the top of the skull. *Face and Muzzle*—The face, measured from the front of the cheekbone to the tip of the nose, should be extremely short, the muzzle being very short, broad, turned upward and very deep from the corner of the eye to the corner of the mouth. *Nose*—The nose should be large, broad and black, its tip set back deeply between the eyes. The distance from bottom of stop, between the eyes, to the tip of nose should be as short as possible and not exceed the length from the tip of nose to the edge of underlip. The nostrils should be wide, large and black, with a well-defined line between them. Any nose other than black is objectionable and a brown or liver-colored nose shall *disqualify*. *Lips*—The chops or "flews" should be thick, broad, pendant and very deep, completely overhanging the lower jaw at each side. They join the underlip in front and almost or quite cover the teeth, which should be scarcely noticeable when the mouth is closed. *Bite—Jaws*—The jaws should be massive, very broad, square and "undershot," the lower jaw projecting considerably in front of the upper jaw and turning up. *Teeth*—The teeth should be large and strong, with the canine teeth or tusks wide apart, and the six small teeth in front, between the canines, in an even, level row.

**Neck, Topline, Body**—*Neck*—The neck should be short, very thick, deep and strong and well arched at the back. *Topline*—There should be a slight fall in the back, close behind the shoulders (its lowest part), whence the spine should rise to the loins (the top of which should be higher than the top of the shoulders), thence curving again more suddenly to the tail, forming an arch (a very distinctive feature of the breed), termed "roach back" or, more correctly, "wheel-back." *Body*—The brisket and body should be very capacious, with full sides, well-rounded ribs and very deep from the shoulders down to its lowest part, where it joins the chest. It should be well let down between the shoulders and forelegs, giving the dog a broad, low, short-legged appearance. *Chest*—The chest should be very broad, deep and full. *Underline*—The body should be well ribbed up behind with the belly tucked up and not rotund. *Back and Loin*—The back should be short and strong, very broad at the shoulders and comparatively narrow at the loins. *Tail*—The tail may be either straight or "screwed" (but never curved or curly), and in any case must be short, hung low, with decided downward carriage, thick root and fine tip. If straight, the tail should be cylindrical and of uniform taper. If "screwed," the bends or kinks should be well defined, and they may be abrupt and even knotty, but no portion of the member should be elevated above the base or root.

**Forequarters**—*Shoulders*—The shoulders should be muscular, very heavy, widespread and slanting outward, giving stability and great power. *Forelegs*—The forelegs should be short, very stout, straight and muscular, set wide apart, with well developed calves, presenting a bowed outline, but the bones of the legs should not be curved or bandy, nor the feet brought too close together. *Elbows*—The elbows should be low and stand well out and loose from the body. *Feet*—The feet should be moderate in size, compact and firmly set. Toes compact, well split up, with high knuckles and very short stubby nails. The front feet may be straight or slightly out-turned.

**Hindquarters—*Legs*—**The hind legs should be strong and muscular and longer than the forelegs, so as to elevate the loins above the shoulders. Hocks should be slightly bent and well let down, so as to give length and strength from the loins to hock. The lower leg should be short, straight and strong, with the stifles turned slightly outward and away from the body. The hocks are thereby made to approach each other, and the hind feet to turn outward. *Feet*—The feet should be moderate in size, compact and firmly set. Toes compact, well split up, with high knuckles and short stubby nails. The hind feet should be pointed well outward.

**Coat and Skin—*Coat*—**The coat should be straight, short, flat, close, of fine texture, smooth and glossy. (No fringe, feather or curl.) *Skin*—The skin should be soft and loose, especially at the head, neck and shoulders. ***Wrinkles and Dewlap*—**The head and face should be covered with heavy wrinkles, and at the throat, from jaw to chest, there should be two loose pendulous folds, forming the dewlap.

**Color of Coat—**The color of coat should be uniform, pure of its kind and brilliant. The various colors found in the breed are to be preferred in the following order: (1) red brindle, (2) all other brindles, (3) solid white, (4) solid red, fawn or fallow, (5) piebald, (6) inferior qualities of all the foregoing. *Note:* A perfect piebald is preferable to a muddy brindle or defective solid color. Solid black is very undesirable, but not so objectionable if occurring to a moderate degree in piebald patches. The brindles to be perfect should have a fine, even and equal distribution of the composite colors. In brindles and solid colors a small white patch on the chest is not considered detrimental. In piebalds the color patches should be well defined, of pure color and symmetrically distributed.

**Gait—**The style and carriage are peculiar, his gait being a loose-jointed, shuffling, side-wise motion, giving the characteristic "roll." The action must, however, be unrestrained, free and vigorous.

**Temperament—**The disposition should be equable and kind, resolute and courageous (not vicious or aggressive), and demeanor should be pacific and dignified. These attributes should be countenanced by the expression and behavior.

**SCALE OF POINTS**

| General Properties | | | Body, Legs, etc. | | |
|---|---|---|---|---|---|
| Proportion and symmetry | 5 | | Neck | 3 | |
| Attitude | 3 | | Dewlap | 2 | |
| Expression | 2 | | Shoulders | 5 | |
| Gait | 3 | | Chest | 3 | |
| Size | 3 | | Ribs | 3 | |
| Coat | 2 | | Brisket | 2 | |
| Color of coat | 4 | 22 | Belly | 2 | |
| Head | | | Back | 5 | |
| Skull | 5 | | Forelegs and elbows | 4 | |
| Cheeks | 2 | | Hind legs | 3 | |
| Stop | 4 | | Feet | 3 | |
| Eyes and eyelids | 3 | | Tail | 4 | 39 |
| Ears | 5 | | | | |
| Wrinkle | 5 | | | | |
| Nose | 6 | | | | |
| Chops | 2 | | | | |
| Jaws | 5 | | | | |
| Teeth | 2 | 39 | TOTAL | | 100 |

**DISQUALIFICATION**

*Brown or liver colored nose.*

Approved July 20, 1976
Reformatted November 28, 1990

Acceptable coat lengths of the Chinese Shar-Pei range from the extremely short "horse coat" to the "brush coat", not to exceed 1" in length at the withers.

Each of the coat lengths has a unique look. Since the harsh coat is one of the distinguishing features of the breed, it is important that the harsh texture be maintained. Due to the popularity of the brush coat in recent years, some of the coats may soften or lengthen after generations of breeding brush to brush. Breeding back to a horse coat every second or third generation strengthens the harshness of the coat and keeps the length within the guidelines of the standard.

# Chinese Shar-Pei

The Chinese Shar-Pei, an ancient and unique breed, is thought to have originated in the area around the small village of Tai Li in Kwantung province, and has existed for centuries in the southern provinces of China, apparently since the Han dynasty (c. 200 B.C.). Statues bearing a strong resemblance to the Shar-Pei have been discovered and dated to this period. More recently, a Chinese manuscript of the 13th century has been translated; it refers to a wrinkled dog with characteristics much like those of the Shar-Pei.

The name "Shar-Pei" itself literally means "sand-skin," but translates more loosely as "rough, sandy coat" or "sand-paper-like coat" and refers to two distinctive qualities of the Shar-Pei coat—roughness and shortness—which make the breed unique in the dog world. The Shar-Pei shares another distinctive characteristic with only one other breed, the Chow-Chow, in having a blue-black tongue, which may indicate an ancestor common to both breeds. However, proof of such a relationship is difficult to confirm.

The history of the Chinese Shar-Pei in modern times is incomplete. However, it is known that, following the establishment of the People's Republic of China as a communist nation, the dog population in China was essentially eliminated. No dogs were seen in the cities, and few dogs remained in the countryside. During this period a few Chinese Shar-Pei were bred in Hong Kong, BCC, and in the Republic of China (Taiwan).

The breed was recognized and registered by the Hong Kong Kennel Club until about 1968. Subsequently the Hong Kong and Kowloon Kennel Association established a dog registry and registered the Shar-Pei. This organization still registers the breed today as do other registries in Taiwan, Japan, and Korea, as well as organizations in Canada, Great Britain and some European countries.

In the United States, the documented history of the breed goes back to 1966 when a few dogs were imported from stock registered with the Hong Kong Kennel Club. The American Dog Breeders Association registered a Chinese Shar-Pei for J.C. Smith on October 8, 1970. Strong interest in the breed increased in 1973 when Matgo Law of Down-Homes Kennels, Hong Kong, appealed to dog fanciers in the United States to "Save the Chinese Shar-Pei." The response was enthusiastic, and because of their rarity, a limited number of Shar-Pei arrived in the United States in the fall of 1973. The recipients of these dogs corresponded with each other and decided to form a national dog club and registry. The Chinese Shar-Pei Club of America, Inc., held its first organizational meeting in 1974, and the club has been in continuous existence since that time. The first annual National Specialty Show was held in 1978 and successive national shows have been held each year.

The CSPCA maintained the stud book registry and actively promoted this uniquely appealing and devoted family dog. By May 1988, when the Shar-Pei was accepted into the AKC's Miscellaneous Class, there were 29,263 registered dogs. The Chinese Shar-Pei won full AKC recognition in October of 1991 and was placed in the Non-Sporting Group.

## Official Standard for the Chinese Shar-Pei

**General Appearance**—An alert, dignified, active, compact dog of medium size and substance, square in profile, close-coupled, the well proportioned head slightly but not overly large for the body. The short, harsh coat, the loose skin covering the head and body, the small ears, the "hippopotamus" muzzle shape and the high set tail impart to the Shar-Pei a unique look peculiar to him alone. The loose skin and wrinkles covering the head, neck and body are superabundant in puppies but these features may be limited to the head, neck and withers in the adult.

**Size, Proportion, Substance**—The preferred *height* is 18 to 20 inches at the withers. The preferred *weight* is 40 to 55 pounds. The dog is usually larger and more square bodied than the bitch but both appear well proportioned. *Proportion*—The height of the Shar-Pei from the ground to the withers is approximately equal to the length from the point of breastbone to the point of rump.

**Head**—Large, slightly but not overly, proudly carried and covered with profuse wrinkles on the forehead continuing into side wrinkles framing the face. *Eyes*—Dark, small, almond-shaped and sunken, displaying a scowling expression. In the dilute colored dogs the eye color may be lighter. *Ears*—Extremely small rather thick, equilateral triangles in shape, slightly rounded at the tips, edges of the ear may curl. Ears lie flat against the head, are set wide apart and forward on the skull, pointing toward the eyes. The ears have the ability to move. Pricked ears are a disqualification. *Skull*—Flat and broad, the stop moderately defined. *Muzzle*—One of the distinctive features of the breed. It is broad and full with no suggestion of snipiness. (The length from nose to stop is approximately the same as from stop to occiput.) *Nose*—Large and wide and darkly pigmented, preferably black but any color nose conforming to the general coat color of the dog is acceptable. In dilute colors, the preferred nose is self-colored. Darkly pigmented cream Shar-Pei may have some light pigment either in the center of their noses or on their entire nose. The lips and top of muzzle are well padded and may cause a slight bulge at the base of the nose.

**Tongue, Roof of Mouth, Gums and Flews**—Solid bluish-black is preferred in all coat colors except in dilute colors, which have a solid lavender pigmentation. A spotted tongue is a major fault. A solid pink tongue is a disqualification. (Tongue colors may lighten due to heat stress; care must be taken not to confuse dilute pigmentation with a pink tongue.) *Teeth*—Strong, meeting in a scissors bite. Deviation from a scissors bite is a major fault.

**Neck, Topline, Body**—*Neck*—Medium length, full and set well into the shoulders. There are moderate to heavy folds of loose skin and abundant dewlap about the neck and throat. *Topline*—The topline dips slightly behind the withers, slightly rising over the short, broad loin. *Chest*—Broad and deep with the brisket extending to the elbow and rising slightly under the loin. *Back*—Short and close-coupled. *Croup*—Flat, with the base of the tail set extremely high, clearly exposing an uptilted anus. *Tail*—The high set tail is a characteristic feature of the Shar-Pei. The tail is thick and round at the base, tapering to a fine point and curling over or to either side of the back. The absence of a complete tail is a disqualification.

**Forequarters**—*Shoulders*—Muscular, well laid back and sloping. *Forelegs*—When viewed from the front, straight, moderately spaced, with elbows close to the body. When viewed from the side, the forelegs are straight, the pasterns are strong and flexible. The bone is substantial but never heavy and is of moderate length. Removal of front dewclaws is optional. *Feet*—Moderate in size, compact and firmly set, not splayed.

**Hindquarters**—Muscular, strong, and moderately angulated. The metatarsi (hocks) are short, perpendicular to the ground and parallel to each other when viewed from the rear. Hind dewclaws must be removed. Feet as in front.

**Coat**—The extremely harsh coat is one of the distinguishing features of the breed. The coat is absolutely straight and offstanding on the main trunk of the body but generally lies somewhat flatter on the limbs. The coat appears healthy without being shiny or lustrous. Acceptable coat lengths may range from extremely short "horse coat" up to the "brush coat," not to exceed one inch in length at the withers. A soft coat, a wavy coat, a coat in excess of 1" in length at the withers or a coat that has been trimmed is a major fault. The Shar-Pei is shown in its natural state.

**Color**—Only solid colors are acceptable. A solid colored dog may have shading, primarily darker down the back and on the ears. The shading must be variations of the same body color (except in sables) and may include darker hairs throughout the coat. The following colors are a disqualifying fault:

Not a solid color, i.e.: Albino; Brindle; Parti-colored (patches); Spotted (including spots, ticked or roaning); Tan-Pointed Pattern (including typical black and tan or saddled patterns).

**Gait**—The movement of the Shar-Pei is to be judged at a trot. The gait is free and balanced with the feet tending to converge on a center line of gravity when the dog moves at a vigorous trot. The gait combines good forward reach and a strong drive in the hindquarters. Proper movement is essential.

**Temperament**—Regal, alert, intelligent, dignified, lordly, scowling, sober and snobbish, essentially independent and somewhat standoffish with strangers, but extreme in his devotion to his family. The Shar-Pei stands firmly on the ground with a calm, confident stature.

### MAJOR FAULTS

1. Deviation from a Scissors Bite.
2. Spotted Tongue.

3. A Soft Coat, a Wavy Coat, a coat in excess of 1″ in length at the withers or a coat that has been trimmed.

DISQUALIFICATIONS

*Pricked Ears.*
*Solid Pink Tongue.*
*Absence of a Complete Tail.*
*Not a solid color, i.e.: Albino; Brindle; Parti-colored (patches); Spotted (including spots, ticked or roaning); Tan-Pointed Pattern (including typical black and tan or saddled patterns).*

Approved October 8, 1991

# Chow Chow

**D**ue in great measure to the ruthlessness with which Chinese emperors destroyed the works of art and the literature of their predecessors, it is difficult to secure evidence of the antiquity of that lordly, aloof dog, the Chow Chow. Still, a bas-relief was discovered not so very long ago that dates back to the Han dynasty, about 150 B.C., which definitely places the Chow as a hunting dog in that period. While this establishes the breed as more than 2000 years old, it is believed by many authorities that the Chow goes back much farther; that it is, indeed, one of the oldest recognizable types of dog.

The theory has been advanced that the Chow originated through a crossing of the old Mastiff of Tibet and the Samoyed, from the northern parts of Siberia. Certainly the Chow evinces some of the characteristics of both breeds. Refutation lies in the fact that the Chow possesses a blue-black tongue. On this score, some maintain that the Chow is one of the basic breeds, and that he may have been one of the ancestors of the Samoyed, the Norwegian Elkhound, the Keeshond, and the Pomeranian, all of which are of somewhat similar type.

In modern times the Chow Chow has become a fashionable pet and guard dog, but there is plenty of evidence available in China to prove that for centuries he was the principal sporting dog. Perhaps the most unusual and lavish kennel in all history was the one maintained by a T'ang emperor about the 7th century A.D. It was so extensive that the emperor could not have availed himself of a fraction of the facilities for sport it afforded. It housed 2500 couples of "hounds" of the Chow type, and the emperor had a staff of 10,000 huntsmen.

Apparently the Chow has been an unusually gifted breed of dog, since his uses have run the gamut of work done by nearly all recognized breeds. Credited with great scenting powers, with staunchness on point, and with cleverness in hunting tactics, he has been used frequently on Mongolian pheasant, and on the francolin of Yunnan, and on both has received great praise for his speed and stamina.

Undoubtedly the Chow Chow is of far northern origin, but he has always been found in greatest number in the south of China, particularly in the district centering about Canton. In that region of China where he is considered indigenous, he is usually called the "black-tongue," or the "black-mouthed" dog. In the north, as in Peking, he is called *lang kou* (wolf dog), *hsiung kou* (bear dog) or, the more sophisticated *hei she-t'ou* (black tongued) or Kwantung *Kou*, i.e. the dog of Canton.

The name Chow Chow has little basis for its origin in China; it is believed that expression evolved from the pidgin-English term for articles brought from any part of the Oriental empire during the latter part of the 18th century. It meant knickknacks or bric-a-brac, including curios such as porcelain and ivory figurines, and finally what is described today as "mixed pickles," whether of the edible variety or not. It was far easier for the master of a sailing vessel to write "chow chow" than it was to describe all the various items of his cargo. So, in time, the expression came to include the dog.

The first Occidental description of the Chow Chow was penned by the Reverend Gilbert White, rector of Selborne, England, and this was published later in the *Natural History and Antiquities of Selbourne*. The description, which is a most complete one, indicates that the dogs were not very different from specimens of modern times. It was a neighbor of the rector who in 1780 brought a brace of Chows from Canton on a vessel of the East India Company.

The importation of Chows into England did not begin, however, until about 1880, and the breed started toward its present popularity after Queen Victoria took an interest in it. The first specialty club was formed in England in 1895. The dog was exhibited for the first time in the United States in 1890 when a specimen named Takya, and identified as a Chinese Chow Chow owned by Miss A. C. Derby, took a third prize in the Miscellaneous Class at the Westminster Kennel Club show in New York.

The AKC officially recognized the breed in 1903. The Chow Chow Club of America was admitted as an AKC member club in 1906. Today, it is one of America's firmly established breeds.

# Official Standard for the Chow Chow

**General Appearance**—*Characteristics*—An ancient breed of northern Chinese origin, this all-purpose dog of China was used for hunting, herding, pulling and protection of the home. While primarily a companion today, his working origin must always be remembered when assessing true Chow type. A powerful, sturdy, squarely built, upstanding dog of Arctic type, medium in size with strong muscular development and heavy bone. The body is compact, short coupled, broad and deep, the tail set high and carried closely to the back, the whole supported by four straight, strong, sound legs. Viewed from the side, the hind legs have little apparent angulation and the hock joint and metatarsals are directly beneath the hip joint. It is this structure which produces the characteristic short, stilted gait unique to the breed. The large head with broad, flat skull and short, broad and deep muzzle is proudly carried and accentuated by a ruff. Elegance and substance must be combined into a well balanced whole, never so massive as to outweigh his ability to be active, alert and agile. Clothed in a smooth or an offstanding rough double coat, the Chow is a masterpiece of beauty, dignity and naturalness, unique in his blue-black tongue, scowling expression and stilted gait.

**Size, Proportions, Substance**—*Size*—The average height of adult specimens is 17 to 20 inches at the withers but in every case consideration of overall proportions and type should take precedence over size. *Proportions*—Square in profile and close coupled. Distance from forechest to point of buttocks equals height at the highest points of the withers. *Serious Fault*—Profile other than square. Distance from tip of elbow to ground is half the height at the withers. Floor of chest level with tips of elbows. Width viewed from the front and rear is the same and must be broad. It is these proportions that are essential to true Chow type. In judging puppies, no allowance should be made for their failure to conform to these proportions. *Substance*—Medium in size with strong muscular development and heavy bone. Equally objectionable are snipy, fine boned specimens and overdone, ponderous, cloddy specimens. In comparing specimens of different sex, due allowance must be made in favor of the bitches who may not have as much head or substance as do the males. There is an impression of femininity in bitches as compared to an impression of masculinity in dogs.

**Head**—Proudly carried, large in proportion to the size of the dog but never so exaggerated as to make the dog seem top-heavy or to result in a low carriage. *Expression* essentially scowling, dignified, lordly, discerning, sober and snobbish, one of independence. The scowl is achieved by a marked brow with a padded button of skin just above the inner, upper corner of each eye; by sufficient play of skin to form frowning brows and a distinct furrow between the eyes beginning at the base of the muzzle and extending up the forehead; by the correct eye shape and placement and by the correct ear shape, carriage and placement. Excessive loose skin is not desirable. Wrinkles on the muzzle do not contribute to expression and are not required. *Eyes* dark brown, deep set and placed wide apart and obliquely, of moderate size, almond in shape. The correct placement and shape should create an Oriental appearance. The eye rims black with lids which neither turn in nor droop and the pupils of the eyes clearly visible. *Serious Faults*—Entropion or ectropion, or pupils wholly or partially obscured by loose skin. *Ears* small, moderately thick, triangular in shape with a slight rounding at the tip, carried stiffly erect but with a slight forward tilt. Placed wide apart with the inner corner on top of the skull. An ear which flops as the dog moves is very undesirable. *Disqualifying Fault*—Drop ear or ears. A drop ear is one which breaks at any point from its base to its tip or which is not carried stiffly erect but lies parallel to the top of the skull. **Skull**—The top skull is broad and flat from side to side and front to back. Coat and loose skin cannot substitute for the correct bone structure. Viewed in profile, the toplines of the muzzle and skull are approximately parallel, joined by a moderate stop. The padding of the brows may make the stop appear steeper than it is. The muzzle is short in comparison to the length of the top skull but never less than one-third of the head length. The muzzle is broad and well filled out under the eyes, its width and depth are equal and both dimensions should appear to be the same from its base to its tip. This square appearance is achieved by correct bone structure plus padding of the muzzle and full cushioned lips. The muzzle should never be so padded or cushioned as to make it appear other than square in shape. The upper lips completely cover the lower lips when the mouth is closed but should not be pendulous. **Nose** large, broad and black in color with well opened nostrils. *Disqualifying Fault*—Nose spotted or distinctly other color than black, except in blue Chows which may have solid blue or slate noses. **Mouth** and **Tongue**—Edges of the lips black, tissues of the mouth mostly black, gums preferably black. A solid black mouth is ideal. The top surface and edges of the tongue a solid blue-black, the darker the better. *Disqualifying Fault*—The top surface or edges of the tongue red or pink or with one or more spots of red or pink. **Teeth** strong and even with a scissors bite.

**Neck, Topline, Body**—**Neck** strong, full, well muscled, nicely arched and of sufficient length to carry the head proudly above the topline when standing at attention. **Topline** straight, strong and level from the withers to the root of the tail. **Body** short, compact, close coupled, strongly muscled, broad, deep and well let down in the flank. The body, back, coupling and croup must all be short to give the required square build. **Chest** broad, deep and muscular, never narrow or slab-sided. The ribs close together and well sprung, not barrel. The spring of the front ribs is somewhat narrowed at their lower ends to permit the shoulder and upper arm to fit smoothly against the chest wall. The floor of the chest is broad and deep extending down to the tips of the elbows. The point of sternum slightly in front of the shoulder points. *Serious Faults*—Labored or abdominal breathing (not to include normal panting), narrow or slab-sided chest. **Loin** well muscled, strong, short, broad and deep. **Croup** short and broad with powerful rump and thigh muscles giving a level croup. **Tail** set high and carried closely to the back at all times, following the line of the spine at the start.

**Forequarters**—**Shoulders** strong, well muscled, the tips of the shoulder blades moderately close together; the spine of the shoulder forms an angle approximately 55 degrees with the horizontal and forms an angle with the upper arm of approximately 110 degrees resulting in less reach of the forelegs. Length of upper arm never less than length of shoulder blade. Elbow joints set well back alongside the chest wall, elbows turning neither in nor out. **Forelegs** perfectly straight from elbow to foot with heavy bone which must be in proportion to the rest of the dog. Viewed from the front, the forelegs are parallel and widely spaced commensurate with the broad chest. **Pasterns** short and upright. Wrists shall not knuckle over. The dewclaws may be removed. *Feet* round, compact, catlike, standing well up on the thick toe pads.

**Hindquarters**—The rear assembly broad, powerful, and well muscled in the hips and thighs, heavy in bone with rear and front bone approximately equal. Viewed from the rear, the legs are straight, parallel and widely spaced commensurate with the broad pelvis. *Stifle Joint* shows little angulation, is well knit and stable, points straight forward and the bones of the joint should be clean and sharp. *Hock Joint* well let down and appears almost straight. The hock joint must be strong, well knit and firm, never bowing or breaking forward or to either side. The hock joint and metatarsals lie in a straight line below the hip joint. *Serious Faults*—Unsound stifle or hock joints. *Metatarsals* short and perpendicular to the ground. The dewclaws may be removed. *Feet* same as front.

**Coat**—There are two types of coat; rough and smooth. Both are double coated. *Rough*—In the rough coat, the outer coat is abundant, dense, straight and offstanding, rather coarse in texture; the undercoat soft, thick and woolly. Puppy coat soft, thick and woolly overall. The coat forms a profuse ruff around the head and neck, framing the head. The coat and ruff generally longer in dogs than in bitches. Tail well feathered. The coat length varies markedly on different Chows and thickness, texture and condition should be given greater emphasis than length. Obvious trimming or shaping is undesirable. Trimming of the whiskers, feet and metatarsals optional. *Smooth*—The smooth coated Chow is judged by the same standard as the rough coated Chow except that references to the quantity and distribution of the outer coat are not applicable to the smooth coated Chow, which has a hard, dense, smooth outer coat with a definite undercoat. There should be no obvious ruff or feathering on the legs or tail.

**Color**—Clear colored, solid or solid with lighter shadings in the ruff, tail and featherings. There are five colors in the Chow: red (light golden to deep mahogany), black, blue, cinnamon (light fawn to deep cinnamon) and cream. Acceptable colors to be judged on an equal basis.

**Gait**—Proper movement is the crucial test of proper conformation and soundness. It must be sound, straight moving, agile, brief, quick, and powerful, never lumbering. The rear gait short and stilted because of the straighter rear assembly. It is from the side that the unique stilted action is most easily assessed. The rear leg moves up and forward from the hip in a straight, stilted pendulum-like line with a slight bounce in the rump, the legs extend neither far forward nor far backward. The hind foot has a strong thrust which transfers power to the body in an almost straight line due to the minimal rear leg angulation. To transmit this power efficiently to the front assembly, the coupling must be short and there should be no roll through the midsection. Viewed from the rear, the line of bone from hip joint to pad remains straight as the dog moves. As the speed increases the hind legs incline slightly inward. The stifle joints must point in the line of travel, not outward resulting in a bowlegged appearance nor hitching in under the dog. Viewed from the front, the line of bone from shoulder joint to pad remains straight as the dog moves. As the speed increases, the forelegs do not move in exact parallel planes, rather, incline slightly inward. The front legs must not swing out in semicircles nor mince or show any evidence of hackney action. The front and rear assemblies must be in dynamic equilibrium. Somewhat lacking in speed, the Chow has excellent endurance because the sound, straight rear leg provides direct, usable power efficiently.

**Temperament**—Keen intelligence, an independent spirit and innate dignity give the Chow an aura of aloofness. It is a Chow's nature to be reserved and discerning with strangers. Displays of aggression or timidity are unacceptable. Because of its deep set eyes the Chow has limited peripheral vision and is best approached within the scope of that vision.

**Summary**—Faults shall be penalized in proportion to their deviation from the standard. In judging the Chow, the overall picture is of primary consideration. Exaggeration of any characteristic at the expense of balance or soundness shall be severely penalized. Type should include general appearance, temperament, the harmony of all parts, and soundness especially as seen when the dog is in motion. There should be proper emphasis on movement which is the final test of the Chow's conformation, balance and soundness.

### DISQUALIFICATIONS

*Drop ear or ears. A drop ear is one which breaks at any point from its base to its tip or which is not carried stiffly erect but lies parallel to the top of the skull.*

*Nose spotted or distinctly other color than black, except in blue Chows which may have solid blue or slate noses.*

*The top surface or edges of the tongue red or pink or with one or more spots of red or pink.*

Approved November 11, 1986
Reformatted August 21, 1990

Samoyed — *Ludwig*

St. Bernard

Portuguese Water Dogs — *Prangley*

Newfoundland

Airedale Terrier — *Ludwig*

West Highland White Terriers — *Cumbers*

Australian Terrier — *courtesy, Purina*

Bedlington Terrier — *Allen*

Border Terrier — *Roslin-Williams*

Smooth Fox Terrier — *Yuhl*

Wire Fox Terrier — *Anderson*

Dandie Dinmont Terrier — *Allen*

Skye Terrier — *Goodman*

Irish Terriers — *Cumbers*

Soft-Coated Wheaten Terrier

Sealyham Terriers — *Cumbers*

Scottish Terriers — *Cumbers*

Miniature Schnauzer — *Allen*

Kerry Blue Terrier — *Ashbey*

Norfolk Terrier — *Thompson*

Norwich Terrier — *Thompson*

Cairn Terriers — *Cumbers*

Staffordshire Bull Terriers — *Cumbers*

Affenpinscher — *Anderson*

Papillon — *Ashbey*

Miniature Pinschers — *Dakan*

Japanese Chin - *Cumbers*

**XLVII**

Maltese — *Allen*

Italian Greyhounds — *McCauley*

Pomeranians

Pug — *Allen*

Chihuahua

Shih Tzu — *Allen*

Brussels Griffon
— *Kohler*

Toy Manchester Terrier — *Gilbert*

Pekingese — *Thompson*

Yorkshire Terrier — *Kinsey*

Chow Chow — *Anderson*

Bulldog — *Anderson*

Keeshond
— *Anderson*

Bichon Frises — *Cumbers*

Boston Terrier — *Thompson*

French Bulldog — *Allen*

Lhasa Apso

Dalmatian — *Callea*

Tibetan Terriers — *Cumbers*

Standard Poodles

*— Ludwig*

*— Ashbey*

Tibetan Spaniel — *Langdon*

Pulik — *Cumbers*

Australian Cattle Dog

German Shepherd Dogs — *Troy*

Belgian Sheepdog — *Thornton*

Belgian Tervuren — *Kelley*

Belgian Malinois

Shetland Sheepdogs — *Krook*

Collie — *Desmond*

Bearded Collies — *Thompson*

Old English Sheepdogs — *Anderson*

Cardigan Welsh Corgi — *McInnes*

Pembroke Welsh Corgi puppies — *Callea*

# Dalmatian

No breed has a more interesting background or a more disputed heritage than that dog from long ago, the Dalmatian. His beginning is buried so deep in the past that researchers cannot agree as to his origin. As to the great age of the breed, and the fact that it has come through many centuries unchanged, investigators are in complete agreement.

Models, engravings, paintings, and writings of antiquity have been used with fair excuse but no certainty to claim the spotted dog first appeared in Europe, Asia, and Africa. Perhaps some of the divergencies in opinion as to the original home of the Dalmatian can be accounted for by the fact that the dog has frequently been found in bands of Romanies, and that like his gypsy masters, he has been well known but not located definitely in any one place. Authoritative writers place him first as a positive entry in Dalmatia, a region in west Yugoslavia, along the Adriatic, which had before (1815 to 1919) been a province of Austria. Though he has been credited with a dozen nationalities and has as many native names—the English have nicknamed him the English Coach Dog, the Carriage Dog, the Plum Pudding Dog, the Fire House Dog, and the Spotted Dick—it is from his first proved home that he takes his correct name, the Dalmatian. We find references to him as a Dalmatian in the middle

18th century. There is no question whatsoever that his lineage is as ancient, and his record as straight, as that of other breeds.

His activities have been as varied as his reputed ancestors. He has been a dog of war, a sentinel on the borders of Dalmatia and Croatia. He has been employed as a draught dog, and as a shepherd. He is excellent on rats and vermin. He is well-known for his heroic performances as a fire-apparatus follower and as a fire house mascot. As a sporting dog he has been used as a bird dog, a trail hound, a retriever, and in packs for boar and stag hunting. His retentive memory has made him one of the most dependable performers in circuses and on the stage. Down through the years, his intelligence and willingness have qualified him for virtually every role that useful dogs are called upon to perform.

But most important among his talents has been his status as the original, one and only coaching dog. The imaginative might say that his coaching days go back to an engraving of a spotted dog following an Egyptian chariot. Even the practical minded will find no end of proof, centuries old, of the Dalmatian with ears entirely cropped away and padlocked brass collar, plying his natural trade as follower and guardian of the horse-drawn vehicle.

He is physically fitted for road work. In his make-up, speed and endurance are blended to a nicety. His gait has beauty of motion and swiftness, and he has the strength, vitality, and fortitude to keep going gaily till the journey's end. The instinct for coaching is bred in him, born in him, and trained in him through the years. The Dalmatian takes to a horse as a horse takes to him, and that is to say, like a duck to water. He may work in the old way, clearing the path before the Tally Ho with dignity and determination, or following on with his ermine spottings in full view to add distinction to an equipage. He may coach under the rear axle, the front axle, or, most difficult of all, under the pole between the leaders and the wheelers. Wherever he works, it is with the love of the game in his heart and with the skill which has won him the title of the only recognized carriage dog in the world. His penchant for working is his most renowned characteristic, but it in no way approaches his capacity for friendship.

There is no dog more picturesque than this spotted fellow with his slick white coat gaily decorated with clearly defined round spots of jet black, or, in the liver variety, deep brown. He does not look like any other breed, for his markings are peculiarly his own. He is strong-bodied, clean-cut, colorful, and distinctive. His flashy spottings are the culmination of ages of careful breeding.

His aristocratic bearing does not belie him, for the Dalmatian is first of all a gentleman. He is a quiet chap, and the ideal guard dog, distinguishing nicely between barkings for fun or with purpose. His courtesy never fails with approved visitors, but his protective instinct is highly developed and he has the courage to defend. As a watchdog he is sensible and dependable. He is not everyone's dog—no casual admirer will break his polite reserve, for he has a fine sense of distinction as to whom he belongs. Fashion has not distorted the Dalmatian. He is born pure white, develops quickly and requires no cropping, docking, stripping, or artifices of any sort. He is all ready for sport or the show ring just as nature made him. He is extremely hardy, an easy keeper, suited to any climate. He requires only the minimum of care, for he is sturdy and neat and clean.

# Official Standard for the Dalmatian

**General Appearance**—The Dalmatian is a distinctively spotted dog; poised and alert; strong, muscular and active; free of shyness; intelligent in expression; symmetrical in outline; and without exaggeration or coarseness. The Dalmatian is capable of great endurance, combined with fair amount of speed. Deviations from the described ideal should be penalized in direct proportion to the degree of the deviation.

**Size, Proportion, Substance**—Desirable height at the withers is between 19 and 23 inches. Undersize or oversize is a fault. Any dog or bitch over 24 inches at the withers is disqualified. The overall length of the body from the forechest to the buttocks is approximately equal to the height at the withers. The Dalmatian has good substance and is strong and sturdy in bone, but never coarse.

**Head**—The head is in balance with the overall dog. It is of fair length and is free of loose skin. The Dalmatian's *expression* is alert and intelligent, indicating a stable and outgoing temperament. The *eyes* are set moderately well apart, are medium sized and somewhat rounded in appearance, and are set well into the skull. Eye color is brown or blue, or any combination thereof; the darker the better and usually darker in black-spotted than in liver-spotted dogs. Abnormal position of the eyelids or eyelashes (ectropion, entropion, trichiasis) is a major fault. Incomplete pigmentation of the eye rims is a major fault. The *ears* are of moderate size, proportionately wide at the base and gradually tapering to a rounded tip. They are set rather high, and are carried close to the head, and are thin and fine in texture. When the Dalmatian is alert, the top of the ear is level with the top of the skull and the tip of the ear reaches to the bottom line of the cheek. The top of the skull is flat with a slight vertical furrow and is approximately as wide as it is long. The *stop* is moderately well defined. The cheeks blend smoothly into a powerful *muzzle,* the top of which is level and parallel to the top of the skull. The muzzle and the top of the skull are about equal in length. The *nose* is completely pigmented on the leather, black in black-spotted dogs and brown in liver-spotted dogs. Incomplete nose pigmentation is a major fault. The *lips* are clean and close fitting. The teeth meet in a *scissors bite.* Overshot or undershot bites are disqualifications.

**Neck, Topline, Body**—The *neck* is nicely arched, fairly long, free from throatiness, and blends smoothly into the shoulders. The *topline* is smooth. The *chest* is deep, capacious and of moderate width, having good spring of rib without being barrel shaped. The brisket reaches to the elbow. The underline of the rib cage curves gradually into a moderate tuck-up. The *back* is level and strong. The *loin* is short, muscular and slightly arched. The flanks narrow through the loin. The *croup* is nearly level with the back. The *tail* is a natural extension of the topline. It is not inserted too low down. It is strong at the insertion and tapers to the tip, which reaches to the hock. It is never docked. The tail is carried with a slight upward curve but should never curl over the back. Ring tails and low-set tails are faults.

**Forequarters**—The *shoulders* are smoothly muscled and well laid back. The *upper arm* is approximately equal in length to the shoulder blade and joins it at an angle sufficient to insure that the foot falls under the shoulder. The *elbows* are close to the body. The *legs* are straight, strong and sturdy in bone. There is a slight angle at the *pastern* denoting flexibility.

**Hindquarters**—The *hindquarters* are powerful, having smooth, yet well defined muscles. The *stifle* is well bent. The *hocks* are well let down. When the Dalmatian is standing, the hind legs, viewed from the rear, are parallel to each other from the point of the hock to the heel of the pad. Cowhocks are a major fault.

**Feet**—*Feet* are very important. Both front and rear feet are round and compact with thick, elastic pads and well arched toes. Flat feet are a major fault. Toenails are black and/or white in black-spotted dogs and brown and/or white in liver-spotted dogs. Dewclaws may be removed.

**Coat**—The *coat* is short, dense, fine and close fitting. It is neither woolly nor silky. It is sleek, glossy and healthy in appearance.

**Color and Markings**—*Color and markings* and their overall appearance are very important points to be evaluated. The ground color is pure white. In black-spotted dogs the spots are dense black. In liver-spotted dogs the spots are liver brown. Any color markings other than black or liver are disqualified. *Spots* are round and well-defined, the more distinct the better. They vary from the size of a dime to the size of a half-dollar. They are pleasingly and evenly distributed. The less the spots intermingle the better. Spots are usually smaller on the head, legs and tail than on the body. Ears are preferably spotted. *Tri-color* (which occurs rarely in this breed) is a disqualification. It consists of tan markings found on the head, neck, chest, leg or tail of a black- or liver-spotted dog. Bronzing of black spots, and fading and/or darkening of liver spots due to environmental conditions or normal processes of coat change are not tri-coloration. *Patches* are a disqualification. A patch is a solid mass of black or liver hair containing no white hair. It is appreciably larger than a normal sized spot. Patches are a dense, brilliant color with sharply defined, smooth edges. Patches are present at birth. Large color masses formed by intermingled or overlapping spots are not patches. Such masses should indicate individual spots by uneven edges and/or white hairs scattered throughout the mass.

**Gait**—In keeping with the Dalmatian's historical use as a coach dog, gait and endurance are of great importance. Movement is steady and effortless. Balanced angulation fore and aft combined with powerful muscles and good condition produce smooth, efficient action. There is a powerful drive from the rear coordinated with extended reach in the front. The topline remains level. Elbows, hocks and feet turn neither in nor out. As the speed of the trot increases, there is a tendency to single track.

**Temperament**—Temperament is stable and outgoing, yet dignified. Shyness is a major fault.

**SCALE OF POINTS**

| | | | |
|---|---|---|---|
| General Appearance | 5 | Feet | 5 |
| Size, proportion, substance | 10 | Coat | 5 |
| Head | 10 | Color and markings | 25 |
| Neck, topline, body | 10 | Gait | 10 |
| Forequarters | 5 | Temperament | 10 |
| Hindquarters | 5 | TOTAL | 100 |

**DISQUALIFICATIONS**

*Any dog or bitch over 24 inches at the withers.*
*Overshot or undershot bite.*
*Any color markings other than black or liver.*
*Tri-color.*
*Patches.*

Approved July 11, 1989

# Finnish Spitz

Suomenpystykorva, the Finnish Cock-eared Dog, was known in earlier times as the Finnish Barking Birddog. Now called the Finnish Spitz, it is the national dog of Finland.

The history of spitz-type dogs can be traced back several thousand years, to an era when the Finno-Ugrian peoples inhabited Central Russia. As various tribes migrated to different areas, they bred their dogs according to need, thus developing separate strains. One clan made its way to the far northern regions where, isolated among 60,000 lakes, the Finnish Spitz emerged as a pure breed and an invaluable asset to the hunter.

As centuries passed and advanced methods of transportation brought diverse populations and their dogs together, the original Finnish Spitz were mated with other breeds, until by 1880 they were nearly extinct. About that time two sportsmen from Helsinki, hunting in the northern forests, observed the pure native dogs, realized their many virtues, and returned home with superior specimens in an effort to salvage the breed.

One of the pioneers, Hugo Roos, became directly involved with the dogs and bred them for over 30 years; later he retired to devote his talents to judging. Another pioneer, Hugo Sandberg, launched an impressive rescue campaign in 1890, though he never actually bred Finnish Spitz himself. At the first Helsinki dog show, held in 1891, Mr. Sandberg judged and on that historic day five Finnish Spitz were awarded ribbons.

With the advent of dog shows, it became necessary to draw up a standard. Due to the success of Mr. Sandberg's promotion, the Finnish Kennel Club recognized the breed in 1892, with a standard based on his observations. In 1897, when the standard was revised in detail, Finnish Spitz became the official breed name.

In 1927 the first Finnish Spitz arrived in England, a pair brought back by Sir Edward Chichester following a hunting trip to Scandinavia. Among the early British devotees was Lady Kitty Ritson, who was instrumental in forming the breed club. It was she who coined the nickname "Finkie" by which the dogs are affectionately known in several countries. By 1935, the breed had sufficient adherents to warrant registration with the Kennel Club. Perhaps the most recognizable name among English supporters is that of Mrs. Griselda Price, whose Cullabine prefix is shared by many top winning dogs worldwide.

A native Finn, Ray Rinta, is credited with piloting the breed to Canadian Kennel Club recognition—the CKC admitted the Finnish Spitz to its stud book in 1974. Mrs. Joan Grant's dogs (Jayenn prefix) have been a major force in the breed's popularity "north of the border."

The first known Finnish Spitz imported to the United States was Cullabine Rudolph, from Mrs. Price's kennel in England, in 1959. It is believed, however, that breeding of the Finnish Spitz in the U.S. commenced in the mid-sixties from Finnish imports belonging to Henry Davidson of Minnesota and Alex Hassel of Connecticut.

The Finnish Spitz Club of America was founded in 1975 by Richard and Bette Isacoff with Margaret Koehler. The American standard for the breed was formulated by Mrs. Koehler and Mrs. Isacoff in 1976, based on the standard of the country of origin.

In November 1983, the breed was accepted into the Miscellaneous Class. The Board of Directors of the AKC opened the stud book for registration of the Finnish Spitz on August 1, 1987. Assigned to the Non-Sporting Group, the breed became eligible to compete at AKC licensed shows January 1, 1988.

Except in his native land, the Finnish Spitz is primarily a house dog, a faithful companion with particular fondness for children. In Finland, however, he is still a worker. He has functioned since earliest times as a natural bark pointer, who directs a hunter to the location of treed game by a distinctive ringing bark or yodel, and points at the prey with his head and muzzle when the hunter approaches. Ranging far into the forest, he seeks out the *capercaillie* (akin to our wild turkey) using sight, scent and sound, all the while keeping audio contact with the hunter. Flushing it from the bush, he follows it until it settles into a tree. Soft at first, then building to a crescendo, the dog's vocalizing alerts the hunter and draws him to the site. As he approaches, the dog gently sways his tail to and fro—this has a mesmerizing effect on the bird which has already been distracted by the barking. In Finland the hunting ability of the breed is so prized that no Finnish Spitz can earn a conformation championship without first proving his worth in the field. Of particular importance is the quality of his bark, and contests are held annually to select a King Barker.

## Official Standard for the Finnish Spitz

**General Appearance**—The Finnish Spitz presents a fox-like picture. The breed has long been used to hunt small game and birds. The pointed muzzle, small erect ears, dense coat and curled tail denote his northern heritage. The Finnish Spitz' whole being shows liveliness, which is especially evident in the eyes, ears and tail. Males are decidedly masculine without coarseness. Bitches are decidedly feminine without over-refinement. The Finnish Spitz' most important characteristics are his square, well-balanced body that is symmetrical with no exaggerated features, his glorious red-gold coat and his bold carriage and brisk movement. Any deviation from the ideal described in the standard should be penalized to the extent of the deviation. Structural faults common to all breeds are as undesired in the Finnish Spitz as in any other breed, even though such faults may not be specifically mentioned in the standard.

**Size, Proportion, Substance**—*Size*—The dog is considerably larger than the bitch. Height at the withers in dogs: 17½ to 20 inches; in bitches, 15½ to 18 inches. *Proportion*—Square, length from forechest to buttocks equal to height from withers to ground. *Substance*—Substance and bone in proportion to overall dog.

**Head**—Clean cut and fox-like. Longer from occiput to tip of nose than broad at widest part of skull in a ratio of 7:4. More refined with less coat or ruff in females than in males, but still in the same ratio. A muscular or coarse head, or a long or narrow head with snipy muzzle, is to be penalized. *Expression*—Fox-like and lively. *Eyes*—Almond-shaped with black rims. Obliquely set with moderate spacing between, neither too far apart nor too close. Outer corners tilted upward. Preferably dark in color with a keen and alert expression. Round, light, running or weepy eyes are to be penalized. *Ears*—Set on high. When alert, upward standing, parallel, open toward the front with tips directly above the outer corner of the eyes. Small, erect, sharply pointed and very mobile. Ears set too high or low or too close together, long or excessive hair inside ears is to be penalized. *Skull*—Flat between ears with some minimal rounding ahead of earset. Forehead a little arched. Skull to muzzle ratio is 4:3, with slightly longer skull in males and slightly shorter skull in females acceptable. *Stop*—Pronounced. *Muzzle*—Narrow as seen from above and the side; of equal width and depth where it insets to the skull. Tapering somewhat, equally from all angles, so that the circumference of the muzzle where the nose begins is 80% of the circumference of the muzzle at its origin. *Nose*—Black. Any deviation is to be penalized. *Lips*—Black; thin and tight. *Bite*—Level mouth with scissors bite. Any deviation is to be penalized.

**Neck, Topline, Body**—*Neck*—Well set; muscular. Clean without excess skin below muzzle. Appearing shorter in males due to their heavier ruff. *Topline*—Level and strong from withers to croup. *Body*—Muscular, square. *Chest*—Deep. Brisket reaches the elbow. Ratio of chest depth to distance from withers to ground is 4:9. *Ribs*—Well sprung. *Tuck-up*—Slightly drawn up. *Loin*—Short. *Tail*—Set on just below level of topline, forming a single curl falling over the loin with tip pointing towards the thigh. Plumed, curving vigorously from its base in an arch forward, downward, and backward, pressing flat against either thigh with tip extending to middle part of thigh. When straightened the tip of the tail bone reaches the hock joint. Low or high tailset, too curly a tail, or a short tail is to be penalized.

**Forequarters**—*Shoulders*—The layback of the shoulders is thirty degrees to the vertical. *Legs*—Viewed from the front, moderately spaced, parallel and straight with elbows close to the body and turned neither out nor in. Bone strong without being heavy, always in proportion to the overall size of the dog. Fine bone, which limits endurance, or heavy bone, which makes working movement cumbersome, is to be penalized. *Pasterns*—Viewed from the side, slope slightly. Weak pasterns are to be penalized. *Dewclaws*—May be removed. *Feet*—Tight and catlike; preferably round.

**Hindquarters**—Angulation in balance with the forequarters. *Thighs*—Muscular. *Hocks*—(Rear pasterns) One-third or less the height of the dog. Straight and parallel. *Dewclaws*—Removed. *Feet*—As in front.

**Coat**—The coat is double with a short, soft, dense undercoat and long, harsh straight guard hairs measuring approximately one to two inches on the body. Hair on the head and legs is short and close; it is longest and most dense on plume of tail and back of thighs. The outer coat is stiffer and longer on the neck and back, and in males considerably more profuse at the shoulder, giving them a more ruffed appearance. Males carry more coat than females. No trimming of the coat except for feet is allowed, not even the whiskers. Silky, wavy, curly, long or short coat is to be penalized.

**Color**—Varying shades of golden-red ranging from pale honey to deep auburn are allowed, with no preference given to shades at either extreme so long as the color is bright and clear. As the undercoat is a paler color, the effect of this shading is a coat which appears to glow. White markings on the tips of the toes and a quarter-sized spot or narrow white strip, ideally no wider than ½ inch, on the forechest are permitted. Black hairs along lipline and sparse, separate black hairs on tail and back permitted. Puppies may have a good many black hairs which decrease with age, black on tail persisting longer. Muddy or unclear color, any white on the body except as specified, is to be penalized.

**Gait**—The Finnish Spitz is quick and light on his feet, steps out briskly, trots with lively grace, and tends to single-track as the speed increases. When hunting he moves on his toes at a gallop. The angulation called for permits him to break into a working gait quickly. Sound movement is essential for stamina and agility.

**Temperament**—Active and friendly, lively and eager, faithful; brave, but cautious. Shyness, any tendency toward unprovoked aggression is to be penalized.

Approved June 9, 1987

# French Bulldog

**W**hile there has been a difference of opinion as to the origin of the French Bulldog, it seems pretty well established that one ancestor must have been the English Bulldog—probably one of the toy variety, of which there were a great number in England around 1860. These toy Bulldogs, not finding favor with the English, were sent in large numbers into France. There they were crossed with various other breeds, and finally became popular in fashionable circles, particularly with women. It was then that they were given the name *Boule-Dog Français*, although later on England scoffed at the idea of applying the word *Français* to a breed so clearly showing a strong strain of English Bulldog. At that time there was little uniformity of type, and one found dogs with rose ears, while others had bat ears which have since come to be recognized as an outstanding feature of the French Bulldog.

There are two distinctive features in French Bulldogs: one, the bat ear, as above mentioned; the other, the skull. The correctly formed skull should be level, or flat, between the ears, while directly above the eyes, extending almost across the forehead, it should be slightly curved, giving a domed appearance. Both of these features add much to the unusual appearance of the French Bulldog.

The preservation of the bat ear as a distinct feature has been due to the persistent efforts of American fanciers, since in the early days of breeding these dogs in Europe the tendency was toward the rose ear. Had this movement not been opposed by America, the breed would eventually have lost the feature that so strongly accentuates its individuality, and the result would have been practically a miniature English Bulldog.

This controversy over type was directly responsible for the formation of the French Bulldog Club of America, the first organization in the world devoted to the breed. Fanciers gave a specialty show in the ballroom of the Waldorf-Astoria in 1898, this being the first of its kind to be held in such deluxe quarters. The affair proved a sensation, and it was due, no doubt, to the resulting publicity that the quaint little chaps became the rage in society. Show entries increased until the peak was reached about 1913, when there were exactly 100 French Bulldogs benched at Westminster, while the following specialty shows had even more.

Unquestionably the dog that did the most toward the establishment of the breed in America was Ch. Nellcote Gamin, imported in 1904 by Mr. and Mrs. Samuel Goldenberg. With the addition of Gamin to the splendid stock already in this country, we were made independent of further importation in order to produce the finest Frenchies in the world.

While bred principally as pets and companions, Frenchies are remarkably intelligent and serve as good watchdogs. They are affectionate, sweet-tempered, and dependable. Alert and playful, they are not noisy and, as a rule, bark very little. Their size is another advantage in considering them as indoor pets, and the smooth, short coat is easily kept clean.

## Official Standard for the French Bulldog

**General Appearance**—The French Bulldog has the appearance of an active, intelligent, muscular dog of heavy bone, smooth coat, compactly built, and of medium or small structure. Expression alert, curious, and interested. Any alteration other than removal of dewclaws is considered mutilation and is a *disqualification*. *Proportion and Symmetry*—All points are well distributed and bear good relation one to the other; no feature being in such prominence from either excess or lack of quality that the animal appears poorly proportioned. *Influence of Sex*—In comparing specimens of different sex, due allowance is to be made in favor of bitches, which do not bear the characteristics of the breed to the same marked degree as do the dogs.

**Size, Proportion, Substance**—*Weight* not to exceed 28 pounds; over 28 pounds is a *disqualification*. *Proportion*—Distance from withers to ground in good relation to distance from withers to onset of tail, so that animal appears compact, well balanced and in good proportion. *Substance*—Muscular, heavy bone.

**Head**—*Head* large and square. *Eyes* dark in color, wide apart, set low down in the skull, as far from the ears as possible, round in form, of moderate size, neither sunken nor bulging. In lighter colored dogs, lighter colored eyes are acceptable. No haw and no white of the eye showing when looking forward. *Ears*—Known as the bat ear, broad at the base, elongated, with round top, set high on the head but not too close together, and carried erect with the orifice to the front. The leather of the ear fine and soft. Other than bat ears is a *disqualification*. The top of the **skull** flat between the ears; the forehead is not flat but slightly rounded. The **muzzle** broad, deep and well laid back; the muscles of the cheeks well developed. The *stop* well defined, causing a hollow groove between the eyes with heavy wrinkles forming a soft roll over the extremely short nose; nostrils broad with a well defined line between them. **Nose** black. Nose other than black is a *disqualification*, except in the case of the lighter colored dogs, where a lighter colored nose is acceptable but not desirable. *Flews* black, thick and broad, hanging over the lower jaw at the sides, meeting the underlip in front and covering the teeth, which are not seen when the mouth is closed. The *underjaw* is deep, square, broad, undershot and well turned up.

**Neck, Topline, Body**—The **neck** is thick and well arched with loose skin at the throat. The **back** is a roach back with a slight fall close behind the shoulders; strong and short, broad at the shoulders and narrowing at the loins. The **body** is short and well rounded. The *chest* is broad, deep, and full; well ribbed with the belly tucked up. The **tail** is either straight or screwed (but not curly), short, hung low, thick root and fine tip; carried low in repose.

**Forequarters**—**Forelegs** are short, stout, straight, muscular and set wide apart. Dewclaws may be removed. **Feet** are moderate in size, compact and firmly set. Toes compact, well split up, with high knuckles and short stubby nails.

**Hindquarters**—**Hind legs** are strong and muscular, longer than the forelegs, so as to elevate the loins above the shoulders. Hocks well let down. **Feet** are moderate in size, compact and firmly set. Toes compact, well split up, with high knuckles and short stubby nails; hind feet slightly longer than forefeet.

**Coat**—Coat is moderately fine, brilliant, short and smooth. Skin is soft and loose, especially at the head and shoulders, forming wrinkles.

**Color**—Acceptable colors—All brindle, fawn, white, brindle and white, and any color except those which constitute disqualification. All colors are acceptable with the exception of solid black, mouse, liver, black and tan, black and white, and white with black, which are *disqualifications*. Black means black without a trace of brindle.

**Gait**—Correct gait is double tracking with reach and drive; the action is unrestrained, free and vigorous.

**Temperament**—Well behaved, adaptable, and comfortable companions with an affectionate nature and even disposition; generally active, alert, and playful, but not unduly boisterous.

### DISQUALIFICATIONS

*Any alteration other than removal of dewclaws.*

*Over 28 pounds in weight.*

*Other than bat ears.*

*Nose other than black, except in the case of lighter colored dogs, where a lighter colored nose is acceptable.*

*Solid black, mouse, liver, black and tan, black and white, and white with black. Black means black without a trace of brindle.*

Approved June 10, 1991

# Keeshond

## (kayz-hawnd)

It took a national political turnover in Holland to bring the Keeshond (*pl.* Keeshonden) to wide attention in the latter part of the 18th century, but the breed had been one of the favorite dogs of the Dutch people for several hundred years before that. Never a hunter, and never used for any of the specialized forms of work that have characterized so many other breeds, the Keeshond had managed by the very force of his personality to win a high place in the affections of a nation.

The events leading up to the recognition of the Keeshond as the national dog of Holland were concerned with the social unrest that seemed to be spreading like a prairie fire throughout the world in the years immediately preceding the French Revolution. Holland was divided into two great camps, the *Prinsgezinden* or partisans of the Prince of Orange, and the *Patriotten* or Patriots.

The Patriots, consisting principally of the people of the lower and upper middle classes, were led by a man named Kees de Gyselaer, who lived in Dordrecht. Like most of his countrymen, de Gyselaer was a dog lover, and at the time he owned a little dog that he called Kees. This dog gave the breed its name, for it became the symbol of the Patriots. It appeared in countless pictures and cartoons made in those days of civil strife. The men who composed the party were firmly of the opinion that their own spirit was typified in the dog. He was a dog of the people.

Histories are rather vague as to what name the Keeshond bore prior to its adoption as a symbol by the Patriots, but it was known mainly as the barge dog. The breed had served for countless years on the *rijnaken*, or small vessels that were found in great numbers on the Rhine River. These vessels seldom were larger than 200 tons at the time when the Keeshond enjoyed its greatest popularity in Holland, and consequently would not accommodate a very large dog. There probably were more of this breed of dog kept as pets and watchdogs throughout the Netherlands than there were dogs on the barges. It was only natural that the dogs of the barges became better known, for they were continually moving up and down the river, coming in contact with more people.

The origin of the Keeshond is Arctic, or possibly Sub-Arctic, and it is of the same strains that produced the Samoyed, the Chow Chow, the Norwegian Elkhound, the Finnish Spitz, and the Pomeranian. It seems the most closely related to the Pomeranian. Some authorities believe that the Pomeranian was produced by selective breeding of the Keeshond.

The Keeshond has changed little in the past two centuries, for the earliest descriptions represent it as nearly identical with the dog of today. There also are a number of old paintings and drawings that prove how well the old Keeshond type has been preserved. A drawing, made in 1794, shows the children and the dog of a burgomaster mourning beside his tomb. The dog clearly resembles today's Keeshonden. Other evidence is found in the paintings of that famous Dutch artist, Jan Steen.

The close link between the Keeshond and the Patriots in the latter part of the 18th century almost proved the dog's undoing. He was so much in the public eye as the symbol of the Patriots that when the Prince of Orange established his party as the dominant one, few people wanted the dog that stood for the opposition. Many who owned Keeshonden disposed of them quietly; and only the most loyal maintained the breed. And then, the type of vessel used on the rivers gradually changed. Each year they seemed to get larger, until, eventually, they were quite pretentious and had plenty of room for large dogs. This affected the popularity of the Keeshond considerably.

The breed was at very low ebb until 1920, at which time the Baroness van Hardenbroek became so interested in the old breed that she undertook an investigation to see how much of the old stock still survived. The results of this search were very surprising. Whereas the breed had passed from public attention, it was still kept in its original form by certain captains of riverboats, by farmers, and by truckmen. There were many excellent specimens. Some owners even had maintained their own crude stud books.

The Baroness began breeding Keeshonden and spread their story throughout Europe. Within ten years she brought the breed to such a solid position that the Dutch Keeshond Club was established, and in 1933 *De Raad van Beheer op Kynologisch Gebeid in Nederland* accepted the standard for judging the breed.

As early as 1925, Keeshonden were in England and making a very good impression. The breed was accepted for registration by the American Kennel Club in 1930, and early development in this country, with few exceptions, was based on imports from England, which were in turn the product of British importations from Holland and Germany.

A handsome dog of well-balanced, medium size, with alert carriage and intelligent expression, the Keeshond is a hardy breed—with a "fur" coat that is easily taken care of. One of the most affectionate and lovable of all dogs, he has been bred for centuries as an "ideal family companion" and sensible watchdog.

## Official Standard for the Keeshond

**General Appearance**—The Keeshond (pronounced *kayz-hawnd*) is a natural, handsome dog of well-balanced, short-coupled body, attracting attention not only by his coloration, alert carriage, and intelligent expression, but also by his stand-off coat, his richly plumed tail well curled over his back, his foxlike expression, and his small pointed ears. His coat is very thick around the neck, fore part of the shoulders and chest, forming a lion-like ruff—more profuse in the male. His rump and hind legs, down to the hocks, are also thickly coated, forming the characteristic "trousers." His head, ears, and lower legs are covered with thick, short hair.

**Size, Proportion, Substance**—The Keeshond is a medium-sized, square-appearing, sturdy dog, neither coarse nor lightly made. The ideal height of fully matured dogs when measured from top of withers to the ground is 18 inches for males and 17 inches for bitches—a one inch variance either way is acceptable. While correct size is very important, it should not outweigh that of type.

**Head**—*Expression*—Expression is largely dependent on the distinctive characteristic called "spectacles"—a combination of markings and shadings in the orbital area which must include a delicate, dark line slanting from the outer corner of each eye toward the lower corner of each ear coupled with expressive eyebrows. Markings (or shadings) on face and head must present a pleasing appearance, imparting to the dog an alert and intelligent expression. *Very Serious Fault:* Absence of dark lines which form the "spectacles." *Eyes*—Eyes should be dark brown in color, of medium size, almond shaped, set obliquely and neither too wide apart nor too close together. Eye rims are black. *Faults:* Round and/or protruding eyes or eyes light of color. *Ears*—Ears should be small, triangular in shape, mounted high on head and carried erect. Size should be proportionate to the head—length approximating the distance from the outer corner of the eye to the nearest edge of the ear. *Fault:* Ears not carried erect when at attention. *Skull*—The head should be well-proportioned to the body and wedge-shaped when viewed from above—not only the muzzle, but the whole head should give this impression when the ears are drawn back by covering the nape of the neck and the ears with one hand. Head in profile should exhibit a definite stop. *Faults:* Apple head or absence of stop. *Muzzle*—Of medium length, neither coarse nor snipy, and well proportioned to the skull. *Mouth*—The mouth should be neither overshot nor undershot. Lips should be black and closely meeting—not thick, coarse or sagging—and with no wrinkle at the corner of the mouth. *Faults:* Overshot, undershot or wry mouth. *Teeth*—The teeth should be white, sound and strong meeting in a scissors bite. *Fault:* Misaligned teeth.

**Neck, Topline, Body**—The *neck* should be moderately long, well-shaped and well set on shoulders. The body should be compact with a short, straight back sloping slightly downward toward the hindquarters; well ribbed, barrel well rounded, short in loin, belly moderately tucked up, deep and strong of chest. *Tail*—The tail should be moderately long and well feathered, set on high and tightly curled over the back. It should lie flat and close to the body. The tail must form a part of the "silhouette" of the dog's body, rather than give the appearance of an appendage. *Fault:* Tail not lying close to the back.

**Forequarters**—Forelegs should be straight seen from any angle. Pasterns are strong with a slight slope. Legs must be of good bone in proportion to the overall dog. Shoulder to upper arm angulation is between slight to moderate.

**Hindquarters**—Angulation in rear should be between slight to moderate to complement the forequarters, creating balance and typical gait. Hindquarters are well muscled with hocks perpendicular to the ground.

**Feet**—The feet should be compact, well rounded, catlike. Toes are nicely arched, with black nails.

**Coat**—The body should be abundantly covered with long, straight, harsh hair standing well out from a thick, downy undercoat. Head, including muzzle, skull and ears, should be covered with smooth, soft, short hair—velvety in texture on the ears. The neck is covered with a mane—more profuse in the male—sweeping from under the jaw and covering the whole of the front part of the shoulders and chest, as well as the top part of the shoulders. The hair on the legs should be smooth and short, except for feathering on the front legs and "trousers" on the hind legs. Hind legs should be profusely feathered down to the hocks—not below. The hair on the tail should form a rich plume. Coat must not part down the back. The Keeshond is to be shown in a natural state with trimming permissible only on feet, pasterns, hocks and—if desired—whiskers. TRIMMING OTHER THAN AS DESCRIBED TO BE SEVERELY PENALIZED. *Faults:* Silky, wavy, or curly coats. Part in coat down the back.

**Color and Markings**—A dramatically marked dog, the Keeshond is a mixture of gray, black and cream. This coloration may vary from light to dark. The hair of the outer coat is black tipped, the length of the black tips producing the characteristic shading of color. Puppies are often less intensely marked. The undercoat is very pale gray or cream, never tawny. *Head*—The muzzle should be dark in color. "Spectacles" and shadings, as previously described, are characteristic of the breed and must be present to some degree. Ears should be very dark—almost black. *Ruff, Shoulders and "Trousers"*—The color of the ruff and "trousers" is lighter than that of the body. The shoulder line markings of light gray must be well defined. *Tail*—The plume of the tail is very light in color when curled on the back, and the tip of the tail should be black. *Legs and Feet*—Legs and feet are cream. *Faults*: Pronounced white markings. Black markings more than halfway down the foreleg, penciling excepted. White foot or feet. ***Very Serious Faults:*** Entirely black or white or any solid color; any pronounced deviation from the color as described.

**Gait**—The distinctive gait of the Keeshond is unique to the breed. Dogs should move boldly and keep tails curled over the back. They should move cleanly and briskly; the movement should be straight and sharp with reach and drive between slight to moderate.

**Temperament**—Temperament is of primary importance. The Keeshond is neither timid nor aggressive but, instead, is outgoing and friendly with both people and other dogs. The Keeshond is a lively, intelligent, alert and affectionate companion.

Approved November 14, 1989

# Lhasa Apso

$\mathbf{B}$eyond the northern boundary of India, where the mighty Mount Everest stands like a guardian sentinel, is the mysterious land of Tibet. It is a country of huge mountains and deep valleys, with a climate of intense cold and great heat, a country where conditions are hard on man and beast. This is the home of the Lhasa Apso, known in that land as *Abso Seng Kye*, the "Bark Lion Sentinel Dog." Small wonder, then, that these members of dogdom should be of such hardy and vigorous constitution.

Since danger threatened from without and within in this strange land, a huge Mastiff was chained to a post beside the outer door to prevent intruders from entering, while Lhasa Apsos were kept as special guards inside the dwellings. For this work the little dogs were peculiarly adapted by their intelligence, quick hearing, and finely developed instinct for distinguishing intimates from strangers.

The Lhasa Apso, from the lamaseries and villages around the sacred city of Lhasa, is one of three breeds native to Tibet that are in the Non-Sporting Group. The others are the Tibetan Terrier and the Tibetan Spaniel. The breeds have two characteristics in common, namely, the heavy coat of hair to protect them from the rigors of the climate and the tail upcurled over the back.

Of the three, the Lhasa was the first admitted to AKC registration—in 1935. It was originally shown in the Terrier Group, then reassigned to the Non-Sporting in 1959.

C. Suydam Cutting, naturalist, world traveler and compatriot to some of the

**519**

more noteworthy men of his generation, is singularly credited with the establishment and reputation of the Lhasa Apso in America. During a trip to Tibet, Mr. Cutting was able to arrange an audience with the then 13th Dalai Lama, and a lasting friendship was formed. The Cuttings' first pair of Lhasas arrived in 1933 as a gift from the Dalai Lama.

The little Lhasa Apso has never lost his characteristic of keen watchfulness, nor has he lost his hardy nature. These two features should always be developed, since they are of outstanding merit. We have found that these dogs are easily trained and responsive to kindness. To anyone they trust they are most obedient, and their beautiful dark eyes are certainly appealing as they wait for some mark of appreciation for their efforts.

## Official Standard for the Lhasa Apso

**Character**—Gay and assertive, but chary of strangers.

**Size**—Variable, but about 10 inches or 11 inches at shoulder for dogs, bitches slightly smaller.

**Color**—All colors equally acceptable with or without dark tips to ears and beard.

**Body Shape**—The length from point of shoulders to point of buttocks longer than height at withers, well ribbed up, strong loin, well-developed quarters and thighs.

**Coat**—Heavy, straight, hard, not woolly nor silky, of good length, and very dense.

**Mouth and Muzzle**—The preferred bite is either level or slightly undershot. Muzzle of medium length; a square muzzle is objectionable.

**Head**—Heavy head furnishings with good fall over eyes, good whiskers and beard; skull narrow, falling away behind the eyes in a marked degree, not quite flat, but not domed or apple-shaped; straight foreface of fair length. Nose black, the length from tip of nose to eye to be roughly about one-third of the total length from nose to back of skull. *Eyes*—Dark brown, neither very large and full, nor very small and sunk. *Ears*—Pendant, heavily feathered.

**Legs**—Forelegs straight, both forelegs and hind legs heavily furnished with hair. *Feet*—Well feathered, should be round and catlike, with good pads.

**Tail and Carriage**—Well feathered, should be carried well over back in a screw; there may be a kink at the end. A low carriage of stern is a serious fault.

Approved July 11, 1978

# Poodle

$F$ew dogs have climbed to such high favor in so many different countries as has the Poodle, but it appeared so early in various parts of the world that there is some doubt as to the land of its origin.

It is supposed to have originated in Germany, where it is known as the *Pudel* or *Canis Familiaris Aquatius*. However for years it has been regarded as the national dog of France, where it was commonly used as a retriever as well as a traveling-circus trick dog. In France it was and is known as the *Caniche*, which is derived from *chien canard* or duck dog. Doubtless the English word poodle comes from the German *pudel* or *pudelin*, meaning to splash in the water. The expression "French Poodle" was in all probability a somewhat later cognomen, bestowed as a result of the dog's great popularity in France.

At any rate, the Poodle undoubtedly originated as a water retriever. In fact the unclipped Poodle of today bears strong resemblance in type to the old Rough-haired Water Dog of England as painted by Reinagle at the beginning of the 19th century; and except that the Irish Water Spaniel is born with short hair on its face and tail, there is little difference between this ancient Irish dog and the Poodle.

Authorities concede that the large, or Standard, Poodle is the oldest of the three varieties, and that the dog gained special fame as a water worker. So widely was it used as retriever that it was shorn of portions of its coat to further facilitate progress in swimming. Thence came the custom of clipping to pattern which so enhanced the style and general appearance that its sponsors, particularly in France, were captivated by it.

All of the Poodle's ancestors were acknowledged to be good swimmers, although one member of the family, the truffle dog (it may have been of Toy or Miniature size), it is said never went near the water. Truffle hunting was widely practiced in England, and later in Spain and Germany, where the edible fungus has always been considered a great delicacy. For scenting and digging up the fungus, the smaller dogs were favored, since they did less damage to the truffles with their feet than the larger kinds. So it is rumored that a terrier was crossed with the Poodle to produce the ideal truffle hunter.

Despite the Standard Poodle's claim to greater age than the other varieties, there is some evidence to show that the smaller types developed only a short time after the breed assumed the general type by which it is recognized today. The smallest, or Toy variety, was known in England in the 18th century, when the White Cuban became popular there. This was a sleeve dog attributed to the West Indies from whence it traveled to Spain and then to England. Queen Anne, we are told, admired a troupe of performing dogs that danced to music in almost human fashion. And this penchant, by the way, Poodles of all sizes have carried down the years intact.

**Standard Poodle**

**Miniature Poodle**

But the Continent had known the Poodle long before it came to England. Drawings by the German artist, Albrecht Durer, establish the breed in the 15th and 16th centuries. How long the dog had been known in Spain is problematical, but it was the principal pet dog of the latter 18th century, as shown by the paintings of the Spanish artist Goya. And France had Toy Poodles as pampered favorites during the reign of Louis XVI at about the same period.

There is scarcely a pure-bred dog of this day that can claim so many references in art and literature going back into time. Bas-reliefs dating from the first century, found along the shores of the Mediterranean, portray the Poodle very much as it is in this 20th century. Clipped to resemble the lion, it is not unlike some of the specimens seen at the earliest dog shows. Possibly long ago there was a link between the dog attributed to the Island of Melita—now known as the Maltese—and the Toy Poodle. Similarly there may have been a relationship between the Poodle and the dog of Spain—the spaniel. If they do not come from the same progenitor, at least the paths of their ancestors must have crossed at some remote time.

The universal esteem in which the Poodle has been held since the beginning of modern history is attested by its interesting variations in size and color. In accordance with present-day show classification, we have three sizes as well as an array of colors to suit almost anyone's taste. We have white ones, black ones, brown, cream, and blue ones, gray, apricot and so on; any solid color is allowed. Some are pink-skinned, some blue- or silver-skinned, others cream-skinned. Hence he who fancies a Poodle is never at a loss: he may choose a big dog to guard and protect, a medium-sized one to fit into restricted quarters, or a tiny tot to serve only as "comforter." And he can pick a color to match whatever his decor may happen to be. Surely such an unusual selection may have played at least some part in the Poodle's continued rise to fame. But even more, the dog's innate intelligence and his ability to learn are considered exceptional.

It should be kept in mind that the words, *Standard, Miniature, and Toy* are used to denote size only. All are one breed, governed by the same standard of perfection.

In addition to differences in size and color, the Poodle enjoys another characteristic unique among doggy kinds, namely, a coat which lends itself to a choice of hair styling. The top coat is very profuse indeed, wiry in texture and composed of thick, close curls, and the undercoat is woolly and warm. If allowed to grow unhindered the top coat forms thin, cylindrical mats which form a mass of ropelike cords: thus the curly Poodle becomes what used to be known in the old days as the Corded Poodle. This style, though, went out long ago; it was impractical for everyday living and difficult to keep in condition.

The various clips are of course a matter of taste insofar as the average owner is concerned. If he plans to exhibit in the show ring, however, he must choose in accordance with the specifications enumerated under Coat in the official AKC standard.

# Official Standard for the Poodle

**General Appearance, Carriage and Condition**—That of a very active, intelligent and elegant-appearing dog, squarely built, well proportioned, moving soundly and carrying himself proudly. Properly clipped in the traditional fashion and carefully groomed, the Poodle has about him an air of distinction and dignity peculiar to himself.

**Size, Proportion, Substance**—*Size*—The **Standard Poodle** is over 15 inches at the highest point of the shoulders. Any Poodle which is 15 inches or less in height shall be *disqualified* from competition as a Standard Poodle. The **Miniature Poodle** is 15 inches or under at the highest point of the shoulders, with a minimum height in excess of 10 inches. Any Poodle which is over 15 inches or is 10 inches or less at the highest point of the shoulders shall be *disqualified* from competition as a Miniature Poodle. The **Toy Poodle** is 10 inches or under at the highest point of the shoulders. Any Poodle which is more than 10 inches at the highest point of the shoulders shall be *disqualified* from competition as a Toy Poodle. As long as the Toy Poodle is definitely a Toy Poodle, and the Miniature Poodle a Miniature Poodle, both in balance and proportion for the Variety, diminutiveness shall be the deciding factor when all other points are equal. **Proportion**— To insure the desirable squarely built appearance, the length of body measured from the breastbone to the point of the rump approximates the height from the highest point of the shoulders to the ground. **Substance**—Bone and muscle of both forelegs and hind legs are in proportion to size of dog.

**Head and Expression (a)** *Eyes*—very dark, oval in shape and set far enough apart and positioned to create an alert intelligent expression. *Major Faults: Eyes round, protruding, large or very light.* **(b)** *Ears* hanging close to the head, set at or slightly below eye level. The ear leather is long, wide and thickly feathered; however, the ear fringe should not be of excessive length. **(c)** *Skull* moderately rounded, with a slight but definite stop. Cheekbones and muscles flat. Length from occiput to stop about the same as length of muzzle. **(d)** *Muzzle* long, straight and fine, with slight chiseling under the eyes. Strong without lippiness. The chin definite enough to preclude snipiness. *Major fault: Lack of chin.* **Teeth** white, strong and with a scissors bite. *Major faults: Undershot, overshot, wry mouth.*

**Neck, Topline, Body**—*Neck* well proportioned, strong and long enough to permit the head to be carried high and with dignity. Skin snug at throat. The neck rises from strong, smoothly muscled shoulders. *Major fault: Ewe neck.* The **topline** is level, neither sloping nor roached, from the highest point of the shoulder blade to the base of the tail, with the exception of a slight hollow just behind the shoulder. *Body* **(a)** Chest deep and moderately wide with well sprung ribs. **(b)** The loin is short, broad and muscular. **(c)** Tail straight, set on high and carried up, docked of sufficient length to insure a balanced outline. *Major faults: Set low, curled, or carried over the back.*

**Forequarters**—Strong, smoothly muscled shoulders. The shoulder blade is well laid back and approximately the same length as the upper foreleg. *Major fault: Steep shoulder.* **(a)** *Forelegs* straight and parallel when viewed from the front. When viewed from the side the elbow is directly below the highest point of the shoulder. The pasterns are strong. Dewclaws may be removed.

**Feet**—The feet are rather small, oval in shape with toes well arched and cushioned on thick firm pads. Nails short but not excessively shortened. The feet turn neither in nor out. *Major faults: Paper or splay foot.*

**Hindquarters**—The angulation of the hindquarters balances that of the forequarters. (a) *Hind legs* straight and parallel when viewed from the rear. Muscular with width in the region of the stifles which are well bent; femur and tibia are about equal in length; hock to heel short and perpendicular to the ground. When standing, the rear toes are only slightly behind the point of the rump. *Major fault: Cow-hocks.*

**Coat**—(a) *Quality*— (1) Curly: of naturally harsh texture, dense throughout. (2) Corded: hanging in tight even cords of varying length: longer on mane or body coat, head, and ears; shorter on puffs, bracelets, and pompons. (b) *Clip*— A Poodle under 12 months may be shown in the "Puppy" clip. In all regular classes, Poodles 12 months or over must be shown in the "English Saddle" or "Continental" clip. In the Stud Dog and Brood Bitch classes and in a non-competitive Parade of Champions, Poodles may be shown in the "Sporting" clip. A Poodle shown in any other type of clip shall be *disqualified.*

(1) *"Puppy"*: A Poodle under a year old may be shown in the "Puppy" clip with the coat long. The face, throat, feet and base of the tail are shaved. The entire shaven foot is visible. There is a pompon on the end of the tail. In order to give a neat appearance and a smooth unbroken line, shaping of the coat is permissible. (2) *"English Saddle"*: In the "English Saddle" clip, the face, throat, feet, forelegs and base of the tail are shaved, leaving puffs on the forelegs and a pompon on the end of the tail. The hindquarters are covered with a short blanket of hair except for a curved shaved area on each flank and two shaved bands on each hind leg. The entire shaven foot and a portion of the shaven leg above the puff are visible. The rest of the body is left in full coat but may be shaped in order to insure overall balance. (3) *"Continental"*: In the "Continental" clip, the face, throat, feet and base of the tail are shaved. The hindquarters are shaved with pompons (optional) on the hips. The legs are shaved, leaving bracelets on the hind legs and puffs on the forelegs. There is a pompon on the end of the tail. The entire shaven foot and a portion of the shaven foreleg above the puff are visible. The rest of the body is left in full coat but may be shaped in order to insure overall balance. (4) *"Sporting"*: In the "Sport- ing" clip, a Poodle shall be shown with face, feet, throat, and base of tail shaved, leaving a scissored cap on the top of the head and a pompon on the end of the tail. The rest of the body and legs are clipped or scissored to follow the outline of the dog, leaving a short blanket of coat no longer than one inch in length. The hair on the legs may be slightly longer than that on the body.

In all clips the hair of the topknot may be left free or held in place by elastic bands. The hair is only of sufficient length to present a smooth outline. "Topknot" refers only to hair on the skull, from stop to occiput. This is the only area where elastic bands may be used.

**Color**—The coat is an even and solid color at the skin. In blues, grays, silvers, browns, cafe-au-laits, apricots and creams the coat may show varying shades of the same color. This is frequently present in the somewhat darker feathering of the ears and in the tipping of the ruff. While clear colors are definitely preferred, such natural variation in

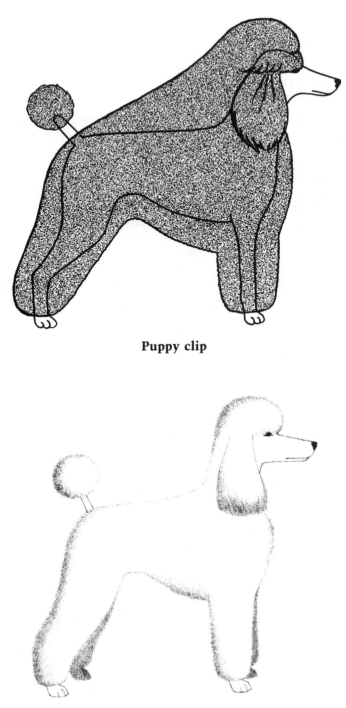

**Puppy clip**

**Sporting clip**

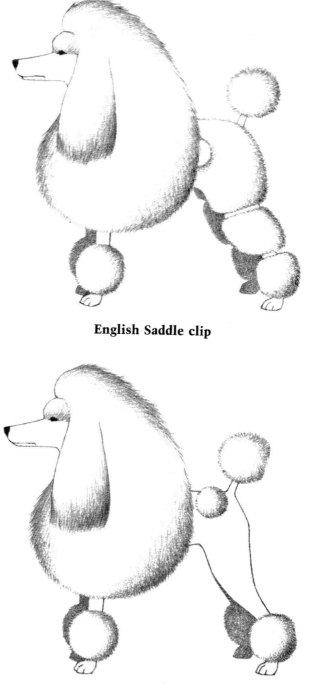

**English Saddle clip**

**Continental clip**

the shading of the coat is not to be considered a fault. Brown and cafe-au-lait Poodles have liver-colored noses, eye rims and lips, dark toenails and dark amber eyes. Black, blue, gray, silver, cream and white Poodles have black noses, eye rims and lips, black or self colored toenails and very dark eyes. In the apricots while the foregoing coloring is preferred, liver-colored noses, eye rims and lips, and amber eyes are permitted but are not desirable. *Major faults: Color of nose, lips and eye rims incomplete, or of wrong color for color of dog.*

Parti-colored dogs shall be *disqualified*. The coat of a parti-colored dog is not an even solid color at the skin but is of two or more colors.

**Gait**—A straightforward trot with light springy action and strong hindquarters drive. Head and tail carried up. Sound effortless movement is essential.

**Temperament**—Carrying himself proudly, very active, intelligent, the Poodle has about him an air of distinction and dignity peculiar to himself. *Major faults: Shyness or sharpness.*

**Major Faults**—Any distinct deviation from the desired characteristics described in the Breed Standard.

### VALUE OF POINTS

| | |
|---|---|
| General appearance, temperament, carriage and condition | 30 |
| Head, expression, ears, eyes, and teeth | 20 |
| Body, neck, legs, feet and tail | 20 |
| Gait | 20 |
| Coat, color and texture | 10 |

### DISQUALIFICATIONS

**Size**—*A dog over or under the height limits specified shall be disqualified.*
**Clip**—*A dog in any type of clip other than those listed under Coat shall be disqualified.*
**Parti-colors**—*The coat of a parti-colored dog is not an even solid color at the skin but of two or more colors. Parti-colored dogs shall be disqualified.*

Approved August 14, 1984
Reformatted March 27, 1990

# Schipperke

The Schipperke originated in the Flemish provinces of Belgium and is sometimes erroneously described as a Dutch dog, due perhaps to a misconception regarding the location of Flanders (a part of which extends into northern France) and to the fact that previous to 1832 Belgium and Holland were at times united. Charles Huge, the Belgian judge, says: "The Schipperke is not derived from the Spitz or Pomeranian but is really a diminutive of the black sheepdog commonly called the *Leauvenaar*, which used to follow the wagons along our old highways in the provinces. The proof of this is that those specimens that are born with a tail carry it like the Groenendael."

In the mid-19th century some of these 40-pound sheepdogs were still herding sheep in the neighborhood of Louvain, and from these both the Schipperke and the Groenendael have descended. The herd dog was gradually bred larger, and the Schipperke bred down to become that "excellent and faithful" little watchdog that we know.

The Schipperke has been known for several hundred years; in fact, it may claim the first known "specialty show," given for any breed. In 1690 a show for Schipperkes of the Guild workmen was held in the Grand Palace of Brussels; the men were invited to bring their dogs and the hammered brass collars which even at that time custom had ordered for the Schipperke.

The breed was called Spits or Spitske then; the name Schipperke was given it only after the forming of the specialty club in 1888. The name is Flemish for "little captain" and is properly pronounced "sheep-er-ker" (the last *r* almost silent). It was chosen as being a more distinctive name, and, as a compliment to Mr. Renssens, known as "the father of the Schipperke" because of his efforts to gain recognition for the breed. He was the owner of a canalboat line operating between Brussels and Antwerp and had observed that there were many Schipperkes used as guards on these boats. Though called a canalboat dog, the Schipperke was as popular with shoemakers and other workmen as it was on the canals.

The legend of the Schipperke relates that the custom of cutting the tails arose in 1609, and it tells the story of a shoemaker who, angered by the repeated thieving of his neighbor's dog, cut off its tail—thereby showing the improved appearance soon copied by others and continued to this day. There is no evidence that the breed was ever born tail-less; in fact, it seems that more dogs are born without tails now than earlier in their history. The Belgian Schipperkes Club has an amusing etching illustrating the legend "The Tail of the Schipperke."

The career of the Schipperke as a fashionable pet began in 1885 when Queen Marie Henriette, wife of Leopold II, saw a Schipperke at a Brussels show and acquired it. Before this time it had been the companion of the lower classes.

The first dog in America is believed to have been imported in 1888 by Walter J. Comstock of Providence. A few years later Frank Dole began showing Schips in the Miscellaneous Class. A specialty club was founded here about 1905, but died out during World War I. There was little interest until, after several years of effort by a few fanciers, the present Schipperke Club of America was founded in 1929.

The general appearance of the Schipperke is very distinctive, resembling no other breed closely. It has a short and thick-set body with foxy head—the whole suggesting a dog with plenty of coat and an outstanding ruff and long culotte. He has an intelligent, keen expression (not at all mean). His close undercoat keeps him warm even in American winters—the latter are far colder than those of his native land—and it sheds water and needs very little attention to keep it in order.

Temperament is considered important in judging this breed in France and Belgium and means what we in America would call pep—a Schip without this is not true to type. A judge of the breed for fifty years has said that the most important thing in judging is the correct silhouette: "I first look to see if the dog has the correct silhouette. If not, he is nothing and I look no further. If he has, I look into further details beginning with the bone structure."

This breed is usually long-lived for a small one, many instances of dogs living to 15 and 16 years old being recorded; one dog, bred in Rothesay, Scotland, was reputed to have lived 21 years.

The Schipperke is often called "the best house dog" (*le meilleur chien de maison*). Schips are very fond of children and in some cases have served as guards; they have taken the place, to some extent, of human nurses, so devoted are they to their small charges.

The dogs have been used to hunt, and one well-known breeder of the past wrote that he used them with great success on coons and possums in Minnesota. While usually an excellent ratter, the Schip is not a powerful fighter, though he can hold his own with most dogs of his weight and will tackle anything in defense of his household or of his master. He is not aware of the limitations of his size. As Caesar said: "the bravest of these were the Belgians."

## Official Standard for the Schipperke

**General Appearance**—The Schipperke is an agile, active watchdog and hunter of vermin. In appearance he is a small, thickset, cobby, black, tailless dog, with a fox-like face. The dog is square in profile and possesses a distinctive coat, which includes a stand-out ruff, cape and culottes. All of these create a unique silhouette, appearing to slope from shoulders to croup. Males are decidedly masculine without coarseness. Bitches are decidedly feminine without overrefinement.

Any deviation from the ideal described in the standard should be penalized to the extent of the deviation. Faults common to all breeds are as undesirable in the Schipperke as in any other breed, even though such faults may not be specifically mentioned in the standard.

**Size, Proportion, Substance**—*Size*—The suggested height at the highest point of the withers is 11–13 inches for males and 10–12 inches for bitches. Quality should always take precedence over size. *Proportion*—Square in profile. *Substance*—Thickset.

**Head**—*Expression*—The expression is questioning, mischievous, impudent and alert, but never mean or wild. The well proportioned head, accompanied by the correct eyes and ears, will give the dog proper Schipperke expression. *Skull*—The skull is of medium width, narrowing toward the muzzle. Seen in profile with the ears laid back, the skull is slightly rounded. The upper jaw is moderately filled in under the eyes, so that, when viewed from above, the head forms a wedge tapering smoothly from the back of the skull to the tip of the nose. The stop is definite but not prominent. The length of the muzzle is slightly less than the length of the skull. *Eyes*—The ideal eyes are small, oval rather than round, dark brown, and placed forward on the head. *Ears*—The ears are small, triangular, placed high on the head, and, when at attention, very erect. A drop ear or ears is a disqualification. *Nose*—The nose is small and black. *Bite*—The bite must be scissors or level. Any deviation is to be severely penalized.

**Neck, Topline, Body**—*Neck*—The neck is of moderate length, slightly arched and in balance with the rest of the dog to give the correct silhouette. *Topline*—The topline is level or sloping slightly from the withers to the croup. The stand-out ruff adds to the slope, making the dog seem slightly higher at the shoulders than at the rump. *Body*—The chest is broad and deep, and reaches to the elbows. The well sprung ribs (modified oval) are wide behind the shoulders and taper to the sternum. The forechest extends in front of the shoulders between the front legs. The loin is short, muscular and moderately drawn up. The croup is broad and well-rounded with the tail docked. No tail is visually discernible.

**Forequarters**—The shoulders are well laid back, with the legs extending straight down from the body when viewed from the front. From the side, legs are placed well under the body. Pasterns are short, thick and strong, but still flexible, showing a slight angle when viewed from the side. Dewclaws are generally removed. Feet are small, round and tight. Nails are short, strong and black.

**Hindquarters**—The hindquarters appear slightly lighter than the forequarters, but are well muscled, and in balance with the front. The hocks are well let down and the stifles are well bent. Extreme angulation is to be penalized. From the rear, the legs extend straight down from the hip through the hock to the feet. Dewclaws must be removed.

**Coat—*Pattern***—The adult coat is highly characteristic and must include several distinct lengths growing naturally in a specific pattern. The coat is short on the face, ears, front of the forelegs and on the hocks; it is medium length on the body, and longer in the ruff, cape, jabot and culottes. The ruff begins in back of the ears and extends completely around the neck; the cape forms an additional distinct layer extending beyond the ruff; the jabot extends across the chest and down between the front legs. The hair down the middle of the back, starting just behind the cape and continuing over the rump, lies flat. It is slightly shorter than the cape but longer than the hair on the sides of the body and sides of the legs. The coat on the rear of the thighs forms culottes, which should be as long as the ruff. Lack of differentiation in coat lengths should be heavily penalized, as it is an essential breed characteristic. ***Texture***—The coat is abundant, straight and slightly harsh to the touch. The softer undercoat is dense and short on the body and is very dense around the neck, making the ruff stand out. Silky coats, coats over three inches in length or very short harsh coats are equally incorrect. ***Trimming***—As the Schipperke is a natural breed, only trimming of the whiskers and the hair between the pads of the feet is optional. Any other trimming must not be done.

**Color**—The outercoat must be black. Any color other than a natural black is a disqualification. The undercoat, however, may be slightly lighter. During the shedding period, the coat might take on a transitory reddish cast, which is to be penalized to the degree that it detracts from the overall black appearance of the dog. Graying due to age (seven years or older) or occasional white hairs should not be penalized.

**Gait**—Proper Schipperke movement is a smooth, well coordinated and graceful trot (basically double tracking at a moderate speed), with a tendency to gradually converge toward the center of balance beneath the dog as speed increases. Front and rear must be in perfect balance with good reach in front and drive in the rear. The topline remains level or slightly sloping downward from the shoulders to the rump. Viewed from the front, the elbows remain close to the body. The legs form a straight line from the shoulders through the elbows to the toes, with the feet pointing straight ahead. From the rear, the legs form a straight line from the hip through the hocks to the pads, with the feet pointing straight ahead.

**Temperament**—The Schipperke is curious, interested in everything around him, and is an excellent and faithful little watchdog. He is reserved with strangers and ready to protect his family and property if necessary. He displays a confident and independent personality, reflecting the breed's original purpose as watchdog and hunter of vermin.

### DISQUALIFICATIONS

*A drop ear or ears.*
*Any color other than a natural black.*

Approved November 13, 1990

# Tibetan Spaniel

$T$he history of Tibet is important to the understanding of the early Tibetan Spaniel. The country has always been an isolated one and has little contact with the outside world except for neighboring China and India. The seclusion of Tibetan society, its political isolation, the loneliness of the nomadic life of its people, even the remoteness of villages within the country, together with the rise of Buddhism which did not permit the killing of animals, are all factors leading to the importance of dogs in the lives of the Tibetans.

Independent since 217 B.C. except for short periods of Chinese imperialism, Tibet became a Buddhist country in the 17th century. The Tibetans were a deeply religious, peace-loving nation, with their own Lamaist form of the Buddhist religion, in which the symbolic lion played an even more important role than it had in the Chinese and Indian interpretations. The lion represented the power of the Lord Buddha over violence and aggression, since Buddha had trained the lion to be tame and to "follow at his heels like a faithful dog." The small monastery dogs, thought to be early representatives of the Tibetan Spaniel, loyally trailed behind their Lama masters and came to be regarded as "little lions," thus giving them even greater value and prestige.

As the breed became more highly regarded, the practice of sending the dogs as gifts to the palaces of China and other Buddhist countries grew significantly and in reciprocity, more "lion dogs" were presented back to Tibet. This practice is believed to have continued until as late as 1908. Through exchange of Tibetan Spaniels between palaces and monasteries, the breed is likely to have common ancestors with a number of the Oriental breeds, including the Japanese Chin and the Pekingese.

The villages were a primary location for breeding and these village-bred Tibetan Spaniels varied greatly in size and type, probably because of little understanding of the value of breeding like to like. Size ranged from 4 to 16 pounds and the smaller puppies were usually given as gifts to the monasteries. In turn, these smaller dogs used in the monastery breeding programs were probably combined with the more elegant Tibetan Spaniel-type dogs brought from China, eventually producing a more refined dog of greater quality and elegance than their village relatives. Those bred in the monasteries closer to the Chinese borders were characterized by shorter muzzles, similar to the Chinese breeds from which they were descended. The purest ancient Tibetan type was found west of Lhasa, for fewer Chinese dogs had found their way to this area. The tremendous distances between monasteries and villages must account for the great difference in type in the early dog and it is not surprising to find other Tibetan breeds occasionally producing Tibetan Spaniel-type puppies. The true Tibetan Spaniel is the only one of all Tibetan breeds to have a hare foot instead of the round or cat foot. They closely resemble the Tibetan Mastiff in outline.

There is no doubt the Buddhist religion made an impact on the prominence of this breed in Tibetan society. Not only did Buddhism forbid the killing of animals, but the Buddhists had great faith in the doctrine of reincarnation. They believed that in previous lives they may have been animals and may be so again in the future. This theory, in addition to the belief that no essential spiritual differences exist between man and dog, encouraged kindness and humane treatment to animals in Tibet. To carry this doctrine even further, the Buddhists placed numerous representations of Tibetan Spaniel-type dogs made from pottery and clay within early Chinese tombs. This practice was believed to result in continued service from the dogs in the lives to come.

Further documentation of the breed's early origins can be found in the Tibetan Spaniel-type dogs frequently depicted in early Eastern art. The breed can be found on bronzes dating from the Shang Dynasty in 1100 B.C. and on finely carved jade representations of the Fu Lin dogs of China, some before the Manchu Dynasty which began in 1644 A.D.

Not only was the Tibetan Spaniel prized as a pet and companion, but it was considered a very useful animal by all classes of Tibetans. During the day, the dogs would sit on top of the monastery walls keeping a steady watch over the countryside below. Their keen eye and ability to see great distances, as well as their persistent barking, made them exceptionally good watchdogs. The Tibetan Spaniels were always quick to respond to the approach of wolves to the flocks grazing below them, in addition to the arrival of a stranger or an intruder. In this case, the dogs would let out continuous shrill barking, thus alerting a nearby Tibetan Mastiff. The larger Mastiff would then keep watch over the visitors. Evidently, this habit of sitting on high places and surveying the area below is still enjoyed by the Tibetan Spaniel of today.

Sometime in the late 1800s, the Hon. Mrs. McLaren Morris brought the first Tibetan Spaniel to England. In the 1920s, Dr. Agnes R. H. Greig, a medical missionary in the East, sent several of the dogs to her mother, Mrs. A. R. Greig, who exhibited them and started a breeding program. Sadly, the only dog from this line who survived World War II was Skyid who appears in some of today's pedigrees.

At the start of the War, Sir Edward and Lady Wakefield, an English couple living in Sikkim, received a gift of a bitch in 1938 from a Dr. Khanshi Ram, a trade agent in Western Tibet. The Wakefields obtained the use of a male, Tashi, from the Tashi Gong monastery for the purpose of breeding their bitch, Mughiwuli, and in 1940, the first of several litters of these two Tibetans was whelped. In 1941, a male, Garpon, and a litter sister, Potala, from one of these matings were brought to England by Colonel and Mrs. Hawkins. In the meantime, with the help of the King of Sikkim, the Wakefields obtained another bitch puppy, Dolma, who together with Lama, a son of Mughiwuli, formed the nucleus of the English "dynasty" of Tibetans commencing from 1947. The Tibetan Spaniel Association was formed in 1958 and by 1960 the Kennel Club awarded Challenge Certificates. By 1980, there were 114 recorded English champions.

Recognition moved a bit slower for American devotees. The first authenticated reference we find to Tibetan Spaniels in this country is a litter bred by a Mr. Harrington of New York state in 1965 out of two imported dogs from a Tibetan monastery. There is sufficient evidence to substantiate the existence of a number of these dogs scattered throughout the United States prior to 1968 but the first definite step toward popularizing the breed here could be credited to Leo Kearns, the Sexton of the Trinity Lutheran Church in New Haven, Connecticut. He purchased a bitch puppy from an antiques dealer who frequented the United Kingdom and the puppy was such a hit with the parishioners that Mr. Kearns ferreted out some of the English breeders and after considerable correspondence, Ms. M. C. Hourihane of the Amcross Kennels in Wilts, England sent him a male, Eng. Ch. Yakrose Chiala of Amcross. This dog was bred to his bitch, Doghouse Dream Baby, and on April 9, 1968, the first known American bred litter of Tibetan Spaniels was whelped. The puppies were quickly acquired by the parishioners and Mr. Kearns soon after imported over a dozen more Tibetan Spaniels from Amcross.

Among those who became interested in the breed was Mrs. Jay Child, who purchased an imported bitch from Kearns named Ciceter Norbu (Pandara). Although Kearns had actively imported stock from England, much credit must go to Mrs. Child for her singular determination to establish the breed in the United States.

In January 1971, the Tibetan Spaniel Club of America was formed with 14 charter members and Mrs. Child was named president. After a period in the Miscellaneous classes, the Tibetan Spaniel was accepted for AKC registration and became eligible to compete as a Non-Sporting breed effective January 1, 1984.

The Tibetan Spaniel possesses a unique personality, described by many as "cat-like." The breed is known to be extremely intelligent, sweet-natured and affectionate, family-oriented and very trusting of other dogs and people.

The litters are small, averaging about three puppies, and the bitches have only one estrus per year. It is a very "natural" breed, presented in the show ring in a completely unaltered condition. Grooming is minimal; they drop their undercoat in late spring and require only occasional brushing and bathing.

## Official Standard for the Tibetan Spaniel

**General Appearance**—Should be small, active and alert. The outline should give a well balanced appearance, slightly longer in body than the height at withers. *Fault*—Coarseness of type.

**Size, Proportion, Substance**—*Size*—Height about 10 inches. Body slightly longer from the point of shoulder to root of tail than the height at withers. Weight 9–15 pounds being ideal.

**Head**—Small in proportion to body and proudly carried, giving an impression of quality. Masculine in dogs but free from coarseness. *Eyes* dark brown in color, oval in shape, bright and expressive, of medium size set fairly well apart but forward looking, giving an apelike *expression.* Eye rims black. *Faults*—Large full eyes; light eyes; mean expression. *Ears* medium size, pendant, well feathered in the adult and set fairly high. They may have a slight lift from the skull, but should not fly. Large, heavy, low set ears are not typical. *Skull* slightly domed, moderate width and length. *Faults*—Very domed or flat wide skull. *Stop* slight, but defined. Medium length of *muzzle,* blunt with cushioning, free from wrinkle. The *chin* should show some depth and width. *Faults*—Accentuated stop; long, plain down face, without stop; broad flat muzzle; pointed, weak or wrinkled muzzle. Black *nose* preferred. *Faults*—Liver or putty-colored pigmentation. *Mouth* ideally slightly undershot, the upper incisors fitting neatly inside and touching the lower incisors. *Teeth* should be evenly placed and the lower jaw wide between the canine tusks. Full dentition desired. A level mouth is permissible, providing there is sufficient width and depth of chin to preserve the blunt appearance of the muzzle. Teeth must not show when mouth is closed. *Faults*—Overshot mouth; protruding tongue.

**Neck, Topline, Body**—*Neck* moderately short, strong and well set on. Level *back.* Well ribbed with good depth. *Tail* set high, richly plumed and carried in a gay curl over the back when moving. Should not be penalized for dropping tail when standing.

**Forequarters**—Shoulder well placed. The bones of the forelegs slightly bowed but firm at shoulder. Moderate bone. *Faults*—Very bowed or loose front. Dewclaws may be removed. *Feet* hare-footed, small and neat. *Fault*—Cat feet.

**Hindquarters**—Well made and strong. Stifle well developed, showing moderate angulation. Hocks well let down and straight when viewed from behind. *Faults*—Straight stifle; cow hocks. Dewclaws may be removed. *Feet* as in front.

**Coat**—Double coat, silky in texture, smooth on face and front of legs, of moderate length on body, but lying rather flat. Ears and back of forelegs nicely feathered, tail and buttocks well furnished with longer hair. Neck covered with a mane or "shawl" of longer hair which is more pronounced in dogs than bitches. Feathering between toes often extending beyond the feet. Should not be over-coated and bitches tend to carry less coat and mane than dogs. *Presentation*—In the show ring it is essential the Tibetan Spaniel be presented in an unaltered condition with the coat lying naturally with no teasing, parting or stylizing of the hair. Specimens where the coat has been altered by trimming, clipping, or by artificial means shall be so severely penalized as to be effectively eliminated from competition. Dogs with such a long coat that there is no rectangle of daylight showing beneath, or so profuse that it obstructs the natural outline, are to be severely penalized. Whiskers are not to be removed. Hair growing between the pads on the underside of the feet may be trimmed for safety and cleanliness.

**Color**—All colors and mixtures of colors allowed. *Feet*—White markings allowed.

**Gait**—Quick moving, straight, free, positive.

**Temperament**—Gay and assertive, highly intelligent, aloof with strangers. *Fault*—Nervousness.

Approved May 10, 1983
Reformatted February 7, 1989

# Tibetan Terrier

As the name indicates, Tibetan Terriers came from the land of Tibet where, so it is said, they were bred and raised in the monasteries by the lamas almost 2,000 years ago. Originating in the Lost Valley ("lost" when the access road was destroyed in the 14th century by a major earthquake) they were prized as companions and "luck bringers" for those fortunate enough to own them.

So inaccessible was the Lost Valley, so hazardous the journey to and from it, that the occasional visitor was often given a dog to safeguard him on the return trip to the outside world. No dog of this kind was ever sold, as no family would tempt fate by selling part of their "luck," but they were presented as a mark of esteem or a measure of gratitude for favors or services rendered.

Thus it came about that the late Dr. A. R. H. Greig, a practising physician in India in the 1920s, was given a dog by a grateful Tibetan whose ailing wife she had treated. Dr. Greig subsequently bred and raised a number of Tibetan Terriers in India, many of them descended from puppies sent to her by His Holiness the Dalai Lama in appreciation of her interest in their cherished breed. When Dr. Greig returned to England, she established the famous Lamleh Kennel there. Recognized in India in the 1920s and in England in 1937, the breed is now exhibited at shows almost the world over.

Dr. And Mrs. Henry S. Murphy of Great Falls, Virginia, brought the first "official" Tibetan Terrier to the United States in 1956, an import from the Lamleh Kennel in England with a Kennel Club (London) pedigree. Since then the breed has attracted fanciers from Canada to Florida, and from coast to coast.

The Tibetan Terrier is not actually a "terrier." He does not have the terrier disposition, nor does he burrow into the earth ("la terre" in French) as terriers were originally expected to do. This breed was called "terrier" because it was of a size widely associated with terriers. The Tibetan people called them "Luck Bringers" or "Holy Dogs," neither of which seemed suitable as a breed name in the Western world of dogs.

Tibetan Terriers were neither guard dogs nor herding dogs in Tibet. They were valued as companions, and were treated like children of the family. Like the children, they eagerly assisted in taking care of the family's property, their flocks and their herds, but these dogs were not raised for utilitarian purposes. The breed was kept pure-bred, as any mismating might bring bad luck to the family and might even be blamed for any village misfortune.

This is an exceptionally healthy breed, probably as a result of the rigorous natural selection process in their recent homeland. Tibet has one of the most difficult populated terrains in the world, and one of the most dramatic climates. Lhasa, for example, is exceedingly cold in the winter but often reaches 85° in the summer. The Tibetan Terrier is prepared to enjoy a blizzard, thanks to his profuse double coat, facial fur to protect his eyes from snow, and "snowshoe" feet, well furnished and suited for walking on the crust. Surprisingly, they do not seem to be at all upset by a hot, humid summer—simply relaxing for a nap during the worst part of such days.

The people of Tibet made no effort to eliminate any of the many colors found in this breed, believing that good health and a delightful temperament were far more important than coat color. It is hoped that Western breeders will continue this sensible breeding program, and that the Tibetan Terrier will continue to be an exceptional companion and friend of man—healthy, gay, intelligent and affectionate.

The Tibetan Terrier was admitted to registration in The American Kennel Club Stud Book on May 1, 1973, and to regular show classification in the Non-Sporting Group at AKC shows October 3, 1973.

## Official Standard for the Tibetan Terrier

The Tibetan Terrier evolved over many centuries, surviving in Tibet's extreme climate and difficult terrain. The breed developed a protective double coat, compact size, unique foot construction, and great agility. The Tibetan Terrier served as a steadfast, devoted companion in all of his owner's endeavors.

**General Appearance**—The Tibetan Terrier is a medium-sized dog, profusely coated, of powerful build, and square in proportion. A fall of hair covers the eyes and foreface. The well-feathered tail curls up and falls forward over the back. The feet are large, flat, and round in shape producing a snowshoe effect that provides traction. The Tibetan Terrier is well balanced and capable of both strong and efficient movement. The Tibetan Terrier is shown as naturally as possible.

**Head**—*Skull*—Medium length neither broad nor coarse. The length from the eye to the tip of the nose is equal to the length from eye to the occiput. The skull narrows slightly from ear to eye. It is not domed but not absolutely flat between the ears. The head is well furnished with long hair, falling forward over the eyes and foreface. The cheekbones are curved but not so overdeveloped as to bulge. *Muzzle*—The lower jaw has a small amount of beard. *Stop*—There is marked stop but not exaggerated. *Nose*—Black. *Teeth*—White, strong and evenly placed. There is a distinct curve in the jaws between the canines. A tight scissors bite, a tight reverse scissors bite or a level bite are equally acceptable. A slightly undershot bite is acceptable. *Eyes*—Large, set fairly wide apart, dark brown and may appear black in color, neither prominent nor sunken. Eye rims are dark in color. *Ears*—Pendant, falling not too close to the head, heavily feathered with a "V" shaped leather proportionate to the head. *Faults*—Weak pointed muzzle. Any color other than a black nose. Overshot bite or a very undershot bite or a wry mouth. Long narrow head. Lack of fall over the eyes and foreface.

**Neck, Topline, Body**—*Neck*—Length proportionate to the body and head. *Body*—Compact, square and strong, capable of both speed and endurance. *Topline*—The back is level in motion, *Chest*—Heavily furnished. The brisket extends downward to the top of the elbow in the mature Tibetan Terrier. *Ribs*—The body is well ribbed up and never cloddy or coarse. The rib cage is not too wide across the chest and narrows slightly to permit the forelegs to work free at the sides. *Loin*—Slightly arched. *Tail*—Medium length, heavily furnished, set on fairly high and falls forward over the back, may curl to either side. There may be a kink near the tip.

**Forequarters**—*Shoulders*—Sloping, well muscled and well laid back. *Legs*—Straight and strong when viewed from the front. Heavily furnished. The vertical distance from the withers to the elbow equals the distance from the elbows to the ground. *Feet*—The feet of the Tibetan Terrier are unique in form among dogs. They are large, flat, and round in shape producing a snowshoe effect that provides traction. The pads are thick and strong. They are heavily furnished with hair between the toes and pads. Hair between the toes and pads may be trimmed level with the underside of the pads for health reasons. The dog should stand well down on its pads. *Dewclaws*—May be removed.

**Hindquarters**—*Legs*—Well furnished, with well bent stifles and the hind legs are slightly longer than the forelegs. *Thighs*—Relatively broad and well muscled. *Hocks*—Low set and turn neither in nor out. *Feet*—Same as forefeet. *Dewclaws*—May be removed.

**Coat**—Double coat. Undercoat is soft and woolly. Outer coat is profuse and fine but never silky or woolly. May be wavy or straight. Coat is long but should not hang to the ground. When standing on a hard surface an area of light should be seen under the dog. The coat of puppies is shorter, single and often has a softer texture than that of adults. A natural part is often present over the neck and back. *Fault*—Lack of double coat in adults. Sculpturing, scissoring, stripping or shaving are totally contrary to breed type and are serious faults.

**Color**—Any color or combination of colors including white are acceptable to the breed. There are no preferred colors or combinations of colors.

**Gait**—The Tibetan Terrier has a free, effortless stride with good reach in front and flexibility in the rear allowing full extension. When gaiting the hind legs should go neither inside nor outside the front legs but should move on the same track approaching single tracking when the dog is moved at a fast trot. The dog with the correct foot and leg construction moves with elasticity and drive indicating that the dog is capable of great agility as well as endurance.

**Size**—Average weight is 20 to 24 pounds, but the weight range may be 18 to 30 pounds. Proportion of weight to height is far more important than specific weight and should reflect a well-balanced square dog. The average height in dogs is 15 to 16 inches, bitches slightly smaller. The length, measured from the point of shoulder to the root of tail, is equal to the height measured from the highest point of the withers to the ground. *Faults*—Any height above 17 inches or below 14 inches.

**Temperament**—The Tibetan Terrier is highly intelligent, sensitive, loyal, devoted and affectionate. The breed may be cautious or reserved. *Fault*—Extreme shyness.

Approved March 10, 1987

# HERDING DOGS

## Australian Cattle Dog

Australians owe a great debt to all the persons involved in the development of the Australian Cattle Dog, for without it the beef industry of Australia would undoubtedly have had great difficulty in developing into the important industry that it has become.

During the early colonization of Australia, the population was mainly confined to what is now the Sydney metropolitan area, the land holdings were relatively small, and the distances involved in taking stock to market were not very far. The stock contained on these properties were used to seeing men and dogs around them, and so were rather quiet and controllable. Working dogs that were brought out from other countries by the early settlers, although suffering a bit from the warmer climate, are believed to have worked these quiet cattle satisfactorily.

Eventually, settlers began spreading. In 1813, vast grazing lands were opened

**543**

up to the west. Here, landholdings were often hundreds, and even thousands of square miles, and were mostly unfenced. Cattle turned loose on these properties became wild and uncontrollable.

The most popular dog used by the early drovers and cattle owners was a working dog breed brought out from England known as the Smithfield. It was a big black, square-bodied, bobtail dog, with a long rough coat and a white frill around the neck. The head was shaped like a wedge, with long saddle flap ears, and the dog had a very cumbersome gait. Like the other working dogs of that time, the Smithfield found the high temperature, rough terrain, and long distances to market, more than it could handle. These early working dogs all had a trait of barking and heading while working stock. This is desirable for working sheep and even acceptable with quiet cattle, but only made the wild stock on the big cattle stations stampede and run off their condition.

It soon became obvious that a dog with more stamina, that would work quietly but more forcefully, was needed to get the wild cattle to the saleyards in Sydney. Around 1830, a drover named Timmins tried crossing the Smithfield with a native breed, the Dingo, with the aim of producing a silent working dog with more stamina. The progeny from this mating were red, bobtail dogs, which were named Timmins biters. Unlike the Smithfield, these dogs were silent workers but proved to be too headstrong, and severe with their biting. Although this crossbreed was used for a while, it gradually died out. Other crossbreeding was tried, such as the Rough Collie-Bull Terrier cross, but all these proved to be unsuccessful for working cattle.

In the year 1840, a land owner named Thomas Hall imported a pair of smooth-haired, blue merle Highland Collies from Scotland. They were good workers, but barked and headed. Hall crossed progeny from this pair with the Dingo, which produced silent workers that became known as Hall's Heelers. The color of the dogs from this cross were either red or blue merle, with most of them having pricked ears, and Dingo-shaped head with brown eyes, and they were generally of the Dingo type. Hall's dogs were a big improvement on any other available working dogs, and became much sought after by cattle men.

Another land owner, George Elliott, in Queensland, was also experimenting with Dingo–blue merle Collie crosses. Elliott's dogs produced some excellent workers. Cattle men were impressed with the working ability of these dogs, and purchased pups from them as they became available. Two brothers, Jack and Harry Bagust, of Canterbury in Sydney, purchased some of these dogs and set about improving on them. Their first step was to cross a bitch with a fine imported Dalmatian dog. This cross changed the merle to red or blue speckle. The pups were born white, developing their coloring at about three weeks of age. The Bagusts' purpose in this cross was to instill the love of horses, and faithfulness to master into their dogs. This characteristic was obtained and made these Bagust dogs useful for minding the drover's horse and gear, but some of the working ability was lost. Admiring the working ability of the Black and Tan Kelpie, which is a sheepdog, the Bagusts experimented in crossing them with their Speckle dogs. The result was a compact active dog, identical in type and build to the Dingo, only thicker set and with peculiar markings found on no other dog in the world. The blue dogs had black patches around the eyes, with black ears and brown eyes, with a small white patch in the middle of the forehead. The body was dark blue, evenly speckled with a lighter blue, having the same tan markings on legs, chest and head as the Black and Tan Kelpie. The red dogs had dark red markings instead of black, with an allover even red speckle.

Only the pups closest to the ideal were kept and these became the forebears of the present-day Australian Cattle Dog. The working ability of the Bagusts' dogs was outstanding, retaining the quiet heeling ability and stamina of the Dingo, with the faithful protectiveness of the Dalmatian. As the word spread on the ability of these dogs to work cattle, they became keenly sought after by property owners and drovers. The blue colored dogs proved to be more popular, and became known as Blue Heelers. These cattle dogs became indispensable to the owners of the huge cattle runs in Queensland, where they were given the name tag of Queensland Heelers or Queensland Blue Heelers.

After the Black and Tan Kelpie cross, no other infusion of breeds was practiced with any success. The breeders of the day concentrated on breeding for working ability, type and color. In 1893 Robert Kaleski took up breeding the Blue Heelers, and started showing them in 1897.

Mr. Kaleski drew up his standard for the Cattle Dog and also for the Kelpie and Barb in 1902. He based the Cattle Dog standard around the Dingo type, believing that this was the type naturally evolved to suit the conditions of this country. Even today the resemblance to the Dingo is evident, except for the color of the blues and the speckle in the reds. After much opposition from careless breeders, Kaleski finally had his standard endorsed by them and all the leading breeders of the time. He then submitted his standard to the Cattle and Sheep Dog Club of Australia, and the original Kennel Club of New South Wales for their approval. The standard was approved in 1903.

The breed became known as the Australian Heeler, then later the Australian Cattle Dog, which is now accepted throughout Australia as the official name for this breed. However, even today, some people can be heard calling them Blue Heelers or Queensland Heelers.

After a period as a Miscellaneous breed, the Australian Cattle Dog was accepted for registration by the American Kennel Club as of May 1, 1980, and became eligible to be shown in the Working Group as of September 1, 1980. It was transferred to the Herding Group when that was formed, effective January 1, 1983.

## Official Standard for the Australian Cattle Dog

**General Appearance**—The general appearance is that of a sturdy, compact, symmetrically-built working dog. With the ability and willingness to carry out any task however arduous, its combination of substance, power, balance and hard muscular condition to be such that must convey the impression of a great agility, strength and endurance. Any tendency to grossness or weediness is a serious fault.

**Characteristics**—The utility purpose is assistance in the control of cattle, in both wide open and confined areas. Ever alert, extremely intelligent, watchful, courageous and trustworthy, with an implicit devotion to duty, making it an ideal dog. Its loyalty and protective instincts make it a self-appointed guardian to the stockman, his herd, his property. Whilst suspicious of strangers, must be amenable to handing in the show ring.

**Head**—The head, in balance with other proportions of the dog, and in keeping with its general conformation, is broad of skull, and only slightly curved between the ears, flattening to a slight but definite stop. The cheeks are muscular, but not coarse nor prominent, the underjaw is strong, deep and well-developed. The foreface is broad and well filled in under the eye, tapering gradually to a medium length, deep and powerful muzzle. The lips are tight and clean. The nose is black irrespective of the color of the dog. **Teeth**—The teeth should be sound, strong, and regularly spaced, gripping with a scissors-like action, the lower incisors close behind and just touching the upper. Not to be undershot nor overshot. **Eyes**—The eyes should be oval shaped of medium size, neither prominent nor sunken, and must express alertness and intelligence. A warning or suspicious glint is characteristic. Eye color is dark brown. **Ears**—The ears should be of moderate size, preferably small rather than large, broad at the base, muscular, pricked and moderately pointed (not spoon nor bat eared). Set wide apart on the skull, inclined outwards, sensitive in their use, and firmly erect when alert. The inside of the ear should be fairly well furnished with hair.

**Neck**—The neck is of exceptional strength, muscular, and of medium length broadening to blend into the body and free from throatiness.

**Forequarters**—The shoulders are broad of blade, sloping, muscular and well angulated to the upper arm, and at the point of the withers should not be too closely set. The forelegs have strong round bone, extending to the feet without weakness at the pasterns. The forelegs should be perfectly straight viewed from the front, but the pasterns should show a slight angle with the forearm when regarded from the side.

**Hindquarters**—The hindquarters are broad, strong and muscular. The rump is rather long and sloping, thighs long, broad and well-developed, with moderate turn to stifle. The hocks are strong and well let down. When viewed from behind, the hind legs, from the hocks to the feet, are straight and placed neither close nor too wide apart.

**Feet**—The feet should be round and the toes short, strong, well-arched and held together. The pads hard and deep, and the nails must be short and strong.

**Body**—The length of the body from the point of the breast bone, in a straight line to the buttocks, is greater than the height at the withers, as 10 is to 9. The topline is level, back strong, with ribs well sprung and ribbed back. (Not barrel ribbed.) The chest is deep and muscular, and moderately broad, loins are broad, deep and muscular with deep flanks strongly coupled between the fore and hindquarters.

**Tail**—The set on of the tail is low, following the contours of the sloping rump, and at rest should hang in a slight curve of a length to reach approximately to the hock. During movement and/or excitement it may be raised, but under no circumstances should any part of the tail be carried past a vertical line drawn through the root.

**Coat**—The weather resisting outer coat is moderately short, straight and of medium texture, with short dense undercoat. Behind the quarters the coat is longer, forming a mild breeching. The tail is furnished sufficiently to form a good brush. The head, forelegs, hind legs from hock to ground, are coated with short hair.

**Color (Blue)**—The color should be blue or blue-mottled with or without other markings. The permissible markings are black, blue or tan markings on the head, evenly distributed for preference. The forelegs tan midway up the legs and extending up the front to the breast and throat, with tan on jaws; the hindquarters tan on inside of hind legs, and inside of thighs, showing down from the front of the stifles and broadening out to the outside of the hind legs from hocks to toes. Tan undercoat is permissible on the body providing it does not show through the blue outer coat. Black markings on the body are not desirable.

**Color (Red Speckle)**—The color should be a good even red speckle all over including the undercoat (not white or cream) with or without darker red markings on the head. Even head markings are desirable. Red markings on the body are permissible but not desirable.

**Size**—The desirable height at the withers to be within the following dimensions— Dogs: 18 to 20 inches. Bitches: 17 to 19 inches. Dogs or bitches over or under these specified sizes are undesirable.

**Movement**—Soundness is of paramount importance. The action is true, free, supple and tireless, the movement of the shoulders and forelegs with the powerful thrust of the hindquarters, in unison. Capability of quick and sudden movement is essential. Stiltiness, loaded or slack shoulders, straight shoulder placement, weakness at elbows, pasterns or feet, straight stifles, cow or bow hocks, must be regarded as serious faults.

Approved June 12, 1979

# Bearded Collie

Sometimes known as the Highland Collie, the Mountain Collie, or the Hairy Mou'ed Collie, the Bearded Collie is one of Britain's oldest breeds. While some have theorized that the Beardie was around to greet the Romans when they first invaded Britain, the current theory is that like most shaggy haired herding dogs, the Bearded Collie descends from the Magyar Komondor of central Europe.

As with most breeds not used by the nobility, there are few early records on this humble herdsman's dog. The earliest known pictures of Bearded Collies are a 1771 Gainsborough portrait of the Duke of Buccleigh and a 1772 Reynolds portrait of that peer's wife and daughter accompanied by two dogs. With Reinagle's more easily recognizable "Sheepdog" published in Taplin's 1803 *Sportsman's Cabinet,* and a description of the breed published in an 1818 edition of *Live Stock Journal,* the existence of the breed as we know it is firmly established.

At the end of the Victorian era, Beardies were fairly popular in southern Scotland, both as working and as show dogs. When Bearded Collie classes were offered at shows, usually in the area about Peebleshire, they were well supported. However, there was then no official standard, since no breed club existed to establish one and each judge had to adopt his own criteria. The lack of a strong breed club proved quite a misfortune. The local popularity of the breed continued until World War I, during which there were few dog shows. By the 1930s there was no kennel breeding Bearded Collies for show purposes.

That Beardies did not die out rests on their ability as workers and the devotion of the Peebleshire shepherds and drovers to the breed. They are still highly valued as a sheepdog, due to their ability to turn in a good day's work in south Scotland's misty, rainy and cold climate, and their adeptness on the rough, rocky ground.

The Bearded Collie's other major use is as a drover. They work with little direction from the butchers and drovers who find them very valuable in moving troublesome cattle. The shepherds and drovers have valued Beardies to such an extent that they have been more than reluctant to sell any puppies (especially bitches) unless they could be sure the puppies would actually be worked.

After World War II, Mrs. G. O. Willison, owner of the Bothkennar Kennels, saved the Beardie from further chance of extinction when she began to breed them for show purposes. She spearheaded the establishment of the Bearded Collie Club in Britain in 1955. After much travail, in 1959 the Kennel Club in England allowed Bearded Collies to be eligible for Challenge Certificates and championships and the popularity of the breed began to steadily increase.

Bearded Collies were introduced into the United States in the late 1950s, but none of these dogs were bred. It wasn't until 1967 that the first litter of Bearded Collies was born in this country. By July 1969, there was enough interest for the Bearded Collie Club of America to be founded.

The breed became eligible to be shown in the Miscellaneous Class as of June 1, 1974. The AKC Stud Book was opened to Bearded Collie registrations on October 1, 1976, and the breed became eligible to compete in the Working Group on February 1, 1977. It became a breed of the Herding Group when that group was established, effective January 1983.

## Official Standard for the Bearded Collie

**Characteristics**—The Bearded Collie is hardy and active, with an aura of strength and agility characteristic of a real working dog. Bred for centuries as a companion and servant of man, the Bearded Collie is a devoted and intelligent member of the family. He is stable and self-confident, showing no signs of shyness or aggression. This is a natural and unspoiled breed.

**General Appearance**—The Bearded Collie is a medium sized dog with a medium length coat that follows the natural lines of the body and allows plenty of daylight under the body. The body is long and lean, and though strongly made, does not appear heavy. A bright inquiring expression is a distinctive feature of the breed. The Bearded Collie should be shown in a natural stance.

**Head**—The head is in proportion to the size of the dog. The skull is broad and flat; the stop is moderate; the cheeks are well filled beneath the eyes; the muzzle is strong and full; the foreface is equal in length to the distance between the stop and occiput. The nose is large and squarish. A snipy muzzle is to be penalized. *(See Color section for pigmentation.)* **Eyes**—The eyes are large, expressive, soft and affectionate, but not round nor protruding, and are set widely apart. The eyebrows are arched to the sides to frame the eyes and are long enough to blend smoothly into the coat on the sides of the head. *(See Color section for eye color.)* **Ears**—The ears are medium sized, hanging and covered with long hair. They are set level with the eyes. When the dog is alert, the ears have a slight lift at the base. **Teeth**—The teeth are strong and white, meeting in a scissors bite. Full dentition is desirable.

**Neck**—The neck is in proportion to the length of the body, strong and slightly arched, blending smoothly into the shoulders.

**Forequarters**—The shoulders are well laid back at an angle of approximately 45°; a line drawn from the highest point of the shoulder blade to the forward point of articulation approximates a right angle with a line from the forward point of articulation to the point of the elbow. The top of the shoulder blades lie in against the withers, but they slope outwards from there sufficiently to accommodate the desired spring of ribs. The legs are straight and vertical, with substantial, but not heavy, bone and are covered with shaggy hair all around. The pasterns are flexible without weakness.

**Body**—The body is longer than it is high in an approximate ratio of five to four, length measured from point of chest to point of buttocks, height measured at the highest point of the withers. The length of the back comes from the length of the ribcage and not that of the loin. The back is level. The ribs are well sprung from the spine but are flat at the sides. The chest is deep, reaching at least to the elbows. The loins are strong. The level back line blends smoothly into the curve of the rump. A flat croup or a steep croup is to be severely penalized.

**Hindquarters**—The hind legs are powerful and muscular at the thighs with well bent stifles. The hocks are low. In normal stance, the bones below the hocks are perpendicular to the ground and parallel to each other when viewed from the rear; the hind feet fall just behind a perpendicular line from the point of buttocks when viewed from the side. The legs are covered with shaggy hair all around. **Tail**—The tail is set low and is long enough for the end of the bone to reach at least the point of the hocks. It is normally carried low with an upward swirl at the tip while the dog is standing. When the dog is excited or in motion, the curve is accentuated and the tail may be raised but is never carried beyond a vertical line. The tail is covered with abundant hair.

**Feet**—The feet are oval in shape with the soles well padded. The toes are arched and close together, and well covered with hair including between the pads.

**Coat**—The coat is double with the undercoat soft, furry and close. The outercoat is flat, harsh, strong and shaggy, free from wooliness and curl, although a slight wave is permissible. The coat falls naturally to either side but must never be artificially parted. The length and density of the hair are sufficient to provide a protective coat and to enhance the shape of the dog, but not so profuse as to obscure the natural lines of the body. The dog should be shown as naturally as is consistent with good grooming but the coat must not be trimmed in any way. On the head, the bridge of the nose is sparsely covered with hair which is slightly longer on the sides to cover the lips. From the cheeks, the lower lips and the under chin, the coat increases in length towards the chest, forming the typical beard. An excessively long, silky coat or one which has been trimmed in any way must be severely penalized.

**Color—*Coat:*** All Bearded Collies are born either black, blue, brown or fawn, with or without white markings. With maturity, the coat color may lighten, so that a born black may become any shade of gray from black to slate to silver, a born brown from chocolate to sandy. Blues and fawns also show shades from dark to light. Where white occurs, it only appears on the foreface as a blaze, on the skull, on the tip of the tail, on the chest, legs and feet and around the neck. The white hair does not grow on the body behind the shoulder nor on the face to surround the eyes. Tan markings occasionally appear and are acceptable on the eyebrows, inside the ears, on the cheeks, under the root of the tail, and on the legs where the white joins the main color. ***Pigmentation:*** Pigmentation on the Bearded Collie follows coat color. In a born black, the eye rims, nose and lips are black, whereas in the born blue, the pigmentation is a blue-gray color. A born brown dog has brown pigmentation and born fawns a correspondingly lighter brown. The pigmentation is completely filled in and shows no sign of spots. ***Eyes:*** Eye color will generally tone with the coat color. In a born blue or fawn, the distinctively lighter eyes are correct and must not be penalized.

**Size—**The ideal height at the withers is 21–22 inches for adult dogs and 20–21 inches for adult bitches. Height over and under the ideal is to be severely penalized. The express objective of this criterion is to insure that the Bearded Collie remains a medium sized dog.

**Gait—**Movement is free, supple and powerful. Balance combines good reach in forequarters with strong drive in hindquarters. The back remains firm and level. The feet are lifted only enough to clear the ground, giving the impression that the dog glides along making minimum contact. Movement is lithe and flexible to enable the dog to make the sharp turns and sudden stops required of the sheepdog. When viewed from the front and rear, the front and rear legs travel in the same plane from the shoulder and hip joint to pads at all speeds. Legs remain straight, but feet move inward as speed increases until the edges of the feet converge on a center line at a fast trot.

### SERIOUS FAULTS

*Snipy muzzle.*
*Flat croup or steep croup.*
*Excessively long, silky coat.*
*Trimmed or sculptured coat.*
*Height over or under the ideal.*

Approved August 9, 1978

# Belgian Malinois

The Belgian Malinois is one of four types of Belgian sheepherding dogs registered in Belgium and France as the *Chien de Berger Belge*. It shares a common foundation with the Belgian Sheepdog and Belgian Tervuren whose historical sections in this book provide additional information on the beginnings of the breed. One of the first short-coated Belgian shepherds registered by the Societe Royale Saint-Hubert was Charlot, born in 1891, which was later used as a model of the Belgian Malinois by the Belgian artist, A. Clary.

While the shorthaired, fawn dogs with black mask which we know today as the Belgian Malinois shared the beginnings with many coat colors and lengths, it quickly established itself as an identifiable type. Bred basically around the city of Malines from whence the name is derived, the Belgian Malinois was bred by a dedicated group of trainers and working competitors. They prized the abilities of this breed and concerned themselves with the breeding of excellent working character. Because of this, the Belgian Malinois has historically been the favorite type of Belgian Shepherd in its native Belgium. Professor Adolphe Reul, one of the dedicated leaders in the breed formation, owned and bred many fine subjects, including the famous Mastock.

Because the early breeders were concerned with type and character, many cross-variety breedings took place. The Belgian Malinois was the superior competition dog, and many used it to add strength to their varieties. We still see the effects of those breedings today when longhaired puppies are born in our registered Belgian Malinois litters. Through the offspring with long hair and from cross-variety breedings, the Belgian Malinois has intertwined its history with the other Belgian Sheepdogs. The Belgian Tervuren, especially, owes a great deal to the function of Belgian Malinois blood.

There have been two periods of Belgian Malinois activity in the United States. Starting in 1911 when the first shorthaired Belgian Shepherds (Belgian Blackie and Belgian Mouche) were registered with AKC until World War II, the Belgian Malinois enjoyed American popularity. Many subjects from the best Belgian bloodlines were imported and bred. There was some renewed interest after the war, but the breed did not flourish. Before 1959, the Belgian Malinois was relegated to the Miscellaneous Class (even though it enjoyed individual AKC Stud Book registration) because there were not enough subjects to provide competition for championships.

The second period of importation and popular support began in 1963. Progressing slowly, the first ten years saw only 107 individual Belgian Malinois registrations. By June of 1965, however, sufficient numbers had been registered by AKC so the Belgian Malinois was moved into the Working Group and was eligible to compete for championships. Importations from Belgium, France and Switzerland, as well as increased breeding activity since 1973, have given rise to a new era of relative popularity. While still numerically one of AKC's smallest breeds, the Belgian Malinois is beginning to make its presence felt in the Herding Group, formed effective January 1983.

The adopted standards recognized by AKC differ somewhat for the three Belgian Shepherd breeds, but the basic dog is the same for each. In Europe and elsewhere in the world, they share a common standard.

The main qualities which make the Belgian Malinois such a desirable breed are the easy-care coat, the medium size, and the keen intelligence. The breed has always been known for its trainability, and many owners today are finding pleasure in training their Belgian Malinois for conformation, obedience, schutzhund, herding, sledding and tracking as well as to be family companions.

## Official Standard for the Belgian Malinois

**General Appearance**—The Belgian Malinois is a well balanced, square dog, elegant in appearance with an exceedingly proud carriage of the head and neck. The dog is strong, agile, well muscled, alert and full of life. He stands squarely on all fours and viewed from the side, the topline, forelegs, and hind legs closely approximate a square. The whole conformation gives the impression of depth and solidity without bulkiness. The male is usually somewhat more impressive and grand than his female counterpart, which has a distinctly feminine look.

**Size, Proportion, Substance**—Males are 24 to 26 inches in height; females are 22 to 24 inches; measurement to be taken at the withers. Males under 23 inches or over 27 inches and females under 21 inches or over 25 inches are to be disqualified. The length, measured from the point of the breastbone to the point of the rump, should equal the height, but bitches may be slightly longer. A square dog is preferred. Bone structure is moderately heavy in proportion to height so that the dog is well balanced throughout and neither spindly or leggy nor cumbersome and bulky.

**Head**—The head is clean-cut and strong without heaviness; overall size is in proportion to the body. The *expression* should indicate alertness, attention and readiness for activity, and the gaze is intelligent and questioning. The *eyes* are brown, preferably dark brown, medium size, slightly almond shaped, not protruding. Eye rims are black. The *ears* approach the shape of an equilateral triangle and are stiff, erect, and in proportion to the head in size. The outer corner of the ear should not come below the center of the eye. Ears hanging as on a hound, or semi-prick ears are disqualifications. The top of the *skull* is flattened rather than rounded with the width approximately the same as the length but no wider. The stop is moderate. The *muzzle* is moderately pointed, avoiding any tendency to snipiness, and approximately equal in length to that of the topskull. The planes of the muzzle and topskull are parallel. The jaws are strong and powerful. The nose is black without discolored areas. The lips are tight and black with no pink showing on the outside. The Belgian Malinois has a full complement of strong, white teeth, that are evenly set and meet in a scissors or level *bite.* Overshot and undershot bites are a fault. An undershot bite in which two or more of the upper incisors lose contact with two or more of the lower incisors is a disqualification. One or more missing teeth is a serious fault.

**Neck, Topline, Body**—The *neck* is round and of sufficient length to permit the proud carriage of the head. It should taper from the body to the head. The *topline* is generally level. The withers are slightly higher and slope into the back which must be level, straight and firm from withers to hip joint. The croup is medium long, sloping gradually. The *body* should give the impression of power without bulkiness. The chest is not broad but is deep with the lowest point reaching the elbow. The underline forms a smooth ascendant curve from the lowest point of the chest to the abdomen. The abdomen is moderately developed, neither tucked up nor paunchy. The loin section, viewed from above, is relatively short, broad and strong, and blends smoothly into the back. The *tail* is strong at the base, the bone reaching to the hock. In action it is raised with a curve, which is strongest towards the tip, without forming a hook. A cropped or stumped tail is a disqualification.

**Forequarters**—The forequarters are muscular without excessive bulkiness. The shoulder is long and oblique, laid flat against the body, forming a sharp angle with the upper arm. The legs are straight, strong, and parallel to each other. The bone is oval rather than round. Length and substance are well in proportion to the size of the dog. The pastern is of medium length, strong, and very slightly sloped. Dewclaws may be removed. The feet are round (cat footed) and well padded with the toes curved close together. The nails are strong and black except that they may be white to match white toe tips.

**Hindquarters**—Angulation of the hindquarters is in balance with the forequarters; the angle at the hock is relatively sharp, although the Belgian Malinois should not have extreme angulation. The upper and lower thigh bones should approximately parallel the shoulder blade and upper arm respectively. The legs are in proportion to the size of the dog; oval bone rather than round. Legs are parallel to each other. The thighs should be well muscled. Dewclaws, if any, should be removed. Metatarsi are of medium length, strong, and slightly sloped. The hind feet may be slightly elongated, with toes curved close together and well padded. Nails are strong and black except that they may be white to match white toe tips.

**Coat**—The coat should be comparatively short, straight, hard enough to be weather resistant, with dense undercoat. It should be very short on the head, ears, and lower legs. The hair is somewhat longer around the neck where it forms a collarette, and on the tail and backs of the thighs. The coat should conform to the body without standing out or hanging down.

**Color**—The basic coloring is a rich fawn to mahogany, with black tips on the hairs giving an overlay appearance. The mask and ears are black. The underparts of the body, tail and breeches are lighter fawn, but washed-out fawn color on the body is a fault. Color should be considered a finishing point, not to take precedence over structure or temperament. The tips of the toes may be white, and a small white spot on the breastbone/prosternum is permitted, not to extend to the neck. White markings, except as noted, are faulted.

**Gait**—The movement is smooth, free and easy, seemingly never tiring, exhibiting facility of movement rather than a hard driving action. The Belgian Malinois single tracks at a fast gait, the legs, both front and rear, converging toward the center line of gravity, while the topline remains firm and level, parallel to the line of motion with no crabbing. The breed shows a marked tendency to move in a circle rather than a straight line.

**Temperament**—Correct temperament is essential to the working character of the Belgian Malinois. The breed is confident, exhibiting neither shyness nor aggressiveness in new situations. The dog may be reserved with strangers but is affectionate with his own people. He is naturally protective of his owner's person and property without being overly aggressive. The Belgian Malinois possesses a strong desire to work and is quick and responsive to commands from his owner. Faulty temperament is strongly penalized.

**Faults**—The degree to which a dog is penalized should depend upon the extent to which the dog deviates from the standard and the extent to which the particular fault would actually affect the working ability of the dog.

### DISQUALIFICATIONS

*Males under 23 inches or over 27 inches and females under 21 inches or over 25 inches. Ears hanging as on a hound, or semi-prick ears.*
*An undershot bite in which two or more of the upper incisors lose contact with two or more of the lower incisors.*
*A cropped or stumped tail.*

Approved July 10, 1990

# Belgian Sheepdog

The Belgian Sheepdog is known as the *Groenendael*, or *Chien de Berger Belge* in most parts of the world. Its origin can be traced to the late 1800s when it was listed, both in stud books and at dog shows, among many other shepherds as the *Chien de Berger de Races Continentales* (Continental Shepherds). By pedigree we can identify many of the Continental Shepherds not only as the Belgian Shepherds (Groenendael, Malinois, Tervuren, and Laekenois), but also as German Shepherds, Hollander Herders, Beauceron, Bouvier des Flandres, and Briards.

As the European countries developed a sense of pride and a spirit of nationalism, many individuals worked to develop animals which would be identified with their own countries. In Belgium, in the late 1800s, efforts were made to determine if there was a true shepherd dog representative only of Belgium, and in September 1891, the *Club du Chien de Berger Belge* (Belgian Shepherd Club) was formed for this purpose. A commission of club members was established which contacted veterinarians and others throughout the provinces. In November, 1891, under the direction of the veterinarian Professor Adolphe Reul, a gathering was held at Cureghem, on the outskirts of Brussels, to examine the shepherd dogs of that area. From the 117 dogs exhibited, Professor Reul and his panel of judges concluded that for this Brabant Province there was a consistent type of sheepdog. They were anatomically identical but differed in hair textures, colors, and hair-lengths. What Professor Reul described was a square, medium-sized sheepdog, with well-set triangular ears and very dark brown eyes. The *Club de Chien de Berger Belge* devoted its efforts to similar exhibitions in the remaining eight provinces, and found similar results. Between 1891 and 1901, when the Belgian Shepherds were registered as a breed by the *Societe Royale Saint-Hubert*, efforts were directed toward developing a standard, improving type, and exhibiting.

The longhaired black Belgian Shepherds primarily owe their existence to Nicolas Rose, restaurateur and owner of the Chateau Groenendael, outside of Brussels. He purchased what are considered to be the foundation couple of the longhaired blacks, Picard d'Uccle and Petite, and established a thriving kennel which can be traced to 1893, the year the *Club du Chien de Berger Belge* adopted the first standard for the Belgian Shepherds. Picard d'Uccle was bred to Petite, producing the outstanding Pitt, Baronne, and Duc de Groenendael, as well as to his daughters and others in the area, who are to be found in the pedigrees of our current dogs. This stock formed the basis of these beautiful longhaired blacks, officially given the name Groenendael in 1910.

Interest in the Belgian Shepherds developed very quickly after they were recognized as a breed. Prior to World War I it had become apparent that, although called a shepherd or sheepdog, the Groenendael was a versatile animal and, with its keen intelligence and easy trainability, it could perform a variety of functions. The Paris Police utilized the Groenendael in the first decade of the 20th Century, as did the New York police who, in 1908, imported four Belgian Sheepdogs to work alongside an American-bred Groenendael.

In the same period, Belgian Customs officers employed the Groenendael for border patrols, and their efforts in capturing smugglers were greatly praised. The Groenendael were also used for herding, watchdogs, faithful companions, and became outstanding participants in the popular European "working trials," from the local trial through international competitions. The Groenendael, Jules du Moulin, demonstrated this versatility by earning his World Championship at the defense trials in France in 1908. Repeating his victories in 1909, 1910, and 1912, he also earned his International Championship at the police trials of Belgium and France for four straight years, 1909–1912.

During World War I, Belgian Sheepdogs distinguished themselves on the battlefields, serving as message carriers, ambulance dogs, and even pulling machine guns. Although first registered in the United States as early as 1911, their fame really took hold after the war. The Belgian Sheepdog Club of America was formed in 1919, and it was not uncommon to see 10 or 12 Belgian Sheepdogs exhibited at the larger Eastern shows in the 1920s. By 1926 the Belgian Sheepdog was ranked 42nd of the 100 breeds recognized by the AKC.

The "Great Depression" had a marked effect on the Belgian Sheepdog. Its popularity dropped to 97th place, and the American club ceased to function. World War II again found the Belgian Sheepdog serving as a war and defense dog, and many were utilized to guard military installations. Interest in the breed was rekindled after the war and the current Belgian Sheepdog Club of America was formed in 1949. Since then, many Groenendael have been imported and the interest in the breed has continued to grow.

Through an AKC decision, effective July 1, 1959, only the Groenendael can be registered as Belgian Sheepdogs, and must have three generations of Groenendael ancestors.

Throughout their history Belgian Sheepdogs have earned their reputation as truly well-rounded dogs, and to this day they continue to captivate our hearts. Their elegance of carriage and balanced movement are a pleasure to behold. Their talents in obedience, tracking, schutzhund, herding and as sled dogs have kept even the most activity-minded of us satisfied. Their skills in police work, search and rescue and as guide and therapy dogs have proven very valuable to society. These dogs have found their greatest value, however, in the hearts of their owners as gentle and devoted companions willing to give all to those they love.

## Official Standard for the Belgian Sheepdog

**General Appearance**—The first impression of the Belgian Sheepdog is that of a well balanced, square dog, elegant in appearance, with an exceedingly proud carriage of the head and neck. He is a strong, agile, well muscled animal, alert and full of life. His whole conformation gives the impression of depth and solidity without bulkiness. The male dog is usually somewhat more impressive and grand than his female counterpart. The bitch should have a distinctively feminine look. *Faults*—Any deviation from these specifications is a fault. In determining whether a fault is minor, serious, or major, these two factors should be used as a guide: 1. The extent to which it deviates from the standard. 2. The extent to which such deviation would actually affect the working ability of the dog.

**Size, Proportion, Substance**—Males should be 24–26 inches in height and females 22–24 inches, measured at the withers. Males under 22½ or over 27½ inches in height and females under 20½ or over 25½ inches in height shall be disqualified. The length, measured from point of breastbone to point of rump, should equal the height. Bitches may be slightly longer. Bone structure should be moderately heavy in proportion to his height so that he is well balanced throughout and neither spindly or leggy nor cumbersome and bulky. The Belgian Sheepdog should stand squarely on all fours. Side view— The topline, front legs, and back legs should closely approximate a square.

**Head**—Clean-cut and strong, overall size should be in proportion to the body. *Expression* indicates alertness, attention, readiness for activity. Gaze should be intelligent and questioning. *Eyes* brown, preferably dark brown. Medium size, slightly almond shaped, not protruding. *Ears* triangular in shape, stiff, erect, and in proportion to the head in size. Base of the ear should not come below the center of the eye. Ears hanging (as on a hound) shall disqualify. *Skull*—Top flattened rather than rounded. The width approximately the same, but not wider than the length. *Stop* moderate. *Muzzle* moderately pointed, avoiding any tendency to snipiness, and approximately equal in length to that of the topskull. The jaws should be strong and powerful. *Nose* black without spots or discolored areas. The *lips* should be tight and black, with no pink showing on the outside. *Teeth*—A full complement of strong, white teeth, evenly set. Should not be overshot or undershot. Should have either an even bite or a scissors bite.

**Neck, Topline, Body**—*Neck* round and rather outstretched, tapered from head to body, well muscled, with tight skin. *Topline*—The withers are slightly higher and slope into the back, which must be level, straight, and firm from withers to hip joints. *Chest* not broad, but deep. The lowest point should reach the elbow, forming a smooth ascendant curve to the abdomen. *Abdomen*—Moderate development. Neither tucked up nor paunchy. The *loin* section, viewed from above, is relatively short, broad and strong, but blending smoothly into the back. The *croup* is medium long, sloping gradually. *Tail* strong at the base, bone to reach hock. At rest the dog holds it low, the tip bent back level with the hock. When in action he raises it and gives it a curl, which is strongest toward the tip, without forming a hook. Cropped or stump tail shall disqualify.

**Forequarters**—*Shoulder* long and oblique, laid flat against the body, forming a sharp angle (approximately 90°) with the upper arm. *Legs* straight, strong and parallel to each other. Bone oval rather than round. Development (length and substance) should be well proportioned to the size of the dog. Pastern medium length, strong, and very slightly sloped. *Feet* round (cat footed), toes curved close together, well padded. Nails strong and black, except that they may be white to match white toe tips.

**Hindquarters**—*Legs*—Length and substance well proportioned to the size of the dog. Bone oval rather than round. Legs are parallel to each other. *Thighs* broad and heavily muscled. The upper and lower thigh bones approximately parallel the shoulder blade and upper arm respectively, forming a relatively sharp angle at stifle joint. The angle at the hock is relatively sharp, although the Belgian Sheepdog does not have extreme angulation. Metatarsus medium length, strong and slightly sloped. Dewclaws, if any, should be removed. *Feet* slightly elongated. Toes curved close together, well padded. Nails strong and black, except that they may be white to match white toe tips.

**Coat**—The guard hairs of the coat must be long, well fitting, straight and abundant. They should not be silky or wiry. The texture should be a medium harshness. The undercoat should be extremely dense, commensurate, however, with climatic conditions. The Belgian Sheepdog is particularly adaptable to extremes of temperature or climate. The hair is shorter on the head, outside of the ears, and lower part of the legs. The opening of the ear is protected by tufts of hair. *Ornamentation*—Especially long and abundant hair, like a collarette, around the neck; fringe of long hair down the back of the forearm; especially long and abundant hair trimming the hindquarters, the breeches; long, heavy and abundant hair on the tail.

**Color**—Black. May be completely black, or may be black with white, limited as follows: Small to moderate patch or strip on forechest. Between pads of feet. On *tips* of hind toes.

On chin and muzzle (frost—may be white or gray). On *tips* of front toes—allowable, but a fault. ***Disqualification***—Any color other than black, except for white in specified areas. Reddening due to climatic conditions in an otherwise correct coat should not be grounds for disqualification.

**Gait**—Motion should be smooth, free and easy, seemingly never tiring, exhibiting facility of movement rather than a hard driving action. He tends to single track on a fast gait; the legs, both front and rear, converging toward the center line of gravity of the dog. The backline should remain firm and level, parallel to the line of motion, with no crabbing. He shows a marked tendency to move in a circle rather than a straight line.

**Temperament**—The Belgian Sheepdog should reflect the qualities of intelligence, courage, alertness and devotion to master. To his inherent aptitude as a guardian of flocks should be added protectiveness of the person and property of his master. He should be watchful, attentive, and always in motion when not under command. In his relationship with humans, he should be observant and vigilant with strangers, but not apprehensive. He should not show fear or shyness. He should not show viciousness by unwarranted or unprovoked attack. With those he knows well, he is most affectionate and friendly, zealous of their attention, and very possessive. Viciousness is a disqualification.

### DISQUALIFICATIONS

*Males under 22½ or over 27½ inches in height and females under 20½ or over 25½ inches in height.*
*Ears hanging (as on a hound).*
*Cropped or stump tail.*
*Any color other than black.*
*Viciousness.*

Approved December 11, 1990

# Belgian Tervuren

The Belgian Tervuren is known in its country of origin as the *Chien de Berger Belge.* This variety is distinguished by its coat color and length as "longhaired other than black" in comparison to the Groenendael with long black hair, the Malinois with a short coat, and the wire-haired Laekenois. The variety designation, Tervuren, owes its name to the Belgian village of Tervuren, the home of M. F. Corbeel, an early devotee of the breed. Mr. Corbeel bred the fawn colored Tom and Poes, commonly considered the foundation couple of the breed, to produce the fawn colored Miss. In turn, Miss was bred to the black Duc de Groenendael, to produce the famous fawn Milsart, who in 1907 became the first Tervuren champion.

Prior to the Industrial Age, the rural farmers of Belgium had a great need for a general purpose herding and guard dog. The protective instinct of these dogs provided security for the farm and the family, and their herding abilities assisted with the daily maintenance of the stock. The mental development of the breed as a versatile helper and attentive companion paralleled the physical evolution of a medium-sized, well-balanced animal with strength and stamina. With industrialization, the rural farm dog became less important, but the beauty and loyalty of the breed made them well appreciated as family companions.

Very little written information is available on the origins of the breed before

**561**

the establishment of the Belgian Shepherd Club in 1891. Professor Adolphe Reul's documentation of the exhibitions held to determine breed type, leading to the first written standard in 1893, and the breed's recognition by the *Societe Royale Saint-Hubert* in 1901, are considered the important historical landmarks in the development of the Belgian Shepherd. In May of 1892, the first Belgian Shepherd Specialty was held in Cureghem, Belgium and was won by a registered Tervuren, Duc II, owned by Arthur Meul. This same Duc, a brown-brindle born in 1890, served as the model for the Belgian Tervuren in the famous painting done by A. Clarys in 1910.

In these early years, differing opinions on the color of the Tervuren allowed for a range of colors. While the breed was established without regard for color, the development of the varieties within the breed led to some breeders advocating a charcoaled fawn with a black mask, others preferring a plain fawn with no mask, and still others breeding for the silver color. Currently, any longhaired Belgian Shepherd that is not black is considered a Tervuren. In the United States the preferred colors range from fawn to mahogany, all with a black masking and a blackened overlay, as detailed in the Standard.

From the establishment of the Belgian Shepherd breed, there were only a few breeders dedicated to the production of the Tervuren, and breeding continued on a modest scale until after World War II. The outstanding reproducers of the 1900s were General, a direct descendant of Milsart, as well as Minox and Colette ex Folette, who were from Malinois parents, and who produced Jinox, Noisette, and Lakme. These dogs figure heavily in the ancestry of the Belgian Shepherds of the 1940s and 1950s who brought about the revival of the Tervuren as we know it today.

It was only after World War II that the Tervuren gained in popularity. In 1948, at the kennel of P. Daniel in Normandy, the pale fawn Willy de la Garde Noire was born, of Groenendael parents. As a pup he was sold to Gilbert Fontaine of the Clos St. Clair kennel. Although the longhaired fawns were generally not preferred at the time, Willy was of such excellent type and structure that he was able to compete equally with the best of the Groenendael and Malinois of the day. He won numerous CACIBs in both Belgium and France, including the 1950, 1953, and 1954 Paris shows. His record as a producer was no less spectacular, and it is because of Willy that the renaissance of the Tervuren began, primarily in France, but eventually extending to the rest of Europe and the United States. The development of the Tervuren during this time is a distinct reminder of the intricate interweavings of the genetics of the Belgian Shepherd. The Tervuren was literally created after World War II, from the longhaired puppies in Malinois litters and the fawn-grey puppies in the Groenendael litters. These dogs were eventually bred to a few remaining postwar Tervuren, producing what is now the most popular variety of Belgian Shepherd in parts of Europe and America.

The first Tervuren was registered with the AKC in 1918. Registrations at this time were sparse and by the time of the Depression the variety had disappeared from the AKC stud books. It was not until 1953 that the blackened fawn longhaired dogs were again imported, through the efforts of Rudy Robinson, Robert and Barbara Krohn, and Marge Coyle. Prior to 1959 these dogs were registered and shown as Belgian Sheepdogs. In that year the AKC granted the separate breed classification designating the Belgian Tervuren as a distinct breed.

The Belgian Tervuren has retained the characteristics of their working ancestors that made them so valued in times past—qualities that make them equally important to their owners today. By virtue of the quick intelligence and unwavering devotion they are precious personal companions. Their versatility is still highly appreciated on a par with their graceful elegance and eye-catching appearance. They have remained useful in herding and are now exhibiting their talents as therapy dogs and companions to the disabled. It is not at all unusual for them to compete equally in the breed and Obedience rings, and many breed champions also have earned Obedience degrees. They have been trained in sports as diverse as schutzhund and sledding. Truly, they have earned our respect for their adaptability, their exuberant personalities and distinctive beauty, and they have captivated our hearts with their love.

## Official Standard for the Belgian Tervuren

**General Appearance**—The first impression of the Belgian Tervuren is that of a well balanced medium size dog, elegant in appearance, standing squarely on all fours, with proud carriage of head and neck. He is strong, agile, well muscled, alert and full of life. He gives the impression of depth and solidity without bulkiness. The male should appear unquestionably masculine; the female should have a distinctly feminine look and be judged equally with the male. The Belgian Tervuren is a *natural* dog and there is no need for excessive posing in the show ring. The Belgian Tervuren reflects the qualities of intelligence, courage, alertness and devotion to master. In addition to his inherent ability as a herding dog, he protects his master's person and property without being overtly aggressive. He is watchful, attentive, and usually in motion when not under command. The Belgian Tervuren is a herding dog, and faults which affect his ability to herd under all conditions, such as poor gait, bite, coat or temperament should be particularly penalized.

**Size, Proportion, Substance**—The ideal male is 24 to 26 inches in height and female 22 to 24 inches in height measured at the withers. Dogs are to be penalized in accordance to the degree they deviate from the ideal. Males under 23 inches or over 26.5 inches or females under 21 inches or over 24.5 inches are to be disqualified. The body is square; the length measured from the point of shoulder to the point of the rump approximates the height. Females may be somewhat longer in body. Bone structure is medium in proportion to height, so that he is well balanced throughout and neither spindly or leggy nor cumbersome and bulky.

**Head**—Well chiseled, skin taut, long without exaggeration. *Expression* intelligent and questioning, indicating alertness, attention and readiness for action. *Eyes* dark brown, medium size, slightly almond shape, not protruding. Light, yellow or round eyes are a fault. *Ears* triangular in shape, well cupped, stiff, erect, height equal to width at base. Set high, the base of the ear does not come below the center of the eye. Hanging ears, as on a hound, are a disqualification. **Skull and muzzle** measuring from the stop are of equal length. Overall size is in proportion to the body, top of skull flattened rather than rounded, the width approximately the same as, but not wider than the length. **Stop** moderate. The topline of the muzzle is parallel to the topline of the skull when viewed from the side. Muzzle moderately pointed, avoiding any tendency toward snipiness or cheekiness. **Jaws** strong and powerful. **Nose** black without spots or discolored areas. *Nostrils* well defined. **Lips** tight and black, no pink showing on the outside when mouth is closed. **Teeth**—Full complement of strong white teeth, evenly set, meeting in a scissors or a level bite. Overshot and undershot teeth are a fault. Undershot teeth such that contact with the upper incisors is lost by two or more of the lower incisors is a disqualification. Loss of contact caused by short center incisors in an otherwise correct bite shall not be judged undershot. Broken or discolored teeth should not be penalized. Missing teeth are a fault.

**Neck, Topline, Body**—*Neck* round, muscular, rather long and elegant, slightly arched and tapered from head to body. Skin well fitting with no loose folds. *Withers* accentuated. *Topline* level, straight and firm from withers to croup. *Croup* medium long, sloping gradually to the base of the tail. *Chest* not broad without being narrow, but deep; the lowest point of the brisket reaching the elbow, forming a smooth ascendant curve to the abdomen. **Abdomen** moderately developed, neither tucked up nor paunchy. Ribs well sprung but flat on the sides. *Loin section* viewed from above is relatively short, broad and strong, but blending smoothly into the back. *Tail* strong at the base, the last vertebra to reach at least to the hock. At rest the dog holds it low, the tip bent back level with the hock. When in action, he may raise it to a point level with the topline giving it a slight curve, but not a hook. Tail is not carried above the backline nor turned to one side. A cropped or stump tail is a disqualification.

**Forequarters**—*Shoulders* long, laid back 45 degrees, flat against the body, forming a right angle with the upper arm. Top of the shoulder blades roughly two thumbs width apart. *Upper arms* should move in a direction exactly parallel to the longitudinal axis of the body. **Forearms** long and well muscled. *Legs* straight and parallel, perpendicular to the ground. Bone oval rather than round. *Pasterns* short and strong, slightly sloped. Dewclaws may be removed. **Feet** rounded, cat footed, turning neither in nor out, toes curved close together, well padded, strong nails.

**Hindquarters**—*Legs* powerful without heaviness, moving in the same pattern as the limbs of the forequarters. Bone oval rather than round. *Thighs* broad and heavily muscled. **Stifles** clearly defined, with upper shank at right angles to hip bones. **Hocks** moderately bent. *Metatarsi* short, perpendicular to the ground, parallel to each other when viewed from the rear. Dewclaws are removed. **Feet** slightly elongated, toes curved close together, heavily padded, strong nails.

**Coat**—The Belgian Tervuren is particularly adaptable to extremes in temperature or climate. The guard hairs of the coat must be long, close fitting, straight and abundant. The texture is of medium harshness, not silky or wiry. Wavy or curly hair is undesirable. The undercoat is very dense, commensurate, however, with climatic conditions. The hair is short on the head, outside the ears, and on the front part of the legs. The opening of the ear is protected by tufts of hair. ***Ornamentation*** consists of especially long and abundant hair, like a collarette around the neck, particularly on males; fringe of long hair down the back of the forearm; especially long and abundant hair trimming the breeches; long heavy and abundant hair on the tail. *The female rarely has as long nor as ornamented a coat as the male. This disparity must not be a consideration when the female is judged against the male.*

**Color**—*Body* rich fawn to russet mahogany with black overlay. The coat is characteristically double pigmented wherein the tip of each fawn hair is blackened. Belgian Tervuren characteristically become darker with age. On mature males, this blackening is especially pronounced on the shoulders, back and rib section. Blackening in patches is undesirable. Although allowance should be made for females and young males, absence of blackening in mature dogs is a serious fault. Washed out predominant color, such as cream or gray is to be severely penalized. *Chest* is normally black, but may be a mixture of black and gray. A single white patch is permitted on the chest, not to extend to the neck or breast. *Face* has a black mask and the ears are mostly black. A face with a complete absence of black is a serious fault. Frost or white on chin or muzzle is normal. The underparts of the body, tail, and *breeches* are cream, gray, or light beige. The *tail* typically has a darker or black tip. *Feet*—The tips of toes may be white. Nail color may vary from black to transparent. Solid black, solid liver or any area of white except as specified on the chest, tips of toes, chin and muzzle are disqualifications.

**Gait**—Lively and graceful, covering the maximum ground with minimum effort. Always in motion, seemingly never tiring, he shows ease of movement rather than hard driving action. He single tracks at a fast gait, the legs both front and rear converging toward the center line of gravity of the dog. Viewed from the side he exhibits full extension of both fore and hindquarters. The backline should remain firm and level, parallel to the line of motion. His natural tendency is to move in a circle, rather than a straight line. Padding, hackneying, weaving, crabbing and similar movement faults are to be penalized according to the degree which they interfere with the ability of the dog to work.

**Temperament**—In his relationship with humans he is observant and vigilant with strangers, but not apprehensive. He does not show fear or shyness. He does not show viciousness by unwarranted or unprovoked attack. He must be approachable, standing his ground and showing confidence to meet overtures without himself making them. With those he knows well, he is most affectionate and friendly, zealous for their attention and very possessive.

### DISQUALIFICATIONS

*Males under 23 inches or over 26.5 inches or females under 21 inches or over 24.5 inches.*
*Hanging ears, as on a hound.*
*Undershot teeth such that contact with the upper incisors is lost by two or more of the lower incisors.*
*A cropped or stump tail.*
*Solid black, solid liver or any area of white except as specified on the chest, tips of the toes, chin and muzzle.*

Approved September 11, 1990

# Bouvier des Flandres

(Boovay duh Flawn-druh)

$D$r. Adolphe Reul, of the Veterinary School of Brussels, was the first to call the attention of breeders to the many good qualities of the Bouvier. At that time, the Bouvier was a dog of great size (about 26 inches high at the shoulder), with a heavy cylindrical body, rough gray, dark hair, and a rough appearance. It was found in Southwest Flanders and on the French northern plain. As a rule, it was owned by people who occupied themselves with cattle, for the dog's chief aptitude seemed to be cattle driving.

Most of the early Bouvier breeders were farmers, butchers, or cattle merchants not particularly interested in breeding pedigreed dogs. All they wanted was help in their work. No one is surprised that the first Bouviers were not absolutely uniform in size, weight, and color. Nevertheless, they all had enough characteristics in common to be recognized as Bouviers. They had different names—*Vuilbaard* (dirty beard), *koehond* (cow dog), *toucheur de boeuf* or *pic* (cattle driver).

The Societe Royale St. Hubert took cognizance of the breed when it appeared on the show benches at the International dog show of May, 1910, in Brussels. The two Bouviers shown there were Nelly and Rex, belonging to a

Mr. Paret of Ghent. However, a standard of the Bouvier type was not adopted until 1912. That was accomplished by a Frenchman, Mr. Fontaine, vice-president of the Club St. Hubert du Nord. At that time a society of Bouvier breeders, founded in Roules (West) Flanders, invited many of the most famous Belgian experts to a meeting in August of that year. Those attending drew up a standard of perfection which became the first official standard to be recognized by the Societe Royale St. Hubert.

From then on, the Bouvier des Flandres grew to be more and more appreciated, and were listed in the L.O.S.H. (the stud book of the Society Royale St. Hubert).

The breed was making rapid progress when World War I broke out. The areas where the Bouvier was most largely bred and where it was becoming popular were entirely destroyed; the people left the country, and most of the dogs were lost. Many were abandoned and died, others were acquired by the Germans. However, a few men succeeded in keeping their dogs all through the war.

The dog whose progeny afterwards did much to revive the Bouvier in Belgium lived in the Belgian army as the property of Veterinarian Captain Barbry. This dog, Ch. Nic de Sottegem, was shown in 1920 at the Olympic show in Antwerp, where the judge, Charles Huge, said: "Nic is the ideal type of Bouvier. He has a short body, with well-developed ribs, short flanks, strong legs, good feet, long and oblique shoulders. His head is of a good shape, with somber eyes and an ideal courageous expression. His hair is dry and dark. The tail should not have been cut so short. I hope that this dog will have numerous progeny."

Mr. Huge's hope was realized. When Nic died in 1926, he left many descendants whose names appear in almost every pedigree. Among those worthy of mention are Prince D'Or, Ch. Draga, Coralie de Sottegem, Goliath de la Lys, Lyda, Nora, Ch. Dragon de la Lys, etc. From these dogs, gathered together one day at Ghent, a group of experts, including Charles Huge, V. Tenret, V. Taeymans, Count de Hemptinne, Captain Binon and A. Gevaert, after examining and measuring each one carefully, established a more comprehensive Standard.

The Bouvier was recognized by the AKC in 1929, and admitted to the stud book in 1931. American fanciers imported dogs regularly from Europe until World War II. At the end of the war interest revived, and the American Bouvier des Flandres Club was established in 1963.

Breeders do not forget that the Bouvier is first of all a working dog, and although they try to standardize its type, they do not want it to lose the early qualities which first called attention to its desirability. For that reason, in Belgium a Bouvier cannot win the title of champion unless he has also won a prize in a work-competition as a police, defense, or army dog.

# Official Standard for the Bouvier des Flandres

The Bouvier des Flandres is a powerfully built, compact, short-coupled, rough-coated dog of notably rugged appearance. He gives the impression of great strength without any sign of heaviness or clumsiness in his overall makeup. He is agile, spirited and bold, yet his serene, well-behaved disposition denotes his steady, resolute and fearless character. His gaze is alert and brilliant, depicting his intelligence, vigor and daring. By nature he is an equable dog.

His origin is that of a cattle herder and general farmer's helper, including cart pulling. He is an ideal farm dog. His harsh coat protects him in all weather, enabling him to perform the most arduous tasks. The coat may be trimmed slightly only to accent the body line. Overtrimming which alters the natural rugged appearance is to be avoided.

He has been used as an ambulance and messenger dog. Modern times find him as a watch and guard dog as well as a family friend, guardian and protector. His physical and mental characteristics and deportment, coupled with his olfactory abilities, his intelligence and initiative enable him to also perform as a tracking dog and a guide dog for the blind.

**Head**—The head is impressive in scale, accentuated by beard and mustache. It is in proportion to body and build. **Skull**—Well developed and flat, slightly less wide than long. When viewed from the side, the top lines of the skull and the muzzle are parallel. It is wide between the ears, with the frontal groove barely marked. The stop is more apparent than real, due to upstanding eyebrows. The proportions of length of skull to length of muzzle are 3 to 2. **Eyes**—The expression is bold and alert. They neither protrude nor are sunken in the sockets. Their shape is oval with the axis on a horizontal plane, when viewed from the front. Their color is a dark nut brown. The eye rims are black without lack of pigment and the haw is barely visible. Yellow or light eyes are to be strongly penalized, along with a walleyed or staring expression. **Ears**—Placed high and alert. They are rough-coated. If cropped, they are to be a triangular contour and in proportion to the size of the head. The inner corner of the ear should be in line with the outer corner of the eye. Ears that are too low or too closely set are serious faults. **Muzzle**—Broad, strong, well filled out, tapering gradually toward the nose without ever becoming snipy or pointed. The cheeks are flat and lean, with the lips being dry and tight fitting. A narrow, snipy muzzle is faulty. **Nose**—Large, black, well developed, round at the edges, with flared nostrils. A brown, pink or spotted nose is a serious fault. **Jaws and Teeth**—The jaws are powerful and of equal length. The teeth are strong, white and healthy, with the incisors meeting in a scissors bite. Overshot or undershot bites are to be severely penalized.

**Neck**—The neck is strong and muscular, widening gradually into the shoulders. When viewed from the side, it is gracefully arched with upright carriage. A short, squatty neck is faulty. No dewlap.

**Body or Trunk**—Powerful, broad and short. The length from the point of the shoulder to the tip of the buttocks is equal to the height from the ground to the highest point of the withers. The chest is broad, with the brisket extending to the elbow in depth. A long-lined, rangy dog should be faulted. **Ribs**—The ribs are deep and well sprung. The first ribs are slightly curved, the others well sprung and very sloped nearing the rear, giving proper depth to the chest. Flat ribs or slabsidedness is to be strongly penalized. **Back—** Short, broad, well muscled with firm level topline. It is supple and flexible with no sign of weakness. **Flanks and Loins—**Short, wide and well muscled, without weakness. The abdomen is only slightly tucked up. **Croup or Rump—**The horizontal line of the back should mold unnoticeably into the curve of the rump, which is characteristically wide. A sunken or slanted croup is a serious fault. **Tail—**Is to be docked, leaving 2 or 3 vertebrae. It must be set high and align normally with the spinal column. Preferably carried upright in motion. Dogs born tailless should not be penalized.

**Forequarters—**Strong boned, well muscled and straight. **Shoulders and Upper Arms—** The shoulders are relatively long, muscular but not loaded, with good layback. The shoulder blade and humerus are approximately the same length, forming an angle slightly greater than 90 degrees when standing. Straight shoulders are faulty. **Elbows—**Close to the body and parallel. Elbows which are too far out or in are faults. **Forearms—**Viewed either in profile or from the front are perfectly straight, parallel to each other and perpendicular to the ground. They are well muscled and strong boned. **Wrists—**Exactly in line with the forearms. Strong boned. **Pasterns—**Quite short, slightly sloped forward. Dewclaws may be removed. **Feet—**Both forefeet and hind feet are rounded and compact turning neither in nor out; the toes close and well arched; strong black nails; thick tough pads.

**Hindquarters—**Firm, well muscled with large, powerful hams. They should be parallel with the front legs when viewed from either front or rear. **Thighs—**Wide and muscular. The upper thigh must be neither too straight nor too sloping. There is moderate angulation at the stifle. **Legs—**Moderately long, well muscled, neither too straight nor too inclined. **Hocks—**Strong, rather close to the ground. When standing and seen from the rear, they will be straight and perfectly parallel to each other and perpendicular to the ground. In motion, they must turn neither in nor out. There is a slight angulation at the hock joint. Sickle or cowhocks are serious faults. **Metatarsi—**Hardy and lean, rather cylindrical and perpendicular to the ground when standing. If born with dewclaws, they are to be removed.

**Coat—**A tousled, double coat capable of withstanding the hardest work in the most inclement weather. The outer hairs are rough and harsh, with the undercoat being fine, soft and dense. **Topcoat—**Must be harsh to the touch, dry, trimmed, if necessary, to a length of approximately 2½ inches. A coat too long or too short is a fault, as is a silky or woolly coat. It is tousled without being curly. On the skull, it is short, and on the upper part of the back, it is particularly close and harsh, always, however, remaining rough. **Undercoat—**A dense mass of fine, close hair, thicker in winter. Together with the topcoat, it will form a water-resistant covering. A flat coat, denoting lack of undercoat is a serious fault. **Mustache and Beard—**Very thick, with the hair being shorter and rougher on the upper side of the muzzle. The upper lip, with its heavy mustache and the chin with its heavy and rough beard gives that gruff expression so characteristic of the breed. **Eyebrows—**Erect hairs accentuating the shape of the eyes without ever veiling them.

**Color—**From fawn to black, passing through salt and pepper, gray and brindle. A small white star on the chest is allowed. Other than chocolate brown, white, or parti-color, which are to be severely penalized, no one color is to be favored.

**Height**—The height is measured at the withers—Dogs, from 24½ to 27½ inches; bitches, from 23½ to 26½ inches. In each sex, the ideal height is the median of the two limits, i.e., 26 inches for a dog and 25 inches for a bitch. Any dog or bitch deviating from the minimum or maximum limits mentioned shall be severely penalized.

**Gait**—The whole of the Bouvier des Flandres must be harmoniously proportioned to allow for a free, bold and proud gait. The reach of the forequarters must compensate for and be in balance with the driving power of the hindquarters. The back, while moving in a trot, will remain firm and flat. In general, the gait is the logical demonstration of the structure and build of the dog. It is to be noted that while moving at a fast trot, the properly built Bouvier will tend to single-track.

**Temperament**—As mentioned under general description and characteristics, the Bouvier is an equable dog, steady, resolute and fearless. Viciousness or shyness is undesirable.

**Faults**—The foregoing description is that of the ideal Bouvier des Flandres. Any deviation from this is to be penalized to the extent of the deviation.

Approved June 10, 1975

# Briard

## (Bree-arrd)

The Briard is a very old breed of French working dog. Depicted in 8th century tapestries and mentioned in records of the 12th century, the breed is accurately described in the 14th and 16th centuries. In early times, Briards were used to defend their charges against wolves and poachers, but the dividing up of the land and the increase in population which followed the French Revolution gradually transformed their work into the more peaceful tasks of herding the flocks, keeping the sheep within the unfenced boundaries of the pastures and guarding their masters' property.

In an article written in 1809, these dogs were referred to as the *Chien Berger de Brie* (Shepherd Dog of Brie) and they were entered as such in dog shows in the latter part of the century. Briards do not necessarily originate in the Province of Brie, as the name may imply. Many authorities claim that *Chien de Brie* is a distortion of the name *Chien d'Aubry* from a 14th century legend pointing to Aubry de Montdidier as having erected a cathedral in memory of his valiant dog (believed to be a Briard) that saved his son's life.

The first known standard for the Briard was written in 1897 by a club of shepherd dog breeders. Then, in 1909, a French society called *Les Amis du Briard* was founded. Although this club disbanded during World War I, it was formed again in 1923 and established a more precise standard for the Briard in 1925. This standard, with slight modification, was adopted by the Briard Club of America, founded in 1928.

The history of the Briard in the Americas is not well documented. Some credit the Marquis de Lafayette with the introduction of the breed to this country. However, writings of Thomas Jefferson indicate that he also brought representatives of the breed to this continent at about the same time. It was not until 1922 that a litter of Briards was registered with the American Kennel Club. Barbara Danielson of Groton, Massachusetts, was the breeder.

The many remarkable qualities that have helped the Briard to withstand the test of time have been passed down through centuries. The French shepherd, being a practical and frugal man, kept only the dogs with superior abilities and the Briard breeders of today carefully strive to preserve these highly valued traits. Intelligent, loyal and obedient, even the companion Briard will display the instinct to herd whatever is at hand, often pushing his master with his head to direct him, alerting his people to anything unusual, and enthusiastically carrying out any task he thinks has been delegated to him. The Briard is still not inclined to wander away from his property and he may decide that the young children in the family must also remain within these boundaries. The breed is prized in the United States, as well as in France, by those who use them for herding, although this occupation is now less common on both continents.

Distinctive in appearance, the Briard has eyebrows and beard, which give the typical expression of the breed and the tail has a small hook at the end, called a *crochet*. The correct coat is slightly wavy, of moderate length and the texture is such that mud and dirt do not cling to it. Another distinctive characteristic is that two dewclaws are required on each rear foot, a traditional trait on most French sheepdogs.

Briards learn readily and training should begin at a young age. Although Briards have been used primarily as guarding and herding dogs, they are usually versatile. They also have served successfully as tracking and hunting dogs and they have a splendid record as war dogs. In this capacity, they served as sentries at advanced posts, where their acute hearing proved to be invaluable. They accompanied patrols, carried food, supplies and even munitions to the front. Reports from the medical corps tell of the Briard's excellent ability to lead corpsmen to the wounded on the battlefield.

Admirable dog that he is, described as "a heart wrapped in fur," the Briard is not the ideal dog for every home. The remarkable character of the breed can only be developed by a willingness on the part of the owner to devote time and affection. He is by nature reserved with strangers. His coat requires regular grooming or the hair that is shed will cause matting, which is difficult to remove. But for those who have time and love to give, he is a loyal and unselfish friend who returns every kindness given to him many times over.

## Official Standard for the Briard

**General Appearance**—A dog of handsome form. Vigorous and alert, powerful without coarseness, strong in bone and muscle, exhibiting the strength and agility required of the herding dog. Dogs lacking these qualities, however concealed by the coat, are to be penalized.

**Size, Proportions**—*Size*—males 23 to 27 inches at the withers; bitches 22 to 25½ inches at the withers. *Disqualification*—all dogs or bitches under the minimum. *Proportions*—the Briard is not cobby in build. In males the length of the body, measured from the point of the shoulder to the point of the buttock, is equal to or slightly more than his height at the withers. The female may be a little longer.

**Head**—The head of a Briard always gives the impression of length, having sufficient width without being cumbersome. The correct length of a good head, measured from the occiput to the tip of the nose, is about forty percent (40%) of the height of the dog at the withers. There is no objection to a slightly longer head, especially if the animal tends to a longer body line. Viewed from above, from the front or in profile, the fully-coated silhouette gives the impression of two rectangular forms, equal in length but differing in height and width, blending together rather abruptly. The larger rectangle is the skull and the other forms the muzzle. The head joins the neck in a right angle and is held proudly alert. The head is sculptured in clean lines, without jowls or excess flesh on the sides, or under the eyes or temples. *Expression*—the gaze is frank, questioning and confident. *Eyes*—the eyes set well apart with the inner corners and outer corners on the same level. Large, well-opened and calm, they must never be narrow or slanted. The color must be black or black-brown with very dark pigmentation of the rim of the eyelids, whatever the color of the coat. *Disqualification*—yellow eyes or spotted eyes. *Ears*—the ears should be attached high, have thick leather and be firm at the base. Low-set ears cause the head to appear to be too arched. The length of the natural ear should be equal to or slightly less than one-half the length of the head, always straight and covered with long hair. The natural ear must not lie flat against the head and, when alert, the ears are lifted slightly, giving a square look to the top of the skull. The ears when cropped should be carried upright and parallel, emphasizing the parallel lines of the head; when alert, they should face forward, well open with long hair falling over the opening. The cropped ear should be long, broad at the base, tapering gradually to a rounded tip. *Skull*—the width of the head, as measured across the skull, is slightly less than the length of the skull from the occiput to the stop. Although not clearly visible on the fully-coated head, the occiput is prominent and the forehead is very slightly rounded. *Muzzle*—the muzzle with mustache and beard is somewhat wide and terminates in a right angle. The muzzle must not be narrow or pointed. *Planes*—the topline of the muzzle is parallel to the topline of the skull, and the junction of the two forms a well-marked stop, which is midway between the occiput and the tip of the nose, and on a level with the eyes. *Nose*—square rather than round, always black with nostrils well opened. *Disqualification*—any color other than black. *Lips*—the lips are of medium thickness, firm of line and fitted neatly, without folds or flews at the corners. The lips are black. **Bite** *Teeth*—strong, white and adapting perfectly in a scissors bite.

**Neck, Topline and Body**—*Neck*—strong and well constructed. The neck is in the shape of a truncated cone, clearing the shoulders well. It is strongly muscled and has good length. *Topline*—the Briard is constructed with a very slight incline, downward from the prominent withers to the back which is straight, to the broad loin and the croup which is slightly inclined. The croup is well muscled and slightly sloped to give a well-rounded finish. The topline is strong, never swayed nor roached. *Body*—the chest is broad and deep with moderately curved ribs, egg-shaped in form, the ribs not too rounded. The breastbone is moderately advanced in front, descending smoothly to the level of the elbows and shaped to give good depth to the chest. The abdomen is moderately drawn up but still presents good volume. *Tail*—uncut, well feathered, forming a crook at the extremity, carried low and not deviating to the right or to the left. In repose, the bone of the tail descends to the joint of the hock, terminating in the crook, similar in shape to the printed "J" when viewed from the dog's right side. In action, the tail is raised in a harmonious curve, never going above the level of the back, except for the terminal crook. *Disqualification*—tail non-existent or cut.

**Forequarters**—Shoulder blades are long and sloping forming a 45-degree angle with the horizontal, firmly attached by strong muscles and blending smoothly with the withers. *Legs*—the legs are powerfully muscled with strong bone. The forelegs are vertical when viewed from the side except the pasterns are very slightly inclined. Viewed from the front or rear, the legs are straight and parallel to the median line of the body, never turned inward or outward. The distance between the front legs is equal to the distance between the rear legs. The construction of the legs is of utmost importance, determining the dog's ability to work and his resistance to fatigue. *Dewclaws*—dewclaws on the forelegs may or may not be removed. *Feet*—strong and rounded, being slightly oval in shape. The feet travel straight forward in the line of movement. The toes are strong, well arched and compact. The pads are well developed, compact and elastic, covered with strong tissue. The nails are always black and hard.

**Hindquarters**—The hindquarters are powerful, providing flexible, almost tireless movement. The pelvis slopes at a 30-degree angle from the horizontal and forms a right angle with the upper leg bone. *Legs*—viewed from the side, the legs are well angulated with the metatarsus slightly inclined, the hock making an angle of 135 degrees. *Dewclaws*—two dewclaws are required on each rear leg, placed low on the leg, giving a wide base to the foot. Occasionally the nail may break off completely. The dog shall not be penalized for the missing nail so long as the digit itself is present. Ideally the dewclaws form additional functioning toes. *Disqualification*—anything less than two dewclaws on each rear leg. *Feet*—if the rear toes turn out very slightly when the hocks and metatarsus are parallel, then the position of the feet is correct.

**Coat**—The outer coat is coarse, hard and dry (making a dry rasping sound between the fingers). It lies down flat, falling naturally in long, slightly waving locks, having the sheen of good health. On the shoulders the length of the hair is generally six inches or more. The undercoat is fine and tight on all the body. The head is well covered with hair which lies down, forming a natural part in the center. The eyebrows do not lie flat but, instead, arch up and out in a curve that lightly veils the eyes. The hair is never so abundant that it masks the form of the head or completely covers the eyes.

**Color**—All uniform colors are permitted except white. The colors are black, various shades of gray and various shades of tawny. The deeper shades of each color are preferred. Combinations of two of these colors are permitted, provided there are no marked spots and the transition from one color to another takes place gradually and symmetrically. The only permissible white: white hairs scattered throughout the coat and/or a white spot on the chest not to exceed one inch in diameter at the root of the hair. *Disqualification*—white coat, spotted coat, white spot on chest exceeding one inch in diameter.

**Gait**—The well-constructed Briard is a marvel of supple power. His movement has been described as "quicksilver," permitting him to make abrupt turns, springing starts and sudden stops required of the sheepherding dog. His gait is supple and light, almost like that of a large feline. The gait gives the impression that the dog glides along without touching the ground. Strong, flexible movement is essential to the sheepdog. He is above all a trotter, single-tracking, occasionally galloping and he frequently needs to change his speed to accomplish his work. His conformation is harmoniously balanced and strong to sustain him in the long day's work. Dogs with clumsy or inelegant gait must be penalized.

**Temperament**—He is a dog at heart, with spirit and initiative, wise and fearless with no trace of timidity. Intelligent, easily trained, faithful, gentle, and obedient, the Briard possesses an excellent memory and an ardent desire to please his master. He retains a high degree of his ancestral instinct to guard home and master. Although he is reserved with strangers, he is loving and loyal to those he knows. Some will display a certain independence.

### DISQUALIFICATIONS

*All dogs or bitches under the minimum size limits.*
*Yellow eyes or spotted eyes.*
*Nose any color other than black.*
*Tail non-existent or cut.*
*Less than two dewclaws on each rear leg.*
*White coat.*
*Spotted coat.*
*White spot on chest exceeding one inch in diameter.*

Approved February 8, 1975
Reformatted January 12, 1992

**Collie (Rough)**

**Collie (Smooth)**

# Collie

There are two varieties of Collie, the rough-coated being by far the more familiar. However, many fanciers have increased their breeding of the smooth-coated variety and many smooths of excellent type are now being exhibited.

Although the exact origin of the Collie remains an enigma, both varieties existed long ago in the unwritten history of the herding dogs of Scotland and northern England.

Since sheepherding is one of the world's oldest occupations, the Collie's ancestors date far back in the history of dogs. The smooth Collie, which for as long as there have been written standards for the breed has been bred to the same standard except for coat, was considered principally as a drover's dog used for guiding cows and sheep to market, not for standing over and guarding them at pasture. Until the last two centuries, both varieties were strictly working dogs without written pedigrees. Their untutored masters saw no need for pedigrees, if indeed they were capable of keeping stud books.

The earliest illustrations known to bear a resemblance to both varieties are found as woodcuts in *The History of Quadrupeds* by Thomas Bewick, ante-dating 1800. The rough dog was described as a "Shepherd's Dog" and the smooth as a "ban dog." The rough was described as being only 14 inches at the shoulder and the smooth was said to be much larger and descended from the Mastiff. (Mastiff in this sense does not refer to the breed we know today by that name but was something of a generic term used basically to describe a common type dog.) It is well established that the roughs at that time were not only much smaller but had shorter, broader heads and were usually black or black and white in color.

From early in the 19th century, when some dog fanciers began to take interest in these dogs, and the keeping of written pedigrees began, the breed progressed rapidly, becoming not only larger in stature but also more refined. The dog "Old Cockie" was born in 1867 and he is credited with not only stamping characteristic type on the rough Collie but he is believed by usually reliable authorities to be responsible for introducing to the breed the factors which led to the development of the sable coat color in the Collie. A short time later Collies were seen of almost every imaginable color, including red, buff, mottle of various shades and a few sables. At that time the most frequently seen colors were black, tan and white, black and white (without tan) and what are now called blue merles, but which were known then as "tortoise shell."

The early pedigrees were very much abbreviated, as compared with our present breed records. In fact, the first volume of the English stud book showed 78 "sheep dogs and Scotch Collies" registered up to 1874. Fifteen of them had written pedigrees but only three extended beyond sire and dam. Proof that pride of ownership was given priority over written records is found in the fact that it was in 1860 that the first classes for "Scotch Sheep Dogs" were offered at the second dog show ever held in England, that of the Birmingham Dog Society. Both varieties competed in the same classes.

Shortly thereafter, Queen Victoria visited Balmoral and saw her first Collies. They captivated her and she enthusiastically began to sponsor them. There was a marked surge in the popularity of the breed which found itself not only the indispensable helpmate of the humble shepherd but the treasure and the playmate of the royal and the rich.

Collie type was well enough "fixed" by 1886 so that the English breeders have never seen fit to change the height and weight established in their standard at that time. Numerous clarifying changes have taken place in the United States standard over the ensuing years but except for recognizing that the Collie has become slightly larger and heavier on this side of the Atlantic there is no fundamental difference, even today, from that 1886 description of the ideal Collie.

Many of the early settlers in the new world brought dogs with them to herd their sheep and cattle in the Colonies but it was not until May of 1877, 17 years after their show ring debut in England, that they were shown here, at the second show of the Westminster Kennel Club in New York. Classes were offered for "Shepherd Dogs, or Collie Dogs" and a few were entered. The next year, however, was to see great interest and excitement. Two Collies imported from Queen Victoria's Royal Balmoral Kennel had been entered! Soon Collies were to be found as prized possessions of the wealthy and socially elite. Kennels were established by the well-known fancier J. P. Morgan and his financial contemporaries, and many fashionable estates up the Hudson River and on Long Island had Collie kennels. English dogs were imported for what were then considered to be exorbitant prices. It is interesting to note that about a half century later almost the reverse situation was occurring. The Collie became a highly desired breed in Japan and there was great persuasion to convince some of the American breeders to export some of their top dogs. By this time, the importation of Collies from England had become exceedingly rare.

Being no longer in great demand as a herder, today's Collie has transferred these abilities to serving as a devoted family dog where he shows a particular affinity for small children. For many years his general popularity has placed him among the top twenty of the favorite dogs registered by the American Kennel Club. Elegant and beautiful in appearance, loyal and affectionate in all his actions, self-appointed guardian of everything he can see or hear, the Collie represents, to his many admirers, the ideal family companion.

The Collie has been the beneficiary of a "good press." Its parent club, The Collie Club of America, Inc. was organized in 1886, two years after the establishment of the American Kennel Club and was the second parent club to join the AKC. Very active in promoting the interest of the breed, the parent club now has a membership numbering well over 3500 and its annual specialty show attracts over 400 Collies from all over the United States. Great impetus to the breed's popularity was provided by the famous Collie stories of Albert

Payson Terhune. His "Lad: A Dog" was followed by many more volumes that have been eagerly read by several generations of Americans. More recently the television exploits of "Lassie" brought to children and their parents a strong desire to have for their very own "a lovely dog like that."

## Official Standard for the Collie

### ROUGH

**General Character**—The Collie is a lithe, strong, responsive, active dog, carrying no useless timber, standing naturally straight and firm. The deep, moderately wide chest shows strength, the sloping shoulders and well-bent hocks indicate speed and grace, and the face shows high intelligence. The Collie presents an impressive, proud picture of true balance, each part being in harmonious proportion to every other part and to the whole. Except for the technical description that is essential to this Standard and without which no Standard for the guidance of breeders and judges is adequate, it could be stated simply that no part of the Collie ever seems to be out of proportion to any other part. Timidity, frailness, sullenness, viciousness, lack of animation, cumbersome appearance and lack of over-all balance impair the general character.

**Head**—The head properties are of great importance. When considered in proportion to the size of the dog the head is inclined to lightness and never appears massive. A heavy-headed dog lacks the necessary bright, alert, full-of-sense look that contributes so greatly to expression. Both in front and profile view the head bears a general resemblance to a well-blunted lean wedge, being smooth and clean in outline and nicely balanced in proportion. On the sides it tapers gradually and smoothly from the ears to the end of the black nose, without being flared out in backskull ("cheeky") or pinched in muzzle ("snipy"). In profile view the top of the backskull and the top of the muzzle lie in two approximately parallel, straight planes of equal length, divided by a very slight but perceptible stop or break. A mid-point between the inside corners of the eyes (which is the center of a correctly placed stop) is the center of balance in length of head.

The end of the smooth, well-rounded muzzle is blunt but not square. The underjaw is strong, clean-cut and the depth of skull from the brow to the under part of the jaw is not excessive. The teeth are of good size, meeting in a scissors bite. *Overshot or undershot jaws are undesirable, the latter being more severely penalized.* There is a very slight prominence of the eyebrows. The backskull is flat, without receding either laterally or backward and the occipital bone is not highly peaked. The proper width of backskull necessarily depends upon the combined length of skull and muzzle and the width of the backskull is less than its length. Thus the correct width varies with the individual and is dependent upon the extent to which it is supported by length of muzzle. Because of the importance of the head characteristics, *prominent head faults are very severely penalized.*

**Eyes**—Because of the combination of the flat skull, the arched eyebrows, the slight stop and the rounded muzzle, the foreface must be chiseled to form a receptacle for the eyes and they are necessarily placed obliquely to give them the required forward outlook. Except for the blue merles, they are required to be matched in color. They are almond-shaped, of medium size and never properly appear to be large or prominent. The color is dark and the eye does not show a yellow ring or a sufficiently prominent haw to affect the dog's expression. The eyes have a clear, bright appearance, expressing intelligent inquisitiveness, particularly when the ears are drawn up and the dog is on the alert. In blue merles, dark brown eyes are preferable, but either or both eyes may be merle or china in color without specific penalty. A large, round, full eye seriously detracts from the desired "sweet" expression. *Eye faults are heavily penalized.*

**Ears**—The ears are in proportion to the size of the head and, if they are carried properly and unquestionably "break" naturally, are seldom too small. Large ears usually cannot be lifted correctly off the head, and even if lifted, they will be out of proportion to the size of the head. When in repose the ears are folded lengthwise and thrown back into the frill. On the alert they are drawn well up on the backskull and are carried about three-quarters erect, with about one-fourth of the ear tipping or "breaking" forward. *A dog with prick ears or low ears cannot show true expression and is penalized accordingly.*

**Neck**—The neck is firm, clean, muscular, sinewy and heavily frilled. It is fairly long, carried upright with a slight arch at the nape and imparts a proud, upstanding appearance showing off the frill.

**Body**—The body is firm, hard and muscular, a trifle long in proportion to the height. The ribs are well-rounded behind the well-sloped shoulders and the chest is deep, extending to the elbows. The back is strong and level, supported by powerful hips and thighs and the croup is sloped to give a well-rounded finish. The loin is powerful and slightly arched. *Noticeably fat dogs, or dogs in poor flesh, or with skin disease, or with no undercoat are out of condition and are moderately penalized accordingly.*

**Legs**—The forelegs are straight and muscular, with a fair amount of bone considering the size of the dog. A cumbersome appearance is undesirable. *Both narrow and wide placement are penalized.* The forearm is moderately fleshy and the pasterns are flexible but without weakness. The hind legs are less fleshy, muscular at the thighs, very sinewy and the hocks and stifles are well bent. *A cowhocked dog or a dog with straight stifles is penalized.* The comparatively small feet are approximately oval in shape. The soles are well padded and tough, and the toes are well arched and close together. When the Collie is not in motion the legs and feet are judged by allowing the dog to come to a natural stop in a standing position so that both the forelegs and the hind legs are placed well apart, with the feet extending straight forward. Excessive "posing" is undesirable.

**Gait**—Gait is sound. When the dog is moved at a slow trot toward an observer its straight front legs track comparatively close together at the ground. The front legs are not out at the elbows, do not "cross over," nor does the dog move with a choppy, pacing or rolling gait. When viewed from the rear the hind legs are straight, tracking comparatively close together at the ground. At a moderate trot the hind legs are powerful and propelling. Viewed from the side the reasonably long, "reaching" stride is smooth and even, keeping the back line firm and level.

As the speed of the gait is increased the Collie single tracks, bringing the front legs inward in a straight line from the shoulder toward the center line of the body and the hind legs inward in a straight line from the hip toward the center line of the body. The gait suggests effortless speed combined with the dog's herding heritage, requiring it to be capable of changing its direction of travel almost instantaneously.

**Tail**—The tail is moderately long, the bone reaching to the hock joint or below. It is carried low when the dog is quiet, the end having an upward twist or "swirl." When gaited or when the dog is excited it is carried gaily but not over the back.

**Coat**—The well-fitting, proper-textured coat is the crowning glory of the rough variety of Collie. It is abundant except on the head and legs. The outer coat is straight and harsh to the touch. *A soft, open outer coat or a curly outer coat, regardless of quantity is penalized.* The undercoat, however, is soft, furry and so close together that it is difficult to see the skin when the hair is parted. The coat is very abundant on the mane and frill. The face or mask is smooth. The forelegs are smooth and well feathered to the back of the pasterns. The hind legs are smooth below the hock joints. Any feathering below the hocks is removed for the show ring. The hair on the tail is very profuse and on the hips it is long and bushy. The texture, quantity and the extent to which the coat "fits the dog" are important points.

**Color**—The four recognized colors are "Sable and White," "Tri-color," "Blue Merle" and "White." There is no preference among them. The "Sable and White" is predominantly sable (a fawn sable color of varying shades from light gold to dark mahogany) with white markings usually on the chest, neck, legs, feet and the tip of the tail. A blaze may appear on the foreface or backskull or both. The "Tri-color" is predominantly black, carrying white markings as in a "Sable and White" and has tan shadings on and about the head and legs. The "Blue Merle" is a mottled or "marbled" color predominantly blue-gray and black with white markings as in the "Sable and White" and usually has tan shadings as in the "Tri-color." The "White" is predominantly white, preferably with sable, tri-color or blue-merle markings.

**Size**—Dogs are from 24 to 26 inches at the shoulder and weigh from 60 to 75 pounds. Bitches are from 22 to 24 inches at the shoulder, weighing from 50 to 65 pounds. *An undersize or an oversize Collie is penalized according to the extent to which the dog appears to be undersize or oversize.*

**Expression**—Expression is one of the most important points in considering the relative value of Collies. *Expression,* like the term "character" is difficult to define in words. It is not a fixed point as in color, weight or height and it is something the uninitiated can properly understand only by optical illustration. In general, however, it may be said to be the combined product of the shape and balance of the skull and muzzle, the placement, size, shape and color of the eye and the position, size and carriage of the ears. An expression that shows sullenness or which is suggestive of any other breed is entirely foreign. The Collie cannot be judged properly until its expression has been carefully evaluated.

SMOOTH

The Smooth Variety of Collie is judged by the same Standard as the Rough Variety, except that the references to the quantity and the distribution of the coat are not applicable to the Smooth Variety, which has a short, hard, dense, flat coat of good texture, with an abundance of undercoat.

Approved May 10, 1977

# German Shepherd Dog

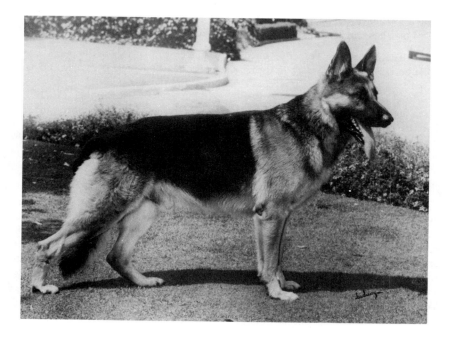

Derived from the old breeds of herding and farm dogs, and associated for centuries with man as servant and companion, the German Shepherd Dog has been subject to intensive development. Sponsored by the *Verein fur Deutsche Schaferhunde*, the parent club of the breed founded in 1899 in Germany, the cult of the Shepherd spread rapidly from about 1914 onward in many parts of the world. Interest in the breed has been fostered by specialty clubs in many lands as it has been in the United States by the German Shepherd Dog Club of America.

First, last and all the time a working dog, the German Shepherd Dog has been developed both temperamentally and structurally through selective breeding, through judging which on the whole has been of a conservative character, and through specialized training.

Considering first the more important side of the dog, its character, the Shepherd is distinguished for loyalty, courage, and the ability to assimilate and retain training for a number of special services. He should be of equable disposition, poised, unexcitable, and with well-controlled nerves. For his typical work as a herding sheepdog, he must not be gun-shy and must have courage to protect his flock from attacks, either animal or human. For his work as a police dog, a development which followed upon his natural aptitude for training, he must have this courage and in addition must be able to make use of the excellent nose which he usually possesses. In his work as a leader of the blind, the Shepherd must and does exhibit a high order of intelligence and discrimination involving the qualities of observation, patience, faithful watchfulness, and even, to a certain degree, the exercise of judgment.

These qualities, which have endeared the German Shepherd Dog to a wide public in practically every country of the globe, are those of the companion, protector, and friend. The German Shepherd is not a pugnacious brawler, but a bold and punishing fighter if need be. In his relation to man he does not give affection lightly; he has plenty of dignity and some suspicion of strangers, but his friendship, once given, is given for life.

On the physical side, the German Shepherd Dog has been developed to a point of almost ideal fitness for the work he is called upon to do. He is a dog of middle size with enough weight to be effective as herder or patrolman, but not enough to be cumbersome or unwieldy.

By careful selective breeding, the naturally easy trot of the German Shepherd Dog has been brought to a high pitch of nearly effortless motion. Essentially a trotting animal, his structure has been modified so as to increase the power, elasticity and length of his gait. Other things being equal, the best-moving Shepherd is the one which covers the maximum amount of ground with the minimum expenditure of energy. So well coordinated and harmonious is this gait when properly exemplified that the dog seems to glide forward without visible effort—suspended, one might almost think, from the firm beam of his back.

The impression of the dog as a whole is one of ruggedness combined with nobility, of power combined with agility. There should be a sense of balance, forequarters and hindquarters compensating each other in their development. The outline should be smooth and flowing, and the topline of the dog, from the ear to the tip of the full tail, a single sweeping succession of unbroken curves. The German Shepherd Dog is a natural dog, unchanged for any whim of the show ring.

## Official Standard for the German Shepherd Dog

**General Appearance**—The first impression of a good German Shepherd Dog is that of a strong, agile, well muscled animal, alert and full of life. It is well balanced, with harmonious development of the forequarter and hindquarter. The dog is longer than tall, deep-bodied, and presents an outline of smooth curves rather than angles. It looks substantial and not spindly, giving the impression, both at rest and in motion, of muscular fitness and nimbleness without any look of clumsiness or soft living. The ideal dog is stamped with a look of quality and nobility—difficult to define, but unmistakable when present. Secondary sex characteristics are strongly marked, and every animal gives a definite impression of masculinity or feminity, according to its sex.

**Size, Proportion, Substance**—The desired *height* for males at the top of the highest point of the shoulder blade is 24 to 26 inches; and for bitches, 22 to 24 inches. The German Shepherd Dog is longer than tall, with the most desirable *proportion* as 10 to 8½. The length is measured from the point of the prosternum or breastbone to the rear edge of the pelvis, the ischial tuberosity. The desirable long proportion is not derived from a long back, but from overall length with relation to height, which is achieved by length of forequarter and length of withers and hindquarter, viewed from the side.

**Head**—The *head* is noble, cleanly chiseled, strong without coarseness, but above all not fine, and in proportion to the body. The head of the male is distinctly masculine, and that of the bitch distinctly feminine. The *expression* keen, intelligent and composed. *Eyes* of medium size, almond shaped, set a little obliquely and not protruding. The color is as dark as possible. *Ears* are moderately pointed, in proportion to the skull, open toward the front, and carried erect when at attention, the ideal carriage being one in which the center lines of the ears, viewed from the front, are parallel to each other and perpendicular to the ground. A dog with cropped or hanging ears must be *disqualified.* Seen from the front the forehead is only moderately arched, and the *skull* slopes into the long, wedge-shaped muzzle without abrupt stop. The *muzzle* is long and strong, and its topline is parallel to the topline of the skull. *Nose* black. A dog with a nose that is not predominantly black must be *disqualified.* The lips are firmly fitted. Jaws are strongly developed. *Teeth*—42 in number—20 upper and 22 lower—are strongly developed and meet in a scissors bite in which part of the inner surface of the upper incisors meet and engage part of the outer surface of the lower incisors. An overshot jaw or a level bite is undesirable. An undershot jaw is a *disqualifying fault.* Complete dentition is to be preferred. Any missing teeth other than first premolars is a *serious fault.*

**Neck, Topline, Body**—The *neck* is strong and muscular, clean-cut and relatively long, proportionate in size to the head and without loose folds of skin. When the dog is at attention or excited, the head is raised and the neck carried high; otherwise typical carriage of the head is forward rather than up and but little higher than the top of the shoulders, particularly in motion. *Topline*—The *withers* are higher than and sloping into the level back. The *back* is straight, very strongly developed without sag or roach, and relatively short. The whole structure of the *body* gives an impression of depth and solidity without bulkiness. *Chest*—Commencing at the prosternum, it is well filled and carried well down between the legs. It is deep and capacious, never shallow, with ample room for lungs and heart, carried well forward, with the prosternum showing ahead of the shoulder in profile. *Ribs* well sprung and long, neither barrel-shaped nor too flat, and carried down to a sternum which reaches to the elbows. Correct ribbing allows the elbows to move back freely when the dog is at a trot. Too round causes interference and throws the elbows out; too flat or short causes pinched elbows. Ribbing is carried well back so that the loin is relatively short. *Abdomen* firmly held and not paunchy. The bottom line is only moderately tucked up in the loin. *Loin*—Viewed from the top, broad and strong. Undue length between the last rib and the thigh, when viewed from the side, is undesirable. *Croup* long and gradually sloping. *Tail* bushy, with the last vertebra extended at least to the hock joint. It is set smoothly into the croup and low rather than high. At rest, the tail hangs in a slight curve like a saber. A slight hook—sometimes carried to one side—is faulty only to the extent that it mars general appearance. When the dog is excited or in motion, the curve is accentuated and the tail raised, but it should never be curled forward beyond a vertical line. Tails too short, or with clumpy ends due to ankylosis, are *serious faults.* A dog with a docked tail must be *disqualified.*

**Forequarters**—The shoulder blades are long and obliquely angled, laid on flat and not placed forward. The upper arm joins the shoulder blade at about a right angle. Both the upper arm and the shoulder blade are well muscled. The forelegs, viewed from all sides, are straight and the bone oval rather than round. The pasterns are strong and springy and angulated at approximately a 25-degree angle from the vertical. Dewclaws on the forelegs may be removed, but are normally left on. The *feet* are short, compact with toes well arched, pads thick and firm, nails short and dark.

**Hindquarters**—The whole assembly of the thigh, viewed from the side, is broad, with both upper and lower thigh well muscled, forming as nearly as possible a right angle. The upper thigh bone parallels the shoulder blade while the lower thigh bone parallels the upper arm. The metatarsus (the unit between the hock joint and the foot) is short, strong and tightly articulated. The dewclaws, if any, should be removed from the hind legs. Feet as in front.

**Coat**—The ideal dog has a double coat of medium length. The outer coat should be as dense as possible, hair straight, harsh and lying close to the body. A slightly wavy outer coat, often of wiry texture, is permissible. The head, including the inner ear and foreface, and the legs and paws are covered with short hair, and the neck with longer and thicker hair. The rear of the forelegs and hind legs has somewhat longer hair extending to the pasterns and hock, respectively. *Faults* in coat include soft, silky, too long outer coat, woolly, curly and open coat.

**Color**—The German Shepherd Dog varies in color, and most colors are permissible. Strong rich colors are preferred. Pale, washed-out colors and blues or livers are *serious faults.* A white dog must be *disqualified.*

**Gait**—A German Shepherd Dog is a trotting dog, and its structure has been developed to meet the requirements of its work. *General Impression*—The gait is outreaching, elastic, seemingly without effort, smooth and rhythmic, covering the maximum amount of ground with the minimum number of steps. At a walk it covers a great deal of ground, with long strides of both hind legs and forelegs. At a trot the dog covers still more ground with even longer stride, and moves powerfully but easily, with coordination and balance so that the gait appears to be the steady motion of a well-lubricated machine. The feet travel close to the ground on both forward reach and backward push. In order to achieve ideal movement of this kind, there must be good muscular development and ligamentation. The hindquarters deliver, through the back, a powerful forward thrust which slightly lifts the whole animal and drives the body forward. Reaching far under, and passing the imprint left by the front foot, the hind foot takes hold of the ground; then hock, stifle and upper thigh come into play and sweep back, the stroke of the hind leg finishing with the foot still close to the ground in a smooth follow-through. The over-reach of the hindquarter usually necessitates one hind foot passing outside and the other hind foot passing inside the track of the forefeet, and such action is not faulty unless the locomotion is crabwise with the dog's body sideways out of the normal straight line. **Transmission**—The typical smooth, flowing gait is maintained with great strength and firmness of back. The whole effort of the hindquarter is transmitted to the forequarter through the loin, back and withers. At full trot, the back must remain firm and level without sway, roll, whip or roach. Unlevel topline with withers lower than the hip is a *fault*. To compensate for the forward motion imparted by the hindquarters, the shoulder should open to its full extent. The forelegs should reach out close to the ground in a long stride in harmony with that of the hindquarters. The dog does not track on widely separated parallel lines, but brings the feet inward toward the middle line of the body when trotting, in order to maintain balance. The feet track closely but do not strike or cross over. Viewed from the front, the front legs function from the shoulder joint to the pad in a straight line. Viewed from the rear, the hind legs function from the hip joint to the pad in a straight line. Faults of gait, whether from front, rear, or side, are to be considered *very serious faults*.

**Temperament**—The breed has a distinct personality marked by direct and fearless, but not hostile, expression, self-confidence and a certain aloofness that does not lend itself to immediate and indiscriminate friendships. The dog must be approachable, quietly standing its ground and showing confidence and willingness to meet overtures without itself making them. It is poised, but when the occasion demands, eager and alert; both fit and willing to serve in its capacity as companion, watchdog, blind leader, herding dog, or guardian, whichever the circumstances may demand. The dog must not be timid, shrinking behind its master or handler; it should not be nervous, looking about or upward with anxious expression or showing nervous reactions, such as tucking of tail, to strange sounds or sights. Lack of confidence under any surroundings is not typical of good character. Any of the above deficiencies in character which indicate shyness must be penalized as *very serious faults* and any dog exhibiting pronounced indications of these must be excused from the ring. It must be possible for the judge to observe the teeth and to determine that both testicles are descended. Any dog that attempts to bite the judge must be *disqualified*. The ideal dog is a working animal with an incorruptible character combined with body and gait suitable for the arduous work that constitutes its primary purpose.

### DISQUALIFICATIONS

*Cropped or hanging ears.*
*Dogs with noses not predominantly black.*
*Undershot jaw.*
*Docked tail.*
*White dogs.*
*Any dog that attempts to bite the judge.*

Approved February 11, 1978
Reformatted March 16, 1989

# Old English Sheepdog

**W**hile as compared with some other kinds of dogs the Old English Sheepdog cannot boast the same antiquity, there is nevertheless ample evidence that it can trace its origin to the early 19th century or at least 150 years back, thus proving that among recognized breeds it is no mere upstart. As to its real origin, there are conflicting ideas based on premises obscured by the passage of time. A painting by Gainsborough of a Duke of Buccleuch, from which engravings were struck off in 1771, shows the peer with his arms clasped about the neck of what appears to be a fairly good specimen of present-day Old English Sheepdog. This is the earliest picture known that in any manner depicts the breed. What, however, the pictured dog was supposed to be at that period is not certain.

In all probability the breed was first developed in the west of England, in the counties of Devon and Somerset and the Duchy of Cornwall, although from what breeds it was produced is a matter of conjecture. Some maintain that the Scotch Bearded Collie had a large part in its making; others claim for one of its progenitors the Russian Owtchar.

At all events, in the beginning of the 18th century, we read of a "drover's dog" which was used largely for driving sheep and cattle into the markets of the metropolis. These drover's dogs were exempt from taxes and, to prove their occu-

**587**

pation, they were docked. Some believe that the nicknames "bob" and "bobtail" trace to this custom. It is not true, or course, that the practice of removing the tail has produced a breed naturally bobtailed or tailless. In fact, few specimens of the breed are whelped without tails, or with tails long or comparatively short. According to the Standard, the tail should be removed at the first joint, when the puppy is three or four days old, and it should never be longer than one and one-half or two inches in length at maturity. Seldom is an Old English Sheepdog seen in the show ring today with more than a mere thickening of the skin where the tail has been removed. Since this dog has been used more for driving than for herding, the lack of a tail to serve as a rudder, so to speak, has in no wise affected its working ability with heavier kinds of sheep and cattle.

For years after the breed's introduction into this country, fanciers did considerable harm by misinterpreting "profuseness" of coat as "excessiveness." This misled the public into believing that the Old English Sheepdog was difficult to care for, when as a matter of fact a dog with typical coat of the right texture is no harder to keep in shape than is any other longhaired dog. Furthermore, it is homeloving, not given to roaming and fighting, and it is extremely agile; because of its intelligence, affection, and lack of boisterousness, it makes an ideal house dog. It has a tender mouth and can be trained as a retriever; it makes a first-class sledge dog, and is satisfactory as a companion equally at home in apartment, large house, drawing room, and practically anywhere else.

In seeking a good representative of the breed, points to look for include a body practically square; good bone, deep brisket, chest, and spring of rib; strong foreface, dark or walleyes, level teeth; straight forelegs, well-let-down hocks; and a hard coat with good underjacket. Markings are not important. The dogs do well under almost any climatic conditions, their coats serving as insulation against heat, cold, and dampness. A marked characteristic of the breed is its gait, which is quite like the shuffle of a bear.

The Old English Sheepdog Club of America was started by W. A. Tilley in 1904, and received official recognition by AKC the following year.

## Official Standard for the Old English Sheepdog

**General Appearance**—A strong, compact, square, balanced dog. Taking him all around, he is profusely, *but not excessively coated,* thickset, muscular and able-bodied. These qualities, combined with his agility, fit him for the demanding tasks required of a shepherd's or drover's dog. Therefore, *soundness is of the greatest importance.* His bark is loud with a distinctive "pot-casse" ring in it.

**Size, Proportion, Substance**—Type, character and balance are of greater importance and are on no account to be sacrificed to size alone. *Size*—Height (measured from top of withers to the ground), Dogs: 22 inches (55.8 cm) and upward. Bitches: 21 inches (53.3 cm) and upward. *Proportion*—Length (measured from point of shoulder to point of ischium [tuberosity]) practically the same as the height. Absolutely free from legginess or weaselness. *Substance*—Well muscled with plenty of bone.

**Head**—A most intelligent expression. **Eyes**—Brown, blue or one of each. If brown, very dark is preferred. If blue, a pearl, china or wall-eye is considered typical. An amber or yellow eye is most objectionable. **Ears**—Medium sized and carried flat to the side of the head. **Skull**—Capacious and rather squarely formed giving plenty of room for brain power. The parts over the eyes (super-orbital ridges) are well arched. The whole well covered with hair. **Stop**—Well defined. **Jaw**—Fairly long, strong, square and truncated. *Attention is particularly called to the above properties as a long, narrow head or snipy muzzle is a deformity.* **Nose**—Always black, large and capacious. **Teeth**—Strong, large and evenly placed. The bite is level or tight scissors.

**Neck, Topline, Body**—*Neck*—Fairly long and arched gracefully. **Topline**—Stands lower at the withers than at the loin with no indication of softness or weakness. *Attention is particularly called to this topline as it is a distinguishing characteristic of the breed.* **Body**—Rather short and very compact, broader at the rump than at the shoulders, ribs well sprung and brisket deep and capacious. Neither slab-sided nor barrel-chested. The loin is very stout and gently arched. **Tail**—Docked close to the body, when not naturally bobtailed.

**Forequarters**—Shoulders well laid back and narrow at the points. The forelegs dead straight with plenty of bone. The measurements from the withers to the elbow and from the elbow to the ground are practically the same.

**Hindquarters**—Round and muscular with well let down hocks. When standing, the metatarses are perpendicular to the ground when viewed from any angle.

**Feet**—Small and round, toes well arched, pads thick and hard, feet pointing straight ahead.

**Coat**—Profuse, but not so excessive as to give the impression of the dog being overly fat, and of a good hard texture; not straight, but shaggy and free from curl. *Quality and texture of coat to be considered above mere profuseness.* Softness or flatness of coat to be considered a fault. The undercoat is a waterproof pile when not removed by grooming or season. Ears coated moderately. The whole skull well covered with hair. The neck well coated with hair. The forelegs well coated all around. The hams densely coated with a thick, long jacket in excess of any other part. Neither the natural outline nor the natural texture of the coat may be changed by any artificial means except that the feet and rear may be trimmed for cleanliness.

**Color**—Any shade of gray, grizzle, blue or blue merle with or without white markings or in reverse. *Any shade of brown or fawn to be considered distinctly objectionable and not to be encouraged.*

**Gait**—When trotting, movement is free and powerful, seemingly effortless, with good reach and drive, and covering maximum ground with minimum steps. Very elastic at a gallop. May amble or pace at slower speeds.

**Temperament**—An adaptable, intelligent dog of even disposition, with no sign of aggression, shyness or nervousness.

Approved February 10, 1990

**Puli (Groomed coat)**

**Puli (Corded coat)**

# Puli

## (Poo-lee)

The Puli (plural Pulik), or drover, has been an integral part of the lives of Hungarian shepherds for more than 1000 years. When the Magyars came into Hungary they brought their sheepdogs with them. There were larger kinds similar to the Komondor and the Kuvasz, and a smaller kind which resembled the Puli. Except in color, the Puli was quite similar to the Tibetan Terrier, which may well have been its foundation stock.

Invaders decimated Hungary during the 16th century. People from western Europe, along with their merino sheep and sheepdogs, began to repopulate Hungary in the 17th century. The Puli intermingled with the sheepdogs of France and Germany and the Pumi was the result. The names Puli and Pumi were used interchangeably for many years, and the Puli breed was nearly lost.

In 1912, Emil Raitsits began a program to reconstitute the Puli. Two types of coats were noted: shaggy and curly. The first standard for the Puli was written in 1915 and, in 1924, the standard was approved by FCI (Federation Cynologique Internationale).

The newly reconstituted Puli was shown at the Budapest dog show in August, 1923. The breed was divided into three classes: ancestral or working Pulik with shaggy coats, luxury or show Pulik, and dwarf Pulik. The 1934 standard divided the Puli according to height: large (19.7 inches or larger); medium (15.7 to 17.7 inches); and dwarf (13.8 inches or smaller). In the Hungarian Stud Book dated January 9, 1935, the Puli is recorded in four size classifications: large police Puli, medium or working Puli, small Puli and dwarf Puli. The medium size appeared to be the most popular.

Color and size both played a part in the development of Hungary's sheepdogs, each for its particular type of work. The more easily seen, lighter-colored kinds guarded herds and flocks from robbers and wild animals at night, while the smaller, darker-colored Puli was used to drive and herd the sheep during the day. There was ample reason for this, since sheep take direction more certainly from dark dogs than from light-colored ones. Moreover the dark dog was more distinctive to the shepherd's eye, as it worked among the flocks rounding them up and even, so it is claimed, jumping on them or running over their backs to cut off or turn back a runaway.

The dark color has always been recognized as truly characteristic of the Puli. Ordinarily it is called black, but it is a black so unlike that of any other breed as to warrant explanation. It is dull; in some cases bronze-tinged, in others just barely grayed like a weather-worn old coat faded by the sun. An outdoor life on the hillside, in all weathers but particularly under a constant glaring sun, robbed the black of its intensity and its sheen. This was the black

**591**

prized as typical of the breed in its homeland. There are, in addition, Pulik both gray and white. Any shade of gray is allowed so long as it is solid gray. The Puli is first and last a solid-colored dog. There may be some intermixture of hair of different colors usually present in the grays, and this is acceptable if the general appearance of solid color is maintained.

The Puli coat, too, is unique. There is nothing exactly like it in all dogdom. The undercoat is soft, woolly, very dense; the outer coat long and profuse. The puppy coat is tufted, but with growth the under coat tangles with the top coat in such a manner as to form long cords. This matting and cording is the natural protector of the working Puli, with the overall effect, as in other Hungarian sheepdogs, best described as unkempt.

The Puli was accepted for AKC registration in 1936, with the first AKC standard for the breed being based on the 1936 Hungarian standard. The Puli Club of America was formed in 1951.

Of course in this country more dogs are kept as guards, watchdogs, and companions than as sheepherders, hence we may find the groomed coat preferred to the uniquely corded coat which is the Puli's rightful heritage. But whatever the style of his hair, the Puli's vigor, versatility, and intelligence fit him as well for the home as for the hills.

He is a medium-sized dog averaging 17 inches height and 30 pounds or so weight, and so striking in appearance that it would be impossible to confuse him with any other kind of dog. His shaggy hair covers his head like an umbrella, and falls all over his body to the very tip of his uncurled tail in such profusion that he seems larger than he actually is. He is keen and quick, and he moves with a gait almost as springy as a bouncing ball, a trait that is perhaps a hand-me-down from those dogs of long ago whose dazzling footwork was the admiration of the shepherd boy with his sheep.

## Official Standard for the Puli

**General Appearance**—The Puli is a compact, square appearing, well balanced dog of medium size. He is vigorous, alert and active. Striking and highly characteristic is the shaggy coat which, combined with his light-footed, distinctive movement, has fitted him for the strenuous work of herding flocks on the plains of Hungary. Agility, combined with soundness of mind and body, is of prime importance for the proper fulfillment of this centuries-old task.

**Size, Proportion, Substance**—Ideally, males are 17 inches measured from the withers to the ground; bitches, 16 inches. An inch over or under these measurements is acceptable. The tightly knit body approximates a square measured from withers to the ground and point of shoulder to point of buttock. Medium boned.

**Head**—The *head* is of medium size in proportion to the body. The almond shaped *eyes* are deep set, rather large, and dark brown with black or slate gray eye rims. The *ears,* set on somewhat higher than the level of the eyes, are hanging, of medium size, V-shape, and about half the head length. The **skull** slightly domed and medium broad. The **stop** is defined, but not abrupt. The **muzzle** is strong and straight, a third of the head length, and ends in a nose of good size. The **nose** is always black. Flews and gums are black or slate gray. Flews are tight. A full complement of **teeth,** comparatively large, meet in a scissors bite.

**Neck, Topline, Body**—The **neck** is strong, muscular, of medium length and free of throatiness. The **back** is level and strong, of medium length, with croup sloping slightly. The **chest** is moderately broad and deep—the ribs well sprung. The **loin** is short, strong and moderately tucked up. The **tail** is carried over, and blends into the backline.

**Forequarters**—The shoulders are well laid back. Upper arm and scapula are approximately equal in length and form an angle of 90 degrees. The forelegs are straight, strong and medium boned with strong and flexible pasterns. Dewclaws, if any, may be removed. The round, compact **feet** have well arched toes and thick cushioned pads. The Puli stands well up on his pads. The pads and nails are black or slate gray.

**Hindquarters**—The hindquarters are well developed and muscular with well bent stifles, the rear assembly balancing that of the front. The hocks are perpendicular to the ground and well let down. Dewclaws, if any, may be removed. Feet as in front.

**Coat**—The dense, weather resistant coat is profuse on all parts of the body. The outer coat is wavy or curly, but never silky. The undercoat is soft, woolly and dense. The coat clumps together easily, and if allowed to develop naturally, will form cords in the adult. The cords are wooly, varying in shape and thickness, either flat or round, depending on the texture of the coat and the balance of undercoat to outer coat. The Puli may be shown either corded or brushed. It is essential that the proper double coat with correct texture always be apparent. With age the coat can become quite long, even reaching to the ground; however, only enough length to properly evaluate quality and texture is considered necessary so as not to penalize the younger or working specimens.

**Color**—Only the solid colors of rusty black, black, all shades of gray, and white are acceptable; however, on the chest a white spot of not more than 2 inches is permissible. In the black and the gray dogs an intermixture of some gray, black or white hairs is acceptable as long as the overall appearance of a solid color is maintained. The fully pigmented skin has a bluish or gray cast whatever the coat color.

**Gait**—The Puli is typically a lively, acrobatic dog; light, quick, agile and able to change directions instantly. At a collected, or contained trot the gait is distinctive: quick-stepping and animated, not far reaching, yet in no way mincing or stilted. When at a full trot, the Puli covers ground smoothly and efficiently with good reach and drive, the feet naturally tending to converge toward a median line of travel as speed increases. His distinctive movement is essential to the Puli's herding style.

**Temperament**—By nature an affectionate, intelligent and home-loving companion, the Puli is sensibly suspicious and therefore an excellent watchdog. Extreme timidity or shyness are *serious faults.*

## FAULTS

*Any deviation from the foregoing should be considered a fault, the seriousness of the fault depending upon the extent of the deviation.*

Approved February 12, 1983
Reformatted June 19, 1990

# Shetland Sheepdog

The Shetland Sheepdog, as its name implies, is a working Collie in miniature. There is little doubt that the small working Collie, from which came the modern show Collie evolving on larger lines, was likewise the progenitor of the Shetland Sheepdog evolving on smaller ones. It was assisted in the process by the environment of the Islands, which produced diminutiveness in all its stock, and by crosses with other breeds residing in, if not indigenous to, the Islands.

The Shetland Islands themselves are not conducive to abundance of fodder or flock, made up as they are of rugged rocks on which only meager vegetation can survive and surrounded by the sea, which brews frequent and severe storms. Small wonder that only the hardiest of both man and beast, and the smaller, could find subsistence. The actual origin of the breed cannot be traced by reference to records, as none were ever written. Tradition makes the dogs as old as the working Collies of Scotland, which frequently came to Shetland as the breed's forebears, and as old as the Islands themselves.

As the Islands were isolated from the trend of travel, the little dogs were a long time coming to the ken of dog-loving folk. Thus the breed did not take its place on the show bench until well along in the present century. The year 1909 marked the initial recognition of the Sheltie by the English Kennel Club. Not until 1914 did the breed obtain separate classification as Shetland Sheepdogs, and not Shetland Collies, because of pressure brought to bear by the Collie

**595**

breeders. The first Challenge Certificate was awarded to the breed in 1915, after which World War I put a stop to all progress for the next few years.

The first Shetland Sheepdog registered by the American Kennel club (1911) was Lord Scott, a golden brindle imported from Shetland by John G. Sherman, Jr. of New York. The American Shetland Sheepdog Association, parent club of the breed, was organized at the Westminster Kennel Club show in 1929, and held its first specialty in 1933.

The history of the several clubs catering to the breed reflects the struggle of breeders to fix and perpetuate the proper type and size. The Shetland Sheepdog Club in the Islands, founded in 1908, was, of course, the oldest. They asked for a rough Collie in miniature, height not exceeding 15 inches. The Scottish Shetland Sheepdog Club, a year later, asked for first an "ordinary Collie in miniature" and finally a "modern show Collie in miniature," ideal height 12 inches, and eventually 13½. The English Shetland Sheepdog Club, founded in 1914, was an offshoot of the Scottish requiring "approximately a show Collie in miniature," height (ideal) first 12 inches and finally from 12 to 15, the ideal being 13½. The British Breeders' Association came into being for a time as the offspring of the English Club and asked for a "show Collie in miniature," maintaining the same heights. In 1930 the Scottish and English Clubs revised their standards jointly to read "should resemble a Collie (Rough) in miniature." The American Shetland Sheepdog Association, youngest in years, tried to profit by the experience of its predecessors by combining the best of each in its standard.

On the subject of size, the current American standard specifies that the Shetland Sheepdog should stand between 13 and 16 inches at the shoulder. Importantly, it calls for disqualification for heights above or below this range.

The breed characteristics common to all Shelties can be used for two purposes pertaining to their working propensities or their companionship qualities. It is their nature to obey, willingly and naturally, with few or no lessons needed, an instinct coming no doubt from the many generations of obediently trained dogs behind them. This responsiveness has helped to make them one of the most successful of all breeds in Obedience trial competition. The instinct to guard property or places and to give watchdog warning makes them invaluable for work as farm helpers or home protectors, a heritage of the constant vigilance required to protect the crofters' cottages, flocks, and herds from invaders of all kinds. Their ability to run swiftly and gracefully, and jump with agility over obstacles, makes them a delight in fields and woods as well as in farm work. But what most endears them to everybody is their devoted, docile natures and their keen and all but human intelligence and understanding.

## Official Standard for the Shetland Sheepdog

**General Appearance**—*Preamble*—The Shetland Sheepdog, like the Collie, traces to the Border Collie of Scotland, which, transported to the Shetland Islands and crossed with small, intelligent, longhaired breeds, was reduced to miniature proportions. Subsequently crosses were made from time to time with Collies. This breed now bears the same relationship in size and general appearance to the Rough Collie as the Shetland Pony does to some of the larger breeds of horses. Although the resemblance between the Shetland Sheepdog and the Rough Collie is marked, there are differences which may be noted. The Shetland Sheepdog is a small, alert, rough-coated, longhaired working dog. He must be sound, agile and sturdy. The outline should be so symmetrical that no part appears out of proportion to the whole. Dogs should appear masculine; bitches feminine.

**Size, Proportion, Substance**—The Shetland Sheepdog should stand between 13 and 16 inches at the shoulder. Note: Height is determined by a line perpendicular to the ground from the top of the shoulder blades, the dog standing naturally, with forelegs parallel to line of measurement. *Disqualifications*—Heights below or above the desired size range are to be disqualified from the show ring.

In overall appearance, the body should appear moderately long as measured from shoulder joint to ischium (rearmost extremity of the pelvic bone), but much of this length is actually due to the proper angulation and breadth of the shoulder and hindquarter, as the back itself should be comparatively short.

**Head**—The **head** should be refined and its shape, when viewed from top or side, be a long, blunt wedge tapering slightly from ears to nose. *Expression*—Contours and chiseling of the head, the shape, set and use of ears, the placement, shape and color of the eyes combine to produce expression. Normally the expression should be alert, gentle, intelligent and questioning. Toward strangers the eyes should show watchfulness and reserve, but no fear. *Eyes* medium size with dark, almond-shaped rims, set somewhat obliquely in skull. Color must be dark, with blue or merle eyes permissible in blue merles only. *Faults*—Light, round, large or too small. Prominent haws. *Ears* small and flexible, placed high, carried three-fourths erect, with tips breaking forward. When in repose the ears fold lengthwise and are thrown back into the frill. *Faults*—Set too low. Hound, prick, bat, twisted ears. Leather too thick or too thin. *Skull* and *Muzzle*—Top of skull should be flat, showing no prominence at nuchal crest (the top of the occiput). Cheeks should be flat and should merge smoothly into a well-rounded muzzle. Skull and muzzle should be of equal length, balance point being inner corner of eye. In profile the top line of skull should parallel the top line of muzzle, but on a higher plane due to the presence of a slight but definite stop. Jaws clean and powerful. The deep, well-developed underjaw, rounded at chin, should extend to base of nostril. *Nose* must be black. *Lips* tight. Upper and lower lips must meet and fit smoothly together all the way around. *Teeth* level and evenly spaced. Scissors *bite.*

*Faults*—Two-angled head. Too prominent stop, or no stop. Overfill below, between, or above eyes. Prominent nuchal crest. Domed skull. Prominent cheekbones. Snipy muzzle. Short, receding, or shallow underjaw, lacking breadth and depth. Overshot or undershot, missing or crooked teeth. Teeth visible when mouth is closed.

**Neck, Topline, Body**—*Neck* should be muscular, arched, and of sufficient length to carry the head proudly. *Faults*—Too short and thick. *Back* should be level and strongly muscled. *Chest* should be deep, the brisket reaching to point of elbow. The ribs should be well sprung, but flattened at their lower half to allow free play of the foreleg and shoulder. Abdomen moderately tucked up. *Faults*—Back too long, too short, swayed or roached. Barrel ribs. Slab-side. Chest narrow and/or too shallow. There should be a slight arch at the loins, and the **croup** should slope gradually to the rear. The hipbone (pelvis) should be set at a 30-degree angle to the spine. *Faults*—Croup higher than withers. Croup too straight or too steep. The **tail** should be sufficiently long so that when it is laid along the back edge of the hind legs the last vertebra will reach the hock joint. Carriage of tail at rest is straight down or in a slight upward curve. When the dog is alert the tail is normally lifted, but it should not be curved forward over the back. *Faults*—Too short. Twisted at end.

**Forequarters**—From the withers, the shoulder blades should slope at a 45-degree angle forward and downward to the shoulder joints. At the withers they are separated only by the vertebra, but they must slope outward sufficiently to accommodate the desired spring of rib. The upper arm should join the shoulder blade at as nearly as possible a right angle. Elbow joint should be equidistant from the ground or from the withers. Forelegs straight viewed from all angles, muscular and clean, and of strong bone. Pasterns very strong, sinewy and flexible. Dewclaws may be removed. *Faults*—Insufficient angulation between shoulder and upper arm. Upper arm too short. Lack of outward slope of shoulders. Loose shoulders. Turning in or out of elbows. Crooked legs. Light bone. **Feet** should be oval and compact with the toes well arched and fitting tightly together. Pads deep and tough, nails hard and strong. *Faults*—Feet turning in or out. Splay feet. Hare feet. Cat feet.

**Hindquarters**—The thigh should be broad and muscular. The thighbone should be set into the pelvis at a right angle corresponding to the angle of the shoulder blade and upper arm. Stifle bones join the thighbone and should be distinctly angled at the stifle joint. The overall length of the stifle should at least equal the length of the thighbone, and preferably should slightly exceed it. Hock joint should be clean-cut, angular, sinewy, with good bone and strong ligamentation. The hock (metatarsus) should be short and straight viewed from all angles. Dewclaws should be removed. *Faults*—Narrow thighs. Cow-hocks. Hocks turning out. Poorly defined hock joint. **Feet** as in forequarters.

**Coat**—The coat should be double, the outer coat consisting of long, straight, harsh hair; the undercoat short, furry, and so dense as to give the entire coat its "standoff" quality. The hair on face, tips of ears and feet should be smooth. Mane and frill should be abundant, and particularly impressive in males. The forelegs well feathered, the hind legs heavily so, but smooth below the hock joint. Hair on tail profuse. *Note:* Excess hair on ears, feet, and on hocks may be trimmed for the show ring. *Faults*—Coat short or flat, in whole or in part; wavy, curly, soft or silky. Lack of undercoat. Smooth-coated specimens.

**Color**—Black, blue merle, and sable (ranging from golden through mahogany); marked with varying amounts of white and/or tan. *Faults*—Rustiness in a black or a blue coat. Washed-out or degenerate colors, such as pale sable and faded blue. Self-color in the case of blue merle, that is, without any merling or mottling and generally appearing as a faded or dilute tri-color. Conspicuous white body spots. Specimens with more than 50 percent white shall be so severely penalized as to effectively eliminate them from competition. *Disqualification*—Brindle.

**Gait**—The trotting gait of the Shetland Sheepdog should denote effortless speed and smoothness. There should be no jerkiness, no stiff, stilted, up-and-down movement. The drive should be from the rear, true and straight, dependent upon correct angulation, musculation, and ligamentation of the entire hindquarter, thus allowing the dog to reach well under his body with his hind foot and propel himself forward. Reach of stride of the foreleg is dependent upon correct angulation, musculation and ligamentation of the forequarters, together with correct width of chest and construction of rib cage. The foot should be lifted only enough to clear the ground as the leg swings forward. Viewed from the front, both forelegs and hind legs should move forward almost perpendicular to ground at the walk, slanting a little inward at a slow trot, until at a swift trot the feet are brought so far inward toward center line of body that the tracks left show two parallel lines of footprints actually touching a center line at their inner edges. *There should be no crossing of the feet nor throwing of the weight from side to side.*

*Faults*—Stiff, short steps, with a choppy, jerky movement. Mincing steps, with a hopping up and down, or a balancing of weight from side to side (often erroneously admired as a "dancing gait" but permissible in young puppies). Lifting of front feet in hackney-like action, resulting in loss of speed and energy. Pacing gait.

**Temperament**—The Shetland Sheepdog is intensely loyal, affectionate, and responsive to his owner. However, he may be reserved toward strangers but not to the point of showing fear or cringing in the ring. *Faults*—Shyness, timidity, or nervousness. Stubbornness, snappiness, or ill temper.

### SCALE OF POINTS

| General Appearance | | | Forequarters | | |
|---|---|---|---|---|---|
| Symmetry | 10 | | Shoulder | 10 | |
| Temperament | 10 | | Forelegs and feet | 5 | 15 |
| Coat | 5 | 25 | Hindquarters | | |
| *Head* | | | Hip, thigh and stifle | 10 | |
| Skull and stop | 5 | | Hocks and feet | 5 | 15 |
| Muzzle | 5 | | *Gait* | | |
| Eyes, ears and expression | 10 | 20 | Gait—smoothness and lack | 5 | 5 |
| *Body* | | | of waste motion when | | |
| Neck and back | 5 | | trotting | | |
| Chest, ribs and brisket | 10 | | | | |
| Loin, croup and tail | 5 | 20 | TOTAL | | 100 |

### DISQUALIFICATIONS

*Heights below or above the desired size range, i.e. 13–16 inches. Brindle color.*

Approved May 12, 1959
Reformatted July 18, 1990

# Welsh Corgi, Cardigan

The Cardigan Welsh Corgi, the Corgi with the tail, is the older of the two Corgi breeds, and one of the earliest breeds in the British Isles.

(The data upon which this summerized history is written was collected over a period of twenty years by W. Lloyd-Thomas of Mabws Hall, Llanrhystyd, Cardiganshire, South Wales.)

In the beginning, the Corgi came to the high country now known as Cardiganshire with the tall, tawny-headed Celts from Central Europe. The migration of this warrior tribe to Wales is placed, roughly, at about 1200 B.C., which means that the Corgi has been known in the land whence its name comes for more than 3000 years. The dog was a member of the same family that has produced the Dachshund.

The village of Bronant in Mid-Cardiganshire became the especial stronghold of those early Celts. The vigilance and intelligence of the Corgi must of been a great asset to the Celts, and tales handed down from father to son for generations identify him always as a valued member of the family circle. His uses were many and varied, not the least of which were his guardianship of the children and his aid in beating out game, which in those times was of more than ordinary importance.

Still, the occupation which made the Corgi worth his weight in gold to those Welsh hillmen came at a much later period, but still hundreds of years ago. This was when the Crown owned practically all land, and the tenant farmers, or crofters, were permitted to fence off only a few acres surrounding their dooryards. The rest was open country, known as common land, on which the crofter was permitted to graze his cattle, one of the chief sources of his meager income. It can be imagined that there was great competition among the crofters to secure as much as possible of this pasture land for their own uses, and the task would have been difficult had it not been for the Corgi. The little dog which had been with this Celtic people so long, and which had come to be of almost human intelligence, was trained to perform a service the opposite of that done by the herding dog.

Instead of herding the cattle, the Corgi would nip at their heels and drive them as far afield as desired. Often the crofter called upon his dog to clear "his" ground of the neighbor's cattle. The dog worked the same way in either case. The crofter would stand by his gate and give a soft whistle of two notes, one high, one low. Many times the dog could not see the cattle he was to chase, but he would keep going as long as he could hear that whistle. His speed was remarkable, considering his short legs with their out-turned feet, but the length of his back gave him added spring. When the dog had scattered the cattle by biting their hocks—avoiding death only by ducking close to the ground when they kicked—the crofter would give the recall signal, a shrill, long-drawn-out whistle made by placing the fingers in the mouth. The dog would return at once.

The division of the Crown lands, their subsequent sale to the crofters, and the appearance of fences, removed the usefulness of the Corgi. He was still retained as guard and companion by some of the hillmen, but to most he was a luxury they could not afford. In many instances he was succeeded by the red herder and by the brindle herder. The original type of Corgi known in Bronant since time immemorial became very scarce, and it is due only to the greatest care on the part of modern breeders that the old strains have been preserved.

Needless to say, stud books were unknown to the Celts and to the early Welsh farmer-descendants of the old warrior tribe. But if there were no records, there was a rigid policy of selective breeding unsurpassed in this present day. The original Corgis had to be proficient workers, and no mating was consummated without due consideration.

After the breaking up of the Crown lands, and the introduction of the new breeds, there was a certain amount of experimentation with crosses. The ancient dog of Bronant was crossed with the red herder, but it did not prove very successful and was not attempted many times. The brindle herder, however, made a rather fortuitous cross. The progeny followed the dominant characteristics of the Corgi, and gained a little through the finer coat and the color of the brindle herder. Crossed later with the Collie, there was produced the breed known as the heeler.

The principal strains of the Cardigan Welsh Corgi of today go back to the old Bronant Corgi with a slight infusion of brindle herder blood. This dog approximates as nearly as possible the dog that enjoyed his greatest popularity in Cardiganshire a century and more ago.

The two Corgi breeds were regarded officially in England as one breed divided into two types until 1934, when they were recognized as separate breeds. Up until that time they had been interbred to some extent, and sorting out the two breeds became a difficult task. In 1934, 250 Pembrokes were registered to only 59 Cardigans. The Cardigan was considered to be less uniform in type at that time and the breed nearly disappeared in its native Wales.

The first pair of Cardigans imported to the United States (by Mrs. Robert Bole of Boston) arrived in June, 1931. The breed was admitted for AKC registration in 1935.

## Official Standard for the Cardigan Welsh Corgi

**General Appearance**—Low set with moderately heavy bone and deep chest. Overall silhouette long in proportion to height, culminating in a low tail set and fox-like brush. *General Impression*—A handsome, powerful, small dog, capable of both speed and endurance, intelligent, sturdily built but not coarse.

**Size, Proportion, Substance**—Overall balance is more important than absolute size. Dogs and bitches should be from 10.5 to 12.5 inches at the withers when standing naturally. The length should be between 36 and 43 inches from tip of nose to tip of tail. Back length (from the base of neck to the base of the tail) should be approximately 1.5 times greater than the height. Ideally, dogs should be from 30 to 38 pounds; bitches from 25 to 34 pounds. Lack of overall balance, oversized or undersized are *serious faults.*

**Head**—The *head* should be refined in accordance with the sex and substance of the dog. It should never appear so large and heavy nor so small and fine as to be out of balance with the rest of the dog. *Expression* alert and gentle, watchful, yet friendly. *Eyes* medium to large, not bulging, with dark rims and distinct corners. Widely set. Clear and dark in harmony with coat color. Blue eyes (including partially blue eyes), or one dark and one blue eye permissible in blue merles, and in any other coat color than blue merle are a *disqualification.* *Ears* large and prominent in proportion to size of dog. Slightly rounded at the tip, and of good strong leather. Moderately wide at the base, carried erect and sloping slightly forward when alert. When erect, tips are slightly wide of a straight line drawn from the tip of the nose through the center of the eye. Small and/or pointed ears are *serious faults.* Drop ears are a *disqualification.* *Skull*—Top moderately wide and flat between the ears, showing no prominence of occiput, tapering towards the eyes. Slight depression between the eyes. *Cheeks* flat with some chiseling where the cheek meets the foreface and under the eye. There should be no prominence of cheekbone. *Muzzle* from the tip of the nose to the base of the stop should be shorter than the length of the skull from the base of the stop to the high point of the occiput, the proportion being about three parts muzzle to five parts skull; rounded but not blunt; tapered but not pointed. In profile the plane of the muzzle should parallel that of the skull, but on a lower level due to a definite but moderate *stop.* *Nose* black, except in blue merles where black noses are preferred but butterfly noses are tolerated. A nose other than solid black in any other color is a *disqualification*. **Lips** fit cleanly and evenly together all around. **Jaws** strong and clean. Underjaw moderately deep and well formed, reaching to the base of the nose and rounded at the chin. **Teeth** strong and regular. Scissors bite preferred; i.e., inner side of upper incisors fitting closely over outer side of lower incisors. Overshot, undershot, or wry bite are *serious faults*.

**Neck, Topline, Body**—*Neck* moderately long and muscular without throatiness. Well developed, especially in males, and in proportion to the dog's build. Neck well set on; fits into strong, well shaped shoulders. **Topline** level. **Body** long and strong. **Chest** moderately broad with prominent breastbone. Deep brisket, with well sprung ribs to allow for good lungs. Ribs extending well back. **Loin** short, strong, moderately tucked up. Waist well defined. **Croup**—Slightly downward slope to the tail set. **Tail** set fairly low on body line and reaching well below hock. Carried low when standing or moving slowly, streaming out parallel to ground when at a dead run, lifted when excited, but never curled over the back. High tail set is a *serious fault*.

**Forequarters**—The moderately broad chest tapers to a deep brisket, well let down between the forelegs. **Shoulders** slope downward and outward from the withers sufficiently to accommodate desired rib-spring. Shoulder blade (scapula) long and well laid back, meeting upper arm (humerus) at close to a right angle. Humerus nearly as long as scapula. **Elbows** should fit close, being neither loose nor tied. The **forearms** (ulna and radius) should be curved to fit spring of ribs. The curve in the forearm makes the wrists (carpal joints) somewhat closer together than the elbows. The **pasterns** are strong and flexible. Dewclaws removed. The **feet** are relatively large and rounded, with well filled pads. They point slightly outward from a straight-ahead position to balance the width of the shoulders. This outward point is not to be more than 30 degrees from center line when viewed from above. The toes should not be splayed. *The correct Cardigan front* is neither straight nor so crooked as to appear unsound. Overall, the bone should be heavy for a dog of this size, but not so heavy as to appear coarse or reduce agility. Knuckling over, straight front, fiddle front are *serious faults*.

**Hindquarters**—Well muscled and strong, but slightly less wide than shoulders. Hipbone (pelvis) slopes downward with the croup, forming a right angle with the femur at the hip socket. There should be moderate angulation at stifle and hock. Hocks well let down. Metatarsi perpendicular to the ground and parallel to each other. Dewclaws removed. **Feet** point straight ahead and are slightly smaller and more oval than front. Toes arched. Pads well filled. Overall, the hindquarters must denote sufficient power to propel this low, relatively heavy herding dog efficiently over rough terrain.

**Coat**—Medium length but dense as it is double. Outer hairs slightly harsh in texture; never wiry, curly or silky. Lies relatively smooth and is weather resistant. The insulating undercoat is short, soft and thick. A correct coat has short hair on ears, head, the legs; medium hair on body; and slightly longer, thicker hair in ruff, on the backs of the thighs to form "pants," and on the underside of the tail. The coat should not be so exaggerated as to appear fluffy. This breed has a shedding coat, and seasonal lack of undercoat should not be too severely penalized, providing the hair is healthy. Trimming is not allowed except to tidy feet and, if desired, remove whiskers. Soft guard hairs, uniform length, wiry, curly, silky, overly short and/or flat coats are not desired. A distinctly long or fluffy coat is an extremely *serious fault*.

**Color**—All shades of red, sable and brindle. Black with or without tan or brindle points. Blue merle (black and gray; marbled) with or without tan or brindle points. There is no color preference. White flashings are usual on the neck (either in part or as a collar), chest, legs, muzzle, underparts, tip of tail and as a blaze on head. White on the head should not predominate and should never surround the eyes. Any color other than specified and/or body color predominantly white are *disqualifications*.

**Gait**—Free and smooth. Effortless. Viewed from the side, forelegs should reach well forward when moving at a trot, without much lift, in unison with driving action of hind legs. The correct shoulder assembly and well fitted elbows allow for a long free stride in front. Viewed from the front, legs do not move in exact parallel planes, but incline slightly inward to compensate for shortness of leg and width of chest. Hind legs, when trotting, should reach well under body, move on a line with the forelegs, with the hocks turning neither in nor out, and in one continuous motion drive powerfully behind, well beyond the set of the tail. Feet must travel parallel to the line of motion with no tendency to swing out, cross over, or interfere with each other. Short choppy movement, rolling or high-stepping gait, close or overly wide coming or going, are incorrect. This is a herding dog which must have the agility, freedom of movement, and endurance to do the work for which he was developed.

**Temperament**—Even-tempered, loyal, affectionate, and adaptable. Never shy nor vicious.

### DISQUALIFICATIONS

*Blue eyes, or partially blue eyes, in any coat color other than blue merle.*
*Drop ears.*
*Nose other than solid black except in blue merles.*
*Any color other than specified.*
*Body color predominantly white.*

Approved December 13, 1983
Reformatted March 14, 1991

# Welsh Corgi, Pembroke

**A**lthough all evidence seems to point to the fact that the Pembroke Welsh Corgi is a much younger dog than the Cardigan Welsh Corgi, it is still true that the Corgi from Pembrokeshire is a breed of considerable antiquity. No breed that traces its origin back to A.D. 1107 can be regarded as an especially new type of dog.

In modern times there has been an effort to link the two types of Corgi under the heading of a single breed. This is far from the truth, according to W. Lloyd-Thomas, the Welsh authority who has spent so many years digging out the history of these small cattle dogs. He has given some interesting information, that, while it tends to divorce the two Corgis definitely, still gives the Pembroke a colorful past.

The direct ancestors of the Pembroke were brought across the Channel by the Flemish weavers who had been induced by Henry I of England to take up their abode in Wales. This occurred in 1107, and it stands as a sturdy cornerstone upon which the development of a breed has been built. While weaving was one of their occupations, these Flemish people were also of an agrarian nature, and they soon had transferred to the southwest corner of Wales, at Haverfordwest, the replicas of the model homes and farms in their native land. The dog fitted into this scheme.

This early progenitor of the Pembroke Welsh Corgi of today has been described as having a noticeable resemblance to the old Schipperkes. It sprang from the same family that includes the Keeshond, the Pomeranian, the

**605**

Samoyed, the Chow Chow, the Norwegian Elkhound, and the Finnish Spitz. It has little or nothing of the Dachshund characteristics.

In relation to the Cardigan, the Pembroke is shorter in body; the legs are straighter and lighter-boned, while the coat is of finer texture. Two of the most noticeable differences are in the ears and the tail. Cardigan ears are rounded, while the Pembroke's are pointed at the tip and stand erect. The Cardigan has a long tail, and the Pembroke a short one. In disposition, the Pembroke is more restless, more easily excited. If one could see specimens of the early members of both breeds at the same time, the differences would be very marked. In modern times they have become more similar. The whole development of the Pembroke evinces a desire on the part of its breeders to produce a lower, stockier dog. It also may be noted that the head has grown stronger, while in these times, good sized, round-tipped ears are not unusual.

The manner in which the Pembroke and the Cardigan have approached each other in appearance is not merely a matter of chance or of selective breeding. It is known, rather definitely, that the two were crossed before the middle of the 19th century.

The story comes direct from one of the old crofters, a man of nearly ninety years, who spent his whole lifetime in Bronant. It seemed that in his youth, many of the young people in that village found a manner of increasing their pocket money. There were always plenty of the Cardigan puppies; in fact, the majority were a burden on the poor tenant farmers. If these puppies were retained, they would cost money to feed. One day an enterprising young man tucked a couple of Corgi puppies under his arm and set forth into a neighboring shire. When he returned there was the jingle of coins in his pocket. Thereafter, other young men followed the example. The old hillman who relates this incident says that he sold puppies to the farmers in Carmarthenshire and in Pembrokeshire.

It is not known whether any Cardigan Corgis had gone into Pembrokeshire at an earlier date, but it is quite possible, and it is only logical that if the two breeds were in the same section they would be bred together at some time. So far as known, the Pembroke was not taken into Cardiganshire up to the time of World War I, although since then there have been many instances of inter-matings.

The two breeds of Corgi were mated together frequently at the time when these dogs first came to the consciousness of the bench-show fanciers. Little was known about either dog, and crossings were common. This practice has been stopped and breeders today are determined to keep the Pembroke distinct from the Cardigan.

The Pembroke is one of the most agreeable of small house dogs. It has an affectionate nature, but does not force its attentions upon those unwilling to accept them. Its intelligence is undoubted, and it is a remarkably alert, ever-vigilant guard of the fireside.

# Official Standard for the Pembroke Welsh Corgi

**General Appearance**—Low-set, strong, sturdily built and active, giving an impression of substance and stamina in a small space. Should not be so low and heavy-boned as to appear coarse or overdone, nor so light-boned as to appear racy. Outlook bold, but kindly. Expression intelligent and interested. Never shy nor vicious.

**Size and Proportions**—Moderately long and low. The distance from the withers to base of tail should be approximately 40 percent greater than the distance from the withers to the ground. *Height* (from ground to highest point of withers) should be 10 to 12 inches. *Weight* is in proportion to size, not exceeding 30 pounds for dogs and 28 pounds for bitches. In show condition, the preferred medium-size dog of correct bone and substance will weigh approximately 27 pounds, with bitches approximately 25 pounds. Obvious oversized specimens and diminutive toylike individuals must be very seriously penalized.

**Head and Skull**—Head to be foxy in shape and appearance, but not sly in expression. Skull to be fairly wide and flat between the ears. Moderate amount of stop. Very slight rounding of cheek, and not filled in below the eyes, as foreface should be nicely chiseled to give a somewhat tapered muzzle. Distance from the occiput to center of stop to be greater than the distance from stop to nose tip, the proportion being five parts of total distance for the skull and three parts for the foreface. Muzzle should be neither dishfaced nor Roman-nosed. *Nose*—Black and fully pigmented. *Eyes*—Oval, medium in size, not round nor protruding, nor deep-set and piglike. Set somewhat obliquely. Variations of brown in harmony with coat color. Eye rims dark, preferably black. While dark eyes enhance the expression, true black eyes are most undesirable, as are yellow or bluish eyes. *Ears*—Erect, firm, and of medium size, tapering slightly to a rounded point. Ears are mobile, and react sensitively to sounds. A line drawn from the nose tip through the eyes to the ear tips, and across, should form an approximate equilateral triangle. Bat ears, small catlike ears, overly large weak ears, hooded ears, ears carried too high or too low, are undesirable. Button, rose or drop ears are very serious faults. *Mouth*—Scissors bite, the inner side of the upper incisors touching the outer side of the lower incisors. Level bite is acceptable. Lips should be tight, with little or no fullness, and black. Overshot or undershot bite is a very serious fault. *Neck*—Fairly long, of sufficient length to provide over-all balance of the dog. Slightly arched, clean and blending well into the shoulders. A very short neck giving a stuffy appearance, and a long, thin or ewe neck, are faulty.

**Body**—Rib cage should be well sprung, slightly egg-shaped, and moderately long. Deep chest, well let down between forelegs. Exaggerated lowness interferes with the desired freedom of movement and should be penalized. Viewed from above, the body should taper slightly to end of the loin. Loin short. Firm level topline, neither riding up to nor falling away at the croup. A slight depression behind the shoulders caused by heavier neck coat meeting the shorter body coat is permissible. Round or flat rib cage, lack of brisket, extreme length or cobbiness, are undesirable.

**Forequarters**—Legs short; forearms turned slightly inward, with the distance between the wrists less than between the shoulder joints, so that the front does not appear absolutely straight. Ample bone carried right down into the feet. Pasterns firm and nearly straight when viewed from the side. Weak pasterns and knuckling over are serious faults. Shoulder blades long and well laid back along the rib cage. Upper arms nearly equal in length to shoulder blades. Elbows parallel to the body, not prominent, and well set back to allow a line perpendicular to the ground to be drawn from the tip of the shoulder blade through to elbow.

**Hindquarters**—Ample bone, strong and flexible, moderately angulated at stifle and hock. Exaggerated angulation is faulty as too little. Thighs should be well muscled. Hocks short, parallel, and when viewed from the side are perpendicular to the ground. Barrel hocks or cowhocks are most objectionable. Slipped or double-jointed hocks are very faulty.

**Tail**—Docked as short as possible without being indented. Occasionally a puppy is born with a natural dock, which if sufficiently short, is acceptable. A tail up to two inches in length is allowed, but if carried high tends to spoil the contour of the topline.

**Feet**—Oval, with the two center toes slightly in advance of the two outer ones. Turning neither in nor out. Pads strong and feet arched. Nails short. Dewclaws on both forelegs and hind legs usually removed. Too round, long and narrow, or splayed feet are faulty.

**Movement**—Free and smooth. Forelegs should reach well forward, without too much lift, in unison with the driving action of hind legs. The correct shoulder assembly and well-fitted elbows allow the long, free stride in front. Viewed from the front, legs do not move in exact parallel planes, but incline slightly inward to compensate for shortness of leg and width of chest. Hind legs should drive well under the body and move on a line with the forelegs, with hocks turning neither in nor out. Feet must travel parallel to the line of motion with no tendency to swing out, cross over, or interfere with each other. Short, choppy movement, rolling or high-stepping gait, close or overly wide coming or going, are incorrect. This is a herding dog which must have the agility, freedom of movement, and endurance to do the work for which he was developed.

**Color**—The outer coat is to be of self colors in red, sable, fawn, black and tan, with or without white markings. White is acceptable on legs, chest, neck (either in part or as a collar), muzzle, underparts, and as a narrow blaze on head. *Very Serious Faults—Whitelies*—Body color white with red or dark markings. *Mismarks*—Self colors with any area of white on back between withers and tail, on sides between elbows and back of hindquarters, or on ears. Black with white markings and no tan present. *Bluies*—Colored portions of the coat have a distinct bluish or smoky cast. This coloring is associated with extremely light or blue eyes and liver or gray eye rims, nose and lip pigment.

**Coat**—Medium length; short, thick, weather-resistant undercoat with a coarser, longer outer coat. Over-all length varies, with slightly thicker and longer ruff around neck, chest and on the shoulders. The body coat lies flat. Hair is slightly longer on back of forelegs and underparts, and somewhat fuller and longer on rear of hindquarters. The coat is preferably straight, but some waviness is permitted. This breed has a shedding coat, and seasonal lack of undercoat should not be too severely penalized, providing the hair is glossy, healthy, and well groomed. A wiry, tightly marcelled coat is very faulty, as is an overly short, smooth and thin coat. *Very Serious Fault—Fluffies—* A coat of extreme length with exaggerated feathering on ears, chest, legs and feet, underparts and hindquarters. Trimming such a coat does not make it any more acceptable.

The Corgi should be shown in its natural condition, with no trimming permitted except to tidy the feet, and, if desired, remove the whiskers.

### OVER-ALL PICTURE

Correct type, including general balance and outline, attractiveness of headpiece, intelligent outlook and correct temperament, is of primary importance. Movement is especially important, particularly as viewed from the side. A dog with smooth and free gait has to be reasonably sound and must be highly regarded. A minor fault must never take precedence over the above desired qualities.

A dog must be very seriously penalized for the following faults, regardless of whatever desirable qualities the dog may present: Whitelies, Mismarks or Bluies; Fluffies; Button, Rose or Drop Ears; Overshot or Undershot Bite; Oversize or Undersize.

*The judge shall dismiss from the ring any Pembroke Welsh Corgi that is vicious or excessively shy.*

Approved June 13, 1972

# The Miscellaneous Class

Authorities acknowledge that in total throughout the world there are several hundred distinct breeds of pure-bred dog. Those officially recognized for registration in the Stud Book of the American Kennel Club are presented in the body of this book. The AKC, however, provides for a regular method of development for a new breed which may result in that breed's full recognition.

Briefly stated, the requirement for admission to the Stud Book is clear and categorical proof that a substantial, sustained nationwide interest and activity in the breed exists. This includes an active parent club, with serious and expanding breeding activity over a wide geographic area.

When in the judgment of the Board of Directors such interest and activity exists, a breed is admitted to the Miscellaneous Class. Breeds in the Miscellaneous Class may compete in AKC obedience trials and earn obedience titles. They may also compete at conformation shows, but here are limited to competition in the Miscellaneous Class and are not eligible for championship points.

When the Board of Directors is satisfied that a breed is continuing a healthy, dynamic growth in the Miscellaneous Class, it may be admitted to registration in the Stud Book and the opportunity to compete in regular classes.

Presently, the breeds in the Miscellaneous Class are:

**Australian Kelpies**
**Australian Shepherds**
**Border Collies**
**Canaan Dogs**
**Cavalier King Charles Spaniels**
**Greater Swiss Mountain Dogs**
**Shiba Inus**
**Spinoni Italiani**

# Healthy Dog

## Keeping Your Dog
## Healthy, Happy and Well-Behaved

AKC gratefully acknowledges the cooperation of the faculty of the School of Veterinary Medicine at the University of Pennsylvania in preparing this discussion of canine health care. M. Josephine Deubler, V.M.D., M.S., Ph.D., coordinated the review of the material by the veterinary specialists at the University. We want to especially thank: Gustavo D. Aguirre, V.M.D.; Kenneth C. Bovee, D.V.M., M. Med. Sc.; Lawrence Glickman, V.M.D., Dr. P.H.; K. Ann Jeglum, V.M.D.; Rebecca Kirby, D.V.M.; Carl E. Kirkpatrick, V.M.D., Ph.D.; David H. Knight, D.V.M.; David S. Kronfeld, Ph.D., D. Sc., M.V. Sc., M.R.C.V.S.; Meryl P. Littman, V.M.D.; John E. Martin, V.M.D.; Vicki Meyers-Wallen, V.M.D.; William Miller, V.M.D.; Charles D. Newton, D.V.M.; Joan B. O'Brien, V.M.D.; Donald F. Patterson, D.V.M., Ph.D.; and Sheldon A. Steinberg, V.M.D., D.Sc.

Good dog care is the dog owner's responsibility. A healthy dog requires proper nutrition, regular grooming and exercise sessions, training for good behavior, vaccinations, and plenty of love. Although dogs can't come right out and announce how they feel, the alert owner can always tell something is not quite right by changes in the dog's normal appearance or behavior. This chapter describes signs of a healthy dog and suggests ways to maintain health which should be practiced by every dog owner. Then, because illness may strike every organism at some point in its life, information about the kinds of illnesses which may affect your dog is presented with a section on canine first aid.

These pages are not meant to replace the care of a veterinarian. Use this information to help recognize a problem when it arises and to give preliminary care before consulting a veterinarian. Throughout your dog's life, you and your veterinarian form an effective team for maintaining your dog's top condition.

## The Healthy Dog (description)

Every dog is an individual, with his own characteristic appearance and personality. What may be normal for one dog may not be for another; only the dog's owner and veterinarian know what is normal for any particular case. Get acquainted with the way your dog acts and looks from day to day. Changes in his appearance or behavior—something best known to the dog's owner—could be clues of possible illness. In general, however, the following describes the physical state of a healthy dog:

**SKIN:** Healthy skin is smooth and flexible, ranging from pale pink to brown or black. Spotted skin is normal in dogs with both spotted and solid colored coats. No scales, scabs, growths or areas of redness should be visible. Check to see that your dog does not have fleas, ticks, lice or other external parasites by running your hand against the grain of his coat; some pests are stationary while others, like fleas, may scurry away as soon as they are exposed. Signs of fleas are itching with the presence of small black and white specks on the skin, which are flea dirt or feces. It's a good idea to check the skin of longhaired dogs in several places. Dogs have seasonal shedding cycles, which may occasionally change. A healthy coat, however, is glossy and pliable, without dandruff, excessive oiliness, or areas of baldness.

**EYES:** A healthy dog has bright, shiny eyes free from excessive watering or discharge. Eyelashes and hair should not rub against the eyeball; owners of longhaired breeds should especially take note. Examine the moist pink inner lining of the eyelids (the *conjunctiva*) by placing your thumb near the edge of the eyelid and pulling gently upward or downward. This smooth membrane should not be inflamed, swollen, or have a yellow discharge. The "whites" of the eyes should not appear yellowish. In the inner corner of the eye is the dog's third eyelid, a light pink membrane. The extent to which the third eyelid is visible on the surface of the eye varies from breed to breed.

**EARS:** The skin inside the dog's ears is light pink, clean and lightly covered with hair. A small amount of yellow, brown or black wax may be present in the ear canals, but an overabundance of this wax is abnormal. The outside of the ear flap is covered with hair like the rest of the body. Healthy ears do not emit a bad smell; they are not red, swollen, itchy or painful to the dog, or exude discharge.

**MOUTH, TEETH, GUMS:** To examine the inside of your dog's mouth, grasp his muzzle with your fingers on one side and thumb on the other. While this hand holds the dog's head, use the other hand to pull down on the lower jaw. Healthy gums will appear pink or pigmented (black or spotted) and will feel firm. The edges of healthy gums surround the teeth, which are free from soft white matter and hard white, yellow or brown material. Your dog should not have unpleasant smelling breath. Young dogs have white, smooth teeth which tend to darken with age. The average puppy has 23 baby teeth with no molars. The figure for adult dogs is normally 42 permanent teeth, although some breeds have less teeth because of the construction of their jaw. Baby teeth should not remain once adult teeth have emerged, and sometimes have to be removed. A dog may have a scissors bite (upper front teeth just overlapping the lower teeth), overbite or underbite. The type of bite which is preferable in a particular breed is described in the breed's standard.

**NOSE:** A dog's nose is normally cool and moist. Secretions from the nose are clear and watery, not cloudy, yellow or green, thick or foul-smelling. Black noses are most common, though a variety of colors and even spots are normal. The nose should not be red or irritated, the possible result of an injury, disease, or sensitivity to sunlight. Many people mistakenly believe that the condition of a dog's nose is the best indicator of his health. A sick dog, however, may have either a warm dry nose or a cold wet one and owners are advised to use a rectal thermometer to correctly determine the possibility of a fever.

**TEMPERATURE:** The normal temperature range for a dog, taken with a rectal thermometer, is from 101 to 102.5 degrees F (38.3° C–39.2° C). Begin by shaking down the thermometer and lubricating the bulb with vaseline, mineral or vegetable oil. Lift the dog's tail and gently slide the thermometer into the anus—the distance depends on the size of the dog. Half the thermometer may be required on a large dog, while an inch may do in a small dog. This is best done while the dog is in a standing position. Remove the thermometer after three minutes to read the temperature.

**HEARTBEAT AND PULSE:** The heartbeat in a healthy dog depends on his size and condition. Normally the heart beats about 50 to 130 times per minute in a resting dog. It is faster in puppies and small dogs, slower in large dogs or those in good physical condition. The heartbeat and pulse are the same. To determine the heartbeat, place your fingertips or palm against the left side of the dog's chest just behind the elbow, or place your ear against the chest over the heart. The pulse is taken by pressing on the artery which lies on the inside of the thigh where the leg joins the body.

**ELIMINATION:** Urine excreted by a healthy dog is yellow and clear. Most adult dogs move their bowels once or twice per day; the stools are well-formed and generally brown. The amount of stools produced by your dog and their color may be affected by the kind of diet that is fed. Large amounts of odorous, loose, or unusually colored stools are abnormal.

It is most important that the dog owner regard persistent diarrhea, difficult elimination, or a change in the frequency or amount of urination as signs of possible illness which should be brought to the attention of a veterinarian.

**WEIGHT:** Even if your dog appears fine in every other way, he can't receive a clean bill of health if he is underweight or, more commonly, overweight. Obesity is usually the fault of the owner and can be corrected by changing the dog's diet after a visit to the veterinarian has ruled out a hormonal imbalance or other problem.

## The Healthy Dog (maintenance)

Keeping a dog healthy and content is neither as easy nor as difficult as many people think. What it takes is an owner who is willing to devote the necessary time and energy to exercise, train, groom and attend to the other needs of his pet. Conscientious dog care actually begins before the purchase of the dog, by realistically evaluating the time one has to spend on a dog and opting for a breed whose needs do not outstrip his owner's resources.

Don't forget that even a well-cared-for, healthy dog needs to be examined and vaccinated regularly by a veterinarian.

### GROOMING

The grooming routine includes attention to the coat, teeth, nails, and ears. How often and how much time is necessary to do the job depends upon the breed and condition of the dog, its size and its coat. Prime examples of the results of good grooming, along with proper nutrition and training, are the beautiful dogs one sees at a dog show. Maybe every dog can't look like an aspiring champion, but good grooming helps a dog look and feel his best.

## Coat

In addition to enhancing the natural beauty of any dog, regular grooming helps keep the coat and skin healthy. Coat color, length and texture vary with breed and therefore, so do the extent and kind of care required to maintain a tidy dog. Short-haired dogs should be brushed to remove dead hairs and distribute the skin's oils; longhaired dogs need regular combing and brushing, with occasional attention to mats, tangles and other coat problems. A terrier's coat requires periodic plucking to remove dead hair and give the dog a trim appearance, with brushing and combing needed between pluckings.

Brushing several times a week will keep the average dog neat and clean, although daily attention is better. Brush all the way down to the skin, letting the massaging action stimulate blood circulation and also loosen and remove flakes of dandruff.

The kind of equipment you will need to groom a dog's coat depends on the breed, coat texture, and purpose. Pin brushes, with long, round-ended stainless steel or chrome-plated pins, are recommended for long-haired breeds. Bristle brushes, recommended for short, medium or long coated breeds, have nylon and/or natural bristles. Slicker brushes, with bent wire teeth set close together to remove mats and dead hair, are made in three sizes for small, medium, and large dogs. A pin palm brush is an oval rubber pad set with round-tipped pins used to brush out facial and leg furnishings of terriers. There is also a rubber brush with soft, flexible rubber bristles to polish smooth coats and remove dead hair. In addition to these items, one can purchase clippers, stripping knives, hair dryers (never used on hot), and other equipment to keep a dog's coat clean and beautiful. All of these tools, however, must be used properly or they may damage the dog's skin and hair.

Depending on where you and your dog reside, a variety of grooming obstacles crop up in the shape of ice, salt, mud, tar, tree sap and burrs. Never use gasoline, turpentine, kerosene, or similar chemical substances to remove tar or paint from your dog's coat. If you choose not to trim the tainted hair away, affected areas may be treated by soaking in vegetable or mineral oil for 24 hours, then washing with soap and water.

In areas where burrs and other stubborn plant materials flourish, owners should frequently check for and remove such harmful objects from between the toes, under the legs, and around the ears and genitals. On the fauna side, that lasting reminder of your dog's encounter with an unfriendly skunk can be eliminated by bathing the dog in soap and water, followed by soaking the coat in tomato juice and doing a final rinse. You may have to repeat the process before the dog smells sweet again.

Mats, solid masses of hair found most often behind the ears and under the legs in long-haired dogs, are a common and often exasperating problem. Sometimes they can be teased apart using only one or two teeth in a comb. If they must be cut out, be extremely careful not to cut the skin at the same time. Cutting leaves a bare, gouged area in the coat, a potential disaster for a show dog. If the mat must be removed by cutting, try to work the comb all the way through the mat but close and parallel to the skin, then cut the mat off outside the comb.

Shedding can be an annoying problem in dogs with long hair or which seem to shed constantly. Vigorous and frequent grooming can help remove this dead hair, and plucking can remove any dead hair tufts.

A dog should be bathed as seldom as possible. Usually baths are needed only when the dog is excessively dirty or contaminated with something offensive. Frequent washing removes natural oils and causes the coat to become dry and harsh. When necessary, bathing should be done with a mild soap, baby shampoo, or coconut-oil shampoo. Stand the dog in a tub or basin, plug his ears with cotton, and place a gentle ophthalmic ointment or a few drops of mineral oil in his eyes. Longhaired dogs should be combed out before bathing to make grooming easier later. Wet the dog with water, apply soap or shampoo and work up a good lather. Rinse well when finished, and try to get a towel around the dog before he lets out his first shake. Bathing can be done outdoors in fine summer weather, but be sure during chilly or windy days to keep the dog indoors until he is thoroughly dry. This process may be hastened by vigorously rubbing the dog with rough towels. Brushing and combing should be performed regularly thereafter to keep the dog as clean as possible.

## Nails

Nails should be trimmed so that they just clear the floor. (This may not be necessary in dogs who wear their nails down through exercise on rough surfaces.) Longer nails may cause the foot to splay or spread, or they may even grow back into the dog's skin. This is most likely to happen in the case of neglected dewclaws, which do not touch the ground and may be hidden under long hair. Dewclaws are usually removed by a veterinarian soon after a puppy is born (however, the Briard and Great Pyreness breed standards require dewclaws be left intact).

To trim your dog's nails, purchase a specially designed nail trimmer at a pet shop. Do not use ordinary scissors. Make the cut just outside the pink blood line visible in white nails; in dark nails, remove only the hook-like part of the nail which turns down.

## Ears

Your dog's ears should be cleaned approximately once every month, more often if he is prone to ear problems. Using your finger covered by a damp towel or a soft cloth, or a cotton swab soaked in mineral oil or alcohol, clean only the part of the outer ear that you can see. There is no need to remove every bit of wax from the ear, since a small amount naturally protects the ear canal. Do not try to clean out an infected ear; seek and follow the advice of your veterinarian instead.

The ears of some dogs contain quite a bit of hair, which may block air circulation and contribute to ear infections. If your veterinarian recommends that you pluck the hair from the ear to free up air circulation, use your fingers or a tweezer to remove only the hairs that come out easily.

### Eyes

Always be careful during grooming and bathing to avoid getting any irritating substances in the eyes. Make sure, especially in breeds with large protruding eyes and long hair, that hairs are not rubbing against the eyeball. Constant irritation can produce a chronic infection, and the dog may appear red-eyed, with a slight discharge in the corner. For mild irritations, you can wash the eye with warm boric acid solution (caution: boric acid is poisonous if taken internally). After the eyes are thoroughly cleaned, cotton or cloth patches can be soaked in warm water and held in place over the eyes for 5 to 10 minutes. More serious irritations, that can result from foreign particles, turned-in eyelashes, or misaligned eyelids, must be brought to the attention of a veterinarian.

### Teeth

Just because dogs don't eat sweets doesn't mean they are free from dental problems. Dogs develop plaque and tartar just like people, which can lead to periodontal (gum) disease, a painful condition and cause of tooth loss. Tartar is recognizable as a hard yellow-brown or gray-white deposit on the teeth which can't be removed by brushing or scraping with a fingernail. Once present, tartar should be removed by a veterinarian.

Because tartar begins its destructive life as plaque, a soft white or yellow substance, regular at-home tooth cleaning sessions can prevent many harmful problems.

Dog owners should clean their pet's teeth once or twice a week; the only tools required are a child's toothbrush or a gauze pad. If you're using the latter, for example, wrap the moist gauze round your finger and dip it in dog toothpaste, or a solution of baking soda. Vigorously scrub teeth from gum to crown. You don't need to clean the inner surfaces of the teeth since the dog's tongue will do most of that work for you.

Also, some veterinarians feel that feeding your dog dry food and offering him hard things to chew on reduce the incidence of tartar formation by abrasion. This does not, however, eliminate the need to do additional teeth-cleaning, or periodic scaling by a veterinarian.

If, despite your efforts, your dog's gums bleed, look red, or recede from the teeth, begin home treatment with a daily gum massage and check with your veterinarian.

## Anal Sacs

Anal sacs are located on either side of the lower half of your dog's anus. They secrete a thick, liquid substance with a powerful odor. Sometimes, especially in small dogs, the fluid inside the anal sacs becomes impacted. This prompts the dog to drag his rear on the ground and lick his anus. In this event, the anal sacs will need to be emptied, which is something you may wish to do at home. If your efforts fail, however, see a veterinarian.

To express the anal sacs, raise the dog's tail with one hand and hold a piece of gauze or tissue in the other hand. Grasp the skin outside of the anal area with your thumb and forefinger (in eight and four o'clock position respectively), then push in and squeeze gently. The anal sac material should exude from the two gland ducts on the anus, which you can then wipe away. If you can't express both glands at once, you can do them individually by placing your gloved forefinger inside the rectum and then pressing the sac between your thumb and forefinger. Impacted anal sacs can become infected, in which case they need to be treated by the veterinarian. The discharge from an infected anal sac will appear bloody or pus-like, and the area will be painful to the dog.

# Preventive Care

$W$e live in an age when some potentially devastating diseases can be prevented by vaccinations. Dogs should receive a series of vaccinations early in life, followed by yearly visits to the veterinarian for booster shots. Controlling parasites is also a lifetime commitment, but one which can save your dog from great discomfort and safeguard the health of the human community as well.

### Vaccinations: What and When

Serious canine diseases such as rabies, distemper, parvovirus, hepatitis and leptospirosis can be prevented by having your dog vaccinated regularly by a veterinarian. These five diseases are extremely dangerous and potentially fatal to your dog and some (rabies and leptospirosis) are dangerous to humans as well. A vaccination is also available for kennel cough, a respiratory problem which generally affects young dogs. While not life threatening in itself, kennel cough is very stressful and can lead to other, more serious illnesses.

A puppy's first vaccinations should ideally take place at five to six weeks of age but if this is not possible, they can be started at eight to nine weeks of age. Over a period of several weeks, a dog should receive a series of vaccinations to build his immunity to disease. Afterward, yearly booster shots to provide ongoing protection are imperative throughout life. Be sure that you understand, especially in the crucial vaccination series during puppyhood, when your dog needs to return to the veterinarian for his next vaccination. And during that vulnerable time when he is waiting to complete the vaccination program, do not allow him to play with strange dogs or visit public parks or similar places where he may be exposed to disease before immunity is insured.

## INTERNAL PARASITES

### Heartworms

Following the bite of an infected mosquito, young heartworms enter the bloodstream of the dog and actually mature within the canine heart where they may reach a length of 5 to 12 inches. Infected dogs may tire easily, have a chronic cough, and lose weight. Needless to say, heartworms present a very serious, life-threatening problem.

Heartworm infection occurs throughout the United States, but is particularly common in warm, mosquito-infested areas. Dogs already infected with heartworms may be treated with drugs to destroy the worms, but preventive medicine is a much better means of control. There are two things you can do:

screen your dog against mosquitoes, and regularly give him heartworm preventive pills available from the veterinarian, who will first want to examine a blood sample to make sure your dog is not already infected.

### Hookworms

Hookworms commonly occur in puppies, but dogs of any age can be seriously infested. Dogs may contract hookworms by swallowing the parasite's larvae, or the larvae can penetrate the dog's skin. Puppies can receive hookworms from their mother before birth, or while nursing. Debilitated dogs are an easy target, and a heavy infestation can cause death.

The parasite's eggs can be identified under the microscope in a fresh stool sample. Treatment is routine, but you can help avoid infection by keeping the dog's environment sanitary: remove feces frequently from the area, keep lawns short and relatively dry, and wash down paved areas with disinfectants.

### Roundworms

Roundworms, or ascarids, are also very common in puppies. Most infected puppies show no signs, but still shed millions of eggs that are infective for other dogs and children. Roundworms look like white, firm, rounded strips of thin spaghetti about one to three inches long, and often curl or coil like springs. Adult dogs who become infested may be tolerant or immune to roundworms and show no signs of infection. Your veterinarian will prescribe medication to treat roundworm infection, but to help prevent it, sanitary conditions like those described in the prevention of hookworms are recommended, and you should try to control rodent populations.

### Tapeworms

Tapeworm segments may be seen in the hair around the dog's anus, in his bedding, or in the stool itself. Alive, the tapeworm segments are off-white, flat, and wave back and forth; when dried out, they may become yellow, translucent, and look like grains of rice. An infected dog may suffer weight loss and occasional diarrhea. If your dog shows signs of being infected with tapeworms, have a veterinarian examine a stool sample and prescribe the proper medication.

### Whipworms

Whipworms inhabit the dog's lower intestinal tract. Some dogs will not show any signs of infestation, so your veterinarian will have to diagnose the problem by checking stool samples. Other dogs will show intermittent, often watery diarrhea, anemia, weight loss, weakness, and a generally poor condition. Medication is necessary for treatment. Because dogs acquire whipworms by licking or sniffing contaminated ground, it is important to keep the kennel area dry and sanitary, as mentioned previously.

If you suspect that your dog has been infested with hookworms, round-worms, tapeworms or whipworms, microscopic examination of one or more stool samples is necessary to accurately determine the nature and extent of the problem and to evaluate the effect of treatment. Never simply take deworming into your own hands; improper deworming can do as much damage to the dog as the worms themselves. Your veterinarian will need to determine if worms are indeed the problem and, if so, what variety; he will also need to assess your dog's physical condition before the correct type and amount of deworming medicine can be prescribed. In fact, the examination of a sample of your dog's stool for parasite eggs should be a part of your dog's annual physical examination, so bring a specimen with you when you visit your veterinarian.

## EXTERNAL PARASITES

### Fleas

Because fleas are such a common problem, you may think they are annoying but inconsequential. Don't! Fleas, a couple or an army, are very unhealthy. An infested dog suffers from blood loss and itchy skin, and can even contract tapeworms, which spend part of their lifecycle in the flea. Dogs with fleas may lose areas of hair, especially in the lower back, neck, and inner thighs. You and your family may also be victimized by hungry fleas in search of a meal. More-over, allergic reactions to flea bites are common in dogs. This is quite painful, with sore skin frequently irritated to the point of rawness.

Although wingless, fleas are expert jumpers. You may actually see them moving quickly through the dog's hair as you part it to examine his skin. Other signs of the presence of fleas are small black and white specks (flea feces or eggs) on the dog's skin. These eggs are not attached to the skin, and easily drop off into the dog's bedding, the carpet, your furniture, and anywhere else the dog has been, where they hatch into a new crop in eight to ten days. Therein lies a great deal of the problem in eradicating fleas from your dog and home.

As for those fleas on your dog, you can kill them by bathing him in a commercial dog shampoo containing an insecticide, or by using a flea dip, spray, powder, or collar, which kill fleas on contact. All of these products should be used only after you have carefully read the package instructions. If you use a flea dip, sponge it over his coat, avoiding his eyes, and do not use it in areas of open sores. Sometimes dogs are sensitive to the flea-killing ingre-dients in flea collars so be alert for reddening around the neck or hair loss. If this happens, remove the collar at once. Also, do not think you are killing twice the amount of fleas by using two products simultaneously. One product is enough; more may harm the dog. Seek advice from a veterinarian, especially if your dog has signs of a flea allergy.

Now you can tackle the problem of the eggs and larval stages of the flea. If you don't, the new generation will soon start the cycle all over again. Thorough vacuuming will remove some eggs from the floor and carpet; washing or burning infested bedding will also have a positive effect. For large areas, or more serious infestations, you may have to fumigate with a commercial insecticide or hire a professional exterminator.

### Ticks

Ticks can cause anemia, tick paralysis, or serious diseases such as Lyme disease. Be sure to check your dog's entire body for ticks *daily* if you live in or visit areas where ticks are prevalent, and to remove the tick as soon as you discover it. Better yet, prevent tick infestation by treating the dog with a flea and tick powder, spray, or dip.

The correct way to remove a tick is to grasp it with a pair of tweezers and firmly (though gently) pull it straight out. Although it's not necessary, first soaking the tick (avoiding the dog's skin) with alcohol or nail polish remover (not gasoline, kerosene or the like) may make removal easier. Don't worry if the whole tick doesn't detach; it will not grow back, and rarely will the area become infected. Once it is removed, you can kill the tick by burning it with a match, but only after dog and tick are separated—never run the risk of burning the dog! You can also use a commercial dog dip to combat numerous ticks and to guard temporarily against further infestation. Tick collars work only on the areas around the dog's head and neck, so don't neglect the possibility of infestation occurring elsewhere on his body, and double-check around the ears.

### Lice

Lice, which cause intense itching, are spread by direct contact with another infested animal. Lice infestation is unusual, but once the tiny, pale-colored parasites move onto your dog, he becomes their permanent home as well as a source of nourishment and a nursery for eggs which attach to the dog's hair. Lice can be killed by giving your dog a good bath, then using a dip or other insecticidal product that is effective against ticks and fleas.

### Mites

Different kinds of mites inhabit different areas of the dog, but the problem caused by any of these pests is generally known as "mange."

Ear mites (*Otodectes cynotis*) live and feed in the dog's ear canals. A dog with ear mites will vigorously shake his head and scratch his ears, and you may see an abundance of dark-colored wax inside his ear. The mites themselves are tiny, mobile white specks that should be eliminated by cleaning the ear and treating with an oily insecticidal liquid formulated specifically for this purpose (see *Grooming* and *Administering Medicine*). Your veterinarian should teach you how to perform this treatment at home.

Scabies, *Sarcoptes scabei,* a condition which spreads rapidly between dogs and which also affects humans, is caused by a microscopic mite that burrows beneath the dog's skin. Scabies is characterized by intense itching and hair loss, especially in the areas of the ears, elbows, legs and face. Left untreated, your dog's entire body can become affected.

To diagnose scabies, veterinarians study skin scrapings under the microscope. Once scabies has been confirmed, your dog will need to be treated several times with an insecticide, possibly in conjunction with an antibiotic-steroid medication to help relieve the itching until the mites are eradicated.

The *Demodex canis* mite, a microscopic mite that lives in hair follicles can cause hair loss and thick red skin. Eventually, it can cause the formation of pustules in infected hair follicles. The first signs of demodectic mange in young puppies are small patches of hair loss around the forehead, eyes, muzzle, and forepaws. For a diagnosis, a veterinarian will examine hair roots and skin scrapings under the microscope. Medicated dips are commonly used to destroy the mites. Dogs with demodectic mange should not be used for breeding.

Dogs that enjoy prowling in wooded areas may become infested with chiggers (red or Harvest mites). A microscopic examination of a skin scraping may be necessary for diagnosis. Although they can attack any part of the dog's body, chiggers usually prefer the abdomen, neck and head (especially the ear flaps and canals); their burrowing causes severe redness and itching. The treatment for ear chiggers is the same as for ear mites. Your veterinarian will tell you what kind of insecticide to use for other body areas, and whether or not to use an antibiotic-steroid medication to control itching.

Puppies are usually targets for the "walking dandruff" mite *Cheyletiella yasguri.* A highly contagious condition, suspect this problem if your puppy has dandruff on his head, back and neck. He may be bothered by mild itching. The mite may be visible when a magnifying glass is used. Insecticidal shampoos, dips, sprays or powders are used to control an infestation. These mites may produce itchy red spots on humans (similar to fleas and scabies) who have handled infected dogs. Control of the mites on the dog usually clears up this problem.

**Flies**

Fly bites give a dog's skin, especially the face and ears, a scabbed, crusty appearance. Prick-eared dogs are especially vulnerable to attack. When you know they are apt to be a problem, prevent fly bites by applying insect repellent to your dog's vulnerable areas, carefully avoiding the eyes.

Another problem posed by flies is that they may sometimes lay eggs in dirty, infected skin and ears. Hatched eggs release maggots, which thrive on the dog's own flesh. If maggots appear on your dog, make sure every single one is removed and the area is cleaned and treated for infection. You can also help prevent maggots by prompt cleaning and treating of all wounds, and clipping away mats created by unattended long hair, particularly around the anus.

Parasitic infestations of the dog, internal or external, are very unpleasant but relatively common and easily treated, if caught soon enough. Neglect can turn an easily cured problem into a serious situation. Never let obvious symptoms go untreated.

# Administering Medicine

It shouldn't be difficult to make a dog accept either solid or liquid medication. Just remember to be firm; don't get frustrated or give up before the medicine is safely on its way to its destination.

### Pills and Liquid Medication

The easiest way to make a dog accept medication is by disguising it in the dog's food or milk. This is not the best method, however, since the dog may not receive the entire dose or, in the case of some pills, may not digest them in the correctly timed sequence. Even so, palatable medicines or those without taste such as cod liver oil, mineral oil, and milk of magnesia are often given this way. Pills may be crushed first into a powder (you can use the bowl of a spoon, for example) because most dogs will immediately reject a pill as soon as it is discovered in a mouthful of food.

A much more positive and effective method of giving medication orally is to force the dog to take it. Capsules, pills, and other solid forms can be given by standing along the dog's right side, grasping his muzzle over the top of his nose so that the fingers of your left hand press in on the lips, and squeezing your fingers against his teeth. This will usually start the dog opening his mouth. As he does so, his lips will curl inward around the points of his teeth; this protects your fingers should the dog attempt to close his mouth. Tilt his head upward slightly. The pill is held in the fingers of the right hand and is pushed deep into the dog's throat. Quickly withdraw your hand and allow him to close his mouth; keep his head elevated and tap his nose or stroke his throat. Usually a dog will lick his nose when he has swallowed the capsule. If he spits it out, repeat the process until you are successful.

Liquids are best administered from an eyedropper, vial or small bottle; spoons are usually too awkward to be useful. It is essential that someone hold the dog's head steady and slightly elevated. Insert two fingers inside the corner of the lips and pull outward away from the teeth. This forms a funnel-like pouch into which the medicine is poured. It will trickle between the teeth and as the dog tastes it, he will usually swallow. If not, try tapping his nose with your finger or jiggling the pouch slightly. Some dogs clench their teeth and prevent the medicine from entering between them. In this case, insert the handle of a spoon between the teeth. Once a dog starts to swallow, he usually takes in the rest of the medicine satisfactorily.

### Eye Medication

Eye ointment is most easily applied to the area of the conjunctiva (see *Eyes*, page 612). With your thumb or forefinger, roll the lower eyelid gently downward and squeeze the ointment into the space between the eyelid and eyeball. When putting eyedrops into the dog's eyes, elevate his head slightly. Grasp his muzzle and hold the lower eyelid open with one hand. The other hand should keep the upper lid open and drop in the medication. Do not touch the end of the bottle or tube to the eye, to prevent injury or possible contamination of the medication.

## Ear Medication

Most veterinarians recommend putting medication in a dog's ear daily for a few weeks after his ears have been cleaned. Many ear ointment tubes have a long nozzle, which you can place into the ear canal; liquids can just be dropped right into the canal. Once the medication is inside, locate the cartilage just below the opening of the ear and vigorously massage it up and down. This should produce a sloshing sound as the medication spreads down inside the ear canal and goes to work.

# Nutrition and Feeding

Food and water are two of the most important items in a dog's life. From food he receives the necessary energy to grow, to maintain a healthy body, to reproduce, and to fight infection. All dogs need to ingest a balanced amount of carbohydrates, protein, fats, vitamins, and minerals. These are contained (in differing amounts) in reputable commercial dog foods, or you can prepare an adequate diet in your own kitchen. What proportion of each key ingredient is needed, and in what overall quantity of food, depends on the individual dog. Is the dog young or old? Is he in good physical shape or does he spend most of his time lying around? Does he live in a hot or cold climate, outside or inside the house? Is he subjected to special demands such as strenuous work? Or do you have a pregnant bitch? Each of these cases has its own nutritional demands.

Every dog should have its own food dish and access to a dish of fresh water. Keep the dishes clean, as well as the utensils you use to open or prepare the food. Regularity is also important: feed at regular times in regular amounts, and feed a stable, uniform diet to achieve the most satisfactory results.

## Puppies

Puppies need more calories and essential nutrients than do adult dogs. Food quality is as important as quantity, especially in the period just after weaning. (Weaning usually takes place at five to seven weeks old if the puppies have received a little solid food three to four weeks after whelping). Eggs, milk, meat and cottage cheese are fine foods for puppies since they are palatable, digestible, and contain abundant protein of good quality. Foods with a very high fiber content are less desirable during the period of rapid growth. If you prefer a commercial dog food, choose one which is specially formulated for puppies, or supplement an adult food with the high protein foods mentioned above.

Three feedings a day help to satisfy the high daily food intake for puppies, although you may prefer to feed four times per day for the first month, and continue with three thereafter. This schedule should continue until the puppy reaches four to six months of age, when the stomach can hold food for longer periods of time. However, be careful to avoid oversupplementing the puppy during those early months. Overfeeding young dogs may cause problems due to disproportionate development of the skeleton and muscles. The pup should be weighed at weekly intervals and the rate of growth compared with published charts for its breed. The amount of food should be adjusted to conform with that for an average rate of growth rather than a maximum one. Plenty of exercise is important at this time, but make sure that the ground is not slippery or too hard in order to avoid mechanical injuries.

Most dogs of small breeds approach maturity when they are seven to ten months old, at which time their total nutrient requirements will begin gradually to decrease. Be alert for this change. Needs at this time gradually diminish and approach those for maintenance. Maturity arrives later in large breeds which develop more slowly.

Don't be alarmed if your dog skips an occasional meal or eats only part of it. It could mean that a feeding can be eliminated or the quantity reduced. Most dogs should finish their meal in twenty minutes, although this is not necessary. Always remember to provide fresh water, even if you feed foods which seem to contain a large amount of moisture. Snacks between meals should be avoided except for an occasional treat for good behavior.

## Adult Dogs

The primary purpose of careful feeding is to meet the nutritional needs of the dog throughout his life. Here is a general guide to the caloric requirements for maintenance of the average adult dog, but the amount of food your dog actually needs may be more or less depending on his size, activity, temperament, metabolism, and other factors. A dog that works hard or lives outside in a cold climate needs more food for energy than one who is basically sedentary or lives in a temperature-controlled apartment, for example.

### DAILY RATIONS IN OUNCES

| Dog's Weight (lb) | Kcal Needed/lb Body Weight | Dry Type | Semi-Moist | Canned |
|---|---|---|---|---|
| 2 | 65 | 1.3 | 1.7 | 3.4 |
| 5 | 52 | 2.5 | 3.2 | 7.00 |
| 10 | 44 | 4.3 | 5.5 | 10.75 |
| 15 | 39 | 6.1 | 7.8 | 15.25 |
| 20 | 37 | 7.5 | 9.7 | 18.75 |
| 30 | 33 | 10.0 | 12.8 | 25.0 |
| 45 | 30 | 14.0 | 18.0 | 35.0 |
| 75 | 26 | 20.4 | 26.2 | 51.0 |
| 110 | 24 | 25.0 | 32.2 | 62.5 |

(Caloric Requirements—Maintenance—and recommended daily food intakes of *average* adult dogs of various body weights. Individuals may require one-quarter more or less than these averages.)

There are three types of dog foods: dry, semi-moist, and canned. One kind or brand is difficult to recommend over another since all contain adequate amounts of carbohydrates, fats, protein, minerals and vitamins. The selection of any diet, however, should depend on three main influences—the nature of the dog, performance desired by the owner, and overall management. Whether or not the diet you feed your dog is suitable may be indicated by the dog himself. First, observe his stools. Large amounts of waters or foamy stools, pale or the color of the food, indicate poor digestion. Smaller, darker, denser stools, on the other hand, suggest superior digestion. Also, the proper diet will help to keep most dogs' coats pliant, glossy and clean-looking. As for the amount of food, adjust the volume of food so that your dog is neither too thin nor too fat. A dog is overweight if you can't feel his ribs when you run your hands over his sides as you stand above his body.

Many people prefer to serve adult dogs a good dry food, served without additional moisture, once or twice daily. Most dogs seem more content if fed twice a day, although once may be more convenient for the dog owner. In regard to two daily meals, feed the heavier meal at night if you want him to sleep quietly or if he has to work hard the next day. The lighter meal should be given at night if the dog is used at that time as a watchdog.

### Pregnant and Lactating Bitches

If you plan to breed your bitch, first make sure she is in good condition. Pregnancy is not the proper time to start rebuilding her depleted body reserves, and may result in complications at the time of whelping.

Prior to breeding, feed her a complete, balanced diet slightly above her usual maintenance intake. A good way to do this is to add a little protein supplement to her usual daily food.

After breeding, return her at once to her usual amount and type of food. A bitch in good condition should continue into pregnancy with the same caloric intake that she had during adult maintenance. Her food intake should be increased only as her body weight increases, beginning about the last five weeks before whelping. Daily food intake should be increased gradually until, at the time of whelping, she may eat 35 to 50% more than the amount of food she consumed before breeding.

If you have been feeding your bitch a well-balanced diet of good quality, you will not need to supplement the diet during pregnancy. Some breeders, however, disagree. If you do choose to supplement your bitch's diet during gestation, give a natural protein supplement, such as evaporated milk, small quantities of lightly cooked eggs, tidbits of meat, or raw liver. These supplements should never represent more than 10% of her daily food intake. As her weight and food intake increase, begin dividing and spacing her feedings more frequently to avoid the discomfort that larger meals might cause, especially in a small dog. The feeding routine during the last third of pregnancy should anticipate the peak needs during lactation.

Some bitches consume little food for the first day or two after whelping. Then their appetites and need for all nutrients rise sharply and peak in about three weeks.

During this entire period, adequate calcium, phosphorus, and vitamin D must be fed to avoid the occurrence of eclampsia. These nutrients already should be present in optimal amounts in a sound diet, so further supplementation should be unnecessary. Eclampsia is a condition caused by temporary derangement of calcium metabolism and characterized by nervousness, whimpering, an unsteady gait and spasms. More commonly a problem in Toy breeds, eclampsia can be readily cured by proper treatment if caught in time.

After whelping, the bitch ideally should be about the same weight as when she was bred, or not more than 5 to 10% heavier. For three weeks after whelping, she will need two or three times the food intake that was necessary for maintenance. This food should be divided into three or four meals, following the pattern established in pregnancy but increasing the amount of food per meal. The composition of the food should be the same during the last third of pregnancy and during lactation, only the amount per day should change.

Nursing puppies should be allowed to eat a little of their mother's food soon after they have normal sight and locomotion. As weaning progresses, start limiting food intake in the bitch so that she will have fewer problems at time of complete weaning.

On the first day of weaning, do not offer the bitch any food at all, although plenty of water should always be available. On the second day, feed one-fourth of her normal maintenance diet; on the third day, one-half; on the fourth day, three-fourths; and then return to the diet to which she was accustomed before breeding. This will help decrease milk production and help prevent problems in the breasts.

Lastly, even if you have followed recommended feeding practices during pregnancy and lactation, many bitches deplete body reserves of nutrients during lactation. Therefore, carefully observe the bitch and be sure she is fed a good quality diet, one that is digested well and has a high content of essential nutrients, until she has reached the same body condition and nutritional status that she enjoyed before breeding.

### Hand-Feeding Newborn Puppies

A puppy whose mother is either unable or unwilling to nurse must be hand-fed. For a description of the suitable environment and other needs of newborn puppies, see the *Reproduction and Breeding* section in this chapter.

Cow's milk doesn't make a good substitute for bitch's milk, which is more concentrated and has twice the level of protein, almost double the caloric content, and more than twice the content of calcium and phosphorus. For feeding puppies, cow's milk may be supplemented with a hen's egg (one egg stirred into two-thirds of a cupful of milk). Evaporated cow's milk should be diluted with only one-fifth of its volume of water (instead of an equal volume as for human use). A good puppy formula can be made at home, but we recommend commercial puppy formulas like Esbilac® for greater ease and accuracy.

The caloric content and nutritive quality of the formula you select in turn dictate the feeding schedule. A dilute formula will either force the puppy to consume larger quantities at each feeding or to be fed more frequently. Otherwise, substandard growth will occur. On the other hand, overfeeding may induce diarrhea, especially in the young, and too rapid growth in older pups. The best policy is to follow manufacturer's recommendations. You may like to underfeed slightly during the period when the puppy is most susceptible to digestive disturbance, then to increase the caloric intake gradually to near full feeding after three weeks of age.

To simplify the feeding program, the following average caloric intakes are recommended:

**First Week:** 60–70 calories per pound body weight per day.
**Second Week:** 70–80 calories per pound body weight per day.
**Third Week:** 80–90 calories per pound body weight per day.
**Fourth Week:** 90+ calories per pound body weight per day.

An individual puppy may require one-quarter more or less of these average daily intakes of calories.

For example, the average daily needs of a formula for a ten-ounce puppy (weighed on a sensitive scale for accuracy) of an average-sized breed would be estimated as follows:

Because the recommended caloric intake is 60 calories per pound body weight per day, for a ten-ounce or 2/3-pound puppy, 2/3 of 60 or 40 calories would be needed. If the formula supplies 30 calories per ounce, the amount needed would be approximately 1.5 ounces of formula.

Not more than three feedings a day are necessary if a formula is fed that approaches the composition of bitch's milk in the amounts just outlined. Thus, for a 10 ounce puppy, the daily allowance of 1.5 ounces of formula could be divided into three feedings of 1/2 ounce each, fed at exactly eight-hour intervals.

Use common sense as you follow the hand-feeding regimen. Start the above puppy, for example, with 1/4 to 1/2 ounce each feeding on the first day, then increase the amount gradually so that he is eating 1/2 ounce per feeding the fourth and fifth days. Continue to increase this as he gains weight and responds favorably to feeding. A steady weight gain and well-formed feces are the best evidence of satisfactory progress.

If diarrhea develops, immediately reduce intake to 1/2 the amount previously fed, then gradually increase it again to the recommended level. Keeping the puppies in separate compartments with clean diapers (see *Reproduction and Breeding* section) allows careful fecal observations for individual puppies.

Never prepare more formula than is required for any 48-hour period, since milk provides a wonderful medium for bacterial growth. Furthermore, maintain clean and sanitary conditions at all times. Divide the formula into portions approximately the size required for each feeding, and keep it refrigerated. Before feeding, warm the formula to about 100 degrees F, or near body temperature. Using a Pyrex baby-nursing bottle and nipple, hold the bottle so that the puppy does not ingest air. Do not let him nurse too rapidly. The hole in the nipple should be enlarged slightly with a hot needle, to let the milk slowly ooze from the nipple when the bottle is inverted. Reasonably vigorous sucking is required by the puppy, however.

### Older Dogs

In the older dog, the activity level and metabolism rate slow down, diminishing the amount of calories required for maintenance. Therefore, to avoid obesity, you must reduce the amount of food usually by one-quarter or one-third. Although caloric requirements clearly are lower now than those for growing puppies and younger adults, the oldster continues to have the usual demands for essential nutrients, so it may need a more nutritious diet than is needed for maintenance. Protein should be of high biological value. Also, since the digestive process and absorption of food take longer, you may try feeding smaller, more frequent meals. Many older dogs suffer from various problems and may benefit from specialized diets while under the supervision of a veterinarian. Diets are now available that are specifically formulated for the needs of older dogs.

### Mealtime Mistakes

Thanks to increased knowledge concerning nutrition and efforts of reputable manufacturers to offer a large number of palatable and nutritionally sound diets, nutritional deficiencies are rare in dogs today. When they do occur, they are often the result of overly anxious owners who mistakenly unbalance an already balanced diet. A common mistake is to add extra fats to increase the energy intake or to improve palatability of a diet. Too much fat will cause caloric needs to be met before enough balanced food is consumed to provide the protein, minerals, or vitamins necessary for good health.

Oversupplementation with additional mineral and vitamin preparations, such as calcium and vitamin D, during the periods of growth and reproduction, is another common source of difficulty. An excess of minerals and vitamins or imbalances among them may cause problems that are more complex and difficult to diagnose or treat than simple deficiencies.

### A Bone to Pick

Finally, a word about giving bones to your dog. Dogs love bones, but in your eagerness to give your pet a special treat, make sure you give him the right kind. Bones to be avoided are turkey or pork bones, or any others that can splinter. Sharp, needle-like pieces of bone can penetrate the stomach or intestines and have a disastrous effect. Better bones are those which are large and hard, such as knuckle or marrowbones. Before you give them to your dog, parboil them to destroy harmful parasites. Then make sure your dog only chews on the bone, and take it away if you see him actually start to eat it.

### The Overweight Dog

Too much food and not enough exercise translate into fat. Fortunately for dogs, the amount of food they have access to can be controlled. Check with your veterinarian to make sure excess food is the actual problem and then put your overweight dog on a strict diet until he reaches the desired weight. This means feeding slightly less than the amount of calories he needs for daily maintenance (and no treats or table scraps!) and increasing exercise. Weight loss will occur when the dog uses more calories than he takes in from food.

### Weighing a Dog

It's a good idea to weigh a dieting dog once a week to determine the progress. You should also weigh growing puppies regularly, and dogs on medication (you may need to gauge dosage according to weight).

Most dogs will not stand quietly on the bathroom scale until you have read their weight. So, weigh yourself, then weigh yourself again with the dog in your arms, and then subtract the first from the second. The difference is the weight of the dog alone.

# Reproduction and Breeding

You may eventually wish to breed your bitch or use your dog at stud. Bringing about the creation of new life should never be taken lightly. The problem of unwanted dogs has reached overwhelming proportions; don't let your enthusiasm for breeding aggravate the situation further. You must have plans for your puppies before they are even conceived.

Many people find breeding an exciting, challenging, and rewarding activity. Others, however, are amazed at how time-consuming, expensive, and occasionally heartbreaking breeding can be. Please research the project thoroughly by talking with an experienced breeder and a veterinarian before you make the decision to breed. This small effort can save you and your dog a lot of work before you find out—the hard way—that breeding just isn't for you.

### Genetically Speaking

Though you may select a mate for your dog on the basis of its physical attributes, you are really choosing the animal's genetic make-up. Genes are the basic units of inheritance. Each parent passes a set of genes to the puppies and chance decides which genes will be chosen when the offspring is formed.

Selection and mutation also influence the genetic outcome of a breeding. Dog breeders participate in the selection process when they subjectively choose a sire and dam to produce a litter. This has been the process that gradually turned the domesticated wolf of some 12,000 years ago into the numerous different dog breeds of today.

Genetic defects can occur in any breed and affect any organ system in the body. Some genetic diseases afflict many breeds (cataracts and deafness, for example); some occur in only one or a few breeds (Collie eye, e.g.). Before you breed your dog, you should discuss your plans and the possibility of genetic defects in your breed with both a knowledgeable breeder and a veterinarian.

In diseases with a dominant pattern of inheritance, only one member of the pair need be of the mutant type. That is, only one parent is affected and transmission of the condition is observed from one generation to the next. Some individuals may be only mildly affected with the condition, making it difficult to detect without careful examination. In such cases, the condition can mistakenly be thought to skip generations.

Diseases with a recessive pattern of inheritance differ in that they require two abnormal genes in the pair, producing a *homozygous* individual. Dogs with one mutant and one normal gene are *heterozygous carriers*, who are outwardly normal but can pass the abnormal gene to their offspring. Recessive mutant genes can be passed through many generations before coming to light in the offspring of two dogs who carry the same gene mutation.

**633**

Polygenic disorders result from the cumulative action of a number of different genes rather than from an abnormality in a single pair. The exact number of genes involved and their individual functions are difficult to determine, and the pattern of inheritance tends to vary from family to family. Polygenic inheritance can sometimes mimic either dominant or recessive inheritance on superficial examination, and this feature may lead to erroneous conclusions regarding the type of underlying genetic abnormality.

Chromosomal anomalies are also responsible for genetic disease in the dog. This refers to the chromosome number and structure. In the dog, there are 39 pairs of chromosomes (as compared to 23 in man), on which the genes are located. Defects in single genes and polygenic defects cannot be identified at present by existing methods of observing the chromosomes because the changes are too small to be visible. It has been recognized, however, that major abnormalities in chromosome number and structure do occur in dogs, often producing serious defects in the individual.

Whether you inbreed or linebreed may have an effect on the incidence of genetic disease in the litters you produce. *Inbreeding* is the mating of two individuals who are related to each other through one or more common ancestors. The most severe form of inbreeding involves parent-offspring and brother-sister matings. *Linebreeding* is a form of inbreeding which usually involves mating more distantly related dogs. Polygenic and recessive inherited diseases tend to increase with inbreeding, since the chance that the two animals will carry the same mutation is greater when the dogs are related. Inbreeding is a common practice among breeders since the population of registered dogs is limited, and because a dog with highly desirable traits may be used at stud frequently, resulting in many puppies with common blood.

### Reproductive Physiology

The age at which your dog reaches maturity depends on its breed. Small breeds tend to mature faster than large breeds. In general, the male puppies become fertile after six months of age and reach mature fertility by twelve to fifteen months. Healthy stud dogs may remain sexually active and fertile up to eight to ten years old. During the period of fertility, the adult male is able to mate at any time.

Bitches have their first estrus (also known as "season" and "heat") sometime after six months of age, although this can occur as late as 18 months of age. Estrus recurs at intervals of 7 months on the average, until late in life. During estrus, the female will accept the male and is fertile.

The bitch's cycle is divided into four periods:

(1) *Proestrus*, during which the female is attractive to the male, has a bloody vaginal discharge, and the vulva is swollen. Proestrus lasts approximately nine days; the female, however will not allow coitus at this time.

(2) *Estrus* also lasts approximately nine days, when the female will accept the male. Ovulation usually occurs in the first 48 hours; however, this is extremely variable. Fertilization takes place during estrus.

(3) *Diestrus* (60–90 days) follows estrus when the reproductive tract is under control of the hormone progesterone. This occurs whether the dog becomes pregnant or not. False pregnancy (*pseudocyesis*), a condition in which the bitch shows all the symptoms of being pregnant although she has not conceived, is occasionally seen during diestrus.

(4) *Anestrus* is the period following diestrus when no sexual activity takes place. It lasts between three and four months.

### Breeding

If you do not wish to breed your bitch, various forms of contraception are available. The most effective and permanent form of contraception is the surgical removal of the ovaries and uterus (spay) in the female or castration (neutering) in the male. Oral contraceptives are also available, which offer the advantage of maintaining fertility if subsequent breeding is desired. The advantages and disadvantages of each method should be discussed with a veterinarian.

The other way to prevent pregnancy is to isolate your bitch during estrus. However, constant vigilance is necessary to make sure no dogs reach her. Estrogen administration can prevent pregnancy after unwanted breeding, but the use of this hormone is inadvisable.

On the other hand, if you decide to breed your bitch, it is customary not to breed at the first heat to avoid placing the stress of pregnancy and lactation in a young growing animal. Most breeders also avoid breeding a bitch on consecutive heats, to allow sufficient time for recuperation between pregnancies, although this is unnecessary if the bitch is otherwise healthy. Both breeding at the first heat and on consecutive heats, when observed, should be accompanied by excellent feeding and management to avoid potential problems.

At least one month prior to breeding, the bitch should have a pre-breeding examination by a veterinarian. She should be brought up-to-date on her vaccinations. The bitch should be in good condition, but not overweight. Some nutritionists believe that steady weight increase for three weeks, beginning just prior to breeding, may increase fertility. A bitch should be tested for parasites before she is bred and treated accordingly; afterward, a control program for both internal and external parasites should be enforced at all times (see *Preventive Care*).

Bitches may also be tested for brucellosis prior to breeding. Brucellosis is a bacterial disease that can cause sterility, or spontaneous abortion between the 45th and 55th days of pregnancy. A male dog should be tested for brucellosis also, but if he breeds many females, a test before he mates with each is impractical. If the stud is kept separate from pregnant, whelping or nursing bitches and tested twice yearly, this should be sufficient.

Breeding management varies among breeders and breeds. Most commonly, dogs are bred between the 10th and 14th day after the onset of proestrus. While the bitch will stand for the male, every other day for two or three breedings total is considered good management for most dogs. In some bitches, the signs of heat are less obvious. In these cases, microscopic examination of vaginal smears by a veterinarian can be a useful guide to the peak fertile period.

Females are usually less inhibited by a new environment, so the bitch is best taken to the stud. The first time a young male is used, breeding will be less tedious if the bitch is experienced.

During breeding, the male will mount the female from the rear and clasp her middle with his front legs. He will then rapidly thrust his pelvis until intromission and ejaculation take place. After his pelvis thrusts cease, the dogs will not separate for 10–30 minutes. This is called a "tie" and it is perfectly normal. It results from the swelling of a section of the penis called the bulbus glandis. During the tie, the male may move around so that he and the female are positioned rear to rear. Do not try to separate the male and female during the tie, which can injure either or both animals.

Artificial insemination is a relatively simple procedure which can be used if a natural breeding is impractical. When performed by a veterinarian under controlled conditions, artificial insemination is approved by the American Kennel Club (allowing registration of the offspring).

## Pregnancy

Pregnancy in the bitch lasts approximately 63 days. Signs of pregnancy include an increase in appetite, weight and breast size. Bitches with "false pregnancy" may also show these symptoms, however. A diagnosis can be made by a veterinarian through abdominal palpation at 28 days, or by ultrasonics and/or X-ray later. Special feeding requirements of the pregnant bitch are described in the section on Nutrition. This is a good time, however, to talk with your veterinarian about how to care for the bitch throughout pregnancy and whelping, and what to do in the case of an emergency.

A few days before the bitch is ready to give birth, she may refuse to eat and start to build her "nest," where she plans to have her puppies. Unless you accustom her beforehand to a whelping box, she may choose your closet, the space under your bed, or another place you may find inappropriate for a delivery room. A whelping box should have ample room for the bitch to stretch out comfortably. It should have low sides and be placed in a warm, dry, draft-free, secluded place. Towels or other soft material may be placed in the bottom of the whelping box for comfort and cleanliness, but newspapers are better because they are easy to remove and replace when they become soiled. Once whelping is over, however, you should replace the newspapers with something that provides better footing for the puppies.

Shortly before the time of whelping arrives, the bitch's body temperature will drop to 99 degrees or lower. Approximately 24 hours later she can be expected to go into the first stage of labor, when the cervix dilates and opens the birth canal for passage of the puppies. At this time, she will pant, strain, appear restless, and perhaps vomit. Vomiting is normal at the onset of labor, but persistent vomiting may be a sign of illness. The next stage of labor involves actual straining of the abdomen and passage of puppies and membranes.

### Birth

A normal, healthy bitch usually gives birth easily, without the need of additional help. Each puppy emerges in its own placental membrane, which must be removed before the puppy can breathe. The bitch usually accomplishes this promptly, and then severs the umbilical cord. After delivery, she will lick the puppies to clean them and consequently to stimulate their respiration. Frequent licking, which continues for three weeks or so, also serves another vital function: it stimulates the excretory organs.

A placenta follows each puppy after a few minutes. The dam may or may not eat each placenta as it emerges. Some people believe eating one or more placentas is beneficial for the bitch, while others do not share this belief. They may cause a digestive upset later. At any rate, you should always keep track of how many placentas are delivered and make sure the number delivered matches the number of puppies, since a retained placenta may cause problems later.

Usually all goes well, and after the whole litter is born, cleaned and allowed to nurse, the bitch will be happy, proud, and tired. Suggestions for feeding the lactating bitch are given in the *Nutrition* section of this book.

Occasionally, a bitch may neglect to remove a placental membrane or sever an umbilical cord, or she may be unable to do the job herself. In that case, you should be prepared to handle the situation quickly. A puppy can remain inside a placental sac after birth for only eight minutes before its oxygen supply is depleted. You can remove the puppy from the sac by tearing the membrane first in the region of the puppy's head and working backward. Then clean any mucus or fluids from the puppy's mouth and nose, and stimulate its circulation by rubbing it briskly with a towel. The umbilical cord can be tied with unwaxed dental floss, and cut about two inches from the abdomen. Apply iodine to the cut end to prevent infection.

### When to Call the Veterinarian

If the events during delivery take a turn that make you feel the situation is beyond your capabilities and the bitch's life is in danger, don't hesitate to call the veterinarian for assistance. Abnormal conditions which signify trouble include:

- indications of extreme pain
- straining in labor for over three hours without passing a puppy, whether one or no puppies have been delivered previously

- trembling, shivering, or collapse
- passage of a dark green or bloody fluid before the birth of the first puppy (after the first puppy, this is normal)

Also, it is advisable to have a veterinarian check the bitch and her litter within a day of the delivery.

### Newborn Puppies

The newborn puppy is unable to control its body temperature and must be kept in an environmental temperature of 85 degrees F. Chilling during these early days of life will stress the puppy and predispose it to infectious disease. You can keep the puppy's environment warm by using a well-insulated electric heating pad, an electric bulb, or a bowl of warm water covered with a towel.

The first milk produced by the bitch after whelping is known as the "colostrum." Every puppy should have colostrum as early as possible after birth, and certainly during the first 24 hours of life. Colostrum contains a number of substances beneficial to the puppy, including immunoglobulins which protect the puppy against all of the infectious diseases to which the mother is immune. The reason that puppies must have colostrum as soon as possible after birth is because absorption of intact immunoglobulins decreases and becomes impossible within a few days following birth. For more information about feeding puppies, refer to the section on *Nutrition and Feeding*.

Sometimes a bitch is unable or unwilling to care for her puppies. When that happens, you must be her substitute: you must feed the puppies, stimulate them, and provide a warm environment. Keeping the puppies in constant warmth, free from chilly air or drafts, is essential. The temperature should be kept between 85 and 90 degrees F during the period from birth to the fifth day. From the seventh to the tenth day, the temperature can be reduced gradually to 80 degrees with further reduction to 75 degrees by the end of the fourth week. You will probably need an incubator to maintain this suitable environment (see if your veterinarian can suggest a place to rent one, if necessary).

Individual compartments in the incubator are desirable for several reasons. Unless orphaned puppies are separated during the first two or three weeks of life, they will suckle or perhaps chew and mutilate one another. All newborn puppies should be kept as free as possible from any disturbance or handling. The bottom of each individual compartment should be lined with a soft, clean, folded diaper. These should be changed whenever necessary, and examined for evaluation of quantity and quality of each puppy's feces after you have stimulated the pups to perform this function.

Many people do not realize that for the first few days of life, both defecation and urination must be stimulated after each feeding. This can be accomplished by gentle massage of the anal region with a piece of cotton that has been dipped in warm water. Observe the puppy's daily habits, and stimulate only as necessary. By keeping the puppies separated and on diapers, this should not be difficult. For a discussion on formula and feeding techniques in hand-rearing puppies, refer to the *Nutrition and Feeding* section.

Regular gentle massage is quite beneficial in the daily routine of a hand-reared puppy. This is a form of passive exercise, stimulating circulation and thoroughly awakening it, and is best done by gentle stroking of the sides and back with a folded, soft diaper. The best time for such treatment seems to be during the awakening period, just before feeding, while the formula is being warmed.

Simple grooming is also best done at feeding time and should be done only as deemed necessary. At first, grooming consists only of wiping the puppies' eyes with ophthalmic boric acid solution and occasionally rubbing the skin with baby oil because conditions in an incubator or similarly warm environment may tend to dry the coat. Grooming or handling should not be overdone at an early age.

### Weaning

Puppies should begin the weaning process at two to three weeks of age. Begin by offering the puppies a pan of formula. When they adjust to this, replace the formula with a combination of Pablum and formula. Hand-fed puppies may be removed from the bottle at this time, and meat or high quality canned dog food may be offered in addition to the Pablum/formula mixture. At five weeks, delete Pablum from the gruel and replace the formula with evaporated milk mixed 1:1 with water. In addition to the meat and canned food, a good commercial dry or moist dog food can be introduced into the feeding program. All changes in food or feeding schedules should be made gradually to allow the digestive system to adjust.

# Illness: Signs and Symptoms

*The following section was written by Elizabeth M. Bodner, D.V.M.*

Illness strikes every dog at some point in its life. With good care, however, your dog has as much protection against illness as possible. He can fight infections and parasites and, through vaccinations, avoid potentially fatal diseases. These are as close to guarantees of good health as a dog owner is apt to find.

When dogs become ill, they communicate that something is wrong in every way but words. Be alert for clues in your dog's body language. If you see one or more of the following symptoms or any deviation in your dog's usual behavior or appearance, bring them to the attention of your veterinarian:

- constipation
- shivering
- fever
- watery eyes
- runny nose
- coughing
- loss of appetite (or ravenous appetite without weight gain)
- vomiting
- increased urination
- restlessness
- straining to urinate
- labored breathing
- weight loss
- increased water intake
- lameness, paralysis
- obvious pain or nervous symptoms

The following section describes illnesses commonly seen by veterinarians, grouped according to the general area primarily affected. Each is characterized by the kinds of symptoms it is likely to produce. But first, a few words of warning. Time is often a deciding factor in the ability to treat an illness. Therefore, we urge you to use this section as a source of information, not as a guide to diagnosing your own dog. A specific disease may or may not manifest itself according to the symptoms you find in this or any other reference book. Never underestimate the seriousness of a problem and let it slip by to the point where treatment is ineffective. Only a veterinarian can provide accurate diagnosis and prescribe the proper treatment, and the sooner he or she can make these judgments, the better.

## Skin Problems

The SKIN protects the organs and tissues within the body from invasions by foreign substances, changing temperatures, and dehydration. Its contribution to the body includes synthesizing essential vitamins and providing a site where information about the external world can be processed through sensation.

Symptoms which may indicate a SKIN PROBLEM are:

| | | |
|---|---|---|
| • itching | • scabs | • swelling |
| • red, sore, moist patches | • hair loss | • purulent discharge |
| • scaling or dandruff | • discoloration | • lumps or bumps |

**Allergy:**  Pollen, dust, mold, insect bites, flea collars, and even certain foods are common canine allergens. Allergic dogs typically have severely itchy skin which, during the course of scratching to relieve discomfort, may become red and sore. Hives and swelling also may be seen in response to insect bites, poison ivy (rare), or nettles. Other uncommon signs of allergies are a runny nose, sneezing, and watery eyes. Vomiting and diarrhea may also accompany an allergic reaction.

Once you have discovered what triggers an allergic reaction in your dog, try to alleviate the problem by keeping him a good distance from the offensive item. If a flea collar is the culprit, remove it at once and thoroughly bathe the dog. Nasal sensitivity to a plastic food dish is solved by replacing it with a glass or metal dish. If you find that the dog is allergic to flea bites (a very common occurrence), cure the infestation and prevent future infestations from happening (see *Preventive Care*). A seriously allergic dog may need medical and/or hyposensitization therapy.

**Parasites:**  Fleas, lice, flies, ticks and mites can cause a great deal of discomfort in dogs and initiate more serious complications. For a description of these parasites and recommendations on how to eradicate them, see the discussion on parasites in *Preventive Care*.

**Seborrhea:**  Seborrheic skin is flaky and scaly, or covered with greasy, yellow-brown scales. An abnormality in the production of skin cells causes this condition and, despite bathing, dogs often have an unpleasant rancid smell. Seborrhea is usually incurable, but it can be controlled by regular baths using a special shampoo.

**Ringworm:**  Despite its name, ringworm is caused by a fungus that lives on the skin surface. Dogs with ringworm often have circular, scaly lesions where hair has fallen out. Stubby bits of broken grayish hair often are found within and along the edges of these areas. Severely affected dogs can have scaling, redness and hair loss over large areas of the body. Heavy crust formations may be seen especially in young dogs. If your veterinarian has examined a skin scraping and found ringworm, he or she will prescribe an antifungal medication and suggest that you treat all household pets and immediately clean the dog's environment to remove ringworm spores. Treating ringworm is especially important since humans are susceptible to catching the fungus through close contact with infected animals.

**Infections:**   When skin is damaged by a cut, puncture, or scrape, it needs to be cleaned adequately and perhaps stitched, depending upon its severity. In either case, bacteria in the wound site can cause inflammation, which makes the area appear red and swollen, feel warm to the touch, and seem painful to the dog. Inflammation usually does not persist for more than a few days. If these signs progressively worsen and are accompanied by the presence of unhealthy-looking tissue and/or pus, the condition has probably progressed to an infection, which needs to be treated by a veterinarian.

**Pemphigus Vulgaris:**   Pemphigus vulgaris is one of several autoimmune diseases in which cells destroy the body's own tissue, as if they were foreign substances themselves. Here the tongue, gums, lips, eyelids, anus, vulva, nail-beds, and nose are affected with ulcers, erosions and crusting blisters.

**Abscess:**   An abscess is a collection of pus under the skin, usually caused by a bite or puncture wound. The area often appears swollen and red, and painful. Abscesses may feel warm and the fluid inside may be apparent. They may open and drain spontaneously, or may need lancing and thorough cleansing before proper healing can take place. Never try to break an abscess open by squeezing. As with other potentially serious conditions, see your veterinarian.

**Cushing's Syndrome:**   Cushing's Syndrome results from an abnormality with the adrenal glands. Dogs gradually lose hair from the flanks and neck. The skin becomes thin, scaly, dry and darkened. Calcium deposits may form in the skin of the groin, neck and back. You may notice an increase in your dog's thirst, appetite and frequency of urination. Many dogs develop a pot-bellied appearance because the liver enlarges and the muscles of the abdominal wall weaken. Affected individuals are more susceptible to infections, especially of the skin, respiratory tract, and urinary tract.

Treatment for Cushing's Syndrome depends on its underlying cause. Surgery or medical therapy may be warranted.

**Hypothyroidism:**   The thyroid glands secrete a hormone which controls the basic metabolic rate of the entire body. Inadequate hormone levels reset the body to function at a lower metabolic level. In that case, dogs fatten easily on a normal diet, become sluggish, and are easily chilled. Hair changes are most noticeable and include loss of hair from the flanks and back, increased pigmentation of the skin, scaling and seborrhea. Secondary bacterial infection of the skin is common. The ears may also be affected, filling with thick, yellow greasy material which may predispose the dog to ear infections. Blood tests will determine the level of thyroid function and tablets of thyroid hormone can treat the condition. Improvement is generally noted within three to four weeks, although the seborrhea and hair loss may take several months to resolve.

**Jaundice:**  Jaundice—yellowing of the skin, eyes, gums, or ears—is not a disease in itself, but a signal of other problems in the body. Leptospirosis, canine hepatitis, and other diseases which damage the liver can cause jaundice, as well as disorders which involve red blood cell destruction. Jaundice usually is accompanied by other signs of illness, all of which mean your dog should be brought to your veterinarian.

**Hot Spots:**  Hot spots are a common problem of dogs, especially heavy-coated breeds. These round patches of painful, moist swollen skin can appear without warning anywhere on the dog's body and progress in size and severity until the dog is in misery. Hot spots need to be treated by a veterinarian (clipped, cleaned and medicated) before they grow, and the source of the problem—fleas, impacted anal glands, etc.—must be identified and resolved.

**Warts:**  Warts, or papillomas, are caused by a virus and are usually found either around the lips or in the mouths of young dogs. Warts on puppies usually appear in groups; in older dogs, they generally occur as individual growths. Highly contagious, warts often spread throughout a litter of puppies or even affect an entire kennel. These round or cauliflower-like, gray fibrous projections can vary in size from less than an eighth of an inch to nearly two inches in diameter. Warts do not invade the skin or spread to other parts of the body. They usually clear up spontaneously with time, but if they cause discomfort or are slow to regress, surgical removal should be considered. Dogs that recover rarely become infected again.

**Calluses:**  Calluses frequently occur in large dogs and appear wherever skin comes into contact with hard or rough surfaces such as concrete. Most are found on the elbows, outside of the hocks, buttocks, and the sides of the legs, where the skin is thick, gray, wrinkled and hairless. If left untreated, calluses may develop into open, infected sores. The best way to stop calluses from occurring is to provide soft bedding for the dog.

**Tumors:**  Tumors are those lumps and bumps you may find in, on, or under your dog's skin. If the tumors have grown slowly, are encapsulated, and do not seem to multiply or affect other parts of the body, they are usually benign. Benign tumors will not recur once they have been removed. Malignant tumors, by contrast, are cancerous. They appear suddenly, grow rapidly, and affect the surrounding tissues, perhaps breaking the skin and bleeding. These tumors may be hard and fixed to a particular site on the dog's body. You should also be wary of colored bumps or moles on the surface of the skin which suddenly begin to spread or bleed. Another form of skin cancer is indicated by sores which do not heal in an appropriate amount of time. All lumps and bumps should be checked by a veterinarian promptly.

## Respiratory Problems

The RESPIRATORY system includes those organs involved in the breathing process. This means the organs and muscles inside the dog's body as well as those which you can see, the nose and mouth.

Symptoms which may indicate a RESPIRATORY PROBLEM are:

- nasal discharge
- sneezing
- coughing
- noisy or difficult breathing
- voice change or loss
- abnormal sounds within the chest

**Kennel Cough:** Kennel cough, otherwise known as infectious canine tracheobronchitis, readily spreads from one dog to another. This disease is thought to be caused by several viruses and *Bordatella bronchiseptica*, a bacteria. Symptoms include an intermittent dry, hacking cough, which is sometimes accompanied by nasal discharge, but dogs usually appear fine in other respects. Kennel cough is not life-threatening in itself: most dogs recover within a few weeks. Affected puppies and small dogs, however, need special care. Any individual with kennel cough should be kept in a warm, humid environment, isolated from other dogs. Your veterinarian may prescribe antibiotics to prevent complications. A vaccination is also effective against some of the kennel cough viruses (see the section on *Vaccinations* for more information).

**Bronchitis:** Bronchitis can develop after a bout with kennel cough or another debilitating respiratory infection. The dog has a persistent dry, rough cough and may retch following a coughing episode, or bring up foamy-appearing saliva. His temperature may not read above normal, but he may look poor in general. Good nursing care and the appropriate medication can restore him to good health.

**Foreign Body (Windpipe):** A sudden, intense fit of coughing may be caused by something lodged in the windpipe. This can occur immediately after the dog has vomited, or more rarely, when he has accidentally inhaled a foreign body. Dogs usually clear the air passage by coughing the irritant back up, but when this is unsuccessful, you must quickly take him to the veterinarian to have the object removed.

**Laryngitis:**  Like an overwinded speaker, a dog who vocalizes or coughs excessively can wind up with a hoarse or faint bark. Resting his voice for a while and treating his cough should clear up the condition. A chronic case of laryngitis, however, may arise from a different and more serious source.

**Laryngeal Paralysis:**  Laryngeal paralysis occurs in large breeds during their middle to old age and is seen congenitally in Siberian Huskies and Bouvier des Flandres. It is indicated by noisy breathing, which starts after the dog is physically or emotionally taxed. Surgery can alleviate the problem. Otherwise, the dog faces the possibility of future laryngeal collapse, which will further block his limited air supply. A dog who suffers from this serious condition needs immediate veterinary attention.

**Collapsing Trachea:**  A collapsing trachea is a birth defect which occurs in small dogs. These dogs have occasional noisy, labored breathing and they are prone to coughing. This condition is rarely life-threatening but sometimes surgery is warranted to correct the defect. You can help the dog by maintaining his proper weight, since obesity aggravates the problem, and by keeping him calm.

**Cleft Palate:**  Cleft palate, another birth defect, leaves an opening between the oral and nasal cavities. This often prevents a puppy from nursing. A nasal discharge is one of the first signs of a cleft palate. If not too deformed, the palate can be corrected by surgery.

**Elongated Soft Palate:**  Dogs with an elongated soft palate, often members of short-faced breeds, have a nasal discharge and breathe noisily because their air passages are obstructed by the soft palate. You may notice that a dog with an elongated soft palate breathes through his mouth, produces snorting noises, or snores when he is asleep. These problems are exacerbated by demands such as hot weather or physical exertion, when the dog needs to draw deep breaths. In most cases, surgery can correct an overlong soft palate and restore normal breathing.

**Rhinitis:**  Nose infections, or rhinitis, can cause a thick greenish and unpleasant smelling nasal discharge. Rhinitis irritation of the nasal mucous membranes is either bacterial or fungal in origin. Treatment depends on the source. After foreign bodies, masses, or infected maxillary teeth are removed, antibiotics are administered to clear up the infection.

**Stenotic Nares:**  Another defect in short-nosed puppies is stenotic or narrowed nostrils. When these dogs inhale, their nostrils collapse and air is blocked. A foamy-looking nasal discharge is typical. Dogs with stenotic nares will breathe through the mouth when aroused. Surgery may be indicated in these cases to enlarge the nostrils.

**Foreign Bodies (Nose):** Dogs can easily inhale foreign matter or get stuck in the nose with a sharp object as they investigate their surroundings. In their discomfort, they will paw at their nose and sneeze violently. You will notice a nasal discharge, with occasional bleeding. The offensive item needs to be removed as soon as possible before it can pass further up the nasal canal. Do not attempt to retrieve the object from this delicate area yourself—let a veterinarian remove it and prescribe an antibiotic to fight possible infection.

**Pneumonia:** A dog with pneumonia coughs, breathes rapidly, has a high fever and a quick pulse, and may produce a rattling or bubbling noise within his chest. An infection of the lungs, pneumonia can be caused by a virus, bacteria, allergy, or parasite. To make breathing easier, a dog with pneumonia will usually sit with his head outstretched and his elbows turned out. Although this is a serious illness, most dogs recover once they are placed on the medication specifically prescribed to combat the factor which initiated the pneumonia.

**Tumors:** Tumors of the respiratory tract can also cause noisy, difficult breathing or coughing. This is something your veterinarian will have to investigate and treat.

**Allergy:** Sneezing and coughing are possibly your dog's reaction to an allergy. Dust, insect bites, foods, or an inhalant allergy or irritant can be the root of the problem. Other typical symptoms of an allergic attack are watery eyes, itching, and possibly vomiting and diarrhea. The way to cope with your dog's allergy depends on its source. For more information about allergies, see the section on *Skin Problems.*

## Musculoskeletal Problems

The MUSCULOSKELETAL system supports, protects, and moves the dog's body. Furthermore, the bones provide a site for mineral and fat storage, and for the production of red blood cells.

Symptoms which may indicate a MUSCULOSKELETAL PROBLEM are:

- limping
- weakness
- pain
- stiffness
- unusual gait
- swollen joints

**Lameness:** Dogs commonly limp when their limbs are painful or weak due to such things as trauma, nutritional imbalance, congenital defects or infection. The problem may be located by palpation or X-rays of the affected area. In the case of a mild injury, the injury may heal by itself within a few days. More serious problems (sprains, fractures, dislocations, and bone disease, for example) need prompt veterinary attention and possibly surgery.

**Sprain:**   When ligaments suddenly stretch or tear slightly during activity, a sprain is said to occur. Although the joint is swollen and painful, it may heal within three to four days with strict rest. If not, or if the situation worsens, the veterinarian should check the dog's limb for a more serious problem such as a ligament tear or a fracture.

**Fractures:**   Most fractures are from trauma (i.e., being hit by a car). They are classified as being either "closed" or "open." The latter is more serious, since the ends of the bones rupture the skin, involving extensive tissue damage and a potential for infection. All fractures need to be treated immediately by a veterinarian. Most are treated with splints, casts, or internal fixation devices like screws, pins, or wires. For more information about restraining an injured dog and temporarily splinting a broken limb, see the discussion of *First Aid*.

**Dislocation:**   Dislocated joints are usually the result of a major trauma. Often, a displaced bone makes one limb appear shorter than its mate. Veterinarians check for additional injuries and restore the joint. Sometimes this requires surgery. See *First Aid* for suggestions on what to do in this emergency situation until the veterinarian is seen.

**Cranial Cruciate Ligament Injury:**   Two criss-crossed ligaments within the knee help hold the joint in place. One of these ligaments (the cranial one) is especially vulnerable to a sudden tear during activity. Once injured, the knee joint no longer moves smoothly and left untreated, it is painful and can lead to arthritis. Rupturing of the cranial cruciate ligament is more common in overweight dogs over one and a half years old. Oddly enough, many older dogs who tear one ligament experience trouble with the other one within a year. Many owners mistake a ruptured cruciate ligament for a sprain when their dog suddenly begins to limp after a romp outside. Be sure to consult your veterinarian if any lameness does not improve within a few days. Surgical repair for the torn ligament is a common procedure, usually restoring full use of the leg if performed soon after the injury.

**Hip Dysplasia:**   Canine hip dysplasia, a congenital defect, is a common source of lameness, especially in large dogs. Basically, dysplastic dogs have an abnormal hip joint. Signs of hip dysplasia usually appear when the dog is four to nine months old, although affected dogs may or may not show signs of disease. Obvious signs include hip pain, a limp or swaying gait, hopping when running, and difficulty in rising from a sitting or lying position. Dogs with this disease commonly develop arthritis of the hip joint due to the abnormal stress on the joint. You can help prevent further aggravation by maintaining the dog's proper weight, controlling his exercise, and keeping his living area warm and dry. Aspirin or a prescription pain reliever can help keep him comfortable. In severe cases, surgery can help alleviate the dog's pain. Breeds known to be susceptible to hip dysplasia should be X-rayed (the recommended age for X-raying by OFA is 2 years old). Only healthy dogs should be used for breeding.

**Disc Disease:**   Disc disease, which is more common in some breeds than others, is a frequent cause of severe neck or back pain. Normally, the job of the discs is to absorb shock for the spinal cord. When material from the disc abnormally protrudes into the spinal cord area, however, the dog experiences a great deal of pain and possibly neurological dysfunction. Signs may include a stiff neck, leg weakness, and a gradual reduction of activity. Prolonged or severe pressure on the spinal cord can lead to paralysis of the hind legs and loss of bladder and/or bowel control. Immediately limit the dog's freedom of movement if you suspect disc protrusion and *see a veterinarian.* Veterinarians typically will need to treat this problem with anti-inflammatory drugs and pain relievers. Surgery is sometimes effective in severe cases.

**Arthritis:**   The most common form of arthritis in the dog is osteoarthritis, a degenerative joint disease which causes pain, lameness, and stiffness in the joints. Arthritis sometimes simply sets in with old age. Large dogs are affected more often than small ones, and the symptoms of the disease are more severe in obese dogs whose joints are forced to support excess weight. Pain relievers help keep most dogs comfortable. Moderate activity, soft bedding, and housing in a warm, dry environment are recommended to sustain pliability in the joints.

## Heart Problems

The HEART is a pump which circulates blood to the body. Blood contains vital nutrients including oxygen and hormones which regulate body functions. An adequate circulation of blood is also needed to eliminate the waste products of metabolism, including carbon dioxide. Poor cardiac performance compromises all other organ functions.

Signs which may indicate a HEART PROBLEM are:

- coughing and short-
  ness of breath
- lethargy and weakness
- fainting
- weight loss

- stunted growth
- bluish gums
- distended abdomen
  and swollen limbs

- irregular and/or persis-
  tently fast heartbeat
- palpable vibrations
  over the heart

**Congestive Heart Failure:**   Heart failure occurs when the heart is unable to deliver oxygenated blood in sufficient quantity to meet body needs. The term "congestive" applies when fluid, resulting from normal compensatory mechanisms to support the cardiovascular system, accumulates outside the vascular compartment. When fluid accumulates in the lungs, coughing and shortness of breath occur. Dogs with congestive heart failure show less tolerance toward exercise and in certain cases the abdomen may become distended with fluid. Infrequently, the limbs also swell. A veterinarian listening to the heart may hear abnormal heart sounds and fluid within the lungs. X-ray pictures of the heart and an electrocardiogram may be needed to fully diagnose the problem. Drugs can strengthen the contractions of the heart and promote excretion of retained fluids from the body. Feeding a low salt diet will also help lessen fluid retention, and limiting the dog's exercise reduces the stress on his heart.

## ACQUIRED HEART DISEASES

**Cardiomyopathy:** Canine dilated (congested) cardiomyopathy is a disease which especially affects large and giant breeds, usually developing between the first and sixth year. The heart muscle weakens and degenerates, making the blood flow sluggishly and resulting in generalized congestive heart failure. The heart itself is greatly enlarged and is predisposed to irregularities in the heart rate. In such cases, some heart beats may fail to eject blood and generate a pulse. Signs of cardiomyopathy include fatigue, coughing, a distended abdomen, weight loss and sometimes swollen legs and collapse. Drugs can help prolong the dog's life but for only a short while since they cannot reverse the change in the heart itself.

**Chronic Valvular Disease:** Chronic valvular disease is one of the most common forms of heart disease in the dog. For an unknown reason, the valves between the pumping chambers become thick and fail to seal tightly, allowing blood to leak backwards. Little by little, the heart becomes unable to pump blood adequately to the body and heart failure eventually occurs. Signs of this insufficiency are a cough, difficult or noisy breathing, and restlessness at night. A heart murmur usually is detectable. A dog with chronic valvular disease and which is showing clinical signs should be seen by a veterinarian immediately.

**Heartworm:** Microscopic heartworm larvae develop within mosquitoes and enter a dog's body through the puncture wound of the mosquito's bite. After molting twice in the tissues, the adult stage parasite gains access to the venous circulation and is deposited in the arteries of the lung. The worms reach lengths of five to twelve inches and both physically obstruct blood flow and damage the pulmonary arteries, making it difficult for the heart to pump blood through the lungs. Heart failure and severe lung damage can occur in heavily infected dogs. Heartworm infection is most commonly detected by looking for the heartworm embryos in the blood. The infection can be eradicated with drugs. Better yet, dogs can be protected with drugs to prevent infection. Adult heartworms grow only from larvae introduced with the bite of a mosquito.

## CONGENITAL HEART DISEASES

**Ventricular Septal Defects:**   A ventricular septal defect is an opening in the muscular wall separating the two major pumping chambers of the heart. This opening is usually quite small, and has little effect on the general circulation, but it can span practically the entire length of the interventricular septum and cause signs of heart failure. The abnormal blood flow caused by this defect produces a heart murmur. Surgical correction may be attempted at some teaching institutions.

**Patent Ductus Arteriosus:**   A fetus has a short, broad vessel (the *ductus arteriosus*) which connects the pulmonary artery with the aorta and conducts most of the blood directly from the right ventricle to the aorta, bypassing the lungs. Shortly after birth, this vessel should close naturally. When it fails to do so, a patent ductus arteriosus is said to be present. This is one of the most common congenital cardiovascular defects in the dog. A distinctive murmur is indicative of this anomaly. The only effective treatment is surgical closure of the ductus.

**Pulmonic Stenosis:**   This defect, where blood flow between the right ventricle and the pulmonary artery is abnormal, increases the cardiac workload and may cause heart failure. Dogs with pulmonic stenosis have conspicuous heart murmurs. Some types of stenosis can be partially relieved by surgery.

## Gastro-Intestinal Problems

The GASTRO-INTESTINAL system receives and processes the food which provides the necessary ingredients and energy for sustaining life. This includes the entire passageway which begins with the mouth and ends with the anus.

Symptoms which may indicate a GASTRO-INTESTINAL PROBLEM are:

- regurgitation
- vomiting
- diarrhea
- blood or mucus with stool
- constipation
- straining

- distended, painful abdomen
- restlessness
- flatulence
- anal irritation, scooting
- drooling

- excessive drinking and urination
- appetite and weight loss
- jaundice
- white stools
- black tarry stools

**Vomiting:**   Vomiting is not an actual disease in itself, it is an indication of other problems. If your dog vomits once or twice but seems healthy in every other way, there is probably no need to worry. Frequent, forceful, or unusual vomiting (containing blood, fecal-type matter, worms or foreign objects), or vomiting accompanied by other signs of illness (diarrhea, lethargy, weight loss, dull coat, etc.) needs to be checked by a veterinarian at once.

But most often, vomiting is the result of having eaten something irritating to the stomach: garbage, grass, paper or another indigestible item, for example. First the dog will vomit his food and later he will bring up a frothy, clear or yellow liquid. In such a case, do not feed your dog for the next 12 to 24 hours, and offer him ice cubes in place of water. Giving him a stomach-soothing medication like Kaopectate or Pepto-Bismol may also help. If his vomiting subsides, begin him on a bland diet of such foods as soft-boiled eggs, cottage cheese, baby food or a mixture of boiled rice and boiled hamburger. Give these foods in small portions for the first day, and continue with the ice cubes. If the vomiting does not recur, feed bland food in normal portions the next day and then you can return the dog's usual diet. If the dog's condition persists or worsens, needless to say, see the veterinarian. Vomiting can be due to infections, obstructions, tumors, pancreatitis, renal failure, liver failure, adrenal failure, and other sources of illness.

**Regurgitation:**   Regurgitation occurs when food rolls up and out of the esophagus, not the stomach. This act requires little or no effort, unlike vomiting. Several conditions can cause this problem, including esophageal disease, obstruction, or a generalized muscle disease.

**Diarrhea:**   The production of loose, soft, and often abundant stools, is a common symptom in dogs. Your veterinarian can learn a lot about the cause of the diarrhea by examining the color, consistency, odor and frequency of the stool itself. Mild diarrhea, unassociated with other problems, is usually treatable at home. However, if diarrhea persists for over 24 hours, contains blood or is accompanied by vomiting, fever, or other signs of distress, see your veterinarian immediately.

As in the case of vomiting, the consumption of irritating and indigestible material, like garbage, is a common cause of diarrhea. Diarrhea can also develop after an emotional upset such as a change in the dog's normal routine or a trip away from home. So can a sudden change in the dog's diet or even a switch to unfamiliar water. In addition, your dog may simply be unable to tolerate certain foods. Intestinal parasites, viruses, bacteria and other organisms can also trigger the onset of diarrhea. Many of the diseases that cause vomiting also cause diarrhea.

To treat diarrhea at home, withhold food from your dog for 24 hours and restrict him to ice cubes. Give him Kaopectate to coat his intestinal tract. On the second day, offer him small amounts of bland foods such as those described to treat vomiting. Continue in this way for three days, even if the condition seems to have cleared up, and then return to his normal diet.

**Constipation:** Be aware of how often your dog normally moves his bowels. If a day or two passes without his having to defecate, he may be suffering from constipation.

Constipation can be caused by a variety of factors, such as being fed a diet low in fiber, or by bones, grass, paper, or other indigestible substances. Dogs with impacted feces may seem listless, lose their appetite, or vomit. Sometimes they may pass blood-tinged or water-brown stools reminiscent of diarrhea, despite the fact that the real problem is constipation. Dogs with long hair are prone to *pseudo-coprostasis*, where feces become trapped in the hair over the anus, and blocks defecation. In still other cases, an enlarged prostate gland, colon problem, or perineal hernia can interfere with the dog's normal elimination process.

Changing your dog's diet can help. A laxative may be necessary. In the case of impacted feces, an enema may need to be administered. Always keep the hindquarters of long-haired dogs clean and free of mats.

**Bloat:** Bloat, otherwise known as acute gastric dilation-torsion, can rapidly kill a dog with no prior history of problems. Large, deep-chested dogs are most often affected. Prior to bloating, these dogs typically ate a big meal, drank large quantities of water and exercised within two or three hours after eating. Their stomachs then filled with gas and/or fluids, swelled, and then may have twisted. Bloat is a very serious, life-threatening situation. Death can occur in just a few hours if the dog is not treated by a veterinarian.

Signs of bloat include extreme restlessness, salivation and drooling, and unsuccessful attempts to vomit. The abdomen is severely distended. Depending on the duration of the condition, the dog may go into shock. Immediate surgery to decompress the stomach and correct the torsion by repositioning the stomach provides the best chance for survival. Owners of bloat-susceptible dogs may wish to: (1) Feed a diet high in fat, allowing the stomach to empty slower after meals. (2) Feed small meals, two or three times daily, instead of one large meal or make dry food available at all times. (3) Restrict water intake after feeding. (4) Never exercise the dog immediately after he has eaten. If dry food is fed 2–3 times per day, add water to it first, let the dry food get soggy so the dog's stomach feels full faster and he won't drink as much.

**Pancreatitis:** Acute pancreatitis usually occurs in overweight dogs over two years of age who are fed fatty foods. The first signs of acute pancreatitis occur several hours after eating and include vomiting and diarrhea. A dog in this condition can become severely dehydrated, or even go into shock, and should be seen by a veterinarian as soon as possible.

**Flatulence:**   Feeding onions, beans, cauliflower, cabbage, soybeans and other highly fermentable foods causes flatulence. So does a diet which includes a lot of milk or meat. Changing the dog's diet should improve the situation; if not, the veterinarian may prescribe medication to control gas formation within the digestive tract. Digel (simethicone containing antacids) may help to control gas.

**Proctitis:**   Diarrhea, impacted anal glands, hard stools, insect bites or worms can cause soreness and irritation in the dog's anal region. He may lick or bite at his rear, or drag himself over the ground in an attempt to relieve his discomfort. Clean the area and apply Vaseline or a similar soothing ointment while the source of the problem is eliminated.

**Eating Stools (*Coprophagia*):**   Some dogs are attracted to the taste of fecal material, an objectionable and unhealthy habit (they can ingest harmful germs and parasites). A change of diet can solve the problem. Sprinkling meat tenderizer on the dog's food may also help by altering the taste of the feces. If all else fails, your veterinarian can provide you with something that imparts a bitter taste to the feces. If coprophagia persists, have your veterinarian conduct a thorough physical exam; occasionally, an organic problem is at fault.

**Swallowing Foreign Bodies:**   Dogs often make the mistake of swallowing things, especially during their puppy stage. Since an object can block or puncture the stomach or intestines, this is an emergency situation. The dog may vomit, retch or cough; he may bleed, or have abdominal pain. When the esophagus is affected, the dog drools, swallows painfully, and may regurgitate food and water. Immediate veterinary attention is necessary to find out what course of treatment is needed. If your dog is lucky and the object is small enough to simply pass out through the GI system on its own, this may be the end of the problem. On the other hand, surgery may be necessary to remove a larger and more potentially dangerous object.

**Pancreatic Insufficiency:**   When the pancreas is unable to produce the necessary enzymes, food passes through the stomach and intestines without proper digestion and absorption. This is known as pancreatic exocrine insufficiency (PEI). The dog will have an enormous appetite, yet loses weight. His stools are characteristically light in color and may appear oily and greasy due to high amounts of undigested fats and proteins. Large amounts of water are present in the feces, giving them a soft to liquid appearance. There is also an increase in the volume of stool produced. Pancreatic exocrine insufficiency is treated with lifelong supplementation of pancreatic enzymes, along with a low fat, moderate protein diet.

**Canine Gastroenteritis (*Corona Virus*):**   Corona virus gastroenteritis is characterized by a sudden attack of bloody, foul-smelling diarrhea and vomiting which can result in dehydration. It is a highly contagious viral disease, probably spread by contact with infectious feces. Dogs suspected of having gastroenteritis should be treated symptomatically for the diarrhea and vomiting without delay.

**Distemper:** Vomiting and diarrhea are among the symptoms of canine distemper. For more information regarding this disease, see the section on *Multi-System Problems.*

**Coccidiosis:** A protozoan infection of the intestinal tract, coccidiosis can cause diarrhea, with or without blood, and a generally poor appearance. In addition, the dog may suffer from a cough, runny nose, and discharge from the eyes. Puppies seem to be the hardest hit.

Stool samples are checked for evidence of this disease; antibiotics clear it up. Keeping the dog's living area clean and dry is the best way to avoid an infection of coccidiosis.

**Giardiasis:** The disease is caused by a microscopic intestinal parasite, *Giardia canis,* and is contracted by ingesting infected water. Giardiasis is a problem mainly in young dogs, which suffer from diarrhea (sometimes containing bloody mucus) when afflicted with the disease. A diagnosis of giardiasis is made by examining a stool sample.

# Head Problems

The HEAD contains organs which participate in sensory functions. The eyes, ears, nose and mouth, for example, reveal a great deal about the dog's physical environment through the senses of sight, hearing, smell and taste. The mouth is also vital for the obvious purpose of ingesting the food which provides energy for the body.

## THE EYE

Symptoms which may indicate an EYE PROBLEM are:

- abnormal discharge
- excessive or inadequate tearing
- inflamed tissues
- vision loss
- unusual growths in or around the eye

- whiteness or opaqueness in the eye
- depressions on the surface of the eye
- swelling
- sensitivity to light
- fluttering of the iris

**Epiphora (Watery Eyes):** Excessive tearing is a problem particularly of small dogs. The tears leave a brown stain in the area of the eyes and down the sides of the face, and the skin may become inflamed and infected. Watery eyes have a variety of causes, such as eye pain or inadequate tear drainage. Removing the source of the irritation, treating the infection with antibiotics, or flushing the nasolacrimal drainage system can help.

**Distichiasis (Extra Eyelashes):**   Some dogs are born with extra or misplaced eyelashes located on the inner edge of the lids. When these hairs rub against the cornea, the eye can become irritated. The irritation may not become serious until the dog reaches maturity. Offending eyelashes are often removed permanently through surgery.

**Entropion:**   An abnormal condition in which the eyelid (typically the lower one) rolls in toward the eye, entropion is usually a congenital defect. The inversion of the lid permits the lashes to rub against the cornea and irritate this sensitive structure. Watery eyes, infection, even a corneal ulcer, can occur. Surgical correction is required.

**Ectropion:**   Ectropion is the opposite of entropion; the margin of the lower eyelid rolls away from the eyeball. Ectropion commonly occurs in dogs with loose facial skin. The condition is caused by heredity, injury, or loss of muscle tone in the older dog. Insufficiently protected by the gaping eyelid, the eyes are susceptible to irritation. Reconstructive surgery can restore the eyelids to their proper place.

**"Cherry Eye":**   The tear gland on the inner surface of the third eyelid can prolapse in some individuals, becoming visible in the inner corner of the dog's eye as a red, cherry-like growth. Antibiotics and anti-inflammatory drugs may help relieve a very mild case of "cherry eye," but surgery is necessary to permanently repair most cases.

**Conjunctivitis:**   Conjunctivitis is an inflammation of the membrane which lines the eyelids and covers part of the eyeball. Swelling and a discharge from the eye result. A clear or watery discharge suggests the cause is an allergy, foreign body, or physical irritant such as a blast of wind. A pus-like, yellowish, or thick discharge indicates the presence of a bacterial infection. Conjunctivitis is treated by eliminating the cause and administering an ophthalmic antibiotic.

**Glaucoma:**   Glaucoma occurs when there is increased pressure within the eyeball. This pressure destroys tissues within the eye, particularly the retina and optic nerve. Complete or partial loss of vision is the outcome, which occurs suddenly or gradually. Glaucoma can be congenital or can be associated with other eye disease or damage. The dog with glaucoma may squint or have a blank expression; his eyes are enlarged, with hazy or opaque corneas. The eyes are painful and watery. Pupils are widely dilated and do not respond well to light. Glaucoma is an emergency which needs immediate or surgical attention.

**Corneal Ulcer:** Ulceration of the cornea often produces a cloudy appearance in the affected portion of the eye, or a depression in the corneal surface may be apparent. A thin, watery discharge which later becomes purulent is also present. The eye is painful; it is frequently held shut. Many cases begin as a small scratch by a cat or a foreign body e.g., or as a result of a corneal irritant such as a misplaced eyelash. Ulcers should be treated as soon as possible to prevent serious complications.

**Keratitis:** Keratitis is an inflammation of the cornea. A gradual loss of transparency is noted as the cornea becomes more and more cloudy, and finally appears milky, bluish, or relatively opaque. The eyelids may look swollen, and the dog will squint. His eyes will water or exude a pus-like discharge. Left untreated, keratitis can lead to partial or complete blindness. Bring the dog to the veterinarian as soon as you notice a dull cast to the cornea.

Pannus, a form of keratitis, is most common in German Shepherd Dogs. Both eyes may be affected by a pink fleshy membrane which starts to grow across the cornea. The eye may be watery, and the eyelids inflamed. Affected dogs are usually over two years old. Medical treatment and eye surgery are effective in controlling the disease, but there is no permanent cure.

**Keratitis Sicca:** Lack of adequate tear production can cause the cornea to become dry and damaged. This can be caused by a problem with the tear gland or as a side effect of some medications. Frequent administration of a lubricating solution, or surgery to replace the fluids that bathe the external eye, are solutions to this condition.

**Cataracts:** A cataract describes any opacity which occurs on the lens within the eye. Very common in older dogs, cataracts can also go hand in hand with diabetes. Inherited cataracts can occur in dogs of all ages. The degree of vision loss caused by cataracts varies from individual to individual. In the case of profound blindness, surgical removal of the lens can restore good, functional vision.

**Lens Luxation:** Dislocation of the lens can occur with glaucoma or as an inherited weakness of the tissues that ordinarily hold the lens in place. One sign of this displacement is fluttering of the iris. The lens can fall into other areas of the eyeball. Surgical removal of the lens may be necessary.

**Progressive Retinal Atrophy (PRA):** Progressive retinal atrophy is a genetic disease in which the cells of the retina gradually degenerate, leading to the loss of sight. Many breeds of dogs are affected by PRA. The age of onset of this disease varies with the breed and is usually breed specific. For example, Irish Setters become blind by 8–12 months of age but Miniature Poodles remain visual until 5–6 years of age. The first sign of the disease is a loss of night vision. The dog may undergo a variety of behavioral changes, especially in situations in which light is limited. PRA occurs over a period of months or years, and will lead to blindness. There is no treatment for this disease.

**Central Progressive Retinal Atrophy (CPRA):**   Another inherited retinal disease, central progressive retinal atrophy (CPRA) affects the pigment cells at the center of the retina, the area responsible for the dog's best vision. Because of this cell destruction, the dog has difficulty in seeing stationary objects although he is still able to see objects in motion which are detected by cells in the peripheral areas of the retina.

**Prolapsed Eyeball:**   A serious injury can cause the eyeball to come out of its socket. This is especially common in dogs with large, protruding eyes. A prolapsed eyeball is an emergency situation; the eye needs to be replaced at once if vision is to be saved. Keep the eye moistened with water, and be ready to treat the dog for shock, if necessary, as you seek veterinary assistance immediately. Do not force the eyeball back into place, as you can make the eye swell even more and cause greater damage. If you cannot get to a veterinarian within an hour, lubricate the eyeball with a few drops of olive or mineral oil and gently draw the lids outward and over the eyeball. Never use force of any kind as you try to replace the eye.

### THE EAR

Symptoms which may indicate an EAR PROBLEM are:

- abnormal discharge or wax accumulation
  - foul odor
- scratching
- swelling and/or tenderness
- inflammation
- scabs or crusts
- hearing loss
- head tilt
- head shaking

**External Ear Infection (*Otitis Externa*):**   Infection of the external ear canal is common, especially in dogs with large drop ears which support a dark moist environment suitable for fungal or bacterial growth. Soap in the ear, water parasites, foreign bodies or an excess of hair or wax can also spur an infection, as can an allergy. Also, certain breeds are simply more prone to ear infections than are others. An infected ear is tender; inside, it is often red and swollen. Frequently an abundance of wax or a pus-like discharge is visible in the ear canal. An unpleasant odor is readily apparent. Bring the dog to a veterinarian to have the problem treated before the situation worsens. Treatment includes a thorough cleaning of the ear. Topical and/or oral antibiotics may be administered. Chronic ear infections may be helped by surgery to allow better drainage and air flow.

**Parasites:**   Tiny "ear mites" can make any dog miserable. Scratching at the ears and head shaking seem irrepressible. Sarcoptic mites make the tips of the dog's ears quite crusty and cause an intense case of scratching. Ticks may be found anywhere in or on the ear; remove them carefully, taking care not to disturb the ear canal. See the section on parasite control for more information about parasites. In addition, dogs are susceptible to annoying fly bites. Use insect repellent to keep flies away from the dog's face and ears.

**Hematoma:**   Dogs with long, hanging ears may develop a sudden swelling on the ear flap which is actually an accumulation of blood. The problem will resolve on its own, but the cartilage of the ear will be deformed. Surgery to remove the blood clot and close the defect will result in a normal ear after recovery.

**Deafness:**   Dogs become deaf because of trauma, infection, distemper, drugs, loud noises, or simply old age. Some are born deaf or gradually lose their hearing because of a congenital defect. One or both ears can be affected. Signs of deafness include difficulty in awakening your dog, or failure to respond to a loud noise which is made outside the dog's field of vision. Some cases are curable, such as a bacterial infection of the middle or inner ear, or a resolvable tumor in the external ear canal. Also, deafness from trauma or loud noises may clear up with time.

### THE MOUTH AND THROAT

Symptoms which can indicate a MOUTH or THROAT PROBLEM are:

- unusual drooling or discharge from the mouth
- inflammation of the lips, mouth, tongue, gums or throat
- pawing at the mouth
- head shaking
- scabs
- appetite loss
- bad breath
- unusual growths
- bleeding
- dysphagia (trouble swallowing)
- coughing/gagging
- swelling beneath eye

**Cheilitis:**   Cheilitis is an inflammation of the lips and lip folds. A thorn or burr embedded in the lips, or an injury sustained from a fight or from chewing on a sharp object can cause the initial irritation. Cheilitis can also develop from an infection within the mouth or ears. Even licking an infected area elsewhere on the body can result in cheilitis. The lip folds of individuals with heavy jowls often trap food and saliva, which provides the perfect medium for the growth of harmful bacteria. Dogs with cheilitis will paw at their lips and their mouth area smells unpleasant. They may drool or stop eating. Crust forms at the edges of the lips over raw, sensitive skin. Areas affected with cheilitis should be kept clean and dry, and should be treated with antibiotics.

**Stomatitis:**   An inflammation of the mouth, stomatitis is a painful condition in which dogs typically paw at the mouth and shake their heads. Drooling is noticed, especially when eating, although many dogs eat less food or none at all. An affected dog may drink more than usual. The gums are red, swollen, and tender and may bleed when touched (indications of gingivitis). The breath has an unpleasant odor and, in severe instances, a thick brown discharge may be produced from the mouth. Treatment depends upon the source of the inflammation: broken or diseased teeth; gingival disease; systemic illness; foreign bodies; or a tumor, for example.

**Glossitis:**   Glossitis, or inflammation of the tongue, can also be associated with other diseases present in the body. Excessive tartar on the teeth, foreign bodies, cuts, burns, or insect stings are common causes for glossitis. The dog will refuse to eat and will drool. The edges of the tongue may look red and swollen. In severe cases, the tongue may bleed or exude a thick, brown malodorous discharge.

**Burns:**   Oral burns are not uncommon since dogs use their mouths to investigate many new and seemingly tasty objects. Mild burns, such as those that can result from chewing on an electric wire, usually heal themselves. Feeding the dog a soft diet will help. If the burn is more serious, or the tissue continues to look unhealthy, a veterinarian's help is necessary. Burns which result from ingesting chemical substances should be treated as specified in the *First Aid* section.

**Oral Papillomatosis:**   These benign warts appear individually or in groups in and around the mouth, usually in puppies. They are not considered dangerous unless they interfere with the dog's ability to eat or they become infected through injury. See *Skin Problems* for more information.

**Foreign Bodies:**   Foreign bodies are often a problem in the mouth, especially in those dogs who catch, or chew on, sticks. Slivers of wood can easily penetrate the lips, gums or palate; they can wedge between the teeth or even across the roof of the mouth. The same holds true for any sharp object found inside or outside the home. Signs of an oral foreign body are gagging, coughing, drooling or refusal to eat. The dog may paw at his mouth or shake his head in discomfort. If you can't remove the object yourself, seek a veterinarian's help since, left untreated, an infection or other problem can easily occur.

**Gingivitis and Periodontal Disease:**   Gingivitis (inflammation of the gums) is usually caused by poor oral hygiene; it can be prevented by taking good care of your dog's teeth and gums (see *Grooming*). Instead of looking pink and feeling firm, the inflamed gums are red and swollen. They are sensitive to the touch and may bleed easily when you rub them. The breath takes on an unpleasant odor. From this stage, a pocket starts to form between the teeth and gums where food and bacteria collect. This clears the way for periodontal disease to step in. The area becomes infected, and the gums recede even further. This is a very unhealthy situation which may lead to serious oral problems such as root infection. Make sure calculus or tartar is removed from the teeth before gingivitis has the chance to develop, and help your dog preserve his teeth for old age.

**Pharyngitis:**   Sore throats are common in dogs. They often are associated with a respiratory infection. The throat will appear red and inflamed, and the dog will cough or gag, and lose his appetite. He may be feverish. In severe cases, breathing sounds are rough, complicated by swollen lymph tissues in the back of the throat. Veterinarians will typically put patients on antibiotics and suggest a soft diet during recuperation.

**Tonsillitis:**   A painful inflammation of the tonsils, this condition usually affects young dogs and may be associated with a respiratory infection. Symptoms are similar to those for a sore throat except fever is more pronounced. Short-faced breeds are prone to chronic tonsillitis. Antibiotics are used to treat tonsillitis; surgical removal of the tonsils is performed when recurrent attacks of tonsillitis are a problem or the tonsils interfere with normal breathing or swallowing.

**Drooling:**   Abnormal drooling can occur for a variety of reasons: drugs or poisons; local irritation or inflammation; nervousness or fear; infectious disease; or a problem with the salivary glands themselves. The correct treatment for drooling largely depends upon discovering the cause for the problem.

**Salivary Mucoceles:**   Soft swellings under the jaw and neck could be due to a traumatized salivary gland causing a collection of saliva beneath the skin. See your veterinarian.

**Nose:**   For illnesses involving the nose, refer to the section on *Respiratory Problems*.

# Neurological Problems

The NERVOUS system is encompassed of the brain, spinal cord, and peripheral nerves. It receives, conducts, and interprets sensory information and sends controlling messages to muscles and other organs.

Signs which may indicate a neurological problem include:

- seizures
- sudden and bizarre behavior
- incoordination
- progressive weakness
- changes in muscle tone
- sensory abnormalities
- paralysis

**Tetanus:**  Tetanus is characterized by the gradual onset of generalized muscle stiffness that often begins with spasms of the jaw and head muscles and progresses to a stiff "sawhorse" gait. A dog with tetanus has difficulty swallowing and his tail often becomes rigid. Spasms worsen until the dog breathes laboriously and is exhausted. The tetanus bacteria lives in soil, feces, and putrifying material, and enters the body through injured tissue. Dogs with tetanus require hospitalization; their chances for recovery improve once a week has passed after symptoms begin. Recuperation generally requires four weeks or longer.

**Rabies:**  Rabies is caused by a virus which is transmitted by contact with infected saliva, usually from the bite of a rabid animal (skunks, foxes, bats and raccoons are typical carriers). There is little chance of survival once the virus starts reproducing within the body. Dogs are a primary direct source of rabies in man, so you *must* maintain current rabies vaccinations in your dog. The first sign of rabies in an infected animal is a marked personality change. In contrast to his ordinary behavior, the dog may seem overly affectionate or shy; he may appear restless, or become aggressive. Light seems to bother his eyes; the pupils are often dilated. A rabid dog progressively shuns your attention, and finally resists handling. In addition, he may have a fever, diarrhea, or may vomit. Rabies is manifested in two possible forms: "furious" and "paralytic." A dog may have one form of the disease or a combination of both. In the case of the former type, the dog indiscriminately bites at anything he sees. His facial muscles twitch, his teeth are bared, and his movements are uncoordinated. "Paralytic" rabies causes loss of muscle control, causing the dog's mouth to drop open and the tongue to hang out. He may drool, cough, paw at his mouth and demonstrate a voice change. Eventually the dog loses coordination, collapses, becomes comatose and dies. There is no treatment for rabies in the dog. Vaccination is for his protection, as well as for your own.

**Seizures:**  During a typical seizure a dog will fall over, paddle the limbs uncontrollably, vocalize, urinate, and/or defecate. Following the episode, the dog returns to normal. The causes include viral, bacterial and fungal infection of the brain, brain tumors, intoxication, and head trauma. Metabolic disease, e.g., low blood sugar, or an irregular heart beat can also cause convulsions. If no cause for the seizures is definable, the condition is called "idiopathic epilepsy." Certain breeds, such as the German Shepherd Dog, St. Bernard, Irish Setter, Poodle and Beagle, are thought by some to have a higher incidence of epilepsy than other breeds. Treatment with oral anti-epileptic drugs can prevent seizures or lessen their severity. However, if the dog suffers from continuous convulsions or seizures so frequent that recovery between episodes is impossible, coma and death may occur. For information about what to do during an epileptic seizure, see the section in *First Aid*.

**Tick Paralysis:** Tick paralysis occurs when a dog is poisoned by a toxin contained in the saliva of the common female wood tick. The disease usually develops after a heavy infestation. Although the dog does not seem to be in any pain, he grows progressively weaker until he becomes paralyzed. Death may occur because the dog cannot breathe. Immediate veterinary attention is absolutely necessary. To learn more about preventing a heavy tick infestation and removing individual ticks, refer to the section of *Preventive Care*.

**Distemper:** One of the symptoms of distemper, a highly contagious viral disease, is the appearance of neurological problems. Specifically, these include seizures, incoordination and uncontrollable twitching, and paralysis. More information regarding distemper may be found in the section describing *Respiratory Problems*.

**Tumors:** As with other tissues of the body, components of the nervous system—the brain, spinal cord and peripheral nerves—can be affected by tumors. Tumors usually occur in older dogs, although they may affect a dog of any age, or they may metastasize to the nervous system from other parts of the body. Signs vary depending on the site.

## Urinary Problems

The URINARY system includes the kidneys, ureters, bladder, prostate (in male dogs) and urethra. The major organ is the kidney which maintains correct water and mineral balance and excretes waste products of metabolism.

Symptoms which may indicate a URINARY PROBLEM are:

| | | |
|---|---|---|
| • excessive drinking and urination | • inability to urinate | • hunched-up posture |
| • straining to urinate | • uncontrollable urination | • weight and appetite loss |
| • frequent urination in small amounts | • blood or pus in the urine | |
| | • vomiting | |

**Chronic Kidney Failure:** The kidneys clear the body of many of its metabolic waste products. Kidney failure occurs when the kidneys cannot adequately perform their job. Chronic kidney failure, the most common form of kidney failure, can occur in any breed at any age. The first signs of this disorder are excessive drinking and urination, weight and appetite loss, and vomiting. A great deal of damage to the kidneys may already exist at the time of diagnosis. If the disease is slowly progressive, anemia develops and the gums and lips appear pale. Waste products begin to accumulate in the dog's blood and he appears listless, weak and depressed. He may be dehydrated. Death is inevitable, but with treatment and support, you can prolong his remaining time. Recognizing the signs of kidney failure before they are allowed to progress and obtaining the proper veterinary help can make treatment more effective. Dogs with chronic kidney failure should be allowed to drink as much water as they wish.

**Renal Dysplasia, Hypoplasia:**    These congenital renal defects are associated with abnormal development in the kidneys, and may be observed in early life. Later, you may notice signs such as excessive drinking and urinating, listlessness, depression, loss of appetite, and ammonia-smelling breath. The dog's growth may be stunted. Treatment for these conditions is similar to that for chronic renal failure.

**Bladder Stones:**    Bladder stones are fairly common in both male and female dogs. Some breeds, such as the Pekingese, Dachshund and Cocker Spaniel, are more prone to forming bladder stones than other breeds. Some, like the Dalmatian, have an inherited enzyme defect that subjects them to forming specific types. In male dogs, small stones can pass into the urethra and cause a urinary blockage. Signs indicative of bladder stones include straining to urinate, frequent urination of small amounts, blood in the urine, and malodorous urine. A blockage is suggested by the inability to pass urine while straining, or dribbling urine. Bladder stones may be caused by an an infection, so treatment for this problem is essential. Stones may need to be surgically removed, and medication or diet changes can prevent new ones from forming.

**Bladder Infection (Cystitis):**    Cystitis is a bacterial bladder infection common in both male and female dogs. Individuals with cystitis urinate frequently and there may be blood in the urine. Urination may appear difficult and/or painful. A female dog may also have a vaginal discharge and lick the vulva often. Antibiotics are needed.

**Prostate Infection (Prostatitis):**    Male dogs have a gland at the base of the bladder known as the prostate. When an infection of the prostate occurs, dogs typically have difficult, painful urination. They may also be feverish and stand in a hunched-up manner. An unusual secretion is often present on the penis. Prostatitis, a bacterial infection, is treated with the appropriate antibiotics, but it can be a chronic problem.

# Reproductive Problems

The REPRODUCTIVE system includes those organs of the male and female dog which contribute to the production of offspring.

Symptoms which may indicate a REPRODUCTIVE PROBLEM are:

- abnormal discharge from the penis or vulva
- swelling of the scrotum, testicles, or vulva
- abortion or failure to conceive
- inflammation and pain in the genital or breast area
- undescended testicles
- distended abdomen
- loss of appetite and energy
- excessive drinking and urination
- vomiting and/or diarrhea
- unusual soft or hard tumors in the genital or breast area

**Brucellosis:** Brucellosis is a bacterial disease which can cause sterility in both sexes at any age. Common signs of infection in females are abortion, failure to whelp, and enlargement of the lymph nodes. In male dogs, swelling or atrophy of the testicles may be observed. Individuals with brucellosis have a poor coat, seem slightly depressed, and have swollen, painful joints. However, infected animals may also show no sign of illness at all—a bitch may appear perfectly normal before and following the expulsion of dead or live puppies—but can infect other dogs with whom they have had contact. Commonly spread through sexual intercourse, the bacteria circulate in the blood of infected animals for over a year. Aborted tissues and vaginal excretion, in which large populations of bacteria are present, are also highly contagious to other dogs. When a bitch aborts, she and any other dogs in the kennel should be blood-tested for brucellosis. Any male who has been associated with the infected female needs to be examined as well.

**Infection of the Penis (*Balanoposthetitis*):** Most intact mature male dogs have a small amount of white or yellowish discharge on the skin covering the penis, known as the prepuce. If your dog licks at the prepuce often, or if he has an excessive, discolored, or foul-smelling discharge, suspect an infection. The penis may appear intensely red, with small bumps. An irritating foreign object or prolonged sexual intercourse may have caused the infection. See your veterinarian for an accurate diagnosis and a method of treatment.

**Undescended Testicles:** The canine testicles are usually descended by ten days after birth, but if one or both have not descended by the time the puppy is six months old, take him to the veterinarian. Cryptorchid dogs, those with only one testicle in the scrotum, run a higher risk of developing testicular tumors. These dogs should not be used for breeding if they are fertile, since the defect can be passed to the offspring. Neutering is advised.

**Inflammation of the Testicle (*Orchitis*):** Orchitis may be caused by an injury or disease, and can cause infertility. The inflamed testicles appear firm, enlarged and painful. The dog may have difficulty in walking normally and may prefer to sit on cold surfaces. Orchitis should be treated by a veterinarian soon after it is discovered if fertility is to be preserved.

**Vaginal Infection (*Vaginitis*):** Females who lick excessively at the vulva and have an abnormal vaginal discharge which stains the hair around the vulva may have vaginitis. These bitches may also seem unusually attractive to male dogs. In young females, the infection may be characterized by only a small amount of discharge and painful urination. Antibiotics and douches may be used to treat the vaginitis. A urinary tract infection may accompany this condition; seek veterinary attention.

**Pyometra:** Pyometra is a very serious uterine infection which may occur in unspayed females. Pus collects in the uterus and may or may not be released through the cervix. In those cases where this odorous pus exudes from the vulva, it appears thick and bloody. Typically, an infected bitch loses her appetite and her energy; she drinks and urinates more frequently than usual. Vomiting and fever sometimes accompany the infection, and the abdomen may appear enlarged. Pyometra can be fatal when it is not treated promptly. Surgery is usually performed to remove the infected uterus. Other methods of treatment are occasionally used in an attempt to save the bitch for future breeding.

**Metritis:** Metritis, another serious uterine infection, is similar to pyometra in that the dog is depressed, loses her appetite, vomits, has diarrhea, and drinks more than usual. A discharge from the vulva, when present, has a strong odor and is either reddish and watery or dark and purulent. The infection may arise during or after estrus, or post-partum. A retained placenta or fetus, or the use of contaminated whelping instruments are some possible causes for the disease. It is a life-threatening condition, and surgical removal of the uterus may be necessary if the condition is not responsive to other methods of therapy.

**Canine Herpesvirus:** Signs of canine herpesvirus are usually so mild in adult dogs that the disease goes unnoticed, or a mild case of vaginitis may be observed in an adult bitch. The virus is fatal to newborn puppies, however, who may become infected with the disease from their mother during birth or by exposure to infective saliva. In that case, apparently healthy puppies suddenly die after only a brief period of illness, usually lasting less than 24 hours. No vaccine against herpesvirus is presently available. A bitch who has lost a litter of puppies from this infection, however, is capable of giving birth to normal puppies at a later time.

**Canine Venereal Granulomas:**   This disease is characterized by the appearance of soft tumors in the dog's genital area. Both sexes and all breeds seem susceptible. Sexual intercourse or licking an infected individual seems to spread the disease from one dog to another. An infected bitch can pass the disease to her offspring. Sometimes the tumors caused by venereal granulomata disappear spontaneously; they can also be removed by surgery. In the case of transmissible venereal tumors, radiation therapy is also very successful.

**Mammary Tumors:**   Mammary tumors are the most common neoplasm in the bitch; about half are benign and half are malignant. These small, firm, typically mobile lumps appear in the area of the nipples, usually involving the rear glands. They can also arise as multiple nodules that form a rapidly growing mass. Malignant mammary tumors tend to metastasize to the lymph nodes and the lungs. Bitches that are spayed before two and a half years of age are less likely to develop mammary tumors (especially if they are spayed prior to their first heat), so if you do not plan to breed your bitch you may wish to consider an ovariohysterectomy for her as a preventative against breast cancer. In any case, make a habit of inspecting your dog, especially during her middle and old age, for signs of mammary tumors and consult your veterinarian immediately if you suspect this problem. An X-ray of the chest and a biopsy to determine whether the tumor is benign or malignant are usually performed. Since benign tumors may develop a malignancy later on, this problem is usually treated by removal of the tumor. In addition, a veterinarian may combine surgery with immunotherapy to kill remaining cancer cells after surgery and prolong the dog's life.

# Multi-System Problems

**Distemper:**   The distemper virus spreads readily from one dog to another. The first signs of distemper are a loss of appetite, a thick, yellow discharge from the nose and eyes, and a dry cough. The dog may also suffer from vomiting and/or diarrhea. Later, the dog may develop neurological symptoms. These include head shaking, drooling, and uncontrollable chewing motions. Seizures may also occur, or twitching. The virus can also attack the skin of the feet and nose, causing these surfaces to harden.

A dog may or may not recover during the first stage of distemper, but his chances of recovery once the brain is involved are poor. Distemper is a universal disease, and remains the principal cause of disease and death in unvaccinated dogs. Make sure your dog receives this and other vital vaccinations early in life.

**Toxoplasmosis:** Toxoplasmosis, a common protozoa disease of warm-blooded animals, often produces no signs in the dog. Dogs that become clinically ill usually are suffering from another infection such as distemper. Young animals are more commonly and seriously affected than older ones, but severe or fatal primary toxoplasmosis is rare. Signs of illness, when present, include coughing, labored breathing, fever, apathy, loss of appetite and weight, enteritis, and disturbances of the nervous system such as tremors, incoordination, and paralysis.

**Canine Hepatitis Virus:** A highly contagious virus, hepatitis usually spreads to a susceptible dog through contact with a sick individual's urine, stool or saliva. The infected dog develops a fever, red eyes, and a discharge from the eyes, mouth and nose. In severe cases, the dog stops eating and enters a coma. Within six to ten days after infection, a dog either dies or quickly recovers. After recovery, some dogs show a temporary opacity of the eyes, known as "blue eyes." All dogs should receive a canine infectious hepatitis vaccine.

**Canine Parvovirus:** Canine parvovirus is a viral disease that attacks the body's rapidly reproducing cells, such as the bone marrow, lymph nodes, heart (only in very young puppies) and the lining of the gastrointestinal tract. There are two forms of the disease: the "enteric," or diarrhea form, and the "myocardial" or cardiac form. Dogs affected with enteric parvovirus appear depressed and have an appetite loss. Vomiting and diarrhea, frequently containing blood, follow in variable severity. Fevers are common, especially in young dogs. Ordinarily, puppies are the exclusive victims of myocardial parvovirus. The onset and progression of the disease are rapid. Puppies may suddenly die, or die soon after taking sick. A puppy who has recovered from myocarditis can develop a chronic form of congestive heart failure which may lead to premature death.

Because it is so contagious and deadly, parvovirus is the nightmare of breeders. The virus spreads from one dog to another by way of contaminated feces, easily carried from place to place on the feet of humans or canines. Once infection is present, the dog's living area should be thoroughly washed with a 1:30 chlorine bleach solution to inactivate the virus, and sick dogs should be isolated from other dogs. Nevertheless, the only practical method for the control of parvovirus infection is vaccination.

**Leptospirosis:** Leptospirosis is a bacterial disease which is spread through contact with contaminated urine. The infected dog weakens and becomes depressed. Some show abdominal pain. Typically, dogs drink and urinate more often and in greater amounts. Painful ulcers form in the mouth or on the tongue, which may also develop a thick brown coating. The whites of the eyes may appear red or jaundiced. Diarrhea, often bloody, and vomiting are also frequent symptoms shown by infected dogs.

In fatal cases, death occurs five to ten days after symptoms first appear. Dogs do not recover rapidly from leptospirosis due to the damage of the digestive tract, liver and kidneys. Because infected dogs can potentially transmit the disease to humans and, even after they recover, to other dogs through their urine, it is especially important to vaccinate dogs against this disease.

**Diabetes Mellitus:**   Diabetes mellitus, or "sugar diabetes," is characterized by uncontrolled blood sugar levels. Dogs with diabetes drink and urinate more than normal, and suffer weight loss although they may have large appetites. Occasionally, cataracts cloud the dog's vision.

Furthermore, diabetic dogs can develop a condition called *ketoacidosis*, which is caused by a build-up of waste products in the blood from excessive protein breakdown. These dogs appear nauseated; they may vomit and you may notice a sweet odor on their breath. They become dehydrated, develop rapid, labored breathing, and can go into a hyperglycemic coma. Intravenous fluids, insulin administration and control of acidosis are necessary to prevent death.

The non-ketotic diabetic dog can lead a long and happy life through dietary control, exercise, and regular insulin injections to maintain a suitable blood glucose level. Intact females should be spayed.

# First Aid

First aid is the first step a dog owner should take in an emergency situation before you can reach a veterinarian. It can prevent injuries from worsening, can alleviate pain, or can even save your dog's life. First aid, however, is *preliminary* action; it can never replace professional care.

What kind of injuries might warrant first aid? Cuts, ingestion or exposure to poisons, eye injury, blunt trauma and heat stroke are just a few of the many types of emergencies that may require first aid at home. In short, first aid is appropriate in the case of any life-threatening or traumatic incident that requires immediate care and attention. However, always use good judgment, appropriate to the specific case.

Before you read on to the rest of this section, we would like to stress the importance of preparation. Familiarize yourself with the basics in this first aid primer *before* an actual emergency situation requiring its use arises. Also, be sure to have the telephone number of your veterinarian or veterinary emergency hospital readily available, preferably placed with other home emergency numbers such as those of your physician, police, and fire department. In case of an emergency, notify the veterinarian that you are on your way with an injured animal and describe the nature of the problem so that he or she can prepare for your arrival. Preparations such as these can greatly improve the probability of a favorable outcome.

## Restraint

In its pain and fright, even a well-loved and trusted pet can become violent while being helped. Muzzling an injured dog is the quickest and easiest way to ensure your safety. Panty hose, a cotton bandage, necktie or piece of rope about two feet long will make a good muzzle. Tie a loose knot in the middle, leaving a large loop. Slip the loop over the dog's nose and tighten the knot over the bridge of the nose. Bring the ends down under the chin, tie a knot there, then bring the ends around back of the ears and tie again. If the dog is short-nosed, take one of the ends from behind the ears, pass it over the forehead and slip it under the noose around the nose. Bring it back over the forehead, and tie firmly with the remaining end. The muzzle will not interfere with breathing if tied in this manner.

## Transporting an Injured Dog

An injured dog should be carried in such a way as not to cause further injury. Very large dogs can sometimes be placed on a large firm surface, such as a plywood board, and be lifted and carried in this fashion. (This method is actually useful for any size dog.) A large towel or blanket can also be used in a supportive fashion to help move a large dog. A smaller dog, i.e., less than 50 pounds, is much easier to move when injured. One method of successful transportation is to gently place the dog in an appropriately sized box. Another option is to use a blanket, picked up by the four corners. Small dogs may also be wrapped gently in a blanket or towel and carried in one's arms.

Always exercise caution when attempting to pick up and support an injured animal. Remember, that you could be bitten (muzzle first, for safety), or you can worsen the extent of the dog's injury through improper handling.

### Artificial Respiration

This maneuver is necessary when a dog has stopped breathing. Be extremely careful since your face will be in very close proximity to the mouth of the dog. Even in respiratory arrest, dogs can close, reflexively, their jaws without warning. It is helpful to already be familiar with the normal appearance of your dog's oral cavity (i.e., the relative position of the teeth, tongue, and laryngeal structures) before you resort to artificial respiration.

First, open the dog's mouth and check for obstructions. Extend the tongue and look into the throat to make sure the passage is clear. Remove any mucous or blood from the mouth, then shut it and hold it gently closed.

Now inhale. Completely cover the dog's nose with your mouth and exhale gently; don't blow hard! Carefully force air into the lungs and watch the dog's chest for expansion. Repeat every five to six seconds, or ten to twelve breaths per minute.

### Heart Massage

Heart massage should be performed when you cannot detect a dog's heart beat (see "Heart Beat and Pulse" in the *Healthy Dog description* section). It must be combined with artificial respiration to approximate a technique known as cardiopulmonary resuscitation (CPR). When performed properly, CPR can help restore breathing and cardiac function in an emergency situation. A basic course in CPR will help you to better understand and perform this lifesaving technique.

Lay the dog on his right side, place your hands over the heart area, and press firmly about 70 times per minute. With small dogs, place one hand on either side of the chest wall near the elbow. Compress about 70 times per minute. The chest diameter should compress approximately 20–30%. Be cautious about breaking ribs!

### Bleeding

You can slow or stop external bleeding by applying a pressure dressing. Use several pieces of clean gauze to cover the wound and bandage snugly, applying pressure evenly on the limb. Watch for swelling of the limb below the pressure pack, a sign of blocked circulation. If this should happen, you must loosen or remove the bandage. Avoid, if possible, using elasticized tape or bandages. If you do not have any bandages available, place a pad or even your clean hand on the wound and press firmly.

When an artery has been severed, blood may spurt from the wound. If applying direct pressure to the region does not decrease the rate of bleeding, you may need to apply a tourniquet in addition to a pressure bandage. However, improper use of tourniquets can lead to greater problems than they solve, so you must use them *very carefully*. Place the tourniquet, a loop of rope, gauze or cloth, on the extremity between the injury and the heart. It should be gently, but firmly, tightened to the extent that bleeding is visibly decreased at the wound site. The tourniquet must be loosened every ten minutes or so to supply blood to the tissue and keep it viable.

For obvious reasons, internal bleeding is much more difficult for people to detect. Internal bleeding can result from trauma, severe irritation or the presence of certain toxins. The dog may have a painful or distended abdomen, pale or white gums, or may cough or vomit blood. Presence of blood in the urine, stool, saliva or nasal discharge is also a possible indication of internal bleeding. Internal hemorrhage is very serious and a veterinarian should be consulted without delay.

### Shock

Shock is a generalized term for a condition characterized by collapse of the cardiovascular system, i.e., the heart and blood vessels. Animals in shock are usually depressed, have a rapid, weak heart beat, dilated pupils, subnormal temperature and muscle weakness. In addition, they usually have pale mucous membranes which are slow to return to a normal pink color when pressed with one's finger. Normal canine gums regain a pink color within one to two seconds after digital pressure is applied. Dogs in shock classically take greater than 2½–3 seconds for gum color to return.

If you believe a dog is in shock, it is important to respond at once. If feasible, begin treatment for the cause (apply a pressure bandage in case of hemorrhage, for example). Keep the animal quiet and warm while transporting it to an emergency facility as fast as possible.

### Fractures

Severe fractures and dislocations are usually self-evident; the affected limb is held in an unnatural position or, in the case of an open fracture, the bone is actually visible through the skin. The sooner the fracture or dislocation is examined by a veterinarian, the less injurious the aftereffects may be. For simple and multiple fractures, muzzle the dog and place him on a board or use another non-traumatic method of transportation to bring him to the veterinarian. Move him as little as possible during the journey and try to keep the limb supported at all times—even a cushion or a hand will help.

Compound fractures, which are more serious and more susceptible to infection, need immediate care. Be sure to tell the veterinarian that bone fragments were seen. In more severe cases, a clean handkerchief, bandage or pad tied over the area is the best preliminary action before you can get professional help.

The preceding material has been presented as an overview. It should be used as a preliminary step until consultation with a veterinarian is possible. Again, it is advisable to familiarize yourself with these first aid principles *prior* to the time when they need to be applied.

The following material is directed toward specific treatment of some of the more common emergency situations requiring first aid.

## Fish Hooks

The only appropriate way to remove fish hooks is to push the hook through the skin until the barb emerges and clip it off with pliers or wire cutters. This may be attempted at home if the hook is relatively small and is lodged in an area which is not extremely sensitive, such as the skin of the legs or body. This becomes a very difficult procedure if the hook is caught in the areas around the face or feet unless the dog is sedated. Occasionally dogs will also catch themselves on lures with multiple hooks. It is not uncommon for the dog to try and scratch or chew at the multiple hook lure and become hooked again. If a multiple hook lure becomes attached, cover it with a cloth or towel so that you and the dog are protected from the exposed barbs.

Baited hooks are sometimes swallowed by dogs. Do not attempt to pull on the string. This will only increase the probability of lodging the barbed hook in the esophagus or stomach and increase the difficulty of its removal by a veterinarian. The best procedure if a dog has swallowed a hook is to cut the line as short as possible and immediately consult your veterinarian.

## Heatstroke

Heatstroke is a common malady that occurs in warm climates, usually brought about by one of the following situations: confining dogs in cars with the windows rolled up on a hot day; kenneling dogs in confined or poorly ventilated areas; or exercising them in hot, humid weather. The classic signs of heatstroke are rapid, shallow breathing, rapid heart beat, very high body temperatures (above 104 degrees) and collapse. It is important that animals suffering from heatstroke be cooled as quickly as possible and treated immediately by a veterinarian. The most effective way to cool an animal suffering from heatstroke is by spraying him with cool water, packing ice in the areas of the groin and around the head and neck, and wrapping cold, wet towels around the dog. It is important to seek professional help after instituting first aid due to the many complications usually caused by elevated temperatures. Cooling procedures must be discontinued when the patient's temperature reaches 103 degrees.

To prevent heatstroke, make sure an animal has adequate ventilation, adequate shade and access to water during hot weather. If you must leave your pet in a car, leave windows open to provide fresh air, or leave the air-conditioner on.

### Poisons

Always have the telephone number of your local Poison Control center readily available to contact prior to instituting First Aid.

Poisons fall into a few basic classes; each is treated in a somewhat different manner. The basic premise in the treatment of poisoning is to neutralize the poison and/or eliminate it from the animal. If detected soon enough, many poisons may be eliminated without need for extensive treatment or antidotal preparations. If, however, a dog has absorbed adequate amounts of a toxic substance, the patient must be treated with medications for an extended time period.

Insecticides and parasite medication are the most common types of intoxications seen in dogs. The most common signs of toxicoses are muscle trembling and weakness, increased salivation, vomiting, and loss of bowel control. The signs may vary in seriousness. If the animal's history indicates exposure to these types of chemicals, any flea collars or other chemical-containing material should be removed from the dog's environment; consult a veterinarian immediately. Many times toxicoses of this nature are caused by over-zealous use of flea or tick preparations in combination with oral deworming medications. Be sure to carefully check the labels of all medications and consult your veterinarian if you are in doubt concerning a drug's use.

Oral rodenticides, such as rat poison, are usually based on a blood anti-clotting factor that reacts rather slowly. If a dog can be induced to vomit within a short time (less than 30 minutes) after ingestion of most rat poisons, the chances of serious toxicity are greatly decreased. Some rodenticides (gopher poison, e.g.) have a strychnine base. This acutely toxic substance is rapidly absorbed into the animal's system and can cause convulsions and death in a short period of time.

Acids, alkalis and petroleum products cause special problems if ingested. Since inducement of vomiting is contraindicated, it is best to immediately consult your veterinarian. If a veterinarian is not available, give antacids (Milk of Magnesia, Pepto-Bismol) in case of acid poisoning (approximately two teaspoons per five pounds body weight is considered a safe dose). In case of alkali ingestion, a one part vinegar–four parts water mixture may be given at the same dosage. Mineral or vegetable oil sometimes helps to protect the gastrointestinal tract in petroleum distillate toxicoses; one tablespoon per five pounds body weight is a reasonably safe dose.

It is important to provide the veterinarian with the poison's label. Some poisons take time to work, so you should consult your veterinarian as soon as possible if exposure to a chemical has occurred.

Antifreeze is another substance which is very toxic to dogs. It causes severe kidney damage after ingestion of a very small quantity. If your dog has eaten even a small quantity of antifreeze, your veterinarian must be consulted immediately since medical treatment is important.

### Topical Irritants

Do not try to remove paint with turpentine or gasoline. These substances are extremely irritating and may cause severe reactions. Vegetable oil will work quite well to remove tar and grease. This can be followed by a gentle wash with a mild hand soap.

Thermal burns are best treated by clipping the hair away from the burned area, gently washing the area with a mild soap, and then applying a topical antibiotic steroid ointment. Extensive thermal burns may be life-threatening, and require a veterinarian's attention.

"Hot spots," localized areas of severe skin irritation, occur commonly in dogs. These areas are usually very red, moist and painful to the animal. In addition, they are usually worsened, even in a short time, by the dog's constant licking or chewing at the area. The seriousness of these lesions should not be underestimated and veterinary consultation should be sought. See *Hot Spots* under the topic of *Skin Problems* in the *Illness: Signs and Symptoms* chapter.

### Dog Fights

Disputes over territory, social hierarchy, or a female in heat are common causes for a dog fight. Despite all the noise and commotion, they usually stop shortly after they begin when one dog indicates submission to the other.

Once a fight has begun, you will have to think and act *quickly*. First consider what kind of action will effectively separate the dogs without causing any injury to yourself. This depends a great deal on the size and strength of the two fighters. You may have to let two large dogs simply settle the dispute themselves and hope for the best. If there are other dogs around, however, remove them as quickly as possible to eliminate any additional impetus for violence. Throwing water over the dogs is a good way to stop the fight, although water is not always around when you need it. If the dogs are small enough, you can always grab them, but guard your own safety at all times. The important element is *time;* the faster you can put an end to the fight, the less damaging it is likely to be.

Dog fights can sometimes result in severe injury to the combatants. The amount of injury may run from a few scratches to extensive internal damage and death. Many times when a fight occurs, the smaller of the combatants sustains serious injuries that are not externally evident. Small puncture wounds on the surface may be but a small indication of extensive damage to muscle and other tissues below. Bite wounds are also usually contaminated with large quantities of oral bacteria and are prone to infection. Flush the wounds with water or hydrogen peroxide and seek veterinary attention as soon as possible. Many of the bite wounds, if left untreated, will abscess.

### Vomiting and Diarrhea

Usually vomiting and diarrhea are signs of an underlying problem that is manifesting itself via the digestive system. Vomiting and diarrhea can quickly dehydrate an animal, especially the very young and old. Appropriate management of these signs can greatly decrease the severity of dehydration and improve the probability of overcoming the underlying cause of the problem. Advice on care for the case of simple diarrhea and vomiting can be found in the section on *Digestive Problems*. If diarrhea or vomiting persists for more than 24 hours or if additional signs of illness arise, a veterinarian's consultation should be sought as soon as possible.

### Seizures

Seizures are most often characterized by generalized loss of muscle control. The best course of action to take with a dog having convulsions is to protect him from injuring himself via falling or hitting his head on floors or walls. A large blanket or towel can be used to protect the dog's head and limbs. Care should be taken when handling the animal's head since reflex biting may occur even in the most docile of pets. Time the duration of the seizure and relay this information to the veterinarian. It is important to consult your veterinarian if your dog has seizures, as many times this is an indication of an otherwise unapparent disease process.

The preceding material is but a small sampling of the many types of situations requiring first aid that can arise during the life of a dog. A comprehensive description of all possible emergency situations is beyond the scope of this text. In summary, the best way to detect abnormalities in your pet's health is to familiarize yourself with his normal anatomy and physiology while he is healthy. Become accustomed to looking in his mouth, feeling his heart beat and pulse, and observing the color and character of his eyes, to help you become a competent judge of abnormalities. At the first sign of any problem, call your veterinarian. He or she is there to help you and your pet.

# Training

When man took the dog from the wild as his companion, the necessity for training arose to make life together tolerable. Every civilized dog should know at least five basic commands: *heel, sit, down, stay* and *come.* If you do not teach your dog these basic commands, you are heading for trouble. Remember it is your responsibility to train your dog. No dog can become a well-behaved member of the household without training.

Training gives you a more controlled dog at home and in public, who neither bothers the neighbors nor balks at grooming procedures; it stimulates the dog's intelligence and lends stability to his life by letting him know what you expect of him. In an emergency, training can save your dog's life.

The five commands: "Heel," "Sit," "Down," "Stay," and "Come," are the core of the exercises required for a Companion Dog degree in American Kennel Club Novice obedience competition. They comprise the *minimum requirements* to make a dog a true companion. Home training does not demand the amount of precision that goes into training for competition. Both, however, are based on making one thing absolutely clear to the dog: *he must learn to obey you instantly, with one and only one command.* A sure sign of a barely trained dog is the repeated command, almost always delivered in a rising voice filled with panic which is only reluctantly, if at all, obeyed by the dog.

## Foundation for Training

Dogs are like young children. They are curious and investigative. They test the world in a variety of ways. Once your dog knows you are the source of its needs and wants, he will experiment with different methods of attracting your attention until one or several bring results. You must channel these natural inclinations into paths you desire, those acceptable to you and later those actually useful and helpful.

Thoroughly pragmatic in nature, dogs use modes of behavior which, through minimum discomfort, yield maximum results. Thus, if your dog learns that he gets what he wants by constantly whining (the child analogy holds remarkably well here), he will whine. If he learns he gets attention through refusal to eat, he will refuse to eat. If he learns that relieving himself on your carpet brings less discomfort through discipline than the discomfort of waiting to go out, he will shower the carpet. But if he learns from first contact with you, that your way of doing things results in praise and comfortable relations, while other ways result in firm, unvarying correction, he will opt for the easier way out. Making the easier way the right way (your way, of course) is a fair definition of training.

676

The key words in training are confidence and consistency. This means your dog's confidence in you as well as yours in him. His confidence is established by your consistently responding to a particular action with the same reaction. In training, this means that certain actions are always prohibited, and certain others always encouraged. *Vacillation is the deadliest enemy of good training*, destroying the secure world in which a dog, at any age, seeks to live. A well-trained dog knows what it can do and what it cannot do. This is only established by consistent reenforcement. A dog that is praised when it does right, and corrected when it does wrong, will soon learn acceptable behavior.

## Praise and Correction

Living successfully with a dog means understanding how to correctly use praise and correction. Praise implies more than obvious approval when your dog has done something right. It also means praising your dog after you have corrected or disciplined him, in the interest of maintaining smooth and happy relations. Many home trainers make the basic, and destructive, mistake of prolonging their anger at a "naughty" dog or one who has seemingly been unable to absorb a training session. A dog cannot remember after a few minutes what he did or didn't do; he only knows that you are displeased with him. All of which teaches him nothing except that you're not so easy to get along with.

Correct when wrong. Praise when right. It is best to be able to praise your dog as soon after a correction as possible; just make sure the praise is for correct behavior. Do this no matter how many times you've had to make the identical correction; it takes a few times for any correction to sink in. Praise after correction doesn't lessen the impact of the correction, but it will reassure him that you are still friends, and training can progress without hard feelings on either side.

Corrections should be mild and non-violent. Your voice is your basic corrective tool, and the basic corrective command is, "No!" There must be authority in your correction voice. Loud, yes; authoritative equally important. Panic, anger and annoyance may confuse the dog. In most cases a sufficiently authoritative correction is adequate. Just how harsh the correction has to be depends on the reaction of the dog. If the dog is not responding to your correction, the chances are you are not being sufficiently authoritative.

There can be tremendous variation from breed to breed in the degree of firmness necessary to get the proper response from the dog. Some breeds are far more strong-willed and hard-headed than others. A dog that has been allowed to develop unacceptable behavior and is then subjected to correction will require a stronger hand than the dog that is never allowed to develop incorrect behavior in the first place.

From the time a puppy enters your life it is learning and adapting its behavior to you and its environment. It must learn what is acceptable and what is unacceptable. Some behavior, such as the commands mentioned above, must be taught in relatively structured, regular sessions. Other behavior must be taught as you interact with the dog. Chewing for example. Puppies are going to chew. When you cannot be with the puppy, make certain it has no access whatsoever to anything it should not chew on. When you are with the puppy, correct it with a firm "No!" as soon as it chews on your clothing, hands, or anything else it should not put in its mouth. Once the correction has been made, of course praise the dog immediately. The dog must learn that it will be corrected for doing something wrong and that you will also praise it abundantly for doing what's right.

The basic corrective device used when systematically training is the choke (or training) collar. The choke permits you to instantly correct a dog when it is being trained. A complete discussion of the choke collar and its use is presented below. The choke is an effective training aid. Used correctly it is not inhumane.

Never strike your dog, with one possible exception. That exception is when a dog actually threatens to bite. In this circumstance, you will have to judge, from your knowledge of your own dog, how to handle the situation, and this may mean force. Even then, however, remember to praise and comfort him once the incident is over.

When we say not to hit your dog, we mean using your hand, a rolled-up newspaper, a stick or any other object. Don't threaten him, either. This is almost worse than actually striking him. Such is the cause of "hand shy" dogs, who cringe at the sight of any hand upraised or otherwise. The dog who expects the possibility of being struck whenever a hand is raised has good reason to try to escape to safer ground.

The use of a rolled-up newspaper in correction is so widespread that it warrants additional discussion. The idea is that the noise of the blow, and not its force, punishes the dog by frightening him. This is wrong on three counts. First, training does not occur by scaring a dog into making him do what you want and not do what you find objectionable. Secondly, deliberately teaching a dog to be frightened of sudden loud noises is not good. What about noise, such as thunder, that you can't control? Third, and perhaps most important, is the unlikelihood of having a rolled-up newspaper on hand or even close by at all times. The power of correction lies in its immediate administration, not following a lapse of even a few seconds.

Furthermore, positive and immediate correction must be somehow connected with the dog's act. Constructive corrections must instantly show the dog what he ought to be doing. For example, if you are teaching your dog to sit and he doesn't, you must instantly show him what he should be doing by guiding him into a sitting position with your hands. Disciplinary corrections must be made as fast and be as closely connected with the misdeed as possible. If you do not want your dog to jump on people, for instance, placing your knee so that it throws him off balance as he jumps at you is an excellent correction.

Note that neither of these situations involves any unpleasantness from you to him; no shouting, no hitting or beating, and no recriminations.

You may also have noticed that the word "punishment" does not appear anywhere in our description of training techniques. A dog is never punished; he is corrected. This may seem a fine point to you, but in such fine points lies the difference between good and bad dog training.

Lastly, never, under any circumstances, correct or discipline your dog when you have called him to you or when he has come to you of his own accord. The canine mind makes direct and short-term connections. If he comes to you and you correct or discipline him, he will connect it with coming to you (the most recent thing he did before the roof fell in) and not with what happened previously. After a few episodes, he will be reluctant to come to you and eventually he may not come at all. Here, as in other training situations, it may be a good idea to put yourself in his position. How would you feel if a friend asked you to come to him, then shouted at you when you arrived? Chances are you'd get pretty cautious about approaching him. Your dog feels much the same way. Therefore, if your dog has done something wrong at a distance, either get to where he is for your correction, or forget about it until you have the opportunity to do the job right.

### Housebreaking

The importance of thorough housebreaking cannot be overemphasized. The younger the dog the more difficult the job will be. Some breeds housebreak more readily than others. Unless you do what has to be done, whether directly housebreaking or paper-training as an intermediate step, as discussed below, the dog will not learn. Unhousebroken dogs are unacceptable. All the reasons that make dogs worthwhile, enjoyable companions are destroyed if the dog cannot be trusted in the house.

There are two basic housebreaking techniques, one in which housebreaking is accomplished directly, and one which uses paper-breaking as an intermediate stage. Direct housebreaking is by far preferable, but is not convenient to everyone's lifestyle. If you have a yard of any sort just outside your door, it is not only possible but best to housebreak directly. Apartment dwellers may have to rely on the intermediate paper-breaking method.

Direct housebreaking is simple. Basically, it involves taking the puppy outside frequently, allowing him to relieve himself, and returning him to the house. Once inside, he is confined to either a large sleeping-living box or crate or, if you can keep a close eye on him, loose, but in a restricted space such as the kitchen. In either case, the puppy will be restricted to a small area in which he must play and sleep, an area that he will be extremely reluctant to soil.

If he does soil the area, and accidents will happen, chastise him mildly and take him outside immediately to the area he has used before, to remind him that the only permissible place is there. Remember to be fair to him, though. A young puppy needs to eliminate often, so take him out frequently in the early days before he has built up a measure of control. He must be taken out about an hour after each feeding. With age, he will be able to contain himself for longer periods and the necessary outings will be reduced to approximately four a day, but let him work up slowly.

There is nothing cruel about restricting a puppy to a box or crate, contrary to what many new dog people think. It is actually a kindness to allow the puppy to get housebreaking over and done with efficiently. A majority of housebreaking problems originate with the "kind" owner who lets an untrained puppy have the run of the house. Then the puppy falls into the habit of soiling the floors and furniture, and for years afterward he may be subjected to constant corrections. The choice is between a couple of weeks of close confinement resulting in efficient housebreaking and the possibility of years of dissatisfaction accompanied by non-stop corrections. Furthermore, it's not as if the dog is in solitary confinement; give your puppy plenty of attention and playtime both in and out of his confinement area.

Accustoming a dog to a crate may also be beneficial later, if you decide to travel with him. In addition, many experienced breeders and trainers who give their dogs free access to their crates following housebreaking will tell you that dogs appreciate having a space of their own apart from the hustle and bustle of human life.

Housebreaking in an apartment is a more difficult task. Your veterinarian may advise you not to take the puppy out into the city streets until his shots fully protect him from diseases he might contract there. On the other hand, it may be difficult to make frequent trips down to the street from a high-rise apartment. Such cases call for use of the paper training method.

Cover the entire floor of the paper training room, preferably the kitchen, with several thicknesses of newspaper and confine the puppy to that area. Wait for him to use them, then pick up the soiled papers and replace them. Continue in this fashion for a day or two. Then leave a small corner of the room bare, and hope he doesn't use it. If he does, chastise him mildly and put him on the papers, letting him know that is the one and only place for him to go.

As he seems to understand the paper idea, widen the bare area until you have a papered space equivalent to about two full newspaper sheets. Allow him to use that area until he is old enough to go to the street. Then begin street walks with him until he learns the street is the proper place for elimination, and remove the papers. At that point, watch carefully for any indication of need for relief (he may search frantically for the papers) and take him out immediately.

As with direct housebreaking, keep him absolutely confined (in this case to the paper-breaking area) until the lesson is fully learned.

Also, you can help your puppy control his bladder by limiting water at night. Don't give him water for at least two hours before his bedtime (this is, of course, your bedtime), and make sure he is taken out, or allowed access to the papers, just before the household retires.

### Using a Training Collar and Lead

Serious training should be postponed until your dog is approximately six to eight months old. Until then he will have little power of concentration, and intense lessons will only confuse him. Puppies are continually being trained and preliminary training for the more demanding, structured training described below is possible and a good idea. As a rule of thumb puppies that are still teething are too young for serious training. On the other hand, if your dog is considerably past his puppyhood and you still wish to train him, it's not too late. Contrary to the old adage, a dog can be trained at any age, old age included.

Before you begin training your dog, you will need a training (choke) collar and lead (leash). The collar is of the metal chain-link variety with metal rings at each end. It forms a loop by slipping the chain through one of the rings; the other ring is where the leash is attached. A training lead is made of leather or webbing a half inch to a full inch wide, and is six feet long. Correct size collar is determined by measuring around the largest part of your dog's head and adding one inch.

The proper way to put on a choke collar is with the loose ring at the right of the dog's neck, the chain attached to it having come over the neck and through the holding ring rather than under the neck. A collar in this position will work correctly, as the dog is to be on your left during training.

Training collars are effective because they allow you to exert as much or as little control as you need. You can get your dog's attention or urge him into the right position or direction by giving a light, quick snap on the lead. This momentarily tightens the collar around the neck. Pressure is then released, and, if you have placed the collar on correctly, it will loosen instantly. Thus the correction is made. A slight tug may be all that is required. A more recalcitrant trainee may require greater exertion on the lead. With training the dog will respond to slight correction. Never use the training collar to exert constant pressure on the dog's neck; this will choke him. In the right hands a training collar and lead are a good training technique; in the wrong hands, they can be harmful or even torturous.

Once your equipment is assembled, gently introduce it to the dog. Put the collar on and let him wear it for a day before trying anything further. Then snap the lead onto the collar and let him drag it around for a while to get used to it, watching that he doesn't get tangled on something and become frightened. When you feel he is used to the lead, take up your end of it and walk around with him, applying little or no pressure. Gradually, over a short period, increase your control until he learns that even though the leash restrains him, it is nothing to be afraid of. When you have reached the point where you can persuade him to come along in the general direction you want by gentle snaps on the lead, you are ready to begin the exercise that forms the foundation for all others, heeling.

## Heeling

Training periods should take place regularly once or twice a day, gradually increasing to 15 to 30 minutes. Longer sessions will only tire him and you, and training will suffer. Nothing is worse for training than boredom, resulting from overlong sessions. Be businesslike during training sessions, but don't forget to be friendly and praise him. At the completion of each lesson, take some time to play and romp with your dog, to ease the pressure and make sure your relationship is amiable.

To begin heeling, put the dog more on your left side and start to walk by calling his name and giving the command to heel, "Fido, Heel!" A good training rule is to call the dog's name and then the command for all movement exercises, "Fido, Heel!" or "Fido, Come!" while for commands where the dog is to be still, "Sit!" or "Stay!" give only the command. Give the command just as you take the first step, and simultaneously give him a light snap with the leash to persuade him to come along. Remember also to step with your left leg first. Since you have the dog on your left this is the leg nearest the dog. On commands where the dog is to be stationary and you move away from him, such as "Stay!," step first with your right leg. Use only as much force as necessary to get him moving with you. As you walk along, continue to urge him to walk at your left side, with his neck and shoulder approximately opposite and level with your left leg, by snapping the leash. Each time give the command "Heel!" as you snap. And each time you snap and command, follow it with praise. It need only be a brief word or two, like "That's it, good boy!" It will take a good deal of work before he understands what is going on, for this is the first time he has ever had to perform on command, but if you are kind and patient and skillful he will soon learn, and without rancor.

The secret of successful heeling training is learning the art of snapping the lead and hence tightening and releasing the choke collar. Although called a "choke collar," a training collar is not meant per se to choke the dog, although that's exactly what will happen if you exert a steady pull. The collar is meant to instantly get the dog's attention and correct only when necessary. The less the choke is used with the least amount of force the better. By the same token the choke is a tool to be used. You must use enough force to get the dog to do what he should. Not steady choking pressure, but a series of quick jerks. You must give a quick snap and then release tension.

You must also remember to give praise after each jerk. However mild your corrections, each is a discomfort to the dog and if you praise him immediately, it will remove the sting without removing the lesson.

Practice heeling in brief but lengthening sessions two or more times daily until you have to give only one command as you start walking and do not have to use the lead for correction. Practice moving in circles, around corners, and other maneuvers, keeping the dog at your side with continual snaps and praise, until you are confident that he is walking with you of his own accord. When heeling is well learned you are ready to move on to teaching the sit. Just remember to practice the heeling often as you work on other commands.

Teaching a dog to heel is vital if for no other reason than to be able to walk your dog for exercise and so it can relieve itself. A dog that will not walk on lead is not a good companion. Dogs that pull you along because they want to continue to sniff at an interesting smell are no fun.

Heeling as described in the preceding paragraphs is a highly disciplined, controlled exercise. A frequently asked question is, "How do you walk the dog for exercise and so it can relieve itself as opposed to rigorous heeling?" The best way to do this is not to use the choke collar in its choke mode when walking the dog and you want to permit him to amble along and relieve himself. Either use a regular collar or snap the lead through both rings of the choke. Once a dog is well trained you can use the choke and the dog will be able to discriminate by the commands you give (or don't) the amount of latitude he has.

### Sit

The sit command in obedience training means the dog should sit at the handler's left side, the dog's shoulder square to the handler's knee. The dog should sit pointing straight ahead. In obedience work the dog is taught to take to the sit position as part of heeling. When you stop moving, the dog is to automatically assume the sit position.

This command is taught by having the dog sit when you stop walking while he is heeling at your side. When you stop, give the command, "Sit!" and while your left hand guides his rear down into a sitting position, your right hand holds his head up and in position with the lead. With your hand and the lead, make him stay in the sitting position a moment; then give the heel command and start walking. Again stop, give the sit command, guide him into position, and have him stay seated a little longer.

Gradually, as he gets the idea, you will be able to abandon giving the command, and then the lead and hand correction. He will sit automatically when you come to a stop, waiting either for you to start moving again or for his release through an established release command, such as "Okay!"

Finally, when he has fully learned the meaning of sit, and learned to sit when you stop walking, you are ready to teach the sit from any position. Put the collar and lead on and give him the "Sit!" command, guiding him into position as before. Concentrate on this phrase, continuing the pure sit training until he will sit on command with no corrections, and then begin to introduce the "Stay."

### Stay

During the stay, your dog is required to remain in a seated position until released by you. To teach the stay, begin by placing your dog in a sitting position while he is on lead. Tell him "Stay!" placing the palm of your left hand in front of his muzzle and stepping one step away from him (starting with your right foot). Repeat the command in a coaxing but firm voice and keep your hands on him if necessary to reenforce the command. Don't try to make him stay for more than 10 to 20 seconds before releasing him during the first few times. Slowly increase the time and the distance you step away from him while cutting down on the continued commands, until he will stay on one command for at least three minutes.

Again, the properly trained dog will do what he is told the first *and only* time he is told. During training, as many commands as it takes to get the idea across are acceptable, but you must arrive at the point where you need only one "Heel," "Sit," or "Stay" for him to respond. Once this is accomplished, you should deliver your single command in a firm but pleasant tone and then use the lead and collar to be sure he follows orders. Never plead or give a command in anger, simply be strong and unequivocal.

### Stand-Stay

Once your dog has mastered heeling and sitting, and sitting and staying, he is ready to learn the stand-stay. This is particularly useful when you want to brush and groom him, for example.

The stand-stay is also taught from the heel. While he is heeling, slow down to a halt and give him the command, "Stand!" As you do so, stop his forward motion with the lead and before he has the chance to do the sit as he has learned, block the forward and downward motion of his rear with your left hand, fingers extended, just in front of the top of his right hind leg. Don't grab him; just block him. If he still attempts to sit, don't chastise him, since he's only trying to do what you've already taught him. Simply start walking again with the "Heel!" command and after a few steps, stop again, using your left hand more firmly to prevent him from sitting. He will probably be a little confused at this point, so praise him to reassure him. While he is standing, give him the "Stand!" command repeatedly, to let him know you want him to remain in that position, and also give him the familiar "Stay!" command. He should soon begin to get the idea.

Continue until he will stand firmly at your side until you start heeling again. If he tries to sit, simply start heeling again with the accompanying command. Combine this training with normal sits when you stop walking. He may at first be confused, and you may have to reenforce the sit with commands again for a short while. Soon it will become clear to him that he must sit unless there is a command to the contrary, and to stand when he hears the word.

Now you can begin leaving him alone a little while he is either sitting or standing at the stay. Whichever position he is in, give him a firm command to "Stay!" At the same time, bring your left hand around, fingers extended, and hold it in front on his nose, palm to him, for a second. This is a signal to stay. With the leash still in your hand, take a step away from him starting with your right foot. If he attempts to move or follow you, give him a firm "No!" and then repeat the "Stay!" guiding him back into position with your hands and the lead. Here again he may be confused, since before you wanted him to go with you when you started walking. Continue until he learns that he is now to stay unless given a counter command to heel, or is released. Step away again and move slowly until you are at the distance of the lead. Stay there only a few seconds before returning to praise him and release him. As the training sessions go on, slowly increase the time you are away from him until you can stay away for at least a minute while he holds the stand position, and three minutes while he holds the sit. Then you can begin to move around him while he is sitting or standing. Still holding the lead, walk away from him and circle around him, being careful that the lead neither tugs on him nor drags across his face. Continue this until he will stay quietly and confidently for three minutes, during which you can walk away from him to the front or back or sides and circle him several times. Don't try to stop him from turning his head to watch you, but gently and firmly correct any break from position, then reenforce it with the command again and leave once more.

Remember the necessity of praising your dog after every correction and whenever he does something right by himself. At the risk of taxing your patience, we have not written praise after every sentence in this section, but it should appear in your mind nonetheless. *Praise is an integral part of your dog's learning process; he can never receive too much praise, only too little.* Don't forget that it is to gain your praise that your dog works and strives to please you.

## Down

To teach your dog to lie down on command, sit him at your side. Kneel beside him and reach over his back with your left arm, taking hold of his left front leg near his body with your left hand and his right front leg similarly with your right hand. Tell him "Down!" and put him gently into the down position by lifting his front feet off the ground and easing his body down until he is in a lying position. This way, there is no struggle between you and your dog. He is comforted by the fact that your arm is around him, and he will not feel the need to fight the pressure of a leash or hand by bracing his front legs.

When he is down, release your grasp on him slowly, sliding your left hand around and leaving it on his back, while continually telling him "Down, stay!" Keep him in position for a few seconds. Then release him and get him into sitting position (by command) for another try. Continue this until he goes down at command without your having to lift him, and will stay quietly until released, without any pressure of your left hand on his back. Then give the command without putting your hands into the ready position. After a few days, you should be able to stand erect and give only one command "Down!" to have him lie at your side. From this you can improvise until he goes down when several feet away from you, still on lead.

When he has learned the down, leave him at the stay, as you did before with the sit and stand exercises. First walk away only briefly and then leave him for longer periods, finally circling around him. You will find it will be easier this time, because now he knows the meaning of "Stay!"

### Come

Perhaps the most important basic command your dog must learn is "Come!" It is last on our training schedule because your dog should already know how to work on command and how to heel and sit, both of which are used in the preliminary "come" training.

While your dog is heeling at your side, take a sudden step back and say, "Fido, Come!" As you give the command, snap the lead to turn him around to his right as he is walking, and get him headed back toward you. When he is facing you, keep walking backward, urging him to come toward you with continued gentle snaps of the lead and repetitions of the "Come!" command.

Praise is particularly important here since this is a confusing turn of events for your dog. When he is in full stride toward you, stop, and give the command "Sit!" as he reaches you. It may be necessary to guide him into a sitting position directly in front of you, but there is a very good chance you won't have to. Once he is in position directly in front of and facing you, the first "recall" is completed. Tell him "Stay!" and walk around into position, then start up at heel again for another try.

Continue working this way until you have only to step backward and give the command with no lead urging for him to turn and walk to you, sitting in front without further command. From here, the progression to the recall from a sitting position at a distance is simple. Get him to sit, and step away from him to the end of the lead, then give the "Come!" command. If he hesitates, give him a slight snap on the lead, to let him know what you want, and he will get up, come to you, and sit again in front.

The key to the success of this method is that there is never a contest of brute strength between you and your dog. He is already in motion when you first give him the "Come!" while heeling, and there is no tugging with the lead to get him up from a sit or down when he doesn't yet understand what "Come!" means.

### Beyond Basic Training

Once your dog understands these six basic commands, you are ready for the final step: obedience without the control of the lead, in "off-lead" work. In preparation, you must be absolutely certain that your dog will obey commands without hesitation on lead. This is a common place for training to break down. Many home trainers do not adequately train their dogs and then try it without lead. The outcome is invariably fatal to the training.

If you and your dog have progressed successfully to this point, get him seated at your side as before. Take the lead off and start up with the heel command. You will probably be greatly surprised to find that he heels with you, which should really be no surprise if your previous training has been good. Go through the whole routine: the stands, downs, stays, and recalls, just as if the lead were still there. In most cases, if all has gone well before, all will go well now. If not, put the lead back on for correction whenever necessary. Work on those parts until they are performed properly and then remove the lead and try again. It should work. A word of caution, however: when trying the recall off lead, don't try it from a great distance at first. Try it from only six feet or so, and work up to greater distances slowly. Like everything else in training, gradual progress is the way.

Everyone can have a well-trained dog if you are patient and apply the methods we have outlined here. The only trick is to be consistent and persistent. Of course, confidence is the most important ingredient to good training: confidence in yourself as a trainer and your dog as an intelligent being, not to mention your dog's confidence in you as a kind, fair, and firm master. Training is not accomplished in a day, a week, or even a month, but doing it can be fun, not a chore, if you go about it right. The result will be a dog who responds to your wishes, a joy to own and a true companion.

# Glossary

**Abdomen:** The belly or undersurface between the chest and hindquarters.

**Acetabulum:** The concave lateral portion of the sacrum that articulates with the head (proximal portion) of the femur. Anatomically important in evaluating hip dysplasia.

**Achondroplasia:** A form of genetic dwarfism specifically characterized by arrested development of the long bones. A defect in most breeds and a requisite in others (e.g. Dachshunds, Basset Hounds).

**Action:** A term used to describe component functions of locomotion (e.g. "action of the hocks"), or as a synonym for gait in some standards.

**AKC:** American Kennel Club

**Albino:** A relatively rare, genetically recessive condition (*cc*) characterized by the inability to synthesize melanin, consequently resulting in white hair and pink eyes.

**Almond eyes:** An elongated eye-shape describing the tissue surrounding the eye itself.

**Amble:** A relaxed, easy gait in which the legs on either side move almost, but not quite, as a pair. Often seen as the transition movement between the walk and other gaits.

**Angulation:** The angles formed by the appendicular skeleton, including the forequarters [shoulder (scapula), arm (humerus), forearm (radius, ulna), wrist (carpus), pastern (metacarpus), toes (phalanges)] and hindquarters [hip (pelvis), thigh (femur), second thigh (tibia, fibula), hock (tarsus), rear pastern (metatarsus), toes (phalanges)].

**Ankle:** *See* Hock.

**Ankylosis:** Abnormal immobility and fusion of a joint. Noted as a cause of faulty tails in the German Shepherd Dog standard.

**Anterior:** The portion carried foremost during normal locomotion.

**Apple head:** A domed top skull rounded in all directions.

**Apron:** Longer hair below the neck on the chest. Frill.

**Arm:** The anatomical region between the shoulder and the elbow, including the humerus and associated tissues. Sometimes called the "upper arm."

**Articulation:** The junction between two or more bones, typically held together by ligaments.

**Artificial Insemination:** The introduction of semen into the female reproductive tract by artificial means.

**Babbler:** A hound that gives tongue when not on the trail.

**Back:** The dorsal surface (topline) of the dog extending (usually) from the withers to the croup, including the thoracic and lumbar vertebral regions; infrequently used to refer only to the thoracic region.

**Bad mouth:** Crooked or unaligned teeth; bite over or undershot in excess of standard specifications.

**Balance:** A condition wherein all proportions of a dog are in static and dynamic harmony.

**Bandog:** A dog tied by day, released at night. Tiedog.

**Bandy legs:** Having a bend of leg outward.

**Barrel:** A rib (thoracic) region that is circular in cross-section.

**Barrel hocks:** Hocks that turn out, causing the feet to toe in. Also called "spread hocks."

**Basewide:** Wide footfall, resultant of "paddling" movement, causing body to rock from side to side. *See* Paddling.

**Bat ear:** An erect ear, rather broad at the base, rounded in outline at the top, and with orifice directed to the front (e.g., French Bulldog).

**Bay:** The prolonged bark or voice of the hunting hound.

**Beady:** Eyes that are small, round, and glittering, imparting an expression foreign to the breed.

**Beard:** Thick, long hair growth on the underjaw.

**Beauty spot:** A distinct spot, usually round, of colored hair, surrounded by the white of the blaze, on the topskull between the ears. (Blenheim Spaniel, Boston Terrier.)

**Bee-sting Tail:** A tail relatively short, strong, straight and tapering to a point.

**Beefy:** Overheavy development of the hindquarters.

**Belly:** The ventral (under) surface of the abdomen.

**Belton:** A color pattern in English Setters (named after a village in Northumberland) characterized by either light or dark ticking or roaning, and including blue belton (black and white), tricolor (blue belton with tan patches), orange belton (orange and white), lemon belton (lemon and white), and liver belton (liver and white).

**Bench show:** A dog show at which the dogs are kept on assigned benches when not being shown in competition, thus facilitating the viewing/discussion of the breeds by attendees, exhibitors, and breeders.

**Best in Show:** A dog show award to the dog adjudged best of all breeds.

**Bevy:** A flock of birds.

**Bilateral cryptorchid:** *See* Cryptorchid.

**Bird dog:** A sporting dog bred and trained to hunt game birds.

**Bird of prey eyes:** Light yellowish eyes, usually harsh in outlook. Cited as a fault in German Shorthaired Pointer standard.

**Bitch:** A female canine.

**Bite:** The relative position of the upper and lower teeth when the jaws are closed, including scissors, level, undershot, or overshot.

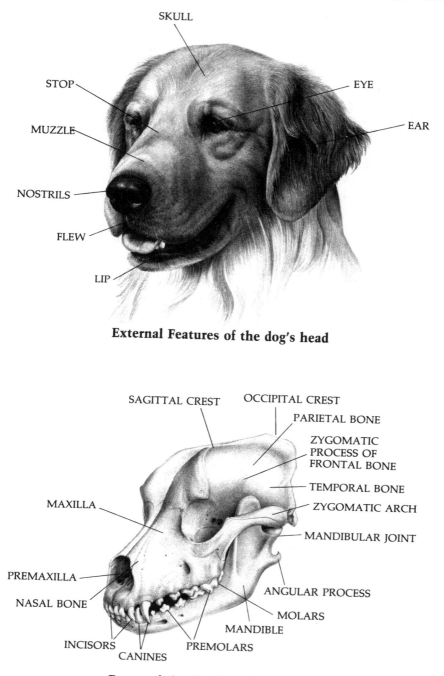

**External Features of the dog's head**

**Bones of the skull and dentition**

**Blanket:** The color of the coat on the back and upper part of the sides, between the neck and the tail.

**Blaze:** A white stripe running up the center of the face usually between the eyes.

**Blinker:** A dog that points a bird and then leaves it, or upon finding a bird, avoids making a definite point.

**Blocky:** Square or cubelike formation of the head.

**Blooded:** A dog of good breeding; pedigreed.

**Bloom:** The sheen of a coat in prime condition.

**Blue:** A dilution of black coat color, due to the recessive dilution (dd) color locus (i.e., BBdd or Bbdd dogs will be blue).

**Blue merle:** A color pattern involving black blotches or streaks on a blue-grey background. *See* Merle.

**Bluies:** Colored portions of the coat have a distinct bluish or smoky cast. This coloring is associated with extremely light or blue eyes and liver or gray eye rims, nose and lip pigment. (Pembroke Welsh Corgi.)

**Board:** To feed, house, and care for a dog for a fee.

**Bobtail:** A naturally tailless dog or a dog with a tail docked very short. Often used as a name for the Old English Sheepdog.

**Bodied up:** Mature, well-developed.

**Body length:** Distance from the prosternum (anterior portion of the Breastbone) to the posterior portion of the pelvic girdle, i.e., the ischial tuberosities.

**Bone:** A type of connective tissue that forms the canine skeleton. Informally used to suggest a quantitative characteristic of limb bones in proportion to overall size of a dog.

**Bossy:** Overdevelopment of the shoulder muscles.

**Brace:** Two specimens of the same breed presented as a pair; a couple.

**Break:** Term used to describe changing of coat color from puppies to adult stages.

**Breastbone:** *See* Sternum.

**Breeching:** Fringing of longish hair at the posterior borders of the thigh regions.

**Breed:** A domestic race of dogs (selected and maintained by man) with a common gene pool and a characterized appearance (phenotype) and function.

**Breeder:** A person who breeds dogs. Under AKC rules the breeder of a dog is the owner (or, if the dam was leased, the lessee) of the dam of the dog when the dam was bred.

**Breeding particulars:** Sire, dam, date of birth, sex, color, etc.

**Brick-shaped:** Rectangular.

**Brindle:** A color pattern specified by the $e^{br}$ allele of the E (extension) locus, resulting in the layering of black pigment in regions of lighter color (usually tan) producing a tiger-striped pattern, e.g. Boxers.

**Brisket:** Usually refers to the sternum, but in some standards it refers to the entire thorax.

**Brock:** A badger.

**Broken color:** Self color broken by white or another color.

**Broken-haired:** A rough, wire coat.

**Broken-up face:** A receding nose, together with a deep stop, wrinkle, and undershot jaw. (Bulldog, Pekingese.)

**Brood bitch:** A female used for breeding. Brood matron.

**Brows:** The ridges formed above the eyes by frontal bone contours. (Superciliary arches or supraorbital ridges.)

**Brush:** A bushy tail; a tail heavy with hair.

**Brushing:** A gaiting fault, when parallel pasterns are so close that the legs "brush" in passing.

**Bullbaiting:** An ancient sport in which the dog baited or tormented the bull.

**Bull neck:** A heavy neck, well-muscled.

**Burr:** The inside of the ear; i.e., the irregular formation visible within the cup.

**Butterfly:** A partially unpigmented nose; i.e., dark, spotted with flesh color.

**Buttocks:** The rump or hips.

**Button ear:** The ear flap folding forward, the tip lying close to the skull so as to cover the orifice.

**Bye:** At field trials, an odd dog remaining after the dogs entered in a stake have been paired in braces by drawing.

**Camel back:** An arched back.

**Canid:** A family (Canidae) of carnivorous animals including dogs. wolves, coyotes, foxes, jackals.

**Canines:** The two upper and two lower large, conical pointed teeth lateral to the incisors and anterior to the premolars.

**Canter:** A gait with three beats to each stride, two legs moving separately and two as a diagonal pair. Slower than the gallop and not as tiring.

**Cap:** Darkly shaded color pattern on the skull of some breeds.

**Cape:** Profuse hair enveloping the shoulder region.

**Carpals:** Bones of the wrist.

**Castrate:** To remove the testicles of the male dog.

**Cat foot:** Round, compact foot, with well-arched toes, tightly bunched or close-cupped.

**Caudal (Coccygeal) Vertebrae:** The only regionally variable number of vertebrae among breeds in the axial skeleton, lying posterior to the sacrum and defining the tail region.

**Cervical Vertebrae:** The seven vertebrae of the region of the neck, articulating anteriorly with the cranium and posteriorly with the thoracic vertebrae.

**CD (Companion Dog):** A suffix used with the name of a dog that has been recorded a Companion Dog by AKC as a result of having won certain minimum scores in Novice Classes at a specified number of AKC licensed or member obedience trials.

**CDX (Companion Dog Excellent):** A suffix used with the name of a dog that

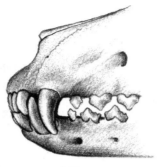

LEVEL

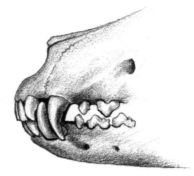

SCISSORS

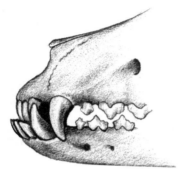

UNDERSHOT

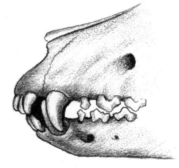

OVERSHOT

**Bites**

ALMOND

OVAL

FULL, ROUND, GLOBULAR

TRIANGULAR

**Eye types**

has been recorded a Companion Dog Excellent by AKC as a result of having won certain minimum scores in Open Classes at a specified number of AKC licensed or member obedience trials.

**Champion (CH):** A prefix used with the name of a dog that has been recorded a Champion by AKC as a result of defeating a specified number of dogs in specified competition at a series of AKC licensed or member dog shows.

**Character:** Expression, individuality, and general appearance and deportment as considered typical of a breed.

**Cheeky:** Cheeks prominently rounded; thick, protruding.

**Chest:** The part of the body or trunk that is enclosed by the ribs; the thoracic cavity.

**China eye:** A clear, flecked or spotted blue, light blue or whitish eye.

**Chippendale front:** Named after the Chippendale chair. Forelegs out at elbows, pasterns close, and feet turned out. *See* Fiddle front.

**Chiseled:** Clean-cut in head, as contrasted with bumpy or bulging outlines; particularly beneath the eyes.

**Choke collar:** A leather or chain collar fitted to the dog's neck in such a manner that the degree of tension exerted by the hand tightens or loosens it.

**Chops:** Jowls or pendulous flesh of the lips and jaw. (Bulldog)

**Chorea:** A nervous jerking caused by involuntary contractions of the muscles (and may be caused by distemper and/or hepatitis).

**Clip:** The method of trimming the coat in some breeds, notably the Poodle.

**Clipping:** When pertaining to gait, the back foot striking the front foot.

**Cloddy:** Low, thickset, comparatively heavy.

**Close-coupled:** Comparatively short from last rib to the commencement of the hindquarters; occasionally used to characterize a comparative shortness from withers to hipbones.

**Coarse:** Lacking refinement.

**Coat:** The dog's hair covering. Most breeds possess two coats, an outer coat and an undercoat.

**Cobby:** Short-bodied, compact.

**Collar:** The markings around the neck, usually white. Also a leather or chain for restraining or leading the dog, when the leash is attached.

**Compact:** Term used to describe the firmly joined union of various body parts. Also to describe a short to medium length coat, very close-lying, with a dense undercoat and giving a smooth outline.

**Companion Dog:** *See* C.D.

**Companion Dog Excellent:** *See* C.D.X.

**Condition:** Health as shown by the coat, state of flesh, general appearance and deportment.

**Conformation:** The form and structure, make and shape; arrangement of the parts in conformance with breed-standard demands.

**Congenital:** Present at birth; may have genetic or environmental causes.

**Corky:** Active, lively, alert.

**Couple:** Two hounds.

**Coupling:** The part of the body between the ribs and pelvis/hindquarters; the loin.

**Coursing:** The sport of chasing prey with Sight Hounds.

**Covering ground:** The distance traveled by a dog with each stride as it gaits.

**Cow-hocked:** Hocks turning in, accompanied by toeing out of rear feet.

**Crabbing:** Dog moves with his body at an angle to the line of travel. Also referred to as "sidewinding."

**Crank tail:** A tail carried down and resembling a crank in shape.

**Crest:** The upper, arched portion of the neck.

**Cropping:** The cutting or trimming of ear leather to permit it to stand erect.

**Crossbred:** A dog whose sire and dam are representatives of two different breeds.

**Crossing over:** Unsound gaiting action which starts with twisting elbows and ends with crisscrossing and toeing out. Also called "knitting and purling" and "weaving."

**Croup:** The region of the pelvic girdle, formed by the sacrum and surrounding tissue.

**Crown:** The dorsal (top) part of the head; the topskull.

**Cry:** The baying or "music" of the hounds.

**Cryptorchid:** The adult whose testicles are abnormally retained in the abdominal cavity. Bilateral cryptorchidism involves both sides; that is, neither testicle has descended into the scrotum. Unilateral cryptorchidism involves one side only; that is, one testicle is retained or hidden, and one descended.

**Culotte:** The longer hair on the back of the thighs.

**Cur:** A mongrel.

**Cushion:** Fullness or thickness of the upper lips. (Pekingese.)

**Cynology:** The study of canines.

**Dam:** The female parent.

**Dapple:** A mottled or variegated coat color pattern. Dachshunds are "dapple" and Collies are "merle," but both determined by the dominant M gene or the M series of multiple alleles.

**Deadgrass:** Tan or dull straw color.

**Dentition:** Forty-two adult teeth, including incisors (I), canines (C), Premolars (P), and molars (M). Formula for dogs is (sequentially on each side): upper jaw—3I-1C-4P-2M; lower jaw—3I-1C-4P-3M.

**Depth of Chest:** An indication of the volume of space for heart and lungs, and commonly referenced to the elbow (i.e., above, at the level of, or below).

**Derby:** Field-trial competition for young, novice sporting dogs usually between one and two years of age.

**Dewclaw:** An extra claw or functionless (vestigial) digit on the inside of the leg; a rudimentary fifth toe.

**Dewlap:** Loose, pendulous skin under the throat and neck.

NORMAL, STRAIGHT

TOO NARROW IN FRONT
AND EAST-WEST FEET

CHIPPENDALE OR
FIDDLE FRONT

OUT AT ELBOW AND
TOO WIDE IN FRONT

STRAIGHT FRONT

KNUCKLED OVER

DOWN IN PASTERN

**Fronts**

**Diagonals:** Right front and left rear legs constitute the right diagonal; left front and right rear constitute the left diagonal. In the trot the diagonals move together.

**Diaphragm:** A muscular sheet that separates the thoracic and abdominal cavities.

**Diehard:** Nickname of the Scottish Terrier.

**Digit:** A synonym for toe.

**Dish-faced:** Slight concaveness of foreface when viewed in profile.

**Dishing:** Weaving. (Cited as a gaiting fault in the standards of the Smooth Fox Terrier and the Wire Fox Terrier.)

**Disqualification:** A decision made by a judge or a bench show committee following a determination that a dog has a condition that makes it ineligible for any further competition under the dog show rules or under the standard for its breed or, an undesirable feature of a dog that results in such action.

**Distemper teeth:** Teeth discolored or pitted as a result of distemper or other disease or deficiency.

**Divergent hocks:** Hocks that turn out. Barrel hocks.

**Dock:** To shorten the tail by cutting.

**Dog:** A male dog; also used collectively to designate both male and female.

**Dog show:** A competitive exhibition for dogs at which the dogs are judged in accordance with an established standard of perfection for each breed.

**Dog Show, All Breed:** *See* Dog Show, Conformation.

**Dog Show, Conformation (Licensed):** An event held under AKC rules at which championship points are awarded. May be for *all breeds*, or for a single breed (Specialty Show).

**Dog Show, Specialty:** *See* Dog Show, Conformation.

**Domed:** Evenly rounded in topskull; convex instead of flat. Domy.

**Domino:** Reverse facial mask pattern on some breeds.

**Dorsal:** The portion of the dog carried farthest from the substratum during normal locomotion (i.e., away from the ground).

**Double coat:** An outer coat resistant to weather and protective against brush and brambles, together with an undercoat of softer hair for warmth and waterproofing.

**Down-faced:** The muzzle inclining downwards from the skull to the tip of the nose.

**Down in pastern:** Weak or faulty pastern (metacarpus) set at an incorrect angle.

**Drag:** A trail prepared by dragging along the ground a bag impregnated usually with animal scent.

**Drawing:** Selection by lot of dogs to be run, and in which pairs, in a field-trial stake.

**Drive:** A solid thrusting of the hindquarters, denoting sound locomotion.

**Drop ear:** One of more than thirty terms used to characterize ears, wherein the leather is folded at least to some degree; contrasted with "erect" or "prick" ears.

**Dropper:** A bird-dog cross.

**Dry neck:** The skin taut; neither loose nor wrinkled.

**Dual champion:** A dog that has won both a bench show and a field trial championship.

**Dudley nose:** Flesh-colored.

**Ear:** The auditory organ consisting of three regions: inner ear, middle ear, and the most important pinna (or leather) which is supported by cartilage and which affects the expression of all breeds.

**East-West front:** Incorrect positioning that causes the feet to turn outwards.

**Elbow:** The posterior region of the articulation between the arm (humerus) and forearm (ulna).

**Elbows out:** Turning out or off from the body; not held close.

**Entire:** A dog whose reproductive system is complete.

**Entropion:** A complex genetic condition that results in the turning in of the upper or lower eyelid, potentially resulting in corneal ulceration.

**Even bite:** Meeting of upper and lower incisors with no overlap, level bite.

**Ewe neck:** A neck in which the topline is concave rather than convex.

**Expression:** The general appearance of all features of the head.

**Eyeteeth:** The upper canines.

**Fall:** Hair overhanging the face.

**Fallow:** Pale cream to light fawn color; pale, pale yellow; yellow-red.

**Fancier:** A person especially interested and usually active in some phase of the sport of pure-bred dogs.

**Fangs:** *See* Canines.

**Fawn:** A brown, red-yellow with hue of medium brilliance.

**Feathering:** Longer fringe of hair on ears, legs, tail, or body.

**Femur:** Thigh bone. Extends from hip to stifle.

**Fetch:** The retrieve of game by the dog; also the command to do so.

**Fibula:** One of the two bones of the leg (i.e., the "lower" thigh, second thigh, or lower leg).

**Fiddle front:** Forelegs out at elbows, pasterns close, and feet turned out. French front.

**Field Champion (Field CH):** A prefix used with the name of a dog that has been recorded a Field Champion by AKC as a result of defeating a specified number of dogs in specified competition at a series of AKC licensed or member field trials.

**Field trial:** A competition for certain Hound or Sporting Breeds in which dogs are judged on ability and style in finding or retrieving game or following a game trail.

**Filled-up face:** Smooth facial contours, free of excessive muscular development.

**Flag:** A long tail carried high. Feathering on tail.

**Flank:** The side of the body between the last rib and the hip. The coupling.

**Flare:** A blaze that widens as it approaches the topskull.

**Flat bone:** Refers to bladed or non-round limb bones.

**Flat-sided:** Ribs insufficiently rounded as they approach the sternum or breastbone.

**Flews:** Upper lip pendulous, particularly at their inner corners.

**Floating rib:** The last, or 13th rib, which is unattached to other ribs.

**Fluffies:** A coat of extreme length with exaggerated feathering on ears, chest, legs and feet, underparts and hindquarters. Trimming such a coat does not make it any more acceptable. (Pembroke Welsh Corgi)

**Flush:** To drive birds from cover, to force them to take flight. To spring.

**Flying ears:** Any characteristic drop ears or semi-prick ears that stand or "fly."

**Flying Trot:** A fast gait in which all four feet are off the ground for a brief second during each half stride. Because of the long reach, the oncoming hind feet step beyond the imprint left by the front. Also called Suspension Trot.

**Foot:** The digits or toes, each consisting of three bones (phalanges; sing phalanx) and a toenail or claw. The ventral surface is cushioned by pads of connective tissue.

**Forearm:** The portion of the forelimb between the arm (humerus) and the wrist (carpels), including the radius and the ulna.

**Foreface:** The anterior portion of the skull (head) that articulates with the cranium (braincase) i.e., the muzzle.

**Forequarters:** The combined front assembly from its uppermost component, the shoulder blade, down to the feet.

**Foster mother:** A bitch used to nurse whelps not her own.

**Foul color:** A color or marking not characteristic for the breed.

**Foxy:** Sharp expression; pointed nose with short foreface.

**French front:** *See* Fiddle front.

**Frill:** *See* Apron.

**Fringes:** *See* Feathering.

**Frogface:** Extending nose accompanied by a receding jaw, usually overshot.

**Front:** The forepart of the body as viewed head on; i.e., forelegs, chest, brisket, and shoulder line.

**Frontal bones:** The anterior bones of the cranium forming the forehead.

**Furnishings:** The long hair on the extremities (including head and tail) of certain breeds.

**Furrow:** A slight indentation of median line down the center of the skull to the stop.

**Futurity Stake:** A class at dog shows or field trials for young dogs which have been nominated at or before birth.

**Gait:** The pattern of footsteps at various rates of speed, each pattern distinguished by a particular rhythm and footfall.

**Gallop:** Fastest of the dog gaits, has a four-beat rhythm and often an extra

CORRECT, STRAIGHT, NORMAL

COW-HOCKED

BANDY OR WIDE

NARROW

NORMAL ANGULATED
HINDQUARTERS

STRAIGHT STIFLES

**Rears**

period of suspension during which the body is propelled through the air with all four feet off the ground.

**Game:** Hunted wild birds or animals.

**Gaskin:** The lower or second thigh.

**Gay tail:** A tail carried above the horizontal; several breed-specific applications.

**Gazehound:** Greyhound or other sight-hunting hound.

**Genealogy:** Recorded family descent. Pedigree.

**Gestation:** A period of sixty-three days in the dog, from fertilization to whelping, characterized by embryonic/fetal development.

**Goose neck:** An elongated, tubular-shaped neck. Also termed swan neck.

**Goose rump:** Too steep or sloping a croup.

**Goose step:** Accentuated lift of the forelimbs.

**Grizzle:** A mixture of black or red hairs with white hairs. Roan. Frequently, a bluish-grey or iron-grey color.

**Groom:** To brush, comb, trim, or otherwise make a dog's coat neat.

**Groups:** The breeds as grouped into seven divisions by the AKC to facilitate judging.

**Guard hairs:** The longer, smoother, stiffer hairs which grow through and normally conceal the undercoat.

**Gun dog:** A dog trained to work with its master in finding live game and retrieving game that has been shot.

**Gun-shy:** When the dog fears the sight or sound of a gun.


**Hackles:** Hairs on neck and back raised involuntarily in fright or anger.

**Hackney action:** A high lifting of the front feet accompanied by flexing of the wrist like that of a hackney horse.

**Hallmark:** A distinguishing characteristic, such as the spectacles of the Keeshond.

**Handler:** A person who handles a dog in the show ring or at a field trial. *Also see* Professional handler.

**Hard-mouthed:** The dog that bites or marks with his teeth the game he retrieves.

**Hare foot:** Foot in which the two center digits are appreciably longer than the outside and inside toes of the foot, and the arching of the toes is less marked, making the foot appear longer overall.

**Harlequin:** Patched or pied coloration usually black or grey on white. (Great Danes.)

**Harness:** A leather strap shaped around the shoulders and chest, with a ring at its top over the withers.

**Haunch Bones:** The anterio-dorsal portion of the pelvic girdle (crest of the ilium); the "hip" bones.

**Haw:** A third eyelid or nictitating membrane on the medial (inside) corner of the eye.

**Head:** The anterior portion of the dog, including the muzzle and the cranium.

**Head planes:** Viewed in profile, the contours of the dorsal (top) portion of the skull from occiput to stop, and of the foreface from stop to tip of nose. Usually spoken of in relation to one another, i.e., parallel, diverging, converging.

**Heat:** Seasonal period of the female. Estrus.

**Heel:** *See* Hock: also a command to the dog to keep close beside its handler.

**Height:** Vertical measurement from the withers to the ground; referred to usually as shoulder height. *See* Withers.

**Hie on:** A command to urge the dog on; used in hunting or in field trials.

**High standing:** Tall and upstanding, with plenty of leg.

**Hindquarters:** Rear assembly of dog (pelvis, thighs, hocks and paws).

**Hock:** The tarsus or collection of bones of the hind leg forming the joint between the second thigh and the metatarsus; the dog's true heel.

**Hocks well let down:** Hock joints close to the ground.

**Hocking out:** Spread hocks.

**Holt:** The lair of the fox or other animal in tree roots, banks, drains or similar hideouts. Lodge.

**Honorable scars:** Scars from injuries suffered as a result of work.

**Hound:** A dog commonly used for hunting by scent or sight.

**Hound-marked:** A coloration composed of white, tan, and black. The ground color, usually white, may be marked with tan and/or black patches on the head, back, legs, and tail. The extent and the exact location of such markings, however, differ in breeds and individuals.

**Hucklebones:** The top of the hipbones.

**Humerus:** The bone of the arm (i.e., the "upper" arm).

**Inbreeding:** The mating of closely related dogs of the same breed.

**Incisors:** The six upper and six lower front teeth between the canines. Their point of contact forms the "bite."

**Interbreeding:** The breeding together of dogs of different breeds.

**Iris:** The colored membrane surrounding the pupil of the eye.

**Isabella:** Fawn or light bay color (e.g., Dobermans).

**Jabot:** The "apron" of the Schipperke, the part situated between the front legs.

**Jowls:** Flesh of lips and jaws.

**Judge:** Official approved by the AKC to judge dogs in conformation, obedience, and/or field trials.

**Keel:** The rounded outline of the lower chest, between the prosternum the posterior portion and of the sternum (breastbone).

**Kennel:** Building or enclosure where dogs are kept.

**Kink tail:** A deformity of caudal vertebrae producing a bent tail.

**Kiss marks:** Tan spots on the cheeks and over the eyes.

**Kneecap:** The stifle, with the bone known as the patella.

**Knee:** *See* Stifle.

**Knee joint:** Stifle joint.

**Knuckling over:** Faulty structure of corpus (wrist) joint allowing it to flex forward under the weight of the standing dog.

**Landseer:** The black and white Newfoundland dog, so-called from the name of the famous painter who used such dogs as models.

**Lateral:** Pertaining to the side.

**Layback:** The angle of the shoulder blade as compared with the vertical plane viewed from the side (laterally).

**Layon:** The angle of the shoulder blade as compared with the vertical plane viewed from the front (medially).

**Lead:** A strap, cord, or chain attached to the collar or harness for the purpose of restraining or leading the dog. Leash.

**Leather:** The flap of the ear; the outer ear supported by cartilage and surrounding tissue.

**Level bite:** When the front teeth (incisors) of the upper and lower jaws meet exactly edge to edge. Pincer bite.

**Level gait:** Dog moves without rise or fall of withers.

**License:** Formal permission granted by AKC to a non-member club to hold a dog show, obedience trial, or field trial.

**Line breeding:** The mating of related dogs of the same breed, within the line or family, to a common ancestor, as, for example, a dog to his granddam or a bitch to her grandsire.

**Lion color:** Tawny (Ibizan Hound).

**Lippy:** Pendulous lips or lips that do not fit tightly.

**Litter:** The puppy or puppies of one whelping.

**Liver:** A color; i.e., deep, reddish brown, produced by recessive (bb) alleles of the B (black) locus.

**Loaded shoulders:** Excessive development of the muscles associated with the shoulder blades (scapulae).

**Loin:** The region of the body associated with the lumbar portion of the vertebrae column (i.e., posterior to the ribs and anterior to the pelvic girdle).

**Loose slung:** Construction in which the attachment of the muscles at the shoulders is looser than desirable.

**Lower thigh:** *See* Second thigh.

**Lumbar Vertebrae:** The seven vertebrae of the loin region, articulating anteriorly with the thoracic vertebrae and posteriorly with the sacrum.

**Lumbering:** An awkward gait.

**Lurcher:** A crossbred hound.

**Luxation:** Dislocation of an anatomical structure, i.e., lens or patella.

**Mad dog:** A rabid dog.

**Making a wheel:** Term given the circling of the tail over the back that is characteristic of the Great Pyrenees when alerted.

**Mandible:** The bone of the lower jaw.

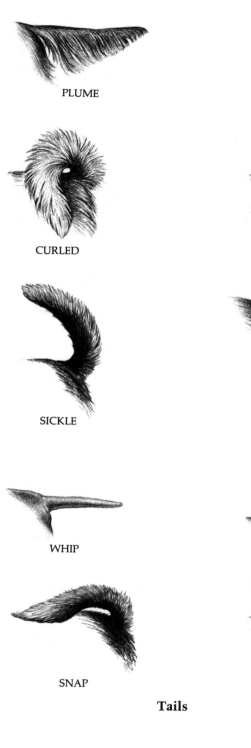

PLUME

GAY

CURLED

DOUBLE CURL

SICKLE

OTTER

WHIP

RING AT END

SNAP

SCREW

**Tails**

**Mane:** Long and profuse hair on top and sides of the neck.

**Mantle:** Dark-shaded portion of the coat on shoulders, back, and sides. (St. Bernard)

**Manubrium:** The first sternabra of the chest. Prosternum.

**Marcel effect:** Regular continuous waves. Named for a French hairdresser. (Specified in American Water Spaniel standard)

**Mask:** Dark shading on the foreface. (Mastiff, Boxer, Pekingese)

**Match show:** Usually an informal dog show at which no championship points are awarded.

**Mate:** To breed a dog and bitch.

**Medial:** Toward the mid-line of the dog.

**Median line:** *See* Furrow.

**Merle:** A color pattern involving a dominant gene (the M or Merling Series) and characterized by dark blotches against a lighter background of the same pigment; e.g., blue merle in Collies and red "dapple" in Dachshunds.

**Metatarsus:** Rear pastern.

**Milk teeth:** First teeth.

**Miscellaneous Class:** Transitory class for breeds attempting to advance to full AKC recognition.

**Mismarks:** Self colors with any area of white on back between withers and tail, on sides between elbows and back of hindquarters, or on ears. Black with white markings and no tan present. (Pembroke Welsh Corgi)

**Molars:** The posterior teeth of the dental arcade, with two on each side in the upper jaw and three on each side in the lower jaw in an adult with correct dentition (42 teeth).

**Molera:** Incomplete, imperfect or abnormal ossification of the skull.

**Mongrel:** A dog whose parents are of two different breeds.

**Monorchid:** A unilateral cryptorchid. *See* Cryptorchid.

**Mottled:** Pattern of dark roundish blotches superimposed on a lighter background, e.g., the blue-mottled variety of the Australian Cattle Dog.

**Moving close:** When the hocks turn in and pasterns drop straight to the ground and move parallel to one another, the dog is "moving close" in the rear. Action places severe strain on ligaments and muscles.

**Moving straight:** Term descriptive of balanced gaiting in which angle of inclination begins at the shoulder, or hip joint, and limbs remain relatively straight from these points to the pads of the feet, even as the legs flex or extend in reaching or thrusting.

**Multum in Parvo:** Latin phrase meaning "much in little," quoted in the Pug standard.

**Music:** The baying of the hounds.

**Mute:** To run mute, to be silent on the trail; i.e., to trail without baying or barking.

**Muzzle:** The head in front of the eyes—nasal bone, nostrils, and jaws. Foreface.

Also, a strap or wire cage attached to the foreface to prevent the dog from biting or from picking up food.

**Muzzle band:** White marking around the muzzle. (Boston Terrier)

**Neck well set-on:** Good neckline, merging gradually with withers, forming a pleasing transition into topline.

**Nick:** A breeding that produces desirable puppies.

**Non-slip Retriever:** The dog that walks at heel, marks the fall, and retrieves game on command; not expected to find or flush.

**Nose:** Organ of olfaction; also, the ability to detect by means of scent.

**Obedience Trial (Licensed):** An event held under AKC rules at which a "leg" toward an obedience degree can be earned.

**Obedience Trial Champion (OTCH):** A prefix used with the name of a dog that has been recorded an Obedience Trial Champion by the AKC as the result of having won the number of points and First Place wins specified in the current Obedience Regulations.

**Obliquely placed eyes:** Eyes with outer corners higher than their inner ones. Requested in Alaskan Malamute and Bull Terrier standards.

**Oblique shoulders:** Shoulders well laid back.

**Occiput:** Dorsal, posterior point of the skull.

**Occipital protuberance:** A prominently raised occiput characteristic of some Sporting and Hound breeds.

**Open bitch:** A bitch that can be bred.

**Open Class:** A class at dog shows in which all dogs of a breed, champions and imported dogs included, may compete.

**Orange belton:** *See* Belton.

**Organized competition:** Competition governed by the rules of a club or society, such as the AKC, organized to promote the interests of pure-bred dogs.

**Otter tail:** Thick at the root, round, and tapering, with the hair parted or divided on the underside.

**Out at elbows:** Elbows turning out from the body as opposed to being held close.

**Out at shoulders:** With shoulder blades loosely attached to the body, leaving the shoulders jutting out in relief and increasing the breadth of the front.

**Outcrossing:** The mating of unrelated individuals of the same breed.

**Oval chest:** Chest deeper than wide.

**Overhang:** A heavy or pronounced brow. (Pekingese)

**Overreaching:** Fault in the trot caused by more angulation and drive from behind than in front, so that the rear feet are forced to step to one side of the forefeet to avoid interfering or clipping.

**Overshot:** The incisors of the upper jaw projecting beyond the incisors of the lower jaw, thus resulting in a space between the respective inner and outer surfaces.

**Pace:** A lateral gait which tends to promote a rolling motion of the body. The left foreleg and left hind leg advance in unison, then the right foreleg and right hind leg.

**Pack:** Several hounds kept together in one kennel. Mixed pack is composed of dogs and bitches.

**Padding:** A compensating action to offset constant concussion when a straight front is subjected to overdrive from the rear; the front feet flip upward in a split-second delaying action to coordinate stride of forelegs with longer stride from behind.

**Paddling:** A gaiting fault, so named for its similarity to the swing and dip of a canoeist's paddle. Pinching in at the elbows and shoulder joints causes the front legs to swing forward on a stiff outward arc. Also referred to as "tied at the elbows."

**Pads:** Tough, shock-absorbing projections on the underside of the feet. Soles.

**Paper foot:** A flat foot with thin pads.

**Parent club:** National club for the breed. Listing with name and address of secretary can be obtained from American Kennel Club, 51 Madison Avenue, New York, NY 10010.

**Parti-color:** Variegated in patches of two or more colors.

**Pastern:** Commonly recognized as the region of the foreleg between the carpus or wrist and the digits, i.e., the metacarpus.

**Peak:** *See* Occiput.

**Pedigree:** The written record of a dog's genealogy of three generations or more.

**Pelvis:** Hip bones, each consisting of three fused bones: an anterior ilium, a ventral pubis, and a posterior ischium; combined with sacrum forming the pelvic girdle.

**Penciling:** Black lines dividing the tan on the toes. (Manchester)

**Peppering:** The admixture of white and black hairs, which in association with some entirely black and some entirely white hairs gives the "pepper and salt" appearance of some Schnauzer breeds.

**Pied:** Comparatively large patches of two or more colors. Piebald, parti-colored.

**Pigeon-breast:** A narrow chest with a protruding breastbone.

**Pigeon-toed:** Toes pointing in toward the mid-line.

**Pig jaw:** *See* Overshot.

**Pile:** Dense undercoat of soft hair.

**Pincer bite:** *See* Level bite.

**Pig Eyes:** Eyes set too close. Specified as a fault in Miniature Pinscher standard.

**Planes:** *See* Head Planes.

**Plume:** Either a long fringe of hair on the tail covering part of the tail only or involving the entire tail, or carried "plumed" over the back.

**Poach:** When hunting, to trespass on private property.

**Point:** The immovable stance of the hunting dog taken to indicate the presence and position of game.

**Points:** Color on face, ears, legs, and tail when correlated—usually white, black or tan. Alternately, credits toward championship status.

**Poke:** To carry the neck stretched forward in an abnormally low, ungainly position, usually when moving.

**Police dog:** Any dog trained for police work.

**Pompon:** A rounded tuft of hair left on the end of the tail when the coat is clipped. (Poodle)

**Posterior:** The portion of the dog carried hindmost (or toward the rear) during normal locomotion.

**Pounding:** Gaiting fault resultant of dog's stride being shorter in front than in the rear; forefeet strike the ground hard before the rear stride is expended.

**Premium list:** An advance-notice brochure sent to prospective exhibitors and containing details regarding a forthcoming show.

**Prick ear:** Carried erect and usually pointed at the tip.

**Professional handler:** A person who shows dogs for a fee.

**Pump handle:** Long tail, carried high.

**Put down:** To prepare a dog for the show ring; also used to denote a dog unplaced in competition.

**Puppy:** A dog under twelve months of age.

**Pure-bred:** A dog whose sire and dam belong to the same breed, and are themselves of unmixed descent since recognition of the breed.

**Quality:** Refinement, fineness, a degree of excellence.

**Racy:** Tall, of comparatively slight build.

**Radius:** One of the two bones of the forearm.

**Ragged:** Muscles appear ragged rather than smooth. (English Foxhound)

**Rangy:** Tall, long in body, high on leg, often lightly framed.

**Rat tail:** The root thick and covered with soft curls; at the tip devoid of hair, or having the appearance of being clipped. (Irish Water Spaniel)

**Reach of front:** Length of forward stride taken by forelegs.

**Rear Pastern:** The metatarsus, the region of the hindquarters between the hock (tarsus) and the foot (digits).

**Register:** To record with the AKC a dog's breeding particulars.

**Retrieve:** A hunting term. The act of bringing back shot game to the handler.

**Ribbed up:** Long ribs that angle back from the spinal column. A reference to a long rib cage.

**Rib cage:** The collection of paired ribs, cartilage, sternum, and associated tissue that define the thoracic region. Among the ribs are pairs 1–9 wherein the cartilage articulates directly with the sternum ("true ribs"), 10–12 wherein the cartilage fuses with anterior cartilage ("false-ribs"), and 13 is not attached ventrally ("floating ribs").

**Ringer:** A substitute for; a dog closely resembling another dog.

**Ring tail:** Carried up and around almost in a circle.

**Roach back:** A convex curvature of the back involving thoracic and lumbar regions.

**Roan:** A fine mixture of colored hairs with white hairs; blue roan, orange roan, lemon roan, etc. (English Cocker Spaniel)

**Rocking horse:** Both front and rear legs extended out from body as in an old-fashioned rocking horse.

**Rolling gait:** Swaying, ambling action of the hindquarters when moving.

**Roman nose:** A nose whose bridge is so comparatively high as to form a slightly convex line from forehead to nose tip. Ram's nose.

**Rose ear:** A small drop ear which folds over and back so as to reveal the burr.

**Rounding:** Cutting or trimming the ends of the ear leather. (English Foxhounds)

**Rudder:** The tail or stern.

**Ruff:** Thick, longer hair growth around the neck.

**Saber tail:** Carried in a semi-circle.

**Sable:** A coat color produced by black-tipped hairs upon a background of silver, gold, grey, fawn, or brown, and determined by the Agouti or A series of multiple alleles.

**Sacrum:** The region of the vertebral column that consists of three fused vertebrae which articulate with the pelvic girdle.

**Saddle:** A black marking over the back, like a saddle.

**Saddle back:** Overlong back, with a dip behind the withers.

**Scent:** The odor left by an animal on the trail (ground-scent), or wafted through the air (air-borne scent).

**Scissors bite:** A bite in which the outer side (anterior portion) of the lower incisors touches the inner side (posterior portion) of the upper incisors.

**Screw tail:** A naturally short tail twisted in more or less spiral formation.

**Second thigh:** That part of the hindquarter from the stifle to the hock, corresponding to the human shin and calf. Lower thigh, including the tibia and fibula.

**Self color:** One color or whole color except for lighter shadings.

**Seeing Eye dog:** A dog trained as a guide for the blind.

**Semi-prick ears:** Ears carried erect with just the tips leaning forward.

**Septum:** The line extending vertically between the nostrils.

**Set up:** Posed so as to make the most of the dog's appearance for the show ring.

**Shelly:** A shallow, narrow body, lacking the correct amount of bone.

**Short back:** *See* Close Coupled.

**Sickle hocked.** Inability to straighten the hock joint on the back reach of the hind leg.

**Sickle tail:** Carried out and up in a semicircle.

**Sight hound:** *See* Gazehound.

**Single tracking:** All footprints falling on a single line of travel. When a dog

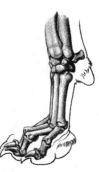

BONES OF THE FOOT

PADS

ROUND OR CAT FOOT

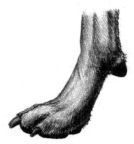

HARE FOOT

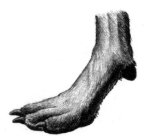

FLAT FOOT OR
DOWN IN PASTERN

SPLAY FOOT

**Feet**

breaks into a trot, his body is supported by only two legs at a time, which move as alternating diagonal pairs. To achieve balance, his legs angle inward toward a center line beneath his body, and the greater the speed, the closer they come to tracking on a single line.

**Sire:** The male parent.

**Skeleton:** Descriptively divided into axial (skull, vertebrae column, chest) and appendicular (forequarters, hindquarters) portions.

**Skully:** Thick and coarse through skull.

**Slab sided:** Flat ribs with too little spring from spinal column.

**Sled dogs:** Dogs worked usually in teams to draw sleds.

**Slew feet:** Feet turned out.

**Sloping shoulder:** The shoulder blade set obliquely or "laid back."

**Smooth coat:** Short hair, close-lying.

**Snatching hocks:** A gaiting fault indicated by a quick outward snatching of the hock as it passes the supporting leg and twists the rear pastern far in beneath the body. The action causes noticeable rocking in the rear quarters.

**Snipy:** A pointed, weak muzzle, lacking breadth and depth.

**Snow nose:** Nose normally solid black, but acquires pink streak in winter. (Specified as acceptable in Siberian Husky standard.)

**Soundness:** The state of mental and physical health when all organs and faculties are complete and functioning normally, each in its rightful relation to the other.

**Spay:** To perform a surgical operation on the bitch's ovaries to prevent conception.

**Speak:** To bark.

**Spectacles:** Shadings or dark markings over or around the eyes or from eyes to ears.

**Spike tail:** Straight short tail that tapers rapidly along its length.

**Splashed:** Irregularly patched, color on white or white on color.

**Splayfoot:** A flat foot with toes spreading. Open foot, open-toed.

**Spread:** Width between the forelegs when accentuated. (Bulldog)

**Spread hocks:** Hocks pointing outward.

**Spring:** *See* Flush.

**Spring of ribs:** Curvature of ribs for heart and lung capacity.

**Square body:** A dog whose measurements from withers to the ground equals that from forechest to the buttocks.

**Squirrel tail:** Carried up and curving more or less forward.

**Stacking:** *See* Set up.

**Stake:** Designation of a class, used in field trial competition.

**Stance:** Manner of standing.

**Standard:** A description of the ideal dog of each recognized breed, to serve as a word pattern by which dogs are judged at shows.

**Standoff coat:** A long or heavy coat that stands off from the body.

**Staring coat:** The hair dry, harsh, and sometimes curling at the tips.

**Station:** Comparative height from the ground, as high-stationed, low-stationed.

**Steep:** Used to denote incorrect angles of articulation. For example, a steep front describes a more upright shoulder placement than is preferred.

**Stern:** Tail.

**Sternum:** Breastbone.

**Stifle:** The joint of the hind leg between the thigh and the second thigh. The dog's knee.

**Stilted:** The choppy, up-and-down gait of the straight-hocked dog. (Chow Chow)

**Stop:** The step up from muzzle to back skull; indentation between the eyes where the nasal bones and cranium meet.

**Straight-hocked:** Lacking appreciable angulation at the hock joints.

**Straight in pastern:** Little or no bend at the wrist.

**Straight shoulders:** The shoulder blades rather straight up and down, as opposed to sloping or "well laid back."

**Stud book:** A record of the breeding particulars of dogs of recognized breeds.

**Stud dog:** A male dog used for breeding purposes.

**Substance:** Bone.

**Superciliary arches:** The ridge, projection, or prominence of the frontal bones of the skull over the eyes; the brow; supraorbital ridges.

**Suspension trot:** *See* Flying trot.

**Swayback:** Concave curvature of the vertebrae column between the withers and the hipbones.

**Symmetry:** Pleasing balance between all parts of the dog.

**Tail set:** How the base of the tail sets on the rump.

**TD (Tracking Dog):** A suffix used with the name of a dog that has been recorded a Tracking Dog as a result of having passed an AKC licensed or member tracking test. The title may be combined with the UD title and shown as UDT.

**TDX (Tracking Dog Excellent):** A suffix used with the name of a dog that has been recorded a Tracking Dog Excellent as a result of having passed an AKC licensed or member tracking dog excellent test. The title may be combined with the UDT title and shown as UDTX.

**Team:** Usually four dogs exhibited by one handler.

**Terrier:** A group of dogs used originally for hunting vermin.

**Terrier front:** Straight front, as found on Fox Terriers.

**Testicles:** The male gonad which produces spermatozoa. AKC regulations specify that a male which does not have two normal testicles normally located in the scrotum may not compete at any show and will be disqualified, except that a castrated male may be entered in obedience trials, tracking tests, field trials (except Beagles) and as Stud Dog in a Stud Dog class.

**Thigh:** The hindquarter from hip to stifle.

**Thoracic Vertebrae:** The thirteen vertebrae of the chest with which thirteen pairs of ribs articulate.

**Throatiness:** An excess of loose skin under the throat.

**Thumb marks:** Black spots on the region of the pastern.

**Tibia:** One of the two bones of the leg (i.e. the "lower" thigh, second thigh, or lower leg).

**Ticked:** Small, isolated areas of black or colored hairs on a white ground.

**Tied at the elbows:** *See* Paddling.

**Tongue:** The barking or baying of hounds on the trail, as to give tongue, to open or speak.

**Topknot:** A tuft of longer hair on top of the head.

**Topline:** The dog's outline from just behind the withers to the tail set.

**Toy dog:** One of a group of dogs characterized by very small size.

**Trace:** A dark stripe down the back of the Pug.

**Trail:** To hunt by following ground scent.

**Triangular eye:** The eye set in surrounding tissue of triangular shape; three-cornered eye.

**Tri-color:** Three-color; white, black, and tan.

**Trim:** To groom the coat by plucking or clipping.

**Triple Champion:** A dog that has won bench show, field trial and obedience trial championships.

**Trot:** A rhythmic two-beat diagonal gait in which the feet at diagonally opposite ends of the body strike the ground together; i.e., right hind with left front and left hind with right front.

**Trousers:** Longish hair at the back of both upper and lower thighs of some breeds.

**Trumpet:** The slight depression or hollow on either side of the skull just behind the orbit or eye socket, the region comparable with the temple in man.

**Truncated:** Cut off. (Old English standard calls for jaw that is square and truncated.)

**Tuck-up:** Characterized by markedly shallower body depth at the loin. Small-waisted.

**Tulip ear:** An ear carried erect with edges curving forward and in.

**Turn-up:** An uptilted foreface.

**Twisting hocks:** A gaiting fault in which the hock joints twist both ways as they flex or bear weight. Also called "rubber hocks."

**Type:** The characteristic qualities distinguishing a breed; the embodiment of a standard's essentials.

**Ulna:** One of the two bones of the forearm.

**UD (Utility Dog):** A suffix used with the name of a dog that has been recorded a Utility Dog by AKC as a result of having won certain minimum scores in Utility Classes at a specified number of AKC licensed or member obedience

**GOOD MOVEMENT
SIDE VIEW
Showing good reach in front
and proper drive in rear**

**POOR MOVEMENT
SIDE VIEW**

trials. The title may be combined with the TD or TDX title and shown as UDT or UDTX.

**Underline:** The combined contours of the brisket and the abdominal floor.

**Undershot:** The front teeth (incisors) of the lower jaw overlapping or projecting beyond the front teeth of the upper jaw when the mouth is closed.

**Unsound:** A dog incapable of performing the functions for which it was bred.

**Unilateral Cryptorchid:** *See* Cryptorchid.

**Upper arm:** The humerus or bone of the foreleg, between the shoulder blade and the forearm and associated tissues.

**Varminty:** A keen, very bright or piercing expression.

**Veil:** The portion of the dog's forelock hanging straight down over the eyes, or partially covering them.

**Vent:** The anal opening.

**Vertebral Column:** The bones of the central axis of the dog posterior to the skull including cervical, thoracic, lumbar, sacral, and caudal vertebrae.

**Walk:** Gaiting pattern in which three legs are in support of the body at all times, each foot lifting from the ground one at a time in regular sequence.

**Walleye:** An eye with a whitish iris; a blue eye, fisheye, pearl eye.

**Webbed:** Connected by a membrane. Webbed feet are important for water-retrieving breeds. (See Chesapeake Bay Retriever and Newfoundland standards.)

**Weedy:** An insufficient amount of bone; light-boned.

**Well let down:** Having short hocks; refers to short metatarsals.

**Wet neck:** Loose or superfluous skin; with dewlap.

**Wheaten:** Pale yellow or fawn color.

**Wheel back:** A marked arch of the thoracic and lumbar vertebrae. Roached.

**Whip tail:** Carried out stiffly straight, and pointed.

**Whiskers:** Vibrissae or sensory organs (hairs) on the sides of the muzzle.

**Whitelies:** Body color white with red or dark markings. (Pembroke Welsh Corgi)

**Wind:** To catch the scent of game.

**Winging:** A gaiting fault where one or both front feet twist outward as the limbs swing forward.

**Winners:** An award given at dog shows to the best dog (Winners Dog) and best bitch (Winners Bitch) competing in regular classes.

**Wirehair:** A coat of hard, crisp, wiry texture.

**Withers:** The region defined by the dorsal portions of the spinous processes of the first two thoracic vertebrae and flanked by the dorsal (uppermost) portions of the scapulae.

**Wrinkle:** Loose, folding skin on forehead and foreface.

**Wry mouth:** Asymmetrical alignment of upper and lower jaws; cross bite.

**Xiphoid process:** Cartilage process of the sternum.

**Zygomatic arch:** A bony ridge extending posteriorly (and laterally) from beneath the eye orbit (i.e., anatomically consists of two processes: zygomatic process of the maxilla and the maxillary process of the zygomatic bone).

# Index